MW00973967

Jim Sloan's

CL Tips & Techniques

DUKE PRESS

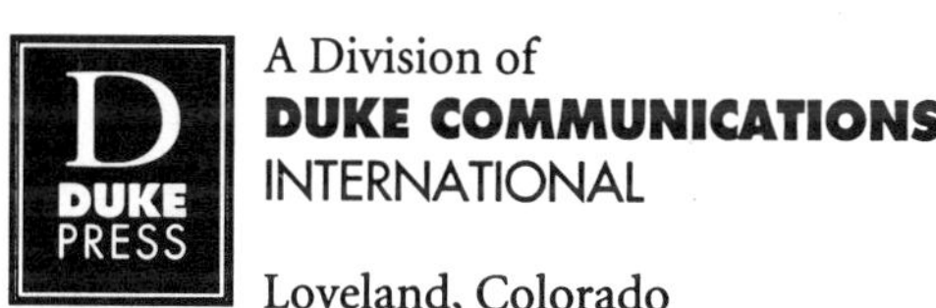

A Division of
DUKE COMMUNICATIONS
INTERNATIONAL

Loveland, Colorado

Library of Congress Cataloging-in-Publication Data

Sloan, Jim, 1936-
[CL tips & techniques]
Jim Sloan's CL tips & techniques : pointers from a IBMer who helped design the CL compiler. — 1st ed.
p. cm.
Includes bibliographical references and index.
ISBN 1-882419-02-2
1. Job Control Language (Computer program language) 2. Compilers (Computer programs) 3. IBM AS/400 (Computer) — Programming.
I. Title. II. Title: Cl tips & techniques. III. Title: CL tips and techniques.
QA76.73.J63S57 1994
005. 4'3—dc20 94-14383
CIP

DUKE COMMUNICATIONS INTERNATIONAL
Loveland, Colorado

This book was printed and bound in the United States of America.

ISBN 1-882419-02-2

2 3 4 5 6 EB 9 8 7 6 5 4

To all the customers and IBMers who have been involved with the AS/400.
Thanks for making it the outstanding midrange commercial system
in the industry. You've made my life a lot more interesting.

Acknowledgments

You only become smarter by listening, asking questions, trying things yourself, and explaining what you know to someone else. As I follow this process, a long list of customers and IBMers have contributed to my knowledge of CL programming. Thanks to you all. And a special thanks to my editor, Dave Bernard, who took my "techie" prose and made it more readable.

Table of Contents

ACKNOWLEDGMENTS ..... **IV**

PREFACE ..... **XVII**

WORKING WITH MESSAGES

CHAPTER 1: MONITORING FOR MESSAGES **1**
Monitoring for Escape Messages 2
Monitoring for the Right Escape Message 2
Escape Messages You Shouldn't Monitor For 3
Using the CHKOBJ Command 5
Monitoring for Multiple Message IDs 5
Monitoring for CPF0000 6
    Misuse of CPF0000 6
    Good Use of CPF0000 8
Monitoring for a Generic Range of Messages 9
The CMPDTA Parameter 9
Negative MONMSG Logic 10
Program-Level Monitoring 11
CL Program Inquiry Message 12
What's Really Happening 14
Exercise A : Error-Handling Conditions from the Command Entry Display 16
Exercise B : CL Program Inquiry Message 18
Exercise C : Monitoring for Messages 21
Exercise D: Logging CL Program Information 22

CHAPTER 2: SENDING MESSAGES **23**
Completion Messages 23
    Placing a Decimal Value in a Message 25
Escape Messages 26
    Using Message ID CPF9898 28
    When Not to Use CPF9898 29
    Using a Library Name in the Message Text 30
    Using a Member Name in the Message Text 31
    Resending an IBM Message 32
Status Messages 34
    How Status Messages Work 34
    Preventing Status Messages from Being Displayed 36

Sending a Message to the Submitter of a Job 36
Exercise A : Simple Completion Messages 38
Exercise B : Using a Count in a Completion Message 40
Exercise C : Sending Basic Escape Messages 40
Exercise D: Sending Escape Messages with Variables 42
Exercise E : Sending a Status Message 43
Exercise F : Shutting Off Status Messages 44
Exercise G: Sending a Message to a Job's Submitter 46

CHAPTER 3: RECEIVING MESSAGES 47
How To Receive Messages 48
Receiving the Last Message 48
Receiving Messages by Message Type 49
Receiving a Message To Remove It 50
Receiving a Message To Resend It 51
Resending a Completion Message 53
Receiving a Message To Extract Data 53
Accessing Data in Binary Format 55
Advanced Topics 56
The Message Key Field 56
Old Versus New Messages 58
Processing in FIFO Order 58
How Do You Know When There Are No More Messages? 58
The RTNTYPE Return Value 59
Writing a RCVMSG Loop 60
Messages You Cannot Access 60
Exercise A : Resending an Escape Message 63
Exercise B : Resending a Completion Message 64
Exercise C : Accessing Message Data Information 66

CHAPTER 4: STANDARD ERROR-HANDLING ROUTINE 69
Duplicating the Standard Error-Handling Routine 69
Basic Program Structure 70
How the Standard Error-Handling Routine Works 71
Modifying the Standard Error-Handling Routine 75
What You Shouldn't Include in the Error-Handling Routine 76
The Cleanup Routine 77
Providing a Program Dump 79
Handling Errors in Production Applications 80
Exercise A : Using Standard Error Handling 82
Exercise B : Adding a Cleanup Routine 85
Exercise C : Adding a CL Program Dump 89

CHAPTER 5: THE JOB LOG 93
The LOG Job Attribute 96
Forcing a Job Log 97
Providing a Temporary Audit Trail 99
Providing a Permanent Audit Trail 100
Cleaning Up the Job Log 101
Reading a Job Log 105
Job Log Review 105
Exercise A : Cleaning Up the Job Log 110
Exercise B : Displaying a Partial Job Log 111

CHAPTER 6: MISCELLANEOUS MESSAGE TECHNIQUES 113
Which Program Called Mine? 113
Which Message File is This Message From? 114
How To Duplicate a Message 115
How To Change a Long Message Text 115
Overriding a Message File 116
Responding to a Message Automatically and Dynamically 118
Converting a Message File to a Database File 120
Providing Multiple-Person Surveillance for the QSYSOPR Message Queue 120
- Capturing Critical System Messages 121
- Managing the QSYSOPR Message Queue 123

Sending Messages to Active Users 125
Using Request Messages 126
- Returning a Command as a Request Message 128

TYPICAL CL PROGRAMMING NEEDS

CHAPTER 7: DATE AND TIME 131
Dates 131
- Date Formats 131
- Date Conversion 133
- Century Support 134
- Choosing a Date Format 134
- My Favorite Date Format 135
- The RTVDAT TAA Tool 137
- The ADDDAT TAA Tool 138
- The CMPDAT TAA Tool 139
- The CHKDAT TAA Tool 140

Time 141

The RTVTIMSTM TAA Tool 142
The CLCTIMDIF TAA Tool 143
Exercise A : Dates 144
Exercise B : Time 148

CHAPTER 8: RETRIEVE COMMANDS 151
Using the RTVMBRD and RTVOBJD Commands 152
The RTNLIB Variable 153
The RTNMBR Variable 154
Using the RTVJOBA Command 154
Emulating the DSP Command OUTPUT Parameter 155
Avoiding SBMJOB if in Batch 156
The BLDCALL TAA Tool 156
Combining the RTVJOBA and CHGJOB Commands 158
Capturing Your Entire Environment 159
QUSRTOOL Retrieve Commands 160
How To Write Your Own RTV Command 160
Exercise A : Using the RTVOBJD Command 162
Exercise B : Using the RTVJOBA Command To Determine Output Form .. 163
Exercise C : Using the CAPJOBA TAA Tool 164

CHAPTER 9: SUBROUTINES 167
A Typical Approach to Subroutines 167
CLPSUBR TAA Tool 169
Reusing Proven Code in Multiple Programs 169
The CPYCL TAA Tool 170
Exercise A : Using a Subroutine 175
Exercise B : Using the CPYCL TAA Tool 176

CHAPTER 10: PASSING PARAMETERS 181
Passing Parameters from a Command Entry Line 182
Adding Meaning to Your Values 183
Submitting a Job with Parameters 184
Using the Right Number of Parameters 185
Using the Local Data Area 186
Passing a Data Structure 186
Passing Really Large Parameters 187
Using the Same Parameter List on SBMJOB and CALL Commands 187
Exercise A : Passing Parameters Longer than 32 Bytes 188
Exercise B : Passing Character Variables Without Quotes 190

CHAPTER 11: ALLOCATING OBJECTS 193

Is a Program Active? 193
Is an Object in Use? 197
Is a Job Active (or on a JOBQ or OUTQ)? 199
Manually Allocating Objects 200
Updating a Data Area 205
Exercise A : Using the CHKACTPGM Command 207
Exercise B : Using the RTVJOBSTS Command 209
Exercise C : Using the ALCOBJ and DLCOBJ Commands 210
Exercise D : Using the CHKACTOBJ Command 215
Exercise E : Using the ADDDTAARA Command 216

CHAPTER 12: ALLOCATION PROBLEMS 219
Object Types 219
Data Areas 220
Display Files 220
Printer Files 220
Spooled Files 221
Programs 221
User Profiles 222
Library Lists 222
Logical Files 222
Source Files 222
Physical Files 224
Physical File SIZE Parameter 225
Functions 226
Authorizations 226
Save/Restore 227
SAVWHLACT (Save While Active) 227
TAA Tools for Saving While Active 229
Restricted State Operations 230
PTFs 232
Installing a New Release 232

CHAPTER 13: COMMUNICATING WITH A WORKSTATION OPERATOR 233
Selective Prompting 233
The Job's External Message Queue (*EXT) 235
TAA Tool PMTOPR 237
Exercise A : Selective Prompting 241
Exercise B : Using the External Message Queue 244
Exercise C : Using the TAA Tool PMTOPR 247

CHAPTER 14: USER-WRITTEN COMMANDS 249
Writing Simple Commands 250
Defining "Command" 250
Command Prompt Text 251
Commands with No Parameters 252
Simple Object Name As a Parameter 253
Using a Qualified Name 254
Required Parameters (MIN Parameter) 257
Special Values for Names 258
Decimal and Character Parameters 259
A Restricted List of Values 259
Relational and Range Checking 260
Duplicating Standard Command Source 260
Other Command Functions 260
Expressions 261
Converting Special Values 262
Generic Names 263
Return Variables 264
Lists 264
Constants in a Command 266
QUSRTOOL Examples 267

WORKING WITH FILES

CHAPTER 15: FILE PROCESSING 269
The DCLF Statement 270
Using a DCLF Statement Without Processing a File 270
Reading a Database File 271
Reading a Spooled File 272
Random Processing 273
WRTSRC TAA Tool 274
Printing from CL 275
Passing Print Lines to an RPG Program 276
PRINT TAA Tool 277
The BLDPRTLIN TAA Tool 278
Exercise A : Reading a Database File 281
Exercise B : Using the WRTSRC TAA Tool 282

CHAPTER 16: DISPLAY FILES AND MENUS 285
Menus 285
Simple Menus 286
Using the GO Command To Access a CL Program 288

Using the DUPSTDSRC TAA Tool To Create Menus **289**
Command Line Processing **290**
Program Message Queue Subfile **291**
Exercise A : Using the Command Line API **293**
Exercise B : Using a Display File Menu **294**
Exercise C : Using the CMDLINE TAA Tool **296**

CHAPTER 17: OUTFILES **297**
Coding Outfiles **297**
The TAA CVT Commands **298**
Creating and Reading an Outfile in the Same Program **299**
The ALCTMPMBR TAA Tool **303**
The DSPJRN Command's Outfile **305**
A Crude Technique for Reusing an Outfile **306**
Exercise A : Using an Outfile **309**
Exercise B : Using the DSPFD Outfile **311**
Exercise C : Using a CVT TAA Tool **314**
Exercise D: Using the RTVPFSRC TAA Tool **316**

CHAPTER 18: OVERRIDES **317**
Controlling the File Open in an HLL Program **324**
Using Unique Printer Files **325**
Overriding Spooled File Attributes **326**
Exercise A : Overrides to the Same File **328**
Exercise B : Overrides to QPRINT at Different Levels **330**
Exercise C : Overrides to a Different File **333**

CHAPTER 19: SEQUENCING AND SELECTION TECHNIQUES **335**
Physical Files **335**
Logical Files **335**
The ADDLFM/RMVM Commands **336**
A Keyed Access Path **337**
A Question of Performance **337**
Where OPNQRYF Fits **338**
Where OPNQRYF Doesn't Fit **339**
To Sort or Not To Sort **339**

CHAPTER 20: OPNQRYF **341**
Important Points To Remember **341**
Typical Errors that "Blow Programmers' Minds" **342**
Typical QRYSLT Examples **343**
The MAPFLD Parameter **348**

Using Key Fields 348
OPNQRYF Performance 350
OPNQRYF Message Feedback 352
The QRYF TAA Tool 352
The CRTPRTPGM TAA Tool 355
The CPYJOBLOG TAA Tool 356
Exercise A : Using OPNQRYF from a Command Entry Display 358
Exercise B : Using OPNQRYF in a CL Program 362
Exercise C : Using the QRYF TAA Tool 364
Exercise D: Using the BLDQRYSLT Command (part of QRYF) 365
Exercise E : Using the CPYJOBLOG TAA Tool 366
Exercise F : Using the CPYFRMQRYF Command 368

CHAPTER 21: DISPLAYING DATA 371
The DSPDB TAA Tool 371
The DSPDBF TAA Tool 373
The CRTPRTPGM TAA Tool 374
Exercise A : Using the DSPDB TAA Tool 377
Exercise B : Using the DSPDBF TAA Tool 379
Exercise C : Using the CRTPRTPGM TAA Tool 379

WORKING WITH CL PROGRAMS

CHAPTER 22: THE PROGRAM STACK 383
The TFRCTL Command 384
Many Ways To Return 385
    Should You Have More than One Return Point? 385
Calling Your Own Program 386
Some Functions End When the Program Ends 386
Request Processor Programs 387
The Program Authority Adoption Function 388
    Advantages of Program Authority Adoption 389
    Disadvantages of Program Authority Adoption 389
The USEADPAUT Parameter 390
Submitting a Job with Adopted Authority 393
Exercise A : Displaying the Program Stack 396
Exercise B : Adopting and Unadopting Authority 397
Exercise C : Creating a Request Processing Program 402

CHAPTER 23: THE CL PROGRAM OBJECT 407
The Program Object 407
The Library Object 409

The CRTCLPGM Command 410
The USRPRF Parameter 410
The Log Parameter 410
The ALWRTVSRC Parameter 411
The TGTRLS Parameter 412
The REPLACE Parameter 412
The CHGPGM Command 415
The RMVOBS Parameter 415
The USRPRF and USEADPAUT Parameters 416
The OPTIMIZE Parameter 416
The CPROBJ Command 417
Displaying a Program's Attributes 417
Retrieving a Program's Attributes 418
Printing a Program's Attributes 419
The RPLPGM TAA Tool 420
Rebuilding an Application 420
The SBMPARMS TAA Tool 421
Squeezing the Size of CL Programs 422
The SQZPGMSIZ TAA Tool 423
Exercise A: Program Options 425
Exercise B: RPLPGM TAA Tool 427
Exercise C: SQZPGMSIZ TAA Tool 428

CHAPTER 24: CL PROGRAM PERFORMANCE 431
Iterative Processing in CL 432
Iterative Use of a CL Function from an HLL Program 435
HLL Program Performance 436

CHAPTER 25: WRITING SECURE PROGRAMS 439
One Way To Break In 439
Controls the Security Officer Should Insist On 440
Menu-Level Security 441
Controlling Programmers 443
Bogus Program Protection 444
Programs That Use Program Authority Adoption 444
Knowing Which Program Called Yours 446
Masking Data 447
Other TAA Tools That Meet Security Needs 447
Exercise A: Authority to Debug 450
Exercise B: SCRAMBLE and OR TAA Tools 452
Exercise C: CHKLMTCPB TAA Tool 454
Exercise D: PRTSECVIL TAA Tool 454

WORKING WITH IBM-SUPPLIED PROGRAMS

CHAPTER 26: QCMDEXC AND QCMDCHK 457
QCMDEXC 457
QCMDCHK 459
Combining the Use of QCMDCHK and QCMDEXC 460
Exercise A : Using QCMDEXC 462

CHAPTER 27: APIs 465
Single-Function Advanced APIs 466
List-Function Advanced APIs 467
Duplicating a Spooled File 471

YOUR ENVIRONMENT AND PROGRAMMING APPROACH

CHAPTER 28: SETTING UP YOUR ENVIRONMENT 473
Personal Library 473
Personal Output Queue 473
Single-Thread Job Queue 473
Job Descriptions 474
Handling Messages at My Workstation 474
Group Jobs 475
PDM Versus the Programmer's Menu 476
User Profile 476
Initial Program 476
Performing Standard Routines 477
Basic Displays 478
Keeping Your Output Queue Clean 478
Backup 479
Displaying Source 479
Printing Source Members 482
Copying Complete Source Members 482
Moving a Source Member 485
Removing Source Members 485
Exercise A : Using the STSMSG TAA Tool 486
Exercise B : Using the ATNPGM TAA Tool 487
Exercise C : Using the DSPLSTCHG TAA Tool 488
Exercise D: Using the PRTSRCF TAA Tool 489
Exercise E : Using the PRTSRCSUM TAA Tool 489
Exercise F : Using the DUPSRC and CNFRMVM Tools 491

CHAPTER 29: DEBUGGING 493
Entering CL Commands via SEU 493

The Compiler Listing 493
Logic Checking 494
Program Dump 495
Display Job Menu 495
System Debug Facility 495
Debugging Large Program Variables 496
Adding Test Statements 496
Exercise A : Using DSPCLPDO 498
Exercise B : Using BKP 498

CHAPTER 30: CROSS-REFERENCE TECHNIQUES 503
Scanning Your Source 504
    The Fastest Way To Scan Source 505
Setting Up a Source Archive for Static Source 506
The PRTCMDUSG Command 508
The DSPPGMREF Command 508
Exercise A : Using SCNSRC 513
Exercise B : Using PRTCMDUSG 514

APPENDICES

APPENDIX A: HOW I CODE 515
Machines Are Relatively Cheap 515
Should You Design a Program? 515
Why Start from Scratch? 516
Using a Standard Heading 516
How I Find the Command I Want 517
Entering Keywords 517
The IF Command 517
The ELSE Command 518
Using Comments 518
External Documentation 519
What My Programs Look Like 519
Taking a Piecemeal Approach 519
My Testing Approach 519
Getting Unstuck 520
What I Do When I Think I'm Done 520
Coding for the Long Term 523

APPENDIX B: QUSRTOOL 525
The Purpose of QUSRTOOL 526
What if QUSRTOOL Is Not on Your System? 526

Unpackaging QUSRTOOL 526
Documentation 527
The DSPTAATOOL Command 527
How To Get Started 528
TAASUMMARY 528
TAA Tools Require the RPG Compiler 530
The CRTTAATOOL Command 530
The CRTFILLIB Parameter 531
Creating All the Tools 531
Steps To Take if CRTTAATOOL Fails 532
The Libraries Used 533
Adding TAATOOL to the Library List 535
Informal Updates to QUSRTOOL 535
What You Should Do on a New Release 536
What if a Tool Doesn't Work? 536
If this Book Doesn't Agree with Your QUSRTOOL 537
The DUPTAPIN Tool 537
The DSPTAACMD Tool 538
The DSPTAAMBR Command 539
Changes to QUSRTOOL 539
Exercise A : Using the CRTTAATOOL Command 541
Exercise B : Using the DSPTAATOOL Command 542
Exercise C : Using the DSPTAACMD Command 544
Exercise D: Using the DSPTAAMBR Command 545

INDEX 547

Preface

For many years, I was a software planner; first on the S/38 and then on the AS/400. I started when the S/38 architecture was no more than notes on a piece of paper and I was involved with many of the major external decisions (e.g., how the command language would look). I remember the early growth pains and the dark days when IBM struggled to deliver the S/38, all of which was overshadowed by the smiling faces I eventually saw as customers began to use and understand the system.

Later, I saw the S/38 architecture teeter on the edge of the junk heap before IBM finally settled on it for the AS/400. And finally, I saw the AS/400 blossom into the finest commercial midrange system in the industry.

As with most things in life, the fun is in getting there. I worked on many aspects of both systems and had the privilege of representing IBM at many conferences and delivering numerous presentations.

Early on in the life of the S/38, I gave presentations that became the source of tools that let the system provide functions not supplied (and possibly never to be supplied) by IBM developers. When the QUSRTOOL library was included in the AS/400 operating system, I had a chance to place my tools where they would be better distributed and better used. I continued to add to the tools as a part of my job with IBM.

In mid-1991, I received an offer I couldn't refuse and retired from IBM. Then I went back to work for IBM part-time to continue to enhance QUSRTOOL.

This book, which focuses on CL programs, is a summary of what I have learned as a software planner and as a developer of the QUSRTOOL tools. You'll not only learn about the techniques I used to create the tools, but you'll also learn how to use many of the tools.

This book is not intended to be a complete course in CL or in the TAA tools. It's written for programmers who can make CL programs work and who are ready to learn what more they can do to improve their programs and to increase their own productivity.

Like many programming topics, most of the subject matter is not difficult, but it takes dedication and practice to be good. I've included exercises at the end of most chapters to assist you in understanding what is important and to give you a chance to try some of the techniques. Real education means that you educate yourself. The book is meant only to stimulate your thinking.

Programming expertise lies somewhere between an art form and a science. To turn out good quality code in a productive manner depends on what you know, what resources exist for you to use, and your work habits. I can't do much about your work habits, but this book attempts to increase how much you know and provide you with more resources (in the form of tips and techniques) to do your job.

Jim Sloan
Rochester, MN

CHAPTER 1

Monitoring for Messages

We don't live in a perfect world where people always do the right thing, where machines always work, or where objects still exist where you left them. Because of this, you probably try to think of as many "what-happens-if" situations as possible when you program and then develop a coding strategy to handle the potential error conditions that might occur. I divide the error conditions into two types.

First are those error conditions known only to your application. For example, a user may enter inappropriate data into a field (i.e., the data doesn't make sense in relation to another field or data record). The system doesn't know this is an error; only your application knows. I am not going to discuss these types of errors, except to say that it can take considerable work to ensure that the application makes sense.

Second are those error conditions known to the system. For example, you may call a program that doesn't exist. These types of errors will cause the system to send an error message to your program. Such system errors include the following:

- Expected errors. I would program for these kinds of errors. Not all applications require programming for expected errors, but sometimes I want my program to take a specific action if, for example, a member exists or does not exist. CL programs support the MONMSG (Monitor Message) command, which provides a great deal of capability for handling error conditions. But using the MONMSG command appropriately is not as easy as it looks; I will use a good portion of this chapter to talk about what to do and what not to do as you use this command.

- Unexpected errors. I would not program for these kinds of errors. Typical unexpected errors would occur when a user is not authorized to a command or an attempt is made to access a damaged object. When an error occurs in a CL program, IBM provides a default (inquiry message CPA0701) if you don't monitor for the error. You can take the default or you can decide on your own error-handling strategy. I prefer not to use the IBM default. Later in this chapter (see "CL Program Inquiry Message") I will discuss the strategy I follow and why.

Technical Tip

It isn't practical to code for all the things that can go wrong in a program. Code for the errors you expect. For unexpected errors, you need an overall error-handling strategy.

MONITORING FOR ESCAPE MESSAGES

When an error occurs in a program, an escape message is sent to the program's message queue. In a CL program, the MONMSG (Monitor Message) command is used to monitor for escape messages — both at the program level and at the command level. Although the AS/400 issues other types of messages (e.g., diagnostic, completion, status, and notify messages), the MONMSG command can monitor only for escape messages. (A few other insignificant message types are also valid.)

When you monitor for an error in a program and the error occurs, you need to be sure that you follow through. If you let your program ignore the error and/or the program does something strange, you can spend a lot of time trying to determine what went wrong. Some of the most difficult situations to debug are those that occur when a program has ignored an error and eventually aborted, or when a program says it finished normally when it did not. You can allow your program to ignore an error, but most of the time you need to write extra code to handle the error.

Technical Tip

If you are going to monitor for an error condition, be sure you do something meaningful (e.g., send an explanatory message or add a member that doesn't exist). In some cases, you can ignore the error; but most of the time you need to do something more than that.

MONITORING FOR THE RIGHT ESCAPE MESSAGE

Most CL commands have a series of escape message IDs that you can monitor for. Some escape message IDs are unique to a particular command; others are general-purpose and can be sent by many different commands. You can find a list of CL commands and their associated escape message IDs in the *Programming: Reference Summary*, (SX41-0028). The manual shows only the first-level text for each message. At that level, the message text may be similar among escape messages and is often ambiguous because the same message is used for more than one error condition. For this reason, I rarely refer to the manual because

I do not trust my ability to correctly interpret the documentation. After working with messages for a long time, I have concluded it is better to work with a small set of escape message IDs I am familiar with so I can get the job done more easily. The following is the short list of CL commands and the escape message IDs I normally monitor for (I probably use these in 95 percent of all my MONMSG statements):

CL Command	Message ID	Message Issued
CHKOBJ	CPF9801	Object not found
	CPF9802	Not authorized to object
	CPF9815	Member not found
ALCOBJ	CPF1002	Cannot allocate
RCVF	CPF0864	End of file condition
DLTF	CPF2105	File not found
DLTPGM	CPF2105	Program not found

Note that escape message CPF9802 occurs when your program tests an object (including *LIB type objects) using the CHKOBJ command and the user is not authorized. You must specify the AUT parameter on the CHKOBJ command to determine whether the user is authorized; otherwise, only the existence of the object is checked. Note also that escape message CPF2105 is not unique to the DLTF and DLTPGM commands; the message ID is sent by most DLT functions if the object does not exist.

If I expect an error might occur, I normally use the CHKOBJ command (more on this command later) to check a function before the program uses it to ensure the objects I need exist and are in the right condition to be used. The other alternative is to execute the function I want and then monitor for the things that can go wrong.

If I can't check the expected error by using a command from my memorized list, I test the function I expect to fail and then determine which escape message is sent when it does fail. Seeing a message after you test the supposed error condition isn't enough. You need to do the following:

- Determine whether or not the message is really an escape message sent to your program
- If it is an escape message, determine whether or not the message ID is meaningful to monitor for (see the following sections)

Escape Messages You Shouldn't Monitor For

You need to be careful not to monitor for general-purpose, ambiguous escape messages — messages that indicate something went wrong in a program but that don't identify the exact problem. In some situations, the AS/400 sends a diagnostic message that defines the problem before it sends the escape message. In other situations, no diagnostic message is sent.

Consider the escape message sometimes sent for the CPYF (Copy File) command: Escape message CPF2817 says only that CPYF failed. A diagnostic message such as CPF2802, sent before the escape message, adds clarification, saying that the From file was not found. As this example demonstrates, monitoring for general-purpose escape messages is not sufficient; you need to consider the diagnostic message as well (when there is one), since the escape message could describe several error conditions. But the AS/400 does not provide you with a list of all diagnostic message IDs associated with a single escape message, and there is no reasonable way to determine the full set of possible error conditions.

Let's look at what might happen if you monitored for a general-purpose escape message. Assume you are going to CALL PGMA and that it might not exist. You could code

```
CALL     PGMA
MONMSG   MSGID(CPF0001) EXEC(DO) /* Does not exist */
  .
  .      /* Error-handling code */
  .
ENDDO    /* Does not exist */
```

The problem with monitoring for escape message CPF0001 (Error found on XXXX command) is that the message is issued in many different cases, including the situation where the program does not exist. CPF0001 also occurs if you have syntax errors in the command, the command itself is misspelled, or the command does not exist when you try to execute it. Although the system will send a diagnostic message explaining the error, accessing the diagnostic message is not easy (see Chapter 3, "Receiving Messages"). I prefer the following approach, which uses the CHKOBJ command to test for the existence of the program (assume I want to initiate an error-handling routine if the program does not exist):

```
CHKOBJ   OBJ(PGMA) OBJTYPE(*PGM)
MONMSG   MSGID(CPF9801) EXEC(DO) /* Does not exist */
  .
  .      /* Error-handling code */
  .
ENDDO    /* Does not exist */
CALL     PGMA
```

By monitoring for escape message CPF9801 (Object XXXX in library XXXX not found), I will know for certain if PGMA is not found. Then if CPF0001 occurs on the CALL command, it won't be because PGMA does not exist. Using this approach, you may still get a CPF0001 someday, but it will be for some unexpected reason.

Using the CHKOBJ Command

I use the CHKOBJ (Check Object) command frequently not only to determine whether or not an object exists, but also to determine a user's authority to the object. Here are a few examples of using the CHKOBJ command:

- Does a file exist?

```
CHKOBJ    OBJ(FILEA) OBJTYPE(*FILE)
MONMSG    MSGID(CPF9801) EXEC(DO) /* No file */
```

- Does a member exist?

```
CHKOBJ    OBJ(FILEA) OBJTYPE(*FILE) MBR(MBR1)
MONMSG    MSGID(CPF9815) EXEC(DO) /* No member */
```

- Is the user authorized to change the object?

```
CHKOBJ    OBJ(FILEA) OBJTYPE(*FILE) AUT(*CHANGE)
MONMSG    MSGID(CPF9802) EXEC(DO) /* Not authorized */
```

You may question whether to use the CHKOBJ command or to monitor for the specific error that occurs on a particular command, because trying the command first does offer some minor performance advantage. But most of the overhead associated with any command is getting the object into main memory, and using both CHKOBJ plus the real command you want does not create much additional overhead. Since CHKOBJ causes the object header to be placed in main memory, the next access, to try the actual command, uses less overhead.

Technical Tip

You don't need to use CHKOBJ on every object you're about to use. A good time to use CHKOBJ is when you expect a problem might occur. I treat most potential problems (e.g., the program doesn't exist) as unexpected errors.

Monitoring for Multiple Message IDs

Sometimes you will want to monitor for multiple error conditions on a single command. You can do this in one of two ways: You can specify up to 50 message IDs on the same MONMSG command:

```
CHKOBJ   OBJ(FILEA) OBJTYPE(*FILE) MBR(MBR1)
MONMSG   MSGID(CPF9801 CPF9815) EXEC(DO)
         /* No file or member */
   .
   .     /* Error-handling code */
   .
ENDDO    /* No file or member */
```

or you can use separate MONMSG commands:

```
CHKOBJ   OBJ(FILEA) OBJTYPE(*FILE) MBR(MBR1)
MONMSG   MSGID(CPF9801) EXEC(DO) /* No file */
   .
   .     /* Error-handling code */
   .
ENDDO    /* No file */
MONMSG   MSGID(CPF9815) EXEC(DO) /* No member */
   .
   .     /* Error-handling code */
   .
ENDDO    /* No member */
```

If you use the first method, you cannot determine explicitly which type of error occurred (i.e., whether the command failed because a file did not exist or a member did not exist). I like to know which type of error occurred, so I normally use the second method to monitor for multiple error conditions.

Monitoring for CPF0000

Monitoring for CPF0000, which allows you to monitor for any escape message, is a very powerful function I use frequently to help me deal with unexpected errors. With CPF0000, you are saying "If anything goes wrong, let me handle it." I monitor for CPF0000 when I know something may go wrong, but I do not want to abort the program when an error occurs. I save the fact that an error occurred and, when my program is ready to end, I end it with an abnormal termination.

Misuse of CPF0000

While monitoring for escape message CPF0000 is very powerful, it is probably one of the most misused functions on the system. Clearly one of the problems with CPF0000 is that some programmers tend to use it all the time rather than take the time to determine the real escape message they should monitor for. But many things can go wrong that are often not considered. For example, normally, when programmers use a command that operates on an object, they often don't think about what would happen if

- The object is damaged
- The user is not authorized to the object
- The user is not authorized to the library
- The user is not authorized to the command
- The object is exclusively allocated

To handle all these conditions, you are forced to do lots of coding. To give you an idea of what can go wrong, let's look at an example of poor coding technique:

```
CLRPFM   FILE(FILEA)
MONMSG   MSGID(CPF0000)
```

Since there is no EXEC parameter, the MONMSG statement ignores any error condition. If anything goes wrong on the CLRPFM command, the program continues with the command that follows the MONMSG command. Monitoring for CPF0000 without the EXEC parameter says that you are not going to abort regardless of what happens. At least 11 different error conditions can occur on CLRPFM, including

- No file found
- No member exists
- Not authorized
- The member is allocated

In addition to the error conditions that can occur specifically for CLRPFM, other more generic errors also can happen. The CLRPFM command itself could have been accidentally deleted, the file or command could be damaged, or the user may not be authorized to the command. It's not likely you are going to want the program to blindly continue if it encounters an error. Probably you will want the program to handle some likely error conditions, but abort if others occur. For example, you might be able to easily work around the fact that a file member doesn't exist when you try to clear it, but it's difficult to program for object damage.

You might want to know the following before executing CLRPFM:

- Does the library exist?
- Is the user authorized to the library?
- Does the file exist?
- Is the user authorized to the file?
- Does the member exist?

- Is the user authorized to clear the member?
- Is the member allocated?

You can easily monitor for all these error conditions using a combination of the CHKOBJ and ALCOBJ commands. The typical escape messages for these two commands are in my memorized list; they are not ambiguous, and I know what to do if the error occurs. If the error is something other than one of these, I prefer to abort. So it would be rare for me to use MONMSG(CPF0000) with CLRPFM. In most of my coding, I would precede CLRPFM with the CHKOBJ and ALCOBJ commands, which handle any of the above conditions, then just let the program abort if CLRPFM does not work correctly. If I cannot clear the member, I might choose to send my own error message instead of letting the system inquiry message occur. I would do this if the error was expected and the system message was not very clear (see Chapter 3, "Receiving Messages").

Technical Tip

Avoid monitoring for CPF0000 unless you really know what you are doing. Use it, for example, when you don't want to abort the program when an error occurs. You probably want to save the fact that an error occurred and abnormally terminate at some later point.

Good Use of CPF0000

Good reasons for monitoring for CPF0000 at the command level include the following:

- You are performing a list of requests and want to complete all you can. For example, you may be copying multiple members and one of them is allocated so it cannot be copied.
- You want to do some cleanup before you end abnormally.
- The function you are performing is not critical to the success of the program. For example, you may be trying to delete something from QTEMP at the end of the program. If some object remains in QTEMP when the program completes, however, you would probably consider the program to be successful.

There also are good reasons for monitoring for CPF0000 at the program level. These include:

- Some escape messages do not start with the prefix CPF. If one of these occurs and you have not monitored for it, the system will turn it into a CPF9999 escape message, which will be caught by CPF0000. Thus, monitoring for CPF0000 is a "catch-all" approach and no error should get past it. Unfortunately, some errors can occur that you can't monitor for. A typical example is where a user is running a program and someone deletes the program or does a restore of the same program. This causes a "destroyed object" error condition, and the job will abnormally terminate even if you are monitoring for CPF0000.

- When you monitor for a message (either on a specific command or at the program level), the inquiry message that says you have an unmonitored escape message will not occur (because everything is monitored for). A program-level MONMSG for CPF0000 prevents the inquiry message from occurring. I use this technique frequently (see Chapter 4, "Standard Error-Handling Routine").

Monitoring for a Generic Range of Messages

A generic message monitor is coded as 'MONMSG CPF9800'. This means that any message from CPF9801 to CPF9899 would be monitored for. Generic message monitors have their place, but I rarely use them because you can't really be sure of the error you think you are experiencing. For example, on CLRPFM, 10 of the 11 escape messages are in the CPF3100 range. That means there is an exception outside the normal range; in addition, all the CPF0001 error types would not be caught if you used a generic monitor for CPF3100. It seems unlikely that you would want to monitor for several error conditions on a single command, process them all in the same manner, and forget about the other potential error conditions.

Technical Tip

If you really want to handle all error conditions when a specific command fails, monitoring for CPF0000 is the safest thing to do. Monitoring for a generic range (something other than CPF0000) will not catch all the errors. If you monitor for CPF0000 on a specific command, be sure you are not dependent on any function that the command might have performed, because if an error occurs the command will not have executed.

The CMPDTA Parameter

Most programmers don't know the CMPDTA parameter exists on the MONMSG command. The CMPDTA parameter specifies comparison data, and it can be very helpful when used with the CPYF (Copy File) command.

If the CPYF command fails, it may do so for a variety of reasons. CPF2817 is issued as a general escape message that says CPYF failed. There should be a preceding diagnostic message that allows you to determine the specific error, but accessing diagnostic messages is not easy to do correctly. To make it easier for you to determine what went wrong, CPYF stores the diagnostic message ID so that it can be used by the CMPDTA parameter of the MONMSG command. The following would be typical coding to handle different errors:

```
CPYF       FROMFILE(FILEA) TOFILE(FILEB)
MONMSG     MSGID(CPF2817) CMPDTA(CPF2802) EXEC(DO)
           /* No FROM file */
   .
   .       /* Error-handling code */
   .
ENDDO      /* No FROM file */
MONMSG     MSGID(CPF2817) CMPDTA(CPF2861) EXEC(DO)
           /* No TO file */
   .
   .       /* Error-handling code */
   .
ENDDO      /* No TO file */
```

When CMPDTA is used, the MONMSG command is not invoked unless the comparison data (the diagnostic message ID) is matched. This can simplify your error-handling of CPYF.

NEGATIVE MONMSG LOGIC

Sometimes the error condition that you must monitor for is really the positive condition. For example, sometimes it is an error if an object exists. I use CHKOBJ to determine whether an object exists, but there is no way to code the MONMSG command for the inverse of an error. Consequently, you must specify a GOTO command on the EXEC parameter of MONMSG. And you must be careful to specify the correct label for the GOTO. My favorite solution is to code a dummy label at the end of the CHKOBJ test with a good comment to go with it. This way I will not accidentally place another command before the end of the block of logic. Assume you want to specify that if data area XXX exists, it is an error. The following is what I would code:

```
                CHKOBJ      OBJ(XXX) OBJTYPE(*DTAARA)
                MONMSG      MSGID(CPF9801) EXEC(GOTO ENDCHK)
                  .
                  .         /* Error logic for the fact that */
                  .         /*  the data area does exist.    */
                  .
    ENDCHK:                 /* XXX data area does not exist  */
                /* Next block of logic */
```

Technical Tip

There is no good way to do negative DO logic following a MONMSG command; you normally need a GOTO command with a label to accomplish this. As a safe approach, I prefer to use a label without a command on it and document what the label is for with a comment to avoid errors when maintaining a program with this type of logic.

Program-Level Monitoring

The MONMSG command is valid at the program level. It must follow the last DCL or DCLF command in the program. The definition of the function is that any escape message not specifically monitored for at the command level can be caught by the program-level monitor. I use this technique all the time with the CPF0000 escape message to say that if any unexpected error occurs in my program, let me gain control. I will discuss this technique further in Chapter 4, "Standard Error-Handling Routine," but here is the basic code:

```
            DCL       ...
            MONMSG    MSGID(CPF0000) EXEC(GOTO STDERR1)
              .
              .           /* Normal coding */
              .
    STDERR1:          /* Standard Error-Handling Routine */
```

When you use the program-level MONMSG, you must either ignore the error (no EXEC parameter), which I prefer not to do, or use a GOTO command in the EXEC parameter. Although the program-level MONMSG also works for specific escape messages, I don't use it for the same reason I rarely use CPF0000 following an individual command. (See the section "Monitoring for CPF0000.")

Technical Tip

A program-level MONMSG for CPF0000 is very powerful, but you have to use it correctly. See Chapter 4, "Standard Error-Handling Routine."

CL Program Inquiry Message

Assume you have the following CL program:

```
PGM
CALL      PGMX
ENDPGM
```

What happens if PGMX does not exist? By default, the system provides an inquiry message (CPA0701) if an unmonitored escape message occurs in your program. As I've discussed previously, almost all my programs use a standard error-handling routine that has a program-level MONMSG command for CPF0000. Consequently, I never see the inquiry message. If you have an unmonitored escape message, the inquiry message is displayed on the screen titled "Display Program Messages." The message text of the message states the error message ID that caused the error. The second-level text of CPA0701 includes the first-level text of the escape message that was unmonitored. The responses you can make to the message include

- C Cancel
- D Dump and cancel
- R Retry
- I Ignore

The CPA0701 inquiry message is controlled by the job value for INQMSGRPY. You can set INQMSGRPY so you will not get the inquiry message by specifying

```
CHGJOB   INQMSGRPY(*DFT)
```

The default for error message CPA0701 is assigned by IBM ('C' for Cancel). You can change the default, but I wouldn't recommend it. If you specify INQMSGRPY(*DFT), the system responds with the default. If 'C' for cancel is taken (because you entered it or the default occurred), what you see on the command entry display is escape message CPF9999 (function check). If you press F10 for low-level messages, you will see the following:

```
  CPD0170   Program PGMX not found    - Diagnostic
  CPF0001   Error on call command     - Escape
  CPA0701   Inquiry message           - Inquiry
? C         (This is the default response)
  CPF9999   Function check            - Escape
```

Some programmers like to see the inquiry message, but I prefer to include a standard error-handling routine in my program so the escape message is sent back to the calling program. If you submit the following program to batch and use the IBM defaults, the CPA0701 message is sent to QSYSOPR.

```
PGM
CALL      PGMX
ENDPGM
```

Personally, I prefer to abort the batch job and look at the job log. What I don't like about the inquiry message is

- It holds the batch queue until the message is answered. Unless you have someone watching the operator's message queue, you can hold up a lot of other work. This is especially true if you have a job queue that handles only one job at a time.
- To make a good "Retry" reply usually means that you had to fix something. This means in the heat of battle you have to make a quick fix and I am not a fan of quick fixes. If the program is complex, you can make a quick fix that will make a bigger mess.
- To make a correct "Ignore" decision, you need to be very familiar with what the program is trying to do, what it has done so far, and how it will react.
- My experience is that people will try the Ignore option hoping that something good will happen without knowing anything about the program. In many cases, choosing the Ignore option may cause more problems than canceling the job.
- For a complex program, it may be impossible to do anything except cancel the job (Ignore and Retry may not be practical).
- If you encourage an environment where people have to make decisions during program execution, you will not achieve an unattended environment. In my opinion, teaching programmers to fix their code so errors do not cause inquiry messages is an appropriate goal.

While handling the inquiry message may be a matter of personal preference for programmers, I feel very strongly about how it should be handled for production end users. Some people prefer that if a problem occurs, their end users receive an inquiry message and then call the DP department to ask how to respond rather than the job aborting automatically. I believe this is inappropriate, and I prefer to abort the job so there is no possibility for someone to ignore the error. (A middle ground says you capture the error, say something intelligent to the operator, and then ensure that the problem is brought to the attention of a programmer. I've included an example of how to do this in Chapter 5, "The Job Log.")

There is another setting for INQMSGRPY that makes sense for production end users, and that is the value *SYSRPYL. If you use this value, the IBM defaults are set to dump the program and then cancel the job (the equivalent of the 'D' response to the CPA0701 message). The dump is useful only if the program has not had its observability removed (see the discussion of the CHGPGM RMVOBS parameter in Chapter 23, "The CL Program Object").

Technical Tip

For programmer test functions, I recommend the JOBD be set to INQMSGRPY(*DFT) or that you use a standard error-handling routine. For production users, I recommend the JOBD be set to INQMSGRPY(*SYSRPYL) or that you use a standard error-handling routine.

What's Really Happening

On the following page is the error-handling logic (Figure 1.1) the system follows to determine what to do when an error occurs. If you followed the discussion so far, this should be just a review. While Figure 1.1 shows that notify and status messages are also handled by MONMSG, from a practical viewpoint, you can ignore these message types.

FIGURE 1.1
Monitor Message Process

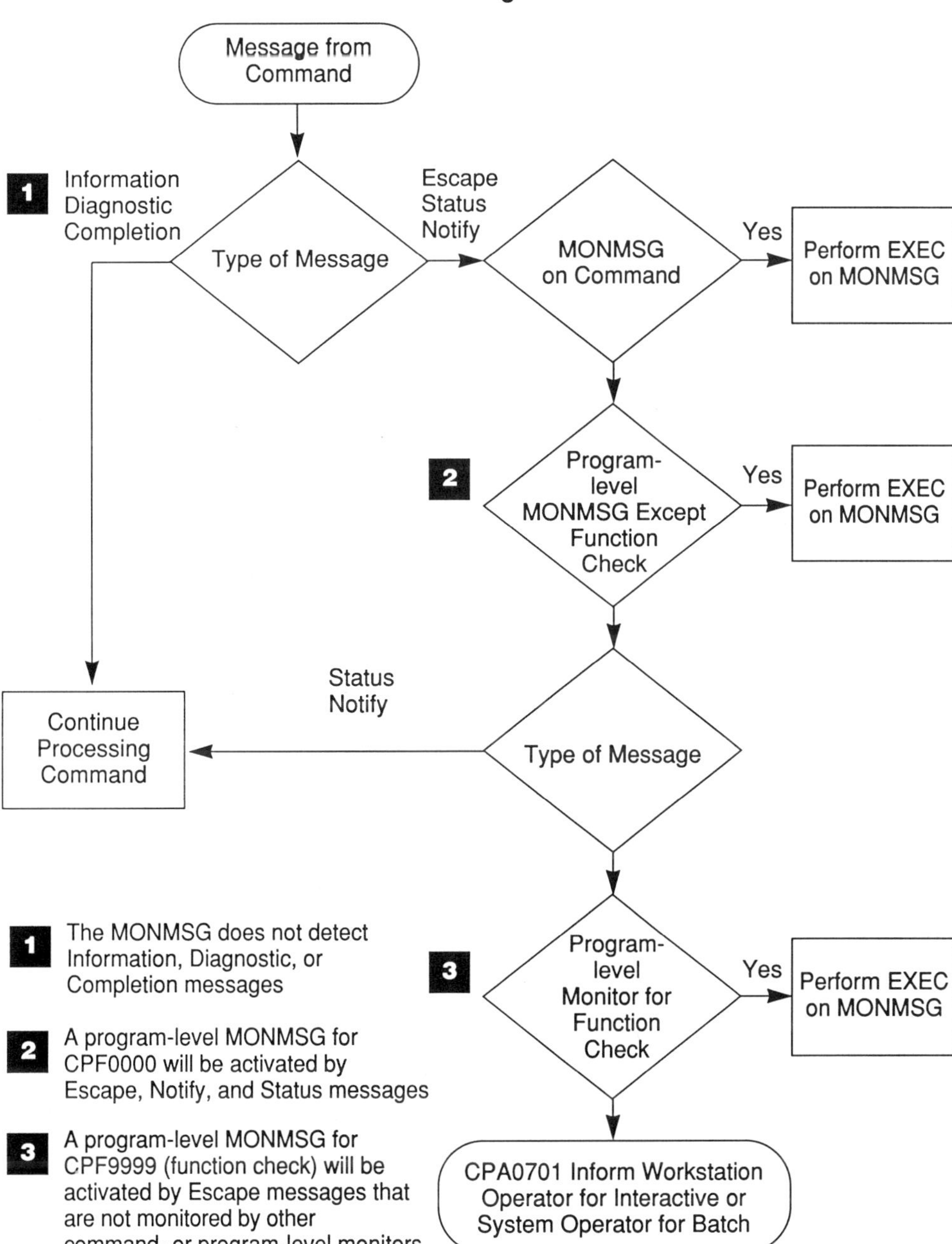

Exercise A Error-Handling Conditions from the Command Entry Display

In this set of exercises you will enter commands interactively to see how the system handles error conditions from the command entry display.

1. Sign on as a user who does not have *ALLOBJ authority.
2. Enter the following command to access the command entry display:

   ```
   CALL   QCMD
   ```

   The command entry display is the place to be when you want to determine what is happening to commands and messages. Many system displays (such as PDM) support a command line that appears to allow the same functions, but the command line isn't really the same. I'll show you some of the differences in these exercises.
3. Use a program name that does not exist in your library list. This name will be ZZXX in the following examples. Enter the command:

   ```
   CHKOBJ     OBJ(ZZXX) OBJTYPE(*PGM)
   ```

   You should receive an escape message stating that the program was not found.
4. Place the cursor on the message and press the Help key. You should see the "Additional Message Information" display. I prefer to work with the "Intermediate Assistance" level of help text. To change the assistance level, press Function key F21. If you use the "Basic Assistance" level of help text, you would press F11 to display message detail information. The message ID should be CPF9801 and the message type should be ESCAPE. The program that sent the message ("From program") is some IBM-supplied internal program (the name starts with a Q). The "To program" is QCMD (the program that you called). The fact that this is an escape message sent to your program means that you can monitor for this message in a CL program with the command

   ```
   MONMSG     MSGID(CPF9801) EXEC(DO) /* Not found */
   ```
5. Enter the command:

   ```
   CHKOBJ     OBJ(QCMD) OBJTYPE(*PGM) AUT(*USE)
   ```

   Since you are on the command entry display, you should be authorized

Exercise A continued

Exercise A continued

to it. CHKOBJ does not send any message when it completes successfully.

6. Enter the command:

```
CHKOBJ     OBJ(QCMD) OBJTYPE(*PGM) AUT(*CHANGE)
```

Unless you have *ALLOBJ authority, you should not be authorized to change QCMD and you should see the escape message CPF9802. You must use the AUT parameter to do any authority checking.

7. Enter the command:

```
CALL       PGM(ZZXX)
```

You should see two messages. Use the cursor and the Help key to examine the messages. The first message should be CPD0170, which is a diagnostic message. The second message is CPF0001, which is sent as an escape message. Monitoring for CPF0001 is not a good practice because there are several errors that all cause CPF0001 to be sent.

8. Enter the command:

```
XXXX       PGM(ZZXX)
```

Assuming the XXXX command does not exist on your system, you should see the CPD0030 diagnostic message followed by the CPF0001 escape message. To understand the specifics of the CPF0001, you need to see the preceding diagnostic message. This is hard to do in a CL program (see Chapter 3, "Receiving Messages").

9. Enter the WRKMBRPDM command to access a source file to enter a test program. You can either

   - enter WRKMBRPDM on the command entry display, or
   - use system request to access another job, or
   - use the attention key to flip-flop between two group jobs (this is described in Chapter 28, "Setting Up Your Environment").

10. On the PDM command line, enter

```
CHKOBJ     OBJ(ZZXX) OBJTYPE(*PGM)
```

You should see a message at the bottom of the display stating the object is not found. Place the cursor on this message and press the

Exercise A continued

Exercise A continued

Help key. You should see that it is the CPF9801 message, but PDM has received it and re-sent it as an informational message. Note the "From" and "To" programs involved in the message.

11. On the PDM command line, enter:

```
XXXX        PGM(ZZXX)
```

The PDM display only has room for one message to be displayed. It is the first message received so you should be looking at CPD0030. PDM has also changed this into an information message. Press the Roll-Up key to see the next message. It is the CPF0001 message, but PDM has changed it to an informational message also. If you operate from PDM, you can get a distorted view of how messages will be sent to a CL program.

Exercise B CL Program Inquiry Message

In this exercise you will see what happens to a CL program when an error occurs that is not monitored for and the CL program inquiry message occurs.

1. Using PDM, create a source member named TRYINQMSG. Describe it as a CLP type program. Enter the following source:

```
PGM
CALL        PGM(ZZXX)
SNDPGMMSG   MSG('The program completed succesfully')
ENDPGM
```

2. Create the program.
3. Return to the command entry display. Enter the command:

```
CALL        PGM(TRYINQMSG)
```

Assuming your job is set to INQMSGRPY(*RQD), you should see the "Display Program Messages" display with a text of "CPF0001 received

Exercise B continued

Exercise B continued

by ... ." Put the cursor on the message and press the Help key. This is the CPA0701 Inquiry Message. Enter 'C' for cancel. You should see the CPF9999 Function check message displayed.

4. Press F10 to display the lower-level messages.

   You should see

CPD0170	Diagnostic	- Program not found
CPF0001	Escape	- Error on CALL command
CPA0701	Inquiry	- CPF0001 received ...
C		- Response
CPF9999	Escape	- Function check

5. Press F10 again and only the CPF9999 message should be displayed. F10 is a toggle between messages sent to QCMD and all messages caused by the command (including all messages from programs that were invoked because of the command).

6. Enter the command:

```
CALL       PGM(TRYINQMSG)
```

   When the inquiry display occurs, enter 'I' for ignore. You should see a message sent by program TRYINQMSG that the program completed successfully. Obviously, it did not. This demonstrates the risk you take in letting anyone answer the CPA0701 inquiry message. It is not easy to tell what the program is going to do; and in this case, it gives a very misleading answer.

7. Assuming you got the inquiry message, now change your job with the following command:

```
CHGJOB     INQMSGRPY(*DFT)
```

8. Enter the command:

```
CALL       PGM(TRYINQMSG)
```

   Instead of the inquiry message, you should now see the function check message. Setting the INQMSGRPY to *DFT causes the system to use the default for the CPA0701 message. Use F10 to display the low-level messages. You should see the same messages as before.

Exercise B continued

Exercise B continued

9. Enter the command:

```
DSPMSGD     RANGE(CPA0701)
```

Use the option to request a display of the message attributes. You may need to use the Roll-Up key, but eventually you will come to the attribute "Default reply." It should be 'C' for cancel. Since you had set your job attribute for INQMSGRPY(*DFT), the system used the default reply of the CPA0701 message.

10. Enter the command to submit TRYINQMSG to batch:

```
SBMJOB      JOB(INQMSG) CMD(CALL TRYINQMSG)
```

11. Assuming the batch job has INQMSGRPY(*RQD) set, the CPA0701 message should go to QSYSOPR. Use DSPMSG of QSYSOPR and answer the message with an 'I' for ignore. You should receive a message back to your workstation message queue that the job completed normally. Obviously, it did not.

12. Enter the command to submit TRYINQMSG to batch and request a default reply:

```
SBMJOB      JOB(INQMSG) CMD(CALL TRYINQMSG) +
            INQMSGRPY(*DFT)
```

13. You should have received a message that the job completed abnormally because the default was received for the inquiry message. There should be a job log for the job. Use WRKSPLF to find the job log and display it. You should see the same messages that you have seen on the command entry display. You don't have to specify INQMSGRPY(*DFT) for every batch job. You can specify it permanently in a job description object.

Exercise C Monitoring for Messages

In this exercise you will see what happens when the MONMSG command is used. The program will check a file for a member name that is passed into the program. If the member exists, it will be cleared. If the member does not exist, the member will be added.

1. Create a file in QTEMP with the command

```
CRTPF   FILE(QTEMP/TRYPFM) RCDLEN(50) MAXMBRS(50)
```

2. Use PDM and create a CLP type member named TRYMONMSG.
3. Enter the following source:

```
PGM         PARM(&MBR)
DCL         &MBR *CHAR LEN(10)
CHKOBJ      OBJ(QTEMP/TRYPFM) OBJTYPE(*FILE) +
            MBR(&MBR)
MONMSG      MSGID(CPF9815) EXEC(DO) /* Not found */
ADDPFM      FILE(QTEMP/TRYPFM) MBR(&MBR)
SNDPGMMSG   MSG('Member ' *CAT &MBR *TCAT ' was added')
RETURN
ENDDO       /* Not found */
                      /* Member already exists, clear it */
CLRPFM      FILE(QTEMP/TRYPFM) MBR(&MBR)
SNDPGMMSG   MSG('Member ' *CAT &MBR *TCAT ' was cleared')
ENDPGM
```

4. Create the program.
5. Call the program:

```
CALL  TRYMONMSG PARM(MBRA)
```

   You should see the message that MBRA was added.

6. Call the program again:

```
CALL  TRYMONMSG PARM(MBRA)
```

   You should see the message that MBRA was cleared.

7. Call the program again with MBRB:

```
CALL  TRYMONMSG PARM(MBRB)
```

   You should see the message that MBRB was added.

Exercise C continued

Exercise C continued

8. Press F10 for detailed messages.

   You should see the escape message CPF9815 when the member did not exist. This is what you monitored for. No message is sent when the member is found by CHKOBJ. You should see a completion message sent by the system when the member was added and when it was cleared. You should also see the messages that were sent from the program.

Exercise D Logging CL Program Information

In this exercise you will turn on CL logging to see how helpful it can be in looking for problems. Logging CL programs gives you more information about what the program is doing and it is a fairly effective debugging aid. The logging function does not cause all CL commands to be logged, but it can be very helpful.

1. Enter the command:

```
CHGJOB      LOGCLPGM(*YES)
```

2. Enter the command:

```
CALL        PGM(TRYMONMSG)
```

   If you still have F10 set to display low-level messages, you should see more information about what the program did. I use the logging function a lot. To save keystrokes in entering the command, a TAA tool exists in QUSRTOOL named LOGCL. It just invokes CHGJOB LOGCLPGM(*YES), but with fewer keystrokes. Prompt for LOGCL. If it is not on your system, you should consider creating it (see Appendix B, "QUSRTOOL").

Technical Tip

The LOGCL tool in QUSRTOOL is a good thing to try when you need more detail about what a program is doing.

CHAPTER 2

Sending Messages

The AS/400 lets you send messages to external message queues and to program message queues. Because sending a message to an external message queue (i.e., a queue that is external to the job, such as a workstation message queue, a user message queue, or the QSYSOPR message queue) is relatively simple to do, I will mostly bypass this subject. In CL programs, it is normal practice to send messages to and receive messages from program message queues and in this chapter I will concentrate on what I think is important about this aspect of CL programming.

When you send messages to a program message queue, you can do so in one of two ways: You can send a predefined message from a message file such as QCPFMSG, or you can send an impromptu message — a message for which you provide the text. Because I prefer to read the message text in the program source code rather than look up the message IDs to determine what the message text is, and because I write for English-reading users, I use impromptu messages most often. Most of the examples in this chapter, then, will illustrate the use of impromptu messages. (If I were going to write a program where messages were translated to a non-English language, I would use predefined messages.)

As you probably are aware, the system supports several different message types, but in my CL coding I predominantly send only three types: completion, escape, and status messages. In the following sections, you will find examples of sending each of these types of messages. In addition, the last section of the chapter will discuss how a batch job can send a message to the submitter of the job.

COMPLETION MESSAGES

I like to know what's happening when I work with the system. For example, if I enter a command and it works correctly, I like to see a message that tells me the function completed normally. Receiving this kind of information is not only helpful when I am working with the system interactively, but also when I am reviewing a job log.

I also like to provide feedback for a user operating from a menu. For instance, when (s)he chooses an option that does not cause a display to appear, I like to provide some feedback that the function worked properly (e.g., if a menu option submits a batch job, I would send a message to the display saying that the batch job was submitted;

the message should keep the operator from choosing the option again just to be sure it worked).

Technical Tip

Sending messages causes overhead. Don't get carried away, but do find a good balance between functionality and performance. A good use of messages is to provide feedback for users. For example, completion messages are helpful when users select an option that does not cause a screen to be displayed (e.g., selecting the SBMJOB command to submit a batch job).

It's easy to send a completion message. When you reach the point in your program where you are ready for the program to return normally, use the MSG parameter of the SNDPGMMSG (Send Program Message) command to send your message:

```
SNDPGMMSG  MSG('The XXX function completed +
                normally.') MSGTYPE(*COMP)
```

Note in the above code that I also use the SNDPGMMSG command's MSGTYPE parameter to specify that this is a completion (*COMP) message. I find it helpful, when reading the job log, to know specifically that a message I am looking at is a completion message. It tells me whether or not a particular command has worked properly. If I use the default (*INFO) for the MSGTYPE parameter, the job log will not provide as clear an audit trail as I would like. When you operate interactively, the system does not make it easy for you to distinguish between *COMP, *INFO, and *DIAG messages. For example, if you received a message while operating from a command entry display, you could determine the message type only by placing the cursor on the message and pressing the Help key. If you use good explanatory text in your completion message, you can provide a good audit trail in the job log.

Technical Tip

Be sure to specify MSGTYPE(*COMP) when you send a completion message. By specifying *COMP, you will find that the job log is more readable when you use it to diagnose problems.

By including variable information in the message, you can make the message as informative as possible. To create a good completion message, you will need to use the *CAT, *TCAT, and *BCAT concatenation operators extensively. Consider the following two examples:

```
SNDPGMMSG  MSG('The PRTDAILY job completed +
              normally using the ' *CAT &FILE *TCAT ' file.')  +
           MSGTYPE(*COMP)

SNDPGMMSG  MSG('The PRTDAILY job completed  +
              normally using member ' *CAT  +
              &MBR *TCAT ' from file ' *CAT +
              &FILE *TCAT ' in ' *CAT &LIB *TCAT '.')  +
           MSGTYPE(*COMP)
```

In the first example, the text would be presented in the job log as a completion message that states "The PRTDAILY job completed normally using the TUESDAY file." In the second example, the job log text would read "The PRTDAILY job completed normally using member MBR1 from file TUESDAY in library QGPL." Obviously, these examples assume that the values (e.g., TUESDAY) are first placed into the corresponding variables. In both instances, the messages give you a clear picture of the job's success.

Technical Tip

Try to place both the function name (e.g., PRTDAILY) and a variable name (e.g., &FILE) in the completion message. When you read the job log, the additional information provided helps clarify what happened.

Placing a Decimal Value in a Message

At times, you might want to include in your completion message a count of how many items were found or how many functions were performed. Unfortunately, impromptu messages don't lend themselves to stating the count clearly, because you can't concatenate a decimal value within the character string of message text. You have to convert the value to a character variable. Then your message might read "000025 objects were moved." But users would prefer an edited and more clearly stated message; for example, "25 objects were moved."

To solve this problem, you can use the EDTVAR (Edit Variable) command (a TAA tool in the QUSRTOOL library — see Appendix B for more information about QUSRTOOL). The EDTVAR command converts a decimal variable to a character variable and edits the data. To use the EDTVAR command, the character field to contain the edited number must be declared as *CHAR LEN(22) and the decimal field must be from 1 to 15 positions long with zero decimal positions. The character length of 22 will handle the largest number of editing characters (e.g., period, comma, hyphen) that the EDTVAR command can add to a 15-digit field.

An option on the EDTVAR command lets you specify where to place a decimal point, if there is one. After the EDTVAR command performs its function, the value is left-adjusted in the character field. You just trim off the trailing blanks with a *TCAT operation. The following code illustrates use of the EDTVAR command:

```
DCL          &COUNT *DEC LEN(5 Ø)
DCL          &COUNTA *CHAR LEN(22)
 .           /* Your code to process */
 .
CHGVAR       &COUNT (&COUNT + 1)
 .
 .
EDTVAR       CHROUT(&COUNTA) NUMINP(&COUNT)
SNDPGMMSG    MSG(&COUNTA *TCAT ' were found ..') MSGTYPE(*COMP)
```

Before trying to use EDTVAR, prompt for the command to see whether it exists on your system. If it does not exist, you should consider creating it. If you would like to see a complete example using EDTVAR, look at the code for the CHGLIBOWN (Change Library Owner) command in QUSRTOOL. To view the code, display the member TAALIBBC in source file QUSRTOOL/QATTCL.

Technical Tip

The EDTVAR command available in QUSRTOOL is very handy for creating a clear and understandable message when you want to include a decimal value.

Escape Messages

The AS/400 is designed so that an escape message is sent when a function does not work. If you write a function that doesn't work (i.e., the task was not completed successfully), you generally want to follow the system convention and send an escape message: You can't count on anyone reading a job log, reading an information type message, or properly handling a return code to determine that the function you provided did not work.

Technical Tip

If a function you write does not work, send an escape message. Sending an escape message is the best way to ensure that someone will know a problem exists.

Here are five important points you should remember when you want to send an escape message:

- You must send an escape message via the SNDPGMMSG command; you cannot use the SNDMSG command.
- You must specify MSGTYPE(*ESCAPE) on the SNDPGMMSG command.
- You don't have to do a RETURN or end your program after you send an escape message. The system automatically ends the program as soon as the escape message is sent. The next CL command in your program will not be executed.
- Normally, you take the default (*PRV) on the TOPGMQ parameter of the SNDPGMMSG command and send the escape message to the program message queue of the program that called your program. In message-handling terminology, the program that called your program is known as the "previous program." Consider the following example:

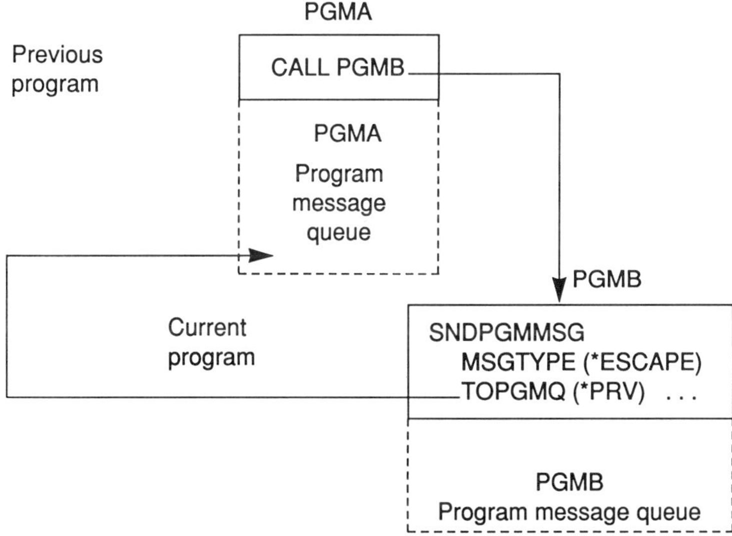

In this example, program PGMB is the current program (i.e., the program at the bottom of the program stack that is executing). Program PGMB would send an escape message to the message queue of the previous program (program PGMA in this example) — that is, the program that called your program and is above your program in the program stack.

- You cannot send an impromptu message as an escape message. An escape message must have a unique message ID and the message must exist in a message file. To send an escape message, you must use the MSGID parameter (not the MSG parameter) on the SNDPGMMSG command. The command would look like this:

  ```
  SNDPGMMSG  MSGID(xxxxxxx) MSGF(yyyyyyy) MSGTYPE(*ESCAPE) ...
  ```

  where xxxxxxx is the MSGID and yyyyyyy is the message file name containing the message description (e.g., message ID CPF9801 in message file QCPFMSG).

The text of an escape message should be as clear as possible, but this isn't as easy to do as it might appear. Messages often can appear out of context. For example, when a user reads a message text, (s)he might not know which program it came from. Messages often can be "bubbled up," the technique I use in my standard error-handling routine (see Chapter 4), where the previous program may resend an escape message to its previous program. To be certain that the message text is clear, you have to put yourself in the place of the user who will read your message.

To add clarity in my escape messages, I like to include the function name in the description of the escape message. For example,

```
SNDPGMMSG  MSGID(CPF9898) MSGF(QCPFMSG) MSGTYPE(*ESCAPE) +
           MSGDTA('Program PGMB requires +
                 the CLEAR parameter to be *YES or *NO')
```

Technical Tip

When you send an escape message, it is good practice to include the name of your program or function in the text. Messages can often appear out of context or be "bubbled up," and when they are, the function name can add clarity.

When you name an object or member in your message text, you want to be as clear as possible about which one you are describing. Two upcoming sections, "Using a Library Name in the Message Text" and "Using a Member Name in the Message Text," provide examples.

Using Message ID CPF9898

Although you cannot send an impromptu message as an escape message, you can get the effect of an impromptu message by using message ID CPF9898. This works well for general error conditions that the previous program would normally not monitor for. For instance, let's say your program accepts a *YES/*NO value as a parameter. If a user calls your program and passes a value of XXXX, your program should send an escape message saying the value must be *YES or *NO.

When you use CPF9898, you can place any character data you want in the MSGDTA parameter of the SNDPGMMSG command and use the concatenation operators to create the message you want. For example, the following code,

```
SNDPGMMSG  MSGID(CPF9898) MSGF(QCPFMSG) MSGTYPE(*ESCAPE)  +
           MSGDTA('File ' *CAT &FILE *TCAT ' cannot be found')
```

will result in an escape message that might say "File FILEX cannot be found." The message would be sent to the previous program's message queue. Note that when you use CPF9898, no specific second-level message text is available for the user. You are limited to 512 bytes of first-level message text.

Technical Tip

Message ID CPF9898 in message file QCPFMSG works very well for sending an impromptu escape message when the previous program does not normally monitor for the specific condition and the user does not need a second level of message text.

When Not to Use CPF9898

Within a complex CL program, several conditions could warrant sending an escape message from the current program to the previous program's message queue. If the current program sends message ID CPF9898 to the previous program in several different situations, the ambiguity created will make it difficult for the current program to handle the error correctly. Because of this, you must be careful not to overuse CPF9898.

For example, assume your program

- accepts a parameter that should be *YES or *NO
- should fail if no records exist in a file

In either situation, you will want to send an escape message, but you may not want to send CPF9898 for both situations.

In some cases within the current program, you may have a specific error condition that the previous program might monitor for. For example, assume your program performs a function that doesn't make sense if there are no records in a file. You want to send an escape message if no records exist, but this is a case where the previous program may want to monitor for this condition. Depending on how the previous program is using your function, the "no records" exception may not be an error to the previous program.

In this instance, the solution is to have a unique message ID that can be sent for each specific error condition that may be handled separately in the previous program. I generally use CPF9898 when I don't expect the previous program to monitor for the error condition. I use a different message ID when I think the previous program might monitor for the error condition. If you expect the previous program might monitor for your escape message, the message ID you send should at least be unique to your program.

Although the system provides no other message like CPF9898, you can find similar message IDs in the QUSRTOOL TAA tools. The CPF9898-like messages are located in message file TAAMSGF in library TAATOOL (if TAAMSGF does not already exist on your system, see Appendix B). The available message IDs are TAA9891, TAA9892, ..., TAA9897. To use message ID TAA9891, for example, you would code

```
SNDPGMMSG  MSGID(TAA9891) MSGF(TAA/TAAMSGF) MSGTYPE(*ESCAPE) +
           MSGDTA('File ' *CAT &FILE *TCAT ' cannot be found')
```

The previous program could monitor for message ID TAA9891 as it would for any escape message:

```
CALL     PGM(PGMB)
MONMSG   MSGID(TAA9891) EXEC(DO)
```

Note that when you monitor for the escape message, you name only the message ID. You don't describe the message file that contains the message.

Technical Tip

If CPF9898 is ambiguous (meaning it could signal one of several problems in the current program) and you want to monitor for the specific error, consider using one of the TAA tool message IDs that have the same format as CPF9898.

You also should not use CPF9898 when you really do need to provide second-level message text with the message. If you are sending a message to a user and the first-level text is not very clear, adding a message to a message file and allowing the user access to second-level message text may be a better solution.

Using a Library Name in the Message Text

The library list function offers significant advantages on an AS/400, but if there are multiple objects of the same name in different libraries and an error occurs, program error messages could potentially be confusing. For example, if you use the library list to search for an object, and the object is not found, sending a message that says something like "Object xxxx not found using *LIBL" usually is sufficient. If, however, the object is found but a problem still exists, your message should say more than "Object xxxx in *LIBL cannot be cleared." That is, you would want the message to tell the user in which library the problem object exists.

Here's how to provide a more meaningful message: After you find the object using the library list function, use the RTNLIB parameter of the RTVOBJD (Retrieve Object Description) command to determine the library name in which the object was found. You can use the same variable name for the actual library used to store the original value of *LIBL:

```
DCL         &LIB *CHAR LEN(10)
 .
 .
 .
IF          (&LIB *EQ '*LIBL') DO /* *LIBL used */
RTVOBJD     OBJ(xxx) OBJTYPE(*FILE) RTNLIB(&LIB)
ENDDO       /* *LIBL used */
```

Note that the code executes the RTVOBJD command only if *LIBL is specified as the &LIB variable.

Technical Tip

When you find an object on the library list, but still need to send an escape message, use the actual library name in the message. Use the RTVOBJD command to retrieve the name of the actual library.

Using a Member Name in the Message Text

If you use files that contain more than one member, it is typical to provide a default of *FIRST for the member name when you provide a command prompt. If you do, you have the same ambiguity problem in your message as in the previous example (specifying *LIBL for the library name). But you also have a similar solution: You can use the RTNMBR parameter of the RTVMBRD (Retrieve Member Description) command to determine the name of the member causing an error. Again, you can use the same variable name for the actual member name returned:

```
DCL        &MBR *CHAR LEN(10)
.
.
.
IF         (&MBR *EQ '*FIRST') DO /* *FIRST used */
RTVMBRD    FILE(xxx) MBR(&MBR) RTNMBR(&MBR)
ENDDO      /* *FIRST used */
```

Note that the code executes the RTVMBRD command only if *FIRST is specified as the member name.

Technical Tip

When you find a member in a file using a default of *FIRST, but still need to send an escape message, use the actual member name in the message. Use the RTVMBRD command to retrieve the actual member.

Resending an IBM Message

In most cases, the program you are writing will become a "middle man" in the program stack. For example, if you execute the CHKOBJ command in your program, an IBM program comes into the program stack as the current program. It is the command processing program (CPP) for the CHKOBJ command. When the CHKOBJ CPP is in the program stack, it will send an escape message if the object is not found. The message is sent to TOPGMQ(*PRV), which is now your program's message queue. The following diagram illustrates the sequence of events that occur:

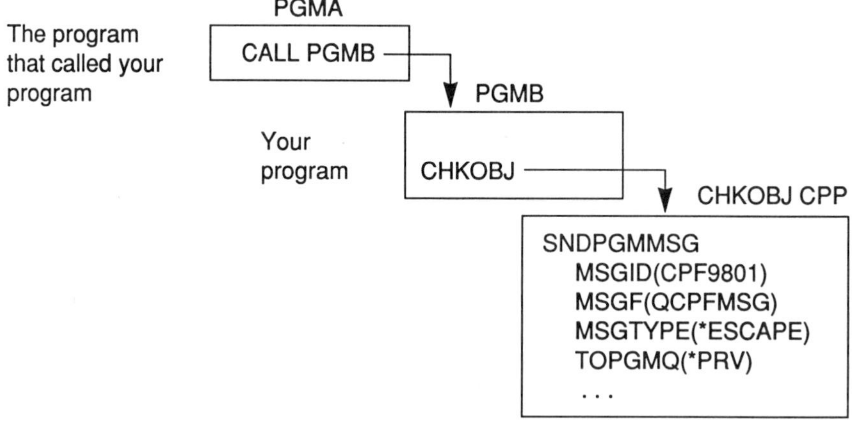

Sometimes you just want to resend the escape message you received from the program, and you want to resend it to the previous program (PGMA in this example). This is not as simple as it might appear because to do it correctly means that you have to define some variables and specify the right parameters. By doing it correctly, I mean that the previous program will receive the same message that was sent to your program. Here is the code I use:

```
DCL       &MSGID     *CHAR  LEN(7)
DCL       &MSGDTA    *CHAR  LEN(512)
DCL       &MSGF      *CHAR  LEN(10)
DCL       &MSGFL     *CHAR  LEN(10)
.
.
.
CHKOBJ    OBJ(&OBJ)  OBJTYPE(*FILE)
MONMSG    MSGID(CPF9801)  EXEC(DO) /* Not found */
RCVMSG    MSGTYPE(*EXCP)  MSGID(&MSGID)       +
          MSGDTA(&MSGDTA)  MSGF(&MSGF) SNDMSGFLIB(&MSGFL)
SNDPGMMSG MSGID(&MSGID)  MSGF(&MSGFL/&MSGF)   +
          MSGDTA(&MSGDTA)  MSGTYPE(*ESCAPE)
ENDDO     /*Not found */
```

In this example, the message you receive with the RCVMSG command will be removed from your program message queue because I took the default (*YES) for the RMV parameter. You might choose to specify RMV(*NO) on the RCVMSG command to keep the message in your program message queue.

Sometimes the message you receive from an IBM command may not say what you want to say in your escape message. For example, the object that is "not found" by the CHKOBJ command may be some internal object to your application that will have no meaning for a user. You can easily send your own message text by coding

```
CHKOBJ    OBJ(PAY135P) OBJTYPE(*FILE)
MONMSG    MSGID(CPF9801) EXEC(DO) /* Not found */
SNDPGMMSG MSGID(CPF9898) MSFG(QCPFMSG) MSGTYPE(*ESCAPE) +
          MSGDTA('Program PGMB did not find +
                the Payroll entry file. Was +
                the Payroll Edit function run?')
ENDDO     /* Not found */
```

Status Messages

Status messages are the messages that wink at you from the bottom of a display when you run certain functions. They are designed to inform you that progress is being made, and they are a good way to tell an end user that a program is doing something worthwhile when the response time will be lengthy. Many system commands (e.g., CPYF, CPYSPLF, OPNQRYF) send status messages. If one of these commands is executed in a CL program, the user will see the status message by default. You don't want to send a status message that will last for such a short duration that a user doesn't have time to read it. This can be more frustrating than seeing no message, so be sure the message is displayed so the user has ample time to read it.

Technical Tip

Send a status message when you have a long-running function so the user knows the program is progressing. And be sure your status message will appear on the display long enough for the user to read it.

How Status Messages Work

Status messages are sent as a special type (*STATUS) to an executing job's external message queue (*EXT). (A job's external message queue, which is temporary, should not be confused with message queues that are external to the job, such as QSYSOPR or workstation message queues.) The AS/400 automatically creates an external message queue for a job when that job starts.

Only one status message at a time can be displayed. When a status message is sent to the external message queue of an interactive job, the system places it on the message line of the display (usually line 24 for 24 X 80 displays). To clear the current status message from the display, you must do one of the following:

- Use one of the IBM commands that sends a new status message (e.g., CPYF).
- Send another status message.
- Send a blank status message. You would use message CPI9801 in message file QCPFMSG for this purpose. CPI9801 contains no message data; blanks are sent to the display.
- Return to a command entry display. The status line is automatically cleared. (Note that the message is not cleared when the CL program that sends it does a return.)

Here are the important things to remember about a status message:

- All *STATUS messages must be predefined as messages in a message file (they cannot be impromptu messages); however, remember that message ID CPF9898 can give you the effect of using an impromptu message.
- A status message must be sent to a job's external message queue by using the SNDPGMMSG command with the parameters TOPGMQ(*EXT) and MSGTYPE(*STATUS).
- If your program sends a status message, it should also get rid of it. (See the previous discussion about removing status messages from the display.)
- You don't have to worry about what happens if status messages are sent during a batch job; the system ignores them.
- A status message never appears in the job log.
- The system allows you to shut off status messages (described in the following section).
- No help text is available to help you determine the message ID of a status message (i.e., you can't place the cursor on a status message and request help).

As an example of using status messages, here is how you would send a status message stating that an outfile is being created:

```
SNDPGMMSG  MSGID(CPF9898) MSGF(QCPFMSG)  +
           TOPGMQ(*EXT) MSGTYPE(*STATUS) +
           MSGDTA('DSPOBJD outfile being created')
DSPOBJD    ... OUTFILE(QTEMP/DSPOBJDP)
SNDPGMMSG  MSGID(CPI9801) MSGF(QCPFMSG)  +
           TOPGMQ(*EXT) MSGTYPE(*STATUS)
```

Note that the program sends message CPI9801 after the function is complete to blank out the previous status message.

Technical Tip

If you send a status message and then want to remove it, you can send message ID CPI9801 to blank out the status message line.

Preventing Status Messages from Being Displayed

You may have a CL program that performs a CPYF or OPNQRYF command for the user. If you want to prevent the user from seeing the status message because it may be confusing, the system supports a job attribute (STSMSG) that lets you do this. Here's what you should do in your code:

- Use the RTVJOBA command to save the current STSMSG value.
- Use the CHGJOB command to set the STSMSG job attribute to *NONE.
- Perform the function that sends a status message.
- Use the CHGJOB command to set the STSMSG job attribute to the saved value (i.e., restore STSMSG to its earlier value).

Your code should look like this:

```
DCL         &STSMSG *CHAR LEN(7)
 .
 .
 .
RTVJOBA     STSMSG(&STSMSG)
CHGJOB      STSMSG(*NONE)
CPYF          ....
CHGJOB      STSMSG(&STSMSG)
```

Technical Tip

You should not stop at changing the value of STSMSG to control it. Save the current value, change it, and then restore it to the saved value when needed.

Sending a Message to the Submitter of a Job

When a batch job ends, the system (by default) sends a message to the submitter of the job. The message goes to the user's message queue (not the workstation message queue). The messages of this type are

- CPF1241 Job completed normally
- CPF1240 Job completed abnormally

When a job completes abnormally, the only information provided is that it failed. The user must look at the job log to determine exactly what happened. To save the user time, you can send a message to the user's message queue that explains why the program ended abnormally, and then end the job. The system will let you retrieve the message queue name and its corresponding library for the user who submitted the job. To send a message to a user's message queue, you would code

```
DCL         &SBMMSGQ *CHAR LEN(10) /* Message queue of +
            submitting user */
DCL         &SBMMSGQL *CHAR LEN(10) /* Message queue library */
  .
  .
  .
RTVJOBA     SBMMSGQ(&SBMMSGQ) SBMMSGQLIB(&SBMMSGQL)
SNDPGMMSG   MSG('File A must exist for PRTDAILY to work.')  +
            TOMSGQ(&SBMMSGQL/&SBMMSGQ)
```

If a batch job completes normally, you might want to send a message that reminds the user of some action (s)he is to take. For example, the user might need to view the results in a spooled file.

Technical Tip

Sending messages from a batch job to the job's submitter can be useful: You can explain why a job ended abnormally or remind the user to take a specific action.

A TAA tool (the SNDMSGSBM command) available in the QUSRTOOL library can make it easier for you to send messages from a batch job to a user's message queue. If you use the SNDMSGSBM command for the above example, you would simply code

```
SNDMSGSBM  MSG('File A must exist for PRTDAILY to work.')
```

The SNDMSGSBM command automatically adds the job name when the message is sent. This is important because there may be several messages in the user's message queue. The message would look like this:

```
From job XXXXXXX - File A must exist for PRTDAILY to work.
```

Note that you don't need any DCL or RTVJOBA statements, and you don't have to tell the message where to go. The SNDMSGSBM command provides a shorthand method for what you would have to code otherwise.

Exercise A Simple Completion Messages

In this exercise we will look at simple completion messages and how they might appear in the job log.

1. Enter the following command to access the command entry display:

   ```
   CALL  QCMD
   ```

2. Enter the following command to create a data area:

   ```
   CRTDTAARA  DTAARA(QTEMP/XXXXX) TYPE(*CHAR) LEN(10)
   ```

   You should see a completion message saying that the data area was created in QTEMP.

3. Place the cursor on the message and press the Help key.

   The help text should tell you that you are looking at message CPC0904 and that it was sent as a completion message.

4. Using PDM, create a source member named TRYCMPMSG with source type CLP. Then enter the following source:

   ```
   PGM        PARM(&FILE)
   DCL        &FILE *CHAR LEN(10)
   SNDPGMMSG  MSG('The function XXX completed successfully +
                 for the ' *CAT &FILE *TCAT ' file.')      +
              MSGTYPE(*COMP)
   ENDPGM
   ```

Technical Tip

I normally don't use the command prompter for many of the commands because I can key faster into the SEU display. If you use the prompter, entering the MSG parameter of the SNDPGMMSG command can be a challenge because of the way the prompter operates on apostrophes. The prompter tends to double up apostrophes when it returns to SEU. You can avoid this by entering parentheses when the prompt is displayed. Start the MSG parameter with a left parenthesis. Then key the text and apostrophes you want. Close the MSG parameter with a right parenthesis and you'll get what you want in SEU.

5. Create the program.

Exercise A continued

Exercise A continued

6. Return to the command entry display. Enter the command:

```
CALL  PGM(TRYCMPMSG) PARM(FILEA)
```

   You should see the completion message sent by your program. Place the cursor on the message and press the Help key. The message type should be COMPLETION. The TRYCMPMSG program should have sent the message (the From program). If you see that the message is not a COMPLETION type and that it was not sent by TRYCMPMSG, you are not on the command entry display. If you operate from PDM or some other display, you will get a distorted view of messages. The command entry display can be accessed by doing a call to QCMD.

7. Submit the program to batch with the command

```
SBMJOB  JOB(TRYCMPMSG) CMD(CALL TRYCMPMSG PARM(FILEA)) +
          LOG(4 Ø *SECLVL)
```

8. When the job completes, look at the job log (use the WRKSPLF command). The job log should include your completion message. Note the difference between the type of message as it appears in the job log. Specifying MSGTYPE(*COMP) can assist you in working with a job log.

Exercise B Using a Count in a Completion Message

In this exercise we will use the TAA tool EDTVAR in QUSRTOOL to edit a count field. You will need to ensure that the tool exists on your system. Prompt for the EDTVAR command. If it is not found, see Appendix B.

1. Using PDM, create a CLP source member named TRYEDTVAR. In this example, a decimal variable will be given a value of 25 to exercise the use of EDTVAR. Enter the following source:

```
PGM
DCL          &COUNT *DEC LEN(5 0)
DCL          &COUNTA *CHAR LEN(22)
CHGVAR       &COUNT 25
EDTVAR       CHROUT(&COUNTA) NUMINP(&COUNT)
SNDPGMMSG    MSG(&COUNTA *TCAT ' of these things were found.') +
             MSGTYPE(*COMP)
ENDPGM
```

2. Create the program.
3. Return to the command entry display. Enter the command:

```
CALL  PGM(KTRYEDTVAR)
```

You should see the completion message you sent with the edited value.

Exercise C Sending Basic Escape Messages

In this exercise we will experiment with message ID CPF9898, first sending it without specifying MSGTYPE, then sending it with MSGTYPE specified as *ESCAPE.

1. Use PDM to create a CLP member named TRYMSG1. Enter the following source:

```
PGM
SNDPGMMSG    MSGID(CPF9898) MSGF(QCPFMSG)      +
             MSGDTA('You need to create FILEA first')
ENDPGM
```

Exercise C continued

Exercise C continued

2. Create the program.
3. Using the command entry display, call the program:

```
CALL  TRYMSG1
```

You should see the message you just sent. Use the Help key to look at the Additional Message Information display. You should see that the message type is informational because the default was taken for MSGTYPE.

4. Use PDM to create a CLP member named TRYMSG2. Enter the following source:

```
PGM
CALL        TRYMSG1
SNDPGMMSG   MSG('TRYMSG2 worked great.') MSGTYPE(*COMP)
ENDPGM
```

5. Create the program.
6. Using the command entry display, call the program:

```
CALL  TRYMSG2
```

If you are excluding detail messages, you should see only the message "TRYMSG2 worked great."

7. Press F10 to see detail messages.

You should see the informational message sent by program TRYMSG1 indicating that a problem has occurred. Because a user would have to look for this error message, I doubt that it will be seen.

8. Use PDM to modify TRYMSG1 (the first program). Add the MSGTYPE(*ESCAPE) parameter to the SNDPGMMSG command. It should look like this:

```
PGM
SNDPGMMSG   MSGID(CPF9898) MSGF(QCPFMSG) MSGTYPE(*ESCAPE)  +
            MSGDTA('You need to create FILEA first')
ENDPGM
```

9. Create the program.

Exercise C continued

Exercise C continued

10. Using the command entry display, call the program:

    ```
    CALL  TRYMSG1
    ```

    The message should look the same as the first time it was sent. Note that the command is left on the command line. This is your indication that an escape message has been sent.

11. Display the details of the message.

    You should see that it is now type (*ESCAPE).

12. Now call the second program:

    ```
    CALL  TRYMSG2
    ```

    Since TRYMSG2 did not handle the escape message sent by TRYMSG1, you should see the function check message (CPF9999). If you use F10 to display detail messages, you should see the escape message that was sent. You should not see the message, "TRYMSG2 worked great," because program TRYMSG2 abnormally terminated before sending the completion message.

Exercise D Sending Escape Messages with Variables

In this exercise we will use message ID CPF9898 and construct a better-looking escape message that includes variables.

1. Use PDM to create a CLP member named TRYESCMSG. The program will use CPF9898 and concatenate some variable names with some literal text for the MSGDTA parameter of SNDPGMMSG. Enter the following source:

```
PGM          PARM(&FILE &MBR)
DCL          &FILE *CHAR LEN(10)
DCL          &MBR *CHAR LEN(10)
SNDPGMMSG    MSGID(CPF9898) MSGF(QCPFMSG)        +
             MSGDTA('Member ' *CAT &MBR *TCAT   +
                   ' must exist in file ' *CAT +
                   &FILE *TCAT ' to use this program')
ENDPGM
```

Exercise D continued

Exercise D continued

2. Create the program.
3. Using the command entry display, call the program:

```
CALL  TRYESCMSG PARM(FILEA MBR2)
```

You should see the message you just sent with concatenated values defined in the MSGDTA parameter. You have to ensure the proper use of *TCAT, *CAT, *BCAT, and blanks to get the text to read properly. It takes some practice to get good at it. Note that a period has appeared at the end of the message text even though there isn't one in your source. The ending period is caused by the fact that the CPF9898 message is coded with a first-level text of '&1.'. It is the period in the message that is added to your replacement text. When you resend an escape message using MSGID CPF9898, you can often have two periods on the end of it because of the embedded period. To avoid this problem, you could use message ID CPF9897, a blank message that does not have an embedded period.

Exercise E Sending a Status Message

In this exercise we will send a status message and blank it out.

1. Use PDM to create a CLP member named TRYSTSMSG. Enter the following source:

```
PGM
SNDPGMMSG MSGID(CPF9898) MSGF(QCPFMSG)  +
          TOPGMQ(*EXT) MSGTYPE(*STATUS) +
          MSGDTA('DSPOBJD outfile being created')
DSPOBJD   OBJ(QGPL/*ALL) OBJTYPE(*JOBD) OUTPUT(*OUTFILE)  +
          OUTFILE(QTEMP/DSPOBJDP)
SNDPGMMSG MSGID(CPI9801) MSGF(QCPFMSG) TOPGMQ(*EXT) +
          MSGTYPE(*STATUS)
ENDPGM
```

2. Create the program.

Exercise E continued

Exercise E continued

3. Using the command entry display, call the program:

```
CALL   TRYSTSMSG
```

You should see the status message appear and then be blanked out. If you don't see the status message, use the CHGJOB command to check the current setting of your job. The job attribute STSMSG should be *NORMAL to test this program.

Exercise F Shutting Off Status Messages

In this exercise we will see how to prevent a status message from appearing to a user.

1. Use PDM to create a CLP member named TRYSTSMSG2. In the first test, we will use a CPYF command, which will cause a status message to be sent during its execution. The following code assumes that you have run the previous exercise, and that file DSPOBJDP still exists in library QTEMP. Enter the following source:

```
PGM
DLTF     FILE(QTEMP/DSPOBJDP2)
MONMSG   MSGID(CPF2105) /* Ignore not found */
CPYF     FROMFILE(QTEMP/DSPOBJDP)  +
         TOFILE(QTEMP/DSPOBJDP2) CRTFILE(*YES)
ENDPGM
```

2. Create the program.
3. Using the command entry display, call the program:

```
CALL   TRYSTSMSG2
```

You should see the CPYF status message appear and then be blanked out.

4. Now modify program TRYSTSMSG2 to prevent the status message from appearing:

Exercise F continued

Exercise F continued

```
PGM
DCL      &STSMSG *CHAR LEN(7)
DLTF     FILE(QTEMP/DSPOBJDP2)
MONMSG   MSGID(CPF2105) /* Ignore not found */
RTVJOBA  STSMSG(&STSMSG)
CHGJOB   STSMSG(*NONE)
CPYF     FROMFILE(QTEMP/DSPOBJDP)  +
         TOFILE(QTEMP/DSPOBJDP2) CRTFILE(*YES)
CHGJOB   STSMSG(&STSMSG)
ENDPGM
```

5. Create the program.
6. Using the command entry display, call the program:

   ```
   CALL  TRYSTSMSG2
   ```

   You should not see a status message.
7. Using the command entry display, call the program created earlier in this exercise.

   ```
   CALL  TRYSTSMSG
   ```

   If you correctly reset the status attribute, you should see the first status message again.

Exercise G Sending a Message to a Job's Submitter

In this exercise we will send a message to the submitter of a batch job. For this program, you will need SNDMSGSBM (a TAA tool in QUSRTOOL). Prompt for SNDMSGSBM. If it does not exist in the TAATOOL library, see Appendix B.

1. Use PDM to create a CLP member named TRYSBMMSG. Enter the following source:

```
PGM
SNDMSGSBM    MSG('Remember to call home with +
               the results of this job')
ENDPGM
```

2. Create the program.
3. Using the command entry display, submit a job:

```
SBMJOB  JOB(SBMMSG) CMD(CALL TRYSBMMSG)
```

   When the job completes, you should see both the message you sent and the CPF1241 completion message in your user message queue.

CHAPTER 3

Receiving Messages

Every time a program is called on the AS/400, the system automatically creates a program message queue for the program. Program message queues are used, among other things, to pass messages between programs on the program stack. Typically, a program lower in the program stack will send a message or messages to the message queue of the program that called it. It does this to communicate information such as whether the called program completed normally or abnormally. If the called program completes normally, it will many times send a completion (*COMP) message to the previous program's message queue. For instances where the called program failed, an escape (*ESCAPE) message is sent to the previous program's message queue. The calling program can then receive the message sent from the lower-level program and take the appropriate action.

A CL program, by its very nature, calls many different programs. CL programs are made up of CL commands, and whenever you execute most CL commands, it causes a command processing program (CPP) to be called. Any of these CPPs, and any programs invoked with the CL CALL command, can send messages to your CL program's message queue. It is perfectly normal for several messages to exist in your program message queue. Messages arriving on your program's message queue are placed into the queue based on their order of arrival, as shown in the following figure:

Program Message Queue

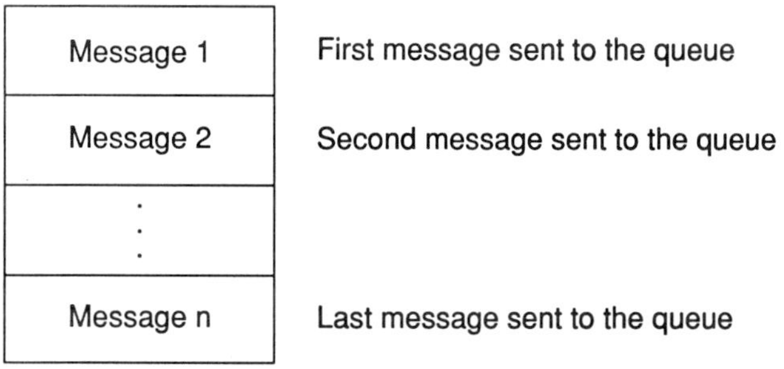

Message 1	First message sent to the queue
Message 2	Second message sent to the queue
. . .	
Message n	Last message sent to the queue

An individual message in a message queue consists of several pieces of information. First, a message key uniquely identifies the message on the queue. Then, several other fields contain information such as the message

ID (e.g., CPF9898), the message file of the message (e.g., QCPFMSG), the message type (e.g., *COMP), the message data used when the message was sent, and information regarding the sender of the message.

In this chapter, I will deal with processing the messages on a program message queue using the RCVMSG command. This command allows your CL program to read messages from the queue, and then take the appropriate action. First, I will deal generally with how to receive messages. Then I will offer more details about how to remove messages, resend messages, and extract message data from the messages.

How To Receive Messages

When you want to receive a message from your program's message queue, you use the RCVMSG command and accept the default PGMQ(*SAME). However, remember that there can be several messages in your program's message queue; you have to know which one you want.

Receiving the Last Message

One way to keep the RCVMSG command simple is to direct your actions to receiving the last message that arrived in your program message queue. Remember that when a new message is sent to your message queue, it goes on the "bottom" of the stack. While there are many reasons why you might want to receive the last message on the queue, a typical use of the function is to receive completion (*COMP) messages. To receive the last message on a queue, you specify the RCVMSG command with the parameter MSGTYPE(*LAST). What I typically want is the completion message associated with a command I just executed, such as the SBMJOB command shown here:

```
SBMJOB  ...
RCVMSG  MSGTYPE(*LAST) ...
```

Here are my two fail-safe rules for receiving the last message when it is a completion message you are looking for (if you don't follow these rules, you will have to know a lot more about message-handling):

- You must know that the command you executed will cause a completion message to be sent to your program. Normally, you would try the command and see what you get. Be sure to place the cursor on the message and press the Help key to determine that you are really looking at a completion message. The SBMJOB command always sends a completion message if it works successfully.
- You must immediately follow the command that causes a completion message to be sent with RCVMSG MSGTYPE(*LAST). Don't use

MSGTYPE(*COMP) because you would be asking the system's message-handler to give you the completion messages in FIFO (first in, first out) order. If other completion messages exist in the program's message queue, you will not get the one you want.'

Technical Tip

The simplest solution for receiving a completion message is to ensure the command is sending one and then immediately follow the command with RCVMSG MSGTYPE(*LAST).

Receiving Messages by Message Type

In most of my coding, I am interested only in receiving two types of messages: escape messages and completion messages. There is a way to receive the others (e.g., information and diagnostic messages), but I will show you that later.

For escape messages, you specify (*EXCP) on the MSGTYPE parameter of the RCVMSG command. You are actually requesting "exception type" messages. If you follow a MONMSG with a request to receive a message with MSGTYPE(*EXCP), you can be assured that you are going to receive an escape message. Not only will it be an escape message, but it will also be the one that caused your MONMSG command to be executed. For example, if you code

```
CHKOBJ  ...
MONMSG  MSGID(CPF9801) EXEC(DO) /* Not found */
RCVMSG  MSGTYPE(*EXCP) ...
```

you will receive the escape message CPF9801 that was sent by the CHKOBJ command.

When you request MSGTYPE(*EXCP), the system looks for the last exception message sent to your program message queue (it uses LIFO — last in, first out — order). You could have several escape messages in your program message queue, but you will receive the one that caused the problem on the command just executed.

The RCVMSG command lets you retrieve information about the message you receive. Thus, if you code

```
DCL      *MSGID *CHAR LEN(7)
.
.
.
CHKOBJ   ...
MONMSG   MSGID(CPF9801) EXEC(DO) /* Not found */
RCVMSG   MSGTYPE(*EXCP) MSGID(&MSGID)
```

the &MSGID variable will contain the message ID of the message received (i.e., CPF9801). It might seem silly to retrieve what you asked for, but it is very normal to code this way. If you want to resend the same message, you can use standard code to both receive and resend the message (examples later in this chapter show you how).

Technical Tip

When you want to receive an escape message generated by a command or a called program, you need to use MONMSG and follow it with RCVMSG MSGTYPE(*EXCP). If you do this, you can be sure of receiving the message that caused the exception.

Many IBM commands will send either an escape message or a completion message. If you wanted to receive both, you would specify

```
SBMJOB   ...
MONMSG   MSGID(CPF0000) EXEC(DO) /* Failed */
RCVMSG   MSGTYPE(*EXCP) MSGID(&MSGID) ...
.
.        /* Your error-handling code */
.
ENDDO    /* SBMJOB failed */
         /* Command worked. Get completion */
RCVMSG   MSGTYPE(*LAST)
```

Now that you understand what "last message" means, let me show you the simple things I do with the last message.

Receiving a Message To Remove It

If you want to remove a message from your program message queue, you simply accept the default (*YES) for the RMV parameter of the RCVMSG command. If you don't remove a message, it will appear in the job log for the job. In Chapter 5 I discuss why I like to keep the job log clean. The two typical things I code are

To remove an escape message:

```
CHKOBJ   ...
MONMSG   MSGID(CPF9801) EXEC(DO) /* Not found */
RCVMSG   MSGTYPE(*EXCP) /* Remove the message */
```

To remove a completion message:

```
SBMJOB   ...
RCVMSG   MSGTYPE(*LAST) /* Remove the message */
```

There are other ways to remove messages from your job log (see Chapter 5, "The Job Log").

Receiving a Message To Resend It

Sometimes, you just want to resend the same message you receive to the previous program (the program that called your program). For example, if you need an object and it doesn't exist, you may want to resend the CHKOBJ escape message that was sent to your program to the previous program. This is called "bubbling up" the message. Here is the code I use to resend an escape message:

```
DCL        &MSGID    *CHAR LEN(7)
DCL        &MSGDTA   *CHAR LEN(512)
DCL        &MSGF     *CHAR LEN(10)
DCL        &MSGFLIB  *CHAR LEN(10)
.
.
.
CHKOBJ     ...
MONMSG     MSGID(CPF9801) EXEC(DO) /* Not found */
RCVMSG     MSTYPE(*EXCP) MSGDTA(&MSGDTA)          +
               MSGID(&MSGID) MSGF(&MSGF) SNDMSGFLIB(&MSGFLIB)
SNDPGMMSG  MSGID(&MSGID) MSGF(&MSGFLIB/&MSGF)     +
               MSGDTA(&MSGDTA) MSGTYPE(*ESCAPE)
ENDDO      /* Not found */
```

The code shown can be used in any CL program; just copy it whenever you want to resend an escape message. This may seem like a lot of code, but it is what you need to do to resend the message correctly. By "correctly" I mean that the code is going to work in almost all conditions and that the previous program is going to get a duplicate of what your program received.

In case you are interested in why this is the correct thing to say, here are some technical comments:

- The MSGDTA field is declared as 512 bytes. This is the largest amount of message data that can be sent. Most commands don't send that much; but if you are receiving a CPF9898 message, the entire text is the message data.

- Receiving the message ID allows the code to work regardless of what message ID you monitor for. For example, if you monitor for message CPF0000, all escape messages would be monitored for, but the message ID of the actual message that caused the exception would be placed into the &MSGID variable. Because a message ID must be used when an escape message is sent, you can be sure that the RCVMSG command will receive a message ID. However, many of the other message types (e.g., *COMP) do not require a message ID. If you use this same technique with completion messages, you must be sure a message ID was used to send the message.

- Rather than receiving the message text (MSG parameter), the code specifies to receive the MSGDTA and resend it along with the message ID. This will allow the previous program to access the message data if it wants to. If the message is sent to a command entry display, the user can place the cursor on the message and get to the second-level text. If the message appears in the job log, the typical logging level will cause the second-level text to appear. If you resend the message with a generic message ID such as CPF9898, you would lose this capability.

- Choosing to use the SNDMSGFLIB parameter rather than the MSGFLIB parameter on the RCVMSG command has to do with how the message was sent. In many cases, a program will send you a message using *LIBL as the message file library on the SNDPGMMSG command. In this case, it is possible that the library containing the message file no longer exists on your library list. This isn't a problem if a message from QCPFMSG in QSYS was sent (QSYS is always on the library list), but it can be a problem if a message file in a separate library was used. If many subprograms are "bubbling up" the same message, it is possible to lose the original library where the message file was contained. If you use MSGFLIB, you might receive *LIBL and your SNDPGMMSG command will fail if it can't find the message ID or message file. Or you could send the same message ID, but from a different message file, and become confused. The SNDMSGFLIB parameter contains the name of the library where the message was actually found. It's the one to use.

Resending a Completion Message

Resending a completion message is quite similar to resending an escape message. You might want to resend a completion message (i.e., bubble it up) if the major purpose of your program is to perform a function that causes a completion message.

An example of this is where the major purpose of your program is to do a CPYF or SBMJOB, and you want to resend the completion message from the IBM command to the previous program. If the user is operating from a command entry display, (s)he won't see the message unless you bubble it up (or (s)he accesses the detailed messages). Here is the code I use:

```
DCL          &MSGID    *CHAR LEN(7)
DCL          &MSGDTA   *CHAR LEN(512)
DCL          &MSGF     *CHAR LEN(10)
DCL          &MSGFLIB *CHAR LEN(10)
 .
 .
 .
SBMJOB       ...
RCVMSG       MSTYPE(*LAST) MSGDTA(&MSGDTA)
                 MSGID(&MSGID) MSGF(&MSGF) SNDMSGFLIB(&MSGFLIB)
SNDPGMMSG    MSGID(&MSGID) MSGF(&MSGFLIB/&MSGF)   +
               MSGDTA(&MSGDTA) MSGTYPE(*COMP)
ENDDO        /* Not found */
```

To understand why I consider this to be the correct technique, see the previous section.

Receiving a Message To Extract Data

Sometimes, you want to access the information you read in a message and bring it into your CL program so you can work with it. For example, the SBMJOB command sends a completion message stating the qualified job name of the batch job that was submitted. Assume that you want to access the information from the completion message so you can store the qualified job name in a database file for further use.

You can receive the message text itself using the MSG parameter on RCVMSG, but this is awkward to use and not very safe (you're more exposed to IBM changing the format of the message text). The better solution is to use the message data sent by the program that did the SNDPGMMSG command.

Each message description in a message file can have message fields described. This allows the program that is sending the message to place variables within the text. If you execute SBMJOB, you see a completion message such as

```
Job 123456/SMITH/QDFTJOBD submitted to ...
```

Looking at the message text, it is obvious that the qualified job name is inserted into the text in the sequence of job number, user, and job name. If you place your cursor on the message and press the Help key, you can see that the message ID is CPC1221 and that it is sent as a completion message. Then, if you enter

```
DSPMSGD  RANGE(CPC1221)
```

you get a menu with the first level of message text at the top. It reads

```
Job &3/&2/&1 submitted to ...
```

This is the message as it exists in the message file. The & values are substitution variables defined in the message description that will be inserted from the message data used on the SNDPGMMSG command. By looking at the message in the message file and the actual message text produced by the SBMJOB command, you can tell that the job number must be &3, the user is &2, and so on. What you need to know now is what the layout of the message data looks like.

In most cases, the message data has more than one substitution variable. When you request a return value of MSGDTA on RCVMSG, you will receive a data structure. You can display the information about the substitution variables by using Option 2 on the DSPMSGD command's menu. The resulting display will tell you the layout of the MSGDTA data structure that was used to send the message. In this case, it says

```
Field      Data Type      Length
&1         *CHAR          10
&2         *CHAR          10
&3         *CHAR           6
.
.
.
```

There is no text description to tell you what the substitution variables stand for, but you can usually determine that by analyzing the message text. In this case, the data structure looks like this:

Position	1 — 10	11 — 20	21 — 26	27 — ...
	Job name	User name	Job number	

This is the same data structure used by the program that used the

SNDPGMMSG command. With RCVMSG you can receive the data structure. If you do, the qualified job name is in the first 26 bytes of the MSGDTA variable.

If you want to access the three fields that make up the qualified job name, you would code

```
DCL      &MSGDTA *CHAR LEN(512)
DCL      &JOB    *CHAR LEN(10)
DCL      &USER   *CHAR LEN(10)
DCL      &JOBNBR *CHAR LEN(6)
  .
  .
  .
SBMJOB   ...
RCVMSG   MSGTYPE(*LAST) MSGDTA(&MSGDTA) RMV(*NO)
CHGVAR   &JOB    %SST(&MSGDTA 1 10)
CHGVAR   &USER   %SST(&MSGDTA 11 10)
CHGVAR   &JOBNBR %SST(&MSGDTA 21 6)
```

Determining the actual layout of the MSGDTA data structure using the DSPMSGD command can be quite confusing. The data structure for messages such as CPC1221 are easy to understand because they have a relatively small number of substitution variables. However, some messages have several variables of differing data types. Sometime you might want to access the MSGDTA for a message where the information you are looking for is in &17 and the prior fields are a combination of binary fields, decimal fields, and so on. The TAA tool DSPMSGDTA in QUSRTOOL can help determine what you need to know. DSPMSGDTA formats the message data and tells you where each of the message data fields begins. To decipher the MSGDTA data structure, DSPMSGDTA offers a much better solution than viewing the information on the DSPMSGD command.

Technical Tip

Except for simple cases, adding up the lengths of the MSGDTA data fields can be challenging. The DSPMSGDTA TAA tool in QUSRTOOL removes the guesswork and helps you determine where each field starts.

Accessing Data in Binary Format

Sometimes, the MSGDTA field you want to access is in a binary format. CL does not work with binary data (it works only with character or decimal data). However, the system does support the CL %BIN function, which lets you convert a binary value to a decimal value and vice versa.

Assume you want to access the number of records copied during execution of a CPYF command. The CPYF completion message is CPC2955. If you use the DSPMSGD command to view the message CPC2955, you can see you want the very first message data field in the message text. Using the TAA tool DSPMSGDTA, you can view the CPC2955 message as stored in the system and determine you really want the &7 message field. DSPMSGDTA will tell you that &7 begins in position 75 and has 4 bytes of binary data. Therefore, you could access the number of records copied from the CPYF completion message with the following code:

```
DCL        &MSGDTA *CHAR LEN(512)
DCL        &CPYFCNT *DEC LEN(9 Ø)
 .
CPYF         ...
RCVMSG     MSGTYPE(*LAST) MSGDTA(&MSGDTA) RMV(*NO)
CHGVAR     &CPYFCNT %BIN(&MSGDTA 75 4)
```

Technical Tip

Even though CL does not support a binary field type, you can get the job done with the %BIN function and convert from a character field that contains binary data to a decimal field and vice versa.

Advanced Topics

Now let me present a few advanced topics on message handling that I occasionally find useful.

The Message Key Field

Messages are assigned an internal key of 4 bytes. Each message has a unique key. You can receive the value for the unique key and use it on certain commands.

The SNDPGMMSG command KEYVAR parameter lets you receive the message key assigned to the message that was sent. All other parameters on SNDPGMMSG are output from your program to the command. KEYVAR is a return variable that must be declared as *CHAR LEN(4); it will contain the unique message key assigned to the message that has been sent. You might want the message key so you can receive the same message at a later point in your program.

The RCVMSG command lets you retrieve the key of the message it receives with the same parameter name of KEYVAR. The one strange thing about the parameter is that the key is only retrieved if you are not removing the message from the message queue (i.e., RCVMSG RMV(*NO)); otherwise, the KEYVAR value is blank.

The RCVMSG command also lets you receive a message by referring to its message key with the MSGKEY parameter. This is an output parameter from your program to the RCVMSG command, rather than a return value from RCVMSG (as is KEYVAR). For example, if you did SNDPGMMSG with KEYVAR and then wanted to receive the message later on, you would refer to it using the RCVMSG command MSGKEY parameter.

Another good use for KEYVAR is when you want to remove certain messages from the program message queue, but not all of them. You must receive the message before you can determine whether to leave it on the program message queue or remove it. To receive the message, use RMV(*NO) and specify the KEYVAR parameter. Then if you decide to remove the message, you use the unique key value on the MSGKEY parameter of RMVMSG. The code would look like this:

```
DCL     &MSGID  *CHAR LEN(7)
DCL     &KEYVAR *CHAR LEN(4)
.
.
.
CHKOBJ  ...
MONMSG  MSGID(CPFØØØØ) EXEC(DO) /* Some error */
RCVMSG  MSGTYPE(*EXCP) RMV(*NO) KEYVAR(&KEYVAR)
IF      (&MSGID *EQ 'CPF98Ø1') EXEC(DO) /* Remove */
RMVMSG  MSGKEY(&KEYVAR)
ENDDO   /* Remove */
```

The KEYVAR value not only lets you say “Give me this key,” but it also lets you say “Give me the one just before or after this key.” This lets you wander up and down the program message queue based on some previous key that you saved, or based on the last message you received. The program message queue is normally processed in FIFO order, but using the MSGKEY parameter along with a MSGTYPE of *NEXT or *PRV, you get to decide in which order you want to process. This only works if you say RMV(*NO). The message key you are referring to must still exist.

You can process the entire queue by receiving the first or last message and then using the KEYVAR value on the first RCVMSG as the MSGKEY value on the next RCVMSG, as well as the MSGTYPE parameter and a value of *NEXT or *PRV.

Old Versus New Messages

The system's message-handling routines assume that after you have received a message, you are done with it. This means if you do not ask for a specific message key, you are not going to receive the ones you have already received (even if you said RMV(*NO)). An old message is one you have already received.

There is no way on a program message queue to reset the old messages so you can get at them again (CHGMSGQ supports the ability to do this, but only on external message queues). Therefore, if you want to receive a message again, you must save the message key and request it specifically.

Processing in FIFO Order

If you don't use MSGTYPE(*LAST), you normally process from the top of the message queue or as the messages came to your program message queue in FIFO order. Because there can be many messages, you normally want to bypass the ones you don't want, to get to the ones you do want.

Normally, if you are going to read through the message queue, it is because you are going to look for some specific message ID. Therefore, you are going to write a loop that keeps reading with RCVMSG. The default for RCVMSG is to ask for the next message in the message queue of any type. The code would look like this:

```
LOOP:      RCVMSG  ...
           .
           .
           .
           GOTO    LOOP
```

How Do You Know When There Are No More Messages?

RCVMSG does not follow the system convention of sending an escape message when the command did not work successfully because there are no more messages. You have to look in one of the return values to determine whether or not you actually received a message. The right way to do this is to use the RTNTYPE return variable. It must be defined as *CHAR LEN(2). You can count on the fact that a blank value means "No more messages exist." Your code would look like this:

```
          DCL      &RTNTYPE *CHAR LEN(2)
          .
          .
          .
LOOP:     RCVMSG   MSGTYPE(*ANY) RTNTYPE(&RTNTYPE) ...
          IF       (&RTNTYPE *NE '  ') DO /* Message received */
          .
          .
          .
          GOTO    LOOP
          ENDDO   /* Message received */
                  /* No more messages exist */
```

In case you are interested, let me tell you about the return values you shouldn't use to determine that no more messages exist:

- Don't trust the MSGID return variable. If you are dealing with an escape message, the MSGID return variable is safe to use, but any other message type can be sent without a MSGID. Thus, you cannot distinguish by looking at a MSGID return value whether there are no more messages or you just received one sent with impromptu text.
- Don't trust the MSGKEY variable. Unless you said RMV(*NO), this variable will be blank.
- Don't trust the MSG, MSGDTA, or SECLVL variables. Not every message has this information and it is possible that a program you call can send you a blank message.

Technical Tip

When you want to test for "No more messages received," you have to check one of the return values. The one to use is RTNTYPE. If it is blank, you have received all the messages.

The RTNTYPE Return Value

In addition to being the value to test to determine whether or not any more messages exist, the RTNTYPE value will tell you the type of message you just received. The following codes are used:

01 Completion
02 Diagnostic
04 Information
05 Inquiry
08 Request
15 Escape

The RTNTYPE value can be very helpful if you don't request a specific message type on the RCVMSG command.

Writing a RCVMSG Loop

Now that you are up on the concepts and pitfalls to avoid, the following is the correct code if you want to read messages in FIFO order and look for message ID CPF1234:

```
         DCL     &RTNTYPE *CHAR LEN(2)
         DCL     &MSGID   *CHAR LEN(7)
         .
         .
         .
LOOP:    RCVMSG  RTNTYPE(&RTNTYPE) MSGID(&MSGID) ...
         IF      (&RTNTYPE *NE '  ') DO /* Message found */
         IF      (&MSGID *NE 'CPF1234) GOTO LOOP
         .
         .       /* Your processing of CPF1234 */
         .
         ENDDO  /* Message found */
```

Messages You Cannot Access

Most of the time, you can get what you want from your program message queue. But sometimes a message you can see in the job log is not in your program message queue. The diagram below illustrates what happens: If PGMB calls PGMC, PGMB is no longer in control. If PGMC causes other programs to come into the program stack, they can send messages to the previous program (PGMC), but unless the messages are bubbled up, PGMB can't get at them with RCVMSG.

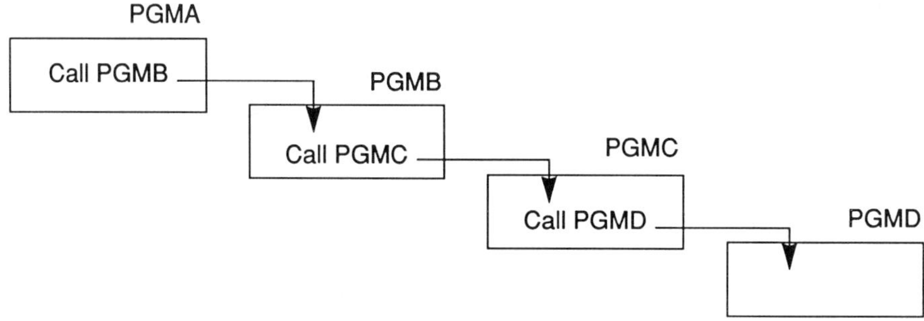

If PGMD sends a message to PGMC and PGMC does not resend the message to PGMB, PGMB cannot access the message with RCVMSG. The message is in the job log and you can see it from the QCMD command entry display (if you use F10 to display detailed messages), but you cannot get at it with RCVMSG. If you want to determine whether or not you can receive a message, look at the program the message was sent to. For you to receive the message, it must have been sent to your program.

Technical Tip

If you see a message in the job log that you want to receive into your program, it must be sent to your program message queue to allow RCVMSG to work. Look at the "To program" the message was sent to. If it isn't yours, you can't use RCVMSG.

It is possible to use DSPJOBLOG to a spooled file, CPYSPLF to a database file, and then read the message. But that would be a lot of work and the process would be slow.

The previous discussion provides some good reasons why you want to bubble up messages from your program. If your previous program might want to access some of the messages you have received, it cannot do so unless you bubble them up.

Note that what you cannot do is receive messages from programs that are no longer active in the program stack (the ones your program called). In many cases, this is what you would really like to do, but it doesn't work. Once the program is no longer active, there is no way to access its messages. Consider the following illustration:

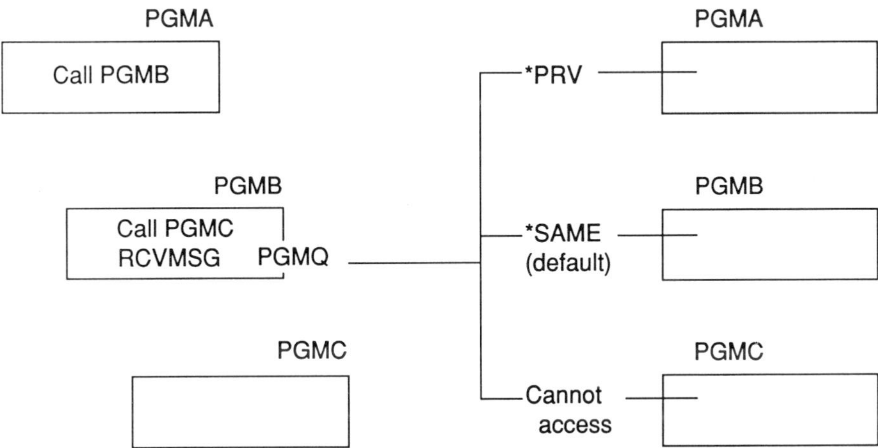

The use of the TOPGMQ and PGMQ parameter is consistent between the SNDPGMMSG, RCVMSG, and RMVMSG commands. TOPGMQ(*PRV) and PGMQ(*PRV) indicate the message queue of a program higher in the invocation stack. TOPGMQ(*SAME) and PGMQ(*SAME) indicate the current program's message queue. When PGMB is in operation, it can access the program message queue of the program higher in the stack. The value *PRV makes it easy to talk to the message queue of the program that invoked your program (it is the default on SNDPGMMSG). When PGMB calls PGMC, PGMC becomes active and a program message queue is created for PGMC. When PGMC ends, the program is no longer active, and its message queue is no longer accessible to your program. PGMB can never access PGMC's program message queue. If PGMC has something important to communicate to PGMB, PGMC should send the message to PGMB's message queue using the SNDPGMMSG command and the default of TOPGMQ(*PRV), which is PGMB's message queue.

Note that PGMB can actually do a RCVMSG from PGMA's message queue. In fact, PGMB could delete some or all of the messages in PGMA's message queue. Although, in general, I haven't found a good use for this function in my applications, I have used the technique a few times to solve an out-of-the-ordinary requirement (e.g., answering the question "What is the name of the program that called my program?").

Exercise A Resending an Escape Message

In this exercise you will resend an escape message. This technique is used commonly in many CL programs.

1. Use PDM to create a CLP member named TRYSNDESC. Enter the following source:

```
PGM        PARM(&FILE)
DCL        &FILE    *CHAR LEN(10)
DCL        &MSGID   *CHAR LEN(7)
DCL        &MSGF    *CHAR LEN(10)
DCL        &MSGFLIB *CHAR LEN(10)
DCL        &MSGDTA  *CHAR LEN(256)
CHKOBJ     OBJ(&FILE) OBJTYPE(*FILE)
MONMSG     MSGID(CPF9801) EXEC(DO) /* Not found */
RCVMSG     MSGTYPE(*EXCP) MSGDTA(&MSGDTA) MSGID(&MSGID)  +
             MSGF(&MSGF) SNDMSGFLIB(&MSGFLIB)
SNDPGMMSG  MSGID(&MSGID) MSGF(&MSGFLIB/&MSGF)    +
             MSGDTA(&MSGDTA) MSGTYPE(*ESCAPE)
ENDDO      /* Not found */
SNDPGMMSG  MSG('Worked great') MSGTYPE(*COMP)
ENDPGM
```

2. Create the program.
3. Access the command entry display. You can do this by calling the program QCMD. Call program TRYSNDESC, supplying as a parameter a file name that exists in your library list (e.g., QCLSRC):

   ```
   CALL  PGM(TRYSNDESC) PARM(QCLSRC)
   ```

   You should see the completion message, "Worked great."
4. Call the program with a file name that does not exist (xxxx in this example):

   ```
   CALL  PGM(TRYSNDESC) PARM(xxxx)
   ```

   If file xxxx does not exist on your system, you should see escape message CPF9801.
5. Place the cursor on the escape message and press the Help key.

Exercise A continued

Exercise A continued

You should see that the escape message was sent by your program, not by CHKOBJ's command processing program.

6. Return to a command entry display and press F10.

   You should see no other messages. Your completion message ("Worked great") should not have been sent because the program terminates as soon as an escape message is sent. The RCVMSG command in the above code took the default for the RMV parameter — RMV(*YES) — which caused escape message CPF9801 to be removed from the message queue automatically. You don't need to remove the escape message to resend it; but if you don't, two messages that say essentially the same thing will exist in the job log.

Exercise B Resending a Completion Message

In this exercise you will learn first-hand what trouble you can get into if you don't receive messages correctly.

1. Use PDM to create a CLP member named TRYSNDCPL. Enter the following source:

```
PGM
DCL         &MSGID    *CHAR LEN(7)
DCL         &MSGF     *CHAR LEN(10)
DCL         &MSGFLIB  *CHAR LEN(10)
DCL         &MSGDTA   *CHAR LEN(256)
DLTDTAARA   DTAARA(QTEMP/XXX)
MONMSG      MSGID(CPF2105) /* Ignore 'not found' */
CRTDTAARA   DTAARA(QTEMP/XXX) TYPE(*CHAR) LEN(10)
SBMJOB      JOB(WRKSYSSTS) CMD(WRKSYSSTS)
RCVMSG      MSGTYPE(*COMP) +
              MSGDTA(&MSGDTA) MSGID(&MSGID) +
              MSGF(&MSGF) SNDMSGFLIB(&MSGFLIB)
SNDPGMMSG   MSGID(&MSGID) MSGF(&MSGFLIB/&MSGF) +
              MSGDTA(&MSGDTA) MSGTYPE(*COMP)
ENDPGM
```

Exercise B continued

Exercise B continued

2. Create the program.
3. Access the command entry display and call the program:

```
CALL  TRYSNDCPL
```

   You should see the completion message sent following creation of a data area. Unfortunately, what you probably wanted to see was the completion message for the SBMJOB command. The above RCVMSG command specifies MSGTYPE(*COMP); and because completion messages are retrieved in FIFO order, you received the first completion message sent to your program's message queue.
4. Call the program again:

```
CALL  TRYSNDCPL
```

   You should now see the completion message for the DLTDTAARA command (it wasn't sent the first time because the data area did not exist).
5. Now let's receive the SBMJOB command completion message correctly. Simply modify the source so that the RCVMSG command requests MSGTYPE(*LAST) instead of MSGTYPE(*COMP).
6. Create the program.
7. Access the command entry display and call the program:

```
CALL  TRYSNDCPL
```

   You should see the completion message for the SBMJOB command.
8. If you press F10 to access the detail messages, you should see other completion messages. You should not see the SBMJOB completion message because the RCVMSG command removed it by default. Again, you don't need to remove the message you received, but doing so avoids having duplicate messages on the job log.

Exercise C Accessing Message Data Information

In this example you will access a CPYF completion message to determine the number of records copied during execution of the CPYF command. You might want to store this information in a database file, but in this case you will just resend the information to the calling program as a test case. To use this example, you will need the TAA tools DSPMSGDTA and EDTVAR; if they are not on your system, see Appendix B.

1. Use a CPYF command on one of your files to create a one-record file in library QTEMP:

```
CPYF  FROMFILE(xxx) TOFILE(QTEMP/TEMP1)  +
        CRTFILE(*YES) FROMRCD(1) TORCD(1)
```

2. By reading the completion message, you can see that the value you want to access (the number of records copied) is at the beginning of the message text. Place the cursor on the message and press Help.

3. You should be looking at message ID CPC2955, which was sent as a completion message. Enter the following TAA tool command:

```
DSPMSGDTA  CPC2955
```

4. DSPMSGDTA provides the same information as DSPMSGD, except that it formats the message data differently. By looking at the first-level message text, you can see you want the value of variable &7 in the message data. Note that & fields occur in both the first- and second-level help text. The question you want an answer to is "Where is variable &7 and what are its attributes?"

5. Scroll through the message information until you see the message data fields. DSPMSGDTA provides a good description of the message data structure. You can see that &7 is a *BIN field of length 4 and that it begins at position 75. This is the information that will be used in the next step to extract the count value.

6. Using PDM, create a CLP source member named TRYCPYMSG. In this exercise an outfile of *JOBD object types will be created from library QGPL. This file will be copied and the number of records copied will be sent in a message. Enter the following source:

Exercise C continued

Exercise C continued

```
PGM
DCL        &CPYCNT *DEC LEN(9 0)
DCL        &CPYCNTA *CHAR LEN(22)
DCL        &MSGDTA *CHAR LEN(512)
DLTF       FILE(QTEMP/JOBD2)
MONMSG     MSGID(CPF2105) /* Ignore not found */
DSPOBJD    OBJ(QGPL/*ALL) OBJTYPE(*JOBD) +
             OUTPUT(*OUTFILE) OUTFILE(QTEMP/JOBD)
CPYF       FROMFILE(QTEMP/JOBD) +
             TOFILE(QTEMP/JOBD2) CRTFILE(*YES)
RCVMSG     MSGTYPE(*LAST) MSGDTA(&MSGDTA) RMV(*NO)
CHGVAR     &CPYCNT %BIN(&MSGDTA 75 4)
EDTVAR     CHROUT(&CPYCNTA) NUMINP(&CPYCNT)
SNDPGMMSG  MSG(&CPYCNTA *TCAT 'records copied')
ENDPGM
```

7. Create the program.
8. From the command entry display, call the program:

   ```
   CALL  TRYCPYMSG
   ```

   You should see the informational message you sent containing the number of records copied.
9. Use F10 to display detailed messages.

   You should see the CPYF completion message with the same count. In this case, the message was not removed.

CHAPTER 4

Standard Error-Handling Routine

A standard error-handling routine provides a standard method of implementing an error-handling procedure within your CL programs. In this chapter, my primary focus will be on the standard error-handling routine that I copy into my CL programs. Note that the type of coding I do may differ from yours. I predominately write short utility functions, many of which are executed by programmers from a command entry display rather than by end users from a menu, and my standard error-handling routine works well for this environment. The routine is not perfect (I will discuss its weaknesses), but it provides a good example of what an error-handling routine should do.

In the last section of this chapter, I will present an alternative error-handling routine; one that I believe is more appropriate for production programs.

My standard error-handling routine for utility programs offers the following advantages:

- The user sees the actual escape message that caused the program to end, rather than "function check" message ID CPF9999. The actual escape message will describe what type of error occurred. The function check message requires that someone look at the detail messages before they can determine the problem.
- If a preceding diagnostic message exists, it is also bubbled up. This is where the weakness is and I'll discuss it later.
- All types of errors are monitored for, so the user will never see the CL Program Inquiry Message. If an unexpected error occurs in the program, it terminates abnormally without anyone having a chance to alter the program's intent.

DUPLICATING THE STANDARD ERROR-HANDLING ROUTINE

Tools are available so that you don't have to key the standard error-handling code into every program. A TAA tool in QUSRTOOL called DUPSTDSRC (Duplicate Standard Source) makes it easy to get started with a new CL program. I'll describe the tool further in Chapter 28, "Setting Up Your Programming Environment." But for the purposes of this chapter, you simply need to code

```
DUPSTDSRC  MBR(xxxx) SRCTYP(*CLP) TEXT('xxxx')
```

DUPSTDSRC copies a CL source program template from a member in QUSRTOOL. The program template includes the standard error-handling routine, a comment with your member name and text as the first statement, and boilerplate code you need in a lot of programs (e.g., how to send a status message, removing messages).

Another alternative, if you want to copy only the standard error-handling code, is to simply copy in the source from member CLPSTDERR in file QATTINFO in library QUSRTOOL.

Basic Program Structure

The following is the standard error-handling code you would copy into your new source member:

```
          DCL       &ERRORSW *LGL        /* Standard error */
          DCL       &MSGID   *CHAR LEN(7)     /* Standard error */
          DCL       &MSG     *CHAR LEN(512)   /* Standard error */
          DCL       &MSGDTA  *CHAR LEN(512)   /* Standard error */
          DCL       &MSGF    *CHAR LEN(10)    /* Standard error */
          DCL       &MSGFLIB *CHAR LEN(10)    /* Standard error */
          DCL       &KEYVAR  *CHAR LEN(4)     /* Standard error */
          DCL       &KEYVAR2 *CHAR LEN(4)     /* Standard error */
          DCL       &RTNTYPE *CHAR LEN(2)     /* Standard error */
          MONMSG    MSGID(CPF0000) EXEC(GOTO STDERR1)
                    /*                  */
                    /* Your program code */
                    /*                  */
          RETURN    /* Normal end of program */
STDERR1:              /* Standard error-handling routine */
          IF        &ERRORSW SNDPGMMSG MSGID(CPF9999)      +
                      MSGF(QCPFMSG) MSGTYPE(*ESCAPE)
          CHGVAR    &ERRORSW '1' /* Set to fail on error */
          RCVMSG    MSGTYPE(*EXCP) RMV(*NO) KEYVAR(&KEYVAR)
STDERR2:  RCVMSG    MSGTYPE(*PRV) MSGKEY(&KEYVAR) RMV(*NO)  +
                      KEYVAR(&KEYVAR2) MSG(&MSG)           +
                      MSGDTA(&MSGDTA) MSGID(&MSGID
                      RTNTYPE(&RTNTYPE) MSGF(&MSGF)        +
                      SNDMSGFLIB(&MSGFLIB)
          IF        (&RTNTYPE *NE '02') GOTO STDERR3
          IF        (&MSGID *NE ' ') SNDPGMMSG             +
                      MSGID(&MSGID) MSGF(&MSGFLIB/&MSGF)   +
                      MSGDTA(&MSGDTA) MSGTYPE(*DIAG)
          IF        (&MSGID *EQ ' ') SNDPGMMSG             +
```

```
                        MSG(&MSG) MSGTYPE(*DIAG)
          RMVMSG      MSGKEY(&KEYVAR2)
STDERR3:  RCVMSG      MSGKEY(&KEYVAR) MSGDTA(&MSGDTA)        +
                        MSGID(&MSGID) MSGF(&MSGF)SNDMSGFLIB(&MSGFLIB)
          SNDPGMMSG   MSGID(&MSGID) MSGF(&MSGFLIB/&MSGF)     +
                        MSGDTA(&MSGDTA) MSGTYPE(*ESCAPE)
          ENDPGM
```

How the Standard Error-Handling Routine Works

Although the code looks complicated, you don't have to understand it to use it. If you are not interested in the details, skip to the next section. To fully understand how the error-handling routine works, you will need to be familiar with the techniques I discussed in Chapters 2 and 3 on sending and receiving messages.

The standard error-handling routine is designed to

- Handle any unmonitored escape message sent to your program.
- Resend the escape message to the calling program using the same message ID, same message file, and same message data.
- Resend a diagnostic message if it was received immediately before the escape message. The routine resends only one diagnostic message.
- Remove from the job log any messages that are re-sent. This prevents two copies of the message from appearing in the job log.

The following discussion highlights some of the important aspects of the standard error-handling routine:

1. `DCL  &MSGDTA *CHAR LEN(512)`

   The MSGDTA field is declared with a length of 512, which will accommodate the majority of escape messages received by your program. It will be rare that your program will receive an escape message where the message data is longer than 512 characters.

2. `MONMSG  MSGID(CPF0000) EXEC(GOTO STDERR1)`

   The program-level MONMSG command will pass control to label STDERR1 if an escape message not specifically monitored for is sent to the program's message queue.

3. ```
   STDERR1:                  /* Standard error-handling routine */
                IF       &ERRORSW SNDPGMMSG MSGID(CPF9999) +
                           MSGF(QCPFMSG) MSGTYPE(*ESCAPE)
                CHGVAR   &ERRORSW '1' /* Set to fail on error */
   ```
   ```

The code at label STDERR1 checks the value of an error switch (a logical variable named &ERRORSW). This ensures that the standard error-handling routine does not get caught in a never-ending loop. For example, if a command you execute in the standard error-handling routine fails (without having a specific MONMSG command for the escape message), the program-level MONMSG command would be invoked and the routine could go into a never-ending loop. The standard error-handling code sets a logical variable to say "I've been here before." If the variable is already set when you enter the routine, it knows a loop is occurring within the error-handling routine and it sends message ID CPF9999 (function check). This is a programmer error and should be corrected.

4. `RCVMSG  MSGTYPE(*EXCP) RMV(*NO) KEYVAR(&KEYVAR)`

   The first real processing the routine does is to receive an escape message. Note that the RCVMSG command specifies that the message is not to be removed and the KEYVAR value is to be returned. At this point, all the other information could be retrieved (e.g., MSGDTA), but the program has coded only one set of DCLs for MSGDTA, MSGF, and so on. These same variables will be shared by both the escape and diagnostic message for different RCVMSG commands. Capturing the KEYVAR value allows the program to refer to it later. This will be used both to receive the previous message (sent before the escape message) and eventually to retrieve the escape message again.

5.
```
STDERR2: RCVMSG  MSGTYPE(*PRV) MSGKEY(&KEYVAR) RMV(*NO)  +
                   KEYVAR(&KEYVAR2) MSG(&MSG)              +
                   MSGDTA(&MSGDTA) MSGID(&MSGID)           +
                   RTNTYPE(&RTNTYPE) MSGF(&MSGF)           +
                   SNDMSGFLIB(&MSGFLIB)
         IF      (&RTNTYPE *NE '02') GOTO STDERR3
         IF      (&MSGID *NE ' ') SNDPGMMSG                +
                  MSGID(&MSGID) MSGF(&MSGFLIB/&MSGF)       +
                   MSGDTA(&MSGDTA) MSGTYPE(*DIAG)
         IF      (&MSGID *EQ ' ') SNDPGMMSG                +
                   MSG(&MSG) MSGTYPE(*DIAG)
         RMVMSG  MSGKEY(&KEYVAR2)
```

   The code at label STDERR2 handles the "bubbling up" of the last diagnostic message (if any). In this section of code lies the weakness of this standard error-handling routine — that you cannot specifically identify a particular diagnostic message as the one you want. I will discuss this weakness and then explain the use of the RCVMSG command.

With the exception of an escape message, it is not possible to relate a message that you receive to a command that you executed. There aren't any marks in the program message queue that tell you where one command begins and ends. If a diagnostic message is found, it isn't possible to determine if it was sent by the same function that caused the escape message. You can determine you received a diagnostic message, but you can only make an intelligent guess within your program about which command sent the message.

Diagnostic messages are normally processed in FIFO order. Rather than receiving all the diagnostic messages and bubbling them up, the routine restricts itself to receiving the message that occurred just before the escape message. If it is a diagnostic message, it is re-sent.

This imperfect solution works well most of the time, but it is possible that the routine will provide misleading information if other functions you are using do one of the following:

- Send multiple diagnostic messages ahead of the escape message. Only the last diagnostic message will be bubbled up.
- Send a diagnostic message without sending an escape message. If the next command that generates a message causes an escape message, the previous diagnostic message will be bubbled up as if it belonged to that escape message. Note that if some other message (other than an escape message) occurs after the diagnostic message, then the other message will be received and neither it nor the diagnostic message will be bubbled up. For example, assume that the following messages are received, in this order, in your program message queue:

  — a diagnostic message
  — a completion message
  — an escape message

  Because the message sent before the escape message is not a diagnostic message, neither it nor the existing diagnostic message will be re-sent.
- Remove an escape message that had an accompanying diagnostic message, and then receive another escape message. For example, assume that

— an executed command fails and sends a diagnostic and an escape message
— your program receives the escape message and removes it
— the next command that sends a message sends an escape message

The standard error-handling routine would bubble up the right escape message, but it would also send the diagnostic message from the previous escape message. This would be misleading.

Also, if the function that fails sends information messages (*INFO) to explain the error (rather than *DIAG messages ahead of the escape message), the *INFO messages will not be bubbled up.

Now let's look specifically at the RCVMSG command used at label STDERR2. For the routine to receive the message sent just before the escape message, the escape message's message key is used as a reference and MSGTYPE(*PRV) is specified. You can only request the previous message (i.e., *PRV) if you have specified a message key. You can't ask specifically for the previous diagnostic message. You first have to receive the previous message and only then can you determine what type it is.

The RCVMSG command also specifies RMV(*NO). If a diagnostic message is received, the program will eventually remove it. If it is not a diagnostic message, the program will not remove it. Note that the KEYVAR parameter is also used on this RCVMSG command. This captures the internal ID of the message received so that it can be used later to remove the message if it is a diagnostic message.

The RCVMSG command also requests the RTNTYPE parameter. The RTNTYPE value contains a code for the type of message received. Each type has a unique code. It could be a diagnostic (code '02'), it could be some other code, or it could be blank, meaning that no message exists prior to the escape message. If it is not a diagnostic message, the program branches to label STDERR3 to resend the escape message.

As described in Chapter 3, it is possible that you will receive a diagnostic message that does not have a MSGID. Since the RTNTYPE is '02', the program knows that a diagnostic message has been received. If the MSGID value for the diagnostic message is not blank, the routine resends the same message ID with the same message file and message data. The MSG value is not used. If the

MSGID value is blank, it means that the SNDPGMMSG command was used with the MSG parameter (not the MSGID parameter) specified. Therefore, the same message text received (MSG value) is re-sent as a diagnostic message. If a diagnostic message is received, the routine removes the message from your program message queue by referring to the message key of the diagnostic message. This avoids the possibility of seeing the same message twice in the job log.

6.
```
STDERR3:  RCVMSG     MSGKEY(&KEYVAR) MSGDTA(&MSGDTA)         +
                       MSGID(&MSGID) MSGF(&MSGF)             +
                       SNDMSGFLIB(&MSGFLIB)
          SNDPGMMSG  MSGID(&MSGID) MSGF(&MSGFLIB/&MSGF)      +
                       MSGDTA(&MSGDTA) MSGTYPE(*ESCAPE)
```

The code at label STDERR3 receives the detail information about the escape message by using the message key that was originally received. The routine then resends the escape message you received as an escape message. Your program doesn't know what the condition is or what the message says. It just "bubbles it up." As soon as the program sends the *ESCAPE message, the system ends the program.

Modifying the Standard Error-Handling Routine

I generally use my standard error-handling routine as is, but there may be times when you want to modify it. For example,

- De-allocation. If you use the ALCOBJ command to allocate an object, you will want to de-allocate it regardless of how the program ends. If you don't de-allocate, the lock remains on the object until the end of your job. The implicit allocations performed by certain CL commands will normally be cleaned up by themselves. For example, the CHGDTAARA command will lock the specified data area before making any change, and then unlock the data area after making the change. (See Chapter 11, "Allocating Objects.")
- Deleting objects. If your program creates objects during its execution, you might want to delete those objects by including code in a standard error-handling routine to perform that task.
- Providing feedback. Sometimes you may want to inform someone that your program has ended abnormally by sending a message to that individual's message queue (for example, you might want to

send a message to the system operator stating that the program ended abnormally).

- Providing a program dump. Including code in the standard error-handling routine that causes a dump of the program (i.e., using the DMPCLPGM command) will let you capture information at the point of program failure. (See the section "Providing a Program Dump" in this chapter.)

WHAT YOU SHOULDN'T INCLUDE IN THE ERROR-HANDLING ROUTINE

Don't include in your standard error-handling routine special commands designed to help your program recover from an external failure (e.g., a power outage or an ENDJOB command). If this type of failure occurs, the error-handling routine will not be invoked and any recovery commands you included will not be executed.

If you need a recovery routine, the typical solution would be to use a data area with a value that can be tested and set from your program. Assume you had created a data area as follows:

```
CRTDTAARA  DTAARA(RECOVSW) TYPE(*CHAR) LEN(10) VALUE(GOOD)
```

Your program would retrieve the value to determine the condition of the program the last time it was run. If recovery was needed, you would execute the required commands and then set the value of the data area to BAD. If the program worked successfully, the data area would be reset to GOOD. The code would look like this:

```
DCL            &RECOVSW *CHAR LEN(10)
.
.
.
RTVDTAARA      DTAARA(RECOVSW) RTNVAR(&RECOVSW)
IF             (&RECOVSW *EQ 'BAD') DO /* Recovery */
.
.              /* Your recovery code */
.
ENDDO          /* Recovery */
CHGDTAARA      DTAARA(RECOVSW) VALUE('BAD')
.
.              /* Your normal processing */
.
CHGDTAARA      DTAARA(RECOVSW) VALUE('GOOD')
ENDPGM
```

Technical Tip

Don't put recovery code into the standard error-handling routine. In some situations (e.g., a power outage, or someone ends your job), you won't get a chance to execute the routine.

In addition, you should not have your error-handling routine remove a lot of messages — that is, don't use the command RMVMSG CLEAR(*ALL). If your program fails, you probably will need all the messages to help you determine what went wrong. You should consider including the command RMVMSG CLEAR(*ALL) as part of your program's normal completion function.

THE CLEANUP ROUTINE

Whatever object de-allocation or cleanup code you need in the error-handling routine, you also need if the program ends normally. Rather than duplicate the cleanup code, which would give you several versions of the same code to maintain, you could create a subroutine that can be used multiple times (see Chapter 9, "Subroutines").

The best place to branch to the subroutine is after your program has received an escape message and just before label STDERR2. For example, your code might look like this:

```
                  .
                  .         /* Normal end of program */
                  .
            CHGVAR      &RTNLOC   'ENDPGM'
            GOTO        CLEANUP
ENDPGM:     RETURN
CLEANUP:                /* Cleanup subroutine */
                  .
                  .     /* Whatever needs to cleaned up */
                  .
            IF          (&RTNLOC *EQ 'ENDPGM') GOTO ENDPGM
            IF          (&RTNLOC *EQ 'STDERR2') GOTO STDERR2
            SNDPGMMSG   MSGID(CPF9898) MSGF(QCPFMSG)          +
                          MSGTYPE(*ESCAPE)                    +
                          MSGDTA('Bad RTNLOC value of '  *CAT +
                          &RTNLOC *TCAT  ' in CLEANUP subr')
STDERR1:                /* Standard error-handling routine */
                  .
                  .
                  .
```

```
            RCVMSG     MSGTYPE(*EXCP)  RMV(*NO)   KEYVAR(&KEYVAR)
            CHGVAR     &RTNLOC 'STDERR2'
            GOTO       CLEANUP
STDERR2:    SNDPGMMSG  MSGTYPE(*PRV)  MSGKEY(&KEYVAR)   RMV(*NO)
              .
              .
```

Placing the GOTO just before label STDERR2 allows your cleanup functions to generate messages without affecting the error-handling routine. Your error-handling routine will have already captured the message key of the escape message, and any diagnostic messages generated by the cleanup routine will not be bubbled up. As with the error-handling routine, your cleanup subroutine should not remove messages. Trying to receive a message that does not exist would cause the cleanup subroutine to abort.

Technical Tip

If you need to de-allocate objects or perform other cleanup functions at the end of your program, as well as in the standard error-handling routine, these functions are best handled as part of a subroutine. You should branch to the subroutine just after your program receives an escape message and right before label STDERR2.

You also should consider monitoring for messages in the cleanup routine. For example, if your program creates an object and you want to delete the object in the cleanup routine, an error will occur if the object you try to delete does not exist. This could happen if the program fails before executing the create command. The purpose of testing the error switch (&ERRORSW) at the beginning of the standard error-handling routine is to prevent looping if something like this happens. The right thing to do is to monitor for expected errors on commands executed within the cleanup routine.

Technical Tip

If you use a cleanup routine in your program, you need to carefully monitor for errors that can occur when the routine executes. And, as with your error-handling routine, don't use the RMVMSG CLEAR(*ALL) function as part of your cleanup routine. You probably will want to see the messages if your program abnormally terminates.

Providing a Program Dump

When an unexpected error occurs in a production program, it can be very helpful to capture as much information as possible at the point of failure. The DMPCLPGM command will dump the program message queue of the program, as well as variable values. The place to insert the DMPCLPGM command into your program is right after the RCVMSG command that receives the escape message, and before any cleanup routine:

```
RCVMSG     MSGTYPE(*EXCP) ...
DMPCLPGM
```

If the observable (debug) information has been removed from the program (via the CHGPGM command), executing a CL dump is not going to provide much information. You would receive only the program message queue, which is part of the job log anyway. A more sophisticated technique would be to check the program's attributes to determine whether or not the program is observable, then execute the DMPCLPGM command only if the program is observable. Your program could send a status message when the dump is taking place.

You can use the RTVPGMA command (a QUSRTOOL TAA tool) to retrieve a program's attributes. The RTVPGMA command lets you retrieve the information that you would see on the DSPPGM display, which includes whether or not the program is observable. To do this, add the following code after the escape message is first received (the code is standard with the exception of the program name specified for the PGM parameter of the RTVPGMA command):

```
             DCL        &OBSERVE *CHAR LEN(5)
              .
              .
STDERR1:                /* Standard error-handling routine */
              .
              .
             RCVMSG     MSGTYPE(*EXCP) RMV(*NØ) KEYVAR(&KEYVAR)
             RTVPGMA    PGM(TRYSTDERR) OBSERVE(&OBSERVE)
             IF         (&OBSERVE *EQ '*NONE') DO /* No observe */
             SNDPGMMSG  MSG('No observability information  +
                          exists to use with DMPCLPGM.')
             ENDDO      /* No observe */
             IF         (&OBSERVE *NE '*NONE') DO /* Use DMP */
             SNDPGMMSG  MSGID(CPF9898) MSGF(QCPFMSG)          +
                          MSGDTA('DMPCLPGM occurring')        +
                          TOPGMQ(*EXT) MSGTYPE(*STATUS)
              DMPCLPGM
```

```
             SNDPGMMSG  MSGID(CPI9801) MSGF(QCPFMSG)          +
                          TOPGMQ(*EXT) MSGTYPE(*STATUS)
             ENDDO      /* Use DMP */
STDERR2:     RCVMSG     ...
```

Technical Tip

Providing a program dump as part of the standard error-handling routine can make a lot of sense for production programs. You can capture the information contained in the program's variables, as well as information contained in the program's message queue.

HANDLING ERRORS IN PRODUCTION APPLICATIONS

The following error-handling routine for production applications protects a program against any unmonitored exception, and it does not have the weakness I pointed out in my standard error-handling routine. Here's the code you would copy into your program:

```
          MONMSG     MSGID(CPF0000) EXEC(GOTO) STDERR)
          .
          .          /* Your program */
          .
          RETURN     /* Normal end of program */
STDERR:              /* Standard error-handling routine */
          SNDPGMMSG  MSGID(CPF9898) MSGF(QCPFMSG)    +
                       MSGDTA('Program aborted on an +
                       unexpected escape message')
          ENDPGM
```

If an unmonitored exception occurs, the program aborts and sends escape message CPF9898. The user does not get a chance to make a decision (right or wrong) about the error condition. I prefer this technique for production programs because

- everything is monitored for; a user of the program will never see inquiry message CPA0701, which was discussed in Chapter 1, "Monitoring for Messages."
- the job log contains the original escape message and the name of the program that sent it. The escape message is not bubbled up (the technique I use in the standard error-handling routine for utility programs) so the user avoids the potential problem of not being able to tell where the error occurred.

- the user is not likely to be confused about how to handle a diagnostic message.

To understand the major difference between this error-handling routine and the one I use as a standard, consider the following scenario: Ten programs are in the program stack, all of which use the same error-handling technique, and the program at the bottom of the stack ends abnormally.

If all 10 programs were using the error-handling routine for production programs, the original escape message sent to the program that ended abnormally, and nine CPF9898 escape messages sent by the other programs as they aborted, would appear in the job log.

If all 10 programs were using my standard error-handling routine for utility programs, the only message to appear in the job log would be the one bubbled up from the bottom program; and it would appear as if the message had been sent by the program highest in the stack. All other versions of the message would be removed. In some cases, this could make it difficult to determine what really happened.

Exercise A Using Standard Error Handling

In this exercise you will use the DUPSTDSRC command from QUSRTOOL to create a new source file member that automatically includes my standard error-handling routine. If the DUPSTDSRC command does not exist on your system, you will need to create it (see Appendix B).

1. Use the DUPSTDSRC command to create a new member in a source file (prompt for the command and enter the SRCFILE parameter, if you want to use something other than the default — QCLSRC). If you use source file QCLSRC, you would code

```
DUPSTDSRC  MBR(TRYSTDERR) SRCTYP(*CLP) +
              TEXT('Standard error-handling test')
```

2. Access the PDM display and request to edit source member TRYSTDERR.
3. Review the other standard source that is created and then delete all the source code you see except the standard error-handling code. You should have left:

   — The DCLs labeled as /* Standard error */
   — The MONMSG labeled as /* Std Err */
   — The STDERR1, STDERR2, and STDERR3 routines at the end

   At this point, the code should be identical to the code introduced in the section "Basic Program Structure."
4. Add a PGM statement at the beginning of the source.
5. After the MONMSG command, add a CPYF command that you know will fail because the FROMFILE will not exist:

```
CPYF  FROMFILE(XXXYX) TOFILE(ZZZZYZ)
```

6. Add a completion message and a RETURN command after the CPYF statement:

```
SNDPGMMSG  MSG('Worked great') MSGTYPE(*COMP)
RETURN     /* Normal end of program */
```

Exercise A continued

Exercise A continued

7. Your code should look like this:

```
          PGM
          DCL        &ERRORSW *LGL            /* Standard error */
          DCL        &MSGID   *CHAR LEN(7)    /* Standard error */
          DCL        &MSG     *CHAR LEN(512)  /* Standard error */
          DCL        &MSGDTA  *CHAR LEN(512)  /* Standard error */
          DCL        &MSGF    *CHAR LEN(10)   /* Standard error */
          DCL        &MSGFLIB *CHAR LEN(10)   /* Standard error */
          DCL        &KEYVAR  *CHAR LEN(4)    /* Standard error */
          DCL        &KEYVAR2 *CHAR LEN(4)    /* Standard error */
          DCL        &RTNTYPE *CHAR LEN(2)    /* Standard error */
          MONMSG     MSGID(CPF0000) EXEC(GOTO STDERR1) /* Std err */
          CPYF       FROMFILE(XXXYX) TOFILE(ZZZZYZ)
          SNDPGMMSG  MSG('Worked great') MSGTYPE(*COMP)
          RETURN     */ Normal end of program */
STDERR1:             */ Standard error-handling routine */
          IF         &ERRORSW SNDPGMMSG MSGID(CPF9999)      +
                       MSG(QCPFMSG) MSGTYPE(*ESCAPE)
          CHGVAR     &ERRORSW '1' /* Set to fail on error */
          RCVMSG     MSGTYPE(*EXCP) RMV(*NO) KEYVAR(&KEYVAR)
STDERR2:  RCVMSG     MSGTYPE(*PRV) MSGKEY(&KEYVAR) RMV(*NO) +
                       KEYVAR(&KEYVAR2) MSG(&MSG)           +
                       MSGDTA(&MSGDTA) MSGID(&MSGID)        +
                       RTNTYPE(&RTNTYPE) MSGF(&MSGF)        +
                       SNDMSGFLIB(&MSGFLIB)
          IF         (&RTNTYPE *NE '02') GOTO STDERR3
          IF         (&MSGID *NE '   ') SNDPGMMSG           +
                       MSGID(&MSGID) MSGF(&MSGFLIB/&MSGF)   +
                       MSGDTA(&MSGDTA) MSGTYPE(*DIAG)
          IF         (&MSGID *EQ '   ') SNDPGMMSG           +
                       MSG(&MSG) MSGTYPE(*DIAG)
          RMVMSG     MSGKEY(&KEYVAR2)
STDERR3:  RCVMSG     MSGKEY(&KEYVAR) MSGDTA(&MSGDTA)        +
                       MSGID(&MSGID) MSGF(&MSGF)            +
                       SNDMSGFLIB(&MSGFLIB)
          SNDPGMMSG  MSGID(&MSGID) MSGF(&MSGFLIB/&MSGF)     +
                       MSGDTA(&MSGDTA) MSGTYPE(*ESCAPE)
          ENDPGM
```

Exercise A continued

Exercise A continued

8. Create the program.
9. From the command entry display (QCMD), call the program:

```
CALL   TRYSTDERR
```

You should see the CPYF escape message CPF2817, indicating that the CPYF command failed, and the diagnostic message CPF2802, indicating that the FROMFILE was not found. If you place the cursor on the messages and request help, you can see that the messages were sent by your program and not by the CPYF Command Processing Program. If you are calling the program from the command line with PDM, the messages will be shown as *INFO type messages and your program name won't be displayed. If you want to see the messages properly, you need to be on the command entry display (QCMD). You should not see the completion message because the program never sent it (the system automatically ends a program when that program sends an escape message). You should not see the CL Program Inquiry Message display because all errors are monitored for. In addition, if you request to see detailed messages (F10), you should not see any duplicated ones. Messages were sent to your program, but they were removed as part of bubbling them up.

10. Next, from the command entry display, key the command:

```
CHGJOB   LOGCLPGM(*YES)
```

This will cause CL commands to be written to the job log as they are executed. You also can use the TAA tool LOGCL to accomplish the same thing.

11. Call program TRYSTDERR again and look at the detailed messages. These now include the commands you executed. You should be able to follow the logic of the program as it tries the CPYF command and then branches to the standard error-handling routine.
12. Now submit program TRYSTDERR to batch:

```
SBMJOB   CMD(CALL TRYSTDERR)
```

The job should abnormally terminate. Look at the job log. You should see the same messages sent by your program that you saw on the command entry display.

Exercise B Adding a Cleanup Routine

In this exercise you will modify the standard error-handling routine to include your own cleanup routine. As part of the exercise, an object will be created in library QTEMP. Assume you want to delete the object (clean up) at the end of the program whether the program ends normally or abnormally.

1. Use PDM to access member TRYSTDERR, created in the previous exercise.
2. Enter the DCL statement:

```
DCL      &RTNLOC *CHAR LEN(8)
```

3. Before the CPYF statement, enter

```
DLTDTAARA   DTAARA(QTEMP/ABC)
MONMSG      MSGID(CPF2105) /* Ignore */
CRTDTAARA   DTAARA(QTEMP/ABC) +
              TYPE(*CHAR) LEN(10)
CPYF        ...
```

4. Following the SNDPGMMSG command for the *COMP message, your code should look like this:

```
            SNDPGMMSG  ... MSGTYPE(*COMP)
            CHGVAR     &RTNLOC 'ENDPGM'
            GOTO       CLEANUP
ENDPGM:
            RETURN     /* Normal end of program */
CLEANUP:               /* Cleanup subroutine */
            DLTDTAARA  DTAARA(QTEMP/ABC)
            MONMSG     MSGID(CPF2105) /* Ignore not found */
            IF         (&RTNLOC *EQ 'ENDPGM') GOTO ENDPGM
            IF         (&RTNLOC *EQ 'STDERR2') GOTO STDERR2
            SNDPGMMSG  MSGID(CPF9898) MSGF(QCPFMSG)        +
                         MSGTYPE(*ESCAPE)                  +
                         MSGDTA('Bad RTNLOC value of ' *CAT +
                         &RTNLOC *TCAT ' in CLEANUP subr')
STDERR1:               ...
```

Exercise B continued

Exercise B continued

5. Just before label STDERR2, set the return location and use a GOTO to the cleanup subroutine:

```
           RCVMSG     MSGTYPE(*EXCP) ...
           CHGVAR     &RTNLOC 'STDERR2'
           GOTO       CLEANUP
STDERR2:   RCVMSG     MSGTYPE(*PRV) ...
```

Your code should now look like this:

```
         PGM
         DCL          &RTNLOC   *CHAR LEN(8)
         DCL          &ERRORSW  *LGL            /* Standard error */
         DCL          &MSGID    *CHAR LEN(7)    /* Standard error */
         DCL          &MSG      *CHAR LEN(512)  /* Standard error */
         DCL          &MSGDTA   *CHAR LEN(512)  /* Standard error */
         DCL          &MSGF     *CHAR LEN(10)   /* Standard error */
         DCL          &MSGFLIB  *CHAR LEN(10)   /* Standard error */
         DCL          &KEYVAR   *CHAR LEN(4)    /* Standard error */
         DCL          &KEYVAR2  *CHAR LEN(4)    /* Standard error */
         DCL          &RTNTYPE  *CHAR LEN(2)    /* Standard error */
         MONMSG       MSGID(CPF0000) EXEC(GOTO STDERR1) /* Std err */
         DLTDTAARA    DTAARA(QTEMP/ABC)
         MONMSG       MSGID(CPF2105) /* Ignore */
         CRTDTAARA    DTAARA(QTEMP/ABC) TYPE(*CHAR) LEN(10)
         CPYF         FROMFILE(XXXYX) TOFILE(ZZZZYZ)
         SNDPGMMSG    MSG('Worked great') MSGTYPE(*COMP)
         CHGVAR       &RTNLOC 'ENDPGM'
         GOTO         CLEANUP
ENDPGM:
         RETURN       */ Normal end of program */
CLEANUP:              */ Cleanup subroutine */
         DLTDTAARA    DTAARA(QTEMP/ABC)
         MONMSG       MSGID(CPF2105) /* Ignore */
         IF           (&RTNLOC *EQ 'ENDPGM') GOTO ENDPGM
         IF           (&RTNLOC *EQ 'STDERR2') GOTO STDERR2
         SNDPGMMSG    MSGID(CPF9898) MSGF(QCPFMSG) MSGTYPE(*ESCAPE)  +
                        MSGDTA('BAD RTNLOC value of ' *CAT  +
                        &RTNLOC *TCAT ' in CLEANUP subr')
STDERR1:              */ Standard error-handling routine */
```

Exercise B continued

Exercise B continued

```
        IF          &ERRORSW SNDPGMMSG MSGID(CPF9999)     +
                      MSG(QCPFMSG) MSGTYPE(*ESCAPE)
        CHGVAR      &ERRORSW '1' /* Set to fail on error */
        RCVMSG      MSGTYPE(*EXCP) RMV(*NO) KEYVAR(&KEYVAR)
        CHGVAR      &RTNLOC 'STDERR2'
        GOTO        CLEANUP
STDERR2: RCVMSG     MSGTYPE(*PRV) MSGKEY(&KEYVAR) RMV(*NO) +
                      KEYVAR(&KEYVAR2) MSG(&MSG)           +
                      MSGDTA(&MSGDTA) MSGID(&MSGID)        +
                      RTNTYPE(&RTNTYPE) MSGF(&MSGF)        +
                      SNDMSGFLIB(&MSGFLIB)
        IF          (&RTNTYPE *NE 'Ø2') GOTO STDERR3
        IF          (&MSGID *NE '  ') SNDPGMMSG            +
                      MSGID(&MSGID) MSGF(&MSGFLIB/&MSGF)   +
                      MSGDTA(&MSGDTA) MSGTYPE(*DIAG)
        IF          (&MSGID *EQ '  ') SNDPGMMSG            +
                      MSG(&MSG) MSGTYPE(*DIAG)
        RMVMSG      MSGKEY(&KEYVAR2)
STDERR3: RCVMSG     MSGKEY(&KEYVAR) MSGDTA(&MSGDTA)        +
                      MSGID(&MSGID) MSGF(&MSGF) NDMSGFLIB(&MSGFLIB)
        SNDPGMMSG   MSGID(&MSGID) MSGF(&MSGFLIB/&MSGF)     +
                      MSGDTA(&MSGDTA) MSGTYPE(*ESCAPE)
        ENDPGM
```

6. Create the program.
7. From the command entry display, call the program:

   ```
   CALL TRYSTDERR
   ```

   You should see the CPYF diagnostic and escape messages. As detailed messages, you should see:

   — The escape message sent by the first DLTDTAARA
   — The completion message sent by CRTDTAARA
   — The completion message sent by DLTDTAARA

8. Do a DSPLIB of LIB(QTEMP).

   You should not see the data area named ABC because your program has deleted it.

Exercise B continued

Exercise B continued

9. Use the TAA tool LOGCL LOG(*NO) or key into the command entry display the following command:

```
CHGJOB    LOGCLPGM(*NO)
```

10. Modify program TRYSTDERR to make a comment line out of the CPYF statement:

```
/* CPYF  FROMFILE(XXXYX) TOFILE(ZZZZYZ) */
```

Commenting out the CPYF statement should cause the program to complete normally.

11. Create program TRYSTDERR.

12. From the command entry display, call the program:

```
CALL TRYSTDERR
```

If you are not displaying detailed messages, you should see only the completion message sent by the program. If detailed messages are displayed, you should see one escape and two completion messages as described previously.

13. Modify program TRYSTDERR to clear all messages sent to the program. You should insert this command — RMVMSG CLEAR(*ALL) — in the normal completion path, just before the RETURN command:

```
ENDPGM:
            RMVMSG  CLEAR(*ALL)
            RETURN  /* Normal end of program */
```

14. Create the program.

15. From the command entry display, call the program:

```
CALL TRYSTDERR
```

You should see only the completion message sent by the program, whether or not you are displaying detailed messages.

Exercise C Adding a CL Program Dump

In this exercise you will see how a program dump is added to the standard error-handling routine. To do this exercise, you will need the RTVPGMA TAA tool from QUSRTOOL. If the command does not exist on your system, you will need to create it (see Appendix B).

1. Use PDM to access member TRYSTDERR, created in the previous exercise.
2. If you had made a comment line out of the CPYF command, remove the comment symbols so the command will execute.
3. Enter the DCL statement:

```
DCL  &OBSERVE *CHAR LEN(5)
```

4. After the receive message of the escape message, enter the code shown earlier in this chapter for using the DMPCLPGM command (it is also included in the STDERR1 routine shown below in the full program):

```
RCVMSG      MSGTYPE(*EXCP) ...
RTVPGMA     ...
            /* Add the other code shown */
```

Your program should now look like this:

```
PGM
DCL            &RTNLOC    *CHAR LEN(8)
DCL            &OBSERVE   *CHAR LEN(5)
DCL            &ERRORSW   *LGL            /* Standard error */
DCL            &MSGID     *CHAR LEN(7)    /* Standard error */
DCL            &MSG       *CHAR LEN(512)  /* Standard error */
DCL            &MSGDTA    *CHAR LEN(512)  /* Standard error */
DCL            &MSGF      *CHAR LEN(10)   /* Standard error */
DCL            &MSGFLIB   *CHAR LEN(10)   /* Standard error */
DCL            &KEYVAR    *CHAR LEN(4)    /* Standard error */
DCL            &KEYVAR2   *CHAR LEN(4)    /* Standard error */
DCL            &RTNTYPE   *CHAR LEN(2)    /* Standard error */
MONMSG         MSGID(CPF0000) EXEC(GOTO STDERR1) /* Std err */
DLTDTAARA      DTAARA(QTEMP/ABC)
MONMSG         MSGID(CPF2105) /* Ignore */
```

Exercise C continued

Exercise C continued

```
          CRTDTAARA      DTAARA(QTEMP/ABC) TYPE(*CHAR) LEN(10)
          CPYF           FROMFILE(XXXYX) TOFILE(ZZZZYZ)
          SNDPGMMSG      MSG('Worked great') MSGTYPE(*COMP)
          CHGVAR         &RTNLOC 'ENDPGM'
          GOTO           CLEANUP
ENDPGM:
          RETURN         */ Normal end of program */
CLEANUP:                 */ Cleanup subroutine */
          DLTDTAARA      DTAARA(QTEMP/ABC)
          MONMSG         MSGID(CPF2105) /* Ignore */
          IF             (&RTNLOC *EQ 'ENDPGM') GOTO ENDPGM
          IF             (&RTNLOC *EQ 'STDERR2') GOTO STDERR2
          SNDPGMMSG      MSGID(CPF9898) MSGF(QCPFMSG)          +
                           MSGTYPE(*ESCAPE)                    +
                           MSGDTA('BAD RTNLOC value of ' *CAT  +
                           &RTNLOC *TCAT ' in CLEANUP subr')
STDERR1:                 */ Standard error-handling routine */
          IF             &ERRORSW SNDPGMMSG MSGID(CPF9999)     +
                           MSG(QCPFMSG) MSGTYPE(*ESCAPE)
          CHGVAR         &ERRORSW '1' /* Set to fail on error */
          RCVMSG         MSGTYPE(*EXCP) RMV(*NO) KEYVAR(&KEYVAR)
          RTVPGMA        PGM(TRYERR) OBSERVE(&OBSERVE)
          IF             (&OBSERVE *EQ '*NONE') DO /* No observe */
          SNDPGMMSG      MSG('No observability information  +
                           exists to use with DMPCLPGM')
          ENDDO          /* No observe */
          IF             (&OBSERVE *NE '*NONE') DO /* Use DMP */
          SNDPGMMSG      MSGID(CPF9898) MSGF(QCPFMSG)          +
                           MSGDTA('DMPCLPGM occurring')        +
                           TOPGMQ(*EXT) MSGTYPE(*STATUS)
          DMPCLPGM
          SNDPGMMSG      MSGID(CPI9801) MSGF(QCPFMSG)          +
                           TOPGMQ(*EXT) MSGTYPE(*STATUS)
          ENDDO          /* Use DMP */
          CHGVAR         &RTNLOC 'STDERR2'
          GOTO           CLEANUP
STDERR2:  RCVMSG         MSGTYPE(*PRV) MSGKEY(&KEYVAR) RMV(*NO)+
                           KEYVAR(&KEYVAR2) MSG(&MSG)          +
```

Exercise C continued

Exercise C continued

```
                        MSGDTA(&MSGDTA) MSGID(&MSGID)        +
                        RTNTYPE(&RTNTYPE) MSGF(&MSGF)        +
                        SNDMSGFLIB(&MSGFLIB)
           IF         (&RTNTYPE *NE '02') GOTO STDERR3
           IF         (&MSGID *NE '  ') SNDPGMMSG           +
                        MSGID(&MSGID) MSGF(&MSGFLIB/&MSGF)  +
                        MSGDTA(&MSGDTA) MSGTYPE(*DIAG)
           IF         (&MSGID *EQ '  ') SNDPGMMSG           +
                        MSG(&MSG) MSGTYPE(*DIAG)
           RMVMSG     MSGKEY(&KEYVAR2)
STDERR3:   RCVMSG     MSGKEY(&KEYVAR) MSGDTA(&MSGDTA)       +
                        MSGID(&MSGID) MSGF(&MSGF)           +
                        SNDMSGFLIB(&MSGFLIB)
           SNDPGMMSG  MSGID(&MSGID) MSGF(&MSGFLIB/&MSGF)    +
                        MSGDTA(&MSGDTA) MSGTYPE(*ESCAPE)
           ENDPGM
```

5. Create the program.

6. From the command entry display, call the program:

   ```
   CALL  TRYSTDERR
   ```

   You should see a status message when the RTVPGMA command is in operation as well as the status message you sent from the program. When the program completes, you should see the same diagnostic and escape message as in the previous exercise. In addition, a spooled file will exist that contains the program dump.

7. Use the WRKSPLF command to find the spooled file and display the program dump. You should see that the program dump contains the values of the variable at the time of the dump, as well as the contents of the program message queue.

8. Remove the observability of the program:

   ```
   CHGPGM  PGM(TRYSTDERR) RMVOBS(*ALL)
   ```

9. Call the program again:

   ```
   CALL  TRYSTDERR
   ```

Exercise C continued

Exercise C continued

You should see a status message when the RTVPGMA command is in operation. The program dump should not occur. When the RTVPGMA command completes, you should see the informational message sent by your program stating that the observable information has been removed from the program so no dump was taken. You should also see the same diagnostic and escape message that you saw in the previous exercise.

CHAPTER 5

The Job Log

The AS/400 job log can be good or bad: It's good to have when a program fails and you need an historical record of the program's processing to help you diagnose the problem. But it can be bad if you have to wade into a 500-page (or 500-pound) job log looking for clues to what went wrong. In this chapter we will discuss techniques that let you keep the job log a manageable size. But before we do, let's review a few facts about the job log.

- Every job on the AS/400 — and that includes the obvious job types (e.g., batch and interactive jobs), as well as the less obvious job types (e.g., group jobs, system request jobs, and system jobs like writers and subsystem monitors) — generates a job log.
- A job log is a combination of program message queues dynamically created by the system. The system creates one external message queue (*EXT) for each job and one program message queue for each program used within the job. While these message queues are logically separate, when combined they form the job's job log. When you display or print a job log, it does not appear in message queue sequence, but in time sequence so that you see the results as they occurred (Figure 5.1).
- Although every job generates a job log, not every job log will be written to a spooled output file. You can control whether or not a job log is spooled with the job attribute LOG, the value of which is determined by the current job's attributes. The system default specifies that, if the job ends normally, the job log will not be spooled. You can override that default either by using the CHGJOB command, by specifying a different value for the LOG parameter on the SBMJOB command, or by using a job description with the LOG attribute specified according to your particular needs.
- The output queue assigned to spooled job logs is controlled by the OUTQ parameter of the QPJOBLOG printer file in library QSYS. You can determine the current value by using the command DSPFD QPJOBLOG. If desired, you can change the value of OUTQ by using the command CHGPRTF QPJOBLOG OUTQ(xxxx). When assigning the OUTQ for QPJOBLOG, you can

FIGURE 5.1
The Job Log's Relationship to Program Message Queues

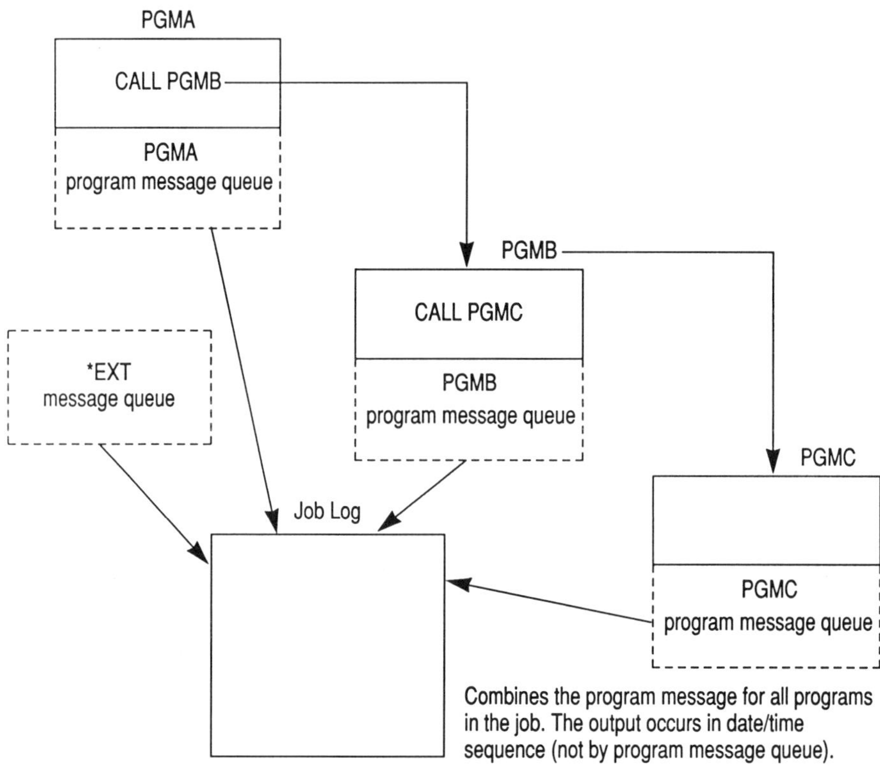

choose any output queue name, or the special value *JOB, which causes the spooled file to be written to the default output queue of the job that generated the job log. Some shops choose to have a different job log output queue for each day of the week. While this requires some user-written programs, it makes locating specific job logs easier. Specifying a single output queue for all job logs, or using a different one for each day of the week, can also be helpful in controlling cleanup (e.g., you can clean up by clearing an entire output queue). Note that if you use Operational Assistant and accept the job log defaults, all job logs will go to a special output queue named QEZJOBLOG in library QUSRSYS.

It is important to understand that the value of the OUTQ parameter for QPJOBLOG controls the fate of every job log on the system. A single job cannot control the output queue to which its job log is spooled. If you use the OVRPRTF command during the job to override the QPJOBLOG file to another output queue, the override will be removed when the job ends. Then the job log is spooled. Therefore, the override will no longer be in effect. If you want to get creative, you could specify OUTQ(*JOB) for the QPJOBLOG file, then you could use the CHGJOB command just before a job ends to output the job log to an output queue of your choice. In this case, you are not using an override command, but rather you are directing the output to the job's default output queue. You could execute the CHGJOB command in any program used by the job, but probably the best place is within a user-written routing program used by the job. Another alternative to control the OUTQ of a job log is to use an OVRPRTF to QPJOBLOG and to execute the command DSPJOBLOG OUTPUT(*PRINT) within the job. (See Exercise B at the end of this chapter.) Assume that your code does the following:

```
OVRPRTF     FILE(QPJOBLOG) OUT(ABC)
DSPJOBLOG   OUTPUT(*PRINT)
```

The partial job log (the job log is not complete because the job has not yet ended) would be spooled to output queue ABC. Now, assuming that the job ends normally, the system's job-ending logic would follow the process illustrated in Figure 5.2.

FIGURE 5.2
The Logic Behind Creating a Spooled File

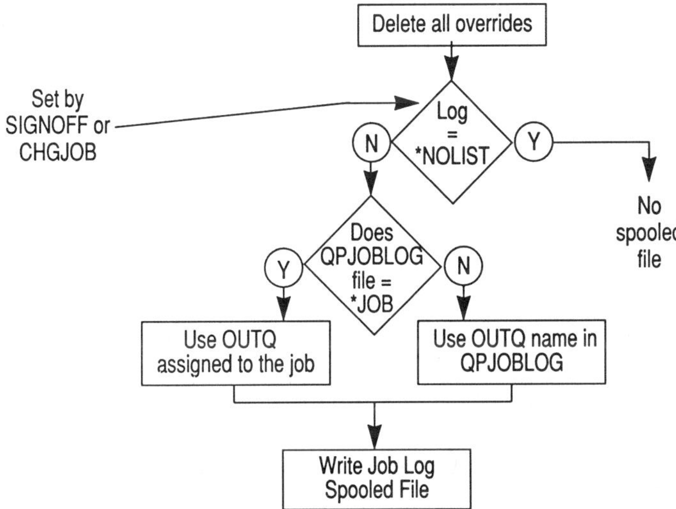

Technical Tip

As an overall system function, placing all job logs in a single output queue (e.g., QEZJOBLOG) or a separate output queue per day seems to provide the best overall solution. The job logs are easier to find and easier to clean up.

- When you want a printed copy of a job log, you can simply move the job log to an output queue that is attached to an active printer.
- The system does not support the capability to save or restore spooled files. But two QUSRTOOL TAA tools — CPYFRMOUTQ and SPLCTL — will let you back up job logs or any spooled files. These tools copy a spooled file to a database file, which can then be saved to tape, if required.

Technical Tip

If you need to back up spooled files regularly, use the TAA tools SPLCTL or CPYFRMOUTQ in QUSRTOOL. They allow you to manage save and restore operations for spooled output files.

- Because job logs (i.e., spooled files) can clutter the system, wasting space and slowing down other system functions, you should have a procedure for regularly cleaning up job logs. Using Operational Assistant offers one solution: It does reasonably well on job log cleanup and it also deletes old system dump spooled files. You control when cleanup occurs and how old the job log must be before it is deleted. To specify cleanup, use the command GO ASSIST and follow the prompts for managing your system and for cleanup tasks. While Operational Assistant handles job logs and dumps, there could be many other old spooled files cluttering up your system. For example, programmers may have their own special output queues where spooled files can lay around forever. Several solutions for cleaning up spooled files exist in QUSRTOOL TAA tools. Consider using the tools SPLCTL, DLTOLDSPLF, or CLNSYS.

The LOG Job Attribute

A job's LOG attribute controls whether or not you will get a job log and, if you do, how detailed it will be. The system default for interactive and batch jobs is LOG(4 0 *NOLIST). Using the default means that if the job ends normally, the job log is not spooled to an output queue. However, if the job ends abnormally, the job log will be spooled and will contain the maximum amount of detail available, including full second-level message text.

I generally use the default, but when I want to ensure that a job log is spooled, I either use a special job description on the SBMJOB command or I specify a CHGJOB command in a CL program. In either case, I specify LOG(4 0 *SECLVL). Specifying *SECLVL causes both first- and second-level message text to be written to the job log and, regardless of how the job ends, the job log will be spooled to an output queue.

Technical Tip

A special job description that specifies LOG(4 0 *SECLVL) can be useful for testing, or for problem determination, because it ensures that you will get a job log with the maximum amount of information.

Forcing a Job Log

Most programmers prefer that a user's interactive job never terminate due to an error condition. However, you cannot always prevent the abnormal termination of an interactive job. For example, some errors, such as deletion of an active program, cannot be monitored for; if such errors occur, the job ends abnormally. But in most cases, you can prevent an interactive job from terminating due to an error. Simply ensure that the highest-level CL program monitors for message ID CPF0000 (i.e., MONMSG CPF0000) to capture all escape messages. Then, if an error occurs, a standard error-handling procedure can take over to explain the problem to the user and suggest that (s)he take appropriate action.

The key concern when this happens is to notify someone in the MIS department that a problem has occurred. The following sample code will inform the user of the problem, capture the job log at the point of program failure, place the job log in a special OUTQ, and inform the programmer that a job log needs to be reviewed.

```
        /* Capturing the job log and continuing */
          PGM
          DCL         &RTNVAR *CHAR LEN(16)
          DCL         &MSG     *CHAR LEN(80)
          DCL         &JOB     *CHAR LEN(10)
          DCL         &USER    *CHAR LEN(10)
          DCL         &JOBNBR *CHAR LEN(6)
          MONMSG      MSGID(CPF0000) EXEC(GOTO ERRHANDL)
BEGIN:                /* The following would be either a */
                      /*    CALL to your menu program or  */
```

```
                        /*    a SNDRCVF to display the menu */
            SNDRCVF     ...
               .
               .
               .
ERRHANDL:   SNDPGMMSG   MSGID(CPF9898) MSGF(QCPFMSG)               +
                          TOPGMQ(*EXT)                             +
                          MSGDTA('An unexpected error occurred.    +
                                Please wait') MSGTYPE(*STATUS)
                        /* Specify your own special OUTQ */
            OVRPRTF     QPJOBLOG OUTQ(xxxxx)
            DSPJOBLOG   OUTPUT(*PRINT)
            RTVJOBA     JOB(&JOB) USER(&USER) NBR(&JOBNBR)
            CHGVAR      &MSG  ('Job ' *CAT &JOBNBR *TCAT '/'  +
                          *CAT &USER *TCAT '/' *CAT &JOB      +
                          *TCAT ' had unexpected error.       +
                          See the job log.')
                        /* Send the msg to as many message */
                        /*   queues as needed.             */
            SNDPGMMSG   MSG(&MSG) TOMSGQ(QSYSOPR)
                        /* Clear the previous status message */
            SNDPGMMSG   MSGID(CPI9801) MSGF(QCPFMSG)        +
                          TOPGMQ(*EXT) MSGTYPE(*STATUS)
                        /* Use TAA tool to communicate      */
                        /*    to the interactive operator   */
            PMTOPR      RTNVAR(&RTNVAR) LEN(1) PROMPT('An   +
                          unexpected error occurred on the +
                          last menu option. It is being    +
                          investigated. Do not use this    +
                          option again until notified.     +
                          Enter one of the following:')    +
                          LINE1('C - Continue')            +
                          LINE2('S - Signoff')
            IF          (&RTNVAR *EQ 'S') SIGNOFF
            GOTO        BEGIN
            ENDPGM
```

In the code above, when an unexpected error occurs, the error-handling routine sends a status message to the user. The DSPJOBLOG command captures information about the problem. Since the job in this example hadn't ended yet, this is a partial job log (more messages will be added later as the job proceeds). The OVRPRTF command directs the job log output to a special OUTQ. The SNDPGMMSG command sends a message describing the problem to the QSYSOPR message queue. You also can use another SNDPGMMSG command to send the same message to a programmer or other responsible person to ensure that the problem will be looked at. The TAA tool PMTOPR gives you an easy way to communicate with the user of an interactive program and elicit a response (i.e., the user can either continue the program or sign off). Chapter 13 provides a detailed description of the PMTOPR command.

PROVIDING A TEMPORARY AUDIT TRAIL

If you need a temporary audit trail to help you diagnose a problem, the job log can be very helpful. For example, you may want to use the SNDPGMMSG command to send some debugging or program progress statements to your program's message queue so they will appear in the job log. For instance, in your program you might be building a command to execute through QCMDEXC. Since commands executed in this manner are not listed in the job log, problems can sometimes be difficult to analyze. Before calling QCMDEXC, you could send a message to your own program message queue documenting the command to be executed. For example,

```
PGM
DCL         &CMD *CHAR LEN(256)
CHGVAR      &CMD ('SAVLIB LIB(' *CAT &LIB *TCAT ')')
SNDPGMMSG   MSG(&CMD) TOPGMQ(*SAME)
CALL        QCMDEXC PARM(&CMD 256)
RMVMSG      CLEAR(*ALL)
ENDPGM
```

Using TOPGMQ(*SAME) sends the message to the current program's message queue. In this case, the message contains the command you are going to execute. If the command executes successfully, the RMVMSG command removes all messages from this program's message queue. If the command fails, the job log will contain both the command you executed and the messages it produced.

Technical Tip

Sending messages to your own program's message queue provides a good temporary audit trail. For example, you can send messages to your program that describe where the program is in its processing.

Although the job log provides an audit trail, its depth of detail can sometimes make it difficult to use for that purpose (i.e., important information can get lost in the clutter of detail). In addition, the job log can be deleted easily because the user of the job has authority to delete any of the spooled files (s)he created. In those instances where a more secure audit trail is required, you should consider establishing a permanent audit trail.

PROVIDING A PERMANENT AUDIT TRAIL

If you want a good permanent audit trail, AS/400 journal support provides an outstanding solution. To collect audit entries for all jobs, you can set up a specific journal or you can use the system job accounting journal (QACGJRN). The advantage of the system job accounting journal is that it automatically includes entries for when the job starts and ends. (Note that the system provides an audit journal, QAUDJRN, but this journal is designed for logging security information and should not be used as a general-purpose audit trail.)

Let's assume that you have set up the job accounting journal (to do this, see IBM's *Work Management Guide*, SC41-8078). Here's the code you would need to add to your program to provide a good permanent audit trail as your application completes its logical steps:

```
      .
      .
      .
CALL      PAY_UPDT
SNDJRNE   JRN(QACGJRN) +
            ENTDTA('The PAYROLL file was updated')
      .
      .
      .
CALL      PAY_SORT
SNDJRNE   JRN(QACGJRN) +
            ENTDTA('The PAYROLL file was sorted')
```

With the job accounting journal active, the system automatically logs information such as the user, the job, the program, and the date/time. These journal entries have two controlling attributes: "code" and "type." User entries written to the journal are uniquely identified as journal code 'U'. You can use your own journal type (see the TYPE parameter on the SNDJRNE command in the CL reference) or take the default (blanks) as shown in the example.

Technical Tip

You can use the job accounting journal to provide a permanent audit trail for your applications. For information about how to set up and work with the job accounting journal, see IBM's *Work Management Guide*, SC41-8078.

Cleaning Up the Job Log

To prevent the creation of a 500-pound job log (i.e., a job log overloaded with messages), you need to add a little code to most CL programs so that you can clean up messages as you go. Fortunately, certain system functions are available to make the task simpler:

- When the RCVMSG (Receive Message) command is used in a program, the received message is, by default, removed from the program message queue. This "scalpel" technique lets you cut one message from the job log each time you use it. Assume that, after using the CHKOBJ command and receiving an escape message on an expected condition (e.g., object not found), you want to remove the escape message. Here's what you would code:

```
CHKOBJ      OBJ(xxxx) OBJTYPE(*FILE)
MONMSG      MSGID(CPF9801) EXEC(DO) /* Not found */
RCVMSG      MSGTYPE(*EXCP) /* Remove it */
ENDDO       /* Not found */
```

- One method of removing one or many messages is to use the RMVMSG (Remove Message) command. The CLEAR parameter of the RMVMSG command lets you remove all messages sent to your program's message queue by specifying

```
RMVMSG  CLEAR(*ALL)
```

  This "meat axe" solution clobbers every message sent to your program's message queue, but it does not clean up all the messages that your program caused to be sent by calling other programs. Unless a lower-level program "bubbled up" its messages to your program's message queue, you can't get rid of them with this technique. For example, if your program calls an HLL program and the HLL program receives a message from some data management function (e.g., buffer is longer than the data received), you can't delete this message with the technique shown (Figure 5.3).

FIGURE 5.3
Using RMVMSG CLEAR (*ALL)

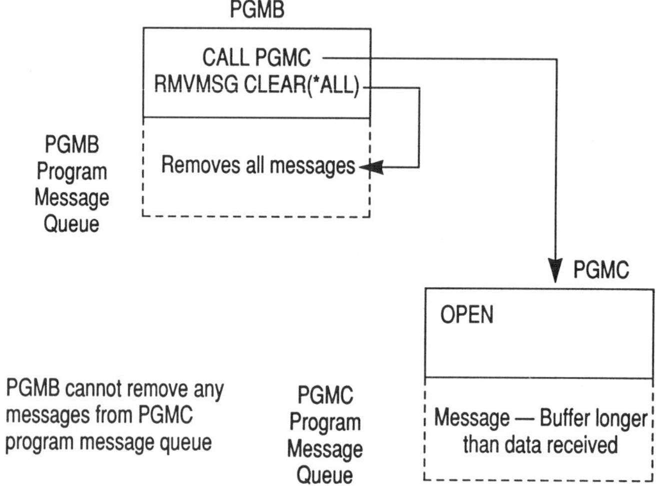

Let's look at how RMVMSG CLEAR(*ALL) can be used effectively. My CL program logic tends to follow a generic design:

- Check the parameters that were received
- Check the existence of objects
- Create temporary objects
- Perform any overrides
- Perform some "do it" function or CALL HLL program
- If successful
    - — Send a completion message
    - — Do a return (RETURN or ENDPGM)

Given this logic, the best place to put the "meat axe" is just before the program completes successfully (e.g., just before the RETURN command). By placing the RMVMSG command here, all the messages will still exist if your CL program fails (the RMVMSG command will not execute). If your CL program is successful, you get rid of any mess that was generated.

Don't use RMVMSG CLEAR(*ALL) after every command in your program; once per program is generally adequate. If your program generated a lot of messages, you may want additional RMVMSG CLEAR(*ALL) statements at logical points just to make it easier to read the job log if an error occurs. If you are testing a program, you may not want to use the RMVMSG CLEAR(*ALL) command until after the program has been thoroughly tested. Retaining the program messages can be helpful during program testing.

Technical Tip

RMVMSG CLEAR(*ALL) is a great technique for minimizing the number of messages contained in a job log. Use RMVMSG CLEAR(*ALL) just before your program executes a return to clean up any messages that were sent to your program. You may prefer to test the program completely before adding this command to your code.

- The command RMVMSG PGMQ(*ALLINACT) lets you remove messages from any program's message queue when the program is no longer active. This system function was created for never-ending programs — programs that might stay active for many days and generate large job logs. But the technique works for any job and should be used more than it is. To use the technique, you would code

  ```
  RMVMSG PGMQ(*ALLINACT) CLEAR(*ALL)
  ```

  Following execution of this command, only messages sent to your program (because it's still active), and messages sent to other active programs in the program stack, would remain in the job log.

  You can use this "bulldozing" technique in an interactive job that is driven from a high-level menu. For example, when the user returns to the high-level menu and all interactive programs have completed successfully, you can safely remove messages caused by the lower-level programs.

  Similarly, if you have a batch job where a main program is in control, the program could specify the following upon successful completion:

  ```
  RMVMSG PGMQ(*ALLINACT) CLEAR(*ALL)
  RMVMSG CLEAR(*ALL)
  SNDPGMMSG  .... MSGTYPE(*COMP)
  ```

  Be aware that you shouldn't use *ALLINACT in a utility program that is called interactively. This can be particularly bothersome to programmers who use the command entry screen (QCMD). You would be "bulldozing" not only the messages caused by your utility, but also any other messages from programs that were no longer active. Almost all the messages in the job log would be wiped out. You could consider including code (i.e., the

RTVJOBA command) in your utility to determine whether the program is running interactively or in batch mode. If the utility were running in batch, you could have the program issue the RMVMSG PGMQ(*ALLINACT) CLEAR(*ALL) command.

Technical Tip

The *ALLINACT function of the RMVMSG command is a winner for cleaning up the job log. But you need to be careful where you use it, because it can clean up more than just the messages generated by your program. Removing messages also removes a good deal of problem determination information from the job log. It is often better to be sure the program works consistently before you start removing any messages.

- Sometimes an HLL program (e.g., RPG or COBOL) can generate messages. These messages (e.g., "Subfile record not found") are normally sent by some database or data management function. Once the HLL program is no longer active, you have no way to delete the messages other than to use the *ALLINACT function of the RMVMSG command. But while the HLL program is active, you can call a CL program that provides the same function as RMVMSG CLEAR(*ALL). The RMVMSG command supports the capability to remove messages from the previous program's message queue with the parameter PGMQ(*PRV). The TAA tool HLRMVMSG, which is a small CL program that contains the code you need, makes it easy to implement this technique in your programs. Simply code

  ```
  CALL  'HLRMVMSG'
  ```

  and all the messages sent to the HLL program's message queue will be deleted. As with RMVMSG CLEAR(*ALL), the place to put the call is at the point where the HLL program has completed successfully and just before the end of the program. Remember that a unique program message queue is created each time a program is called. If it is an RPG program that returns with LR off, or a COBOL program that does not execute a STOP RUN statement, you will need to call HLRMVMSG before every return to keep the job log clean.

Technical Tip

The TAA tool HLRMVMSG makes it simple to clean up the messages that have been sent to an HLL program's message queue.

Reading a Job Log

As mentioned earlier, the job log is written in time sequence. If your program fails, the place to start diagnosing the problem is usually at the end of the job log where the error occurred. This assumes that your program did not try to do a lot of processing after the error occurred. The last message in the job log is the job completion message (CPF1164). Before that you will normally see some messages (CPC2191) issued when the system deleted objects in library QTEMP. This is all perfectly normal.

Technical Tip

If you want to keep the CPC2191 cleanup messages from being generated, you could use the command CLRLIB LIB(QTEMP) just before you end the job. The fewer extraneous messages in the job log, the easier it will be to find the information you need to diagnose a problem.

Ahead of the QTEMP cleanup messages are the messages that your job generated. In many cases you will have several programs in the stack when an error occurs. If this happens, you normally should see a series of CPF9999 function check messages that were issued as each program in the stack aborted. If you keep rolling backward through the job log, you will eventually see the escape message that caused the program on the bottom of the program stack to abnormally terminate. You may need to read a prior diagnostic message, but once you find the real problem, note which program sent the message and which program received it. This is usually a key piece of information if you have to fix something. It tells you which program had the problem (i.e., the one that sent or received the escape message). You can ignore the information in the job log about which instruction was used to perform the send or receive (this information refers to a “machine” instruction and is meaningless when debugging at the CL command level).

Job Log Review

Let’s walk through a series of commands and see how their execution affects the job log. This will give you an idea of what is happening as a program performs its processing. Consider the following two programs:

```
 Program A
PGM
            /* Create XXX data area */
DLTDTAARA   DTAARA(QTEMP/XXX)
MONMSG      MSGID(CPF2105) EXEC(DO) /* Not found */
RCVMSG      MSGTYPE(*EXCP)
CRTDTAARA   DTAARA(QTEMP/XXX) TYPE(*CHAR) LEN(10)
ENDDO       /* Not found */
            /* Create XXX2 data area */
DLTDTAARA   DTAARA(QTEMP/XXX2)
MONMSG      MSGID(CPF2105) EXEC(DO) /* Not found */
RCVMSG      MSGTYPE(*EXCP)
CRTDTAARA   DTAARA(QTEMP/XXX2) TYPE(*CHAR) LEN(10)
ENDDO       /* Not found */
CALL        PGMB
DLTDTAARA   DTAARA(QTEMP/XXX*)
SNDPGMMSG   ('PGMA worked great') MSGTYPE(*COMP)
RMVMSG      CLEAR(*ALL)
ENDPGM

 Program B
PGM
            /* Create YYY data area */
DLTDTAARA   DTAARA(QTEMP/YYY)
MONMSG      MSGID(CPF2105) EXEC(DO) /* Not found */
CRTDTAARA   DTAARA(QTEMP/YYY) TYPE(*CHAR) LEN(10)
ENDDO       /* Not found */
RMVMSG      CLEAR(*ALL)
DLTDTAARA   DTAARA(QTEMP/YYY)
SNDPGMMSG   ('PGMB worked great.') MSGTYPE(*COMP)
ENDPGM
```

1. When you start your job, the system automatically creates an *EXT (external) message queue for the job.
2. When you call PGMA, the system automatically creates a program message queue for the program.
3. The DLTDTAARA command attempts to delete the XXX data area in library QTEMP. The DLTDTAARA CPP (an IBM-supplied command processing program) does the work. The CPP acts as a normal program in that it is in the program stack and can send and receive messages. In this case, the DLTDTAARA CPP sends an

escape message to the previous program (PGMA) stating that the data area does not exist.

4. The MONMSG command in PGMA monitors for an escape message. This command does not cause any messages to be sent to PGMA's message queue.
5. The RCVMSG command defaults to RMV(*YES) to remove the escape message sent by the DLTDTAARA command. This is the "scalpel" technique discussed earlier that removes a single message.
6. The CRTDTAARA command sends a completion message to PGMA's message queue stating that the data area was created successfully. The completion message is left in the program message queue at this point.
7. The same code is repeated to create data area XXX2.
8. The CALL to PGMB occurs, and the system creates a program message queue for PGMB.
9. PGMB executes the DLTDTAARA command for a non-existent data area, which causes an escape message to be sent to PGMB's message queue.
10. PGMB does not remove the escape message from the program message queue.
11. PGMB then creates data area YYY, which causes a completion message to be sent to PGMB's message queue.
12. The RMVMSG CLEAR(*ALL) command executes. This is the "meat axe" technique described earlier that cleans up all messages sent to PGMB's message queue. It causes the escape message and the completion message to be removed, so PGMB's message queue contains no messages at this point. But in this example, the command is in the wrong place. It should be run after the next command (DLTDTAARA) to clean up the completion message.
13. The DLTDTAARA command executes, which causes a completion message to be sent to PGMB's message queue.
14. The SNDPGMMSG command sends a completion message stating that PGMB was successful. By default, this message is sent to the previous program's message queue (PGMA in this case). Note that the message never exists in PGMB's message queue.

FIGURE 5.4
Messages Don't Bubble Up if a Subprogram is Invoked

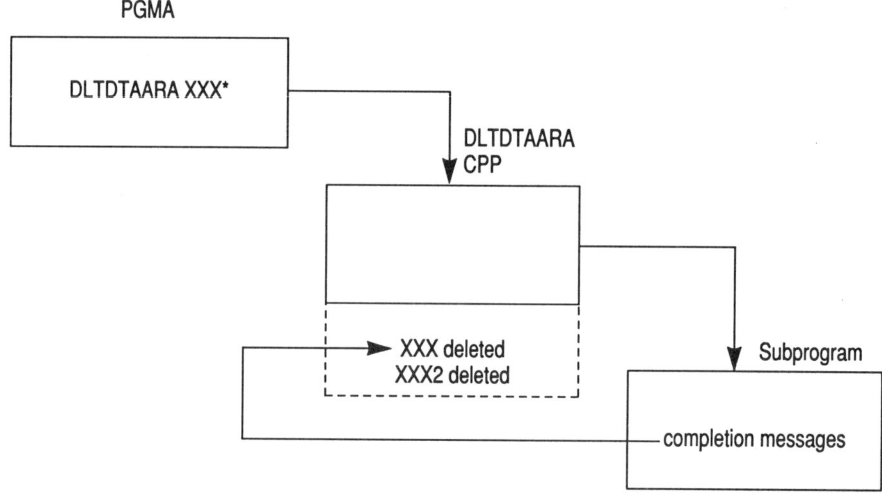

15. PGMB then does a return and the program is removed from the job's program stack.

16. Control is returned to program PGMA.

17. The DLTDTAARA command runs, using the generic name XXX*. The DLTDTAARA CPP recognizes that a generic request exists and calls a subprogram for each object to be deleted. A completion message is sent from the subprogram to the CPP. The CPP does not bubble up the completion messages for the individual deletions. When the generic objects have all been processed, a final completion message is sent stating how many objects were deleted. The final completion message is in PGMA's message queue, but the individual completion messages for each object deleted were sent to the CPP's message queue. Since the CPP did not bubble up these messages, they are in the job log, but cannot be accessed from PGMA (Figure 5.4).

18. The SNDPGMMSG command sends a completion message to the previous program's message queue. If you are working from the command entry display, that program is named QCMD.

19. The RMVMSG CLEAR(*ALL) command deletes all the messages in PGMA's message queue. The messages deleted include

- The two CRTDTAARA completion messages
- The final DLTDTAARA completion message
- The completion message sent by PGMB

The RMVMSG CLEAR(*ALL) command does not clear the low-level messages generated by the DLTDTAARA command executed in PGMA, the DLTDTAARA message generated in PGMB, or the completion message sent by the prior command (SNDPGMMSG) to QCMD's program message queue. They are still in the job log.

The result is that some cleanup of the job log was done, but it was not perfect. The program could have used the *ALLINACT function to get rid of the low-level messages. One of the steps in the Exercises section of this chapter will walk you through using this technique in a batch job.

The following summarizes the chronological order of messages received by the three important program message queues used in this example:

PGMA Program Message Queue

- DLTDTAARA CPP sends escape message for XXX not found
- RCVMSG removes the previous escape message
- CRTDTAARA of XXX completion message
- DLTDTAARA CPP sends escape message for XXX2 not found
- RCVMSG removes the previous escape message
- CRTDTAARA of XXX2 completion message
- Completion message sent by PGMB
- DLTDTAARA completion message for XXX* generic delete
- RMVMSG CLEAR(*ALL) removes all messages in this queue

PGMB Program Message Queue

- DLTDTAARA CPP sends escape message for YYY not found
- CRTDTAARA of YYY completion message
- RMVMSG CLEAR(*ALL) removes all messages in this queue
- DLTDTAARA of YYY completion message

CPP for DLTDTAARA for generic delete in PGMA

- XXX data area deleted
- XXX2 data area deleted

If you want a clean job log, you have to work at it. In general, the RMVMSG *CLEAR(*ALL) command will help, but it won't be perfect. As you can see from the sample we walked through, some commands will invoke subprograms and not bubble up every message.

Exercise A Cleaning Up the Job Log

In this exercise you will see how to keep your job log clean.

1. Use PDM to create the source PGMA and PGMB shown at the end of this chapter.
2. Create both programs.
3. From the command entry display (i.e. CALL QCMD), enter

   ```
   CALL PGMA
   ```

   You should see the completion message sent from PGMA.
4. Press F10 for detail messages.

   You should see the DLTDTAARA completion message of YYY caused by PGMB. You should also see the two individual completion messages indicating that the DLTDTAARA command in PGMA deleted data areas XXX and XXX2.
5. Use the Help key on each of the low-level messages to display more detailed information.

   You should see that the YYY data area message was sent to PGMB from an IBM-supplied program (the DLTDTAARA command's CPP). You should see that the XXX data area message was sent by the CPP, but the CPP is sending the message to itself. In this case, the CPP has actually called itself to delete each of the generic data areas.
6. Use PDM to modify PGMA. Add the following statement right after the PGM statement:

   ```
   CHGJOB    LOG(4 Ø *SECLVL)
   ```

   This will ensure that the job log is spooled.
7. Create the program.
8. From the command entry display, submit the program to batch.

   ```
   SBMJOB    CMD(CALL PGMA)
   ```

9. When the job completes, use the WRKSPLF command to look at the job log.

   You should see the same messages that you saw on the command entry display.

Exercise A continued

Exercise A continued

10. Return to PDM and modify PGMA to include the following command immediately following the existing RMVMSG command:

```
RMVMSG  PGMQ(*ALLINACT) CLEAR(*ALL)
```

11. Create the program.
12. From the command entry display, submit the program to batch.

```
SBMJOB   CMD(CALL PGMA)
```

13. When the job ends, use the WRKSPLF command to look at the job log.

    You should now see that the job log has been cleaned up. You should only see the IBM messages for beginning and end of job and the completion message from PGMA.

14. Return to the display of all your spooled files and note the device or output queue name for the job log you just displayed. As discussed previously, it probably says QEZJOBLOG.

Exercise B Displaying a Partial Job Log

In this exercise you will create two job logs, a full job log and a partial job log that you will be able to display.

1. From the command entry display, enter the following command and assign an output queue other than the one named at the end of Exercise A (a good choice would be your own personal output queue):

```
OVRPRTF  FILE(QPJOBLOG) OUTQ(xxxx)
```

2. Now enter the following command:

```
DSPJOBLOG  JOB(*) OUTPUT(*PRINT)
```

3. Use the WRKSPLF command to display your spooled files. Note the output queue assigned to the partial job log. It should be the one you named.
4. Display the job log. It should look like a normal job log for all the messages from your current job.

Exercise B continued

Exercise B continued

5. Use the PDM display to modify PGMA from Exercise A. Just before the SNDPGMMSG command, enter the following:

```
OVRPRTF    FILE(QPJOBLOG) OUTQ(xxxx)
DSPJOBLOG  JOB(*) OUTPUT(*PRINT)
```

6. Create the program.
7. Submit the program to batch.

```
SBMJOB  CMD(CALL PGMA)
```

When the job ends, two job logs should be created. The first is the partial job log caused by the DSPJOBLOG command. It should be in the output queue that you named. The second job log is the full version created when the job ended. Even though you have overridden QPJOBLOG, the override is no longer in effect at job completion. The full job log is probably in output queue QEZJOBLOG, as described previously.

CHAPTER 6

Miscellaneous Message Techniques

This chapter contains specific solutions to a wide range of problems related to working with messages.

WHICH PROGRAM CALLED MINE?

When you need to know which user called your program, the RTVJOBA command is available to access the name of that user. It's not quite as easy to learn the name of the program that called your program, but it can be done.

A little-used function lets you receive a message from the program message queue of the previous program (i.e., the program higher in the program stack that called your program). First, use the SNDPGMMSG command to send a message (any message will do) to the previous program. Then use the RCVMSG command and specify PGMQ(*PRV) and SENDER(&SENDER) to have the same message returned to your program. The SENDER parameter on the RCVMSG command is the key. It is an 80-byte field that includes information such as the date and time the message was sent and the name of the program it was sent to. Lying in the middle of the SENDER field is the information you want (the name of the program that called your program). Here's the code you need:

```
DCL         &SENDER *CHAR LEN(80)
DCL         &PGM *CHAR LEN(10)
SNDPGMMSG   MSG(DUMMY)
RCVMSG      PGMQ(*PRV) MSGTYPE(*LAST) SENDER(&SENDER)
CHGVAR      &PGM %SST(&SENDER 56 10)
            /* &PGM now contains the name of the */
            /* program that called your program. */
```

Technical Tip

With the RCVMSG command, you can use the SENDER and PGMQ(*PRV) parameters to determine the name of the program that called your program.

Application Programming Interfaces (APIs) also exist that are equivalent to the SNDPGMMSG and RCVMSG commands. The APIs let you send and receive messages to and from programs higher in the program stack (not just the previous program) without knowing a program's name. With the APIs, it is possible to determine the names of the programs in the program stack. (For more information about these APIs and others, see IBM's *System Programmer's Interface Reference*, SC41-8223.)

WHICH MESSAGE FILE IS THIS MESSAGE FROM?

If you answer questions for other programmers or users, you might occasionally be asked to explain what a particular message means. To answer the question, you would first probably use the DSPMSGD command to display the message so you can read it. Most OS/400 operating system messages (those beginning with message prefix CPF) are in the IBM-supplied message file QCPFMSG in library QSYS. The DSPMSGD command defaults to message file QCPFMSG, so it's easy to find these messages. For example, if you want to see the details of message ID CPF1234, you would key

```
DSPMSGD  CPF1234
```

However, not all IBM messages are in message file QCPFMSG. Some of them are in different message files in library QSYS and some are in message files in different libraries. For example, if someone asks you the meaning of message ID PQT0012, which is not contained in message file QCPFMSG, where would you look for the answer? No manual exists that lists all the messages. You could use the DSPOBJD command to find all the *MSGF object types and then search for message ID PQT0012.

But a better solution is to use the DSPMSGTXT command, a QUSRTOOL TAA tool. As with any TAA tool, you need to be sure it exists on your system (if it does not, see Appendix B). Then, all you have to do is specify the message ID:

```
DSPMSGTXT  PQT0012
```

The DSPMSGTXT command examines the first three letters of the message ID and determines the message file and library where the message exists. It then invokes the DSPMSGD command for you. (In case you are curious, message ID PQT0012 is in message file QPQMSGF in library QSYS.) If you are like me, you will find using the DSPMSGTXT command to be a consistently better alternative than using the DSPMSGD command. It only requires that you know the message ID; you don't need to know the name of the message file or the name of the library in which the message file resides.

Technical Tip

The TAA tool DSPMSGTXT can be used any time you need to display an IBM-supplied message. The command has the "smarts" to find the right message file and library for you.

How To Duplicate A Message

The AS/400 does not supply a way to duplicate a message description. But if you work with message files, this is an important function to have: Many messages have similar text and it's no fun to rekey the text over and over. The QUSRTOOL TAA tool DUPMSGD offers a solution. For example, to duplicate message ID CPF1234 in library QSYS in your message file, you would specify

```
DUPMSGD  FROMID(CPF1234) FROMMSGF(QCPFMSG) +
           TOMSGF(xxxx)
```

where xxxx is the name of your message file.

If you write message descriptions, you can use the DUPMSGD command (with the TOID parameter specified) to duplicate one of your own and use it as a base to start a new message ID. The DUPMSGD command's only restriction is that it cannot duplicate validity-checking parameters specified on a message description. If you need these parameters, you will need to enter them manually.

Technical Tip

The TAA tool DUPMSGD is a must if you create your own message descriptions. It allows you to duplicate almost all message attributes.

How To Change A Long Message Text

If you write message descriptions, you may have found that the CL prompter makes it difficult for you to write second-level text longer than 512 bytes. The SECLVL parameter value can be up to 3,000 characters in length, but the CL prompter is limited to 512 bytes for a single parameter. You may find the limitation a real challenge when you want to modify the text of an existing message. The WRKMSGD command supports a good list display that lets you access an existing message description, display it with the CL prompter, and key over the text. But, because you are still using the CL prompter, you will lose any part of your second-level message text that exceeds 512 bytes.

One way to solve this problem is to use the CHGMSGD command, without using the command prompter, and rekey the entire second-level text. You could do this from the command entry display; however, if you have ever done this, you probably don't want to do it again. A better solution is to use the QUSRTOOL TAA tool CHGMSGD2. Using this command, you would specify

```
CHGMSGD2  MSGID(xxxxxxx) MSGF(yyyyy)
```

After entering the command, you will see the CHGMSGD display with most of its parameters supported. You can change any of the displayed parameters. After you press Enter on the CHGMSGD display, you will see a second screen containing 1,500 bytes of second-level text that you can key over. To get the additional 1,500 bytes of text, you would press the F6 command key.

Technical Tip

The TAA tool CHGMSGD2 can be a lifesaver if you need to enter or modify long second-level text fields.

OVERRIDING A MESSAGE FILE

The OVRMSGF (Override Message File) command offers a useful function, although many programmers have never used it. You can use the OVRMSGF command to temporarily change the text or the default of an IBM-supplied message. Let's step through an example that will temporarily change the text of message ID CPF9801 in message file QCPFMSG so that for a specific job the message reads differently. All other jobs would see the standard system text. The first-level text of CPF9801 reads

```
Object &2 in library &3 not found
```

The second-level text uses variable &5 to describe the object type. Assume that you want the first-level text of CPF9801 to read as follows for a specific job:

```
Object &2 of type &5 in library &3 not found
```

First, you need to add a message description with the same message ID to your own message file. The easiest way to do this is to use the QUSRTOOL TAA tool DUPMSGD, as described earlier in this chapter. The DUPMSGD command will not only duplicate the first- and second-level text, but it will also duplicate the field descriptions for the message data. Assuming your message file is MSGF1, you would key

```
DUPMSGD  FROMID(CPF9801) FROMMSGF(QCPFMSG)  +
           TOMSGF(MSGF1)
```

Next, you would modify the first-level message text. To do this, use the WRKMSGD command as follows:

```
WRKMSGD  MSGID(CPF9801) MSGF(MSGF1)
```

Then enter the screen option for the change operation. This will place the current values of the message description in the command prompts so that you can key over them. Simply change the first-level message text to read

```
Object &2 of type &5 in library &3 not found.
```

Now, when you want to use your message text instead of the system version for message ID CPF9801, simply use the OVRMSGF command in your CL program. When you use the OVRMSGF command, the system will first search your message file for the message ID that is being sent. If it can't find the message ID in your message file, it looks in the message file specified on the SNDPGMMSG command.

You don't have to duplicate the entire QCPFMSG message file to change one or more message descriptions. Here are the commands you would include in your CL program to substitute your version of message ID CPF9801 (contained in message file MSGF1) for the system version. First, include the command

```
OVRMSGF  MSGF(QCPFMSG) TOMSGF(MSGF1)
```

and then later in your program when you want to check for an object's existence, include the command

```
CHKOBJ   OBJ(XXX) OBJTYPE(*PGM)
```

Assuming that program XXX is not found in your library list, the system would send message ID CPF9801. It would first attempt to retrieve the message ID from MSGF1 because of your override statement. Since the message description exists in MSGF1, the system would retrieve your message and insert the proper message data.

The OVRMSGF command lets you specify the message file where your customized version of a message exists. You just add message descriptions for the messages you have customized. If the system needs a message description that doesn't exist in your message file, it will look in message file QCPF.

Technical Tip

The OVRMSGF command lets you control what a message says and many of the other attributes of a message. You don't have to live with the IBM defaults.

Another use for modifying a message is to address the fact that sometimes users are confused because a message even exists. You can't prevent the IBM code from sending a message, but under certain circumstances you might want to totally blank out the message text and have the IBM code send blanks. To do this, you just follow the steps we used in the above example and blank out the first- and second-level text for your message description.

A good example of this is message ID CPF1392, which is sent to a user when (s)he has one more opportunity to enter a valid password on the sign-on display. The first-level text of the message, sent based on your setting of the QMAXSIGN system value, states "Next not valid sign-on disables user profile." The message text protects the innocent, but it probably tells the user who is trying to break in exactly what (s)he wants to know.

Responding to a Message Automatically and Dynamically

In previous examples, I've demonstrated how to duplicate a message and how to use the OVRMSGF command to temporarily change a message's first-level message text. Now let's see how you can modify an inquiry message so that, rather than a user or the system operator seeing and responding to the message, your CL program provides a response to the message automatically.

Assume you are writing a CL program that may elicit from the system the inquiry message CPA4034. This message would be sent by the CPYF command to message queue QSYSOPR if a user tried to copy a tape file and the volume mounted was not the first sequence number. For example, assume that you are duplicating a set of tapes. You want to make many duplicates of the first volume, then many duplicates of the second volume, and so on. And you want to ignore message CPA4034, if it occurs.

To accomplish this task, first display message ID CPA4034. You will find that the valid replies to the message are

C - Cancel
I - Ignore
R - Retry

For this example, you want the automatic response to be 'I' for Ignore. If you display the message attributes of CPA4034, you will see that the default reply is 'C'. This means that if you place your job in default reply mode, the response would be 'cancel'. You need to change the default reply to Ignore. Rather than changing the definition of the IBM-supplied message, you can create a customized version of the message, and then make sure that your program uses it in the place of IBM's message.

As in the previous technique, the first step is to duplicate the IBM message in your own message file using the TAA tool DUPMSGD:

```
DUPMSGD  FROMID(CPA4034) FROMMSGF(QCPFMSG)  +
           TOMSGF(MSGF1)
```

Then use the WRKMSGD command

```
WRKMSGD  MSGID(CPA4034) MSGF(MSGF1)
```

and request the change option. Press the RollUp key within the display until you come to the Default Reply Value (DFT parameter). Change this value from 'C' to 'I'. Now you have a customized version of the IBM message in your message file. The next thing to do is code your program. Good coding practice suggests that you would

- Use the OVRMSGF command to ensure that your customized version of the message is found when the program runs
- Use the RTVJOBA command to save the current value of the INQMSGRPY job attribute
- Use the command CHGJOB INQMSGRPY(*DFT) (This will cause the system to automatically respond to the message using the message's default reply.)
- Run the command (e.g., CPYF) that produces the inquiry message
- Use the CHGJOB command to reset the INQMSGRPY job attribute to its original value

The entire set of code would look like this:

```
DCL         &INQMSGRPY *CHAR LEN(10)
  .
  .
OVRMSGF     MSGF(QCPFMSG) TOMSGF(MSGF1)
RTVJOBA     INQMSGRPY(&INQMSGRPY)
CHGJOB      INQMSGRPY(*DFT)
            /* CPYF produces the CPA4034    */
            /*   inquiry message.           */
CPYF        ...
CHGJOB      INQMSGRPY(&INQMSGRPY)
```

Technical Tip

You can place your job in default response mode and control the response you want made to an inquiry message. You don't have to make a user or the system operator respond to the message.

CONVERTING A MESSAGE FILE TO A DATABASE FILE

You can't really process a message file within a program. Although the system provides a few commands that let you work with message descriptions (for example, the DSPMSGD and WRKMSGD commands), you can't read a message file as you can a database file. But you can convert a message file to a database file and then process the database file. If you write your own message descriptions, you might want to write all the messages to a database file so that you could scan the file for certain text or for parameter usage. You can convert a message file to a database file using the QUSRTOOL TAA tool CVTMSGF. The following command will create a database file:

```
CVTMSGF MSGF(xxxx) OUTLIB(yyyy)
```

The database file created will be an externally described file named MSGFP and it will be placed in the library you specify for parameter OUTLIB. You can then use normal database functions to read the file. You should note that modifying the records in the database file does not change the message descriptions. In addition, no command exists to reconvert the database file to a message file.

Technical Tip

The TAA tool CVTMSGF can be used to convert a message file to a database file. If you write your own message descriptions, you might prefer to record their contents in a database file for ease of maintenance or for scanning.

PROVIDING MULTIPLE-PERSON SURVEILLANCE FOR THE QSYSOPR MESSAGE QUEUE

Many AS/400 shops do not have a person solely responsible for watching after the QSYSOPR message queue. For example, a full-time person is normally not needed if no system operator activity (e.g., backup with media changes) is occurring and the volume of messages sent to QSYSOPR is low. Even if a person is given the part-time job of looking after QSYSOPR, that person can be busy or in a meeting when a message arrives that needs attention (e.g., a message that must be responded to before a program continues).

A better approach is to have several people watching over the QSYSOPR message queue. But the problem to be solved is how to alert a list of users when an important message arrives at QSYSOPR (or at any message queue). You can't place a single message queue in break mode for multiple people.

The answer lies in the use of a break-handling program. A break-handling program gains control of a message when it arrives on the message queue and determines how to respond to or act on the message. A break-handling program is specified on the PGM parameter of the CHGMSGQ command.

A solution has already been written for you. The QUSRTOOL TAA tool BRKMSGQN not only provides an example of how to write a break-handling program, but it uses the technique to alert multiple users when a message arrives at a message queue.

BRKMSGQN requires some modification to set up and use. You need to describe a list of users you want to notify. And you may want to be selective about which messages you break on (e.g., only inquiry messages or messages of a certain severity). Documentation accompanying this TAA tool describes how to check only for inquiry messages or messages with a high severity.

Technical Tip

The TAA tool BRKMSGQN allows you to alert a list of users when an important message (e.g., a message that must be answered before a program continues) arrives at the QSYSOPR message queue, or at any message queue.

Capturing Critical System Messages

When the system fails, every user on the system is going to be aware of it and there will be no problem recognizing that something is wrong. But in some cases, the system will warn you that a failure may be imminent and then keep running. The system sends these warning messages (e.g., you are running out of storage, you are running out of addresses (need to IPL), a disk has exceeded its error threshold, you have lost a mirrored device) to the QSYSOPR message queue.

Unless someone pays attention to these warning messages, there could be trouble. No one wants to do a costly IPL in the middle of the day or lose a mirrored device. But some shops manage the QSYSOPR message queue by looking only at inquiry messages. Unfortunately, many of the messages that indicate serious potential problems are not inquiry messages. The system sends a wide variety of messages to the QSYSOPR message queue and critical messages receive no special treatment.

Consequently, even though the system often sends the same message every hour until the problem is fixed, these warning messages can be missed easily, not coming to light until a failure occurs later on.

Fortunately, the system provides a solution. If the optional message queue QSYSMSG in library QSYS exists on your system, critical system messages are sent to the QSYSMSG message queue as well as to the QSYSOPR message queue. To use the QSYSMSG message queue, you first have to create it:

```
CRTMSGQ   MSGQ(QSYS/QSYSMSG)  +
            TEXT('Message queue for critical messages')
```

After you create the QSYSMSG message queue, you must monitor the message queue for critical messages sent by the system. (IBM's *Work Management Guide* contains a discussion of message IDs considered to be critical.) To inform a list of users that a critical message needs attention, you can place the message queue in break mode to a single user or use the previously described BRKMSGQN function. Not every message sent to the QSYSMSG queue indicates that the system is going to fail. For example, messages might be sent stating that mirroring is being resumed or that a security failure has occurred (e.g., an operator exceeding a set number of invalid password attempts). You need to select from the messages sent to the QSYSMSG message queue so that you are sure the "failure critical" messages will be brought to someone's attention.

The QUSRTOOL TAA tool CHKSYSCND (Figure 6.1) offers one solution for ensuring that critical messages are not ignored. The CHKSYSCND command will monitor the QSYSMSG message queue and further select from the messages received so that action is only taken on those that indicate a potential system failure. To use the command, simply specify a list of users you want to receive a break message when a critical message is sent to the QSYSMSG message queue. The following is a sample command:

```
CHKSYSCND USERS(SMITH JONES *FIRSTUSER)
```

You should put the CHKSYSCND command in a CL program and then call the program from the startup program associated with your controlling subsystem (IBM's *Work Management Guide* explains how to modify the startup program). Placing the CHKSYSCND command in a CL program lets you modify the list of users without changing your startup program, and lets you restart the CHKSYSCND command easily if you have to end it. The CHKSYSCND command submits a batch job (to the QINTER subsystem by default) that waits for a message to arrive in the QSYSMSG message queue. It then checks for critical message IDs and if

FIGURE 6.1
CHKSYSCND TAA Tool Prompt Screen

```
                         Check System Condition (CHKSYSCND)

 Type choices, press Enter.

 User profiles to notify . . . .   *FIRSTUSER    Character value...
               + for more values   __________
 Job queue  . . . . . . . . . . .  QINTER____    Name
   Library name . . . . . . . . .    QGPL______   Name
 Job description  . . . . . . . .  QBATCH____    Name
   Library name . . . . . . . . .    QGPL______   Name

                                                                      Bottom
 F3=Exit   F4=Prompt   F5=Refresh   F12=Cancel   F13=How to use this display
 F24=More keys
```

one is found, it alerts the list of users. You can specify two special values for the list of users:

- *FIRSTUSER says that the message will be sent to the user signed on with the highest security classification (e.g., the security officer). If only *USER types (based on the user profile parameter USRCLS) are active, the first user found receives a break message to contact the system administrator immediately.
- *ALLACTIVE says to inform all users signed on that a problem exists.

Technical Tip

The TAA tool CHKSYSCND provides an excellent way to monitor the system and to ensure that you'll be informed if the system senses it might fail. If the CHKSYSCND command can avert just one system failure, it is worth your time to implement it.

Managing the QSYSOPR Message Queue

As mentioned, the QSYSOPR message queue receives a variety of messages. The number of messages sent to the QSYSOPR message queue varies, depending on how much and what type of activity exists on the system. To help you manage the QSYSOPR message queue, you can use the MSGCTL TAA tool in QUSRTOOL. The MSGCTL tool is designed to

- allow unattended operations, or
- allow mostly unattended operations, or
- cut down on the number of messages received by the system operator

Although the MSGCTL tool can be used to manage any message queue, you would normally use it for the QSYSOPR message queue. Here's how the MSGCTL tool works: When a message arrives in a specified message queue, MSGCTL looks up the message ID in a database file. You can enter records into the database file so that based on the message ID, you can respond to an inquiry message, call a program, forward the message to another message queue, or just ignore the message. Parameters on the STRMSGCTL command (Figure 6.2) let you control what happens to a message that arrives on a message queue that does not match a database record.

You would specify on the STRMSGCTL command an alternate message queue (i.e., a message queue other than QSYSOPR) where selected messages would be forwarded. You can decide to automatically respond to some inquiry messages and forward others depending on how much

FIGURE 6.2

STRMSGCTL TAA Tool Prompt Screen

```
                   Start Message Control Function (STRMSGCTL)

Type choices, press Enter.

Message queue . . . . . . . . .    __________    Name
  Library name . . . . . . . . .     *LIBL_____    Name, *LIBL
Default forward MSGQ . . . . . .                 Name
  Library name . . . . . . . . .     *LIBL_____    Name, *LIBL
Job description  . . . . . . . .   *USRPRF___    Name, *USRPRF
  Library name . . . . . . . . .     *LIBL_____    Name, *LIBL
MSGCTLP file library . . . . . .   *LIBL_____    Name, *LIBL
MSGCURP file library . . . . . .   *LIBL_____    Name, *LIBL
MSGHSTP file library . . . . . .   *LIBL_____    Name, *LIBL
MSGINQP file library . . . . . .   *LIBL_____    Name, *LIBL
Msg Severity lvl to ignore . . .   20__          Number
Inq msg polling in secs  . . . .   30__          5-999
Reset LOG ID in MSGCURP  . . . .   *NO_          *YES, *NO
Restart after excess msgs  . . .   *NO_          *YES, *NO


                                                                         Bottom
F3=Exit   F4=Prompt   F5=Refresh   F12=Cancel   F13=How to use this display
F24=More keys
```

you want your system operations to be unattended. You can forward some non-inquiry messages and not others. Several commands are provided as part of the MSGCTL tool. A typical command to start the tool would be

```
STRMSGCTL  MSGQ(QSYSOPR) DFTFWDQ(MSGQ1)
```

The MSGCTL tool also provides a better audit trail of messages received by the QSYSOPR message queue, because MSGCTL places the messages it receives into a database file and associates the reply (if there is one) with the original message. The database file can be queried easily to help you determine how many of each type of message ID have been received.

Technical Tip

The TAA tool MSGCTL lets you automate or semi-automate the QSYSOPR message queue, or any other message queue. If you are trying to run your system in unattended or mostly unattended mode, consider using it.

Sending Messages to Active Users

A system operator sometimes needs to send a message to all users signed on to the system. A typical message might be "Please sign off, we are going down in 5 minutes." The system operator can use the SNDBRKMSG (Send Break Message) command to send this message, but it is not an ideal solution because a break message can be sent only to a specific workstation or to all users. If the message is sent to all users, it is even sent to those users who are not signed on. The next time they sign on, they may find the message quite confusing.

The system operator should send the message only to active users. The Operational Assistant provides a way to do this, but you must work interactively through a few menus before you get to the screen that allows you to send a break message. The TAA tool SNDBRKACT will let you perform the same function from any command line. All you need to code is

```
SNDBRKACT  MSG('Please sign off. We are going down in 5 minutes')
```

SNDBRKACT has the "smarts" to find the active users and send the break message only once if the user has multiple jobs active at the same workstation (e.g., system request or group jobs).

Technical Tip

The SNDBRKACT command in QUSRTOOL provides an easier way than the Operational Assistant to send a break message to all active users.

USING REQUEST MESSAGES

The AS/400 sends a special type of message, called a request message, to execute a command. You can think of a request message as data being sent to the program that executes commands: The command entry program receives the data, interprets it, and executes it.

As IBM has added certain functions to the system over the years, the need to manipulate request messages has diminished. But even though the need has lessened, you can still find practical uses for request messages.

First, to help you understand how you can use request messages, let me give you an example. (While the function I'll describe could be performed by using QCMDEXC, the example provides a basic illustration of the processing performed by request messages). Assume that you want to submit to batch the following program (TRYRQS), which will build a command string, place the command string in a request message, and then have the system execute the command string:

```
PGM         PARM(&PGM)
DCL         &PGM *CHAR LEN(10)
DCL         &CMD *CHAR LEN(100)
CHGVAR      &CMD ('DSPOBJD OBJ(' *CAT  +
              &PGM *TCAT ') OBJTYPE(*PGM)')
SNDPGMMSG   MSG(&CMD) MSGTYPE(*RQS) TOPGMQ(*EXT)
TFRCTL      PGM(QSYS/QCMD)
ENDPGM
```

When you submit a CALL to program TRYRQS, you pass it a parameter containing the name of a program to be displayed using the DSPOBJD command. Program TRYRQS will build the DSPOBJD command, place the command string in a request message (specified as MSGTYPE(*RQS)), and send the request message to the external message queue (TOPGMQ(*EXT)). In this example, the request message is sent to the external message queue because that is the message queue the system uses for commands. After program TRYRQS sends the request message, it transfers control (TFRCTL) to the AS/400 command processor (QCMD) so that it can execute the command.

Now that you have an idea how to use request messages, let's look at a more practical example. Assume that your programmers are submitting RPG compiles using PDM. Let's say that, in certain situations, you want all RPG compile listings to be indented. To do this, you need to modify the CRTRPGPGM command so that it specifies the INDENT parameter. But, if you changed the IBM-supplied command CRTRPGPGM, it would be in effect for all RPG compiles. In this example, we will do it by making a change to the batch subsystem description used for certain compile operations. To do this, you first need to specify that rather than calling QCMD in library QSYS (the default for IBM-supplied subsystems), the subsystem will initiate a routing program you will write. The following is an example of the code you would use to add a routing entry to the subsystem you want to use:

```
ADDRTGE  SBSD(xxxx) SEQNBR(100)    +
           CMPVAL(PGMR)            +
           PGM(yyyy/PCSRQS)
```

In this example, you want program PCSRQS (the routing program you will write) in library yyyy to be called when the RTGDTA value of the SBMJOB command is PGMR. Because of the way PDM option 14 (Create) works, you will have to invent your own PDM user-defined option to get a unique RTGDTA value. (To learn how to modify PDM to add a user-defined option, please refer to the example QUSRTOOL TAA tool SBMPARMS, or to IBM's *PDM User's Guide and Reference* — SC09-1338).

Once you have added the above routing entry, you are ready to write program PCSRQS. The program must receive a request message from the job's *EXT message queue. This request message will be the actual command (e.g., CRTRPGPGM...) that was originally submitted for batch processing.

The following code checks to see if the request message is a CRTRPGPGM command. If it is, and the INDENT parameter was not specified, the parameter is added to the command. The TAA tool SCNVAR is used to check the command string to see if the INDENT parameter exists. SCNVAR returns the position within the command string where the scan was successful. If the INDENT parameter is not found, the position returned is 0 and the INDENT parameter is concatenated onto the command with a value of "—". This will cause a dash (—) to be used as the indentation character.

```
PGM
DCL        &CMD *CHAR LEN(256)
DCL        &LOC *DEC LEN(3 Ø)
RCVMSG     PGMQ(*EXT) MSGTYPE(*RQS) MSG(&CMD)
IF         (%SST(&CMD 1 9) *EQ 'CRTRPGPGM') DO /* RPG */
SCNVAR     RESULT(&LOC) STRING(&CMD) STRINGLEN(256)  +
             PATTERN('INDENT(') PATTERNLEN(7)
IF         (*LOC *EQ Ø) DO /* Not found */
CHGVAR     &CMD (&CMD *BCAT 'INDENT(-)')
ENDDO      /* Not found */
ENDDO      /* End of CRTRPGPGM */
SNDPGMMSG  MSG(&CMD) MSGTYPE(*RQS) TOPGMQ(*EXT)
TFRCTL     PGM(QSYS/QCMD)
ENDPGM
```

Technical Tip

Manipulating request messages and routing entries can really put you in control of a command submitted to batch. By working with request messages, you can do a wide variety of customizing to achieve your special programming requirements.

Returning a Command as a Request Message

Writing your own commands can simplify the use of more complex commands. For example, you might want to provide your programmers with an abbreviated version of the OPNQRYF command. This abbreviated command would specify commonly used parameters that would serve users' needs in most situations. At the same time, you could cause the OPNQRYF command created by the abbreviated command to be returned in full to the command entry display so that a programmer could specify additional parameters, if necessary.

The QUSRTOOL TAA tool QRYF (Figure 6.3) does just that. It provides a front end to the OPNQRYF command that works for many simple cases. The QRYF command executes the OPNQRYF command and then both sends and receives the command as a request message. At the command entry display, you would see the QRYF command as you entered it, and the OPNQRYF command that the QRYF command generated and executed (Figure 6.4). Then, to modify the full OPNQRYF command, you would simply place the cursor on the OPNQRFY command, press F4 to prompt the command, and make whatever changes are necessary.

You could use this same technique to give your users the opportunity to modify a command before it is executed. To illustrate how easy it

FIGURE 6.3
The TAA Tool QRYF

```
                        Front End to OPNQRYF - TAA (QRYF)

Type choices, press Enter.

File name........................> XXXX                 Name
  Library name...................   *LIBL       Name, *LIBL
Selection criteria:
  Factor 1 or *BLANK.............> YYYY
  Operator.......................> *EQ                  *EQ, *LE, *GT, *LT, *GE
  Factor 2 or *BLANK.............> ZZZ
  Character literal..............> F2          *NONE, F1, F2
  Translate table on F1..........  *NONE                Name, *STD, *NONE
  And/Or relation to next select  *AND                  *AND, *OR, *EAND, *EOR
            + for more values
Sequencing criteria:
  Key field...............                              Character value, *FILE
  Sequence................               *ASCEND        *ASCEND, *DESCEND
            + for more values
Member....................               *FIRST         Name, *FIRST
```

would be to implement this technique, let's look at a subset of the code for the QRYF command. In this case, the command won't be executed,

FIGURE 6.4
Command Entry Display After Entering the QRYF Command

```
                              Command Entry

All previous commands and messages:
   > QRYF FILE(XXXX) SELECT((YYYY *EQ ZZZ F2))
   > OPNQRYF FILE((*LIBL/XXXX *N)) QRYSLT('(YYYY *EQ "ZZZ")')











Type command, press Enter.                                            Bottom
===>



F3=Exit    F4=Prompt    F9=Retrieve    F10=Include detailed messages
F11=Display full        F12=Cancel     F13=User support    F16=System main menu
```

but it will be returned to the command line ready to execute. You need to be operating from the command entry display to do this:

```
DCL        &MRK *CHAR LEN(4)
DCL        &CMD *CHAR LEN(512)
 .
 .
           /* Build up command to execute */
CHGVAR     &CMD ('...')
SNDPGMMSG  MSG(&CMD) TOPGMQ(*PRV) MSGTYPE(*RQS) +
             KEYVAR(&MRK)
RCVMSG     PGMQ(*PRV) MSGKEY(&MRK) RMV(*NO)
```

The command is built as a variable. Then, the command is sent as a request message (*RQS) and the internal key to the message is returned to the program with the KEYVAR parameter. The request message is then received by RCVMSG, but not removed. The purpose of receiving the message is to prevent the command entry display from executing it as a command (the command entry program is looking for request messages to process). What you would see on the command entry display is the command that is ready to be executed in a form that you can modify. In this case, the command is not executed, but it could have been executed by using the QCMDEXC command.

Technical Tip

Returning a command to the command entry display before it is executed can be a very handy thing to do when you are creating your own shorthand command. Just follow the technique shown to build up the command. You can optionally execute it and then send and receive it as a request message.

CHAPTER 7

Date and Time

The AS/400 supports certain date and time options, and tools in the QUSRTOOL library provide additional support. In this chapter, as we tackle dates and then time, we will discuss those functions supported by the system and those functions provided by QUSRTOOL tools.

DATES

Most programmers know how to use the RTVSYSVAL command to retrieve the system value for the current date:

```
DCL         &DATE *CHAR LEN(6)
  .
  .
  .
RTVSYSVAL   SYSVAL(QDATE) RTNVAR(&DATE)
```

Separate system values are also available for the day (QDAY), month (QMONTH), and year (QYEAR), or you can use a substring function on the return value for QDATE and pick them out yourself.

When you retrieve the QDATE system value, it is in the format set by another system value, QDATFMT. The default format for QDATFMT in the United States is MDY (MMDDYY).

The system value for date is a dynamic value. If you are in a job that runs past midnight, you can retrieve the new day's date. When a job starts, the system value is used to initialize the job date. The job date can also be changed by the job description used to start the job and by the CHGJOB command. You can retrieve the job date by using the RTVJOBA command.

Date Formats

Although the system date format and the job date format can be specified only as *MDY, *DMY, *YMD, or *JUL, the AS/400 supports other date formats for use in your applications. Most of the additional formats were added to support SQL and they let you develop a long-range strategy for handling year and century fields in your applications.

These additional date formats (shown on the following page) are used predominantly for database support, but you can work with them in CL and you can use the CVTDAT (Convert Date) command with them:

*MDYY = MMDDYYYY
*YYMD = YYYYMMDD
*DMYY = DDMMYYYY
*ISO = YYYY-MM-DD
*USA = MM/DD/YYYY
*EUR = DD.MM.YYYY
*JIS = YYYY-MM-DD

The CVTDAT command also supports another date format, *CYMD (CYYMMDD, where C = century), but this format is not an SQL format (i.e., you cannot specify DATFMT(*CYMD) in DDS).

Here are some important facts to remember about the date formats:

- Because the additional formats cannot be specified for either the system date or the job date, they cannot affect how dates appear in system output. For example, when you use a DSP command to print, only one of the standard job date formats can be used for the date on the spooled output.

- Whatever date formats you use, the RTVSYSVAL command for QDATE follows the rule for the format for the system date (controlled by the system value QDATFMT) and not the job date format. For example, if the system value for the QDATE format is *MDY and your job format is *YMD, the value retrieved by the RTVSYSVAL command will be in *MDY format.

- The job format only sets the default for certain functions (e.g., the CVTDAT command) and how the date appears on some printed output.

- Many system commands provide outfiles that contain dates. In most cases, the date formats placed in outfiles do not vary at the whim of the job. The typical date output format is YYMMDD, with the century as a separate field. But some commands that support outfiles (e.g., some commands developed for the S/38) march to a different drummer. For example, the DSPOBJD (Display Object Description) outfile has several date fields. The job format is used for one of the date fields and a fixed format of MMDDYY is used for other date fields. To work with outfiles, you need to know the format of the date you are working with. In most cases, the field description text will tell you the format. For example, the DSPFD command specified with TYPE(*MBRLIST) uses the model file QAFDMBRL in library QSYS. If you use the DSPFFD command for the model file, it lists each of the fields in the file. By reading the field text descriptions, you can determine that the MLCDAT field (the date the member was created) is in the format YYMMDD.

- Many of the system RTV commands also support dates. Normally, either the command prompt or the help text tells you which format is being used.

Date Conversion

The system provides an excellent function, the CVTDAT command, that lets you convert from one date format to another. The CVTDAT command works with all date formats. For example, you could convert from a format of *MDY to *YMD, or vice versa, or you could convert the system date (regardless of format) to a date with the format YYYYMMDD. To do the latter, you would use the following command:

```
DCL         &DATE *CHAR LEN(6)
DCL         &DATE2 *CHAR LEN(8)
  .
  .
  .
RTVSYSVAL   SYSVAL(QDATE) RTNVAR(&DATE)
CVTDAT      DATE(&DATE) TOVAR(&DATE2) TOFMT(*YYMD) TOSEP(*NONE)
```

The TOSEP(*NONE) value on the CVTDAT command prevents separators from appearing in the new date format. Note that *YYMD is the specification for the format YYYYMMDD.

Although the CVTDAT command can eliminate the need for complicated substring functions in your code, use of the command can be abused. To execute even a simple command like CVTDAT repetitively (e.g., if you had to convert every record read from a database) would require significant performance overhead. In such a situation, a better solution would be to write your own conversion routine using CHGVAR commands.

Technical Tip

Used wisely, the CVTDAT command can be effective. But its use can be abused. For instance, repetitive use of CVTDAT (e.g., converting every record read from a database) can degrade performance. A better solution would be to code your own conversion routine.

Century Support

In a few years a new century will be upon us and many applications will be subject to date comparisons that no longer make sense. You would be wise to include a one-digit century field or a four-digit year field in your applications so you can make comparisons using the full date.

Since many date formats do not include the century, the system has to assume which century you mean when you specify a two-digit year. To determine the century, the system uses the following rules:

Year 40 - 99 = 20th century
Year 00 - 39 = 21st century

When you perform various functions, the system uses these rules to determine what century it is. For example, when you use the CVTDAT command to convert a two-digit year to one that uses a four-digit year or a century digit, the system "invents" a century for you.

Many system functions capture the century so you can retrieve it. If you display an object with DSPOBJD, you see only a two-digit year presented. However, the RTVOBJD command and the outfile supported by the DSPOBJD command provide century support with various dates so you can use them in programming for date comparison.

At some point in the next 45 years, the system will need to be revised to include the 22nd century in its rules, or give you an option so you can decide. For now, the system rules work well in most situations.

Choosing a Date Format

Your choice of date formats will depend on a lot of factors, many of which will probably have more to do with how things have always been done than with any technical arguments. But if you are leaning toward using the new SQL date formats, let me offer a cautionary note about their use in DDS. When you use the DATFMT keyword in DDS, the system uses the information only to externalize the dates. That is, the system stores the dates in a consistent manner (4 bytes) in the internal record and then externalizes the dates to your format (6 to 10 bytes) when the record is passed to a program.

Keeping all the dates in an internal format makes it very easy for the system to compare them with different types of formats and to add and subtract days to the date. But there is system overhead associated with converting from the internal format to the external format, and it adds up every time you read a record (regardless of whether or not you want to access the date field). For most interactive use, you don't read many records, so the little bit of overhead per record is usually not significant.

However, if you process large files in batch, the accumulative overhead can be significant.

If, in a batch environment, you are going to use the SQL date comparison functions extensively (e.g., in Query), using the new DDS DATFMT keyword can be advantageous. But if you use the SQL date comparison functions only occasionally, the performance impact caused by using the DDS DATFMT keyword could be excessive for the benefit gained.

Technical Tip

The DDS DATFMT keyword for dates can affect batch performance considerably. Before specifying DATFMT, you should run tests to weigh the advantages of the function against the cost of the overhead.

My Favorite Date Format

I am a major fan of date fields. From an auditing perspective, they help me determine when work was done. And including in a record a date field that might help me someday doesn't consume much system overhead.

My favorite date format is CYYMMDD, which I place in a packed field of 7 digits and 0 decimals (4 bytes). I describe it as a normal packed field without the use of the DDS DATFMT keyword. You can add the EDTCDE(Y) keyword in DDS (which causes the date to be separated by slash marks) to help format the date. The slashes make the date more readable when using Query or DFU. With this format, the dates would look like the following (no slash mark appears after the century):

```
 92/12/31
101/05/30
```

The CYYMMDD date format offers many advantages; it

- uses little disk space. The cost is 4 bytes per field, which is as low as, if not lower than, any other technique.
- minimizes the system overhead required to move the data to a high-level language. For RPG, if you use the field in the program, this is just a move from one packed field to another. If you don't use the field, there is no overhead (the field is not moved from the buffer unless you have referenced it in the program). The cost of overhead is less than when converting SQL date fields (see the previous section, "Choosing a Date Format").

- is easy to understand and will still be easy to understand at the turn of the century.
- is easy to see which date is most current if you print dates in columns.
- is easy to perform such functions as sort and set lower limit on the date field because the most significant values (century and year) are in the high-order position.
- is easy to use for comparisons in a program. For example, the functions of "less than" or "greater than" make sense.
- can be used for many query functions. The user who is doing a query can specify "less than" or "greater than" or "range" without a lot of training.

The CYYMMDD date format has the following disadvantages:

- You have to build the century identifier as the first numeral of the field. If the year is greater than or equal to 40 and less than or equal to 99, it is the twentieth century (century Ø).
- If you plan to print or display the value, you might need to convert the date so that it follows the standard MM/DD/YY format users are accustomed to. You would incur overhead in your job to do this, but normally the number of dates that need to be converted is small.
- The CYYMMDD format is not an SQL standard. Consequently, there is no help in Query when working with this format; it looks like any numeric field to the user. Note that a user could perform functions such as "range," but (s)he would not be able to use, for example, a selection criteria for a date 30 days greater than a given date — (s)he would have to specify both dates in a range.
- The CYYMMDD format probably will not get a lot of attention from IBM (i.e., don't expect a lot of function to be added). If you use this date format, you probably will have to develop your own application functions forever.

Technical Tip

The date format of CYYMMDD in a packed format provides an efficient form for storage and for most processing needs.

The RTVDAT TAA Tool

The RTVDAT (Retrieve Date) command makes it easy to access the date, either fully spelled out or in other formats. The default for this command is to use the current system date, but you can specify any date you would like.

When you use the RTVDAT command, you can specify one or more return variables for such values as the following:

Option	Typical return value
Full spelling	October 19, 1992
Abbreviated spelling	Oct 19, 1992
Day of the week	Monday
Day in uppercase 3	MON
Day in lowercase 3	Mon
Month	October
Month in uppercase 3	OCT
Month in lowercase 3	Oct
Day of the year	293
Day of the week	2
Week of the year	43
CYYMMDD format	0921019

The RTVDAT command prompt (Figure 7.1) describes how to declare the return values. To access the full spelling of the month, you would specify

FIGURE 7.1
RTVDAT TAA Tool Prompt Screen

```
                         Retrieve Date (RTVDAT)

Type choices, press Enter.

Date in system format . . . . .   *SYSDAT       000001-999999, *SYSDAT
Day of week name            (9)   __________    Character value
Month name                  (9)   __________    Character value
Date:  March 1, 1989       (17)   __________    Character value
Date:  Mar 1, 1989         (12)   __________    Character value
Day in upper case: TUE      (3)   __________    Character value
Day in lower case: Tue      (3)   __________    Character value
Month in upper case: OCT    (3)   __________    Character value
Month in lower case: Oct    (3)   __________    Character value
Day of week as a digit      (1)   __________    Character value
Day of year as digits       (3)   __________    Character value
Week of year as digits      (2)   __________    Character value
Date as YYMMDD              (6)   __________    Character value
Date as CYYMMDD             (7)   __________    Character value
Full year (eg 1995)         (4)   __________    Character value
Century                     (1)   __________    Character value

                                                                   Bottom
F3=Exit   F4=Prompt   F5=Refresh   F12=Cancel   F13=How to use this display
F24=More keys
```

```
DCL          &MTHNAME *CHAR LEN(9)
 .
 .
 .
RTVDAT       MTHNAME(&MTHNAME)
```

Technical Tip

The QUSRTOOL TAA tool RTVDAT makes it easy to access any date in a variety of formats.

The ADDDAT TAA Tool

The ADDDAT (Add Date) command (Figure 7.2) makes it easy to add or subtract a number of days from a given date. For example, you could use the ADDDAT command to calculate a date that is 30 days in the future or 30 days in the past from the current date. The ADDDAT command automatically handles all problems associated with crossing month or year boundaries and with leap years. The default for the command is to use the current date for its calculations, but you can specify any date you want.

A typical example of the ADDDAT command's usefulness is specifying an expiration date on media to be written by a SAV command. The EXPDATE parameter defaults to *PERM, but you can enter a specific date.

FIGURE 7.2

ADDDAT TAA Tool Prompt Screen

```
                           Add Date (ADDDAT)

Type choices, press Enter.

Nbr of days to add/sub    (5 0)    ______      -35000-35000
New date variable           (6)    _________   Character value
Date (sys fmt)            (6 0)    *TODAY__    000000-999999, *TODAY, *JOB
TOVAR date format . . . . . . .    *JOB___     *SYSVAL, *MDY, *DMY, *YMD...
DATE date format . . . . . . . .   *JOB___     *SYSVAL, *MDY, *DMY, *YMD...

                                                                    Bottom
F3=Exit   F4=Prompt   F5=Refresh   F12=Cancel   F13=How to use this display
F24=More keys
```

If you wanted the media to expire in 30 days, you would code

```
DCL         &NEWDAT *CHAR LEN(6)
  .
  .
  .
ADDDAT      DAYS(30) TOVAR(&NEWDAT)
SAVLIB         ... EXPDATE(&NEWDAT)
```

You can also use the ADDDAT command to clean up old objects in your database. Assume that the records in your database contain a date field in CYYMMDD format that represents when each record was created. And let's say you want to delete all records that are 90 days old or older (i.e., you want to delete all records that are equal to or less than a date 90 days earlier than the current date). In your CL program, you would use the ADDDAT command to return the retention date and then pass that date to your program. You would specify

```
DCL         &CYYMMDD *CHAR LEN(7)
  .
  .
  .
ADDDAT      DAYS(-90) TOVAR(&CYYMMDD) +
              TOVARFMT(*CYMD) TOSEP(*NONE)
CALL        PGMX PARM(&CYYMMDD)
```

You can use the ADDDAT command to return the value of the date you want to compare against in a variety of formats, so you normally will not also need to use the CVTDAT command.

Technical Tip

Become familiar with the TAA tool ADDDAT. It can be invaluable when working with relative dates.

The CMPDAT TAA Tool

With the CMPDAT (Compare Date) command you can easily compare two dates, determine if one is greater than the other, and then determine the number of days' difference between the two dates. The dates are input in job format by default. Two return values let you determine which date is more current and the numbers of days between. To compare two dates and determine the number of days' difference between them, you would specify

```
DCL        &DAT1 *CHAR LEN(6)
DCL        &DAT2 *CHAR LEN(6)
DCL        &RTNRES *CHAR LEN(2)
DCL        &DIFF *DEC LEN(5 Ø)
  .
  .
  .
CMPDAT     FROMDATE(&DAT1) TODATE(&DAT2) +
             RTNRES(&RTNRES) RTNDAYS(&DIFF)
IF         (&RTNRES *EG 'GT') DO /* Greater than */
```

Technical Tip

The TAA tool CMPDAT makes it easy to determine the number of days' difference between two dates.

The CHKDAT TAA Tool

The CHKDAT (Check Date) command makes it easy to provide some degree of validity checking when a user passes a date value to your program. You may want to perform validity checking to ensure that the date is

- valid
- not in the past
- not greater than N days from now
- in the current year

For example, assume you want to ensure that a date passed as a parameter to your program is valid and that it is within 365 days from the current date and not in the past. You would code

```
PGM        PARM(&DATE)
DCL        &DATE *CHAR LEN(6)
  .
  .
  .
CHKDAT     DATE(&DATE) DAYLORNG(Ø) DAYHIRNG(+365)
MONMSG     MSGID(CPF9898) EXEC(DO) /* Bad date */
```

Technical Tip

The TAA tool CHKDAT makes it easy to validate a date that is passed into your program. This command lessens the chance of having incorrect dates in your database.

TIME

In this section we will discuss functions the system provides for working with the system time, and then we will discuss two functions for working with system time supported by tools in the QUSRTOOL library.

Most programmers know how to use the RTVSYSVAL command to retrieve the system time from system value QTIME:

```
DCL        &TIME *CHAR LEN(6)
  .
  .
  .
RTVSYSVAL  SYSVAL(QTIME) RTNVAR(&TIME)
```

The time is placed in your program in the format HHMMSS. The system uses military time, so there is no notion of AM and PM. You can access separate system values for hours (QHOUR), minutes (QMINUTE), and seconds (QSECOND), or you can use a substring function to pull the information you want from the QTIME return variable.

If you need to provide a more precise time, you can use an often-ignored feature of system value QTIME. The system time can be returned to a variable longer than 6 bytes (it can be up to 9 bytes long). By specifying a variable 9 bytes long, you can retrieve the system time in milliseconds (HHMMSSMMM):

```
DCL        &TIME *CHAR LEN(9)
  .
  .
  .
RTVSYSVAL  SYSVAL(QTIME) RTNVAR(&TIME)
```

Although retrieving the system time in milliseconds adds precision, it is not precise enough to ensure that the time will be a unique value across multiple jobs. If two users both executed the RTVSYSVAL command at the same time, it is possible that they would both receive the same 9-digit value. If you want a unique value, you need to use a technique such as the TAA tool ADDDTAARA described in Chapter 11, "Allocating Objects."

Technical Tip

While using a 9-character time value for system value QTIME will let you specify a precise time, it will not necessarily provide a unique value across multiple jobs. It is possible that two users could receive the same value on the RTVSYSVAL command. It is also possible that the same user could receive the same 9-character value if (s)he executed two RTVSYSVAL commands in

close sequence. Even if this isn't a problem today, it could be in the future when faster CPUs are available.

Accessing the system time value also can help you provide a better audit trail (i.e., one that provides more information than just current date). Consider establishing a standard heading format for printed output that includes date, time, system name, and page number. You can access the time in a CL program and pass it to your print program, or you can use the RPG TIME operation code at the beginning of the program.

Another system value (QUTCOFFSET) lets you specify the number of hours and minutes your system is offset from Greenwich mean time. With this function, an application attempting to determine an audit trail of events throughout a network of systems can normalize the date/time values reported.

Unfortunately, no corresponding value exists for a job. Therefore, users in time zones different from the host system (e.g., a user in Los Angeles is accessing a system in Chicago) cannot see the correct local time on their displays and printed output. You can write your programs so that the user sees the local time on application output, but any system output would still use the system time.

The RTVTIMSTM TAA Tool

If you want your application to provide a time stamp for messages or transactions, the TAA tool RTVTIMSTM gives you an easy solution. The RTVTIMSTM (Retrieve Time Stamp) command provides a time stamp for you in a variety of formats. For example, the following code:

```
DCL        &TIMESTAMP *CHAR LEN(23)
  .
  .
  .
RTVTIMSTM  DATTIM23(&TIMESTAMP)
```

would return a time value that looks like this:

10/30/92 at 8:44:11 AM

Other time stamp formats you can choose include values such as

10/30 at 8:44 AM and
103092084411

Technical Tip

The TAA tool RTVTIMSTM will provide a time stamp for you in various formats. It is helpful when you want to provide a specific time and date for messages or for identifying transactions.

The CLCTIMDIF TAA Tool

Some system functions ask you to provide a value in seconds (e.g., the WAIT parameter on various commands) and in some situations that may require subtracting one time value from another. For example, you may have an application that receives messages or data queue entries. A user might pass your application a time value in HHMMSS for how long the application should wait before performing its function. Your application then needs to determine the current time and calculate in seconds the difference between the current time and the time passed to your application by the user.

The TAA tool CLCTIMDIF (Calculate Time Difference) will do this for you as long as the time values are all on the same day. Simply code

```
PGM         PARM(&TO)
DCL         &FROM *CHAR LEN(6)
DCL         &TO *CHAR LEN(6)
DCL         &DIFF *CHAR LEN(5)
  .
  .
  .
RTVSYSVAL   SYSVAL(QTIME) RTNVAR(&FROM)
CLCTIMDIF   FROMTIME(&FROM) TOTIME(&TO) +
              SECONDS(&DIFF)
Some cmd    ... WAIT(&DIFF)
```

The &DIFF variable returns the answer in seconds so it is ready to use in several system commands.

Technical Tip

The TAA tool CLCTIMDIF makes it easy to determine the number of seconds between two times.

Exercise A Dates

In this exercise we will use several of the date functions discussed in this chapter to show how the system support and the QUSRTOOL commands can be used together. For this exercise, you will need the TAA tools RTVDAT, ADDDAT, CMPDAT, and EDTVAR. If they are not on your system, see Appendix B.

1. Use PDM to create a CLP member named TRYDAT. This CL program will change the format of the job date. The code assumes that your job date and system date are not currently set in *YMD format. If they are in that format, use a different format (e.g., *MDY) when the coding example used in this exercise specifies *YMD.
2. Enter the following source:

```
PGM
DCL         &DATE *CHAR LEN(6)
DCL         &DATFMT *CHAR LEN(4)
RTVJOBA     DATE(&DATE) DATFMT(&DATFMT)
SNDPGMMSG   MSG('JOBDAT Before chg-' *CAT &DATE)
CHGJOB      DATFMT(*YMD)
RTVJOBA     DATE(&DATE)
SNDPGMMSG   MSG('JOBDAT as *YMD-' *CAT &DATE)
WRKDSKSTS
RTVSYSVAL   SYSVAL(QDATE) RTNVAR(&DATE)
SNDPGMMSG   MSG('System date-' *CAT &DATE)
CHGJOB      DATFMT(&DATFMT)
RTVJOBA     DATE(&DATE)
SNDPGMMSG   MSG('JOBDAT reset-' *CAT &DATE)
ENDPGM
```

3. Create the program.
4. Call the program:

```
CALL  TRYDAT
```

   You should see the WRKDSKSTS display with the date in the upper right-hand corner in *YMD format because your job changed to this format.

5. Press Enter.

Exercise A continued

Exercise A continued

You should see messages sent from the program that show the job date before and after the change. Note that the system value date is retrieved and sent in a message, but it is not affected by the job format. The system date uses the QDATFMT system value to determine how the return value is formatted.

6. Using PDM, create a CLP member named TRYCVTDAT. The program illustrates the use of the CVTDAT command and provides an example of how the system determines century.
7. Enter the following source:

```
PGM
DCL         &TODAY *CHAR LEN(6)
DCL         &MDYY *CHAR LEN(10)
DCL         &CYMD *CHAR LEN(7)
RTVSYSVAL   SYSVAL(QDATE) RTNVAR(&TODAY)
CVTDAT      DATE(&TODAY) TOVAR(&MDYY) TOFMT(*MDYY)
SNDPGMMSG   MSG('Today as *MDYY-' *CAT &MDYY)
CVTDAT      DATE('013199') TOVAR(&CYMD) +
              TOFMT(*CYMD) TOSEP(*NONE)
SNDPGMMSG   MSG('Jan 31, 1999 as *CYMD-' *CAT &CYMD)
CVTDAT      DATE('013100') TOVAR(&CYMD) +
              TOFMT(*CYMD) TOSEP(*NONE)
SNDPGMMSG   MSG('Jan 31, 2000 as *CYMD-' *CAT &CYMD)
ENDPGM
```

8. Create the program.
9. Call the program:

```
CALL    TRYCVTDAT
```

The first message you see should show the current date in *MDYY format. The next two messages should show a 7-digit value in *CYMD format. This shows the system rules in action where a 6-digit date is given and the system has to determine what century it is. Years 00-39 are considered the 21st century.

10. Using PDM, create a CLP member named TRYRTVDAT. This program will demonstrate various date formats that can be retrieved by using

Exercise A continued

Exercise A continued

the TAA tool RTVDAT. Be sure to prompt for RTVDAT when entering the command to see the other parameters you can choose from.

11. Enter the following source:

```
PGM
DCL         &DAY *CHAR LEN(9)
DCL         &MTHNAME *CHAR LEN(9)
DCL         &DIGITDAY *CHAR LEN(3)
RTVDAT      DAYNAME(&DAY) MTHNAME(&MTHNAME) +
              DAYOFYEAR(&DIGITDAY)
SNDPGMMSG   MSG('Day-' *CAT &DAY)
SNDPGMMSG   MSG('Month-' *CAT &MTHNAME)
SNDPGMMSG   MSG('Day of the year-' *CAT &DIGITDAY)
ENDPGM
```

12. Create the program.

13. Call the program:

```
CALL  TRYRTVDAT
```

The first message you see should show the current day of the week. The second message should show the current month fully spelled out. The third message should show the current day of the year.

14. Using PDM, create a CLP member named TRYADDDAT. This program will show you how the TAA tool ADDDAT works.

15. Enter the following source:

```
PGM
DCL         &NEWDAT *CHAR LEN(6)
DCL         &CYMD *CHAR LEN(10)
ADDDAT      DAYS(90) TOVAR(&NEWDAT)
SNDPGMMSG   MSG('90 Days plus-' *CAT &NEWDAT)
ADDDAT      DAYS(-30) TOVARFMT(*CYMD)  +
              TOVAR2(&NEWDAT)
SNDPGMMSG   MSG('30 Days prev as CYMD-' *CAT &CYMD)
ENDPGM
```

16. Create the program.

Exercise A continued

Exercise A continued

17. Call the program:

```
CALL   TRYADDDAT
```

The first message sent from your program should be the date 90 days from the current date displayed in your job's date format. This value is ready to be plugged into a SAV command's EXPDATE parameter, or it could be passed to a high-level language program as a retention date. The second message should be the date 30 days prior to the current date in the format *CYMD. This date is ready to be passed to a program that might perform some cleanup activity on database records that have the same date format.

18. Using PDM, create a CLP member named TRYCMPDAT. This program will show you how the TAA tool CMPDAT can be used to compare two dates.

19. Enter the following source:

```
PGM          PARM(&TODAT)
DCL          &TODAT *CHAR LEN(6)
DCL          &RTNRES *CHAR LEN(2)
DCL          &DIFF *DEC LEN(5 0)
DCL          &CHAR22 *CHAR LEN(22)
CMPDAT       FROMDATE(*TODAY) TODATE(&TODAT) +
               RTNRES(&RTNRES) RTNDAYS(&DIFF)
SNDPGMMSG    MSG('Result-' *CAT &RTNRES)
EDTVAR       CHROUT(&CHAR22) NUMINP(&DIFF)
SNDPGMMSG    MSG('Diff-' *CAT &CHAR22)
ENDPGM
```

20. Create the program.

21. Call the program and pass it a parameter with the value of January 1 of the next year. For example, if it is now 1994 and your job format is *MDY, enter

```
CALL   TRYCMPDAT PARM('010195')
```

The TO date parameter you are passing to program TRYCMPDAT is compared to the FROM date (i.e., the current date). You should see a message stating that the result is LT, meaning the FROM date is "less

Exercise A continued

Exercise A continued

than" the TO date. A second message provides the "differences" value — the number of days separating the two dates. The "differences" value is always positive.

22. Now call the program with a date of January 1 of the current year. For example,

```
CALL  TRYCMPDAT PARM('010194')
```

Assuming that it is not January 1, you should see two messages: one indicating the current date you input is greater than (GT) January 1 and another noting the number of days between the two dates.

Exercise B Time

In this exercise we will use the system time function and show how the system support and QUSRTOOL commands we discussed in this chapter can be used. For this exercise, you will need the TAA tools RTVTIMSTM and CLCTIMDIF. If these commands are not on your system, see Appendix B.

1. Using PDM, create a CLP member named TRYTIM. This program will extract the time value in different formats.
2. Enter the following source:

```
PGM
DCL         &TIME6 *CHAR LEN(6)
DCL         &TIME9 *CHAR LEN(9)
RTVSYSVAL   SYSVAL(QTIME) RTNVAR(&TIME6)
SNDPGMMSG   MSG('Time as 6-' *CAT &TIME6)
RTVSYSVAL   SYSVAL(QTIME) RTNVAR(&TIME9)
SNDPGMMSG   MSG('Time as 9-' *CAT &TIME9)
RTVSYSVAL   SYSVAL(QTIME) RTNVAR(&TIME9)
SNDPGMMSG   MSG('Time as 9-' *CAT &TIME9)
ENDPGM
```

Exercise B continued

Exercise B continued

3. Create the program.
4. Call the program:

```
CALL  TRYTIM
```

You should see the current time displayed in messages as both a 6-character and a 9-character value. The 9-character value is retrieved again and the same message sent. This will let you see how many milliseconds (if any) pass between execution of the commands. As CPUs become faster, the time difference will become smaller and the 9-character value will become less reliable as a unique time stamp.

5. Using PDM, create a CLP member named TRYRTVSTM. This program will show you how to use the TAA tool RTVTIMSTM to provide a time stamp for your applications in a readable form. The time stamp should not be considered to be a unique value (see the previous discussion). Be sure to prompt for RTVTIMSTM when entering the source to see the other format choices on the command.
6. Enter the following source:

```
PGM
DCL         &TIMESTAMP *CHAR LEN(20)
RTVTIMSTM   DATTIM20(&TIMESTAMP)
SNDPGMMSG   MSG(&TIMESTAMP)
ENDPGM
```

7. Create the program.
8. Call the program:

```
CALL  TRYRTVSTM
```

You should see the current date and time presented in a manner that you can use for a time stamp.

9. Using PDM, create a CLP member named TRYCLCTIM. This program will show you how to use the TAA tool CLCTIMDIF to determine the number of seconds between two times.

Exercise B continued

Exercise B continued

10. Enter the following source:

```
PGM        PARM(&TO)
DCL        &FROM *CHAR LEN(6)
DCL        &TO *CHAR LEN(6)
DCL        &DIFF *CHAR LEN(5)
RTVSYSVAL  SYSVAL(QTIME) RTNVAR(&FROM)
CLCTIMDIF  FROMTIME(&FROM) TOTIME(&TO) +
             SECONDS(&DIFF)
SNDPGMMSG  MSG('Diff-' *CAT &DIFF)
ENDPGM
```

11. Create the program.
12. Call the program and enter a parameter value in HHMMSS that is approximately 1 hour later than the current time. For example, if it is now 10:15 AM, enter:

```
CALL  TRYCLCTIM PARM('111500')
```

You should see a difference of approximately 3600 seconds (1 hour). You can try other values, but you are entering the TO time and it must be greater than the current time or message ID CPF9898 will be sent as an escape message.

CHAPTER 8

Retrieve Commands

The AS/400 supports a variety of Retrieve (RTV) commands to assist you in accessing attributes or information external to a program. In this chapter I will provide examples of using the following popular IBM-supplied RTV commands:

RTVJOBA	(Retrieve Job Attribute)
RTVOBJD	(Retrieve Object Description)
RTVMBRD	(Retrieve Member Description)
RTVSYSVAL	(Retrieve System Value)

and then discuss some of the RTV commands that can be found in the QUSRTOOL library.

Because a RTV command returns information into a variable, a RTV command can exist only in a CL program. When you code a RTV command, you must specify one or more return variables. The return variables must be declared correctly (i.e., the correct length and type) to receive the values returned from the command.

You can simplify the task of declaring the variables correctly by prompting for the specific RTV command. For example, if you prompt for the RTVMBRD command, you would see the screen shown in Figure 8.1.

FIGURE 8.1
Retrieve Member Description Prompt

```
           Retrieve Member Description (RTVMBRD)

Type choices, press Enter.

File . . . . . . . . . . . . . .   __________     Name
  Library  . . . . . . . . . . .     *LIBL        Name, *LIBL, *CURLIB
Member:
  Reference member . . . . . . .  *FIRST         Name, generic*, *FIRST
  Relationship . . . . . . . . .  _____          *SAME, *NEXT, *PRN
CL var for RTNSYSTEM       (4) . .  __________     Character value
CL var for RTNLIB         (10) . .  __________     Character value
CL var for RTNMBR         (10) . .  __________     Character value

CL var for TEXT           (50) . .  __________     Character value
CL var for NBRCURRCD    (10 0) . .  __________     Number
```

As you can see, if you want to retrieve the TEXT value on the RTVMBRD command, the prompt shows that you must declare the variable as TYPE(*CHAR) LEN(50). If you want to retrieve the NBRCURRCD value, the prompt shows that you must declare the variable as TYPE(*DEC) LEN(10 0).

Technical Tip

For most RTV commands, simply use the command prompt to determine the attributes of the value you are trying to retrieve.

Most RTV commands let you retrieve one or more values on the same command. An exception to this rule is the RTVSYSVAL command. You can return only one system value at a time with the RTVSYSVAL command and you must know the attributes of the value you want returned. You can find these attributes listed in IBM's *Work Management Guide* (SC41-8078) or *Programming Reference Summary* (SX44-0028). You also can view a table of all the system values and their definitions by prompting for the RTVSYSVAL command, placing the Help key on the RTNVAR prompt, and pressing Enter.

Using the RTVMBRD and RTVOBJD Commands

I frequently use the IBM-supplied RTV commands, and two of my favorites are RTVMBRD and RTVOBJD. The RTVMBRD command retrieves information about an individual database file member. You can use the RTVMBRD command to answer a typical question such as "Are there any records in the file?" You can do this by coding

```
DCL          &NBRRCD *DEC LEN(10 0)
 .
 .
 .
RTVMBRD      FILE(xxx) NBRCURRCD(&NBRRCD)
IF           (&NBRRCD *EQ 0) DO /* No rcds */
```

In addition to the return variable used in this example, the RTVMBRD command supports many other return variables that let you access information about a database file member. Note that if you specify MBR(*FIRST) on the RTVMBRD command, a member must exist in the file; otherwise, your program will receive an escape message.

The RTVOBJD command retrieves descriptive information about a single object. For example, if you wanted to access an object's owner and create date information, you would specify

```
DCL          &OWNER *CHAR LEN(10)
DCL          &CRTDATE *CHAR LEN(13)
  .
  .
  .
RTVOBJD      OBJ(xxx) OBJTYPE(*PGM) +
               OWNER(&OWNER) CRTDATE(&CRTDATE)
```

The CRTDATE value is returned as CYYMMDDHHMMSS. You can use a substring function to pick just the date from the return variable. As with the RTVMBRD command, the RTVOBJD command supports many additional return variables that allow you to obtain information about a specific object.

The RTNLIB Variable

When you work with objects, you often must be specific in your messages and reports about which library you found the object in. The library list is a wonderful thing, but it is also the cause of many errors when objects of the same name exist in multiple libraries.

Many applications are coded to use the library list to access objects. You can use the RTNLIB parameter on the RTVOBJD command to retrieve the name of the library in which the object was found by coding

```
DCL          &LIB *CHAR LEN(10)
  .
  .
  .
RTVOBJD      OBJ(xxx) OBJTYPE(*FILE) +
               RTNLIB(&LIB)
```

If you expect a user to pass your program the name of a library as a special value (e.g., *LIBL or *CURLIB), you would use the following code:

```
DCL          &LIB *CHAR LEN(10)
  .
  .
  .
IF           ((&LIB *EQ '*LIBL') *OR +
               (&LIB *EQ '*CURLIB')) DO /* Get lib */
RTVOBJD      OBJ(&LIB/xxx) OBJTYPE(*FILE) +
               RTNLIB(&LIB)
ENDDO        /* Get library name */
```

Note that the RTNLIB parameter places the value in the same parameter that I tested. If you are going to use the original value later on, this is obviously not a good technique. In most of my coding, I normally don't use the original value after it is input, so I just overlay the input value. The &LIB value can now be used in any messages as the actual library name.

The RTNMBR Variable

Most database files have only a single member. If you use multiple-member files, your program may need to specify MBR(*FIRST). If so, you can use the same technique described above, but using the RTNMBR parameter on the RTVMBRD command to return the name of the first member:

```
DCL          &MBR *CHAR LEN(10)
  .
  .
  .
IF           (&MBR *EQ '*FIRST') DO /* Get member */
RTVMBRD      FILE(xxx) RTNMBR(&MBR)
ENDDO        /* Get member name */
```

The system selects the first member based on the order in which the members were created (i.e., by the date created and not in alphabetical name order).

Using the RTVJOBA Command

The RTVJOBA command is very valuable for writing good CL programs because accessing job attributes allows your program to determine dynamically which functions to perform, or how to perform them. For example, if you have a function that isn't going to work or will work differently depending on whether your program is running in a batch or an interactive environment, you need to know in which environment your program is running. RTVJOBA can give you the answer. Simply code

```
DCL          &TYPE *CHAR LEN(1)
  .
  .
  .
RTVJOBA      TYPE(&TYPE)
IF           (&TYPE *EQ '1') DO /* Interactive job */
```

Unfortunately, the prompt does not describe whether a '1' or '0' is an interactive job (the help text does). If the job type is '1', the job is interactive; if it is '0', the job is batch. I remember it with the phrase, "Good old number 1," meaning the interactive job is more important than the batch job.

Emulating the DSP Command OUTPUT Parameter

Several system DSP commands support an OUTPUT parameter with a default of (*). This means if you operate interactively, the output is displayed. If your job is running in batch, the output is written to a spooled file. You can also force spooled output by specifying OUTPUT(*PRINT). You can use the same approach for your applications.

Several TAA tools also support OUTPUT(*). These tools normally spool the output and then use DSPSPLF if the job is being run interactively. Let me show you how this is done.

The TAA tools normally print to QPRINT using RPG output specifications. An OVRPRTF command is used to override QPRINT and use a different spooled file name. Here's the code to do this:

```
PGM        PARM (&OUTPUT ...)
DCL        &OUTPUT *CHAR LEN(6)
DCL        &JOBTYP *CHAR LEN(1)
 .
 .
 .
OVRPRTF    FILE(QPRINT) SPLFNAME(xxx) HOLD(*YES)
CALL       PGM(yyy) /* Prints to QPRINT */
RTVJOBA    TYPE(&JOBTYP) /* Ø = Batch */
           /* If int and default, do DSPSPLF */
IF         ((&JOBTYP *EQ '1') *AND +
             (&OUTPUT *EQ '*')) DO /* Display */
DSPSPLF    FILE(xxx) SPLNBR(*LAST)
DLTSPLF    FILE(xxx) SPLNBR(*LAST)
ENDDO      /* Display */
           /* If batch or *PRINT, send comp msg */
IF         ((&JOBTYP *EQ 'Ø') *OR +
             (&OUTPUT *EQ '*PRINT')) DO /* Print */
RLSSPLF    FILE(xxx) SPLNBR(*LAST)
SNDPGMMSG  MSG('...') MSGTYPE(*COMP)
ENDDO      /* Print */
```

Note that the OVRPRTF command specifies HOLD(*YES) to prevent the spooled file from being output by a writer. If the DSPSPLF command is used, the spooled file is deleted. If the spooled file is to be kept, the RLSSPLF command is used to allow the spooled file to be output by a writer.

Technical Tip

You can emulate the DSP command OUTPUT(*) function by using the RTVJOBA command and a little bit of standard coding.

AVOIDING SBMJOB IF IN BATCH

Using the SBMJOB command inside a CL program to submit a program (e.g., PGMB) to batch makes sense if the CL program is in an interactive job. However, if the CL program can be called from either a batch or interactive job, you probably do not want your CL program to execute a SBMJOB command if the program is already running in a batch environment. In many cases, you would rather just call PGMB instead of submitting another job to call PGMB.

You can determine in which environment your job is running by using the RTVJOBA command:

```
DCL         &JOBTYPE *CHAR LEN(1)
 .
 .
 .
RTVJOBA     TYPE(&JOBTYPE)
IF          (&JOBTYPE *EQ '1') DO /* If interactive */
SBMJOB      CMD(CALL PGM(PGMB))
ENDDO       /* If interactive */
IF          (&JOBTYPE *EQ '0') DO /* If batch */
CALL        PGM(PGMB)
ENDDO       /* If batch */
```

THE BLDCALL TAA TOOL

In the above example, the CALL to PGMB is simple because there are no parameters to pass to the program. If there are a lot of parameters, your code would look something like this:

```
DCL       &JOBTYPE *CHAR LEN(1)
 .
 .
 .
RTVJOBA   TYPE(&JOBTYPE)
IF        (&JOBTYPE *EQ '1') DO /* If interactive */
SBMJOB    CMD(CALL PGM(PGMB) PARM(&A &B '123' &C *YES &D))
ENDDO     /* If interactive */
IF        (&JOBTYPE *EQ '0') DO /* If batch */
CALL      PGM(PGMB) PARM(&A &B '123' &C *YES &D)
ENDDO     /* If batch */
```

Making sure that the parameter lists on both the SBMJOB and CALL commands are identical is a very error-prone process. Rather than code two identical parameter lists, it is better to code one parameter list as a variable and then use the same variable on both the SBMJOB and CALL commands. Unfortunately, you cannot code the CHGVAR command as

```
CHGVAR  &PARMS (&A *BCAT &B *BCAT '123' ...)
```

and then follow it with

```
CALL     PGM(PGMB) PARM(&PARMS)
 .
 .
 .
SBMJOB  CMD(CALL PGM(PGMB) PARM(&PARMS)')
```

You won't achieve the results you want because the system will interpret the statement on both commands as passing a single variable instead of several. The system does support a way to code a single parameter list that you can use on both commands, but it is very complex. You have to code something like the following:

```
CHGVAR  &CMD ('CALL PGM(PGMB) PARM('          +
             *CAT &A *BCAT &B *BCAT ''''      +
             *CAT '123' *CAT '''' *BCAT       +
             &C *BCAT *YES *BCAT &D *TCAT ')')
```

Then you would code

```
CALL     QCMDEXC PARM(&CMD nnn)
 .
 .
 .
SBMJOB  RQSDTA(&CMD)
```

Although the system-supported method leaves you with one parameter list to maintain, debugging the program could become a difficult task. Fortunately, you can find a reasonable alternative in the QUSRTOOL library. When you want to maintain only a single parameter list, the BLDCALL TAA tool helps you get the job done easily.

With the BLDCALL tool, you name a program and then list the parameters you want to pass to the program. The BLDCALL tool builds the parameter list (or command string) for you and then returns the result in a 256-byte character return variable that you specify on the BLDCALL RQSDTA keyword. Here are the key commands required to use the BLDCALL tool:

```
DCL      &RQSDTA *CHAR LEN(256)
.
.
.
BLDCALL  RQSDTA(&RQSDTA) PGM(PGMB) PARM(&A &B 123 &C *YES &D)
.
.
.
CALL     QCMDEXC PARM(&RQSDTA 256)
.
.
.
SBMJOB   RQSDTA(&RQSDTA)
```

After the BLDCALL tool completes its function, the value of the RQSDTA variable would look like this:

```
CALL  PGM(PGMB) PARM('aaa' 'bbb' '123' 'cc' '*YES' 'dd')
```

The BLDCALL tool inserts the correct number of quote marks and builds the parameter string just as you want it for execution.

The BLDCALL tool makes it easier to maintain a single parameter list, but it does have a restriction: Only character variables of 32 bytes or fewer can be passed. I recommend passing character variables of 32 bytes or fewer any time you want to submit a CALL with parameters (see Chapter 10, "Passing Parameters").

Technical Tip

When you want to be able to use either the SBMJOB or CALL command to execute the same program, and a long parameter list is required, use the BLDCALL TAA tool. This tool makes it much simpler to build a single parameter list that can be easily maintained and can be used by both the SBMJOB and CALL commands.

Combining the RTVJOBA and CHGJOB Commands

I quite often need to combine the functions of the RTVJOBA and CHGJOB commands to control a specific option for a short time. A good example would be to promote a job to a very high priority while your program performs a specific function. You must have the special authority *JOBCTL to change the RUNPTY parameter on the CHGJOB command. If you don't have this special authority, you can adopt *JOBCTL authority by having a programmer who has *JOBCTL authority create the program and specify USRPRF(*OWNER).

To use this technique correctly, you should save the current value of the function you want to control and then reset it when you are done:

```
DCL         &RUNPTY *DEC LEN(2 0)
.
.
.
RTVJOBA     RUNPTY(&RUNPTY)
CHGJOB      RUNPTY(05) /* Set to high priority */
            /*   Do the critical function */
CHGJOB      RUNPTY(&RUNPTY)
```

The RTVJOBA command is nearly a mirror image of the CHGJOB command. The major difference is that the RTVJOBA command works only against the job in which it is run, whereas the CHGJOB command can be used on any job. Most of the parameters that can be specified on the CHGJOB command can be retrieved by the RTVJOBA command.

Capturing Your Entire Environment

The ultimate in capturing your environment is to capture everything and then be able to restore it later on. The QUSRTOOL TAA tool CAPJOBA (Capture Job Attributes) does this for you.

Assume you have a routine that performs a valuable function but when the code completes, some part of your job environment has not been reset (e.g., the library list, logging level).

A solution to this problem is to let the CAPJOBA command capture your entire environment before you call the routine and then reset the environment with the companion command RTNJOBA (Return Job Attributes). Here's what you would code:

```
CAPJOBA     DTAARA(SAV1)
   .
   .          /* Call the routine */
   .
RTNJOBA     DTAARA(SAV1)
```

The CAPJOBA command captures all your job attributes and places them in the data area you name. If the data area does not exist in library QTEMP, it is created. If you want to create the data area first, it must be declared as *CHAR LEN(1000).

The RTNJOBA command uses the CHGJOB command to reset your job attributes. The library list is restored by the CHGLIBL command, which is executed using the QCMDEXC command.

QUSRTOOL Retrieve Commands

The system supports about 20 RTV commands. But if you can't find the system function you want, QUSRTOOL TAA tools offer more than 25 additional RTV commands (and some CHK TAA tools that return variables).

Some of the TAA tool commands let you retrieve into your CL program attributes unique to an existing object type. The system-supported RTVOBJD command only allows you to retrieve the set of attributes common to all objects (e.g., the owner of an object and the object's creation date). If you need to access attributes, such as whether or not a CL program was created with the ALWRTVSRC(*YES) attribute or which output queue is specified in a print file, you may need a TAA tool.

For example, here is the code you would need to use the RTVPGMA TAA tool to access the ALWRTVSRC attribute of a CL program:

```
DCL          &ALWRTVSRC *CHAR LEN(4)
  .
  .
  .
RTVPGMA      PGM(xxx) ALWRTVSRC(&ALWRTVSRC)
IF           (&ALWRTVSRC *EQ '*YES') DO /* Exists */
  .
  .
  .
```

The QUSRTOOL library contains many RTV commands, such as RTVJOBD, RTVPFA, and RTVSPLFA. For a full list of these commands, see the discussion of member TAASUMMARY in Appendix B.

How To Write Your Own RTV Command

Now that we have looked at using existing RTV commands, here are some pointers on writing your own.

The typical error most programmers make when writing their own RTV commands is that they don't handle the situation that occurs when the program that uses the RTV command doesn't specify all the return variables as parameters. Here's why this becomes a problem: When a RTV command is executed, it only creates work areas for the variables that were specified by the program using the command. All the other variables specified by the RTV command are undefined (i.e., work areas for them do not exist). The command processing program (CPP) for the RTV command probably uses CHGVAR commands to move a value to a parameter being returned to the CPP. When a return variable has not been specified as a parameter, the system attempts unsuccessfully to move a value into an undefined work area and then sends escape message MCH3601, which states "Referenced location does not contain a pointer."

The way to keep this error from occurring in the CPP is to monitor for message ID MCH3601 after every CHGVAR command. Assume you have a RTV command that can return two values. The program using the RTV command can specify either one or both of the values. Your CL code would look something like this:

```
PGM          PARM(&RTN1 &RTN2)
DCL          &RTN1 *CHAR LEN(10)
DCL          &RTN2 *CHAR LEN(5)
  .
  .
  .
CHGVAR       &RTN1 &YOURVALUE1
MONMSG       MSGID(MCH3601) /* Ignore */
CHGVAR       &RTN2 &YOURVALUE2
MONMSG       MSGID(MCH3601) /* Ignore */
  .
  .
  .
RMVMSG       CLEAR(*ALL)
RETURN
```

You could monitor for message ID MCH3601 at the program level rather than at the command level, but I prefer not to. By monitoring at the program level, you might mask other escape message MCH3601 errors that could occur in the program. (For more information on this topic, see Chapter 14, "User-Written Commands.")

Technical Tip

When you use a CL program as a CPP for your own RTV command, you should monitor for message ID MCH3601 after every CHGVAR command that moves a value to one of the return parameters.

Exercise A Using the RTVOBJD Command

In this exercise we will extract some information from an object with the RTVOBJD command to see how easy it is to do.

1. Create a data area in a library on your library list as follows:

```
CRTDTAARA  DTAARA(xxx/DTAARA1) TYPE(*CHAR) LEN(10)
```

2. Using PDM, create a CLP member named TRYRTVOBJD.

3. In program TRYRTVOBJD, use the RTVOBJD command to retrieve the following values from data area DTAARA1:

   - The name of the library in which the data area exists
   - The create date
   - The owner

   Your RTVOBJD command should look like this:

```
RTVOBJD  OBJ(DTAARA1) OBJTYPE(*DTAARA) RTNLIB(...) ...
```

   You should be able to look at the command prompt and determine which return variables you want to use. After retrieving the values, send messages for each value:

```
SNDPGMMSG  MSG(&LIB)
SNDPGMMSG  MSG(&CRTDATE)
SNDPGMMSG  MSG(&OWNER)
```

   Enter the code to complete the program. Determine the attributes of the variables to be declared by looking at the RTVOBJD command prompt.

4. Create the program.

5. Call the program:

```
CALL  TRYRTVOBJD
```

   You should see the three messages you sent and the correct values for each.

6. If you don't need DTAARA1 any more, delete it.

Exercise B Using the RTVJOBA Command To Determine Output Form

In this exercise we will extract the type of job (batch or interactive) and use the value to determine how to print.

1. Use PDM to create a CLP member named TRYRTVJOBA.
2. In this program we will make a spooled output file from WRKSYSSTS and then decide whether to display the spooled file or release the spooled file based on parameter input.
3. Enter the following source:

```
PGM        PARM(&OUTPUT)
DCL        &OUTPUT *CHAR LEN(6)
DCL        &TYPE *CHAR LEN(1)
OVRPRTF    FILE(QPDSPSTS) HOLD(*YES)
WRKSYSSTS  OUTPUT(*PRINT)
RTVJOBA    TYPE(&TYPE)
IF         ((&TYPE *EQ '1') *AND +
             (&OUTPUT *EQ '*')) DO /* Interactive */
DSPSPLF    FILE(QPDSPSTS) SPLNBR(*LAST)
DLTSPLF    FILE(QPDSPSTS) SPLNBR(*LAST)
ENDDO      /* Interactive */
IF         ((&TYPE *EQ '0') *OR +
             (&OUTPUT *EQ '*PRINT')) DO /* Batch */
RLSSPLF    FILE(QPDSPSTS) SPLNBR(*LAST)
SNDPGMMSG  MSG('See spooled file QPDSPSTS') MSGTYPE(*COMP)
ENDDO      /* Batch */
ENDPGM
```

4. Create the program.
5. Call the program:

```
CALL  TRYRTVJOBA PARM(*)
```

   You should see the DSPSPLF display of the WRKSYSSTS spooled file.
6. Press Enter.
7. Use the WRKSPLF command to look at your spooled files.

   You should not see the QPDSPSTS file because the program deleted it.

Exercise B continued

Exercise B continued

8. Call the program:

```
CALL   TRYRTVJOBA PARM(*PRINT)
```

   You should see the completion message that says look at the QPDSPSTS spooled file.

9. Use the WRKSPLF command to look at your spooled files.

   You should see the QPDSPSTS spooled file.

10. Do the following SBMJOB:

```
SBMJOB   CMD(CALL TRYRTVJOBA PARM(*)) JOB(TRYRTVJOBA)
```

   The QPDSPSTS spooled file should exist when the job completes and it should be in a RDY status because the program released the file.

Exercise C Using the CAPJOBA TAA Tool

In this exercise we will use the CAPJOBA TAA tool to capture the job environment and then reset the environment by using the companion command RTNJOBA. If the CAPJOBA tool does not exist on your system, see Appendix B.

1. From the command entry display, enter the command:

```
CAPJOBA   DTAARA(MYJOB)
```

   The command captures the attributes about your job using the RTVJOBA command.

2. Prompt for the CHGLIBL command.

3. The prompt should show your library list and current library. Change both these values, but be sure to keep the TAATOOL library on your library list (if that is where your TAA tool commands exist). Press Enter.

4. Prompt for the CHGJOB command.

   The prompt should show the * in the job name.

Exercise C continued

Exercise C continued

5. Press Enter.

   You should see the first display of your job's attributes.

6. Change the Output priority to some other value than what you see.

7. Press Enter.

8. Now let's restore the saved attributes for our job with the command

   ```
   RTNJOBA  DTAARA(MYJOB)
   ```

9. Enter the command:

   ```
   DSPLIBL
   ```

   You should see that both the library list and your current library have their original value.

10. Prompt for the CHGJOB command.

11. Press Enter when the * appears in the job name prompt.

    You should see that the Output priority has its original value.

Technical Tip

The CAPJOBA command and its companion command, RTNJOBA, let you capture and reset your job environment. They are helpful to use when you have some program that needs to change the environment, and does not reset it.

CHAPTER 9

Subroutines

The term "subroutine" is used in many ways. In the normal use of the term, a subroutine describes a set of code that is part of the same program (i.e., you do not do a CALL in the program that is using the subroutine). A subroutine can be code that will be used at multiple points in the same program, or it can be a standard function that will be used in several programs (but normally, only once per program).

Subroutines shouldn't be confused with subprograms. A subprogram is a separately compiled program that requires a CALL from the program that will use it. Subprograms work well when you have a standard function to perform and you can package it in such a way that it is easily called (usually with a parameter list). In CL programming, the more sophisticated form of a subprogram is to provide a user-written command. I use user-written commands extensively, and you will find most of them in QUSRTOOL. With user-written commands, you can avoid the complexity and potential for errors associated with passing parameters.

In this chapter, I will concentrate on situations where subroutines are executed as part of one program, rather than as a part of multiple programs.

Technical Tip

In an upcoming release of OS/400, the CL compiler may become part of the Integrated Language Environment (ILE). If this occurs, you will have additional options for how to call a subroutine. From a performance perspective, code compiled into your program will always provide the fastest solution.

A Typical Approach to Subroutines

Although the CL compiler does not directly support subroutines (I wish it did), you can incorporate subroutines into your CL programs by using IF and GOTO statements. The following is a typical structure you can use whenever you need to include a subroutine in a CL program:

```
             DCL         &RTNLOC *CHAR LEN(10)
              .
              .
              .
                         /* 1st point where you need subr */
             CHGVAR      &RTNLOC 'LOC1'
             GOTO        SUBR
LOC1:                    /* Return from subroutine */
              .
              .
              .
                         /* 2nd point where you need subr */
             CHGVAR      &RTNLOC 'LOC2'
             GOTO        SUBR
LOC2:                    /* Return from subroutine */
              .
              .
              .
                         /* 3rd point where you need subr */
             CHGVAR      &RTNLOC 'LOC3'
             GOTO        SUBR
LOC3:                    /* Return from subroutine */
              .
              .
              .
STRSUBR:                 /* Beginning of code to copy for subr */
             SNDPGMMSG   MSGID(CPF9898) MSGF(QCPFMSG)          +
                           MSGTYPE(*ESCAPE)                    +
                           MSGDTA('Programmer error. You have  +
                           fallen into the subr code           +
                           instead of a GOTO')
SUBR:                    /* Beginning of subr for common code */
              .
              .              /*  Your common code */
              .
                         /* End of common code, branch back   */
             IF          (&RTNLOC *EQ 'LOC1') GOTO LOC1
             IF          (&RTNLOC *EQ 'LOC2') GOTO LOC2
             IF          (&RTNLOC *EQ 'LOC3') GOTO LOC3
             SNDPGMMSG   MSGID(CPF9898) MSGF(QCPFMSG)          +
                           MSGTYPE(*ESCAPE)                    +
                           MSGDTA('Bad RTNLOC value of ' *CAT  +
                           &RTNLOC *TCAT ' in SUBR routine')
```

If you use the label name (in this case, LOC1, LOC2, and LOC3) as the value for the IF test, it's fairly easy to make this approach work. Notice how the code protects itself if the program falls into the subroutine (the first SNDPGMMSG command), or if the RTNLOC value is not one of the expected values (the second SNDPGMMSG command).

Technical Tip

Subroutines can be incorporated into your CL programs fairly easily by using a combination of IF and GOTO commands. Using a consistent approach makes it easier to be productive and simplifies program maintenance.

CLPSUBR TAA Tool

If the concept of subroutines appeals to you, implementing the concept is fairly easy — you don't even have to key any code. You will find the code shown on the previous page in the QUSRTOOL TAA tool CLPSUBR.

Simply enter SEU and select the option (F15) for split-screen browse mode. Then specify member CLPSUBR in file QATTINFO in library QUSRTOOL. Roll through member CLPSUBR until you see the source code shown on the previous page and then copy it into your program. I normally copy all the code and then move pieces of the code to logical points in my program.

Technical Tip

The QUSRTOOL TAA tool CLPSUBR makes it easy for you to bring standard subroutine code into your program. Typically, you would copy all the standard subroutine code contained in CLPSUBR and then move the statements where you want them.

Reusing Proven Code in Multiple Programs

The most productive form of programming is to reuse code that has already been tested, and it is perfectly normal to borrow or steal code from some other program as you write a new application.

The traditional way to include source from another member in your program is to use the SEU split-screen Browse/Copy function. The CPYSRCF (Copy Source File) command or the PDM option for copying source is helpful when you want to duplicate an entire source member. And the QUSRTOOL TAA tool DUPSTDSRC (Duplicate Standard Source) is useful when you want to create a new program from existing code (see Chapter 28, "Setting up Your Environment").

Some compilers support an "include" function such as the RPG /COPY function. An "include" function allows you to maintain separately some standard code that you can "include" in several programs without making it part of your source. Although the CL compiler does not support an "include" function, the QUSRTOOL TAA tool CPYCL provides similar, if not better, support.

The CPYCL TAA Tool

The CPYCL (Copy CL) tool is designed for those times when you want to include some standard source in several different programs. If you use the SEU copy function instead of the CPYCL tool, the copied source becomes a permanent part of your program. Then, when the standard source must be modified, you have to determine where you have used it, fix the source, and re-create all the programs that are involved. Obviously, this could become a major maintenance job.

Another disadvantage of using SEU is that many standard source functions you might want to include in a program will contain both DCL statements and normal commands. You can include both types of statements using SEU, but it requires multiple steps. The CPYCL tool will merge the standard source into your program in the right place (it places the DCL statements from the standard source immediately following the last DCL statement in your program).

Two commands are provided as part of the CPYCL tool:

- The CPYCL command performs the include function based on a special comment that must be placed in your source. You use the CPYCL command at least once before you create the program. It copies your standard source into your program. If your standard source never changes, you never need to use the CPYCL command again on this member.
- The CRTCPYCL command simplifies the steps required when your standard source changes. You just point the CRTCPYCL command to the library that contains your object programs and it finds the programs that used the standard source, refreshes them with the latest version, and then re-creates each program. Compare this to using the RPG /COPY function when the standard source must be changed. With /COPY you have to scan the source for the programs that used the code and recompile each one yourself (there is no tool to find and recompile them).

For CPYCL to work correctly, you must place a special comment (STRCPYCL) into your source so that the CPYCL command knows what to do. You can have multiple STRCPYCL comments in the same member. The rules are strict as to how the STRCPYCL comment must appear. You can specify just a member name, in which case it is assumed that the standard source member you want to copy is in the same source file and library as the source you are currently using; or you can specify a different source file name or qualify the source file with a library name. In addition, the special comment must begin in position 1. Following are the three specifications that would be correct:

```
*...+....1....+....2....+....3....+....4
/*STRCPYCL STDSRC1    */

/*STRCPYCL STDSRC1 QCLSRC */

/*STRCPYCL STDSRC1 LIBX/QCLSRC */
```

Note that no keywords can be used. If you would like to see more detailed information about the rules for inserting the STRCPYCL comment, please refer to the documentation that accompanies the CPYCL tool.

Now let's see how the CPYCL tool works. Assume that you want to copy the following standard source from member STDSRC1:

```
DCL  &VAR *CHAR LEN(8)
CALL PGMB PARM(&VAR2)
IF   (&VAR2 *EQ 'GOOD') DO
.
.
.
ENDDO
```

Assume that you are copying the standard source into source member MBR1. You must place the STRCPYCL comment at the exact point in MBR1 where you want the source from STDSRC1 copied. To accomplish this, your code might look like the following:

```
*...+....1....+....2....+....3....+....4....+....5....+....6
                 DCL        &VAR1 *CHAR LEN(10)
                 CALL       PGM(PGMA)
/*STRCPYCL STDSRC1    */
                 CHKOBJ     ...
```

After you have placed the STRCPYCL comment in your source (MBR1), and before you execute a CRTCLPGM command, you would enter the following CPYCL command:

```
CPYCL  SRCMBR(MBR1) SRCFILE(xxxx)
```

The CPYCL command reads your source and writes it to a temporary source member. When the CPYCL command finds the special comment STRCPYCL, it slightly alters the comment and adds it to the temporary member. Then the CPYCL command reads the STDSRC1 member and adds the statements to the temporary source member. The CPYCL command actually splits your code into three temporary members:

- DCL statements
- program-level MONMSG commands
- all other CL statements

When your standard source is read, the same split occurs and the statements are added to the separate temporary members. This allows the statements to be merged properly so that your standard source can contain DCL statements, program-level MONMSG commands, and normal CL statements.

When the CPYCL command reaches "end of file" on STDSRC1, it adds a special ending comment to the temporary source and then returns to reading source member MBR1. After the CPYCL command writes all of source member MBR1 to the temporary file, and there are no errors, the command first clears source member MBR1 and then copies the temporary source into source member MBR1.

At that point, your source would look like the following:

```
              DCL   *VAR1 *CHAR LEN(10)
/*CPYCL*/     DCL   &VAR2 *CHAR LEN(8)
              CALL PGM(PGMA)
/*STRCPYCL - FOLLOWS - STDSRC1
              CALL PGMB PARM(&VAR2)
              IF    (&VAR2 *EQ 'GOOD') DO
              .
              .
              .
              ENDDO
/*ENDCPYCL
              CHKOBJ     ...
```

Notice that the DCL statement for variable &VAR2 has been merged at the correct point in the program and has been flagged with a preceding comment of /*CPYCL*/.

The purpose of the modified STRCPYCL statement (the text, " - FOLLOWS -," is inserted), the ENDCPYCL statement, and the /*CPYCL*/ comment on the DCL statement is to allow you to run the CPYCL command again against the same source. If you did run the

CPYCL command against the same source, the command would remove all the source statements between the STRCPYCL comment and the ENDCPYCL comment, remove all the /*CPYCL*/ DCL statements, and perform the CPYCL command again (this refreshes the member with the current STRSRC1 source). To allow this function to occur, you should not modify the special comments.

You can use the CPYCL command to "include" source from many different standard source members, but the standard source member cannot contain a STRCPYCL comment. For instance, in our example the STDSRC1 source could not have a STRCPYCL comment within it (nesting is not supported by the CPYCL command).

An option on the CPYCL command controls whether or not comments found within the standard source will be copied. For more information about this option, see the documentation that accompanies the CPYCL tool or the discussion in Exercise B at the end of this chapter.

The STDSRC1 source is now part of your source, and you can create the program when you are ready. You don't need to use the CPYCL tool again on source member MBR1 unless the standard source changes.

If the standard source member is modified, the CPYCL tool makes it easy to implement the changes in any source members in which you have used the standard source. You simply use the CRTCPYCL command and specify the library that contains the program objects using STDSRC1:

```
CRTCPYCL  PGM(LIBX/*ALL) STRCPYCL(STDSRC1)
```

Note that this technique will work only if you have not moved the source that was used to create the object. If you moved the object to a different library (but the source is still in the original library/file/member), the technique will still work.

The CRTCPYCL command does the following:

1. Builds an outfile of the program objects in the library you name.
2. Reads the outfile and selects the CLP types.
3. Determines the source member used to create the program.
4. Ensures the existence of the source member used to create the object program. An option (TAA tool SRCARC) is available that lets you use the source in a source archive if your source member cannot be found.
5. Searches the source member looking for the STRCPYCL comment and the member you named (STDSRC1).
6. If the STRCPYCL comment is not found, the CRTCPYCL command bypasses the object and prints a line noting the fact.

7. If the STRCYPCL comment is found, the CRTCPYCL command uses the CPYCL command to refresh the source. This causes the new source from STDSRC1 to be copied in and the old "include" to be deleted.
8. If the CPYCL command was used, the CRTCPYCL command uses the TAA tool RPLPGM (Replace Program) to re-create the program. The RPLPGM tool does a good job of capturing the current attributes of the program (e.g., LOG, removing observability, security information) and specifying them on the new program.
9. Outputs a spooled file with one line per CLP member that notes whether the member was re-created and whether any errors occurred.

Technical Tip

If you are writing an application for distribution to multiple sites, you might prefer not to have the special comments associated with the CPYCL command in the source. You can eliminate the special comments by naming a "to source file" when using the CPYCL command. The documentation included with the CPYCL command tells you how to do this. However, you probably will have to re-create all the programs for a particular application when you are ready to ship a new version.

Technical Tip

Although not a perfect solution for doing an "include," the CPYCL TAA tool can be used very effectively. The companion command, CRTCPYCL, provides the real power. The CRTCPYCL command re-creates the programs after your standard source has been modified. Together, the CPYCL and CRTCPYCL commands can boost your productivity greatly when you use standard source in several CL programs.

Exercise A Using a Subroutine

In this exercise we will use the same subroutine at three different points within a CL program. For this exercise, you will need the TAA tools EDTVAR and CLPSUBR. If they do not exist on your system, see Appendix B.

1. Use PDM to create a CLP member named TRYSUBR.
2. Enter the following statements:

```
PGM
DCL         &COUNT *DEC LEN(5 0)
DCL         &COUNTA *CHAR LEN(22)
```

3. Request the SEU split-screen browse mode (F15) and specify member CLPSUBR in file QATTINFO in library QUSRTOOL. (Remember that the CLPSUBR tool contains a coding template for using subroutines in a CL program.) When the member is displayed, roll through the member until you see the CL source described in the first part of this chapter. Copy the source code into member TRYSUBR.
4. The following is the subroutine you want to execute from three different points in the program you are creating:

```
CHGVAR      &COUNT (&COUNT + 1)
EDTVAR      CHROUT(&COUNTA) NUMINP(&COUNT)
SNDPGMMSG   MSG('Count = ' *CAT &COUNTA)
```

   Enter the subroutine into member TRYSUBR at the appropriate place. Remember that the places to branch to the subroutine are noted in the source you copied from the CLPSUBR tool.
5. Place a RETURN command after label LOC3.
6. Add an ENDPGM statement.
7. Create the program.
8. Call the program:

```
CALL  TRYSUBR
```

Exercise A continued

Exercise A continued

You should see the messages

Count = 1
Count = 2
Count = 3

You should not see the message, "Programmer error. You have fallen ...". If you do, you need to end the program at the right point with a RETURN command.

Exercise B Using the CPYCL TAA Tool

In this exercise we will use the CPYCL and CRTCPYCL commands to show you the power of these TAA tools. You will need the TAA tool CPYCL (the CRTCPYCL command is part of the same tool). If the CPYCL tool does not exist on your system, see Appendix B.

1. Use PDM to create a CLP source member named TRYSTDSRC1. This will be your standard source. Although you can enter any statements you want because we will not execute the programs created for this exercise, I suggest using the following statements (be sure to place the comments as shown in member TRYSTDSRC1).

```
*...+....1....+....2....+....3....+....4....+....5....+....6
/*CPYCMNT - This is the standard source */
                DCL         &VAR2 *CHAR LEN(8)
                CALL        PGMA
                            /* Comment from TRYSTDSRC1 */
                SNDPGMMSG    MSG(Hi)
```

2. End SEU. You don't need to create this program.
3. Use PDM to create a CLP source member named TRYCPY1. Enter the following statements (be sure the /* starts in position 1 and that there is only a single blank before the member name TRYSTDSRC1):

Exercise B continued

Exercise B continued

```
*...+....1....+....2....+....3....+....4....+....5....+....6
        PGM
        DCL         &VAR1 *CHAR LEN(1)
        CALL        PGMC
/*STRCPYCL TRYSTDSRC1      */
        CALL        PGMD
        ENDPGM
```

4. End SEU. Don't create the program at this time.
5. Using the copy option (3) on PDM, copy TRYCPY1 twice to create two additional CLP source members named TRYCPY2 and TRYCPY3.
6. Use PDM to edit source member TRYCPY3. Delete the STRCPYCL comment. This program will not use the CPYCL function.
7. End SEU. Do not create the program at this time.
8. From a command entry line, use the CPYCL command to include the source that you have described in the STRCPYCL comment:

   ```
   CPYCL  SRCMBR(TRYCPY1) SRCFILE(xxx)
   ```

9. When the command is complete, use PDM to look at source member TRYCPY1.

   You should see that the standard source from TRYSTDSRC1 was copied in and the DCL statement was placed in the proper position. The STRCPYCL comment has been changed so that the text " - FOLLOWS - " has been inserted. You should not see the special comment that was in member TRYSTDSRC1 because the default for CPYCL is to drop the special comments.

10. To see how to control whether or not comments are copied, use the CPYCL command on source member TRYCPY2 and request that no comments be copied:

    ```
    CPYCL  SRCMBR(TRYCPY2) SRCFILE(xxx) CPYCOMMNTS(*NO)
    ```

11. Use PDM to look at source member TRYCPY2.

    You should see that all the comments have been dropped from member TRYSTDSRC1.

Exercise B continued

Exercise B continued

12. This next exercise will work best if you use a unique library. Enter the command:

    ```
    CRTLIB  LIB(TRYCPYCL)
    ```

13. Now you need to create the three programs (TRYCPY1, TRYCPY2, and TRYCPY3) in library TRYCPYCL. You can use PDM, but you must prompt for the create command and specify library TRYCPYCL.
14. When the CRTCLPGM commands are complete, display the library:

    ```
    DSPLIB  TRYCPYCL
    ```

    You should see the three programs you created.
15. Now we will make a change to source member STDSRC1 and show the use of the CRTCPYCL command. Use PDM to edit member TRYSTDSRC1. Before the SNDPGMMSG command, enter the command:

    ```
    CALL  PGMZ
    ```

16. End SEU but don't create the program.
17. Now you need to find all the places you have used the STRCPYCL comment for member TRYSTDSRC1, refresh them with the new source from TRYSTDSRC1, and re-create the programs. The CRTCPYCL command does all of this for you. You get to decide how you want to handle the CPYCOMMNTS parameter in the following command:

    ```
    CRTCPYCL  PGM(TRYCPYCL/*ALL) STRCPYCL(TRYSTDSRC1) +
                CPYCOMMNTS(xxxx)
    ```

    Note: The CRTCPYCL command takes awhile to run. If you were working with a large library, you would want to submit the command to batch. If you execute the CRTCPYCL command interactively, status messages are sent describing the progress.
18. When the CRTCPYCL command completes, use the WRKSPLF command to display the spooled file that was created.

    You should see one line for every CLP program in the library. The entries in the columns describe whether the STRCPYCL value was found and whether the program was re-created successfully.

Exercise B continued

Exercise B continued

19. Use PDM to look at member TRYCPY1.

    You should see that the new source from TRYSTDSRC1 has been included in the member. At this point, the new code has been included in all the programs that used TRYSTDSRC1 in library TRYCPYCL, and the programs have been re-created.

Technical Tip

Reusing well-tested code is the number one technique for gaining productivity. You can probably find several places among your own CL programs where the CPYCL TAA tool can be used effectively.

20. If you have no further use for this exercise, delete the library you created:

```
DLTLIB  LIB(TRYCPYCL)
```

CHAPTER 10

Passing Parameters

The AS/400 offers considerable protection — in the form of error messages — as a programmer performs functions such as entering source, compiling a program, or using externally described data. However, the system provides little protection when a programmer uses the CALL command to pass parameters. Passing parameters can be very error prone, and if you don't pass the parameters correctly, you can spend a lot of time debugging programs.

When you code a parameter list on a CALL command to a CL program, you need to be certain that in both the calling program and the called program

- the same number of parameters exist
- the parameters are listed in the same sequence
- the type and length of corresponding parameters are defined the same

The names of the parameters do not have to be the same.

You can pass parameters in several ways; some ways are more error prone than others.

- Passing parameters from one program to another. The system allows you to pass parameters between different high-level language (HLL) programs; but not all HLLs support all data types, so you need to be careful. For example, passing parameters between RPG and CL programs works well with character or packed-decimal data. But, if you want your program to work correctly the first time, you should convert other RPG data types to character or packed-decimal when passing parameters to a CL program.

- Passing parameters from a command to a Command Processing Program (CPP). When you define a command, the order of the PARM statements determines the order in which the parameters are passed to the CPP. The system automatically generates a CALL command using the parameters you specified on the command you defined.

- Passing parameters to a submitted job. You can pass parameters to a submitted job by using the CMD parameter on the SBMJOB command. This method is similar to passing parameters from a command entry line (see the section "Submitting a Job with Parameters" later in this chapter).

- Passing parameters from a command entry line. This method works well if you pass only character values of 32 bytes or less in length that start with letters (not numbers). For example,

  ```
  CALL  PGMA PARM(FILE1 WEDNESDAY YES)
  ```

  The next section looks more closely at this method of passing parameters.

Passing Parameters from a Command Entry Line

As I indicated previously, you can eliminate a lot of the potential for problems when passing parameters from a command entry line by passing only character values less than 32 bytes long. The system is designed to pass parameters in 32-byte sections. If the parameter value is less than 32 bytes long, the system automatically pads the value to the right with blanks.

If you pass parameters other than character variables of 32 bytes (or fewer) from a command entry line, you need to be concerned with a few rules:

- If you pass a decimal value that will be placed in a character variable, you must enclose the value in quotes. For example,

  ```
  PARM('1' '123192' '1AX')
  ```

  Be particularly careful about passing switches (e.g., 1 or 0) or passing dates that you want to treat as character data. If you want the value placed in a character variable, you must use quotes. If you don't use quotes, the system will attempt to pack the data. The system will assume the value is numeric and it always converts numeric data to packed-decimal data. Even though the system is smart enough to recognize a character value (e.g., 1AX) when it sees one, I still put quote marks around the value just to be safe.

- If you pass a single value such as MILK MAN, which contains a blank, the system will read the value as two parameters rather than one. To be sure the system reads MILK MAN as one parameter, you must use quotes: 'MILK MAN'.

- If you pass a character value that is declared in the called program as longer than 32 bytes, you must pass exactly the number of bytes that you have specified. If the lengths of the corresponding parameters don't match, unpredictable results will occur in your program. In this situation, the system moves into the variable the amount of data required to fill the variable. For example, if a program passes a 30-byte variable to a program that is expecting a 50-byte variable, the system will pad with blanks to 32 bytes and include in the value passed an additional 18 bytes of data — unfortunately, it won't be 18 bytes of data you want your program to use.

- If you pass a numeric value from a command entry line, the called program must declare it as *DEC LEN(15 5). This means that you might have to use the CHGVAR command to move the value to a variable with a correct definition after you receive the value into your program. For example, if you code

  ```
  CALL PGM(PGMA) PARM(22)
  ```

  the value passed to the program will be 22.00000. Because CL always performs decimal alignment, you would code something like the following to move the passed value to a zero decimal field:

  ```
  PGM      PARM(&AMT)
  DCL      &AMT *DEC LEN(15 5)
  DCL      &AMT2 *DEC LEN(5 0)
    .
    .
    .
  CHGVAR   &AMT2 &AMT
  ```

As long as you don't truncate any high-order digits, the CHGVAR command will provide you with a decimal variable containing the value passed on the call. To continue our example, variable &AMT2 would contain the passed value of 22.

Adding Meaning to Your Values

Because 1-byte switches don't provide enough documentation when passed from another program, I prefer to pass 8-byte character values (e.g., PRINT or NOTFOUND) that describe the condition being passed. In addition, RPG allows a simple move or compare of eight characters in Factor 1 or 2. Using an 8-byte switch, then, provides better documentation and is easy to code. The following code illustrates the use of 8-byte switches:

```
DCL        &RTNCDE *CHAR LEN(8)
DCL        &RQSCDE *CHAR LEN(8)
 .
 .
 .
CHGVAR     &RQSCDE 'DETAIL'
CALL       PGM(xxx) PARM(&RQSCDE &RNTCDE)
IF         (&RTNCDE *EQ 'GOOD') DO /* Good one */
 .
 .
 .
ENDDO      /* Good one */
IF         (&RTNCDE *EQ 'NOTFOUND') /* Not found */
 .
 .
 .
ENDDO      /* Not found */
           /* If the code gets to here it is    */
           /*    a bad return code              */
SNDPGMMSG  MSGID(CPF9898) MSGF(QCPFMSG)     +
             MSGTYPE(*ESCAPE)               +
             MSG('Bad return code of ' *CAT +
             &RTNCDE *TCAT ' from xxx')
```

In this example, I use variable &RQSCDE to tell an RPG program what to do, and I use variable &RTNCDE to tell the CL program what the result was. Notice how the code protects itself (the SNDPGMMSG command) if the called program returns a return code that the calling program does not expect.

Technical Tip

Using 8-byte descriptive switches instead of 1-byte switches can improve a program's documentation. Use of more descriptive switches also avoids logic errors caused by trying to remember that "1" is good and "0" is bad.

SUBMITTING A JOB WITH PARAMETERS

On the AS/400, the CMD parameter on the SBMJOB command simplifies the task of submitting a batch job with parameters. But you still need to watch for potential problems — the same problems (discussed earlier) that might occur when passing parameters from a command entry line.

To avoid these potential problems, I practice the following techniques when using the CMD parameter on the SBMJOB command:

- Move any switches or dates to character variables instead of specifying a constant as a parameter. Specify the variable name on the command parameter so it will quote the value properly.
- Move any decimal variables to character variables and pass the character variable. In the batch program, move the data to a decimal variable. This technique may seem odd, but it avoids having to remember what the system will do to your data when it passes it to the batch program. That is, you don't need to remember to declare a receiving variable as LEN (15 5).
- If a program must pass a character variable longer than 32 bytes, you can divide the variable into multiple variables of no more than 32 bytes each and pass the pieces. Then, in the batch program, you can use a concatenate operation to bring the variable back together. For more information about passing large parameters, see the section "Passing Really Large Parameters" later in this chapter.

Technical Tip

My philosophy on passing parameters is to keep it simple and always pass character variables of 32 bytes or fewer. Adding code to both programs that moves variables or divides and then concatenates variables is well worth the effort to reduce the chance of making mistakes.

Using the Right Number of Parameters

Whether or not you need to specify the same number of parameters in both the calling program and the called program depends on which programming language was used to write the called program (i.e., the program to which you are passing parameters).

When you pass parameters to a CL program, you always need to specify in the CL program the same number of parameters specified in the calling program. A CL program does not have the capability to ignore parameters that were defined but not passed.

When you pass parameters to an RPG program, you can pass a shorter parameter list than that specified in the calling program. The object code won't do anything with a parameter unless the program tries to use it. If the RPG program tries to use a parameter that wasn't passed, the program issues an escape message.

System programs are like RPG programs; they have the "smarts" to not check for a missing parameter.

Using the Local Data Area

Although the local data area (LDA) can be used effectively as an alternative to passing parameters, you shouldn't use this technique if you are writing tools for general use. Nothing will prevent a program from overwriting the LDA with whatever data the program needs. For this reason, I don't use the LDA for any of the TAA tools.

Passing a Data Structure

You can pass only 40 parameters on a CALL command. If 40 parameters aren't enough, you can concatenate several variables into a single data structure and pass the data structure as a single variable. Although some programmers think it is good practice to pass only data structures rather than multiple parameters, I rarely use this technique because CL does not support a command to declare data structures. There is a performance consideration that can make this desirable in some cases (see Chapter 24, "CL Program Performance").

For those of you who prefer working with data structures, let me offer a solution to what might be the worst situation you could find yourself in when using this technique: receiving a data structure that contains a packed-decimal field. In this situation, you can retrieve the data by using a substring function, but you can move the data only to a character field (the substring function does not work with decimal fields). You won't find a CL command that lets you specify "Move this character variable to a decimal variable, but don't pack it (because it's already packed)." But the QUSRTOOL TAA tool MOVCHRDEC offers a solution.

If you have a packed-decimal value in a character variable, you would code

```
DCL          &DEC *DEC LEN(5 0)
DCL          &CHAR *CHAR LEN(3)
  .
  .
  .
MOVCHRDEC    DECOUT(&DEC) CHRINP(&CHAR)
```

The MOVCHRDEC command automatically moves the packed-decimal value from the character variable to the decimal variable.

Technical Tip

When passing data structures to a CL program, the MOVCHRDEC TAA tool can be extremely helpful when a data structure contains a packed-decimal field.

Passing Really Large Parameters

You can pass up to 3,000 bytes of data to a batch program using the SBMJOB command. But if 3,000 bytes isn't enough, you might consider using the QUSRTOOL TAA tool CHGBIGPARM. The CHGBIGPARM command lets you store up to 2,000 bytes of data per use of the command. By using the CHGBIGPARM command multiple times, you can pass more than the 3,000 bytes supported by the SBMJOB command.

When the CHGBIGPARM command stores a chunk of data, you identify it by using your unique qualified job name and an optional modifier. Then, instead of passing the data, you pass the qualified job name of the submitting job. The companion command RTVBIGPARM is used in the batch program to access the data in the batch job.

It takes a little bit of work, but the CHGBIGPARM TAA tool allows you to pass an unlimited amount of data to a batch program.

Technical Tip

The QUSRTOOL TAA tool CHGBIGPARM allows you to pass an unlimited amount of data to a batch program.

Using the Same Parameter List on SBMJOB and CALL Commands

Sometimes you might want to use the same parameter list on both the SBMJOB and CALL commands in the same CL program. For example, if your program can execute interactively or in batch, you may not want to submit a job if you are already in batch.

If this (or something similar) is your problem, you may want to code the parameter list only once to minimize maintenance. A good tool to use for this purpose is the BLDCALL TAA tool. It provides the same quoting function as the CMD parameter on the SBMJOB command. For a discussion about how to use the BLDCALL tool, see Chapter 8, "Retrieve Commands."

Exercise A Passing Parameters Longer than 32 Bytes

In this exercise you will see why I recommend that you pass character variables of 32 bytes or fewer when operating from a command entry line or when using the CMD parameter on the SBMJOB command. For program-to-program communication, there is nothing wrong with passing a large parameter. But if you don't define the parameter the same in both the calling and called programs, your program can experience unexpected results. We will use a simple program, first correctly and then incorrectly, to show you what happens when you pass a large parameter.

1. Using PDM, create a CLP member named TRYPARM.
2. Enter the following source:

```
PGM         PARM(&BIG &LITTLE)
DCL         &BIG *CHAR LEN(32)
DCL         &LITTLE *CHAR LEN(5)
SNDPGMMSG   MSG('BIG-' *CAT &BIG)
SNDPGMMSG   MSG('LITTLE-' *CAT &LITTLE)
ENDPGM
```

3. Create the program.
4. Call the program:

```
CALL    PGM(TRYPARM) PARM('Here is the big one' 'ABC')
```

   You should see the two values you entered as parameters in the messages returned to the display. The values are correct even though the value you entered for variable &BIG is fewer than 32 bytes. Because the system passes parameters in 32-byte sections, you will have no problems as long as the variable is 32 bytes or fewer.

5. Call the program again, but this time enter a parameter longer than 32 bytes:

```
CALL    PGM(TRYPARM)  PARM('Here is the big one +
          1234567890 1234567890' 'ABC')
```

   You should see the two values you entered, but the first value will be truncated. The system, however, does not treat the truncated value as an error, making the problem difficult to detect.

Exercise A continued

Exercise A continued

6. Use PDM and change the DCL statement for variable &BIG to LEN(50).
7. Re-create the program.
8. Call the program using the original value for variable &BIG:

```
CALL  PGM(TRYPARM) PARM('Here is the big one' 'ABC')
```

   You should see the two values you entered, but the first variable will contain information from the second variable. To explain what happens in simple terms, the system stores the data passed as parameters in a string and moves as many bytes as it needs to fill up your variable. In this case, the called program expects a 50-byte variable but receives only 21 bytes. The system fills the space between 21 and 32 bytes with blanks and then moves an additional 18 bytes of data into the value. Some, or all, of that data will come from the value of the next variable passed to the program.

9. Use PDM and change the PGM statement so there is only a single parameter:

```
PGM  PARM(&BIG)
```

10. Create the program.
11. Call the program:

```
CALL  PGM(TRYPARM) PARM('Here is the big one')
```

   As in Step 8, you should see the value you entered, but at the end of the first variable you will see "interesting results." Because fewer bytes of data were received by the program than it expected, the system fills in the value with whatever data follows the parameter work area.

Exercise B Passing Character Variables Without Quotes

In this exercise we will demonstrate what happens when you fail to put quote marks around data that you want to be recognized as character data. To do this exercise, you will need the QUSRTOOL TAA tool BKP. If this tool does not exist on your system, see Appendix B.

1. Using PDM, create a CLP member named TRYPARM2.
2. Enter the following source:

```
PGM        PARM(&SWITCH &DATE)
DCL        &SWITCH *CHAR LEN(1)
DCL        &DATE *CHAR LEN(6)
SNDPGMMSG  MSG('SWITCH-' *CAT &SWITCH)
SNDPGMMSG  MSG('DATE-' *CAT &DATE)
ENDPGM
```

3. Create the program.
4. First, call the program and pass quoted values:

```
CALL  TRYPARM2 PARM('1' '120192')
```

   You should see the correct values in the messages displayed.

5. Now call the program and pass the characters A and 12ABCD:

```
CALL  TRYPARM2 PARM(A 12ABCD)
```

   You should see the correct values in the messages displayed. The system looks at the values, determines they are character values, and moves them correctly.

6. Now call the program as you did in Step 4, but without the quote marks:

```
CALL  TRYPARM2 PARM(1 120192)
```

   You should see that the first message doesn't appear to have any value and the second message is garbled because it is trying to display non-displayable data.

7. Use the BKP TAA tool and specify

```
BKP  STMT(400) PGMVAR(SWITCH DATE) PGM(TRYPARM2) OUTFMT(*HEX)
```

Exercise B continued

Exercise B continued

8. Call the program:

```
CALL  TRYPARM2 PARM(1 120192)
```

When the breakpoint display appears, you should see that variable &SWITCH has a hex value of '00'. Nothing is displayed by the SNDPGMMSG command because X'00' is a null value. Variable &DATE has a hex value of '000012019200'. This is close, but not what you want. The system always passes numeric data as if it were defined with a value of LEN(15 5). When it moves it to your variable, you get interesting results.

9. To end this exercise, return to the command entry line and enter the command

```
ENDDBG
```

CHAPTER 11

Allocating Objects

The AS/400 is designed to let multiple jobs simultaneously share the same resources as much as possible. The system allows this resource sharing by automatically placing implicit locks on objects as your job needs them. For example, when your job opens a file, the system places a lock on both the file and the member that was opened. Another job can open the same file to perform the same function, but gaining the implicit lock prevents another job from performing a function that requires exclusive use of the file/member (e.g., removing it or clearing it).

The system also lets you manually allocate specific objects to a job. You might need to do this when an application requires that only one job at a time perform a certain function, or when an application needs to control certain objects for a long period of time so that its access to them is ensured at a later point to complete its function.

You can control objects in one of three ways; the choice depends on how much control you want:

1. Do nothing. You can let the system object allocation defaults occur and share resources as much as possible. This method is the most desirable and the easiest to use.
2. Perform an "If active" test. In this situation, an application does not actually allocate an object; the application only ensures that a single job is using a function at a given time. This method of controlling objects typically would be used with batch programs that update many records in a file. The next three sections in this chapter, "Is a Program Active," "Is an Object Active," and "Is a Job Active," offer techniques for performing an "If active" test on three different object types.
3. Manually allocate an object. This method of controlling objects requires a good knowledge of how object allocation works and how to obtain and release locks. I'll discuss this method in the section "Manually Allocating Objects" later in this chapter.

Is a Program Active?

You may have a program that performs some sensitive function for you (e.g., running all updates in one job). In this situation, you often need a simple way to determine whether or not the program is already executing. The system neither implicitly locks a program object when it is called nor provides a way to determine whether or not a program is in use.

A solution can be found, however, in the QUSRTOOL TAA tool CHKACTPGM (Check Active Program), which lets you call a program and then determine whether or not it is being used (Figure 11.1). To use the CHKACTPGM tool, place the following command inside the program to be tested for activity:

```
CHKACTPGM  /* TAA Tool command */
```

In this case, you are using the default (*LOCK) for the ALLOCATE keyword on the CHKACTPGM command; the other values supported by the keyword are *UNLOCK and *TEST. The CHKACTPGM tool uses the ALCOBJ (Allocate Object) command to attempt to place a lock on the program that is executing. If the allocation attempt is successful, a completion message is issued and the lock remains on the program. If the allocation attempt is unsuccessful, escape message CPF9898 is sent, which in this case reads:

```
Program xxx is already in use by another job and can only be used
   by one job at a time.
```

You could monitor for the message and resend it (or your own text)

Figure 11.1
CHKACTPGM TAA Tool Prompt Screen

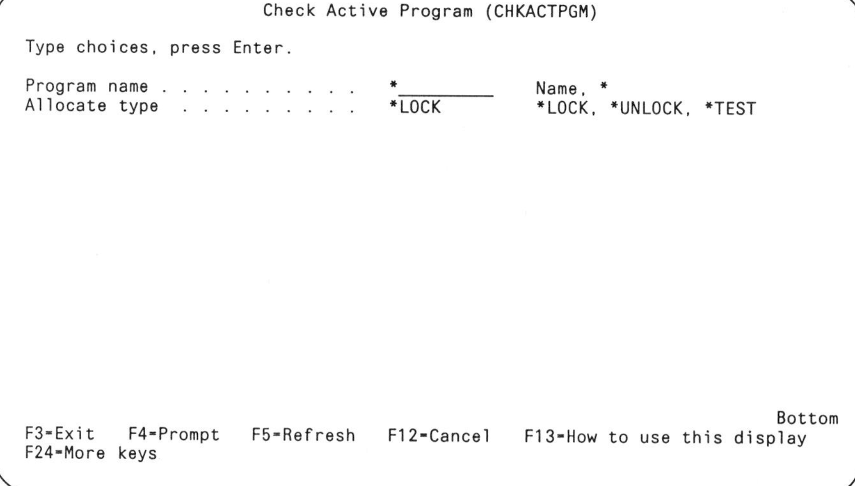
```
                        Check Active Program (CHKACTPGM)

Type choices, press Enter.

Program name . . . . . . . . . .   *_________     Name, *
Allocate type  . . . . . . . . .   *LOCK          *LOCK, *UNLOCK, *TEST

                                                                     Bottom
F3=Exit   F4=Prompt   F5=Refresh   F12=Cancel   F13=How to use this display
F24=More keys
```

to the program that called your program, or you could handle the escape message and do some different processing. If you use the standard error-handling routine described in Chapter 4, you could let the routine take over and resend the escape message automatically.

Note that if the CHKACTPGM command's attempt to allocate a program is successful, your job will have achieved an exclusive (*EXCL) lock on the program. If the program that is locked is the first program called in a batch job, the exclusive lock is probably just what you want. When the job ends, the system releases all the locks held by the job. But if this is a program that is part of a larger application, then you need to release the lock on the program when you are done. As part of your program ending logic, you would specify the following to unlock the program:

```
CHKACTPGM  ALLOCATE(*UNLOCK)
```

The *TEST function allows you to ask the question, "Can a program be locked?". You get a completion message if the program can be locked (although a lock will not actually exist) and an escape message (CPF9898) if it cannot.

The CHKACTPGM PGM keyword defaults to (*), which means that the program you are running will be tested. You can also check a different program. For example, if you were going to submit PGMA to batch, you might want to determine whether or not PGMA is already active; if it is active, you would not submit a job to use the program in batch. To perform this test, you would use the following CHKACTPGM command in PGMA:

```
CHKACTPGM  /* TAA Tool Command */
```

Your interactive program would include the following code:

```
CHKACTPGM  PGM(PGMA) ALLOCATE(*TEST)
MONMSG     MSGID(CPF9898) EXEC(DO) /* In use */
   .
   .       /* Say something to the operator */
   .       /*       Handle the error        */
   .
ENDDO      /* In use */
SBMJOB     CMD(CALL PGMA)
```

When using the CHKACTPGM command, you need to be aware of some potential problems. For example, if two jobs tried to execute the above code at the same instant, both jobs would find that PGMA is not in use and the SBMJOB command would be executed to call PGMA. Whichever batch job executed the CHKACTPGM command first in

PGMA would obtain the lock. The other job would receive an escape message. At a minimum, the CHKACTPGM command would prevent the second job from running PGMA.

A more typical situation, and one more difficult to resolve, would be the following: An interactive job determines that PGMA is not active and executes a SBMJOB command to execute PGMA, but some time may pass before PGMA becomes active and executes the CHKACTPGM command. Between the time the SBMJOB command is executed and the time PGMA executes the CHKACTPGM command, you are exposed to a second job attempting the same thing. The second job submitted to batch would receive escape message CPF9898. You can take the default and abnormally terminate the second job, or you could monitor for the escape message in PGMA and use the DLYJOB (Delay Job) command for some number of seconds and then retry the CHKACTPGM command.

This problem occurs because there is no way to transfer a lock that you establish in one job and pass it to a different job. Therefore, in the case of a program executing a SBMJOB command, you can't set a lock to prevent another job from executing the same command. You can use either of two techniques to prevent the simultaneous submission of the same batch job, but neither of them is perfect:

1. *Data areas.* Some programmers place a value in a data area in the interactive job to indicate that the batch job is "in use." Then they set the data area to blanks when the batch job completes. The exposure with this technique is that the batch job could be cancelled by another job, or end abnormally, before it resets the value in the data area. When using this technique, good programming practice suggests that you have the batch program check the same data area for the "in use" value when the batch program begins. The batch program should reset the value whether or not it ends successfully. In your interactive program, you need to allocate the data area before setting the "in use" value. Unless you allocate the data area, you will be exposed to two jobs trying to perform the same function at the same time (see the section "Updating a Data Area" later in this chapter).

2. *Allocations.* Since there is no way to pass a lock from an interactive job to a batch job, you must use allocation requests in both the interactive job and the batch job. But what should you allocate? The interactive job or the batch job cannot allocate the same object, and there is no guarantee that the interactive job will still exist when the batch job begins. A solution may exist, but it probably is non-trivial to code and test. That is why I prefer the

CHKACTPGM TAA tool discussed earlier. The worst that can happen when using the CHKACTPGM tool is that a second batch job will fail when it attempts to gain a lock.

Technical Tip

The CHKACTPGM TAA tool is a winner for determining whether or not a program is active. It is simple to use and protects the function you want run by a single job. It is not perfect (another batch job can be submitted), but it is safer than most solutions (the second batch job will not run the program if it is still active).

Is an Object in Use?

The typical way to determine whether or not an object is active (i.e., in use) is to try to use the object or to allocate the object. The easiest way to do this is to use the QUSRTOOL TAA tool CHKACTOBJ (Figure 11.2). The CHKACTOBJ tool does for other objects what the CHKACTPGM ALLOCATE(*TEST) function does for programs. It attempts to lock the object to an *EXCL state and then unlocks the object if it is successful. For example, you would use the following command to determine whether a data area is in use:

```
CHKACTOBJ  OBJ(AREA1) OBJTYPE(*DTAARA)
```

FIGURE 11.2
CHKACTOBJ TAA Tool Prompt Screen

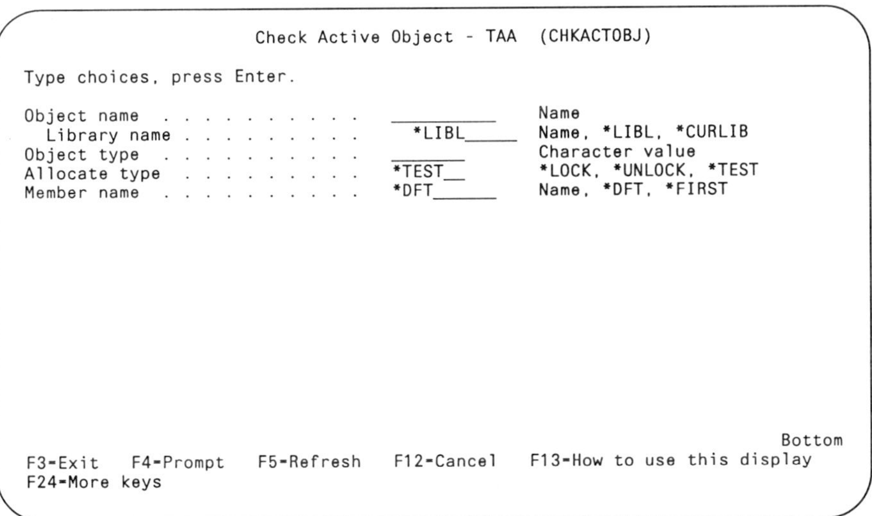

```
                    Check Active Object - TAA  (CHKACTOBJ)

Type choices, press Enter.

Object name . . . . . . . . . . .   __________   Name
  Library name  . . . . . . . . .    *LIBL_____   Name, *LIBL, *CURLIB
Object type . . . . . . . . . . .   ________     Character value
Allocate type . . . . . . . . . .   *TEST__      *LOCK, *UNLOCK, *TEST
Member name . . . . . . . . . . .   *DFT______   Name, *DFT, *FIRST

                                                                  Bottom
F3=Exit   F4=Prompt   F5=Refresh   F12=Cancel   F13=How to use this display
F24=More keys
```

If the command is successful, you know that no one is using data area AREA1. If someone is using the object, you will receive escape message CPF9898. The object types supported by CHKACTOBJ are the same as those supported by the ALCOBJ command, with the following exceptions:

- For *PGM objects, you will get a message that says you should be using the CHKACTPGM TAA tool.
- For *LIB and *DEVD type objects, the system does not support the use of *EXCL so there is no way of determining whether or not they are in use.
- The object you probably want to check is a database file. This is the most complex case, because the file may have many members. The ALCOBJ command puts the requested lock on the member. The file object gets a *SHRRD lock. You normally only lock a single member (you can specify a list, but you cannot specify *ALL). Therefore, if you code

  ```
  CHKACTOBJ  OBJ(FILEA) OBJTYPE(*FILE)
  ```

  you would be checking to see if anyone had the first member of the file allocated. You can specify a particular member name, but you cannot specify a list or *ALL on the CHKACTOBJ command. If you only operate on single member files, the result is exactly what you want.

You can also use the CHKACTOBJ command to lock and unlock objects. The ALLOCATE parameter on the CHKACTOBJ command is similar to the same parameter on the CHKACTPGM command, the exception being that CHKACTOBJ ALLOCATE defaults to *TEST. Note that you don't get to specify the type of lock; the lock is always *EXCL. If you need a different type of lock, use the system command ALCOBJ.

Many system commands require that a lock be placed on an object before the command performs its function. If the required object is already locked by another job at a level that keeps the function from being performed, most system commands simply wait a specified amount of time before attempting the lock again.

For most of these system commands, the default wait time is 30 seconds — a long time if you are operating interactively. The ALCOBJ command lets you control the wait time, but most of the system commands do not. For example, if you want to delete a database file, the DLTF (Delete File) command will attempt to place an *EXCL lock on the file. If the DLTF command cannot get the lock, it will wait, hoping to obtain to lock. Assuming you are taking the default and the file is still locked, a timeout will occur after 30 seconds. You can avoid this long wait by using the CHKACTOBJ command first (it uses a two-second wait time).

Technical Tip

The TAA tool CHKACTOBJ provides a simple solution for determining whether or not an object or member is in use. In many cases it is preferable to know that your function will be successful, rather than trying the function and then failing.

Is a Job Active (or on a JOBQ or OUTQ)?

The system provides an API to help you determine whether or not a specific job is active. When using the API, you can specify an unqualified job name (e.g., PAYROLL) or a qualified job name (e.g., 123456/USERA/PAYROLL or USERA/PAYROLL). APIs are not necessarily easy to work with, but the QUSRTOOL TAA tool RTVJOBSTS (Retrieve Job Status) provides a simple way to invoke the API (Figure 11.3). You would simply code the following:

FIGURE 11.3
RTVJOBSTS TAA Tool Prompt Screen

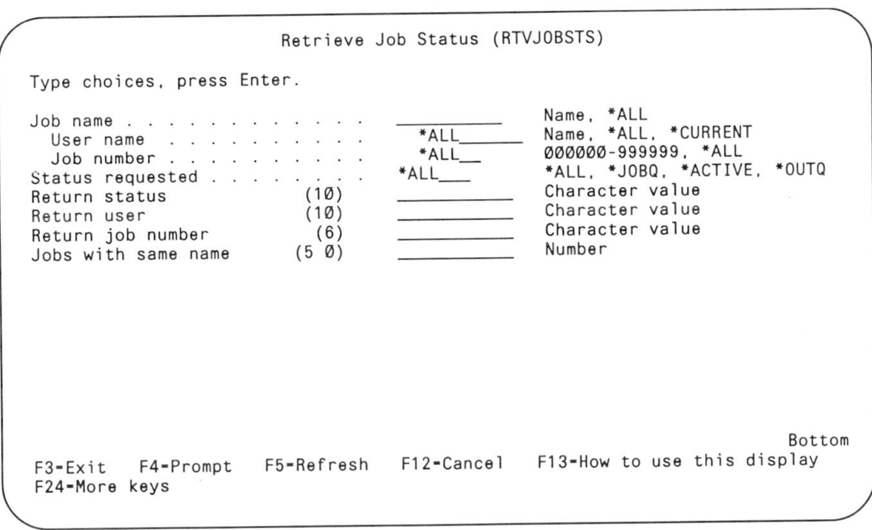

```
                     Retrieve Job Status (RTVJOBSTS)

 Type choices, press Enter.

 Job name . . . . . . . . . . . . .   __________    Name, *ALL
   User name  . . . . . . . . . . .     *ALL______  Name, *ALL, *CURRENT
   Job number . . . . . . . . . . .     *ALL__      000000-999999, *ALL
 Status requested . . . . . . . . .   *ALL___       *ALL, *JOBQ, *ACTIVE, *OUTQ
 Return status              (10)      __________    Character value
 Return user                (10)      __________    Character value
 Return job number           (6)      __________    Character value
 Jobs with same name        (5 0)     __________    Number

                                                                        Bottom
 F3=Exit   F4=Prompt   F5=Refresh   F12=Cancel   F13=How to use this display
 F24=More keys
```

```
RTVJOBSTS  JOB(xxx) STATUS(*ACTIVE)
MONMSG     MSGID(CPF9898) EXEC(DO) /* Not active */
  .
  .
  .
ENDDO      /* Not active */
```

With the RTVJOBSTS NBROFJOBS parameter, you can determine how many jobs of the same name are active. And you can determine whether or not there is a job on a JOBQ or OUTQ of the same job name. Note that the RTVJOBSTS command will work only if you control the job names. For example, a simple test will tell you whether or not the job PAYROLL is active. But if a user submits a job named PAYROLL that is different from your production job, the RTVJOBSTS command will give you misleading results. This problem is less likely to occur if you qualify your request by specifying the user name (assuming the production job is submitted by a single user), as shown by the following example:

```
RTVJOBSTS  JOB(USERA/PAYROLL) STATUS(*ACTIVE)
```

You should not rely on the results of the RTVJOBSTS command to determine whether or not it is safe to submit a job of the same job name. Because the RTVJOBSTS command does not lock an object when it tests whether or not a job is active, you will be exposed to the problem mentioned earlier: two jobs attempting to use the same function at the same time. To minimize your exposure to this potential problem, use two RTVJOBSTS commands. One would check for STATUS(*ACTIVE) and one would check for STATUS(*JOBQ). The RTVJOBSTS command can be helpful, but it should not be misused.

Technical Tip

The TAA tool RTVJOBSTS provides a useful way to determine the status of a job. But you should not use this command to determine whether or not to submit a job of the same job name.

Manually Allocating Objects

IBM's *CL Programmer's Guide* (SC41-8077) provides a good discussion on allocating objects, but it doesn't tell you everything. Let me point out what I think is important:

- When you successfully allocate an object, a lock is placed on the object.

- The different types of locks are explained in detail in the *CL Programmer's Guide.* They are

*SHRRD	Shared read
*SHRNUP	Share no update
*SHRUPD	Shared update
*EXCLRD	Exclusive allow read
*EXCL	Exclusive

- The following chart indicates what you can and cannot do when allocating objects:

If you get this lock:	**Someone else can get one of these locks:** *SHRRD	*SHRNUP	*SHRUPD	*EXCLRD	*EXCL
*SHRRD	X	X	X	X	
*SHRNUP	X	X			
*SHRUPD	X		X		
*EXCLRD	X				
*EXCL					

- Not all object types can be locked and not all lock types are supported for each object type. The major object types not supported (i.e., cannot be locked) are

  *CLS
  *CMD
  *JOBD
  *JOBQ
  *JRN
  *JRNRCV
  *OUTQ
  *TBL

- The system handles *EXCL lock requests in FIFO order. This means that if an object is locked and JOB1 requests the lock before JOB2, JOB1 will get the lock unless it times out. Note that this occurrence is independent of job priority (i.e., JOB2 could have a higher execution priority than JOB1, but JOB2 would still wait its turn). The system handles requests for other types of locks (e.g., *SHRNUP) in an unpredictable manner.

- The ALCOBJ command defaults to use the class wait time before it times out. The default class wait time is 30 seconds — a long time for an interactive job. For batch jobs, the default wait time of 30 seconds might make sense. For interactive jobs, you probably should specify a wait time of no more than 5 seconds using the CHGJOB or CHGCLS command.

- If the ALCOBJ command cannot obtain a requested lock during the wait time specified, it times out and sends escape message CPF1002, which states that a timeout has occurred. Another escape message that can be sent by the ALCOBJ command, CPF1085, should be treated with care. Escape message CPF1085 ("Objects were not allocated, see the previous diagnostic messages") is a general-purpose message that can be sent for a variety of reasons (e.g., your object cannot be found, it is not a valid object type or subtype for ALCOBJ, or the lock type cannot be used). Because of its ambiguity, you should treat escape message CPF1085 as an unexpected error and abort the program. If you are not sure an object exists, use the CHKOBJ command in your program before the ALCOBJ command.
- The ALCOBJ command escape message CPF1002 tells you only that your request had a timeout; it does not tell you who has the lock on the object you want to use. You can determine who has the lock if you use the WRKOBJLCK (Work with Object Locks) command. The WRKOBJLCK command displays a list of all objects allocated to a job and the lock states requested.

  If you need to determine in a CL program which job has a lock on an object, you can use the QUSRTOOL TAA tool CVTOBJLCK (Convert Object Lock). The CVTOBJLCK command uses the WRKOBJLCK command to collect object lock information and then builds an outfile you can read to determine which job has the lock and the type of lock held. For more information about using this technique, see Chapter 17, "Outfiles."

Technical Tip

The TAA tool CVTOBJLCK can be very helpful if you are trying to determine in a CL program which job has a lock on an object.

- To release a lock on an object, you use the DLCOBJ (De-allocate Object) command or end the job (the system removes all your locks when your job ends). The DLCOBJ command should be used if your job is going to be active for some time and you no longer need the lock. The DLCOBJ command only releases a single lock (assuming you only named a single object). But you can have more than one lock on an object and, in this case, you must use the DLCOBJ command for each lock you have achieved.

Separate locks are helpful if you first need a higher lock (e.g., *EXCL) and can downgrade it later on. For example, the following code ensures that you will be able to allocate a *SHRNUP lock to file FILEA when needed:

```
ALCOBJ      OBJ((FILEA *FILE *EXCL))
   .
   .        /* Do your exclusive thing */
   .
ALCOBJ      OBJ((FILEA *FILE *SHRNUP))
DLCOBJ      OBJ((FILEA *FILE *EXCL))
   .
   .        /* Do your 'share no update' thing */
   .
DLCOBJ      OBJ((FILEA *FILE *SHRNUP))
```

If, in this example, a DLCOBJ command was executed before the request for the *SHRNUP lock, another job making a request at the same time could lock the file first.

Technical Tip

It is always important to keep in mind that even though your CL statements may be consecutive, or close together, there may be a significant time gap in the execution of the statements. A higher priority job may interrupt your execution and your next statement may not be processed for some time. When you write a program, you should try to protect against this possibility.

- Both the ALCOBJ and DLCOBJ commands send escape messages if they do not work successfully, but neither command sends a completion message if it is successful. Be aware, though, that the definition of "successful" may not be what you expect. The DLCOBJ command, for example, does not send an escape message if your job does not hold the lock on the object you have specified; the command simply completes normally. Therefore, you must be sure you are attempting to de-allocate the right object.
- The DLCOBJ command will send an escape message if the object cannot be found. The message that will be sent, escape message CPF1005, is a general-purpose error message that points you to the previous diagnostic message. You should not rely on this escape message to determine that no object exists because it is sent for

other reasons as well. If you are not sure an object exists, use the CHKOBJ command in your program before the DLCOBJ command.

- If you place an *EXCL lock on an object, the lock prevents other users from accessing the object. Unfortunately, it does not prevent mistakes from occurring in your job. For example, despite having an *EXCL lock on an object, you can still delete the object accidentally. Another mistake might occur if you locked a program using *EXCL and then used the CRTxxxPGM command to replace the program. When you were done, you would still have a lock on the old version of the program in QRPLOBJ, but you would not have a lock on the new version of the program.
- When you allocate a database file, the default for the ALCOBJ command is to allocate the first member even though you don't specify a member value. No matter what type of lock you request, a *SHRRD lock is placed on the file object and on the member. The lock you requested (e.g., *EXCL) is placed on the data (if it is a physical file). In most cases, having a lock on the file object will prevent other jobs from performing high-level actions against the file object (e.g., deleting or changing the file).
- You must have a member in a database file to use the ALCOBJ command. If no member exists in the database file, you receive escape message CPF1085, an ambiguous general-purpose error message that isn't safe to monitor for. If you are not sure whether the file has a member, use the CHKOBJ command, specifying MBR(*FIRST), followed by the ALCOBJ command. If a member exists in the file, specifying *FIRST will find it.
- You can allocate database files, but not device files (e.g., DSPF and PRTF). Although the system implicitly places a lock on device file objects when they are opened by a job, you cannot specify them on an ALCOBJ command. If you need to know in a CL program whether a non-database file is in use, the QUSRTOOL TAA tool CVTOBJLCK offers a solution.
- The ALCOBJ command lets you specify a list of objects/members on a single ALCOBJ command. The command operates in an all-or-nothing fashion: If the system cannot allocate all the objects you have specified, none of the objects will be allocated. Exercise C at the end of this chapter will show you an example of allocating multiple objects.

- The QUSRTOOL TAA tool ALCDBF (Allocate Data Base File) offers a function not supported by a system command. The ALCDBF command lets you allocate all members of a file with only one command. A companion command, DLCDBF (De-allocate Data Base File), deallocates all the members. If the ALCDBF command can't allocate all the members specified, it sends an escape message and returns with none of the members locked.

Technical Tip

Use the TAA tool ALCDBF (Allocate Data Base File) when you want to allocate all members of a multimember database file.

Updating a Data Area

If you just want to change the contents of a data area, the CL command CHGDTAARA will do it for you. The system will automatically

- lock the data area,
- update the data area, and
- unlock the data area

However, if you need to

- read the data area (RTVDTAARA),
- determine the new value, and
- update the data area (CHGDTAARA)

you are exposed to the possibility of another job trying to do the same thing at the same time. A lock is placed on the object only during execution of the CHGDTAARA command. You need to lock the data area before you retrieve it and then unlock the data area after you have updated it.

If you are trying to add one to a counter kept in a data area, your code should look like this:

```
DCL         &VALUE *DEC LEN(9 Ø)
DCL         &NEWVALUE *DEC LEN(9 Ø)
 .
 .
 .
ALCOBJ      OBJ((xxx *DTAARA *EXCL))
RTVDTAARA   DTAARA(xxx) RTNVAR(&VALUE)
CHGVAR      &NEWVALUE (&VALUE + 1)
CHGDTAARA   DTAARA(xxx) VALUE(&NEWVALUE)
DLCOBJ      OBJ((xxx *DTAARA *EXCL))
```

Typically, you would use this technique when keeping a unique value (e.g., an order number) in a data area. Because you must read the value before updating it, you must be sure that two users are not accessing the same value simultaneously.

The QUSRTOOL TAA tool ADDDTAARA (Figure 11.4) can do what you need in this situation, but with fewer lines of code. Instead of specifying the code shown above, you just code

```
DCL        &VALUE *DEC LEN(9 0)
  .
  .
  .
ADDDTAARA  DTAARA(xxx) RTNAMT(&VALUE) ADDAMT(1) ALLOCATE(*YES)
```

Variable &VALUE will contain the value of the data area before the update.

Technical Tip

The ADDDTAARA TAA tool is good to use for the typical case of adding one to a count kept in a data area. It will handle the task of allocating and deallocating the data area for you.

FIGURE 11.4
ADDDTAARA TAA Tool Prompt Screen

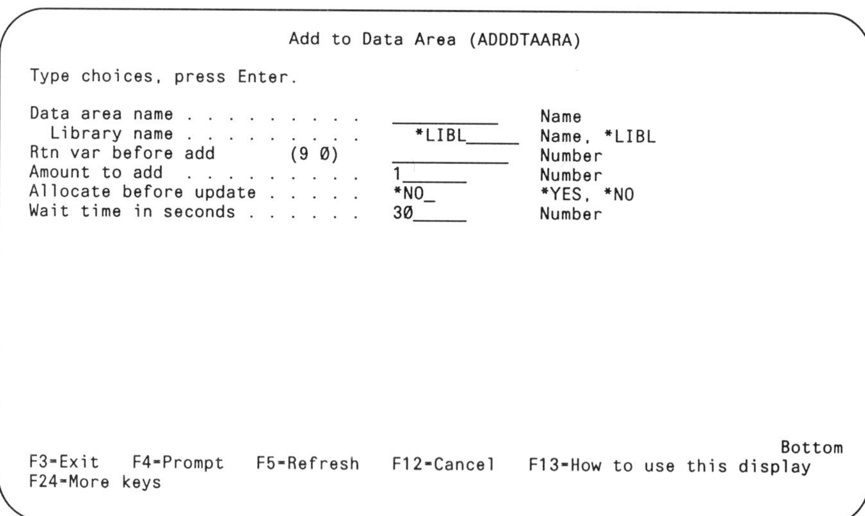

```
                    Add to Data Area (ADDDTAARA)

Type choices, press Enter.

Data area name . . . . . . . . .   __________   Name
  Library name . . . . . . . . .     *LIBL_____   Name, *LIBL
Rtn var before add       (9 0)     ___________  Number
Amount to add  . . . . . . . . .   1_______     Number
Allocate before update . . . . .   *NO_         *YES, *NO
Wait time in seconds . . . . . .   30_____      Number

                                                              Bottom
F3=Exit   F4=Prompt   F5=Refresh   F12=Cancel   F13=How to use this display
F24=More keys
```

Exercise A Using the CHKACTPGM Command

In this exercise you will work with the QUSRTOOL TAA tool CHKACTPGM, which lets you determine whether or not a program is active. You will find that the simplest approach is to place the CHKACTPGM command in the program you want to test. For this exercise, you will need two jobs (either two group jobs or two system request jobs). You will also need the TAA tool DUPSTDSRC. Prompt for the DUPSTDSRC and CHKACTPGM commands. If they do not exist on your system, see Appendix B.

1. Use the DUPSTDSRC TAA tool to create a CLP member named TRYCHKACT.
2. Use PDM to edit the member.
3. Delete all the source code except the standard error-handling routine. Your code should look like the following:

```
             DCL         &ERRORSW *LGL /* Std error */
              .          - other standard error DCLs -
              .
              .
             MONMSG      MSGID(CPF0000) EXEC(GOTO STDERR1)
                         /* Ready for your source to be added */
STDERR1:                 /* Standard error-handling routine */
              .            - rest of the STDERR routine -
              .
              .
             ENDPGM
```

4. Enter the following source before the first DCL statement:

```
PGM         PARM(&TYPE)
DCL         &TYPE *CHAR LEN(7)
```

5. Enter the following source after the program-level MONMSG command:

```
IF          (&TYPE *EQ '*LOCK') DO /* Lock */
CHKACTPGM
SNDPGMMSG   MSG('The program has been locked.')
GOTO        ENDPGM
ENDDO       /* Lock */
```

Exercise A continued

Exercise A continued

```
                IF         (&TYPE *EQ '*TEST') DO /* Test */
                CHKACTPGM  ALLOCATE(*TEST)
                SNDPGMMSG  MSG('The program is not locked.')
                GOTO       ENDPGM
                ENDDO      /* Test */
                IF         (&TYPE *EQ '*UNLOCK') DO /* Unlock */
                CHKACTPGM  ALLOCATE(*UNLOCK)
                SNDPGMMSG  MSG('The program has been unlocked.')
                GOTO       ENDPGM
                ENDDO      /* Unlock */
                SNDPGMMSG  MSGID(CPF9898) MSGF(QCPFMSG) +
                             MSGTYPE(*ESCAPE) +
                             MSGDTA('Bad parm value of ' *CAT &TYPE)
     ENDPGM:               /* End of program */
                RMVMSG     CLEAR(*ALL)
                RETURN     /* Normal end of program */
```

6. Create the program.
7. Call the program as

   ```
   CALL  TRYCHKACT PARM(*LOCK)
   ```

   You should see the message that the program has been locked.
8. Enter the following command:

   ```
   WRKOBJLCK  OBJ(TRYCHKACT) OBJTYPE(*PGM)
   ```

   You should see that your job holds an *EXCL lock on the program.
9. Access a different job (either a group job or a system request job).
10. Enter the command:

    ```
    CALL  TRYCHKACT PARM(*LOCK)
    ```

    You should see the message that the program is already in use. This is the CPF9898 escape message, which you could monitor for.
11. Enter the following:

    ```
    CALL  TRYCHKACT PARM(*TEST)
    ```

    You should again see the escape message that says the program is already in use.

Exercise A continued

Exercise A continued

12. Return to the first job that has the lock and enter the following:

```
CALL   TRYCHKACT PARM(*UNLOCK)
```

You should see the message that says the object has been unlocked.

13. Enter the following:

```
CALL   TRYCHKACT PARM(*TEST)
```

You should see the message that says the object can be locked. The *TEST function first executes an ALCOBJ command; if successful, the function then executes a DLCOBJ command.

14. Enter the following command:

```
WRKOBJLCK  OBJ(TRYCHKACT) OBJTYPE(*PGM)
```

You should see that there are no locks on the object.

Exercise B Using the RTVJOBSTS Command

In this exercise you will work with the QUSRTOOL TAA tool RTVJOBSTS, which lets you determine whether or not a job is active on the system. Prompt for the RTVJOBSTS command. If it does not exist on your system, see Appendix B.

1. Use PDM to create a CLP member named TRYRTVJOBS.
2. Enter the following source (Note that the job name xxxyyy is used. You should not have any jobs with this name on your system.):

```
PGM
RTVJOBSTS  JOB(xxxyyy) STATUS(*ACTIVE)
MONMSG     MSGID(CPF9898) EXEC(DO) /* Not active */
SNDPGMMSG  MSG('No jobs are active.')
RETURN
ENDDO      /* Not active */
SNDPGMMSG  MSG('A job is already active.')
ENDPGM
```

Exercise B continued

Exercise B continued

3. Create the program.
4. Call the program:

```
CALL  TRYRTVJOBS
```

   You should see the message that no jobs are active by this name.

5. In the following SBMJOB command, submit the job to a job queue (we use QINTER in the example) that will let the job become active immediately. Enter the command:

```
SBMJOB  JOB(XXXYYY) CMD((DLYJOB DLY(20)) JOBQ(QINTER)
```

6. Enter the command:

```
CALL  TRYRTVJOBS
```

   Assuming that job XXXYYY is active, you should see the message that a job is already active. In this exercise the RTVJOBSTS command used an unqualified job name and requested the status of active jobs only (this does not include jobs on a job queue or an output queue). Be sure you understand the discussion in this chapter about the RTVJOBSTS command before using it to determine whether or not a job should be submitted.

Exercise C Using the ALCOBJ and DLCOBJ Commands

In this exercise you will use the ALCOBJ and DLCOBJ commands to see how locks are set. For this exercise, you will need two jobs (either two group jobs or two system request jobs).

1. Access the command entry display:

```
CALL  QCMD
```

2. We will use two permanent file objects in this example: TRYFILEA and TRYFILEA2. Assuming that these files do not exist on your system, create them as

Exercise C continued

Exercise C continued

```
CRTPF  FILE(TRYFILEA) RCDLEN(50) TEXT('Used for ALCOBJ exercise')
CRTPF  FILE(TRYFILEA2) RCDLEN(50) TEXT('Used for ALCOBJ exercise')
```

3. Use the ALCOBJ command as follows:

```
ALCOBJ  OBJ((TRYFILEA *FILE *EXCL))
```

4. Enter the command:

```
WRKOBJLCK  OBJ(TRYFILEA) OBJTYPE(*FILE)
```

   You should see that you have a *SHRRD lock on the object even though you requested an *EXCL lock. This is because you are looking at the file object. The *EXCL lock is placed on the data in the member.

5. Enter the command:

```
WRKOBJLCK  OBJ(TRYFILEA) OBJTYPE(*FILE) MBR(*ALL)
```

   You should see that you have a *SHRRD lock on the member and an *EXCL lock on the data, but you can think of the *EXCL lock as being on the member.

6. Enter the command:

```
WRKJOB
```

7. Enter Option 12 to work with locks.

   When the display appears, you will probably have to roll past all the implicit locks placed on objects by your job. One of the last objects displayed should be file TRYFILEA with the lock you placed on it.

8. Enter Option 5 next to file TRYFILEA to display the member locks.

   You should see the same display you saw when you executed the WRKOBJLCK command in Step 5.

9. Return to the Work with Job Locks Display. Enter Option 8 to display the object level locks.

   You should see the same display you saw when you executed the WRKOBJLCK command in Step 4.

10. Return to the command entry display and enter the command:

```
ALCOBJ  OBJ((TRYFILEA *FILE *EXCL))
```

Exercise C continued

Exercise C continued

11. Enter the command:

```
WRKOBJLCK  OBJ(TRYFILEA) OBJTYPE(*FILE)
```

You should see that you have two locks on file TRYFILEA. Each successful use of the ALCOBJ command adds a unique lock.

12. Enter the command:

```
WRKOBJLCK  OBJ(TRYFILEA) OBJTYPE(*FILE) MBR(*ALL)
```

You should see that you have two more locks on the member. You now have two *SHRRD locks on the member and two *EXCL locks on the data.

13. Enter the command:

```
DLCOBJ  OBJ((TRYFILEA *FILE *EXCL))
```

14. Enter the command:

```
WRKOBJLCK  OBJ(TRYFILEA) OBJTYPE(*FILE)
```

You should see that you now have only one lock on the file. Each use of the DLCOBJ command removes only the set of locks caused by a single ALCOBJ command. At the member level, you should have two locks.

15. Access another job and enter the command:

```
ALCOBJ  OBJ((TRYFILEA *FILE *EXCL)) WAIT(0)
```

You should see the message that says, "Cannot allocate objects."

16. Place your cursor on the message and press the Help key.

You should see that the message ID is CPF1002. This is the message you should monitor for to determine whether or not an object cannot be allocated.

17. Return to the command entry display and press F10 for detailed messages.

You should not see any detailed messages, which tells you that escape message CPF1002 is safe to monitor for. When the text of the message describes a specific problem and there are no preceding diagnostic messages, you can assume that monitoring for escape message CPF1002 will not produce ambiguous results.

Exercise C continued

Exercise C continued

18. Enter the following command (we are assuming that file XXXYYY does not exist on your system):

```
ALCOBJ  OBJ((XXXYYY *FILE *EXCL)) WAIT(Ø)
```

You should see the message "Objects not allocated." If you are displaying detailed messages, you should see a previous diagnostic message that says file XXXYYY does not exist.

19. Place your cursor on the escape message and press the Help key.

You should see that this is message ID CPF1085 and that it is a general-purpose message. It is not safe to monitor for this message because it may be sent for errors other than non-existence of the object you are trying to allocate. If you are not sure whether the object exists, use the CHKOBJ command to check for its existence before using the ALCOBJ command.

20. File TRYFILEA is locked to your other job. File TRYFILEA2 is not. Enter the following command to try locking both files at the same time (specify file TRYFILEA2 first in the list):

```
ALCOBJ  OBJ((TRYFILEA2 *FILE *EXCL) (TRYFILEA *FILE *EXCL)) WAIT(Ø)
```

You should see escape message CPF1002, "Cannot allocate objects."

21. Enter the following command for file TRYFILEA2:

```
WRKOBJLCK  OBJ(TRYFILEA2) OBJTYPE(*FILE)
```

As the error message in Step 20 indicated, you should see that there are no locks on the file. The system did not complete your entire list of objects and therefore deallocated any that it had successfully allocated on the same command.

22. Allocate only file TRYFILEA2 as

```
ALCOBJ  OBJ((TRYFILEA2 *FILE *EXCL))
```

23. Enter the command:

```
WRKOBJLCK  OBJ(TRYFILEA2) OBJTYPE(*FILE)
```

You should see the *SHRRD lock on the file.

24. Return to the command entry display and remove the member:

```
RMVM  FILE(TRYFILEA2) MBR(*ALL)
```

Exercise C continued

Exercise C continued

25. Enter the WRKOBJLCK command again:

```
WRKOBJLCK  OBJ(TRYFILEA2) OBJTYPE(*FILE)
```

    You shouldn't see any locks because removing the member removes any locks on it as well as the associated lock on the file. If you delete the file, you also remove the locks.

26. Use the ALCOBJ command to try to lock file TRYFILEA2 again:

```
ALCOBJ  OBJ((TRYFILEA2 *FILE *EXCL))
```

    The command should fail and send escape message CPF1085 with a preceding diagnostic message. The diagnostic message tells you that you can't lock a file that does not have a member. The AS/400 does not provide a way to lock only the file object.

27. Enter the command:

```
ALCOBJ  OBJ((QPRINT *FILE *EXCL))
```

    The requested allocation will fail, and you should see the general-purpose escape message CPF1085 and an accompanying diagnostic message. Place your cursor on the diagnostic message and press the Help key. The diagnostic message should be CPF0984, which will tell you what the problem is: QPRINT is a printer file. You can allocate only database file/members. Even though the system will implicitly lock device files when you open them, you cannot allocate device files ahead of time or test to see if they are in use.

28. When you have finished this exercise, delete files TRYFILEA and TRYFILEA2.

Exercise D Using the CHKACTOBJ Command

In this exercise you will work with the QUSRTOOL TAA tool CHKACTOBJ, which provides a simple way to test whether or not an object is active (i.e., in use). Remember that the CHKACTOBJ command does not work for all object types, and that for program objects you should use the CHKACTPGM command. For this exercise, you will need two jobs (either two group jobs or two system request jobs). Prompt for the CHKACTOBJ command. If it does not exist on your system, see Appendix B.

1. Access the command entry display:

```
CALL  QCMD
```

2. You will need a permanent file object to lock. In this example, we will use file TRYFILEB. Assuming that this file does not exist on your system, create it as

```
CRTPF   FILE(TRYFILEB) RCDLEN(50) +
          TEXT('Used for CHKACTOBJ exercise')
```

3. Enter the CHKACTOBJ command as follows:

```
CHKACTOBJ  OBJ(TRYFILEB) OBJTYPE(*FILE)
```

   You should see a completion message that says no one is using the object.

4. The CHKACTOBJ command can also be used to lock and unlock the object. Lock the object with the command:

```
CHKACTOBJ  OBJ(TRYFILEB) OBJTYPE(*FILE) ALLOCATE(*LOCK)
```

5. Access another job and enter the command:

```
CHKACTOBJ  OBJ(TRYFILEB) OBJTYPE(*FILE)
```

   You should see the escape message that tells you the object is in use.

Technical Tip

The TAA tool CHKACTOBJ is just a front end to the ALCOBJ and DLCOBJ commands. It can make your life easier because it provides better messages and supports the *TEST function to help determine whether or not an object is in use. The CHKACTOBJ always allocates an *EXCL lock; you cannot specify a different choice.

Exercise E Using the ADDDTAARA Command

In this exercise you will work with the QUSRTOOL TAA tool ADDDTAARA, which lets you add a value to a data area and retrieve the previous value of the data area. You will need the TAA tools ADDDTAARA and EDTVAR for this exercise. If these commands do not exist on your system, see Appendix B.

1. The ADDDTAARA command requires that the data area be created as TYPE(*DEC) LEN(9 0). Create a data area with the command

```
CRTDTAARA   DTAARA(QTEMP/TEMP) TYPE(*DEC) LEN(9 Ø)
```

2. Use PDM to create a CLP member named TRYADDDTA.
3. Enter the following source:

```
PGM
DCL         &VALUE *DEC LEN(9 Ø)
DCL         &CHAR22 *CHAR LEN(22)
RTVDTAARA   DTAARA(QTEMP/TEMP) RTNVAR(&VALUE)
EDTVAR      CHROUT(&CHAR22) NUMINP(&VALUE)
SNDPGMMSG   MSG('Before-' *CAT &CHAR22)
ADDDTAARA   DTAARA(QTEMP/TEMP) RTNAMT(&VALUE) ALLOCATE(*YES)
RTVDTAARA   DTAARA(QTEMP/TEMP) RTNVAR(&VALUE)
EDTVAR      CHROUT(&CHAR22) NUMINP(&VALUE)
SNDPGMMSG   MSG('After-' *CAT &CHAR22)
ENDPGM
```

4. Create the program.
5. Call the program:

```
CALL  TRYADDDTA
```

You should see Before and After messages that show the data area has been updated correctly. The default on the ADDDTAARA command is to add 1. The ADDDTAARA command automatically performs the functions you would normally need to code explicitly:

- Allocates the data area
- Retrieves the value of the data area
- Adds the value specified to the original value
- Changes the data area

Exercise E continued

Exercise E continued

- Deallocates the data area
- Returns the original value in the RTNAMT parameter

6. Call the program again:

```
CALL  TRYADDDTA
```

You should see that each use of the ADDDTAARA command increments the data area value.

Technical Tip

The TAA tool ADDDTAARA makes it easy to add a value to a data area. You could do the same thing with individual ALCOBJ and DLCOBJ commands, as described in this chapter, but using the ADDDTAARA command requires significantly less code.

CHAPTER 12

Allocation Problems

In Chapter 11 we discussed how objects are allocated and de-allocated, either implicitly by the system or explicitly by CL or TAA tool commands. Whether you let the system control the lock state of objects, or whether you explicitly allocate objects, you undoubtedly will eventually come face to face with allocation problems.

This chapter will build on what you learned in Chapter 11 by providing additional information about what happens when an object is allocated for specific functions and by suggesting techniques for working around some of the problems caused when objects are allocated.

The discussion is broken into two sections: object types and functions. My intent in this chapter is not to discuss all potential allocation problems, but to touch on the more common ones.

OBJECT TYPES

Before discussing specific system functions and the problems that might occur when allocating objects, let me make four general comments relevant to many system functions:

- Many system functions (excluding database file operations) require a *SHRNUP lock. This means that multiple jobs can perform the same function simultaneously, but a job cannot request a lock that is stronger (e.g., *SHRUPD, *EXCLRD, or *EXCL).
- Authority (e.g., GRT/RVKOBJAUT) locking requirements vary according to object type. For example, for database files, no job can change the authority at the object level if another job has already opened the file.
- When a job places any kind of lock on an object, it precludes another job from moving, deleting, or renaming the object. For example, with database members, a job cannot clear a member if another job has already placed a lock on the member.
- The default lock state for SAV commands is *SHRNUP, which means that no job can open a file for update while another job is trying to save the file (the section "SAVWHLACT (Save While Active)" discusses this further).

Now let's look at potential allocation problems associated with specific object types.

Data Areas

The CHGDTAARA (Change Data Area) command requires a *SHRNUP lock. Consequently, if any job has a lock of *SHRNUP or greater (e.g., *EXCL) on a data area, no other job will be able to use the CHGDTAARA command on that same data area.

If several jobs must be able to change a data area at the same time, each job must explicitly use the ALCOBJ command to allocate the data area. To provide the greatest degree of sharing, you should allocate the data area for a short time (see the discussion on allocating data areas in Chapter 11).

Display Files

You may remember from Chapter 11 that you cannot use the ALCOBJ command on a display file. When a job opens a display file, the system implicitly places a *SHRNUP lock on the file. The *SHRNUP lock prevents another job from deleting the file or using the CHGDSPF (Change Display File) command on the file.

Even though the CHGDSPF command supports the REPLACE parameter, a job cannot re-create a file that another job has opened. To re-create a display file already in use, you first must have the users back off to a point where no one has the file open.

Printer Files

The previous discussion on display files applies to printer files as well (i.e., you can't replace or change a printer file that is open).

In addition, you need to be sure that the number of records specified for your printer file is adequate before writing printing output; otherwise, you might run into problems. The default for the MAXRCDS parameter on the CRT/CHGPRTF commands is 100,000 records. If the limit is reached, the job producing the printer file receives inquiry message CPA4072. Although you can't change the file at that point, the inquiry message provides good options for recovery. For example, you can respond 'NOMAX' to avoid seeing the inquiry message again for this use of the file.

Technical Tip

You can permanently specify a printer file as MAXRCDS(*NOMAX), but I recommend not using this technique. A run-away program (i.e., a program creating output in an endless loop) could fill your system with spooled records. You may want to increase the maximum number of records for a particular printer file, but you should avoid specifying *NOMAX as a general-purpose solution.

Spooled Files

If you generate a spooled file and then decide that you should have changed the attributes of the printer file before you opened it, you will find that most printer file attributes can be changed by using the CHGSPLFA (Change Spooled File Attributes) command. But for those attributes (e.g., lines per inch — LPI) that cannot be changed using the CHGSPLFA command, the QUSRTOOL TAA tool DUPSPLF can be helpful. The DUPSPLF tool allows you to duplicate a spooled file by reprinting it to a different printer file. It supports two commands:

- DUPSPLF. This command uses an API to duplicate the file. The command works fairly quickly and no printer function is lost. You cannot change any of the file's attributes.
- DUPSPLF2. This command uses the CPYSPLF and CPYF commands to duplicate the file. The DUPSPLF2 command works more slowly than the DUPSPLF command, and it is effective only on typical data processing output (i.e., output with no special printing functions). The advantage of the DUPSPLF2 command is that you can reprint to a printer file of your choice, which the DUPSPLF command does not allow you to do.

Technical Tip

The TAA tool DUPSPLF won't solve your allocation problems, but it may help when you want to change a spooled file attribute (e.g., LPI) that can be changed only by duplicating the file.

Programs

The system does not implicitly lock programs when they are called (except for those called in the S/36 Environment). You can manually allocate a program, but this is normally not done.

If the program is not allocated, a job can do anything it wants to the program, even if another job is using it. A job can even delete the program, which would cause the job using the program to abort.

If the program is not allocated, the REPLACE(*YES) function can often be used to replace a program with a newer version while some users are using an older version of it. But you can do things to a program so that REPLACE(*YES) will cause problems. For example, if you need to change the number of parameters or parameter attributes between two programs, REPLACE(*YES) is probably not going to work. Using REPLACE(*YES) is a reasonable function if you are doing something simple such as adding an IF test to your code. See Chapter 23, "CL Program Objects," for more explanation.

User Profiles

User profiles can normally be changed any time, including when the profile is active. However, most changes do not affect an existing job running under the user profile. The user must sign off the system and then sign back on before any changes will take effect.

Library Lists

If a library is specified on a user's library list, you can't delete the library until the user ends his or her job or until (s)he removes the library from the list. If you are performing a cleanup function, you can clear the library, which would at least delete the objects in the library.

Logical Files

Although you can manually allocate a logical file, you normally would not; it's more normal to allocate a physical file. The system implicitly places a *SHRRD lock on the file object when it is opened. If the file is opened for input only, the system places a *SHRRD lock on the member; if the file is opened for update, the system places a *SHRUPD lock on the member.

When a logical file is opened by one job, another job can neither change the file-level attributes nor re-create the file. As with all database files, the job is actually opening the member and not the file. If the logical file has only a single member, you can think of the lock as being at the file level.

Source Files

A source file is like any database file with multiple members. Because source is normally processed using SEU and the compilers, I will focus only on those functions.

When you request SEU to operate on a member, all the source is written to a temporary work space on the system, and editing occurs in that work space. When you end SEU after making changes, you decide on the Exit display whether or not you want to update the member (the default is to update the member).

When you use SEU to edit a member, a *SHRRD lock is placed on the source file and an *EXCLRD lock is placed on the member. Because SEU uses multiple access paths when processing a source member, you will actually see multiple locks at the file and member level. Since the *EXCLRD lock is on a specific member, you can update, add, remove, or clear other members without any allocation problems.

The *EXCLRD lock prevents two users from editing the same source member at the same time, and it allows the compiler to read the source and create a program even though you are making changes. For example, you can end SEU and submit a compile and then immediately start editing the source again while the compiler is reading the old version.

*EXCLRD allows another user to use the CPYF (or CPYSRCF) command on the same source member. The CPYF command is like any database program that only requests to read the file (not update). A "read only" request places a *SHRRD lock on the member. Another user also can use SEU's browse mode (F15) to browse the same source member.

When you modify a source member and then end SEU, the source member is cleared, and then the source from the work space is written to the member. Clearing the source member requires an *EXCL lock on the member. If you are editing a member and try to end the session (write the changes back) while a second user is using SEU to browse the same member, the session will end normally because SEU has released the *EXCLRD lock while in browse mode. However, if another user is executing a CPYF or DSPPFM command on the source member while you are trying to end SEU, you will not be able to write your changes back until the lock is released or you time out (a timeout would cause a message to be sent to the SEU Exit display). The CPYF command does not normally cause a problem because it executes quickly. However, the DSPPFM command, or any function that keeps a *SHRRD lock on a source member for a long period of time, can be a problem.

Technical Tip

Avoid using the DSPPFM to read source data because no one can end an editing session on the same source member while it is being read. Rather, consider SEU's browse mode: It allows one user to browse a source member while another user is editing the same member.

Physical Files

You will find that most allocation problems occur with database physical files. Let's review what happens when a program opens a database file:

- the system places a *SHRRD lock on the file
- if the program opens the file for input only, the system places a *SHRRD lock on the member
- if the program opens the file for update or output only, the system places a *SHRUPD lock on the member

If only one member exists in the database file, any program that opens the file prevents another program from performing functions against the member (e.g., clearing, reorganizing, removing, or renaming the member).

Strange but true is the fact that a program can change member-level options (using the CHGPFM command), such as member text and expiration date, even though another program has opened the member for update (the changes don't affect the other program). But if the file is locked, another program cannot

- change the file-level options (e.g., SIZE)
- delete the file
- rename the file
- move the file
- change the field definitions of the file (a program could not re-create the file, which requires deleting the file first)
- make authorization changes to the file

Here are some things you can do to work around a few of these limitations:

- One job cannot clear a member (using the CLRPFM command) if a another job has placed a lock on the member, but you could use the DELETE operation in an HLL program to delete all the records in the member (assuming you can get a lock on each record). This technique would be extremely crude and slow, and it would be practical only on a very small file.
- You cannot reorganize a file (using the RGZPFM command) if a lock has been placed on the file, but you can avoid the need to reorganize if you use the CRTPF/CHGPF function (the REUSEDLT parameter) for reusing deleted record space. A reorganize does two things:

— it eliminates the space for deleted records

— it lets you sequence the file on the predominantly used access path

REUSEDLT(*YES) may solve the deleted record space problem, but not the sequencing function. If you want to physically resequence the data into a different file, you can use a sort function (see Chapter 20, "OPNQRYF"). If you want to physically rearrange the data in the same file, you need to use the RGZPFM command and you need to wait until the member can be exclusively allocated.

- You cannot use the CHGPF command to change file-level options when another program has a file open (e.g., you might want to change a file's SIZE parameter). But you may be able to work around this problem (see the next section).

Physical File SIZE Parameter

Physical files support the SIZE parameter, which defaults to 10,000 records in a file and allows three increments of 1,000 records. This means that you can write 13,000 records to a file without any problems. When the value is exceeded, a message (CPA5305) is sent to the QSYSOPR message queue explaining the problem and asking if another increment is needed (the message is sent directly to the QSYSOPR message queue and not to the job that caused the problem, because multiple jobs may be causing the problem).

If you have a file that keeps bumping into the SIZE parameter limit, you might want to set your system so that it will automatically respond to "increment" when inquiry message CPA5305 occurs, rather than having the system operator respond to the message manually. To accomplish this, you can use the TAA tool MSGCTL, discussed in Chapter 6. (You may recall that the MSGCTL tool is designed to help you manage the QSYSOPR message queue.)

Let's assume that the MSGCTL tool is operating when your program receives inquiry message CPA5305 for a certain file, and you want the program to respond to the message with 'I' for Ignore (this causes another increment to be added). You would add a record for message ID CPA5305 to the database file the MSGCTL tool searches when a message arrives, and you would use the CMPDTA function to specify the file (or member) name that you want to process. You would specify the REPLY field as 'I' for Ignore and let the MSGCTL tool respond for you.

Note that this is a temporary fix. At some point, you need to use the

CHGPF command to change the problem file's SIZE parameter. You should then remove the record you added to the database file used by the MSGCTL tool.

Technical Tip

If a particular database file hits a SIZE limit that you want the system to ignore automatically, consider using the TAA tool MSGCTL. It will let you provide an automatic response as a temporary solution.

Changing the file to a specific SIZE value is a better option than permanently specifying a physical file as SIZE(*NOMAX). Using some reasonable SIZE value prevents a run-away program from taking over the system and filling your auxiliary storage.

FUNCTIONS

System functions such as move, rename, and delete all require an *EXCL lock on an object, and there is no way to circumvent a lock already placed on an object. System change functions differ in the allocation required, depending on the type of object. For most of the change commands (including change commands for files), you can't make a change at the object level if someone has a lock. For example, you can't use the CHGDSPF command on a file if another user has the file open. The previous section described a few work-around techniques for specific functions. The following techniques offer more general-purpose solutions.

Authorizations

The rules for changing object authority vary according to object type. Sometimes a job can change an object's authority even if another job has a lock on the object. But the rules for database files (the object type that most programmers want to authorize) are very strict: You cannot change the authority at the file level if another user has a lock on the file.

However, you can change an authorization list at almost any time; and this capability provides a good work-around for changing object authority of a file. Simply use the EDTOBJAUT (Edit Object Authority) command to specify an authorization list for a file when no one is using the file.

Technical Tip

When you need to make authority changes while an object is in use, authorization lists provide a good solution.

Save/Restore

How allocation affects restore commands is straightforward. A restore command won't work if a lock has been placed on objects you are trying to restore. The objects that are not locked would be restored and the others would be bypassed. With one major exception, this protects objects that are in use. The exception is program objects: Since the system doesn't lock programs when they are in use, a program can be restored while it is in use. The job that was already using the program would be aborted.

Now let's look at how allocation affects save commands. The normal SAV command (not considering the SAVWHLACT option) requires a *SHRNUP lock. This means that programs, display files, commands, and data areas can be saved unless they have been explicitly allocated as *SHRNUP, *EXCLRD, or *EXCL. It also means that a database file can be saved if it is open for input only.

A multimember database file (e.g., source files), however, cannot be saved unless all the members can be locked to *SHRNUP. In this situation, you can use the CPYSRCF command to work around the problem. Because SEU is doing the editing in a work space, CPYSRCF would copy the version of the source in the member (not the version in the work space). For example, you would use the CPYSRCF command to copy the file the programmers are working on to a file only used for backup. Then you would save the backup file. This is usually a very acceptable solution, and the same concept is used by the TAA tool SRCARC. For physical files, the CPYF command could be used.

If you have a lot of backup to do, the save commands will be faster if executed from a restricted state. This is especially true on larger systems with fast tape drives.

SAVWHLACT (Save While Active)

The SAVWHLACT option on SAV commands supports a useful function: the capability to save objects while they are active. Although the SAVWHLACT function is great, its complexity can lead to misuse. To help you avoid problems when using the SAVWHLACT function, let's look at how it works:

- The SAVWHLACT option first internally seizes the objects in the library you are trying to save. When all objects are seized in the library, the save begins. The internal seize takes time (particularly with a large library) and will most likely cause some users to "hang"; they cannot gain access to the objects in the library until the seize is complete. In a typically sized library, this will be several seconds — longer than your interactive users would like.

An alternative to "hanging" users like this with no warning is to first specify a message queue that will receive a message when the SAVWHLACT seize operation completes, and then get your users to some safe point where the application has no files open for update until the "seize complete" message appears. This means that no user has the file open for update when the save begins; this approach also will avoid splitting transactions that involve updates to multiple files.

- During the seize operation, SAVWHLACT will try to place a *SHRRD lock on every object and member in the library you want to save, and it will retain the lock until the library is saved. If an application has an *EXCL lock on an object in the library you want to save, the object won't be saved. SAVWHLACT is designed to save the objects it can and bypass the rest. Depending on how large the library is and the speed of your save device (e.g., a tape drive), objects and members can be locked for a long time. This same situation occurs during a normal save operation, except the lock requested is *SHRNUP. Don't confuse what I said earlier about the "seize duration" time with the "lock duration" time. The seize time occurs when the SAVWHLACT function first begins and is fairly short. The lock time lasts for the full length of the save.

- If you are *not* using commitment control, a SAVWHLACT request will give you an instantaneous snapshot of the object. The system accomplishes this by doing an internal "seize" of the objects (by library) and establishing a checkpoint. When the checkpoint is complete, the "seize" is released and any changes after that point are not part of the save (What actually happens is that any pages that are about to be changed are placed in a separate area and the save operation is smart enough to save them and not the changed pages). Therefore, you get an instantaneous snapshot, but it is not the same thing as doing a save while no one is using the objects.

  For complex applications, what would appear on the media is close to what would happen if the system crashed and then went through recovery. You would find some transactions that were half-way done, which can be a difficult situation to recover from.

- If you are using commitment control, the system waits until all users reach a specified commitment boundary before performing the SAVWHLACT function. Some active applications may "hang" while the system waits for the commitment boundary to be reached. A timeout value on the SAV command determines how long the system will wait and, depending on the value specified, it is possible that the system can time out and not save anything if the commitment boundary is not reached for a long time.

- Because of the *SHRRD lock on every object and member, no applications can perform a move, rename, delete, or clear function while the library is being saved. If an application attempts one of these functions, it will wait until it either gets the lock or times out.

  A similar problem will occur if programmers using SEU try to edit source files that are being saved with SAVWHLACT. Programmers can edit a member while it is being saved, but they will not be able to end SEU because of the *SHRRD lock. They would just "hang" on the exit screen with a message that says they can't get the lock they need to clear the member.

Technical Tip

If you design your applications and libraries with SAVWHLACT in mind, you can use it effectively. But unless you really know what you are doing or have a very isolated case, you may be better off to avoid the SAVWHLACT function and do your backup in a quiet environment.

TAA Tools for Saving While Active

For saving data files, you could consider using the TAA tool SAVWHLACT. It differs from the system-supported SAVWHLACT function; and even though the TAA tool has problems also, it might be a better solution in some situations. Let's look at some specific points relevant to the use of TAA tool SAVWHLACT:

- To use the TAA tool, you must be journaling the active files you want to save. You also need to create duplicate files in a separate library to which you will copy the files you want to save.
- You can specify multiple files on a single TAA tool SAVWHLACT command. Each file is copied by the CPYF command to the backup library. When the SAVWHLACT command completes, use normal save commands to save the backup library.
- The SAVWHLACT command captures the journal entry IDs when each CPYF starts and ends and when SAVWHLACT starts and ends. These entries are used for recovery.

- To recover, you restore the backup version to the backup library. Then you run the companion command RSTWHLACT. It will copy each file back and then apply the journal entries that occurred during the time the CPYF command was started for each file until the end of the SAVWHLACT command. During the application of journal entries, errors are possible (e.g., a record may already exist when the journal entry says to add it). RSTWHLACT is sensitive to possible errors and masks this type of error if it occurred during the running of the CPYF command used during SAVWHLACT.
- When RSTWHLACT completes, you should see the files back at the point where SAVWHLACT completed.
- The problem of having transactions split may still occur. The TAA tool does not support commitment control. The result is no different than trying to recover from a system crash without commitment control.
- The TAA tool SAVWHLACT avoids most of the locking problems because of the use of CPYF. You can still have some, but they normally don't last as long.
- A definite disadvantage of using the TAA tool is that because RSTWHLACT does a copy back to the original file, any access paths over the file will be rebuilt, which requires more time.

For source files, the TAA tool SRCARC can be a better solution than the system-supported SAVWHLACT option. It would be rare if you saw any allocation problems because it uses a *SHRRD lock only for the time to read each changed member. See the discussion of the source archive in Chapter 28, "Setting up your Environment."

Restricted State Operations

The system must be in a restricted state (i.e., all subsystems are ended and a single interactive job is active in the controlling subsystem) before some functions can be performed. The most typical of these functions are SAVSYS and RCLSTG. Two SAVSYS functions have been split into two other commands (SAVSECDTA and SAVCFG), so the SAVSYS command does not have to run as frequently. With these two commands, you can easily capture most of the changes to objects that SAVSYS would capture. The changes that will be caught only by the SAVSYS command (e.g., Edit Code definition objects) are fairly minor. If you make permanent changes to objects such as edit descriptions in library QSYS, you should place these changes in a CL program. To recover, load the system and rerun your program. Authorization and configuration changes do not have to be included in the program (they can be saved with the SAVSECDTA/SAVCFG commands).

The restricted state can be reached only by a workstation in the controlling subsystem. You can't submit a batch job to execute a SAVSYS or RCLSTG command; the functions must be run interactively. Because SAVSYS and RCLSTG are long-running functions, you probably will want them to run unattended. You may want them to run after the regular unattended batch work has completed, but you probably don't want to come in at 1:00 a.m. to start them.

The solution in this situation is the TAA tool DLYCMD (Figure 12.1). Before you go home at night, prompt for the DLYCMD command at the system console. The DLYCMD lets you specify the command you want to run and the time you want it to run (e.g., at a specific time or when all batch work is done). You also specify that the command run in the restricted state and provide instructions for what happens when the command completes (e.g., start the controlling subsystem or power down).

After you enter your specifications for the DLYCMD and press Enter, a display screen appears so you can verify your entries. Then, while you are home in bed, the system performs the function you specified. If the function is a SAVSYS and the backup will not fit on one volume of media, at least one volume can be done in unattended mode.

FIGURE 12.1
DLYCMD TAA Tool Prompt Screen

```
                           Delay Command (DLYCMD)

 Type choices, press Enter.

 Command to execute or *NONE  . .   ___________________________________________

 ______________________________________________________________________________

 Time of day (HHMMSS) trigger . .   *NONE___      000000-235999, *NONE
    Date   *TODAY *DAY1 *DAY2  . .   *TODAY        *TODAY, *DAY1, *DAY2
 Max act jobs trigger . . . . . .   *NOMAX        0-9999, *NOMAX
    Subsystem for MAXJOBS . . . .   *ALL______    Name, *ALL
               + for more values    __________
 Text description:  . . . . . . .   *NONE______________________________________

 Restricted state required  . . .   *NO_          *YES, *NO
 Power down when complete . . . .   *NO_          *YES, *NO
 Restart after powerdown  . . . .   *NO_          *YES, *NO
 Signoff after completion . . . .   *YES          *YES, *NO
 Wait secs for MAXJOBS  . . . . .   900____       Number


                                                                        Bottom
 F3=Exit   F4=Prompt   F5=Refresh   F12=Cancel   F13=How to use this display
 F24=More keys
```

Technical Tip

The TAA tool DLYCMD lets the system perform functions in a restricted state while unattended. You don't have to be physically present to perform a SAVSYS or RCLSTG function.

PTFs

Not all PTFs require a dedicated system. For example, a licensed product such as RPG can be maintained while the system is up as long as no one is using the RPG compiler. However, the LIC and Operating System can be maintained only when the system is in a dedicated state. Normally, trying to determine what does and does not require a dedicated system is not worth the effort — you won't save much time.

Technical Tip

You can install some PTFs while the system is running, but you probably won't save much time. I prefer to apply everything in a dedicated environment.

Installing a New Release

Some day, you may be able to install a new release of the operating system while other users are running, but you can't do that today. You must shut down all activity and install the release on a dedicated system. Most of the program products can be installed if no one is using them on the current release, but normally they won't work without the new system release. From a practical viewpoint, you have to dedicate the system until all the install work is done.

CHAPTER 13

Communicating with a Workstation Operator

Most interactive applications spend their time communicating with an end user. These applications typically use a display file and when they need to "talk" to an end user, they normally use a display format in the display file. Interactive applications (e.g., utility programs) that need to talk to the system operator or a programmer normally operate from the command entry display and there is no convenient user display file to use. In this chapter we will look at three ways to communicate with a workstation operator (or an end user, in some cases) when you don't have, or don't want to use, a separate display file.

SELECTIVE PROMPTING

The first method is a system-supported function called "selective prompting," which allows you to control the parameters that are displayed when a command is prompted, as well as how those parameters are displayed. Selective prompting is specified by placing special prompting characters immediately before the keyword of parameters selected for prompting. The *CL Programmers Guide* has a good discussion of what the special characters mean. The following table reviews the most frequently used values:

Special Prompting Characters	Value Displayed	Input-Capable
??KWD()	Default value	Yes
??KWD(xxx)	Value specified	Yes
?*KWD()	Default value	No
?*KWD(xxx)	Value specified	No
?-KWD()	Nothing[1]	No
?-KWD(xxx)	Nothing[1]	No

[1] The keyword is not displayed and the user cannot enter a value. Either the command default or the value specified is used.

If you want to do something simple — for example, allow a workstation operator to enter a command during execution of an interactive program — selective prompting can be a good choice. For example, if you wanted the workstation operator to restore an object, you could code the following in your CL program:

```
?RSTOBJ
 MONMSG  MSGID(CPF6801) EXEC(DO) /* Cancelled */
 .
 .
 .
 ENDDO   /* Cancelled */
```

The question mark (?) in front of the command tells the system to display the command prompt for the specified command (in this case, the RSTOBJ command). Note that, as in the above example, you should monitor for error message CPF6801 when you use selective prompting. Error message CPF6801 is issued when the workstation operator keys F3 or F12 to cancel the command for which the command prompt was displayed.

When you specify selective prompting by placing a ? in front of a command, any parameter values you specify are displayed on the prompt and they can be changed. Parameters you do not specify are displayed with the default values, which can also be changed. Because of these points, you may find that this approach to selective prompting is too flexible: A workstation operator could enter any values (s)he wishes. To better control what a workstation operator is able to enter on the prompt screen, you could specify selective prompting characters in front of the parameters. For example, you could code the following so the workstation operator cannot change the values specified for the DEV, ENDOPT, and LABEL parameters on the RSTOBJ command:

```
?RSTOBJ  ??OBJ() ??SAVLIB(ABC) ?*DEV(TAP01) ?*ENDOPT() ?-LABEL()
 MONMSG  MSGID(CPF6801) EXEC(DO) /* Cancelled */
 .
 .
 .
 ENDDO
```

You also can specify selective prompting by placing the special characters only in front of parameters and not in front of the command. When you do not use the ? in front of the command, only the parameters you have specified are prompted for. For example, you could code

```
RSTOBJ   ??OBJ() ??SAVLIB(ABC) ?*DEV(TAP01) ?*ENDOPT()
MONMSG   MSGID(CPF6801) EXEC(DO) /* Cancelled */
.
.
.
ENDDO   /* Cancelled */
```

Note that in this example we cannot use the ?- value (as we did in the previous example) because it is valid only when a ? is placed in front of the command. Not using the ? in front of the command is normally a better solution if you are going to use selective prompting.

Although selective prompting can be useful, it should be used with care for the following reasons: 1) If you specify selective prompting by placing a ? in front of a command, a user may have access to more parameters than you would like; you are exposed to potential problems if a command's parameters change because of a new release of the operating system. 2) Selective prompting is typically a programmer or system operator interface; an end user may not understand the command prompts. 3) Selective prompting works only with commands; if you don't have a command interface, you must use some other solution. 4) Selective prompting provides neither feedback to a program nor good error-handling capability.

Technical Tip

Selective prompting is a simple way for an interactive CL program to communicate with a workstation operator when the program requires that a command be entered. If you require a more complex solution, selective prompting is not appropriate.

The Job's External Message Queue (*EXT)

In addition to selective prompting, you can use a job's external message queue to communicate with a workstation operator. The simplest method is to send an informational message. For example,

```
SNDPGMMSG  MSG('No bananas today') TOPGMQ(*EXT)
```

When you send a message to a job's external message queue, the Display Program Messages display will appear on the workstation operator's terminal. To keep this generally unfriendly display as user-friendly as possible, you should clear the external message queue before you send a message. You can clear the external message queue with the following command:

```
RMVMSG  PGMQ(*EXT) CLEAR(*ALL)
```

Technical Tip

If you are going to use a job's external message queue, you should clear it before sending a message. Clearing the message queue will let the workstation operator concentrate on a single message and will avoid cluttering the Display Program Messages display.

You also can send an inquiry message to a job's external message queue and receive a reply to the inquiry. The easiest way to do this is to use the SNDUSRMSG command, which combines the functions of the SNDPGMMSG and RCVMSG commands. Because it's easy to get into trouble when you use the SNDUSRMSG command, let's look first at a poor implementation of the command:

```
            */ Poor coding example */
DCL         &REPLY *CHAR LEN(1)
RMVMSG      PGMQ(*EXT) CLEAR(*ALL)
SNDUSRMSG   MSG('How about lunch today? Enter Y or N.')  +
              VALUES(Y N) MSGRPY(&REPLY)
IF          (&REPLY *EQ 'Y') DO /* Yes reply */
            .
            .
            .
            ENDDO /* Yes reply */
ELSE        DO    /* Do the following for an "N" response */
            .
            .
            .
            ENDDO /* "N" response */
```

When you use the SNDUSRMSG command, lowercase responses are automatically translated to uppercase (the SNDUSRMSG TRNTBL parameter defaults to QSYSTRNTBL). In addition, the system will prevent the workstation operator from keying in a non-blank character other than Y or N. But the system does not prevent the operator from keying in a blank or from responding to the display with F3 or F12.

Therein lies the problem with the above code: If the operator takes either of these actions, the system sends a null value — denoted by *N — to the program. Because the code specifies a one-byte reply, the system truncates the null value and sends only an * to your program. It appears that the operator replied to the inquiry by keying an *, even though (s)he is prevented from entering an *. The code above treats the * as a "No" response.

What makes the example bad is that in your CL program you think the validity-checking facilities of the SNDUSRMSG command are protecting you. Therefore, you would normally check for only one of the replies; the reply you don't check for in your program automatically becomes the default. Or even worse, you check for both values and, if the reply is not Y or N, you are sent to some strange place in your program. The way to fix this is by providing a value for the DFT keyword on the command, such as

```
SNDUSRMSG  ... DFT(N) ...
```

To do it correctly, you probably want to tell the operator what the default is in the message text:

```
SNDUSRMSG  MSG('How about lunch today? Enter Y or N. Default +
             is N.') VALUES(Y N) DFT(N)
```

Now you can be assured that only an uppercase Y or N will come back to your program and that the logic following the SNDUSRMSG command is straightforward.

Technical Tip

The SNDUSRMSG command is provided by the system to simplify sending an inquiry message to a job's external message queue. The function does work, but you have to be careful what you specify so the workstation operator understands how to respond and so the CL program logic is easier to handle.

TAA Tool PMTOPR

If you want a command that offers the same function as the SNDUSRMSG command but that also enforces validity checking, try the QUSRTOOL TAA tool PMTOPR. The command requires less coding on your part to prompt for and validate responses correctly, offers less chance that an unexpected error will be returned to your CL program, allows your program to validate a response and provide a good error message if necessary, and provides an understandable interface for end users because the default response appears in the input field. To use the PMTOPR command, simply code:

```
DCL      &REPLY *CHAR LEN(16)
.
.
.
PMTOPR   RTNVAR(&REPLY) LEN(1) PROMPT('Would you like to go to +
           lunch?') VALUES(Y N)
IF       (&REPLY *EQ 'Y') DO /* Yes reply */
         .
         .
         .
         ENDDO /* Yes reply */
ELSE     DO /* "No" reply */
         .
         .
         .
         ENDDO /* "No" reply */
```

In this example, specifying a values list ensures that a Y or N will be entered. The operator cannot press F3 to avoid answering or enter something other than Y or N. The RTNVAR value must be declared as *CHAR LEN(16). You can specify that the reply must be a decimal value, which will force validity checking, but the reply is always returned in a 16-byte character variable. The LEN parameter on the PMTOPR command controls the length of the input field the workstation operator can key into. You can provide explanatory text for up to four responses and you can specify a default, which is displayed in the reply field. For example, the following code:

```
PMTOPR   RTNVAR(&REPLY) LEN(1)                          +
           PROMPT('Would you like to go to lunch?')  +
           LINE1('Y - I would like to go to lunch')  +
           LINE2('N - You can lunch by yourself' )   +
           DFT(N) VALUES(Y N)
```

would produce the following prompt display:

```
                         Prompt Operator

Would you like to go to lunch?

Y - I would like to go to lunch
N - You can lunch by yourself

N

Validation performed

Values

  Y      N
```

The PMTOPR command also allows you to request responses other than Y or N (e.g., date, file names, and digit values). The PMTOPR command lets you specify a certain level of validity checking and/or you can perform your own validity checking on the response and use the command again with your error message text shown at the bottom of the display. The code might look like this:

```
DCL      &LIB *CHAR LEN(16)
DCL      &ERRTXT *CHAR LEN(150)
PMT:     PMTOPR  RTNVAR(&LIB) LEN(10)                          +
           PROMPT('Enter the library name to be displayed') +
           DFT(&LIB) ERRTXT(&ERRTXT)
CHKOBJ   OBJ(&LIB) OBJTYPE(*LIB)
MONMSG   MSGID(CPF9801) EXEC(DO) /* Not found */
CHGVAR   &ERRTXT ('The library entered does not exist.')     +
GOTO     PMT
ENDDO    /* Not found */
DSPLIB   LIB(&LIB) ...
```

Note that the library variable is declared as 16 bytes. This is required for the &RTNVAR value. On the first pass, the program displays the default value (blanks) for parameter &LIB. The value subsequently entered by a user is returned to the program when the PMTOPR command completes and then is used by the program when it loops back to the PMTOPR command if the library does not exist. Identical processing takes place for variable &ERRTXT.

Technical Tip

The TAA tool PMTOPR provides a good way to ask a question and receive a single response from a user. And the validity-checking function provided by the PMTOPR command means less coding required for your program.

Exercise A Selective Prompting

In this exercise you will practice using the special selective prompting characters in a CL program.

1. Use PDM to create a CLP member named TRYSELPMT and describe it as "Test Selective Prompting."
2. Enter the following code (in this case we'll send a unique string of message text rather than using the IBM-supplied message text for error message ID CPF6801):

```
  PGM
 ?CRTCLPGM
  MONMSG     MSGID(CPF6801) EXEC(DO) /* Cancel */
  RCVMSG     MSGTYPE(*EXCP) /* Remove message */
  SNDPGMMSG  MSGID(CPF9898) MSGF(QCPFMSG) MSGTYPE(*ESCAPE)  +
               MSGDTA(You cancelled command  +
               prompting with F3 or F12')
  ENDDO      /* Cancel */
  ENDPGM
```

3. Create the program.
4. Access the command entry display.
5. Call the program:

```
CALL  TRYSELPMT
```

6. Press F3 to check the program's exception processing.

   You should see the escape message sent by the program. If you press F10 to see detailed messages, you should not see any because the RCVMSG command removed the CPF6801 message.
7. Call program TRYSELPMT again.
8. Press F9 when the command prompt appears.

   You should see all the parameters for the CRTCLPGM command. Note that the LOG parameter appears on the second display. This form of selective prompting (placing a ? in front of the command) does not restrict the user. (S)he can enter any parameters (s)he wants.

Exercise A continued

Exercise A continued

9. On the command prompt, enter TRYSELPMT as the name of the program name to be created. This is an unusual thing to do, but it illustrates that end users are liable to do anything if you offer them the opportunity. Even though you already called program TRYSELPMT, you can re-create the program you are currently running if the default (*YES) is taken for the REPLACE parameter on the CRTCLPGM command. This means the program you are running (TRYSELPMT) will be moved to library QRPLOBJ while the new version of the program is being created. The system protects current users of a program when it is replaced. The old version of the program continues to live in library QRPLOBJ. This subject is also discussed in Chapter 23, "The CL Program Object."

   Note that the code does not prevent a workstation operator from entering REPLACE(*NO), because all the CRTCLPGM command's parameters are displayed and they are input-capable. If the operator entered REPLACE(*NO), the CL program would not be created because the current program still exists and the program that is running would receive an unexpected escape message. You don't want to give the operator an opportunity to get into trouble with the REPLACE parameter; we will fix that problem in the next series of steps.

10. Press the Enter key to create the program. Then press F10 for detailed messages. You should see the completion message stating that the program was created.

11. Return to PDM and request to edit member TRYSELPMT.

12. Change the CRTCLPGM command as follows:

```
?CRTCLPGM   ??PGM(TRYSELPMT) ??SRCFILE() ?*SRCMBR() ?-LOG(*NO) +
              ?-REPLACE(*YES)
```

13. Create the program from the PDM display.

14. Access the command entry display.

15. Call the program:

```
CALL  TRYSELPMT
```

   You should see 1) that the program name is already filled in, but that it can be changed; 2) that the default is displayed for the SRCFILE

Exercise A continued

Exercise A continued

parameter, but it can be changed; and 3) that the default is displayed for the SRCMBR parameter, but it cannot be changed.

16. Press F9 to see the second half of the CRTCLPGM command prompt. Note that neither the LOG nor the REPLACE parameters appear on the second display. The ?- selective prompting character prevents these parameters from being displayed and causes the values you specified to be used. Preventing the operator from entering REPLACE(*NO) protects him/her from getting into trouble.

17. Create the program using the defaults supplied.

18. Display the program:

```
DSPPGM  TRYSELPMT
```

    You should see that the LOG parameter is specified as *NO.

19. Call program TRYSELPMT again.

20. Enter a program name for a source member that does not exist (e.g., xxxyyyx).

    Note the type of error that occurs. If you are taking the defaults for answering inquiry messages (e.g., see the CHGJOB INQMSGRPY parameter), the Display Program Messages display should present inquiry message CPA0701, which says that error message CPF9801 was received. If you display the message details, you will see what happened. If you enter 'C' for Cancel, the program should function check. See the discussion in Chapter 1, "Monitoring for Messages," about the CL Program Inquiry Message. The point of this exercise is to demonstrate the trouble a user can get into if (s)he has too many choices (see Step 27).

21. Return to PDM and request to edit member TRYSELPMT.

22. Remove the ? from in front of the CRTCLPGM command. When you do not use the ? in front of the command, only the parameters you have specified are prompted for. You can't use the ?- value, but you don't need it. Your command should look like this:

```
CRTCLPGM  ??PGM() ??SRCFILE() ?*SRCMBR()
```

23. Create the program from the PDM display.

Exercise A continued

Exercise A continued

24. Access the command entry display.
25. Call the program:

```
CALL  TRYSELPMT
```

    The command prompt should display a blank input field for the PGM parameter and an input field containing the default value for the SRCFILE parameter. The default value also is used for the SRCMBR parameter, but the value cannot be changed. None of the other parameters are displayed and you can't access them with F9.

26. Use F3 to cancel.

    Selective prompting works well if you keep it simple, but it is difficult to prevent a user from doing something totally unexpected (e.g., replacing the current program). If the validity of a parameter's value is critical, you probably don't want to use selective prompting.

Exercise B Using the External Message Queue

In this exercise you will practice using and clearing the external message queue and using the SNDUSRMSG command.

1. Use PDM to create a CLP member named TRYEXTMSG and describe it as "Test External Message Queue."
2. Enter the following code:

```
PGM
SNDPGMMSG  MSG('No bananas today.') TOPGMQ(*EXT)
ENDPGM
```

3. Create the program.
4. Access the command entry display.
5. Call the program:

```
CALL  TRYEXTMSG
```

Exercise B continued

Exercise B continued

You should see the Display Program Messages display, which shows the messages sent to the program's external message queue.

6. Press Enter to end the program. If you are not displaying detail messages, press F10.

   You should see the same message you saw in Step 5.

7. Place the cursor on the message and press the Help key. You should see that it is an INFO type message (the default of MSGTYPE(*INFO) was used on the SNDPGMMSG command).

8. Call the TRYEXTMSG program again.

   You should see the Display Program Messages display again, but now it has two identical messages: the one sent when you first called the program and the one sent when you called the program the second time. Because two messages are displayed, an end user may be confused about which message applies to the program being run.

9. Press Enter to end the program.

10. Return to PDM and request to edit member TRYEXTMSG.

11. Enter the following command before the SNDPGMMSG command:

    ```
    RMVMSG  PGMQ(*EXT) CLEAR(*ALL)
    ```

12. Create the program from the PDM display.

13. Access the command entry display.

14. Call the program:

    ```
    CALL  TRYEXTMSG
    ```

    Because the RMVMSG command you specified in Step 11 clears the external message queue before a message is sent, you should see only a single message on the Display Program Messages display.

15. Press Enter to end the program.

16. Call the program again.

    You should see only a single message.

17. Press Enter to end the program.

Exercise B continued

Exercise B continued

18. Return to PDM and request to edit member TRYEXTMSG.
19. Revise the code as follows (we'll use a poor example first to show how you can get in trouble using the SNDUSRMSG command):

```
PGM
DCL         &REPLY *CHAR LEN(1)
RMVMSG      PGMQ(*EXT) CLEAR(*ALL)
SNDUSRMSG   MSG('How about lunch today?') +
              VALUES(Y N) MSGRPY(&REPLY)
SNDPGMMSG   MSG('The reply was -' *CAT &REPLY)
ENDPGM
```

20. Create the program from the PDM display.
21. Access the command entry display.
22. Call the program:

```
CALL  TRYEXTMSG
```

23. Enter a lowercase "y". The SNDUSRMSG command defaults to provide the system translation table QSYSTRNTBL, which automatically translates lowercase letters to uppercase. You should see an uppercase "Y" as the reply.
24. Call the program again and enter an uppercase "N". The program should work successfully.
25. Call the program again and enter an *.

    You should see the Display Program Messages display with

    - The message you sent
    - The reply you entered
    - A message stating the reply is not valid (CPD2406)
    - The message you sent
    - The reply line

    The system correctly prevents you from entering a value that does not match the list of values you specified on the SNDUSRMSG command. This capability eliminates the need for a lot of code in your program; but the program is not correct the way it is coded, as the following step demonstrates.

Exercise B continued

Exercise B continued

26. At this point, the system is asking for a value. Just press Enter. Because you did not enter a value, the system returns a null value (*N) to your program. But because a one-byte reply value is specified, the system truncates the N and returns only the *. The same thing happens if you key in a blank and press Enter or just end the display by keying F3 or F12. Although the system prevents you from keying in an *, an * can be returned to your program if you don't code the command correctly.
27. Return to PDM and edit the TRYEXTMSG member.
28. Change the CRTCLPGM command as follows:

```
SNDUSRMSG  MSG('How about lunch today?  +
             Enter Y or N. Default is N.)  +
             VALUES(Y N) DFT(N)
```

29. Create the program from the PDM display.
30. Access the command entry display.
31. Call the program:

```
CALL  TRYEXTMSG
```

You should not be able to fool the program now. Try entering different values.

Exercise C Using the TAA Tool PMTOPR

In this exercise you will practice using the TAA tool PMTOPR. If the PMTOPR command does not exist on your system, see Appendix B.

1. Use PDM to create a CLP member named TRYPMTOPR and describe it as "Test Prompt Operator."
2. Enter the following code:

Exercise C continued

Exercise C continued

```
PGM
DCL        &REPLY *CHAR LEN(16)
PMTOPR     RTNVAR(&REPLY) LEN(1) PROMPT('Would you like +
             to go to lunch?') VALUES(Y N)
SNDPGMMSG  MSG('Reply-' *CAT &REPLY)
ENDPGM
```

3. Create the program.
4. Access the command entry display.
5. Call the program:

```
CALL  TRYPMTOPR
```

You should see the Prompt Operator display with your text and a reply line of a single character. Although the return variable is a 16-character field, the LEN parameter determines the length of the input field and ensures that the user cannot key a longer value.

6. Key in value of "Y". You can enter only an uppercase letter.
7. Call the program again and try an invalid value such as *. Then try entering a blank. The default on the PMTOPR command is RQD(*YES), which means that blanks are not acceptable as a reply.
8. Return to PDM and request to edit member TRYPMTOPR.
9. Modify the PMTOPR command as follows:

```
PMTOPR  RTNVAR(&REPLY) LEN(1) PROMPT('Would you like +
          to go to lunch?') LINE1('Y - I would like +
          to go to lunch') LINE2('N - You can lunch +
          by yourself') DFT(N) VALUES(Y N)
```

10. Create the program from the PDM display.
11. Access the command entry display.
12. Call the program:

```
CALL  TRYPMTOPR
```

You should see the same display with additional text to assist the operator in entering the desired value. Note that the default reply is already entered so the operator just has to press Enter.

Chapter 14

User-Written Commands

I prefer user-written commands for standard functions that require several parameters. I would much rather code a user-written command (i.e., a command interface) than code a CALL command that requires a complex parameter list. Unless you are dealing with one of the following situations:

- a need for high program performance
- a need for an internal program call
- a one-time need for a program

I recommend writing your own command interface.

When compared with a CALL command, command interfaces generally offer the following benefits:

- Some degree of prompting so parameters can be entered correctly
- Defaults for certain parameters
- Improved documentation when keywords are contained in the source
- Better syntax-checking when you enter a command and during execution of the command
- Less chance of error (remembering parameter lists on a CALL command is very error prone and a mistake can be difficult to debug)
- Better productivity (if you can remember the command's name, you often don't need a manual to help you use the command)

User-written commands have the following disadvantages:

- Reduced performance. Executing a user command is not as fast as directly calling the command processing program (CPP). To execute a command, the system must first access the command definition object. The system then must perform validity checking on the parameters and possibly call a validity checking program. Finally, the system calls your CPP. When you use the CALL command, something similar happens, but the path is much more streamlined. If you are writing a CL program as the front end to an application and you are not going to process the same user-written command iteratively, you probably won't see any performance difference.

- Increased time required to code and test a user command. In general, a user command is only worth coding if you are going to use it multiple times. You must invest time and effort to create a good productivity aid.

Writing Simple Commands

My intent in this chapter is not to provide a full course in writing command definition specifications, but to step you through some important points (e.g., the most common types of command definition entries, and how to specify the typical types of command definition entries in CL programs). Writing command definition statements can be quite complex, but if you stick with a few simple command definition functions, you can easily write useful commands without the need to understand the complex functions.

If you've never written a command, the following sections will help you get started. You can key the examples as they are described to begin building a meaningful user-written command.

Defining "Command"

A command normally comprises two objects:

- A command definition object, which defines the parameters, defaults, validity checking, and so on. Command definition source follows CL's syntactical rules for commands and keywords but you do not use CL to write the command definition source. The special statements required can be used only to write the command definition source. To create the command definition source, you use the CRTCMD command; the result is a command definition object (CDO) that has an object type of *CMD.
- A command processing program (CPP). The CPP, normally written in CL, accepts a parameter list according to specifications in the command definition object and does the real work. You specify the name of the CPP on the PGM parameter of the CRTCMD command when you create the CDO.

When you execute a command (either on a command entry display or in a CL program), the system finds the command definition object, validates the parameters, and calls the CPP. For example, let's say you executed command GOODWRK, which has a CPP named GOODWRKC. The process would look like this:

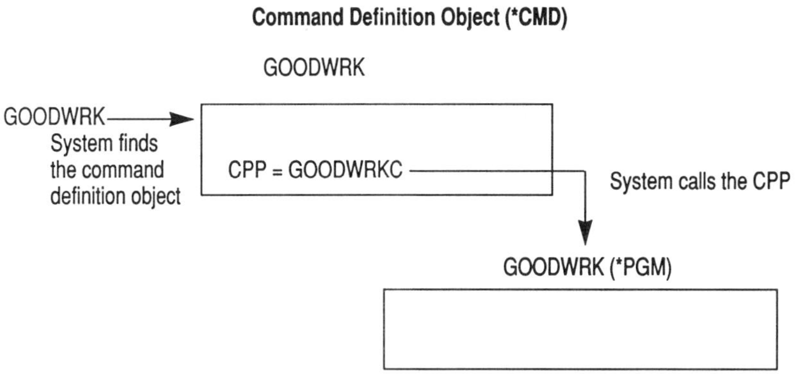

Command Definition Object (*CMD)

GOODWRK

GOODWRK → System finds the command definition object

CPP = GOODWRKC → System calls the CPP

GOODWRK (*PGM)

Command Prompt Text

When a user prompts for a command, the value specified on the PROMPT parameter of the CMD statement appears at the top of the display. The system automatically adds the command name (up to 10 characters long) in parentheses on the same line.

Thus, if you were creating a command named CLR to clear all spooled files in your output queue, you would enter the following command definition source statement:

```
CMD  PROMPT('Clear my Output Queue')
```

If you prompt for the command after you have created it, the following would appear on the command prompt display:

```
Clear my Output Queue (CLR)
```

To help identify your user-written commands, you may want to follow a standard used for the TAA commands. The TAA commands always include the letters TAA in the command prompt. For example,

```
Retrieve Job Description - TAA (RTVJOBD)
```

In this case, by adding TAA to the command description, TAA commands are easily distinguishable from system commands. You can follow this convention to distinguish between commands you have written for systemwide use and commands you have written for your own personal use. For example, you might use the letters USR to identify systemwide user-written commands:

```
CMD  PROMPT('Print Payroll - USR')
```

Or you might use your initials to identify personalized user-written commands.

Commands with No Parameters

You can create a command that has no parameters to perform a specific function. For example, assume you want to create a command named CLR that will clear your output queue. Use SEU to create a CMD source member and enter the following source statement (also assume that your initials are "FDR" and that you want them included as a reminder that this is your command):

```
CMD  PROMPT('Clear Output Queue - FDR')
```

When you create a command, you have to name the CPP in the PGM parameter of the CRTCMD command. For example:

```
CRTCMD  CMD(CLR) PGM(CLRC) TEXT('Clear Output Queue')
```

The CPP does not have to exist at the time the command is created. Your CPP is normally a CL program and, in this case, needs only one line of code (where xxx is the name of your output queue, and yyy is the library in which it exists):

```
CLROUTQ  OUTQ(yyy/xxx)
```

Now let's create a CLP member named CLRC and gradually add functionality. Assume the source is as follows with variables for the queue and library names (when you enter the source, assign values to your output queue using the VALUE keyword):

```
PGM
DCL      &OUTQ *CHAR LEN(10) VALUE(yyy)
DCL      &OUTQL *CHAR LEN(10) VALUE(xxx)
CLROUTQ  OUTQ(&OUTQL/&OUTQ)
ENDPGM
```

If you created the CL program above and the CLR command from the previous example, you could execute the CLR command now (if you don't mind clearing your output queue).

Although the CLR command works, we can add some useful functions to make it better. For example, I prefer commands such as CLR to send completion messages when they end. The CLROUTQ command executed by the CPP does send a completion message, which includes the number of spooled files that the command deleted and the number it could not delete. But this message normally is not seen by the user of the CLR command (unless low-level messages are displayed).

You could modify program CLRC to resend the CLROUTQ completion message (this technique is described in Chapter 2, "Sending Messages"). The code would look like this:

```
DCL        &MSG *CHAR LEN(512)
  .
  .
  .
CLROUTQ    ...
RCVMSG     MSG(&MSG) MSGTYPE(*LAST)
SNDPGMMSG  MSG(&MSG) MSGTYPE(*COMP)
```

The CLROUTQ completion message tells you how many spooled files were deleted and how many were not deleted, but unfortunately it does not tell you which output queue the spooled files were in. You can change the message so that it includes additional information. For example,

```
SNDPGMMSG  MSG('Cleared output queue ' *CAT &OUTQ *TCAT ' in '  +
             *CAT &OUTQL *TCAT '. ' *CAT &MSG) MSGTYPE(*COMP)
```

The other alternative would be to access the message data for the entries deleted and not deleted and place those in your own message (see Chapter 3, "Receiving Messages").

Simple Object Name As a Parameter

Now the message text names the output queue being cleared but the CLR command prompt does not. Let's modify the command definition to include this information.

First let's use an output queue name with no library qualifier. Add the following code to your command definition source:

```
PARM  KWD(OUTQ) TYPE(*NAME) LEN(10) DFT(xxx)  +
        PROMPT('Output queue')
```

The KWD(OUTQ) entry provides a name for the parameter. The TYPE(*NAME) specification prevents the user from entering an invalid name. The DFT parameter is where you would specify the default output queue name (the name of your output queue).

As you modify the CLR command, you could re-create the command each time by using the CRTCMD command; but this requires that you enter the PGM parameter name every time you re-create the command. An alternative is to use the RPLCMD (Replace Command) TAA tool:

```
RPLCMD  CMD(CLR)
```

The RPLCMD command will extract any attributes of the command that you originally specified and use them on the CRTCMD command.

Another alternative is to use the SBMPARMS TAA tool described in

Chapter 23, "The CL Program Object." To use the SBMPARMS command, one of the first statements in your command definition source would specify

```
*...+....1....+....2....+
/*PARMS PGM(CLRC) */
```

Whether or not you use SBMPARMS, it is a good idea to include the parameter values in your source as documentation for the command.

Since we now have a parameter to be passed to the CPP, we have to modify program CLRC. Your first two statements should look like this (be sure to delete the VALUE keyword on the DCL &OUTQ statement):

```
PGM  PARM(&OUTQ)
DCL  &OUTQ *CHAR LEN(10)
```

When you re-create the command and the CL program, you will have a much-improved command. The command prompt will say what the command is going to do and the completion message will say what the command did. A user can either use the default or enter the name of an output queue.

The only thing the command prompt doesn't tell you is which library will be used for the output queue. To provide for this, you need to specify a qualified name.

Using a Qualified Name

To specify a qualified name, modify the PARM statement as follows:

```
PARM  KWD(OUTQ) TYPE(QUAL1) PROMPT('Output queue name')
```

The TYPE(QUAL1) entry refers to QUAL type statements that are normally entered at the end of all parameters. The QUAL statements describe the object and library values (the two pieces of a qualified name).

The QUAL statements would normally be entered after your PARM statements (use your specific output queue name and library for the default values):

```
QUAL1:  QUAL  TYPE(*NAME) LEN(10) DFT(xxx)
        QUAL  TYPE(*NAME) LEN(10) DFT(yyy) PROMPT('Library name')
```

Note that you don't add a PROMPT value to the first piece of the qualified name. This was already specified on the PARM statement.

The command prompt displays one line for the PARM statement and one line for each additional QUAL statement (the first QUAL statement is used for the normal parameter line). The command prompt would appear as

```
                    Clear Output Queue - FDR (CLR)

Type choices, press Enter.

Output queue . . . . . . . . . .   xxx_______       Name
  Library name . . . . . . . . .     yyy_______     Name
```

When you use QUAL statements, you don't specify a DFT value on the PARM statement. Instead, each QUAL statement can have a separate default.

A qualified name is always passed to the CPP as a single field with a length equal to the sum of the lengths of the QUAL fields. In this case, you have two 10-character fields, so the variable in your CL program must be declared as LEN(20).

Although this is the way the name will be passed to program CLRC, it is not the way CL normally lets you work with object and library names. You need separate variables for each name. Therefore, you need to use a substring function to pull the individual names from the 20-character variable and separate them into 10-character variables. The order of the values in the passed variable is the same order as the QUAL statements. Therefore, the object name is in the first 10 bytes. The data in the variable would look like this:

```
Ø         1         2
12345678901234567890
xxx       yyy
```

Note that the values are in fixed positions. The library name will always start in position 11, regardless of how long the object name is.

The beginning of program CLRC should now look like this (be sure to delete the VALUE keyword on the DCL &OUTQL statement):

```
PGM       PARM(&FULLOUTQ)
DCL       &FULLOUTQ *CHAR LEN(20)
DCL       &OUTQ *CHAR LEN(10)
DCL       &OUTQL *CHAR LEN(10)
DCL       &MSG *CHAR LEN(512)
CHGVAR    &OUTQ %SST(&FULLOUTQ 1 10)
CHGVAR    &OUTQL %SST(&FULLOUTQ 11 10)
CLROUTQ   ...
```

At this point, the function of your command is very clear and you have provided a good completion message. A user can take the default, enter his/her own output queue name, use a different library, and so on.

The only thing missing from the command now is a good way to handle errors (e.g., if the output queue specified does not exist). The system command function will automatically reject an invalid output queue name (e.g., ABC*DEF) and provide a reasonable error message. However, if a user specified a valid name for an output queue that did not exist, program CLRC would receive an escape message. To provide a reasonable message for this condition, you should consider adding to program CLRC the code described in Chapter 4, "Standard Error-Handling Routine." The standard error-handling routine would prevent the CL program from ending with a function check message. Here's program CLRC in its final form, with the error-handling routine included:

```
PGM       PARM(&FULLOUTQ &TYPE)
DCL       &FULLOUTQ *CHAR LEN(20)
DCL       &OUTQ *CHAR LEN(10)
DCL       &OUTQL *CHAR LEN(10)
DCL       &TYPE *CHAR LEN(1)
DCL       &ERRORSW *LGL                 /* Standard error */
DCL       &MSGID *CHAR LEN(7)           /* Standard error */
DCL       &MSG *CHAR LEN(512)           /* Standard error */
DCL       &MSGDTA *CHAR LEN(512)        /* Standard error */
DCL       &MSGF *CHAR LEN(10)           /* Standard error */
DCL       &MSGFLIB *CHAR LEN(10)        /* Standard error */
DCL       &KEYVAR *CHAR LEN(4)          /* Standard error */
DCL       &KEYVAR2 *CHAR LEN(4)         /* Standard error */
DCL       &RTNTYPE *CHAR LEN(2)         /* Standard error */
MONMSG    MSGID(CPF0000)  +
            EXEC(GOTO STDERR1) /* Standard error */
CHGVAR    &OUTQ %SST(&FULLOUTQ 1 10)
CHGVAR    &OUTQL %SST(&FULLOUTQ 11 10)
CLROUTQ   OUTQ(&OUTQL/&OUTQ)
```

```
         RCVMSG     MSG(&MSG) MSGTYPE(*LAST)
         SNDPGMMSG  MSG(&TYPE)
         SNDPGMMSG  MSG('Cleared output queue '          +
                      *CAT &OUTQ *TCAT ' IN ' *CAT       +
                      &OUTQL *TCAT '. ' *CAT &MSG) MSGTYPE(*COMP)
         RETURN     /* Normal end of the program */
STDERR1:            /* Standard error-handling routine */
         IF         &ERRORSW SNDPGMMSG MSGID(CPF9999)   +
                      MSGF(QCPFMSG) MSGTYPE(*ESCAPE)
         CHGVAR     &ERRORSW '1' /* Set to fail on error */
         RCVMSG     MSGTYPE(*EXCP) RMV(*NO) KEYVAR(&KEYVAR)
STDERR2: RCVMSG     MSGTYPE(*PRV) MSGKEY(&KEYVAR) RMV(*NO)  +
                      KEYVAR(&KEYVAR2) MSG(&MSG)            +
                      MSGDTA(&MSGDTA) MSGID(&MSGID)         +
                      RTNTYPE(&RTNTYPE) MSGF(&MSGF)         +
                      SNDMSGFLIB(&MSGFLIB)
         IF         (&RTNTYPE *NE '02') GOTO STDERR3
         IF         (&MSGID *NE '  ') SNDPGMMSG             +
                      MSGID(&MSGID) MSGF(&MSGFLIB/&MSGF)    +
                      MSGDTA(&MSGDTA) MSGTYPE(*DIAG)
         IF         (&MSGID *EQ '  ') SNDPGMMSG             +
                      MSG(&MSG) MSGTYPE(*DIAG)
         RMVMSG     MSGKEY(&KEYVAR2)
STDERR3: RCVMSG     MSGKEY(&KEYVAR) MSGDTA(&MSGDTA)         +
                      MSGID(&MSGID) MSGF(&MSGF) SNDMSGFLIB(&MSGFLIB)
         SNDPGMMSG  MSGID(&MSGID) MSGF(&MSGFLIB/&MSGF)      +
                      MSGDTA(&MSGDTA) MSGTYPE(*ESCAPE)
         ENDPGM
```

If you have followed the discussion up to this point, you know enough to write simple, but very helpful commands. In the following sections, we will look at some specific functions you can add to typical commands.

Required Parameters (MIN Parameter)

Sometimes, rather than providing a default for a command, you want to require a user to enter a value. To do this, add the MIN(1) value, which requires that a user enter one value, to the PARM statement:

```
PARM  KWD(OUTQ) TYPE(*NAME) LEN(10) MIN(1) PROMPT('Output queue')
```

If you use a qualified name, the MIN(1) value is normally specified on the PARM statement and not on the QUAL statement. You can't specify

MIN(1) and then use the DFT keyword to supply a default value (it wouldn't make sense).

Special Values for Names

When you prompt for an object or library name, you may have a special value that begins with an * that can be used in place of a name.

Since an * is not valid in a name (the first character must be a letter or some special characters followed by letters or numbers), you must describe the special name values on the SPCVAL keyword. For example, if you wanted a special value of *ALL, you would specify

```
PARM  KWD(OUTQ) TYPE(*NAME) LEN(10) MIN(1) SPCVAL(*ALL)  +
        PROMPT('Output queue')
```

You can make the special value the default:

```
PARM   KWD(OUTQ) TYPE(*NAME) LEN(10) DFT(*ALL) SPCVAL(*ALL)  +
         PROMPT('Output queue')
```

or you can place the special value in a qualified name (the system does this frequently with values such as *LIBL and *CURLIB):

```
        PARM  KWD(OUTQ) TYPE(QUAL1) MIN(1)  +
                PROMPT('Output queue name')
QUAL1:  QUAL  TYPE(*NAME) LEN(10)
        QUAL  TYPE(*NAME) LEN(10) DFT(*LIBL)  +
                SPCVAL(*LIBL *CURLIB) PROMPT('Library name')
```

In the CPP, I prefer to determine whether or not a special value was used and, if so, have the program access the real library name. This technique helps provide messages that clearly state what object was operated on. To do this, you would code the CPP as follows:

```
CHGVAR   &OUTQ %SST(&FULLOUTQ 1 10)
CHGVAR   &OUTQL %SST(&FULLOUTQ 11 10)
CHKOBJ   OBJ(&OUTQL/&OUTQ) OBJTYPE(*OUTQ)
MONMSG   MSGID(CPF9801) EXEC(DO) /* Not found */
.
.
.
ENDDO    /* Not found */
IF       (%SST(&OUTQL 1 1) *EQ '*') DO /* Spc */
RTVOBJD  OBJ(&OUTQL/&OUTQ) OBJTYPE(*OUTQ) RTNLIB(&OUTQL)
ENDDO    /* Special value */
```

In this example, after the object and library name are placed in separate variables, the CHKOBJ command is used to determine that the output queue exists. If the user had entered *LIBL for the library, *LIBL would be used on the CHKOBJ command.

If the object cannot be found when the user specifies *LIBL, the system escape message would refer to *LIBL in the message text. This would be appropriate because the system could not find the object on the library list. However, if the system does find the object, any subsequent messages should identify the library where the object was found.

If an * was used in the first position of the library name, the RTVOBJD command is used to determine the name of the library that contains the output queue. The code works if either *LIBL or *CURLIB is specified. The actual library name is placed into variable &OUTQL so that the code will then operate as if the user had specified the actual library name. If you need to save the original input name, you would use a different variable.

The user can't enter a value such as *ABC as the library name (and have it passed to the CPP) because your command definition statements say that only special values *LIBL or *CURLIB are allowed.

Decimal and Character Parameters

Normally, decimal and character parameters don't require unique coding techniques in CL. You just declare the CL variables to match the corresponding PARM statement. For example, if you wanted parameters for text and number of days, you might code

```
PARM  KWD(TEXT) TYPE(*CHAR) LEN(50) MIN(1)    +
        PROMPT('Text description')
PARM  KWD(DAYS) TYPE(*DEC) LEN(3 0) DFT(10)   +
        PROMPT('Number of days')
```

The DCLs for the CPP would be

```
DCL  &TEXT *CHAR LEN(50)
DCL  &DAYS *DEC LEN(3 0)
```

You can specify a default for either type (with the DFT keyword), or make them required by using MIN(1).

A Restricted List of Values

Another typical approach to user-written commands is to limit a parameter to a restricted list of values. For example, if you ask for a *YES or *NO value, you don't want the user to enter Y or *MAYBE. The following code shows how to require that any value entered must match a value in your list of values:

```
PARM  KWD(DLTSPLF) TYPE(*CHAR) LEN(4) DFT(*YES) RSTD(*YES)  +
        VALUE(*YES *NO) PROMPT('Delete the spooled file')
```

Using the RSTD and VALUE keywords ensures that only a *YES or *NO value will be passed to the CPP.

Relational and Range Checking

If you want the user to enter a number, you normally want to place some restrictions on the value. For example, if the value must be greater than zero, you could code

```
PARM  KWD(DAYS) TYPE(*DEC) LEN(3 0) DFT(10) REL(GT 0)  +
        PROMPT('Number of days')
```

Or you might want to specify both an upper and lower boundary (i.e., a range) with the statement

```
PARM  KWD(DAYS) TYPE(*DEC) LEN(3 0) DFT(10) RANGE(0 180)  +
        PROMPT('Number of days')
```

In this case, the RANGE parameter prevents a user from entering negative values or values too large for your program to support.

Duplicating Standard Command Source

Now that you have a feel for writing commands, let me offer a shortcut. I begin writing a command by copying in command definition source that I have already written. The tool I use, DUPSTDSRC, is available for your use in the QUSRTOOL library. To begin a new command definition source member, just specify

```
DUPSTDSRC  MBR(xxx) SRCTYP(*CMD) TEXT('...') SRCFILE(yyy)
```

You'll find the typical kinds of parameters already coded and ready to use. Simply modify the source for your own needs and you can build a command quickly. You will find more information about the DUPSTDSRC command in Appendix A, "How I Code."

Technical Tip

The DUPSTDSRC TAA tool provides a good starting point when you need to write a new command definition source member. The tool has most typical command functions already coded for you.

Other Command Functions

In this section, we will look at some other things you might want to do when writing your own commands and how what you do might affect the CL program used as the CPP.

Expressions

It can sometimes be helpful to allow a user to key an expression as the value for a parameter. For example, the SNDPGMMSG command's MSG parameter supports an expression such as

```
MSG(&FILE *TCAT ' is missing')
```

Or a user might want to construct names from a constant by adding ever increasing numbers (e.g., MBR001, MBR002, and so on).

To allow a user to enter an expression as the value for a parameter, you must specify EXPR(*YES) on the parameter statement. For example,

```
PARM  KWD(TEXT) TYPE(*CHAR) LEN(50) MIN(1) EXPR(*YES)  +
        PROMPT('Text description')
```

Unless a parameter supports only a restricted list of values (e.g., *YES or *NO), it is a good idea to specify EXPR(*YES) for most parameters. Specifying EXPR(*YES) gives the user of a command in a CL program more flexibility when entering values.

Technical Tip

If you want to allow an expression to be entered as a parameter value, the parameter must be coded as EXPR(*YES). Allowing an expression is almost always a good thing to do.

When you prompt for a command that has a parameter coded as EXPR(*YES), the length of the input line as initially displayed on the command prompt may not be long enough to enter the expression the user wants (the command prompt assumes an expression will not be entered). You can expand the size of the parameter input field by entering & and pressing Enter. Each time you do this, the size of the parameter field increases in length.

Technical Tip

When entering an expression into a command prompt, you can expand the size of the input area for the parameter by entering & and pressing Enter. You can do this multiple times.

Converting Special Values

It is common to allow a user to enter a meaningful value such as *ALL or *YES and then to change that value to A or Y to simplify coding the CPP. You can accomplish this by using IF logic in conjunction with the CHGVAR command in the CPP, or you can use the SPCVAL keyword in the command definition.

For example, assume that you want the user to enter *YES or *NO, but you want to process a one-character value of Y or N in the program. Your command definition statement would look like this:

```
PARM  KWD(DLTSPLF) TYPE(*CHAR) LEN(1)      +
        DFT(*YES) RSTD(*YES)               +
        SPCVAL((*YES Y)(*NO N))            +
        PROMPT('Delete the spooled file')
```

The command processing function will convert what the user specifies to a Y or N. Note that the variable length is specified as 1 byte. When a user prompts for the command, (s)he will see that the default and the size of the input field will be long enough to handle the largest value entered into SPCVAL.

Another form of "special value" is to provide a command prompt similar to that provided by the system for a parameter like FROMRCD on the CPYF command. The default is *START, which means the first record in the file. You can also enter a relative record number.

If you want to write your own FROMRCD parameter, you would use a relational check to prevent a user from entering a 0 or minus value. A special value of *START would be converted to 0 during the command processing. For example,

```
PARM  KWD(FROMRCD) TYPE(*DEC) LEN(13 Ø) +
        DFT(*START) SPCVAL((*START Ø))  +
        REL(*GT Ø) PROMPT('Copy from record number')
```

The user can't enter a 0 and have it passed to your CL program because the REL parameter prevents it. If the user entered a 0, (s)he would receive an error message from the system.

In the CL program, your logic would say if the value is 0, the user specified *START. If the value is greater than 0, the user wants to start at a specific relative record number.

Some commands have several special values in addition to allowing a number to be entered. These can be handled by assigning negative values and protecting what the user can enter with a relational test such as

```
SPCVAL((*START Ø)(*LAST -1)) REL(*GT Ø)
```

In your CL program just test for 0 or -1 to handle the special cases. As with the previous example, a user can't key these values because the REL statement prevents it.

Generic Names

To allow a user to enter a generic name on a command prompt, you would specify the PARM statement as TYPE(*GENERIC). When the variable appears in your program, it could be a name or a generic name.

The TAA tool CHKGENERC (Check Generic) can help you handle generic names returned to the CPP. The command will return a Y or N value to indicate whether the name is a generic value (i.e., the name has an * on the end). You would specify in the CPP

```
DCL        &GENERC *CHAR LEN(1)
.
.
.
CHKGENERC  VAR(&NAME) GENERC(&GENERC)
IF         (&GENERC *EQ 'Y') DO /* Generic */
.
.
.
ENDDO      /* Generic */
```

Two additional return variables are optional with the CHKGENERC command:

- RTNVAR — The name with the * removed. You can use this for a function like RPG's SETLL.
- RTNLEN — The length of the name field without the *. You can use this if you have to compare against records or objects that you are reading.

For example, you could have an application that is similar to many of the system displays that allow a generic name. If a user enters a non-generic name, the application would display only a single record from the database. If the user enters a generic name, the application would display all the database records that match.

To do this, use CHKGENERC as follows:

```
CHKGENERC  VAR(&INPUT) GENERC(&GENERC)  +
             RTNVAR(&INPUT2) RTNLEN(&LEN)
```

Pass these variables to an RPG program that does the following:

- if a non-generic name was specified, the program accesses a single record from the database
- if a generic name was specified, the program
  - uses SETLL, using the value for INPUT2
  - reads a record
  - uses the SUBST operation to substring out the length of the record key for the number of bytes of the &LEN parameter
- compares the result field to the value from the &INPUT2 parameter

When you use the CHKGENERC command, it is easier to code your high-level language program.

Return Variables

If you are writing a RTV command, you need to specify RTNVAL(*YES) for the parameter(s) to be returned. For example,

```
PARM  KWD(TEXT) TYPE(*CHAR) LEN(50) RTNVAL(*YES)  +
        PROMPT('Text description      (50)')
```

The RTNVAL function says that the parameter is not just an input value to the command, but also an output value. The most typical use would be that any input value is ignored and the CPP just returns a value. Note that you can help the user by entering how the DCL statement should be coded at the right end of the PROMPT in parentheses. This is the convention used by most system and TAA commands.

Multiple parameters can be returned. If you have optional return variables, you must monitor for escape message MCH3601 (Pointer error) after each value is placed in the return parameter name (see Chapter 8, "Retrieve Commands").

When you use RTNVAL(*YES), you are restricting the use of the command to a CL program. You must create the command with ALLOW((*IPGM)(*BPGM)).

Lists

If you want to allow a user to enter a parameter such as

```
OBJ(ABC DEF GHI ...)
```

the command definition source is easy to write. Simply specify the maximum number of values you want to allow. For example:

```
PARM  KWD(OBJ) TYPE(*NAME) LEN(10) MIN(1) MAX(40)  +
        PROMPT('Output queue')
```

More complex is the code required for the CPP. A list always begins with a 2-byte binary field (which contains the number of entries made) followed by the list entries specified. For the above example, you would have to declare the CL variable as LEN(402) to handle a maximum of 40 entries of 10 bytes each plus the 2-byte variable.

If the user of the command does not make 40 entries, the remainder of the variable passed to your CL program will be filled with garbage. To handle the CL variable correctly, the program must process the number of entries indicated by the 2-byte binary value.

Even more complex is when you want to allow a user to enter a parameter with a list of lists:

```
OBJ((ABC *FILE)(DEF *DTAARA)(GHI *PGM) ...)
```

To accomplish this, you have to use the ELEM command definition statement to describe the sublist (in this case one ELEM for object and one for object type). When the variable is passed to your CL program, you get 2 bytes for the number of lists entered and then each list has 2 bytes plus the lengths of the ELEM statements. In addition, the list is in inverted order so the last one specified is the first one in the list.

If you want a simple solution for both simple lists and a list of lists, use the EXTLST (Extract List) TAA tool in the QUSRTOOL library. The member EXTLST in file QATTINFO has two sets of skeleton code that can be copied into your CL program source.

The first set is for a simple list (i.e., for lists that do not require coding the ELEM statement). The code would look like this (assume you have a 10-character name in your list and a maximum of 50 entries):

```
         PGM     PARM(&LIST)
         DCL     &LIST *CHAR LEN(502)
         DCL     &CURNBR *DEC LEN(5 0)
         DCL     &ELEMENT *CHAR LEN(100)
LOOP:    EXTLST  LIST(&LIST) ELMLEN(10)          +
                   ELEMENT(&ELEMENT) CURNBR(&CURNBR)
         IF      (&CURNBR *GT 0) DO /* Process element */
         CHGVAR  &xxxx %SST(&ELEMENT 1 10)
         .
         .  Your processing of variable &xxxx
         .
         GOTO    LOOP
         ENDDO   /* Process element */
```

The EXTLST command returns variable &CURNBR, which tells you which element in the list you are processing. The purpose of the parameter is to act as both input and output for EXTLST. You start with a value of 0. EXTLST adds 1 to this value and accesses the first element. The command then returns the number of the element that it processed.

Normally, you won't care which element in the list is being processed; but you want to know when there are no more elements to process. When all elements in a list have been processed, variable &CURNBR will contain the value -1. If you want to process the list again, set variable &CURNBR to 0 and execute another loop.

The second set of code in EXTLST handles the more complex list of lists. Both versions of EXTLST require that a CL variable, &ELEMENT, be defined as 100 bytes, an arbitrary length chosen to meet the command processing function's need for a specific length. As long as the length of your element is 100 bytes or fewer (e.g., the length of your variable or the sum of the ELEM lengths), the EXTLST command will work properly. To see an example of command EXTLST's use, look at the MOVMNYOBJ (Move Many Objects) TAA tool in the QUSRTOOL library. See member TAAOBJBC in file QATTCL.

Technical Tip

The EXTLST TAA tool can greatly simplify the coding required to process user-written commands that support parameters that accept lists or lists of lists as values.

Constants in a Command

Multiple commands can use the same CPP. In this case, you want to pass a parameter to the CPP that identifies the command used. The user does not need to see this parameter.

You can accomplish this by using the CONSTANT parameter on the PARM statement. You must define a unique value for CONSTANT so you can determine which command invoked the CPP. The parameter statement might look like the following (assuming ABCD is the unique value for CONSTANT):

```
PARM  KWD(TYPE) TYPE(*CHAR) LEN(4) CONSTANT(ABCD)
```

Although the user would not see the TYPE keyword when (s)he prompts for the command, the value ABCD would be passed to the CPP just as if (s)he had entered it.

In the CPP you would specify

```
DCL  &TYPE *CHAR LEN(4)
.
.
.
IF   (&TYPE *EQ 'ABCD') DO /* ABCD type */
.
.
.
ENDDO /* ABCD type */
```

QUSRTOOL Examples

You might see a system command that has a parameter similar to one you would like to use in a command you are writing. Unfortunately, the system does not ship the source for its commands so you can't see how the command is coded. To find live examples that you can draw from, however, you need look no further than the QUSRTOOL library.

Source code for the TAA commands are stored in library QUSRTOOL. Once you have found a TAA command that provides an example of what you want to do, execute a DSPCMD command to determine the source member name used for the command definition source. Then execute the DSPTAAMBR command to look at the command definition source or to copy what you want into your own source.

You also might want to see how a parameter for a TAA command was coded in the CPP. For example, assume that you want to see how the CPYJOBLOG TAA tool handles the JOB parameter (a three-part qualified name). You would enter DSPCMD CMD(CPYJOBLOG) to learn the name of the command definition source member (TAASPLA) and the name of the CPP (TAASPLAC — if the CPP ends with a C, a CLP program was probably used as the source). To see the command definition source, specify

```
DSPTAAMBR  MBR(TAASPLA) SRCFILE(*CMD)
```

To see the CPP source, specify

```
DSPTAAMBR  MBR(TAASPLAC) SRCFILE(*CLP)
```

The QUSRTOOL library contains several examples of functions you might like to use in your own commands. For example,

- Qualified job name. See the CPYJOBLOG command.
- Output (* or *PRINT). See the DSPMONGROW command.
- Converting source types (e.g., *CLP) to standard file names. See the PRTSRCF command.

- Job description name with a default of *USRPRF. See the CLNSYS command.
- Prompt override program. See the BKP command.

CHAPTER 15

File Processing

When it comes to file processing, CL is a weak language. You can perform some file processing functions in CL, but mostly you have to live with some severe restrictions. The following are the major restrictions, some of which I discuss in more detail in subsequent sections of this chapter:

- You can use only one file (and, therefore, only one DCLF statement) per CL program. Although there is no architectural reason for CL's inability to process more than one file, system support has not been provided. I know of no way around this restriction and because of it, you sometimes need multiple CL programs to accomplish a single purpose.
- CL cannot add, update, or delete records in database files. However, TAA tool WRTSRC, described later in this chapter, will let you update source members. Another TAA tool, WRTDBF, will let you add records to any database file. But WRTDBF is a crude function and should be used only for very trivial, specific functions. To see how WRTDBF might be used, see Chapter 17, "Outfiles."
- CL can read a keyed file only in key order. CL does not support the capability to access a keyed file in arrival sequence. But you can work around this limitation by creating a logical file that does not specify any key fields and then specifying the logical file on the DCLF statement.
- CL provides minimal support for reading a database file beginning at a random position (either by relative record number or by key value). For more information, see the section "Random Processing."
- When a CL program reading a file reaches "end of file," the system closes the file. The CL program cannot re-open the file. Many programmers have tried all sorts of tricks to avoid this limitation. I know of no direct method that works, but for a crude workaround see the discussion of WRTDBF in Chapter 17. I discuss this topic in more detail in the section "Reading a Database File."
- You cannot access the file feedback area, which contains information such as the relative record number of the record just read.

- CL supports display files, but not subfiles (although it does support a message subfile). Chapter 16, "Display Files and Menus," covers this topic in more detail.
- A CL program cannot print data, but techniques exist to help minimize this limitation (see the section "Passing Print Lines to an RPG Program").

The DCLF Statement

CL supports only one DCLF statement per program. The file (you can name either a database file or a display file) must exist when the program is created. For database files, the same program might create the database file and then read the file. If so, a model file must exist when you create the program. In the program, you would use an override command to specify the real file the program will use. You will find examples of this technique in the section "Reading a Spooled File" in this chapter and in Chapter 17, "Outfiles."

A database file declared in a CL program can be an externally described file or a program-described file. When you create a program-described database file using the RCDLEN parameter on the CRTPF command, the system defines a single field for the entire length of the record and gives the field the same name as the file. For example, if you specify

```
CRTPF  FILE(TEMP132) RCDLEN(132)
```

the file created will have a single field named TEMP132. If you declare file TEMP132 (using a DCLF command) in a CL program, the name of the variable field you process would be &TEMP132. Typically, you would use a substring function to retrieve the information you need from variable &TEMP132.

Using a DCLF Statement Without Processing a File

Sometimes in a CL program you may need to declare many of the same variables that exist in a database file, but you may not need to actually process the database file itself. Assuming you do not need a second DCLF statement in your program, you can use one DCLF statement to name the file and automatically declare all the variables in the file. If you declare a file in the CL compiler, the compiler does not force you to have a processing statement for the file (unlike RPG). You can also create a dummy physical file with fields you want to declare in several CL programs and then use the DCLF statement in each of the programs.

Reading a Database File

CL always reads a file in sequence (i.e., keyed files in keyed order, unkeyed files in arrival order). CL has no way to read a keyed file in arrival order. One way to work around this limitation is to create a logical file with no key fields and then process the logical file.

To read a file, you would use a DCLF statement to declare the file and a RCVF statement to process the file. The code required would look like the following:

```
             DCLF       FILE(xxx)
               .
               .
               .
READ:        RCVF       /* Read a record */
             MONMSG     MSGID(CPF0864) EXEC(GOTO EOF)
               .
               .           /* Your processing */
               .
             GOTO       READ /* Loop back */
EOF:                    /* All records have been read */
```

The first RCVF command executed opens the file. Note that the open is not done by the DCLF statement (the DCLF command is used only at compile time). Since the first RCVF command opens the file, you can specify an override command in the same program that reads the file (just specify the override command before the program executes the first RCVF command). When the program reaches "end of file," the system sends escape message CPF0864, which you normally would monitor for. Once "end of file" is found, the system closes the file. After the file is closed, the program can clear the member and delete the file, but it cannot re-open the file and read it again. The program can add records to the file (by using an outfile function) and it can delete the file and re-create it, but the program still wouldn't be able to read the file again.

Let me explain why this situation occurs, so you can avoid trying to work around the problem. When you specify a RCVF command, the system first determines whether or not the "end-of-file" bit has been set. If it has been set, the system sends escape message CPF0864. If the "end-of-file" bit is not set, the system tries to read a record in the file. Then, when "end of file" is found, the system sets the "end-of-file" bit and sends escape message CPF0864. Nothing in the IBM code resets the end of file bit. You must end the program and call it again to have it reset.

Consequently, there is no way to fool the system into reprocessing the same file. If you attempt to read the file again in the same program, the file acts as if it has no records (even though records exist) and the system sends escape message CPF0864.

Technical Tip

Once a CL program reaches "end of file" when using the RCVF command, the program cannot read the file again. No attempt to fool the system into reprocessing the file will work.

READING A SPOOLED FILE

Sometimes you might need to process information contained in a spooled file. CL cannot read a spooled file directly, but you can convert the spooled file to a database file (using the system CPYSPLF command) and then have the CL program read that database file.

To perform this function, normally you would convert the spooled file to a database file you have created in library QTEMP. Since the file you really want to read in CL won't exist when you create the program, you must create a model file ahead of time that the program will use when compiling. To create the model file, you would specify something like the following:

```
CRTPF  FILE(TEMP136) RCDLEN(136)
```

By specifying a record length of 136, the file will accommodate a 132-byte print line plus the optional control characters supported by the CPYSPLF command (in the following example, no control characters were used).

Assume that you wanted to read spooled file QPDSPSTS created by the WRKSYSSTS (Work with System Status) command. You could specify

```
DCLF        FILE(TEMP136)
  .
  .
  .
DLTF        FILE(QTEMP/SPLF)
MONMSG      MSGID(CPF2105) /* Ignore not found */
CRTPF       FILE(QTEMP/SPLF) RCDLEN(136)
OVRPRTF     FILE(QPDSPSTS) HOLD(*YES)
WRKSYSSTS   OUTPUT(*PRINT)
CPYSPLF     FILE(QPDSPSTS) TOFILE(QTEMP/SPLF) +
              SPLNBR(*LAST)
DLTSPLF     FILE(QPDSPSTS) SPLNBR(*LAST)
OVRDBF      FILE(TEMP136) TOFILE(QTEMP/SPLF)  +
              SECURE(*YES)
```

```
READ:        RCVF        /* Read a record */
             MONMSG      MSGID(CPF0864) EXEC(GOTO EOF)
                         /* Substring to get the data */
             CHGVAR      &VAR1 %SST(&TEMP136 1 10)
                         /* Your processing */
             GOTO        READ
EOF:                     /* All records have been read */
```

Although the CPYSPLF command lets you capture the control characters for printer spacing and skipping, the default was used in the code shown so that no control characters exist in the database record and the data starts in position 1.

Technical Tip

Before you try to copy one of the system spooled files to a database file so you can access some information, see if there is a TAA tool that can do the function for you. There are several RTV and CVT TAA tools that either use APIs or read the spooled file for you. For example, the CVTSYSSTS (Convert System Status) command lets you create an externally described database file for the WRKSYSSTS information.

Random Processing

Unlike an RPG program, CL cannot override a keyed file or a sequential file and process it in arrival sequence. But the OVRDBF command does support the POSITION parameter so you can specify that processing start at a point other than the beginning of a file. For example, if you wanted to begin processing a non-keyed file at relative record number 100, you would code

```
OVRDBF    FILE(xxx) POSITION(*RRN 100)
```

If you wanted to begin processing a keyed file at a specific key (i.e., if you wanted to "set lower limit"), you could do it, but the CL support is very crude. Assume that you want to process FILEA, which has a record format name of FMTA and a single key field, and you want to start processing at the key greater than the value MX. You would specify the OVRDBF command as

```
OVRDBF     FILE(FILEA) POSITION(*KEYA 1 FMTA MX)
```

In this example, we used the value *KEYA, which specifies "key after," but there are several other choices. The "1" indicates that only the first key to the file is being supplied. Then you specify the record format name

(FMTA) and the record key (MX) at which you want processing to start.

If you deal with multiple key fields, and some of them are packed, the POSITION statement can be very difficult to code correctly. In these more complex situations, TAA tool STRKEY can help. The STRKEY command provides a prompt that lets you enter the starting key value for a file. You can read about how to use the STRKEY command in the QUSRTOOL library.

Technical Tip

If you want to position randomly to a keyed file and then read it in CL, take a look at TAA tool STRKEY. It can be very helpful if you have a complex key.

WRTSRC TAA Tool

The WRTSRC TAA tool lets you add to or update source statements in a source member. A good example of when you might use WRTSRC is when you have sort specifications that will be used by the FMTDTA command to select records. Assume you want to select on the current date, but the source specifications don't allow you to request a current date and you can't pass a variable into the sort specifications. What you can do is use the WRTSRC tool to change an existing statement before you execute the FMTDTA command.

Assume you want to sort the output of the DSPOBJD outfile on the object name field (ODOBNM) and select those objects that were created on the current date (the create date field name in the DSPOBJD outfile is ODCDAT). The ODCDAT field is defined as 6 bytes and is always in the format MMDDYY.

If you are not familiar with the sort specifications required by FMTDTA, you can read more about them in the IBM manual, *Sort User's Guide and Reference*, (SC09-1363). The sort specifications use program-described data, so you must know the from-to positions of the fields you want to work with. Assume the specifications are entered into the member SORT1 in the source file QTXTSRC.

```
...+... 1 ...+... 2 ...+... 2 ...+... 4 ...+...
    HFILE     10A        X
    I C 112 117EQC123456             ODCDAT
    FNC  24  33                      ODOBNM
    FDC
```

The sort specifications shown above are ready to be used by the FMTDTA command, except that we need to use the current date instead of the dummy value "123456." You can see that the dummy value is in positions

20-25, so those are the positions we need to modify.

The CL code you need to determine the current date, modify the sort specs, and execute the FMTDTA command would look like the following:

```
DCL         &DATE *CHAR LEN(6)
  .
  .
  .
RTVSYSVAL   SYSVAL(QDATE) RTNVAR(&DATE)
WRTSRC      SRCFILE(QTXTSRC) MBR(SORT1) RELRCD(2)   +
              ACTION(*UPD) POS1(2Ø) TXT1(&DATE)
WRTSRC      SRCFILE(QTXTSRC) MBR(SORT1) ACTION(*END)
FMTDTA      INFILE((DSPOBJDP)) OUTFILE(DSPOBJDP2)   +
              SRCFILE(QTXTSRC) SRCMBR(SORT1)
```

This example assumes that the format of your system date is *MDY. If it is not, then you will also need to use the CVTDAT command to convert the &DATE variable to *MDY, before you place the date into the source file.

The first WRTSRC command updates the second source record beginning at position 20 with the value of the current date, which was retrieved by the RTVSYSVAL command. WRTSRC assumes you are going to do more than one update, so it keeps the source member open. When you are done, you need to close the member, which is what the second WRTSRC command does.

The sort specs have now been changed and the FMTDTA command will sort the file using your selection criteria. Although FMTDTA works, I prefer to use OPNQRYF (see Chapter 20, "OPNQRYF").

Technical Tip

The WRTSRC TAA tool can be helpful when you are trying to make slight modifications to existing source or when you are adding a source statement from CL.

PRINTING FROM CL

Although you cannot print from a CL program, you can use a couple of techniques to work around this limitation:

- If I have mostly high-level language (HLL) work to do, I'll use an RPG program and call a CL program when I need a CL function. This technique does have performance implications, which I discuss in Chapter 22, "Program Stack."

- If I have mostly CL work to do, I'll use a CL program for processing and call an RPG program for printing. The following section offers an example of this technique.
- If I have very simple printing needs, I will use the TAA tool PRINT, which does not require an RPG program. You will find an example of using the PRINT command in the section "PRINT TAA Tool."

Passing Print Lines to an RPG Program

I use this technique when I want to perform mostly CL functions but I need some information printed. When I need to print I'll pass print lines or information to an RPG program.

Here is the CL program structure:

```
             DCL        &REQST *CHAR LEN(8)
             DCL        &PRTLIN *CHAR LEN(132)
              .
              .
              .
LOOP:                   /* Detail printing loop */
             CHGVAR     &REQST 'DETAIL'
             CHGVAR     &PRTLIN 'xxx'
             CALL       PGM(TRYPRTRPG) PARM(&REQST &PRTLIN)
             GOTO       LOOP
FINAL:                  /* Print final lines and end RPG */
             CHGVAR     &REQST 'FINAL'
             CALL       PGM(TRYPRTRPG) PARM(&REQST &PRTLIN)
```

The accompanying RPG program, TRYPRTRPG, looks like this:

```
...+... 1 ...+... 2 ...+... 3 ...+... 4 ...+... 5 ...+... 6
    FQPRINT  O   F      132       OF      PRINTER
    .
    .
    .
    C           *ENTRY    PLIST
    C                     PARM           REQST   8
    C                     PARM           PRTLIN132
    C* Print heading
    C           FSTTIM    IFEQ ' '
    C                     EXCPTHDG
    C                     MOVE 'X'       FSTTIM  1
    C                     ENDIF
    C* DETAIL Request
```

```
C           REQST     IFEQ 'DETAIL  '
C                     EXCPTDETAIL
C   OF                EXCPTHDG
C                     GOTO RETURN
C                     ENDIF
C* Final print line
C           REQST     IFEQ 'FINAL   '
C                     EXCPTFINAL
C                     SETON                     LR
C                     GOTO RETURN
C                     ENDIF
C* If code gets to here its an error (bad request)
C                     SETON                     H1
C* Return point
C           RETURN    TAG
C                     RETRN
OQPRINT  E  206           HDG
O                                 +  8 'Heading info'
O        E  1             DETAIL
O                         PRTLIN   132
O        E 11             FINAL
O                                 +  5 'The end'
```

In this example, the CL program formats the print lines. More realistically, I would probably pass a parameter list for what I want to print and then let the RPG program format the print lines. If you want to format a print line in CL, see the description of the BLDPRTLIN TAA tool later in this chapter.

PRINT TAA Tool

In many cases, what you want to print may be fairly simple and you may not want to code another RPG program just for this function. The PRINT TAA tool is designed for just such a situation.

Here's an example of how to use the PRINT TAA tool:

```
             /* Print heading */
PRINT        ACTION(*OPN) TITLE('Library list') COLHD1('Library  +
               Text description') SPLFNAME(xxx)
  .
  .          /* Your processing loop */
  .
             /* Print detail line */
PRINT        LINE(&LIB *CAT '    ' *CAT &TEXT)
  .
  .
  .
             /* Close print file */
PRINT        ACTION(*CLO)
```

The PRINT command's TITLE parameter lets you describe a title for the report. The ACTION parameter specifies one of the following:

*OPN = Open the printer file
*PRT = Print a line
*PAG = Skip to a new page
*CLO = Close the printer file

You also can specify options for spacing and whether or not to count the *PRT lines (to provide a total of lines printed).

Note that the program formats the print line by inserting blanks between the fields. Formatting the print line in this way can be difficult if the print line has many fields. You could use a substring function instead, but a better approach is to use the BLDPRTLIN TAA tool.

The BLDPRTLIN TAA Tool

The BLDPRTLIN (Build Print Line) TAA tool is designed to work in conjunction with the PRINT TAA tool, but it can be used independently. BLDPRTLIN lets you use a command to format a print line. Using parameters, you describe how the print line should be formatted. You also define a variable for the LINE parameter, which will contain the formatted print line.

All the numeric fields passed to BLDPRTLIN must be declared with 0 decimals. You can specify the number of decimal positions to be shown on BLDPRTLIN. You specify a position for the character fields and then define whether you want to align left or right. Numeric fields are right-aligned to the position you specify.

When you prompt for BLDPRTLIN, the command prompt looks like this:

```
                        Build Print Line (BLDPRTLIN)

   Type choices, press Enter.

   LINE parm to return (132)  . . .   ___________    Character value
   Format for char fields:          _
     Char var or literal(up to 50)    _____________________________

     Print position . . . . . . . .   ____           1-132
     Align left or right (L R)  . .   L              Character value
                  + for more values _
   Format for dec fields:           _
     Dec variable or literal  . . .   ___________
     Units print position . . . . .   ____           2-131
     Number of decimals . . . . . .   0              0-9
     Edit code  . . . . . . . . . .   J              J, K, L, M, W, Y, Z
                  + for more values _
```

The first parameter is the return variable name. It must be declared as *CHAR LEN(132). The next two parameters, one for character fields and one for decimal fields, accept a list of values so you can have multiple fields of each type. Here's an example of what the CL code might look like when you use the BLDPRTLIN command:

```
  .          /* The decimal fields must be declared */
  .          /*        with 0 decimals              */
             /* Build and print heading */
BLDPRTLIN    LINE(&LINE) CHARFLDS(('Number' 001)              +
               ('Customer name' 010) ('Owed' 037 R)           +
               ('Sales' 051 R) ('Last order' 065 R))
PRINT        ACTION(*OPN) TITLE('Customer report')            +
               COLHD1(&LINE) SPLFNAME(CUSTOMERS)
  .
  .          /* Detail print loop */
  .
             /* Build and print detail line */
BLDPRTLIN    LINE(&LINE) CHARFLDS((&NUMBER 001) (&NAME 010))  +
               DECFLDS((&OWED 037 2) (&SALES 051 2)           +
               (&DATE 065 0 Y))
PRINT        LINE(&LINE)
             /* Add up totals */
CHGVAR       &OWEDT (&OWEDT + &OWED)
CHGVAR       &SALEST (&SALEST + &SALES)
```

```
   .
   .
   .
            /* Build and print total line */
BLDPRTLIN   LINE(&LINE) DECFLDS((&OWEDT Ø37 2) (&SALEST Ø51 2))
PRINT       LINE(&LINE) SPCBFR(1) COUNT(*NO)
            /* Close print file */
PRINT       ACTION(*CLO)
```

The combination of the BLDPRTLIN and PRINT commands lets you print from a CL program. This technique is not as efficient as using an RPG program; but if you don't have many print lines, it works adequately.

Exercise A Reading a Database File

In this exercise you will use the RCVF command to read a database file and to look for certain records. The example you will step through sends a message for each *JOBQ object type found in library QGPL.

1. Use the DSPOBJD command to create a database file named DSPOBJ2:

```
DSPOBJD    OBJ(QGPL/*ALL) OBJTYPE(*ALL)  +
             OUTPUT(*OUTFILE)            +
             OUTFILE(xxx/DSPOBJ2)
```

2. Use PDM to create a CLP source member named TRYRCVF.
3. Enter the following:

```
           PGM
           DCLF       FILE(DSPOBJ2)
LOOP:      RCVF
           MONMSG     MSGID(CPF0864) EXEC(GOTO EOF)
           IF         (&ODOBTP *EQ '*JOBQ') DO
           SNDPGMMSG  MSG(&ODOBNM *BCAT &ODOBTP)
           ENDDO
           GOTO       LOOP
EOF:       ENDPGM
```

4. Create the program.
5. Call the program:

```
CALL  TRYRCVF
```

   You should see a message for each *JOBQ object type found.

6. The next series of steps will demonstrate how you can position to a specific relative record number before reading from a file. To do this exercise, you will need to determine which relative record number to use. Use the DSPPFM command to look at file DSPOBJ2:

```
DSPPFM  FILE(DSPOBJ2)
```

7. Roll through the display file until you come to the *JOBQ records. Count about half way through the *JOBQ records to a specific record

Exercise A continued

Exercise A continued

and then estimate which relative record number it is (the record number of the first record on the page appears at the top of the display). On my system, record 10 in the file is about half way through the *JOBQ objects. We'll use this number to override the file and start reading at this position.

8. Use PDM to access the TRYRCVF source and enter the following OVRDBF command ahead of the RCVF statement (the first RCVF executed opens the file, so we want the override done before then).

```
OVRDBF  FILE(DSPOBJ2) POSITION(*RRN 10)
```

9. Re-create the program.

10. Call the program:

```
CALL  TRYRCVF
```

Using the POSITION parameter lets your program start reading from either a relative record number or a keyed position. You don't have to start reading at relative record number 1. In this case, because we started reading the file at relative record number 10, you should see fewer messages than you did earlier.

Exercise B Using the WRTSRC TAA Tool

In this exercise you will use the WRTSRC TAA tool to modify some sort specifications. First, you will use the SORTDB TAA tool to create the sort specifications. Both TAA tools must exist on your system; if they do not, see Appendix B.

1. The SORTDB command can be used to generate sort specifications, or it can be used both to generate the specifications and to execute the FMTDTA command. In this exercise we will just generate the sort specifications. Let's assume that we want a report in size order for a particular object type. For this exercise, you would sort on field ODOBSZ (the object size of file DSPOBJ2, created in Exercise A), and you would select on field ODOBTP (the variable passed into the program for the

Exercise B continued

Exercise B continued

object type). In this exercise, we will use the commands interactively, not in a CL program.

2. Enter the SORTDB command as follows (generate the sort specifications so that they will select the *PGM object types):

```
SORTDB  FILE(DSPOBJ2) SORTFLD(ODOBSZ) SEL1(ODOBTP *EQ *PGM)  +
          EXECSORT(*NO) OUTSRCF(xxx) OUTSRCMBR(TRYSORT)
```

3. Look at the sort specifications that were generated:

```
STRSEU  SRCFILE(xxx) SRCMBR(TRYSORT)
```

You should see that the sort specifications are ready to be used by the FMTDTA command. If we want to change the object type we are going to select on, the statement we want to modify is the second record in the file beginning at position 20.

4. Now let's assume that a value has been passed to the program to select *JOBD object types instead of *PGM object types. We will use the WRTSRC TAA tool to modify the sort specifications and then execute the WRTSRC command interactively instead of in a CL program:

```
WRTSRC  SRCFILE(xxx) MBR(TRYSORT) RELRCD(2) +
          ACTION(*UPD) POS1(20) TXT1(*JOBD)
```

5. The WRTSRC command assumes that you have more than one record to update so we need to execute the command again and tell it to end (i.e., close the file).

```
WRTSRC  SRCFILE(xxx) MBR(TRYSORT) ACTION(*END)
```

6. Now look again at the sort specifications:

```
STRSEU  SRCFILE(xxx) SRCMBR(TRYSORT)
```

You should see that we have modified the object type so it is now *JOBD. If this code was in a CL program, you would be ready to execute the FMTDTA command. Use of the FMTDAT command is described in Chapter 19, "Sequencing and Selection Techniques."

CHAPTER 16

Display Files and Menus

You can use CL to process simple display files, but you really need a high-level language (HLL) program to process complex display files. For example, you cannot use CL to process a display file that

- uses subfiles (but you can use message subfiles)
- needs access to the feedback area

For most interactive applications, you would normally use a HLL program and a display file. If you need to solicit information from an end user, you would use a format in a display file. If you need to solicit information from a system operator or programmer, you may or may not use a display file (see Chapter 13, "Communicating with a Workstation Operator").

When it comes to using CL to process display files, the most typical use is for menus, small front-end programs for user processes, or simple prompts. In this chapter, I will focus on using CL to create and display menus.

MENUS

The system supports several ways to create a menu. For example, the system supports a special object type called a menu object (*MNU), which is created by using the CRTMNU (Create Menu) command, but you don't have to use this method. You can write a display file and program to provide your own solution.

If you write your own solution (i.e., you don't use a *MNU object), you can use DDS or SDA to create a display file. (SDA also has an option that allows you to create a *MNU object.) In DDS, you can use windows support and keywords such as RTNCSRLOC (Return Cursor Location) to process a display file.

If you choose to use the CRTMNU command to create a menu object, to be invoked by the GO command, you must specify the TYPE parameter, for which there are three options:

1. *DSPF — This option indicates that you have already created a display file for the menu and that you also have created a message file that contains the commands you want to execute as menu options. In this case, you don't write a program to create the menu. When

the GO command is issued, an IBM program is used to display your menu. SDA uses this same function when it creates a menu. The advantage of this approach is that it is easy to do. The disadvantages are that you can execute only one command per menu option (it could be a CALL command) and that an error-handling routine exists but you have no control over it (the routine provides a standard solution you may not like in all situations).

2. *PGM — This option means you have written a program that will control the display of your menu; the GO command will call the program you have written. Typically, your program would display a menu that would be a separate object (e.g., a display file). The advantages of this approach are that you allow the use of the GO command for consistency in displaying menus and that you have more control over what happens when the menu is displayed (e.g., you can have multiple commands issued for a menu option or you can provide your own unique error-handling routine).

3. *UIM — This option indicates that you have used the UIM tag language to create the menu. There are advantages to using UIM (e.g., more consistency and built-in functions) but you must learn a different language and you don't have as much flexibility as you have when using a CL program and DDS.

For simple menus, using SDA is a good approach. If you want more control (e.g., better control of function, messages, and error handling), it is easy to write your own CL program. Which method you choose depends on personal preference and whether or not you have an installation standard. You can read more about menus in IBM's *Guide to Programming Displays* (SC41-0011).

Simple Menus

Most programmers know how to code a simple menu in CL. The typical CL code would look like this:

```
              DCLF        FILE(MENU1)
PROMPT:       SNDRCVF     RCDFMT(PROMPT)
F3:           IF          (&IN99 *EQ '1') DO /* F3 */
              RETURN
              ENDDO       /* F3 */
SELECT1:      IF          (&SELECT *EQ '1') DO /* Option 1 */
               .
              ENDDO       /* Option 1 */
SELECT2:      IF          (&SELECT *EQ '2') DO /* Option 2 */
               .
              ENDDO       /* Option 2 */
                          /* All options have been handled */
              GOTO        PROMPT
```

Let's review what is happening:

- The DCLF command accesses the display file, which must exist when you create the program, and generates DCL statements for the input and output fields defined in the file. You don't have to declare any variables already defined in the display file.
- The SNDRCVF command is the equivalent of the RPG EXFMT operation. It does a "put/get," which means it writes ("puts") the record format to the display and waits for ("gets") a response (i.e., the user pressing the Enter key, a Function key, the Print key). It is also possible to use the SNDF and RCVF commands to separate the "put" and the "get" functions. Using the two commands can be helpful if some other processing needs to occur, such as opening files, and yet you want to display the menu quickly.
- In DDS you must assign indicators for the valid command keys, options, and so on. Indicators are assigned names using the format &INxx in the CL program. In this example, indicator 99 is assigned to the F3 command key to end the menu. You can debug the values of these variables as well.
- The value of the &SELECT field, returned from the display file, is examined to determine which option the user chose.

A good technique is to send messages to the display for selections that don't invoke another display (e.g., the SBMJOB command). The simplest way to do this is to define an output field at the bottom of the display and clear the field immediately after the SNDRCVF statement. Your code might look like this:

```
PROMPT:     SNDRCVF     RCDFMT(PROMPT)
            CHGVAR      &MSG ' '
             .
             .
             .
            IF          (&SELECT *EQ '2') DO /* Option 2 */
            SBMJOB      JOB(PAYUPD) ...
            CHGVAR      &MSG ('The PAYUPD job was submitted +
                          to do the payroll update')
            ENDDO       /* Option 2 */
             .
             .
             .
            GOTO        PROMPT
```

When the display appears after the SBMJOB option has been chosen, the message text appears. The variable for the message text is cleared as soon as the next response is received. To make the message more readable, you might fit the &MSG variable over two lines (e.g., a length of 155).

Using the GO Command To Access a CL Program

The GO command only operates against a *MENU object. You can create a *MENU object with the CRTMNU command by specifying TYPE(*PGM) and then name your program in the PGM parameter. The CL program named on the PGM parameter must be a program that will accept the specific parameter list the menu object is looking for, as shown in the following code:

```
PGM         PARM(&MENU &MENUL &ACTION)
DCL         &MENU *CHAR LEN(10)
DCL         &MENUL *CHAR LEN(10)
DCL         &ACTION *CHAR LEN(2)
 .
 .
 .
CHGVAR      &ACTION X'FFFE' /* Set to -2 */
 .
 .
 .
SNDRCVF
```

You don't need to set the &MENU and &MENUL parameters to a particular value, but they must exist. The &ACTION value is a binary return code that tells the menu processing function what to do when your CL program does a return. In this case, we are requesting that the menu itself do a return by setting the &ACTION variable to a binary -2 (X'FFFE').

Once your CL program looks like that shown above, you can specify the program name in the CRTMNU command and create the *MENU object:

```
CRTMNU MENU(ABC) TYPE(*PGM) PGM(yyyy)
```

You can display the menu with the following command:

```
GO  MENU(ABC)
```

You can give the menu the same name as the program or you can use a different name. The intent of the system-supplied GO command is to display a menu, but you don't have to use the command for that purpose. You could name a CL program that performs any function you want. For consistency, you should probably restrict your use to menu-type functions.

Using the DUPSTDSRC TAA Tool To Create Menus

In the previous sections, I've talked about how to code a menu in CL and how to create a menu object. If you like this approach, the skeleton code you need is waiting for you in the QUSRTOOL library as part of the DUPSTDSRC TAA tool.

To use DUPSTDSRC to create a menu, you simply specify the special source types *MNUC and *MNUD. For example, assume that you want to create a menu using CLP program MENU1 and display file MENU1D. You would enter the following commands:

```
DUPSTDSRC    MBR(MENU1D) SRCTYP(*MNUD)   +
               TEXT('...') SRCFILE(xxx)
DUPSTDSRC    MBR(MENU1) SRCTYP(*MNUC)   +
               TEXT('...') SRCFILE(xxx)
```

You can modify the DDS source copied by DUPSTDSRC for source type *MNUD to meet your needs. Simply key over or delete the values you see in the duplicated source.

The CLP source copied for source type *MNUC contains both the code to drive the menu and the code shown earlier that allows you to use the GO command (you must first create a menu object). You only need to fill in the commands you want to execute from the menu. After each command selection, you need a GOTO command to determine what should happen next. The code contains standard label names that you can branch to for the following functions:

- Blank the selection field (normal action — this is the default as coded)
- Place a message on the display and blank the selection field (e.g., for a SBMJOB command)
- Place a message on the display and leave the selection field as it was (e.g., for a situation where an error occurs)
- Execute a DSPJOBLOG command

After you create the display file and the program, you can create a menu object for use with the GO command as described in the previous section.

Technical Tip

The DUPSTDSRC entries for *MNUC and *MNUD make it easy to get the right code in place for a menu. The code is set up for you to quickly create a menu object for use with the GO command.

Command Line Processing

The system supports an API (QUSCMDLN) that lets you place a window containing a command line on any display. For example, to support a Function key on a display that lets a user request a command line, you would code the following:

```
IF          (&IN97 *EQ '1') DO /* Cmd line request */
CALL        QUSCMDLN /* API for command line */
ENDDO       /* Cmd line request */
```

When the user presses the appropriate Function key, a window appears on the display and the user can enter any valid command. Messages sent by the command entered by the user would appear in a one-line message subfile below the command line.

Note that the API can only be called. The API cannot be used to cause a command line to appear permanently on a display. In other words, you can't use the API to make your displays look like IBM menus. But if you do want to emulate IBM menus and their permanent command line, the QUSRTOOL TAA tool CMDLINE will provide the capability. (You also can cause a command line to appear on a display if you use the display file option on the CRTMNU command or choose that option when using SDA to create a menu.)

The CMDLINE tool shows you a sample menu and provides documentation for what you need to do to modify the menu for your specific needs. You can see a demonstration of the function if the CMDLINE tool exists on your system (if it does not, see Appendix B). To call the demonstration program, enter

```
CALL  TAACMDBC
```

The CMDLINE display includes sample options to show you how to handle different types of menu options (e.g., errors). The display also supports the F9 retrieval function. Although the CMDLINE tool supports menus somewhat differently than the system does, the differences are fairly minor, and in some cases (e.g., handling errors) the CMDLINE tool provides better support than the system menu function.

The CMDLINE tool uses a program message queue subfile to display messages. The concept of a message subfile is fairly easy to understand: You enter a command and the messages produced by the command are returned to a subfile and displayed below the command line. More difficult to understand is what you must do to implement a message subfile. Fortunately, you don't have to understand the implementation to follow the instructions for the CMDLINE tool. With a little bit of work, you can easily emulate the IBM menu function.

Program Message Queue Subfile

If you like the way the system menus handle messages, you can use the same technique when writing a CL program to create a menu. To handle messages received on a menu, the system uses UIM, but the concept is similar to how a message subfile works: When a user selects a menu option, messages sent by the command that is executed will be placed in a scrollable area on the display. The user can scroll through the messages. If you want to use a similar approach, you need a message subfile.

To work with a message subfile, let's assume you like the CMDLINE TAA tool's approach to messages, but you don't want a command line on the menu. The easiest solution is to start with the existing code in the CMDLINE tool and throw out the code that performs the command line function (but be sure you have tried demonstration program TAACMDBC and you understand the function before you start throwing out code).

Follow the CMDLINE tool's instructions for copying the code. Read the implementation discussion and use different names for the source members (e.g., TRYLINC, TRYLIND, and TRYLINR).

Your approach to handling errors can vary. For example, you could capture the job log if an error occurs and send a generic message to the user (see Option 3 of the CMDLINE menu). Another approach would be to provide a program-level monitor message such as

```
MONMSG MSGID(CPF0000) EXEC(GOTO DSPMSGS)
```

This would allow the code provided at label DSPMSGS in the CMDLINE source to display whatever messages exist. Or you could code your own error message, in which case you would send your message to TOPGMQ(*SAME).

The message subfile support provides an option to move all the messages in a program message queue to a subfile. This option was not used in the CMDLINE tool because it would have caused all the messages received by your program to be displayed each time a command was entered. If the option had been used in conjunction with the "remove all messages" option, which uses the RMVMSG CLEAR(*ALL) command, you would have no job log audit trail if a problem occurred.

Instead, the CMDLINE tool uses an RPG program to write to the subfile (CL cannot write to the subfile) only the messages that you choose (e.g., you could send your own message in place of a system-supplied message).

I don't use this technique for production end users. Users unfamiliar with entering commands may find it confusing to have to sort through a list of messages and determine what action to take. I use a single variable for message text and write my own text for what should appear on the display.

Technical Tip

My approach for handling messages for production end users is to use the technique described earlier in this chapter (using the DUPSTDSRC TAA tool options of *MNUD and *MNUC). I use a single variable for message text and write my own text for what should appear on the display.

Exercise A Using the Command Line API

In this exercise we will demonstrate (using API QUSCMDLN) how you can add a command line to any display. To perform this exercise, you can be on any system display (including the command entry display).

1. Enter the command:

   ```
   CALL  QUSCMDLN
   ```

   You should see a command line window on the display.

2. Enter a command that will perform some function (e.g., WRKDSKSTS).
3. Press Enter to end the function and return to the command line window.
4. Enter a call to a program that does not exist, such as

   ```
   CALL  XXXYZZZ
   ```

   You should see a one-line message subfile on the display.

5. Place your cursor on the message and press the Help key.

   You should see message CPD0170, sent as a diagnostic message for the QUSCMDLN API.

6. Press Enter and then scroll to the next message in the subfile.

   You should see message CPF0001, also said to be sent as a diagnostic message for the QUSCMDLN API. But this is misleading because the message is really an escape message. The API changes the message type when it resends the message. For more information about why this situation occurs, see Chapter 1, “Monitoring for Messages.”

7. Press F12 to end the QUSCMDLN function.

Exercise B Using a Display File Menu

In this exercise we will create a display file and a CL program to invoke a menu. Then we will modify the program and create a menu object to invoke the menu using the GO command. We will use the DUPSTDSRC TAA tool. If this tool is not on your system, see Appendix B.

1. Use the DUPSTDSRC TAA tool to create the members TRYMNU and TRYMNUD:

```
DUPSTDSRC   MBR(TRYMNUD) SRCTYP(*MNUD) TEXT('...') SRCFILE(xxx)
DUPSTDSRC   MBR(TRYMNU) SRCTYP(*MNUC) TEXT('...') SRCFILE(xxx)
```

2. Use PDM to edit the TRYMNUD display file source.
3. Change the text for the first five options on the display file to read
   1. WRKDSKSTS
   2. SBMJOB
   3. SYSERRMSG
   4. USRERRMSG
   5. JOBLOG
4. Create the display file.
5. Use PDM to edit the TRYMNU CLP source.
6. Change the DCLF statement to specify file TRYMNUD.
7. Roll through the code and read the directions.
8. For Option 1, enter the WRKDSKSTS command to simulate a function that puts up a display.
9. For Option 2, use the following SBMJOB command to simulate a job being submitted to batch (we'll show the completion message on the menu):

```
SBMJOB  JOB(DUMMY) CMD(WRKDSKSTS)
```

10. For Option 3, enter a CHKOBJ command (for a program that doesn't exist) and then monitor for the escape message. Use GOTO RCVEXCP to demonstrate how an escape message is handled:

```
CHKOBJ  OBJ(XXXYYY) OBTYPE(*PGM)
MONMSG  MSGID(CPF9801) EXEC(GOTO RCVEXCP)
```

Exercise B continued

Exercise B continued

11. Using the system message can be confusing to your end user. A better solution would be to send your own message. Enter the following command for Option 4:

```
CHGVAR  'This is my error message'
```

12. Change the label of the GOTO command for Option 4 to DISPLAY. This will prevent the option field from being erased on the display.
13. For Option 5, change the GOTO label to JOBLOG. This will simulate what happens if you want to capture the job log at this point.
14. In the JOBLOG routine later in the program, a message is sent to the QSYSOPR message queue. You could see how this works or delete the SNDPGMMSG statement.
15. Create the program.
16. Enter the following command to create a menu object:

```
CRTMNU  MENU(TRYMNU) TYPE(*PGM)
```

17. Invoke the menu with the GO command:

```
GO  TRYMNU
```

    You should see the menu you created.

18. Try each option for which you entered code.
19. Try an invalid selection (e.g., 99).

    An advantage of using CL programs to create menus is that you have much greater control over error handling. The DUPSTDSRC command can help you build a good menu quickly.

Exercise C Using the CMDLINE TAA Tool

In this exercise we will use the demonstration program supplied with the CMDLINE TAA tool (we won't create anything) to show you how the tool works. If the CMDLINE tool is not on your system, see Appendix B.

1. Enter the following command to demonstrate the CMDLINE tool:

   ```
   CALL  TAACMDBC
   ```

2. Try some of the options, which are handled in a manner similar to the options presented in Exercise B. Option 4 causes error messages. Be sure to roll through the subfile and read the messages.
3. Enter the WRKDSKSTS command on the command line.

   You should see the correct display (i.e., the WRKDSKSTS display).

4. Enter a call to a program that does not exist:

   ```
   CALL  XXXYYY
   ```

   You should see the error subfile in action.

5. Press F9 until the WRKDSKSTS message appears. Execute the command again. The CMDLINE tool emulates how the system handles F9.

CHAPTER 17

Outfiles

The system provides several commands that support an outfile parameter. This system function lets you capture a command's output in a database file. Outfiles are helpful for letting a program make decisions about your objects, members, spooled files, and so on, and for assisting you in automating certain operations.

System APIs also are available that provide function similar to some command outfiles, but outfiles are much easier to use than the APIs. And in performance tests I have run, it appears that outfiles perform as well as, if not better than, APIs. Because of this, I believe little is to be gained by substituting APIs for outfiles in a CL program. Having said that, let me note that some APIs do perform very well. For example, APIs that access an object's attributes (e.g., retrieving the attributes for a job description) are very fast.

CODING OUTFILES

How you code an outfile depends on when you create the outfile. Because you must declare a file name on the DCLF statement to process an outfile in a CL program, you need to know what name to use. If you create the outfile before you code the CL program, you know the name of the file you created (it's the name you specified on the OUTFILE parameter and it's the name you would specify in the DCLF statement in your CL program). If you create the outfile and read it in the same CL program (or the name of the file is passed to the CL program), you need to know the name of the model file associated with the outfile.

Each CL command that has an outfile has its own unique IBM-supplied model file. The model file is nothing more than a database file (which normally does not contain a member) that contains the file's field descriptions. When you request an outfile, the system copies the specified model file and uses it to create the file definition. The system model files are in library QSYS and typically start with the letters QA (e.g., QADSPOBJ, the model file used by the DSPOBJD command).

To find the names of model files, you can refer to IBM's *AS/400 Programming: Reference Summary* (SX41-0028), or you can use the command prompter for most commands with outfile support. Press the Help key at the prompt for the outfile name; the help text will name the model outfile. Once you know this name, you can use the DSPFFD command to display individual field names and descriptions for the file.

It is the name of the model file that you specify on the DCLF statement. Then you use an override command to point to the real file you want the program to use. Some programmers like to use the same name as the model file and specify it in one of their libraries. This approach has some advantages, but I prefer to use a different name for the following reasons:

- Using a name that starts with a Q (as do all the model files) is a bad habit because some of the operating system code is sensitive to names that begin with Q.
- If you forget to specify a library or forget to do the override properly, the system will send an error message indicating that you are trying to read or write to a file that has no member (i.e., the model file in library QSYS). The error message is obvious if you realize what happened, but you also can waste time figuring out what is wrong.

In my code, I use a unique name or TAA tool ALCTMPMBR (Allocate Temporary Member), which automatically handles the need for unique outfile names. I provide an example of using the ALCTMPMBR command later in this chapter.

Most system commands that support outfiles have only a single model file. The DSPFD command is an exception. This command has a separate model file for each type of request you can make. A table provided in the help text for the DSPFD command can help you find the model file you need.

Technical Tip

If I am writing a program to access the members of a source file, I generally specify TYPE(*MBRLIST) on the DSPFD command to create an outfile with one record per member. The other possibility is to specify TYPE(*MBR). The TYPE(*MBR) option provides more information, but requires more system overhead.

THE TAA CVT COMMANDS

Not all system commands support outfiles for the functions you might want. If you don't find an outfile on the command you want, be sure to look at the TAA tool CVT commands (there are about 20) before you go off and do your own thing. You may find what you need here.

No help text is provided for the TAA CVT commands, so you must use the DSPTAATOOL command to read the online tool description. For example, if you read the description for the CVTOUTQ command, you will see that the model file located in library TAATOOL is TAASPLCP and that the format is SPLREC.

Some of the TAA CVT commands use APIs to access the information and some obtain results by 1) writing a spooled file, 2) copying the spooled file to a database file, and then 3) reading the database file to determine the information to be written. If a spooled file is used, it takes longer for the CVT command to work; and the tool is release-dependent, because the format of the spooled file may change. The documentation for each CVT command describes which technique is used.

Creating and Reading an Outfile in the Same Program

The following commands are required when you use an outfile:

- The DCLF command specifies the name of the file your program will use when it compiles. As mentioned, you need to know the name of the model file for the command you are using.
- The DSPxxx command creates the outfile. Typically, you will create the outfile in library QTEMP so that it is not permanent.
- The OVRxxx command overrides the model file (which is used only to compile against) to the real file that you created (typically in library QTEMP). It is a good idea to specify SECURE(*YES) when processing the outfile to keep a program higher in the program stack from directing your program to the wrong file (see Chapter 18, “Overrides”).
- The first RCVF command executed opens the file and reads the first record. Subsequent RCVF commands executed each read one record.
- The MONMSG MSGID(CPF0864) command monitors for the escape message sent when the RCVF command reaches “end of file.” Once “end of file” occurs, any subsequent RCVF command will send escape message CPF0864 to your program’s message queue.

Now that you are aware of the commands required, let’s look at an example using the same CL program to create and read an outfile. Assume that you want to process all the *OUTQ objects found in library QGPL. DSPOBJD is the command to use, and you need to know the model file name (QADSPOBJ) the command uses. Here’s what you would code:

```
             DCLF       FILE(QADSPOBJ) /* DSPOBJD outfile */
             DLTF       FILE(QTEMP/DSPOBJDP)
             MONMSG     MSGID(CPF2105) /* Ignore not found */
             DSPOBJD    OBJ(QGPL/*ALL) OBJTYPE(*OUTQ)           +
                          OUTPUT(*OUTFILE)                      +
                          OUTFILE(QTEMP/DSPOBJDP)
             OVRDBF     FILE(QADSPOBJ) TOFILE(QTEMP/DSPOBJDP) +
                          SECURE(*YES)
READ:        RCVF       /* Read a record */
             MONMSG     MSGID(CPF0864) EXEC(GOTO EOF)
              .
              .         /* Your processing */
              .
             GOTO       READ /* Loop back for next record */
EOF:                    /* All records have been read */
             RCVMSG     MSGTYPE(*EXCP) /* Remove EOF message */
```

If you are creating a program that could run interactively, it would be a good idea to add a status message that would appear when the DSPxxx command is creating the outfile. The status message will let your end user know what's happening (see Chapter 2, "Sending Messages").

You can find the above code, which is the basic code you will need to access an outfile, in the CLPOUTFILE TAA tool. When you want the outfile code in a CL program, use the browse mode (F15) of SEU to access member CLPOUTFILE in file QATTINFO in library QUSRTOOL. The source contained in CLPOUTFILE provides two sets of code: one uses the ALCTMPMBR TAA tool, which I discuss later; the other is the code shown above.

Technical Tip

The CLPOUTFILE TAA tool provides the basic code you will need to access an outfile.

Now that you have seen an example using an outfile, let's review some important points to remember about outfiles:

- The system creates outfiles with LVLCHK(*NO), which means your program most likely will still work if the file format has changed. On a new release, IBM may add additional fields to outfiles. Usually, these fields are placed at the end of the record format. Therefore, any existing programs that read outfiles won't be affected by a new release because the data the programs are reading is still in the same place (i.e., the from/to positions of the fields in the previous format have not changed).

Technical Tip

LVLCHK(*NO) is a reasonable solution for outfiles, but I don't like the concept for normal database files. The default of LVLCHK(*YES) protects you from potential mistakes.

- When you request an outfile, the system first checks to see whether or not the file exists. If it does not exist, the system creates the file using a model file. If the file does exist, the system ensures that the file is in the expected format. If the file is not in the expected format, the system refuses to write the outfile. This situation isn't a problem if you can ensure that your outfile names are unique; otherwise, it can be a problem. For example, assume that you used the name TEMP1 in library QTEMP for the outfile on the DSPOBJD command. If you don't delete the file first, and another file by the same name has been created for a different purpose, the DSPOBJD command will fail because the file format will not be correct. To avoid potential problems, either I delete the file in library QTEMP before writing to the outfile or I use the ALCTMPMBR TAA tool (discussed later).
- The default for outfiles is to clear the member and then start writing records. But you also can use the OUTMBR parameter to specify that you want to add records to an existing outfile. Most commands that support outfiles also support the OUTMBR parameter.
- Because IBM does not guarantee the consistency of outfile formats between releases, you should avoid updating any information in an outfile. Most of the time, you only need to read the outfile. If you need to update an outfile, consider using the CPYF command with FMTOPT(*MAP) to copy the outfile to a permanent file.

Technical Tip

You should avoid updating any information in an outfile. It may work today, but you are somewhat exposed on a new release. A better solution is to use CPYF FMTOPT(*MAP) to copy the outfile to a permanent file.

- In the coding example presented earlier, I specified OVRDBF SECURE(*YES). It would make no sense for the program to process any file other than the one in library QTEMP. Protect yourself by specifying SECURE(*YES). The use of SECURE(*YES) is discussed in detail in Chapter 18, "Overrides."

Technical Tip

When you process an outfile, you almost always want to specify SECURE(*YES) on the override command.

- You don't have to declare the fields used in an outfile because the DCLF command will automatically declare them when you compile the program. You can use the DSPFFD command to see what the fields are for a particular model file, or you can compile the program with the right model file and see what fields are listed on the compiler printout.
- The naming convention used for most outfile field names is to have a unique two-character identifier for the file followed by a unique four-character identifier for the field. Thus, all the field names for the DSPOBJD outfile start with OD. The object name field is ODOBNM. If you happen to be working with the output from two different outfiles in a program, the same field will have two different names. Working with two different outfiles is not a problem with CL programs because you can use only one outfile per program. But you can use multiple outfiles in a HLL program.
- Most commands that support outfiles have nice clean outfiles with all the fields properly defined. One exception is the DSPJRN (Display Journal) command. The outfile for this command defines standard fields and then uses a single field for your data (it does not have the field descriptions of your data record). See the section "The DSPJRN Command's Outfile" later in this chapter for more information about this.
- OPNQRYF can be used effectively with outfiles (see Chapter 20, "OPNQRYF").
- Unlike RPG and COBOL, CL does not support blocked records when sequentially processing a file. This means that every record read by the RCVF command requires a data management call — a call to the database requesting that the next record be placed in the buffer. If you need to read a large outfile (e.g., all object descriptions in a large library or in the entire system), you should consider using a HLL to read the file so you can gain the performance benefit of blocking.

Technical Tip

Specifying an override with a blocking factor does not appear to have any significant benefit in either writing an outfile or reading it in a CL program.

THE ALCTMPMBR TAA TOOL

In the coding example shown previously in this chapter (creating and reading the outfile in the same program), the following processing occurs:

- the program deletes a file and monitors for a "file not found" condition
- the program creates an outfile in library QTEMP (this process creates both a file and a member)
- at "end of job," the system deletes both the file and the member from library QTEMP, unless you have previously deleted them

Having to create and delete database files and members in your CL program does not lead to good performance. The system must perform several forced writes to disk to ensure that the object is correct and to protect the system in case a failure occurs during execution of the command. In most cases, having permanent files that you clear when needed would be a better solution.

In addition, when you need a unique member for a user job, you can't assign a member name using the user name and expect it to work, because a user of the same name may be using the identical function in a different job. For example, the same user may be signed on to multiple workstations, be using batch and interactive at the same time, or be running multiple group jobs or system request jobs. You shouldn't allocate an entire resource such as a work file or member created with the name of the user (in a library other than QTEMP), because you could cause problems for another job.

The ALCTMPMBR (Allocate Temporary Member) TAA tool addresses both the need for permanent files and the need for unique member names. You can use the command for several standard files (e.g., typical outfile usage, work files, files to copy spooled files to). And you can steal the code and use it for your own files.

With the ALCTMPMBR command, you request the type of file you want (e.g., *OBJD, *PHY, *SRC) and the command returns two parameter values for you:

- the name of the member assigned uniquely to you
- the name of the file in library TAATOOL

To process the outfile, you would use these return values in variables rather than using actual names, as we did in the previous coding example. Here's the previous coding example modified to use the ALCTMPMBR command:

```
              DCLF       FILE(QADSPOBJ) /* DSPOBJD outfile */
              DCL        &MBR *CHAR LEN(10)
              DCL        &FILE *CHAR LEN(10)
                         /* TAA Tool command */
              ALCTMPMBR  FILETYPE(*OBJD) RTNMBR(&MBR) +
                           RTNFILE(&FILE)
              DSPOBJD    OBJ(QGPL/*ALL) OBJTYPE(*OUTQ) +
                           OUTPUT(*OUTFILE) +
                           OUTFILE(TAATOOL/&FILE)  +
                           OUTMBR(&MBR *ADD)
              OVRDBF     FILE(QADSPOBJ) TOFILE(TAATOOL/&FILE) +
                           MBR(&MBR) SECURE(*YES)
READ:         RCVF       /* Read a record */
              MONMSG     MSGID(CPF0864) EXEC(GOTO EOF)
               .
               .         /* Your processing */
               .
              GOTO       READ /* Loop back for next record */
EOF:                     /* All records have been read */
              RCVMSG     MSGTYPE(*EXCP) /* Remove EOF message */
              DLCTMPMBR  FILETYPE(*OBJD) ALCMBR(&MBR)
```

When the ALCTMPMBR tool is created, the typical kinds of outfiles you will need are automatically created in library TAATOOL with three members each. Standard member names are used (e.g., MBR1, MBR2). When the ALCTMPMBR command is run, it attempts to allocate the first member of the file. If the command can't allocate the first member, it tries the next member. If all the members are allocated, the command adds a new one. The new member is allocated as *EXCLRD and cleared before the command returns control to your program. Because the member is already cleared, the OUTMBR parameter on the DSPOBJD command was specified as *ADD.

You should use the companion command (TAA tool DLCTMPMBR) when you no longer need the member. Because the DLCTMPMBR command specifies the same file type as we specified in the ALCTMPMBR command, the system knows which member and file to de-allocate. The member is cleared first (to minimize space) and then de-allocated. Another solution is to let the system clean up the object locks when the job ends, but simply removing the locks does not clean up the space used in the members.

The concept used by the ALCTMPMBR command is the same as that used by system spool support: Database file members are used to hold the spooled data and the members are reused rather than re-created each time a member is needed. When using the ALCTMPMBR command, you may find, as you do with system spool support, that you need to periodically clean up the system (many members may have been created but are no longer needed).

The CLNTAATEMP (Clean TAA Temporary Files) TAA tool addresses this problem. The command will clear any members not in use and reduce the number of members that exist based on their last change date. (If you use several members from different jobs regularly, you don't want to keep re-creating them.) The CLNTAATEMP command emulates the same type of support provided by the QRCLSPLSTG system value. Simply include the CLNTAATEMP command in a cleanup program and run it once a week.

Technical Tip

If you create a lot of temporary outfiles or work files that are in QTEMP, you should consider the use of ALCTMPMBR. It's faster to use an existing member than to create a file and member (this is the same technique used by the system spool support).

The DSPJRN Command's Outfile

As mentioned, the system has a few commands such as the DSPJRN command that provide an outfile for you, but the file definition may not be what you'd like. The DSPJRN outfile has standard fields for the journal entry (e.g., the time, the job, the file), but it defines the data as a large entity (a single field). Because the journal may contain several different files, it would be impossible to give the output record the specifics for multiple files.

However, when you use the DSPJRN command to output journal entries for a single file, you might want to include the specific field definitions for that file along with the standard journal entries. Although no system command can do this for you, the RTVPFSRC (Retrieve Physical File Source) TAA tool can help. Assume that you want the DDS for a journal outfile and the DDS for file FILA in a single physical file definition. The DDS source should be placed in member JRNFILA in file QDDSSRC. Here are the steps you would follow:

1. Use the TAA tool RTVPFSRC to retrieve the DDS source for the model file (QADSPJRN) used by the DSPJRN command:

   ```
   RTVPFSRC FILE(QADSPJRN) TOFILE(QDDSSRC) TOMBR(JRNFILA)
   ```

   The RTVPFSRC command generates a reasonable facsimile of what the DDS source looked like originally.

2. Use SEU on the JRNFILA member and delete the statements about the JOESD field (the general-purpose field used for all data). JOESD is the last field described.

3. Use the SEU browse function (F15) to access the DDS for your file FILA. Add just the field specifications (not the format) to the end of the source.

4. Create the file.

5. Use the DSPJRN command to create the outfile for FILA. You have to output to a file using the standard format (let's call it JRNOUTP). You want just the journal entries for records from FILA:

   ```
   DSPJRN  JRN(xxx) FILE(FILA *ALL) ENTTYP(*RCD) +
             OUTPUT(*OUTFILE) OUTFILE(JRNOUTP)
   ```

6. Use the CPYF command and specify *NOCHK to copy the data to your file (you should specify *NOCHK because the system definitions of the files differ; since you know the formats are identical, *NOCHK is safe to use):

   ```
   CPYF  FROMFILE(JRNOUTP) TOFILE(JRNFILA) +
           MBROPT(*ADD) FMTOPT(*NOCHK)
   ```

You would now have the journaled records in an externally described file with the standard journal fields and your field names for the data portion of the record. You can use this file to look for certain problems that may have occurred. For example, assume that you wanted to find all the records in FILA with the key field (KEY1) equal to ABCD and then print a report with certain fields from the file (e.g., who updated it, when they updated it, the value of some other field). You don't even have to code a program. You could use the CRTPRTPGM TAA tool described in Chapter 21, "Displaying Data," and the OPNQRYF command described in Chapter 20, "OPNQRYF."

A Crude Technique for Reusing an Outfile

As you learned in Chapter 15, where I presented the short list of what you can do with files in a CL program and the much longer list of what you cannot do, CL's ability to process files is very weak. Processing an outfile is about as complex a situation as CL can handle. If you ever try to do something fancier (e.g., use the same, or a different, DSPxxx command again with an outfile so you can read the same outfile again), it isn't going to work. For example, you cannot reuse an outfile by coding the following:

```
          /* Incorrect coding */
          DSPFD    ... OUTFILE(xxx)
LOOP:     RCVF
          MONMSG   MSGID(CPF0864) EXEC(GOTO NEXT)
          .
          .
          .
          GOTO     LOOP
NEXT:     DSPFD    ... OUTFILE(xxx)
LOOP2:    RCVF
          MONMSG   MSGID(CPF0864) EXEC(GOTO END)
          .
          .
          .
          GOTO     LOOP2
END:
```

The reason this code will not work is that as soon as the program reaches "end of file," the program will keep on returning escape message CPF0864 upon execution of any subsequent RCVF command.

In many cases, the only way to handle complex processing needs is to use two CL programs. You would use one program to create the files and then call a different program to process each file. However, a crude way to fool the system into reusing a file does exist. In the following code, I use the WRTDBF TAA tool to write a dummy record to the outfile. The record contains only an X in the first position of the record, which is the MLRCEN field. This field is a 1-byte character value for the century in which the data was retrieved. Because a normal record won't contain an X, the program uses this information to cause another outfile to be added to the file and then reads the outfile. Note that the records are added to the outfile (the member is not cleared on each use). This means that the next use of the DSPFD command causes records to be written after the X record and then another X record is added to the file.

The WRTDBF command is specified as ACTION(*WRTCLOSE), which means the member will be opened, the record will be written, and then the file will be closed. The WRTDBF command writes blanks to the file after position 1. This will cause an escape message (CPF0886) when the file is read in a CL program because invalid data exists in the decimal fields. The program checks for this condition and ensures that an X record was read.

As I said, this technique is crude. The technique works because it prevents escape message CPF0864 from occurring. Here's the code to read the outfile from multiple DSPFD commands where a list of members is needed:

```
          PGM
          DCLF      FILE(QAFDMBRL) /* DSPFD Member list */
          DLTF      FILE(QTEMP/MBRLSTP)
          MONMSG    MSGID(CPF2105) / Ignore not found */
          OVRDBF    FILE(QAFDMBRL) TOFILE(QTEMP/MBRLSTP) SECURE(*YES)
          DSPFD     FILE(xxx) TYPE(*MBRLST) OUTPUT(*OUTFILE) +
                      OUTFILE(QTEMP/MBRLSTP) OUTMBR(*FIRST *ADD)
          WRTDBF    FILE(QTEMP/MBRLSTP) RECORD('X') ACTION(*WRTCLOSE)
LOOP1:    RCVF
          MONMSG    MSGID(CPF0886) EXEC(DO) /* Bad data */
          IF        (&MLRCEN *EQ 'X') GOTO NXTFILE
          SNDPGMMSG MSGID(CPF9898) MSGF(QCPFMSG) MSGTYPE(*ESCAPE) +
                      MSGDTA('Bad data in one of the fields')
          ENDDO     /* Bad data */
          .
          .         /* Your processing of the members */
          .
          GOTO      LOOP1
NXTFILE:
          DSPFD     FILE(yyyy) TYPE(*MBRLST) OUTPUT(*OUTFILE) +
                      OUTFILE(QTEMP/MBRLSTP) OUTMBR(*FIRST *ADD)
          WRTDBF    FILE(QTEMP/MBRLSTP) RECORD('X') ACTION(*WRTCLOSE)
LOOP2:    RCVF
          MONMSG    MSGID(CPF0886) EXEC(DO) /* Bad data */
          IF        (&MLRCEN *EQ 'X') GOTO ENDPGM
          SNDPGMMSG MSGID(CPF9898) MSGF(QCPFMSG) MSGTYPE(*ESCAPE) +
                      MSGDTA('Bad data in one of the fields')
          ENDDO     /* Bad data */
          .
          .
          .
          GOTO      LOOP2
ENDPGM:   ENDPGM
```

Exercise A Using an Outfile

In this exercise you will use the standard outfile source that is in TAA tool CLPOUTFILE. We will access the *JOBD objects in library QGPL and then send a message for each one found. For this exercise you will need the ALCTMPMBR TAA tool. If it doesn't exist on your system, see Appendix B.

1. Use PDM to create a CLP member named TRYOUTFILE.
2. When the SEU display appears, use the browse function (F15) and request member CLPOUTFILE in file QATTINFO in library QUSRTOOL. Use the first set of code, which uses the ALCTMPMBR tool.
3. Copy all the code statements into member TRYOUTFILE.

   The code is almost a complete program for using the DSPOBJD outfile to access the *JOBD objects in library QGPL. If this were a production program, I would start with the DUPSTDSRC TAA tool and bring in the standard error-handling routine. Then I would access the CLPOUTFILE command and add the specific source.
4. Add PGM and ENDPGM statements. Note the use of the ALCTMPMBR TAA tool. It requests the *OBJD type file that matches the DSPOBJD outfile format. The ALCTMPMBR command will return the assigned file name and member name in library TAATOOL into variables &FILE and &MBR. The member is allocated to your job and cleared when the command completes (before control is returned to your program). The variables &FILE and &MBR are plugged into the DSPOBJD OUTFILE parameter and specified on the OVRDBF statement.
5. Add a SNDPGMMSG command in the processing loop for every object name read:

   ```
   SNDPGMMSG  MSG(&ODOBNM *CAT &ODOBTP)
   ```
6. Create the program.
7. Call the program:

   ```
   CALL  TRYOUTFILE
   ```

   You should see the status message telling you an outfile is being created. Messages are sent to the display when the command completes.

Exercise A continued

Exercise A continued

8. The ALCTMPMBR command has allocated a member for you in a standard file in library TAATOOL. Use the WRKOBJLCK command to see that this has happened:

```
WRKOBJLCK  OBJ(TAATOOL/TAATMPOBJD) OBJTYPE(*FILE) MBR(*ALL)
```

   You should see that you hold a lock on a member. The member name is just a standard of MBR followed by a 4-digit consecutive number. Note the member name that has been assigned to your job. If you don't remove the lock, it will be held for your entire job. The system would automatically remove the lock when your job ends, but the data that was written into the member by the DSPOBJD command could still exist. Ending your job won't clean up the space used. You can free the lock and clean up the space with the companion command, DLCTMPMBR.

9. Use PDM to access the TRYOUTFILE source member.
10. Add the DLCTMPMBR command to your program after the point at which all database records have been read:

```
DLCTMPMBR  FILETYPE(*OBJD) ALCMBR(&MBR)
```

11. Modify the program so that it accesses only the *OUTQ objects in library QGPL.
12. Create the program.
13. Call the program:

```
CALL  TRYOUTFILE
```

   You should see the *OUTQ objects identified in messages.

14. Use F9 to duplicate the WRKOBJLCK command and try it again.

   You should see that you still have a lock on the member. The member name should be the same as that initially assigned by the ALCTMPMBR command. The reason the lock is still on the member is that each use of the ALCOBJ command causes a separate lock. The first time you ran the program, you got one lock. The next time, you got a second lock and then freed it by using the DLCTMPMBR command. But the first lock still exists. This phenomenon is discussed in

Exercise A continued

Exercise A continued

Chapter 11, "Allocating Objects." Having a lock on the member isn't really hurting anything at this point. The space has been cleaned up and the system will remove your lock when the job ends. If multiple users request the same function, ALCTMPMBR will add new members if it has to. If this is a handful of users, you would never notice the difference. If many users are using the same file from ALCTMPMBR at the same time, you should find a different approach.

Exercise B Using the DSPFD Outfile

In this exercise you will create an outfile containing a list of the members in a source file and look for certain information in the member records. You will need the TAA tools EDTVAR and ALCTMPMBR. If they are not on your system, see Appendix B. Rather than show you all the code for this exercise, I will describe the steps and let you determine some of the coding detail. If you have trouble, refer to the previous exercise.

1. To access a list of members in an outfile, you need to use the DSPFD command. Normally, you would specify the *MBRLIST option if you are accessing basic information (that's all we'll need in this exercise). *MBRLIST is faster than the *MBR option. Prompt for the DSPFD command and determine the name of the model file by using the Help key on the "File to receive output" parameter.
2. In this example we will try to find all the CLP source members that have more than 200 records. If you don't think one of your source files will have any CLP type members with 200 or more records, reduce the number of records to something you believe will work.
3. Use PDM to create a CLP member named TRYMBRLIST.
4. When the SEU display appears, use the browse function (F15) to bring in all the source for the CLPOUTFILE member in file QATTINFO in library QUSRTOOL. You want the set of code that includes ALCTMPMBR.

Exercise B continued

Exercise B continued

5. Add PGM and ENDPGM statements.
6. We want to use DSPFD *MBRLIST, so make the modifications to the program to use the correct DCLF command, the right outfile command, the correct value on ALCTMPMBR, the correct OVRDBF command, and so on.
7. Add a DLCTMPMBR command at the end of the source.
8. You now have a "base" program to process the outfile for the DSPFD member list. At this point it doesn't have any unique code. In this exercise we want to send a message for certain fields in the outfile. You need to determine the field names used for the
   - member name
   - number of records
   - SEU source type

   You can do this by

   - compiling the base program and looking at the listing to determine the field names to use, or
   - using DSPFFD for the model file and determining the field names to use.
9. If you are not looking at field names that start with ML, you have used the wrong model file.
10. There are two fields that describe the source type of a member. MLSEU was the old version when source types were 4 characters or less. The one to use now is MLSEU2.
11. Even if your source file contains only CLP type members, enter an IF statement to bypass any source types that are not CLP.
12. You need to add the logic to bypass the member record if it has fewer than 200 records (don't use OPNQRYF). Use the field name you determined in a prior step for the "number of records."
13. In this exercise we want to send a message for every member that has 200 or more records. The messages should look like this:

```
MBR1          CLP   200
MBR2          CLP   318
```

Exercise B continued

Exercise B continued

To send a message of this type, you will need the EDTVAR TAA tool to convert the decimal field for number of records to a character field so you can include it in the message text. When the EDTVAR command is used, the character field containing the edited result must be declared as *CHAR LEN(22). Thus, your code would look like this:

```
DCL  &RCDSA *CHAR LEN(8)
 .
 .
 .
EDTVAR  CHROUT(&RCDSA) NUMINP(&MLNRCD)
```

Assume that we want a fixed number of blanks (use 3) between the fields. Use the name of the member field and source type you determined from a previous step and the variable you converted to with the EDTVAR command. Your SNDPGMMSG command should look like this:

```
SNDPGMMSG  MSG(&MLNAME *CAT '   ' *CAT &MLSEU2 +
               *TCAT '   ' *CAT &RCDSA)
```

14. Create the program.
15. Call the program:

```
CALL  TRYMBRLIST
```

You should see messages sent for every CLP type member that has 200 or more source statements.

Exercise C Using a CVT TAA Tool

In this exercise we will use a couple of CVT commands from the TAA tools to let you see how easy it is to gain additional outfiles. If the following tools are not on your system, see Appendix B:

- **CVTDSKSTS**
- **CVTOUTQ**
- **DSPDBF**
- **DSPTAACMD**
- **DSPTAATOOL**

1. Use the DSPTAACMD command and request to look at the CVT commands:

   ```
   DSPTAACMD  CMD(CVT)
   ```

   You should see a subfile of commands that start with CVT. Not all the CVT commands create an outfile, but there are several that do. Roll through the subfile to see others.

2. Assuming that you have a few spooled files in a specific output queue, let's try the CVTOUTQ (Convert Output Queue) TAA tool. The command will create one database record for each spooled file that exists in an output queue. It uses the information you see on a WRKSPLF or WRKOUTQ display. The actual implementation of CVTOUTQ is that it uses an API to access the information. When using CVTOUTQ, you must name an output queue. If this is the first time you have used CVTOUTQ, you also must name the library where the OUTQP file will be created by using the OUTLIB parameter:

   ```
   CVTOUTQ  OUTQ(xxx) OUTLIB(yyy)
   ```

3. The OUTQP file should now exist. Use DSPDBF to look at the file:

   ```
   DSPDBF  FILE(OUTQP)
   ```

   You should see an externally described file with individual fields for each of the spooled file attributes.

4. The CVTDSKSTS (Convert Disk Status) TAA tool converts the information you see on WRKDSKSTS to a database file.

Exercise C continued

Exercise C continued

5. Try WRKDSKSTS (the system command) so you are familiar with the information:

```
WRKDSKSTS
```

6. The implementation of CVTDSKSTS is to use WRKDSKSTS OUTPUT(*PRINT) and then read the spooled file to access the information. We use a spooled file approach because the system does not support an API for this function. If you use a spooled file for this technique, you are somewhat exposed to changes on a new release where IBM may change the format. Hopefully, the QUSRTOOL tools are all tested before you get them, but you still have to re-create the objects for the tool on every release to allow for changes. As with CVTOUTQ, if you have never used CVTDSKSTS before, you must name a library for the DSKSTSP file on the OUTLIB parameter:

```
CVTDSKSTS  OUTLIB(xxx)
```

7. The DSKSTSP file should now exist. Use DSPDBF to look at the file:

```
DSPDBF  FILE(DSKSTSP)
```

   You should see the same information you saw on WRKDSKSTS in an externally described file with individual fields for the information.

8. If you wanted to both create and process the DSKSTSP file in the same CL program, you would need the name of the model file used by CVTDSKSTS. The TAA tool commands do not have help text, but the information is online. Just use the DSPTAATOOL command and look for a discussion of the model file that is used:

```
DSPTAATOOL  TOOL(CVTDSKSTS)
```

   You should have found that the model file name is TAASYSFP and that it has a format name of DSRCD. All the TAA tool model files are in the TAATOOL library.

Exercise D Using the RTVPFSRC TAA Tool

In this exercise you will use the RTVPFSRC TAA tool to retrieve a reasonable facsimile of the DDS source that was originally used to create a physical file. Once the DDS source exists, you can do any function you want with it. Prompt for the RTVPFSRC command; if it does not exist, see Appendix B.

1. In this exercise we will use the source for the model file QADSPOBJ in library QSYS, which is used by the DSPOBJD command. This will generate DDS similar to that used by IBM to create the model file.
2. Enter the command:

```
RTVPFSRC  FILE(QSYS/QADSPOBJ) TOSRCFILE(xxxx) TOMBR(OBJDP)
```

3. Use SEU to look at the source:

```
STRSEU  SRCFILE(xxxx) SRCMBR(OBJDP)
```

   You should see a reasonable facsimile of what the original source looked like. RTVPFSRC accesses the file object and generates the DDS. No comments from the original source are placed in the file object so none can be generated. Text descriptions for both the format and fields are part of the object and are retrieved.

4. Create the physical file OBJDP with the command

```
CRTPF  FILE(OBJDP)
```

5. Use DSPOBJD with an outfile to write to this file. This will test to see if the format is identical. Only one record is needed so we'll use the object QCMD in QSYS.

```
DSPOBJD  OBJ(QCMD) OBJTYPE(*PGM) OUTPUT(*OUTFILE) OUTFILE(OBJDP)
```

6. If the command works correctly, you can be sure that the formats are identical.

Technical Tip

RTVPFSRC has several advantages. The obvious one is when you have lost your source. The not-so-obvious one is when you really need the source from an IBM file or some other file for which you have never had the source.

CHAPTER 18

Overrides

One of the most complex chapters to read in IBM's *Data Management Guide* is the chapter on file overrides. Here, I will provide a less complex discussion of what you need to know about overrides. Basically, you can do three things with overrides:

1. You can override an attribute of a file. For example, the following code overrides the number of copies to be printed when a program writes to file QPRINT:

   ```
   OVRPRTF  FILE(QPRINT) COPIES(2)
   ```

   Files have many attributes for which you can specify a value. Many of these attributes cannot be specified in a high-level language (HLL) program such as RPG. You need a CL program to

   — use a CHGxxx command to change a file attribute permanently,

   or

   — use an OVRxxx command to change a file temporarily.

2. You can override to a different file. For example, a CL program containing the following line of code would cause a request to open FILEA to actually open FILEB:

   ```
   OVRDBF  FILE(FILEA) TOFILE(FILEB)
   ```

   The FILE parameter value should always describe the name of the file that you specified in the program.

3. You can use one OVRxxx command to override to a different file and to specify a file attribute. For example, the following code directs a program to FILEB and specifies MBR1 for the MBR file attribute:

   ```
   OVRDBF  FILE(FILEA) TOFILE(FILEB) MBR(MBR1)
   ```

As you work with overrides, you need to remember the following points:

- The file override must occur before the program opens the file. Once the file is open, the file's attributes cannot be changed. If an override is specified after a file has been opened, the system does not issue an error message; it simply saves the override in case the file is opened again. Also, your program will not receive an error message if an override specifies the wrong file (i.e., the wrong file name was specified on the FILE parameter). For example, assume you misspelled FILEA as FILA so that your program contained the override command

```
OVRDBF  FILE(FILA) TOFILE(FILEB)
```

When the program opens FILEA, the override would not take effect and the program would read FILEA. The system does not check the file name specified on overrides until your program opens a file.

- In CL, the first RCVF command executed will open the file. This means that you can create an outfile, override it, open it, and read it all in the same program (you will find an example of this in Chapter 17, "Outfiles").

- The system automatically removes overrides specified within a program when the program is no longer in the program stack. This point is significant if you are using an RPG program to call a CL program that executes an override command. For example, assume you want to use the RPG OPEN operation code to open a file and then read a specific member in the file. Because you cannot specify the member option in RPG, you would need to use an override to specify the member. But you cannot call a CL program to perform the override, then return to the RPG program, expecting the override to still be in effect. Later in this chapter, I'll discuss using QCMDEXC to execute an override in RPG.

- A second override in the same program for the same file takes precedence over the first override. For example, if you specify the following code, program PGMX will read FILEC:

```
OVRDBF     FILE(FILEA) TOFILE(FILEB)
  .
  .
  .
OVRDBF     FILE(FILEA) TOFILE(FILEC)
CALL       PGMX /* Opens FILEA */
```

Understanding this concept is particularly important when working with printer files. For example, the following code might not give you the results you want:

```
OVRPRTF    FILE(QPRINT) COPIES(2)
   .
   .
   .
OVRPRTF    FILE(QPRINT) LPI(8)
CALL       PGMX /* Outputs to QPRINT */
```

In this example, the second override supercedes the first override and the number of copies printed will be the number specified in the file, not the number specified in the first override.

- An override specified in a program higher in the program stack will take precedence over an override specified in a program lower in the stack. To see if you understand the rules for overrides so far, look at the following diagram and determine which file program PGM3 opens when it opens FILEA:

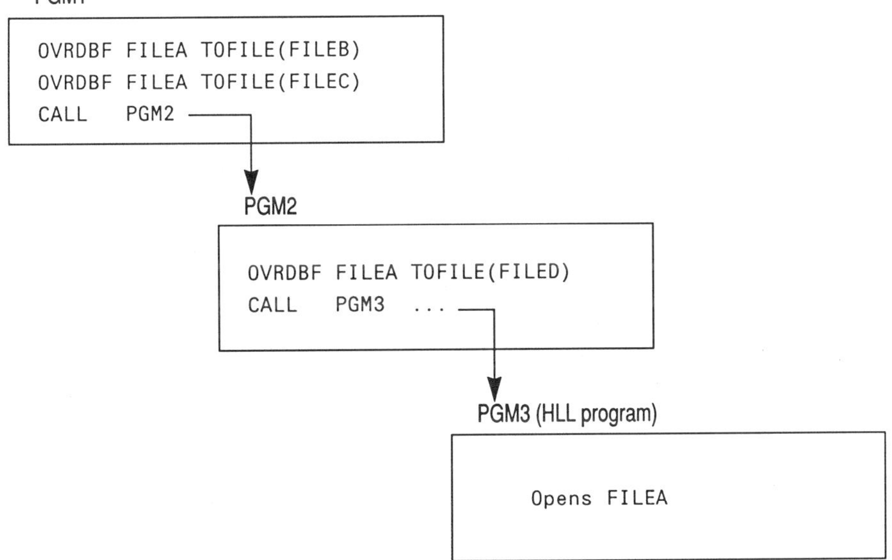

If you said FILEC, move to the head of the class. The second override in PGM1, which specifies TOFILE(FILEC), takes precedence over the first override in the same program. In addition, because program PGM1 is higher in the program stack, the override specified in PGM1 takes precedence over the override in program PMG2.

One of the confusing things about overrides is that there is both a precedence rule and a merging rule. The precedence rule (as shown in previous examples) has to do with what happens when programs at different levels specify the *same* override for the *same* function (e.g., the TOFILE parameter). The merging rule determines what happens when overrides at different levels specify *different* attributes to be overridden. For example, if PGMA contains the following override:

```
OVRPRTF  QPRINT COPIES(2)
```

and PGMA calls PGMB, which contains the override command

```
OVRPRTF  QPRINT SPLFNAME(PAYCHKS)
```

the overrides do not conflict and merging of the attributes occurs (i.e., when file QPRINT is opened, both overridden attributes will be used). I'll discuss more about attribute merging rules later.

When you specify an override command, you can choose whether or not the precedence and merging rules will be followed. Your choice is made by the value you specify for the SECURE parameter, which exists on every OVRxxx command. The default, *NO, allows the precedence and merging rules to occur; if you specify *YES, you prevent both precedence and merging from occurring.

So how do you keep the rules straight, keep yourself out of trouble, and provide programming flexibility? I do it by following two simple guidelines:

1. If I'm working with a device file (e.g., QPRINT), I normally take the default for the SECURE parameter and let precedence/merging occur. I assume that a programmer or user knows what (s)he is doing if (s)he wants to override the file's attributes to print more copies or to print to a different printer file.

2. If I'm working with a database file, I normally specify SECURE(*YES). I assume that it would rarely make sense for my program to operate against a different file.

Here's an example of what might happen if you don't specify SECURE(*YES) on a database file: Assume you have an override that specifies a wait file time for the Accounts Receivable file that you are going to write to

```
OVRDBF  FILE(ACCRVC) WAITFILE(5)
```

A production user somehow accesses a command entry display and issues the following command:

```
OVRDBF  FILE(ACCRVC) TOFILE(PAYROLL) LVLCHK(*NO)
```

Then (s)he calls your program. Your program just wrote the Accounts Receivable data into the PAYROLL file. How would you like to look into that problem and try to figure out what happened? The way to prevent this is to specify SECURE(*YES) and/or prevent production users from accessing the command entry display. To be certain about which file your program will use when you don't need to override any of the attributes, use a simple override command such as the following:

```
OVRDBF  FILE(ACCRCV) SECURE(*YES)
```

Technical Tip

For device files, I prefer the default of SECURE(*NO) to let attributes be merged at various invocation levels. For database files, I prefer SECURE(*YES) unless you have a good reason to differ. In most cases it would make absolutely no sense for a program to read any other file than what you intended when you wrote the program.

- If you specify SECURE(*YES) in a program, it applies to all file opens that occur below your program in the program stack. Thus, a CL program can specify an override such as the following to prevent a program higher in the stack from directing program PGMX to read some other file:

```
OVRDBF  FILE(FILEA) SECURE(*YES)
CALL    PGMX /* Opens FILEA */
```

To understand how SECURE(*YES) works, think of all overrides specified as being in a stack in the same order as the program stack. When a program opens a file, the system starts applying overrides beginning at the bottom of the stack for the file specified. If the system finds a SECURE(*YES) parameter, it stops looking for overrides. Thus, if a series of overrides looked like the following, program PGM3 will read FILEA, not FILEB:

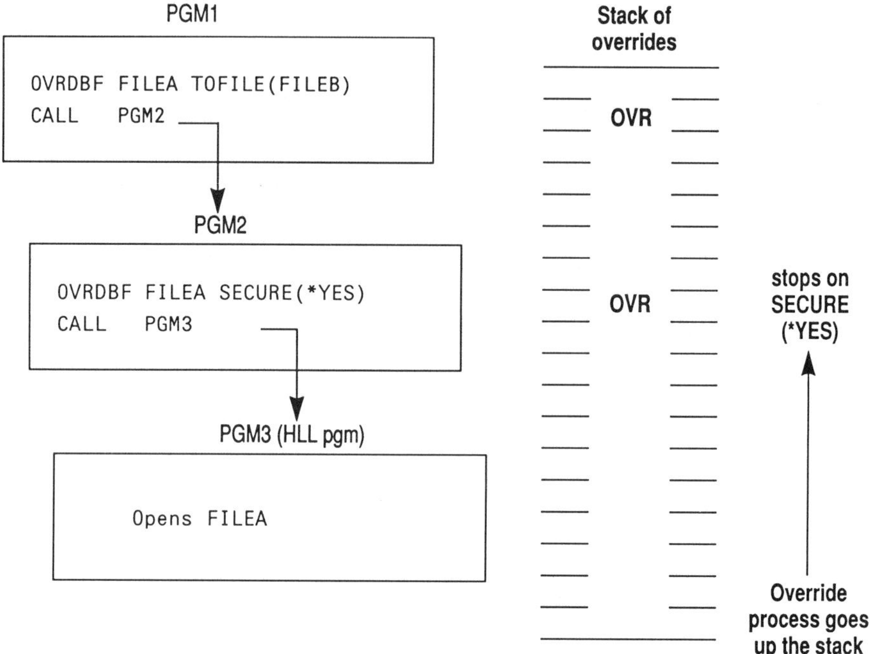

Technical Tip

I don't recommend changing the default for all OVRxxx commands to SECURE(*YES) because of the amount of code that is passed around from one system to another where someone may be relying on the fact that the default is SECURE(*NO). Changing some command defaults is acceptable, but changing the SECURE parameter could definitely affect a program's logic.

- Overrides are ignored by many commands (the list is described in the *Data Management Guide*). For example, CLRPFM ignores any overrides you have specified for a file or member. You cannot, therefore, use overrides in a CL program to specify a file or a member for CLRPFM. If you don't want to hard code which file or member gets cleared, you can use variables on CLRPFM for the file and/or member name.
- Overrides don't cascade within the same program. For example, if you coded the following, program PGMX would read FILEB, not FILEC:

```
OVRDBF      FILE(FILEA) TOFILE(FILEB)
OVRDBF      FILE(FILEB) TOFILE(FILEC)
CALL        PGMX /* Opens FILEA */
```

- Overrides do cascade if specified in different programs at different levels in the program stack. For example, if the following overrides appeared in the series of programs as shown below, PGMZ would open FILEC, not FILEA:

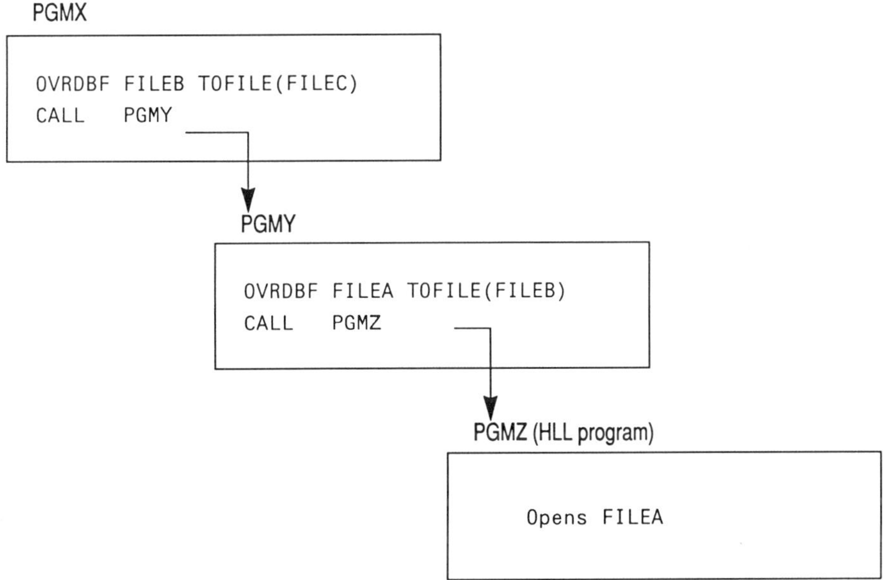

- Overrides merge if specified in programs at different levels of the program stack. For example, in the following series of programs, the overrides specified for file QPRINT would merge when program PGMZ opens the file:

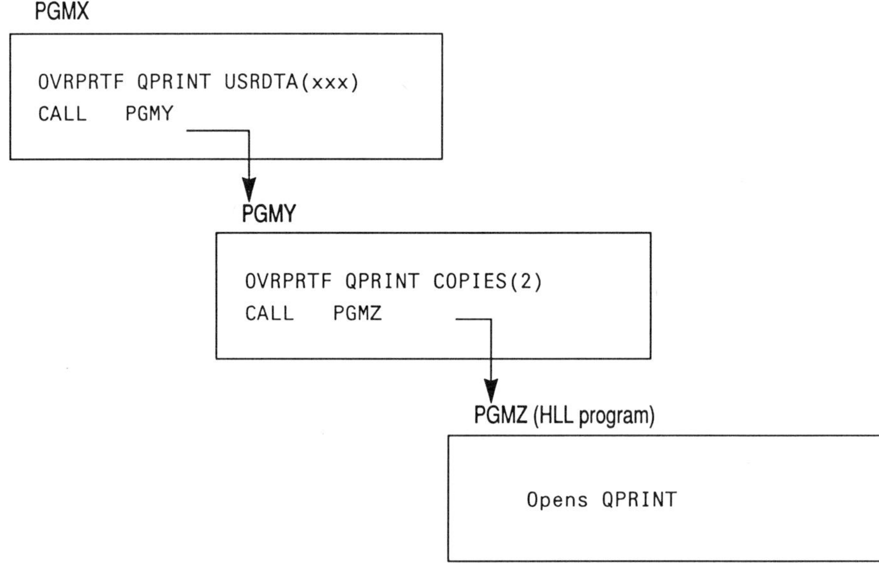

File QPRINT would be printed with USRDTA of xxx and COPIES of 2. If program PGMX had specified the COPIES parameter also, it would have been honored (by default, programs at the top of the stack take precedence). If program PGMY had specified SECURE(*YES), then only the COPIES attribute would be modified and the USRDTA option would come from the file.

Controlling the File Open in an HLL Program

Sometimes you will need to use a "user-controlled" file open in an RPG program. If you are opening and closing the same file multiple times, you probably need to do an override before each open in your RPG program.

However, you cannot call a CL program, perform the override, and then return to the RPG program and do the open. This technique does not work because the system automatically deletes all override commands issued by a program when the program is removed from the program stack. There are two ways to get around this:

1. Use a CL program that calls the RPG program. When the RPG program needs an override, it returns to CL with LR off. CL does the override and calls the RPG program again. This technique is described further in Chapter 24, "CL Performance."
2. Call QCMDEXC within the RPG program and pass it the OVRxxx command you want to execute. You might ask why using

QCMDEXC will work for an override command, when calling a CL program that executes an override does not work. The answer is that the system handles any overrides done through QCMDEXC as a special case and the overrides are not deleted. Handling the override in RPG is messy. Typically, I want the flexibility to read any file and any member. Here is the RPG code that I use (the code is crude, but it works; and you can open any file and member with it):

```
...+... 1 ...+... 2 ...+... 3 ...+... 4 ...+... 5 ...+... 6 ...+... 7 ...+
    FINPUT   IF  F     100             DISK                          UC
    .
    .
    E                        OVR         70  1
    .
    C* Modify override command
    C*     Assemble and move qualified tofile name
    C                         MOVE *BLANKS   QLFNAM 21
    C            TOLIB        CAT  '/':0     QLFNAM
    C            QLFNAM       CAT  TOFILE:0  QLFNAM
    C                         MOVEAQLFNAM    OVR,33
    C*     Move the member name
    C                         MOVEATOMBR     OVR,60
    C* Execute OPEN using QCMDEXC
    C                         CALL 'QCMDEXC'
    C                         PARM           OVR
    C                         PARM 70        LEN     155
    C                         OPEN INPUT                 20
    C* Handle error on open failure with indicator 20
    C            *IN20        IFEQ *ON
    .
    .
    .
    C                         ENDIF
    O*. 1 ...+... 2 ...+... 3 ...+... 4 ...+... 5 ...+... 6 ...+...7 ...
** Array for OVR
OVRDBF  FILE(INPUT     ) TOFILE(                        ) MBR(          )
```

Using Unique Printer Files

During the early days of the S/38, override processing was not as fast as it is today. At one point, IBM encouraged programmers to use more permanent files and fewer overrides. On the AS/400, however, override processing is fairly efficient. Assuming you are performing typical functions, you should not need to define many printer files to avoid overrides.

You can define printer files in two ways:

1. You can use the CRTPRTF command to create a non-DDS printer file. The default for parameter SRCFILE is *NONE. This means that you are going to format the print line in a high-level language program.
2. You can use DDS source to create an externally described printer file.

I prefer to use externally described printer files only when I need a function supported solely by DDS. In most situations, DDS-written printer files are not nearly as performance-efficient as formatting print lines in an RPG program.

Externally described printer files let you print multiple lines from one WRITE operation. Although it sounds good to be able to print multiple lines with one WRITE statement from RPG, the performance is not what you would expect, for two reasons. First, RPG print lines are buffered, so by default you are passing many print lines to data management at one time. Therefore, you may be doing more data management calls with externally described printer files than with the RPG approach. Second, the externally described printer files use a table-driven approach to processing the fields, as opposed to the RPG approach, which generates a set of instructions to format the output lines.

Technical Tip

In most situations, your program's performance will suffer when the program is using printer files written in DDS. If you choose to use DDS to create printer files, you should have a good reason to do so (e.g., when you need a function supported solely by DDS).

Overriding Spooled File Attributes

In addition to the spooled file attributes such as COPIES and LPI that you might normally override, you should be aware of two other useful attributes:

1. SPLFNAME. You can use this attribute to change the name of the spooled file from QPRINT (or whatever name you normally use) to a spooled file name of your choice. Choose a name appropriate for what you are printing, so that you or the system operator can

easily recognize the spooled file. For example, if you are printing payroll checks, you might code:

```
OVRPRTF  FILE(QPRINT) SPLFNAME(PAYCHECKS)
CALL     PGM(xxx) /* Opens QPRINT */
```

Because specifying a value for the SPLFNAME attribute permanently changes the spooled file attribute, you would use the spooled file name you assigned when using the CHGSPLFA or DLTSPLF commands.

2. USRDTA. This attribute is used primarily to provide descriptive information about the spooled file. By default it contains the name of the program that printed the output, but you can specify any information you want. Because the USRDTA value appears on the first display of the WRKSPLF command (if you use the intermediate-level view), specifying a value for USRDTA can help determine what the output is. For example, you could decide that the USRDTA parameter will contain the application area or function and the SPLFNAME will contain a meaningful file name:

```
OVRPRTF  FILE(QPRINT) USRDTA(ACCTG) SPLFNAME(MTHEND)
CALL     PGM(yyy) /* Opens QPRINT */
```

When I write a command that provides printer output, I place the command name in the USRDTA parameter. I place something that relates to what the user specified on the command in the SPLFNAME parameter (e.g., the file name or library name).

Exercise A Overrides to the Same File

In this exercise you will experiment with overrides at various levels to better your understanding of how overrides function.

1. Use PDM to create a CLP member named TRYOVR.
2. Enter the following source:

```
PGM
WRKDSKSTS  OUTPUT(*PRINT)
ENDPGM
```

3. Create the program.
4. Call the program:

```
CALL  TRYOVR
```

5. Use the WRKSPLF command to look at your spooled files.

   You should see the QPWCDSKS spooled file created by the WRKDSKSTS command. Note the attributes for USRDTA and number of copies. (If you don't see these on the first display, you need to be at the intermediate assistance level. Use F21 and change to this level). The USRDTA attribute should be blank and the number of copies should be 1 (the values will be different if your installation has changed the defaults).

6. Using PDM, modify the TRYOVR source by inserting the following OVRPRTF command ahead of the WRKDSKSTS command:

```
OVRPRTF  FILE(QPWCDSKS) USRDTA(XXX)
```

7. Create the program.
8. Call the program:

```
CALL  TRYOVR
```

9. Use the WRKSPLF command to look at your spooled files.

   You should see the QPWCDSKS command with USRDTA of XXX.

10. Enter the following command on the command entry display:

```
OVRPRTF  FILE(QPWCDSKS) USRDTA(YYY)
```

Exercise A continued

Exercise A continued

11. Call the program:

```
CALL  TRYOVR
```

12. Use the WRKSPLF command to look at your spooled files.

    You should see the QPWCDSKS spooled file with USRDTA of YYY. Overrides at a higher level of the program stack take precedence unless you specify SECURE(*YES) in the program lower in the program stack.

13. You can see the overrides in your own job by using the DSPJOB command. Enter the following command:

```
DSPJOB
```

14. When the Display Job menu appears, use option 15.

    You should be looking at the override you specified. Display the details of the override.

15. Return to the command entry display and enter the following command:

```
OVRPRTF  FILE(QPWCDSKS) COPIES(2)
```

16. Call the program:

```
CALL  TRYOVR
```

17. Use the WRKSPLF command to look at your spooled files.

    You should see the QPWCDSKS spooled file with USRDTA of XXX and 2 copies. Another OVRxxx command in the same program overrides the first (the command entry display is a program). The override of USRDTA(YYY) was lost. Note also that the attributes specified at different levels in the program stack have been merged.

18. Using PDM, modify the TRYOVR source by adding the SECURE(*YES) parameter to the OVRPRTF command.

19. Create the program.

20. Call the program:

```
CALL  TRYOVR
```

Exercise A continued

Exercise A continued

21. Use the WRKSPLF command to look at your spooled files.

    You should see the QPWCDSKS spooled file with USRDTA of XXX as specified in your program and the number of copies as 1. SECURE(*YES) prevents any overrides higher in the program stack from taking over. Your program is now in control of its own destiny.

22. Return to the command entry display and delete all your overrides with the command

    ```
    DLTOVR  *ALL
    ```

    When you specify DLTOVR *ALL, it affects any overrides specified in your current level (i.e., where your program is in the stack). The DLTOVR *ALL command has no effect on overrides issued by programs higher in the program stack. Those overrides would still exist. Also, the DLTOVR *ALL does not affect overrides issued by programs lower in the program stack. When the program returns, the system removes the program from the stack and automatically deletes these overrides.

Exercise B Overrides to QPRINT at Different Levels

In this exercise you will create a CL program and a small RPG program. The RPG program, called by the CL program, prints one meaningless line to file QPRINT. If you are a COBOL programmer, write a similar program in COBOL. Using these programs, you will see the effect overrides have when they are executed at different levels in the program stack.

1. Use PDM to create a CLP member named TRYOVR2.
2. Enter the following source (note that you are overriding both the spooled file name and the user data to provide more meaningful descriptions in the output queue):

Exercise B continued

Exercise B continued

```
PGM
OVRPRTF  FILE(QPRINT) USRDTA(ACCRCV) SPLFNAME(REGISTER)
CALL     TRYOVR3
ENDPGM
```

3. Create the program.
4. Use PDM to create an RPG member named TRYOVR3.
5. Enter the following source:

```
...+... 1 ...+... 2 ...+... 3 ...+... 4 ...+... 5 ...+... 7 ...
    FQPRINT  O   F      132      OF      PRINTER
    C                         EXCPTPRINT
    C                         SETON                        LR
    C                         RETRN
    OQPRINT  E  206               PRINT
    O                                      30 'One and only line'
```

6. Create the program.
7. Call the RPG program:

```
CALL  TRYOVR3
```

8. Use the WRKSPLF command to look at your spooled files.

   You should see the QPRINT spooled file name. Also note that the name of the program that created the output (TRYOVR3) is the default value for USRDTA. Some IBM display commands fill in the USRDTA value and some (e.g., WRKDSKSTS) do not.

9. Now call the CL program, which performs the override:

```
CALL  TRYOVR2
```

10. Use the WRKSPLF command to look at your spooled files.

    You should see REGISTER as the spooled file name (rather than QPRINT) because you changed it with the OVRPRTF command. You should also see that the USRDTA value has changed per the OVRDBF command. Specifying values for SPLFNAME and USRDTA help provide meaningful descriptions of spooled files for you or your operators.

Exercise B continued

Exercise B continued

11. Return to the command entry display and issue the following command:

```
OVRPRTF  FILE(QPRINT) SPLFNAME(XXX)
```

12. Now call the CL program:

```
CALL  TRYOVR2
```

13. Use the WRKSPLF command to look at your spooled files.

    You should see the spooled file name is XXX. Overrides specified in programs higher in the program stack take precedence.

14. Using PDM, modify CLP member TRYOVR2 by adding the SECURE(*YES) parameter to the OVRPRTF command.
15. Create the program.
16. Call the CL program:

```
CALL  TRYOVR2
```

17. Use the WRKSPLF command to look at your spooled files.

    You should see the spooled file name is REGISTER again. The SECURE(*YES) parameter prevents the override you entered on the command entry display from taking effect. Note that CL program TRYOVR2 does not open file QPRINT. It is opened in the RPG program. The SECURE(*YES) value protects a file opened after the override command has executed, whether or not the file is in the same program or in a program lower in the program stack.

18. Call the RPG program:

```
CALL  TRYOVR3
```

19. Use the WRKSPLF command to look at your spooled files.

    You should see the spooled file name is XXX again. You are calling the RPG program without the intervening CL program. The CL program ended a long time ago and the system removed the override command with the SECURE(*YES) parameter when the program was removed from the program stack. Therefore, file QPRINT is being opened without the override from the CL program in effect. This makes the override you issued from the command entry display effective and the system uses it.

Exercise B continued

Exercise B continued

20. Delete your overrides:

```
DLTOVR  FILE(*ALL)
```

21. If you used F21 to change your assistance level on the WRKSPLF command, and you want to return to the original assistance level, do so now.

Exercise C Overrides to a Different File

In this exercise you will read a file in CL and then see the effect of overrides.

1. You will need to create two outfiles, so enter the following commands:

```
DSPOBJD  OBJ(QGPL/*ALL) OBJTYPE(*OUTQ) OUTPUT(*OUTFILE)  +
           OUTFILE(QTEMP/TRYOVROUTQ)
DSPOBJD  OBJ(QGPL/*ALL) OBJTYPE(*JOBQ) OUTPUT(*OUTFILE)  +
           OUTFILE(QTEMP/TRYOVRJOBQ)
```

The first file will contain only *OUTQ objects and the second one will contain only *JOBQ objects.

2. Use PDM to create a CLP member named TRYOVR4. This program will declare the file with *OUTQ objects. It will read the first record from the file and then send a message containing the file name and object type.

3. Enter the following source:

```
PGM
DCLF       FILE(TRYOVROUTQ) /* Outfile used by */
RCVF       /* Read a record */
SNDPGMMSG  MSG(&ODOBNM *CAT '  ' *CAT &ODOBTP)
ENDPGM
```

4. Create the program.

Exercise C continued

Exercise C continued

5. Call the program:

```
CALL  TRYOVR4
```

You should see a message that indicates an *OUTQ object was read.

6. Now let's try to override to the *JOBQ file. Enter the following command on the command entry display:

```
OVRDBF  FROM(TRYOVROUTQ) TOFILE(TRYOVRJOBQ)
```

You always override from the file specified in the program to the file you want the program to open.

7. Call the program:

```
CALL  TRYOVR4
```

You should see a message that says a *JOBQ object was read. It is possible to cause a totally different file to be read by entering override commands at a higher level. The way to protect against this is to use the SECURE(*YES) parameter.

8. Using PDM, modify the source for TRYOVR4 by adding the following OVRDBF command ahead of the RCVF command:

```
OVRDBF  FILE(TRYOVROUTQ) SECURE(*YES)
```

The first RCVF command executed will open the file. For the override to be effective, you must specify it before the file is opened.

9. Create the program.

10. Call the program:

```
CALL  TRYOVR4
```

You should see a message that says an *OUTQ object has been read. Specifying SECURE(*YES) prevents override commands higher in the program stack from having any effect. The program with the SECURE(*YES) parameter controls its own destiny.

11. Delete your overrides:

```
DLTOVR  FILE(*ALL)
```

CHAPTER 19

Sequencing and Selection Techniques

You can sequence and select data in a variety of ways on the AS/400. In this chapter we'll look at the options available when you are working with physical or logical files.

PHYSICAL FILES

You can access physical files in two ways:

1. *Keyed sequence.* You would provide this option by defining one or more fields in a file as a key field. You could then access the file randomly by key or sequentially by key. With a keyed physical file, you have no record selection capability; all records are always available.
2. *Arrival sequence.* This is the order in which records are added to a physical file; no key field is specified. You can access the file sequentially (i.e., in arrival sequence) or randomly by relative record number. If you ask for a record by relative record number, the system determines where the record must be by multiplying the record number times the record length.

A physical file can have one or more members. Each physical file member uses the same access path definition, but each member has a unique index that points to its actual records. Most physical files that contain data have a single member. Multimember physical files are primarily source files.

LOGICAL FILES

Although you can specify logical files in several ways (e.g., as multiformat files, with arrival sequence access paths, as joined files) I will focus here on the typical way in which logical files are specified: a keyed access path built over a single member of a single physical file.

When creating a logical file, you need to be aware that the MAINT (type of manintenance) parameter on the CRTLF (Create Logical File) command influences your processing requirements. Here's a rundown on the values you can specify for the MAINT parameter:

- *IMMED (Immediate). If you take the default, *IMMED, the access path will be maintained all the time (whenever a record is added or deleted, or whenever the key field changes). If you want the fastest possible access to a record, specify *IMMED.

- *REBLD (Rebuild). If you specify *REBLD, the access path is maintained only if it is open. When a program opens the file, the access path is built and then maintained until the file is closed. Before the introduction of OPNQRYF and SQL, *REBLD was a popular form for seldom-used (e.g., once a month) logical files. Today, I prefer to use OPNQRYF in a CL program. OPNQRYF has more function and eliminates the need for another object and source member on the system.
- *DLY (Delayed). If you specify *DLY, changes to the access path are buffered and not made until the file is opened. When the file is opened, the changes are applied and the access path is immediately maintained. *DLY is rarely used. Its use makes sense only for applications where there is a small percentage of change (e.g., the file is not opened frequently and then only in batch).

A logical file cannot be in a different ASP (Auxiliary Storage Pool) from the physical file. A logical file's access path is saved and restored only if you follow certain rules: The logical file must exist in the same library as the physical file, and you must specify ACCPTH(*YES) on the SAVLIB command.

The ADDLFM/RMVM Commands

Sometimes, for month-end processing you need an access path on a particular field. If this is a one-time requirement, I prefer to use OPNQRYF to build the access path. But if you are going to use the same access path in multiple jobs (or in several programs in a complex job), you should consider adding the necessary logical file member and then removing the member. For best performance, use the RMVM command to remove the logical file member before performing an update where you add many records, and then use the ADDLFM command to add the member when the update is complete. The access path is built when the member is added. If you add a large number of records to a seldom-used file (at the end of the month, for example), it is actually faster for the system to build a new access path than to maintain an existing access path.

The ADDLFM and RMVM commands let you control when you want the member to exist so you don't need to do as much access path maintenance. Although using these commands is a good idea if you are going to access the data randomly, a sort can be significantly faster if you are going to access the data sequentially.

Technical Tip

While no one likes to build access paths from scratch, don't underestimate the system's ability to build them rapidly as opposed to making a lot of additions (and/or deletions) in a batch program. In terms of performance, having the system maintain access paths as you make many changes is not as efficient as building the access path from scratch.

A Keyed Access Path

When you specify a keyed access path, the system builds a table of entries in keyed value order. Each key value in the table has an associated relative record number. The table, called a binary tree, might look like this:

Key Value	Relative Record number
ABCDE	5
ABCDR	32
ABCDR	112
ABCDZ	55
ABCEX	3
.	.
.	.

When you process a file randomly, a keyed access path gives the system a quick way to find the key value in the table. Once the system locates the key in the table, it has immediate access to the relative record number of the record in the file and can quickly calculate where the record is on disk. To access the data sequentially by key, the system walks through the table beginning at the top.

If you process sequentially by key, the system must access each data record by relative record number. Because the data records are usually in some order other than the order by which you are processing, accessing all records by key generally results in considerable disk arm movement. The worst case is that the system must physically move the disk arm for every data record. Unfortunately, any time the system has to move a disk arm frequently, performance will be relatively slow. Consequently, if you have to read many records (i.e., thousands), you should avoid reading them by key. Arrival sequence processing is a much faster solution.

A Question of Performance

You can consider many factors as you determine the appropriate access path for a particular database file. But after being involved in database planning for many years and listening to many programmers discuss their problems, I would say the choices you have are fairly simple unless you have an unusual situation. These choices involve deciding on the performance level you want when accessing information. I put the choices in three categories, and each category carries responsibilities with it:

- *Fast performance.* You want an answer in two seconds or less. To achieve this goal you must be willing to build the right database files (access paths) and to use application programs to access the data. If you want a page of records (e.g., 20) that belong to a group (e.g., invoices owed by a specific customer), you may have to wait a little longer than two seconds; but the requirement still falls in this category.
- *Good performance.* You are willing to wait longer than two seconds, but you don't want to search the entire file. You are willing to build some database files (access paths), but you rely on either application programs or some form of Query to access the information. The database files must have immediately maintained access paths over the fields that users want to select on (e.g., ZIP code, city, sales amount). If you don't set up anything ahead of time to facilitate the search, the system must read every record in the file to identify all the records that match your selection criteria. For example, if you have not set up an immediately maintained access path on field TYPE, you can't pass a request to the system that says "Find all the records of TYPE = A" and expect the system to rapidly read only type A records.
- *Reasonable performance.* You are willing to search the entire file, but you want to use the best-performing technique. To provide this level of performance, you rely on either application programs or some form of Query.

Where OPNQRYF Fits

OPNQRYF (discussed in more detail in Chapter 20) is a very powerful function. It is mostly just a front end to the common internal support (the optimizer) used by SQL, AS/400 Query, and other functions.

OPNQRYF offers good solutions for two of the performance objective categories I mentioned earlier:

- *Good performance.* OPNQRYF does not have to read the entire file if your selection criteria matches an existing access path. Regardless of what approach OPNQRYF chooses, you can generally rely on its judgment for accessing the data in the fastest possible manner.
- *Reasonable performance.* OPNQRYF will usually do a good job

for you if you have to read the entire file to perform selection and sequencing.

Where OPNQRYF Doesn't Fit

When it comes to fast performance (two seconds or less), OPNQRYF is not a contender because you need immediately maintained access paths and HLL programs.

If your file contains only a handful of records and you want to process some of them, OPNQRYF adds overhead. Just read the file yourself.

To Sort or Not To Sort

Many AS/400 programmers believe that to physically sort data would be to use a technique from the dark ages of data processing. While sorting may seem old-fashioned, you may be missing an outstanding performance advantage if you don't use the capability.

Processing many records in keyed sequence is slow and, as I mentioned earlier, you can gain performance benefits by processing in arrival sequence. And if you process enough volume, you are better off to physically sort the data so you can take advantage of arrival sequence processing of the sorted data. If you are going to process more than 1,000 records, you should consider doing a physical sort.

Technical Tip

A physical sort is a very good performance solution if you want to read a lot of data in sequence. Processing via keyed access paths is not very fast. Consider anything over 1,000 records as a candidate for a physical sort.

You can do a physical sort in one of two ways:

1. Use the FMTDTA command. This approach wouldn't be my first choice. The FMTDTA command uses the same format for source specifications designed for the System/3 card system in 1968. The command does not allow the use of externally described data (you have to name the from/to positions). Although the FMTDTA command was once a favorite of mine, I have switched to OPNQRYF since support was added for a sort.

   If you find that you prefer the FMTDTA command, consider using it in conjunction with the SORTDB TAA tool. The SORTDB command generates the sort specifications for you so you can use externally described field names.

2. Use the OPNQRYF command. The OPNQRYF command has always been a good solution for selecting a small number of records. When selecting a handful of records, keyed processing is more efficient than sorting. Now OPNQRYF lets you sort records. In Version 2, Release 2 of the OS/400 operating system, the *OPTIMIZE value was added to the OPNQRYF ALWCPYDTA parameter.

   When you specify ALWCPYDTA(*OPTIMIZE), you are telling OPNQRYF that it is okay to perform a sort. OPNQRYF probably will perform a sort any time you are going to sequence on more than 1,000 records. Whether or not OPNQRYF performs a sort depends on how many records you select, not on the size of the file.

When OPNQRYF performs a sort, the program that processes the output will be reading data stored in a temporary file. If someone updates a data record during the creation of the temporary file, you might not see the update. For most applications, this won't be a concern.

Technical Tip

OPNQRYF is my favorite solution for selecting and sequencing data. If you are going to sequence many records (more than 1,000) in a file and you want your program to run fast, specify ALWCPYDTA(*OPTIMIZE) on the OPNQRYF command to allow a sort. *OPTIMIZE is not the default; you must specify the value to get the performance option.

CHAPTER 20

OPNQRYF

The OPNQRYF command is one of the most powerful AS/400 commands. The great amount of function provided by OPNQRYF can boost programmer productivity and application performance. However, the command's rich function does not come without complexity, and that complexity can make the command difficult to use. The intent of this chapter is not to provide a full course on the OPNQRYF command. Instead, we will examine the basic implementation of OPNQRYF, and we will present several TAA tools that can make it easier to use OPNQRYF.

IMPORTANT POINTS TO REMEMBER

As you experiment with OPNQRYF, keep the following points in mind:

- OPNQRYF (like SQL and AS/400 Query) is an interface to the internal function (the query optimizer) used by the system when it receives a request to perform a database query function. Unlike SQL, OPNQRYF lets you provide front-end processing for your applications so you can keep high-level language (HLL) programs free of selection and sequencing requirements.
- OPNQRYF requires a shared file. Normally, to ensure that the file to be opened has the SHARE(*YES) value, you would use an OVRDBF command just before executing OPNQRYF to explicitly specify SHARE(*YES). For example,

```
OVRDBF    FILE(xxx) SHARE(*YES)
OPNQRYF   FILE(xxx) ...
```

- Because of the requirement for a shared file, many system functions do not work with OPNQRYF. These functions include:

  CPYF
  DFU
  DSPPFM
  RUNQRY
  AS/400 Query

  These functions require a full open (the first open of a shared file is a full open) and ignore attempts to have them share a file. However, you can use the CPYFRMQRYF (Copy From Query File) command to copy records selected during an OPNQRYF process to the permanent file; then you can use any function to process the file.

- Also because of the requirement for a shared file, you must close the file when you are done and delete the override. For a file named FILEA, the code might look like the following:

```
OVRDBF     FILE(FILEA) SHARE(*YES)
OPNQRYF    FILE(FILEA) ...
CALL       PGM(yyy)
CLOF       OPNID(FILEA)
DLTOVR     FILE(FILEA)
```

- OPNQRYF creates an open data path (ODP). Because the ODP is shared (the OVRDBF command requested that it be shared), the HLL program uses the same ODP built by OPNQRYF. The system assigns an ID to each ODP. By default the ID is the same name as the file name you specified on the OPNQRYF command. Several ODPs could exist for your job at one time, but each ODP must have a unique ID.

Typical Errors that "Blow Programmers' Minds"

When you operate from the command entry display, any escape message will cause an internal RCLRSC (Reclaim Resource) command to occur, which closes all open files. Because of this, if you make a mistake with OPNQRYF or your program, you don't get what you want because the shared file is either already open or it has been closed. OPNQRYF is very unforgiving.

To clarify this point, here are examples of what might go wrong when you use OPNQRYF from the command entry display. Being able to recognize these errors will help you recover more quickly.

- You successfully enter OPNQRYF and then realize you need to change the command. So you enter the command again and receive escape message CPF4174, which says that the OPNID for the file already exists. The message's second-level text tells you to close the file (using the CLOF command). After executing the CLOF command, you receive escape message CPF4520, which tells you that no file with the specified OPNID is open.

  When you enter an OPNQRYF command successfully and then change it before executing your program, anything you do to cause an escape message on the command entry display will close the file. To recover, you should *not* execute CLOF; simply start over by executing the OPNQRYF command again (the third time is the charm). Or you can do what I prefer to do: Enter the X command, which does not exist on my system. When I enter X and press Enter, the system sends me an escape message, which causes the internal RCLRSC command to execute and close all open files. Then I start over by entering the OPNQRYF command again.

Note that prompting for a command and then cancelling with F3 or F12 also causes an escape message to be sent, which invokes the internal RCLRSC command.

- You enter the OPNQRYF command successfully and then call your program using an incorrect name or parameter. The system sends a message explaining the problem. When you correct the CALL command, the program runs but provides results as if OPNQRYF didn't do anything. In this instance, when the CALL command failed on the first try, the command entry function closed the file and the ODP is no longer available. Consequently, you are reading the file without the benefit of OPNQRYF. As in the situation above, you must start over. I like to enter the X command to ensure I have a clean slate and then re-enter the OPNQRYF command.
- After running OPNQRYF and calling your program, you decide to call the program again. The message you receive almost immediately says no records were found. In this situation, when you first called the program, the records were read until "end of file" was reached. When you call the program again, the shared ODP is still available but the file cursor is at "end of file." You can use the POSDBF command to reposition the file cursor before recalling your program, but the simplest approach is to start over.

Technical Tip

Several common errors can occur when you use OPNQRYF. Being able to recognize these errors when they happen, and knowing how to recover from them, can be helpful. In general, if you receive unusual results when using OPNQRYF, close the file, delete the override, and check your specifications — then try again.

Typical QRYSLT Examples

The QRYSLT parameter of the OPNQRYF command provides record selection before record sequencing occurs. The query selection expression can be up to 2,000 characters long, must be enclosed in apostrophes (because it comprises a character string for the command to evaluate), and can consist of one or more logical expressions connected by *AND or *OR. Let's look at some typical ways you might use QRYSLT.

First, assume you have a file named FILEQ that contains a one-character field named CUSCDE and you want to select all the records where CUSCDE = B. You would code the following:

```
OVRDBF      FILE(FILEQ) SHARE(*YES)
OPNQRYF     FILE(FILEQ) QRYSLT('CUSCDE *EQ "B"')
CALL        PGM(xxx)
CLOF        OPNID(FILEQ)
DLTOVR      FILE(FILEQ)
```

If no access path exists for CUSCDE, OPNQRYF will tell the system to read all the records in arrival sequence and to pass to your program only those records that match the specified selection criteria. If an access path does exist for CUSCDE, the system may use that access path.

Whether the system uses an existing access path or arrival sequence depends on internal calculations regarding the percentage of records in the file that will match the selection criteria. If the system calculates that less than 20 percent of the records will match, it will use the access path. If the system calculates that a greater percentage of the records will match, it will ignore the existing access path and use arrival sequence. In this case, the system will read the data in arrival sequence.

Look again at the QRYSLT parameter specified in this example:

```
QRYSLT('CUSCDE *EQ "B"')
```

The entire expression is enclosed in single quotes because the value will be evaluated by the command as a character string. The field name in the file (CUSCDE) is used without an & preceding it. Double quote marks are placed around the literal character B. Also note that the "B" was entered in uppercase. If you entered "b" and your data is stored in uppercase, OPNQRYF won't find any records. The command prompter can make a mess of what you enter into the QRYSLT parameter. I either code without the prompter or enter the following into the prompt:

```
Query selection expression . . . > ('CUSCDE *EQ "B"')
      .
      .
      .
```

When the command is returned, you'll still see the outside parentheses:

```
QRYSLT('CUSCDE *EQ "B"')
```

If you wanted to select all records where the AMT field (a decimal field) is greater than 1000, your QRYSLT statement would be coded as

```
QRYSLT('AMT *GT 1000')
```

Because you are selecting on a decimal field, the value (1000) does not need double quote marks around it.

Technical Tip

The way to remember whether or not to use double quote marks when specifying the QRYSLT parameter is to think about how the field you are selecting on is defined in the database. If it is a character field, you must place double quote marks around the literal to which you are comparing.

Now assume you want to pass a value as a parameter into your CL program and select on it. The variable returned to your program must be concatenated into the QRYSLT character string. To do this correctly, think about the statement as if it was a literal. For example, to meet the requirements of our original QRYSLT statement

```
QRYSLT('CUSCDE *EQ "B"')
```

we would code the following:

```
PGM        PARM(&SELECT)
DCL        &SELECT *CHAR LEN(1)
 .
 .
 .
OPNQRYF    FILE(FILEQ) QRYSLT('CUSCDE *EQ "' *CAT +
             &SELECT *CAT '"')
```

The character string 'CUSCDE *EQ "' would be concatenated with the value passed into the program and then with the double quote character. Thus, after substituting the real value and performing the concatenation for the QRYSLT parameter

```
('CUSCDE *EQ "' *CAT &SELECT *CAT '"')
```

we would end up with

```
('CUSCDE *EQ "B"')
```

When you have a string (a single value) and you use concatenation, the system knows it is still a string. That's why the expression does not always begin or end with a single quote. The second double quote was entered as

```
'"'
```

or single quote, double quote, single quote. You treat the double quote as a literal.

When you prompt for OPNQRYF from SEU, entering this type of an expression can be challenging because the prompter loves to double up the single quotes. To avoid problems, begin and end the expression with a parenthesis. For example,

```
('CUSCDE *EQ "' *CAT &SELECT *CAT '"')
```

When the command is returned to SEU, you'll see exactly what you keyed and you can safely reprompt the command without having a multitude of single quote marks appear in your source.

Technical Tip

When you deal with an expression in SEU and want to prompt for it, put parentheses around the entire expression as you enter it.

If you want to select on a decimal variable, the QRYSLT statement is easier to work with because you don't need the double quote marks. However, you can't concatenate a decimal variable into a character string. Therefore, you must first convert the decimal variable to a character variable. For example, to use the selection criteria AMT *GT 1000, you would specify

```
PGM        PARM(&SELECT)
DCL        &SELECT *DEC LEN(7 0)
DCL        &SELECTA *CHAR LEN(7)
  .
  .
  .
CHGVAR     &SELECTA &SELECT /* Change to *CHAR */
OPNQRYF    FILE(FILEQ) QRYSLT('AMT *GT ' *CAT &SELECTA)
```

Technical Tip

When you want to select on a variable that will be compared to a decimal field, you must convert the variable to a character field so you can concatenate it into the string value required by QRYSLT. Because the field in the database you are comparing to is a decimal field, you don't need double quotes around the variable.

So far, our examples of QRYSLT have used simple selection statements; more complex selection statements follow the same concept. For example, if you want to select on CUSCDE = B and AMT greater than 1000, you simply code a longer expression:

```
OPNQRYF    FILE(FILEQ)  +
             QRYSLT('CUSCDE *EQ "B" *AND AMT *GT 1000')
```

Just as in CL, the system performs the *AND tests first. Therefore, if you coded

```
QRYSLT('CUSCDE *EQ "A" *OR CUSCDE *EQ "B" *AND AMT *GT 1000')
```

you would get the following result:

```
CUSCDE = A
```

or

```
CUSCDE = B and AMT GT 1000
```

To control the and/or logic, you would use parentheses. For example, you might code

```
QRYSLT('(CUSCDE *EQ "A" *OR CUSCDE *EQ "B") *AND AMT *GT 1000')
```

which would give you the following results:

```
CUSCDE = A or CUSCDE = B
```

and

```
AMT GT 1000
```

THE MAPFLD PARAMETER

The MAPFLD parameter on the OPNQRYF command provides considerable function. The mapped field specifications let you derive new fields from fields in the record format being queried. Assume you want to select on the year portion of a field (CHRDAT) that is in MMDDYY format. As the following code shows, you can use a substring function to extract the year from CHRDAT and then create mapped field YY on which to perform your selection criteria:

```
OPNQRYF    FILE((FILEQ)) QRYSLT('YY *EQ "95"') +
             MAPFLD((YY '%SST(CHRDAT 5 2)'))
```

As with the QRYSLT parameter, prompting for the MAPFLD parameter can be a challenge. You must roll through several screens to find the parameter. I often key the parameter without using the prompter; but if you do use the prompter, it should look like this:

```
Mapped field specifications:
  Mapped field . . . . . . . . . > YY             Name, *NONE
  Field definition expression  . > '%SST(ODCDAT 5 2)'


  Mapped field type  . . . . . .   *CALC          *CALC, *BIN2, *BIN4, *FLT4 ...
  Length . . . . . . . . . . . .   _______        0-32766
  Decimal positions  . . . . . .   _______        0-31
  Mapped field CCSID . . . . . .   *CALC          *CALC, *HEX ...
               + for more values   _

    .
    .
    .
```

USING KEY FIELDS

In addition to selecting records, you can establish the order of the records

OPNQRYF presents to your HLL program by entering one or more key fields in the key field specifications. The KEYFLD parameter consists of several elements. You must specify the field name, whether to sequence the field in ascending or descending order, whether or not to use absolute values for sequencing, and whether or not to enforce uniqueness.

For example, here's what you code to process on field CUSCDE in ascending order:

```
OVRDBF     FILE(FILEQ) SHARE(*YES)
OPNQRYF    FILE(FILEQ) KEYFLD(CUSCDE)
CALL       PGM(xxx)
CLOF       OPNID(FILEQ)
DLTOVR     FILE(FILEQ)
```

To specify descending sequence, you would code

```
KEYFLD((CUSCDE *DESCEND))
```

You can also specify multiple key fields. For example,

```
KEYFLD(TERR CUSCDE)
```

The key field also can be a variable. For example,

```
PGM        PARM(&FIELD)
DCL        &FIELD *CHAR LEN(10)
  .
  .
  .
OPNQRYF    FILE(FILEQ) KEYFLD(&FIELD)
```

And you can specify multiple key fields as variables. For example,

```
PGM        PARM(&FIELD1 &FIELD2)
DCL        &FIELD1 *CHAR LEN(10)
DCL        &FIELD2 *CHAR LEN(10)
  .
  .
  .
OPNQRYF    FILE((FILEQ)) KEYFLD(&FIELD1 &FIELD2)
```

A strict rule is that the key field must exist in the record format being queried. Thus, the key field cannot be a mapped field. But you can work around this restriction. Assume you want to sequence a field in MMDDYY format as if it were in YYMMDD format. The easiest solution is to map the field into the order you want and then map the new value into a field that you don't need, but that exists in the record format being queried.

For example, let's say that field CHRDAT is in MMDDYY format and you don't need field CITY in your program. You could use the CITY field for the new format of the date:

```
OPNQRYF     FILE((FILEQ)) KEYFLD(CITY)            +
              MAPFLD((MMDD '%SST(CHRDAT 1 4)') +
              (YY '%SST(CHRDAT 5 2)') (CITY 'YY *CAT MMDD'))
```

If field CITY is read by your program, it would contain the YYMMDD value and not the city name.

The MAPFLD parameter can't refer to a mapped field name without defining it first. For example, it would have been *invalid to* specify

```
OPNQRYF   FILE((FILEQ)) KEYFLD(CITY) MAPFLD((CITY 'YY *CAT MMDD') +
            (MMDD '%SST(CHRDAT 1 4)') (YY '%SST(CHRDAT 5 2)')
```

In this example, the MAPFLD parameter in the command could not define the CITY field because CITY refers to the YY and MMDD fields, which the command has not yet defined.

To define a new field on a mapped field statement, you can specify the characteristics of the new field or you can take the default. In the case of the MMDD mapped field, since you are substringing out 4 characters and don't define the field, the system defaults to define MMDD as a *CHAR LEN(4) field.

OPNQRYF Performance

It is fairly typical to use both selection and sequencing on the same OPNQRYF command. If an access path already exists for the sequencing field, don't be surprised if OPNQRYF builds an access path for you. Normally, OPNQRYF will use an existing access path for selection and then build a temporary access path over the selected records.

In general, OPNQRYF will select the fastest way to read the records, but you should keep a few points in mind:

- If you want quick response time, don't use OPNQRYF. For quick response time, you need an existing access path and a HLL program that accesses a record by key or that starts reading at a specified key.
- In most situations, each use of OPNQRYF causes a full open (the first open of a shared file is a full open). A full open is not one of the fastest performers on the system, so you don't want to abuse the function by using OPNQRYF too often.
- In a few situations, OPNQRYF might make a poor performance choice. One of the internal rules for OPNQRYF involves the use

of join and temporary files. In general, OPNQRYF will attempt to avoid building a temporary file if you are joining files. Because of this, you have to be careful when you are joining a small file to a large file. If you specify a key field on the large file, OPNQRYF will invert the join to avoid building a temporary file. To control the order, you must specify JORDER(*FILE).

- If you have a very small file, OPNQRYF will not bother looking to see if any useable access paths exist. It just assumes some default and runs. This is what you want to happen: You don't want OPNQRYF to spend a lot of time searching for an optimal path when it really won't make a lot of difference.

Technical Tip

When you test OPNQRYF against a small subset of a file, you will see only if the results are correct; you may not see how OPNQRYF will access similar data in the larger file. If a file is very small, OPNQRYF may ignore existing access paths and process in arrival sequence. This could give a misleading impression about how your production version will perform. The true test is to run against your production version.

- For reasonably sized files, OPNQRYF will look at the access paths built over the physical file to see if it can find a good one to use. However, if a lot of access paths have been built over a physical file, OPNQRYF may reach a time-out and not search all the access paths (a time-out is used to prevent OPNQRYF from searching too long). If a time-out occurs, OPNQRYF might not choose the best access path. You can keep this from happening by
  - specifying (on the FILE parameter) the logical file that you know has the best access path (then OPNQRYF will be forced to look at that access path), or
  - specifying OPTALLAP(*YES) on OPNQRYF, which causes all the access paths to be searched (no time-out occurs)
- It used to be faster to physically sort the data if you were going to sequence a lot of records (e.g., 10,000 records or more) than to use OPNQRYF. However, in Version 2 Release 2, OPNQRYF was given the ability to perform the physical sort. This function only works if you specify ALWCPYDTA(*OPTIMIZE).

Technical Tip

If you are going to sequence one thousand records or more and read the records for input (not update), be sure to specify ALWCPYDTA(*OPTIMIZE). This will allow the system to physically sort the records into a temporary file, which will improve performance in your processing program. If you don't specify *OPTIMIZE, the system will not physically sort the data because it tries to avoid temporary files. Instead, OPNQRYF would use a keyed access path, which would lead to slower processing.

- If you have a large database and you want fast queries, you must build access paths over the fields that users normally select on. Otherwise, you force OPNQRYF to process the entire file in arrival sequence.

OPNQRYF Message Feedback

By default, OPNQRYF doesn't send a completion message (status messages are sent if you operate interactively). However, if you are in debug mode, completion messages are sent. To receive the completion messages, simply enter

```
STRDBG
```

By using debug mode, you will know for certain how OPNQRYF accessed your data.

Technical Tip

To better understand what OPNQRYF is doing, use debug mode so you will receive completion messages. The completion messages describe how a result was achieved.

The QRYF TAA Tool

Now that you have seen how OPNQRYF can help you, let's look at three TAA tools that can help you use OPNQRYF: the QRYF TAA tool, the CRTPRTPGM TAA tool, and the CPYJOBLOG TAA tool.

The QRYF (Query File) TAA tool provides two commands: the QRYF command and the BLDQRYSLT command. The QRYF command provides a simple front end to OPNQRYF. For simple queries, you don't need to understand how to enter quote marks in the character string — you don't need quote marks with the QRYF command. The prompt for QRYF looks like this:

```
                 Front End to OPNQRYF (QRYF)

    Type choices, press Enter.

    File name . . . . . . . . . . .   __________      Name
      Library name . . . . . . . . .      *LIBL       Name,  *LIBL
    Selection criteria:                 _
      Factor 1 or  BLANK . . . . . .   __________
      Operator . . . . . . . . . . .   *EQ            *EQ, *LE, *GT, *LT, *GE...
      Factor 2 or  BLANK . . . . . .   __________
      Character literal  . . . . . .   *NONE          *NONE, F1, F2
      Translate table on F1  . . . .   *NONE          Name,  STD, *NONE
      And/Or relation to next select   *AND           *AND, *OR, *EAND, *EOR
                   + for more values _
    Sequencing criteria:                _
      Key field  . . . . . . . . . .   __________     Character value,  FILE
      Sequence . . . . . . . . . . .   *ASCEND        *ASCEND, *DESCEND
                   + for more values
    Member . . . . . . . . . . . . .   *FIRST         Name, *FIRST
                                                          ...
```

Most of the prompts are self-explanatory. When you enter the selection criteria, the important parameter is the prompt for "Character literal." This prompt asks whether Factor 1 or Factor 2 is a character literal. If your select criteria is 'CUSCDE *EQ B', then Factor 2 is a character literal and you need to enter F2 on the prompt screen. When you key in the values, the prompt would look like this:

```
    Selection criteria:                 _
      Factor 1 or  BLANK . . . . . .   CUSCDE____
      Operator . . . . . . . . . . .   *EQ            *EQ, *LE, *GT, *LT, *GE...
      Factor 2 or  BLANK . . . . . .   B_________
      Character literal  . . . . . .   F2             *NONE, F1, F2
```

The QRYF command generates the proper OPNQRYF command and then executes it. The QRYF command also sends the command as a *RQS message and then receives it so that the OPNQRYF command is mostly filled out for you. For instance, if, in this example, we had entered FILEQ as the file name, we would have seen the following on the command entry display:

```
QRYF    FILE(FILEQ) SELECT((CUSCDE *EQ B F2))
OPNQRYF FILE(FILEQ) QRYSLT('(CUSCDE *EQ "B")')
```

If you want to add more parameters or modify the command, place the cursor on the fleshed-out OPNQRYF command and press F4. Note that because we said Factor 2 is a character literal, double quote marks surround the B in the OPNQRYF command.

The QRYF command also supports the KEYFLD and MBR parameters, but not the rest of the parameters supported by OPNQRYF.

The QRYF command is designed to be used when you are operating from the command entry display. You can use it in a CL program; but the companion command, BLDQRYSLT, is preferred for CL programs.

The BLDQRYSLT command uses the same prompt for the QRYSLT parameter as does the QRYF command and it returns a value ready to be used for the QRYSLT parameter. The BLDQRYSLT command prompt looks like this:

```
                Build Query Select (BLDQRYSLT)

Type choices, press Enter.

Query select return var (2000)    __________   Character value, FILE
Selection criteria:               _
  Factor 1 or  BLANK . . . . . .  __________
  Operator . . . . . . . . . . .  *EQ          *EQ, *LE, *GT, *LT, *GE...
  Factor 2 or  BLANK . . . . . .  __________
  Character literal  . . . . . .  *NONE        *NONE, F1, F2
  Translate table on F1  . . . .  *NONE        Name,  STD,  NONE
  And/Or relation to next select  *AND         *AND, *OR, *EAND, *EOR
              + for more values
```

The return variable must be declared as *CHAR LEN(2000). Normally you would assign a variable name such as &QRYSLT. As in the previous example, you simply fill in the blanks to specify the selection criteria.

Let's assume you are in SEU and you prompt for BLDQRYSLT. When the prompt screen appears, you enter &QRYSLT as the return variable. Then you enter 'CUSCDE *EQ B' and specify that Factor 2 is a character literal. When you press Enter, the SEU statement would look like this:

```
BLDQRYSLT  QRYSLT(&QRYSLT) SELECT((CUSCDE *EQ B F2))
```

When you execute the BLDQRYSLT command, it will return the &QRYSLT parameter. The parameter contains the string needed for the QRYSLT parameter on the OPNQRYF command. The full program would look like this:

```
DCL        &QRYSLT *CHAR LEN(2000)
.
.
.
OVRDBF     FILE(FILEQ) SHARE(*YES)
BLDQRYSLT  QRYSLT(&QRYSLT) SELECT((CUSCDE *EQ B F2))
OPNQRYF    FILE((FILEQ)) QRYSLT(&QRYSLT)
CALL       PGM(xxx)
CLOF       OPNID(FILEQ)
DLTOVR     FILE(FILEQ)
```

The real power of BLDQRYSLT occurs when you use a variable name and not a literal: You don't have to mess with all the concatenation functions.

The CRTPRTPGM TAA Tool

You can use the CRTPRTPGM TAA tool, which is discussed in Chapter 21, "Displaying Data," to create a general-purpose print program for use with OPNQRYF. The general-purpose print program is ideal for an *ad hoc* OPNQRYF function or for printing a small amount of data. But the program is not very efficient, so you shouldn't print a lot of records with it.

Assume you want a general-purpose print program to work with FILEQ. To create the program, you would enter

```
CRTPRTPGM  FILEQ
```

This command submits a batch job that creates a general-purpose print program named ZFILEQ. You can then print the data in FILEQ by using the PRTDBF command (the companion command to the CRTPRTPGM command):

```
PRTDBF  PGM(ZFILEQ)
```

This command will print a report that is 132 positions wide. If the data is too long, it is truncated. You can use a combination of QRYF and PRTDBF to handle simple requests:

```
QRYF    FILE(FILEQ)...
PRTDBF  PGM(ZFILEQ)
```

In Chapter 21, the discussion of CRTPRTPGM shows how you can prompt for a list of the fields in your file with the PRTDBF command and select those you want to print and the order. Or you could just key in the command yourself:

```
PRTDBF  PGM(ZFILEQ) FIELDS(CUSCDE CUST NAME CITY)
```

You can also use the KEYFLD function of QRYF and the totaling function, such as

```
QRYF    FILE(FILEQ) KEYFLD((TERR))
PRTDBF  PGM(ZFILEQ) FIELDS(TERR CUST AMT) L1CTL(TERR)
```

You would see a report with the records sequenced on the TERR field and a control break on TERR. Any numeric fields (e.g., AMT) would be totaled.

If you have created the general-purpose print program, the DSPDBD (Display Data Base Definition) command, which is part of the CRTPRTPGM tool, can be used to look at the field descriptions of a file. Simply code

```
DSPDBD  ZFILEQ
```

You would see a display with the field names, attributes, and text.

THE CPYJOBLOG TAA TOOL

As you key several commands interactively, or as you key a difficult command such as OPNQRYF, you may suddenly realize that the commands ought to be in a CL program. You would then have the thrill of rekeying the commands using SEU.

Or you could use the CPYJOBLOG (Copy Job Log) TAA tool to make your life easier. You would enter

```
CPYJOBLOG   MBR(xxx) SRCFILE(yyy)
```

After entering the CPYJOBLOG command, any commands you had entered during the past five minutes (five minutes is the default) would be written to the source member you named. You would then enter SEU and use F4 to prompt for the commands you want, delete what you don't want, add a PGM and ENDPGM statement, and you would have a CL program ready to go.

Technical Tip

The CPYJOBLOG command can save you many keystrokes when you want to capture your command entry commands and place them in a CLP source member.

Exercise A Using OPNQRYF from a Command Entry Display

In this exercise you will create an outfile in a library from the objects in library QGPL and look for certain information in the records. You will need the TAA tool CRTPRTPGM; if it is not on your system, see Appendix B.

1. First, we'll create an outfile of the objects in library QGPL and use CRTPRTPGM to look at the data. Create the outfile:

   ```
   DSPOBJDP  OBJ(QGPL/*ALL) OBJTYPE(*ALL) OUTPUT(*OUTFILE) +
             OUTFILE(xxx/DSPOBJDP)
   ```

2. Use the CRTPRTPGM TAA tool to create a general-purpose print program:

   ```
   CRTPRTPGM  FILE(DSPOBJDP)
   ```

   This command should submit a job named ZDSPOBJDP.

3. You will want to be on the command entry display for these exercises. If you are not already there, enter

   ```
   CALL  QCMD
   ```

4. When the ZDSPOBJDP program has been created, ensure that reasonable output is being produced by entering the following command:

   ```
   PRTDBF  PGM(ZDSPOBJDP)
   ```

   You should see a display of the printed output from the file.

5. Use OPNQRYF interactively to select the *JOBQ objects from the DSPOBJDP file. The field name for the object type is ODOBTP. Use the PRTDBF command to print the results.

6. If you don't get the right answer, review the basic complete program described earlier in this chapter. Did you remember to use the OVR command and specify SHARE(*YES)? Did you remember to double-quote the literal? You need the double-quote character when the field in the database is in character format.

7. Use option 14 of the DSPJOB menu to display the open files.

   You should see that the DSPOBJDP file is open.

Exercise A continued

Exercise A continued

8. Return to the command entry display and use F9 to duplicate the OPNQRYF command and then execute it.

   The command should fail because the ODP is already open.

9. Use option 14 of the DSPJOB menu again to display the open files.

   You shouldn't see file DSPOBJDP because when the second OPNQRYF command failed, an internal RCLRSC command was executed, which causes all files to be closed.

10. Return to the command entry display and use F9 again to duplicate the OPNQRYF command and then execute it.

    This time, OPNQRYF should work because the ODP is not open.

11. Enter the X command (assuming it is not on your system).

    This should produce an escape message that causes the internal RCLRSC command to be executed.

12. Try DSPJOB menu option 14 again to see if your file is open. (The file should not be open.)

13. Use the DSPDBD command (part of the CRTPRTPGM tool) as follows:

    ```
    DSPDBD  ZDSPOBJDP
    ```

    You should see a display of the field names, attributes, and text description of the fields in file DSPOBJDP. Determine the name of the field that has the object size, for use in Step 16.

14. Enter the STRDBG command

    ```
    STRDBG
    ```

    This will cause messages to appear that are produced by OPNQRYF (they appear only in debug mode).

15. Use OPNQRYF to select all the objects in DSPOBJDP where the size of the object is greater than 50,000 bytes.

    If OPNQRYF executed successfully, you should see two *INFO messages that tell you

    — all access paths were considered
    — arrival sequence was used (not a keyed access path)

Exercise A continued

Exercise A continued

16. Use the PRTDBF command for program ZDSPOBJDP and prompt for the fields:

```
PRTDBF  PGM(ZDSPOBJDP) FIELDS(*YES)
```

17. Request to print only the following fields in this order: ODOBNM, ODOBSZ, ODOBTP, ODOBAT. Press Enter to refresh the display and then press Enter again.

    You should see the report you want.

18. Use F9 to duplicate the generated PRTDBF command (the one with all the fields) and then execute it.

    You should see that no records were printed. This occurred because you were already at "end of file" because of the shared open.

19. Use the POSDBF command to reposition the file cursor:

```
POSDBF  OPNID(DSPOBJDP) POSTION(*START)
```

20. Now duplicate the generated PRTDBF command (the one with all the fields) and then execute it.

    You should see the correct report. You can reuse the same ODP created by OPNQRYF, but you need to use the POSDBF command to reposition the cursor after each use.

21. To start another test, use F4 on the previous OPNQRYF command to prompt for the command. Enter ODOBSZ on the KEYFLD parameter. This requests that the data be sequenced according to field size. If you forgot to close the files (e.g., you didn't enter the X command), you should have received the error message that said the OPNID was already open (the OPNID doesn't exist now, so you can use it). If you received this error message, execute the OPNQRYF command again.

    You should see *INFO messages stating that all access paths were considered and an access path was built.

22. Use F9 to duplicate the full PRTDBF command (the one with all the fields) and then execute it.

    You should see that the records have been sequenced correctly.

23. Enter the X command to close the open files.

Exercise A continued

Exercise A continued

24. Use F9 to duplicate the OPNQRYF command and intentionally make an error by placing double quote marks around the value 50000:

```
QRYSLT('ODOBSZ *GT "50000"')
```

25. Execute the command.

    You should see the message

```
Operand for *GT function not valid
```

    The messages are good if you have a reasonable understanding of what is happening. This message tells you that the two operands are not the same type (one is character and one is numeric). If you looked at the second-level text of the message, you would find additional explanation for the error. Let's try a few more typical errors.

26. Enter a field name that doesn't exist in the file:

```
QRYSLT('ODOBXX *GT "50000"')
```

    You should see an appropriate error message.

27. Of course, if you specify a value that doesn't exist, no error will occur, but you won't find any records. Try specifying the QRYSLT parameter as

```
QRYSLT('ODOBTP *EQ "*JBX"')
```

28. Use F9 to duplicate the last PRTDBF command and then press Enter.

    If you notice the status message, it tells you that no records were found. The PRTDBF output will tell you the same thing. Receiving a message that no records exist in the file is a good indication that something is wrong with your QRYSLT statement or that you have not repositioned the file cursor, or that the shared file is closed and you are not executing the results of OPNQRYF.

29. We're now finished with OPNQRYF from an interactive viewpoint. Clean up your environment by using the X command to close the file.

30. Now delete the overrides:

```
DLTOVR  FILE(DSPOBJDP)
```

31. End debug:

```
ENDDBG
```

Exercise B Using OPNQRYF in a CL Program

In this exercise you will use OPNQRYF from a CL program and practice concatenating variables. You'll need the same objects you used in the previous exercise.

1. To ensure that you are not in debug mode, enter

```
ENDDBG
```

2. Use PDM to create a CLP member named TRYQRYF.
3. Enter the following source:

```
PGM
OVRDBF      FILE(DSPOBJDP) SHARE(*YES)
OPNQRYF     FILE(DSPOBJDP) +
              QRYSLT('ODOBTP *EQ "*JOBQ"')
PRTDBF      PGM(ZDSPOBJDP)
CLOF        OPNID(DSPOBJDP)
DLTOVR      FILE(DSPOBJDP)
ENDPGM
```

4. Create the program using PDM.
5. Call the program:

```
CALL  TRYQRYF
```

   You should see the same report you saw earlier. When you use an override command in a CL program, the override is deleted when the program ends. In this simple case, we would not have needed the DLTOVR command. In a more realistic environment, the CL program could be larger or could be invoking other programs after the function was complete. I like to include the DLTOVR command to be sure my program is clean at that point.

6. Now let's pass a parameter for the object type and use it in the QRYSLT statement. Modify your PGM statement and enter a DCL such as

```
PGM   PARM(&TYPE)
DCL   &TYPE *CHAR LEN(7)
```

   Now use the &TYPE parameter in the QRYSLT statement. You might want to refer again to the discussion earlier in this chapter about how to concatenate a character variable.

Exercise B continued

Exercise B continued

7. Create the program.
8. Call the program:

   ```
   CALL   TRYQRYF   PARM(*JOBD)
   ```

   You should see a report listing only the *JOBD objects.
9. Now let's try a numeric variable. Normally, you would be passing in a numeric value from a display or another program. Passing a numeric value from the command entry display is no fun, so let's simulate this by assigning a value of 50000 to the &SIZE parameter. Modify your PGM and DCL statements as follows:

   ```
   PGM
   DCL    &SIZE *DEC LEN(7 0) VALUE(50000)
   ```

   Complete the program with whatever other statements you need to select on the ODOBSZ field from the &SIZE variable.
10. Create the program.
11. Call the program:

    ```
    CALL   TRYQRYF
    ```

    You should see a report listing only the objects that exceed 50,000 bytes. If you can't see the size field, you might want to specify the FIELDS parameter on the PRTDBF command for the fields you want to print. If you can't get the program to work, it is probably because you forgot that you can only concatenate a character variable into the QRYSLT statement and therefore would have had to declare another character variable and use CHGVAR to convert numeric to character. Since you still want to compare against a numeric value, you don't want the double quote marks.
12. Now modify the source again to add the KEYFLD parameter to OPNQRYF to specify the ODOBSZ field.
13. Create the program.
14. Call the program:

    ```
    CALL   TRYQRYF
    ```

    You should see a report listing only the objects that exceed 50,000 bytes in sequence by the size field.

Exercise C Using the QRYF TAA Tool

Now that you can make OPNQRYF work the hard way, lets do it the easy way with QRYF. If the QRYF command is not on your system, see Appendix B.

1. Access the command entry display if you are not already there:

```
CALL  QCMD
```

2. Enter the OVRDBF command:

```
OVRDBF  FILE(DSPOBJDP) SHARE(*YES)
```

3. Prompt for the QRYF command.
4. Enter the parameters for the DSPOBJDP file and request to select on the ODOBTP field for just the *JOBQ objects.
5. When you press Enter, the OPNQRYF command will be executed. If you did it right, you told QRYF that Factor 2 was a character literal (i.e., you entered F2 on the prompt screen). If you forgot that important piece of information, you should see an error message that says that *JOBQ in the expression is not valid. When the QRYF command works correctly, you should see both the QRYF command you specified and the OPNQRYF command that was generated.
6. Enter PRTDBF to see the results:

```
PRTDBF  PGM(ZDSPOBJP)
```

   You should see the report we saw previously.
7. Enter the X command to close the file.
8. Use F4 to prompt for the fleshed-out OPNQRYF command. Add the KEYFLD parameter to sequence on the ODOBTX field. Enter PRTDBF to see the results:

```
PRTDBF  PGM(ZDSPOBJP)
```

   You should see the report sequenced on the text description field.
9. Use the X command to clean up your environment and delete the override to DSPOBJDP.

Exercise D Using the BLDQRYSLT Command (part of QRYF)

1. Use PDM to create a CLP member named TRYBLDSLT.
2. Enter the following source (we will use BLDQRYSLT in the next step):

```
PGM
DCL         &QRYSLT *CHAR LEN(2000)
OVRDBF      FILE(DSPOBJDP) SHARE(*YES)
OPNQRYF     FILE((DSPOBJDP)) QRYSLT(&QRYSLT)
PRTDBF      PGM(ZDSPOBJDP)
CLOF        OPNID(DSPOBJDP)
DLTOVR      FILE(DSPOBJDP)
ENDPGM
```

3. Just before the OPNQRYF statement, enter the command BLDQRYSLT and prompt for the parameters. See if you can correctly enter the parameters to select the ODOBTP field for the *JOBQ objects.
4. Create the program.
5. Call the program:

```
CALL  TRYBLDSLT
```

The report should show only the *JOBQ objects.

6. Now let's modify the program to allow the object type to be a parameter. Change the PGM statement and add a DCL, such as

```
PGM  PARM(&TYPE)
DCL  &TYPE *CHAR LEN(7)
```

Prompt for the BLDQRYSLT command and use the variable &TYPE instead of the literal '*JOBQ'.

7. Create the program.
8. Call the program:

```
CALL  TRYBLDSLT PARM(*OUTQ)
```

The report should show only the *OUTQ objects. Note that you never had to enter the *CAT and double quote symbols; BLDQRYSLT does it all for you.

Exercise D continued

Exercise D continued

9. Now let's try a numeric variable. As in the previous exercise, we'll pretend a value is being passed in. Change the source so that no parameter is passed in and enter the following DCL statement:

```
PGM
DCL   &SIZE *DEC LEN(7 0) VALUE(50000)
```

   See if you can fill in the rest of the code to select only those records where the ODOBSZ field exceeds the value of the &SIZE variable.

10. Create the program.

11. Call the program:

```
CALL  TRYBLDSLT
```

   When you use numeric variables with BLDQRYSLT, you still have to go through the step of converting the value to a character variable so it can be properly concatenated into the QRYSLT return value. A user-written command such as QRYF cannot handle a numeric variable of a varying number of decimal positions.

Exercise E Using the CPYJOBLOG TAA Tool

In this exercise you will need the CPYJOBLOG TAA tool; if it doesn't exist on your system, see Appendix B. You'll do an OPNQRYF interactively and then capture the commands you've entered to place them in a CLP-type source member.

1. Access the command entry display:

```
CALL  QCMD
```

2. Enter the OVRDBF command:

```
OVRDBF  FILE(DSPOBJDP) SHARE(*YES)
```

3. Enter the OPNQRYF command:

```
OPNQRYF  FILE(DSPOBJDP) QRYSLT('ODOBTP *EQ "*JOBQ"')
```

Exercise E continued

Exercise E continued

4. Enter the PRTDBF command:

```
PRTDBF  PGM(ZDSPOBJDP) FIELDS(*YES)
```

When the prompt appears, request that the fields be printed in the following order: ODOBNM, ODOBTP, ODOBSZ.

You should see a report listing only the *JOBQ objects.

5. Enter the X command to close the file.

6. Enter the CPYJOBLOG command and use a member name of TRYCPYLOG:

```
CPYJOBLOG  MBR(TRYCPYLOG) SRCFILE(xxxx)
```

The command submits a batch job that will do a DSPJOBLOG of your current job and read the information. If the member you named does not exist, it will be added. An informational message is written as the first source record. CPYJOBLOG searches for *RQS-type messages in the job log and writes them as source statements.

7. Use PDM to access the TRYCPYLOG source member.

8. Delete the statements you don't need (e.g., you don't need the first PRTDBF command).

9. Use F4 on the statements you do want to format normally.

10. Add the PGM, CLOF, DLTOVR, and ENDPGM statements.

11. Create the program.

12. Call the program:

```
CALL  PGM(TRYCPYLOG)
```

You should see the same results you saw interactively. Sometimes you may be better off to get your OPNQRYF command working interactively and then use CPYJOBLOG to help you create the CL program you really want.

Exercise F Using the CPYFRMQRYF Command

In this exercise you will use the CPYFRMQRYF system command. We'll use the DSPDBF TAA tool to look at data; if it is not on your system, see Appendix B. CPYFRMQRYF allows you to follow an OPQNRYF statement with a function that will copy all the selected records (in the sequence you specified) to a named file. You can either create the file ahead of time or use the CRTFILE(*YES) value on CPYFRMQRYF.

1. Select the *PGM objects from the DSPOBJDP file you have been using and sequence them on the size field:

```
OPNQRYF  FILE(DSPOBJDP) QRYSLT('ODOBTP *EQ "*PGM"') +
           KEYFLD(ODOBSZ)
```

2. Enter the DSPPFM command:

```
DSPPFM  DSPOBJDP
```

   You should see that the entire file was displayed as if the OPNQRYF statement didn't do anything. It did, but DSPPFM didn't. DSPPFM ignores any shared ODPs and does a full open. The only system function that works with the shared ODP is CPYFRMQRYF.

3. Enter the following CPYFRMQRYF command to create a file in library QTEMP from the ODP you just created:

```
CPYFRMQRYF  FROMOPNID(DSPOBJDP) TOFILE(QTEMP/TEMPOBJ) +
              CRTFILE(*YES)
```

4. Use the DSPDBF command to display the records:

```
DSPDBF  FILE(QTEMP/TEMPOBJ)
```

   You should see only *PGM objects that are sequenced by size.

5. Use the DSPPFM command to display the same records:

```
DSPPFM  FILE(QTEMP/TEMPOBJ)
```

   Now you're using DSPPFM against a real file and it shows you what you want to see.

Exercise F continued

Exercise F continued

CPYFRMQRYF is the only system support that will read the contents of an OPNQRYF ODP. Your only other choice is to write an application program to use the ODP or use the general-purpose print program created by CRTPRTPGM (it's just an RPG program) as shown in the previous exercises. As you can see from the DSPPFM step, the subset file you created can now be processed as a normal database file.

CHAPTER 21

Displaying Data

Most of the time, a programmer looks at data in a particular file via application programs. But at times — for example, when a problem occurs or when developing a program — a programmer needs to look directly at the data in a file. Two system-supplied commands — DSPPFM (Display Physical File Member) and RUNQRY (Run Query) — are helpful, but they are not ideal tools.

Most programmers are familiar with the DSPPFM command. This command works well if all the data is in a single field and in character format. But the command's output is more difficult to read if a file contains packed fields or multiple fields (field boundaries are not well-defined).

Although the RUNQRY command is normally thought of as working only with a predefined query object, the command can be used when you don't have a query. This command provides powerful functionality but it is awkward to use. The TAA tool DSPDBF, which I discuss in a subsequent section in this chapter, provides a front end to the RUNQRY command that simplifies its use. In addition, I discuss two other TAA tools that help you display data.

THE DSPDB TAA TOOL

The DSPDB (Display Data Base) TAA tool (Figure 21.1a), designed for use when you need to examine the contents of a single record, can be used effectively on any externally described database file (either physical or logical).

To use the command, simply enter

```
DSPDB  FILE(xxxx)
```

where xxxx is the name of the file you want to access.

The command will present in a readable format all the information that fits on a single display (e..g., field names are highlighted, data is unpacked, decimal points are inserted). By default, you will see the first record in the file. If the file is keyed, the record displayed will be the first record by key value. You can request a specific relative record number or prompt to enter a starting key value. Sample output for a file named FILEQ is shown in Figure 21.1b.

FIGURE 21.1a
DSPDB TAA Tool Command Prompt

```
                    Display Data Base File - TAA (DSPDB)


File name . . . . . . . . . . .     ___________     Name
  Library name  . . . . . . . .       *LIBL______   Name, *LIBL
Relative record number. . . . .     *START_______   1-16000000, *START
Prompt for key to start from. .     *NO__           *YES, *NO
Use minimum char set. . . . . .     *NO__           *YES, *NO
```

FIGURE 21.1b
Sample Output for FILEQ

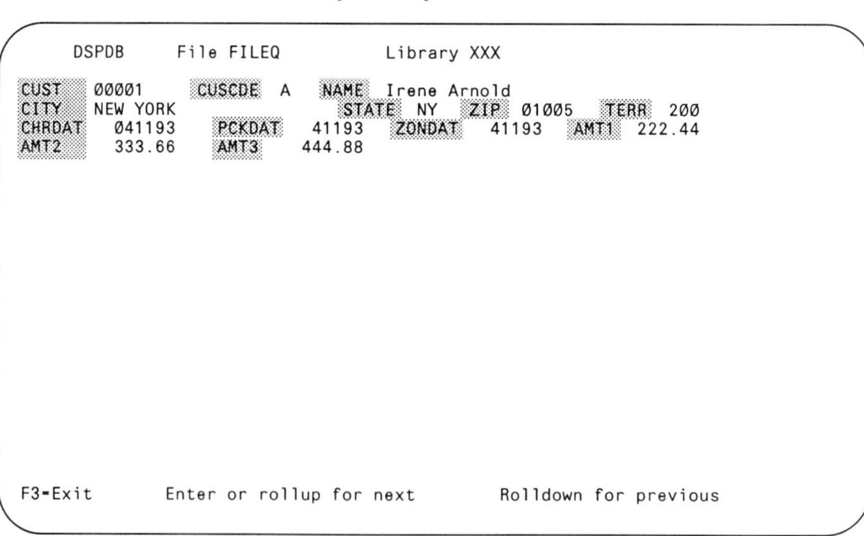

```
     DSPDB      File FILEQ          Library XXX

CUST    00001      CUSCDE  A    NAME  Irene Arnold
CITY    NEW YORK                  STATE  NY   ZIP  01005    TERR  200
CHRDAT    041193    PCKDAT    41193    ZONDAT    41193    AMT1  222.44
AMT2      333.66    AMT3    444.88

F3=Exit       Enter or rollup for next        Rolldown for previous
```

Technical Tip

The DSPDB TAA tool is a good problem-determination aid when you want to look at a few records in a file.

The DSPDBF TAA Tool

Because the prompt screen for the system-supplied RUNQRY command presents several parameters pertaining to a predefined query object (an object created by Query/400), the command can be awkward to use if you want to view the data in a particular database file. To simplify matters, the DSPDBF (Display Data Base File) TAA tool (Figure 21.2a) provides a front end to the RUNQRY command that prompts you only for parameters relevant to a request that does not involve a query object.

Figure 21.2a

DSPDBF TAA Tool Command Prompt

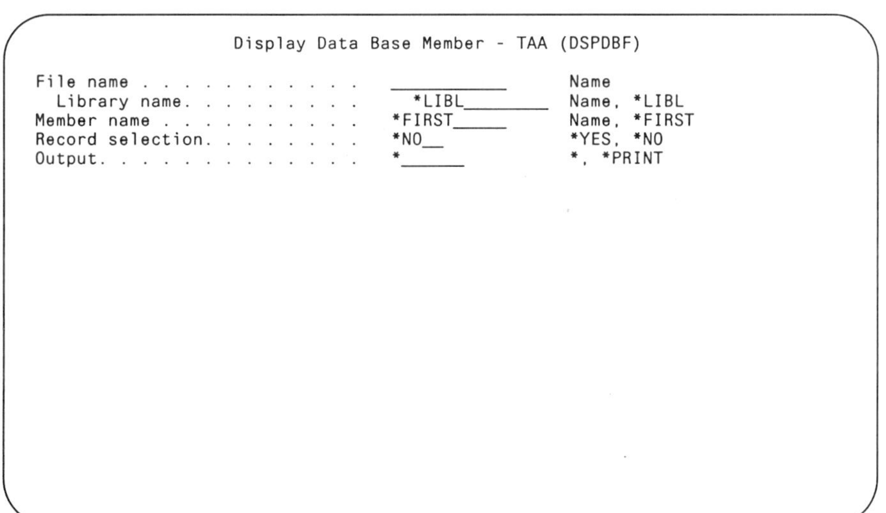

```
                    Display Data Base Member - TAA (DSPDBF)

File name . . . . . . . . . . . .    ___________     Name
  Library name. . . . . . . . . .     *LIBL_______   Name, *LIBL
Member name . . . . . . . . . . .    *FIRST_____     Name, *FIRST
Record selection. . . . . . . . .    *NO__           *YES, *NO
Output. . . . . . . . . . . . . .    *______         *, *PRINT
```

To display a file, you would enter

```
DSPDBF    FILE(xxxx)
```

where xxxx is the name of file you want to view. The display that appears is the same one used by SQL. The screen supports functions such as windowing, screen-splitting, and positioning to a specific line. As the sample output demonstrates (Figure 21.2b), you would see the

FIGURE 21.2b

Sample Output for the DSPDBF TAA Tool

```
                              Display Report

Position to line . . . . . _____
Line    ....+....1....+....2....+....3....+....4....+....5....+..
        Customer  Cust  Customer              Address
        number    code  name

000001  00003     B     Billy Smith           10 W Simpson
000002  00001     A     Irene Arnold          522 Lexington Ave
000003  00002     C     Jennifer Lattis       1900 Wilshire NE
000004  00015     A     Johnny Johnson        200 N Broadway
000005  00017     C     The Really BIG Co     White Gables Court
000006  00025     B     Judy Heimer           300 S Broadway
****** ********   End of report   ********









F3=Exit       F12=Cancel       F19=Left       F20=Right       F21=Sp
```

column headings of the fields as specified in DDS (if there are any) and not the field names.

If you have the IBM Query/400 product installed on your system, you also can specify record-selection criteria on the DSPDBF command.

Technical Tip

The DSPDBF TAA command serves as a front end to the RUNQRY CL command, a powerful system-supplied function. You don't need a predefined query object to use the tool; it works on any database file.

THE CRTPRTPGM TAA TOOL

The CRTPRTPGM (Create Print Program) TAA tool will create a general-purpose RPG print program that lets you print any externally described database file. The companion command PRTDBF (Print Data Base File) prints the data. You decide which fields you want to print and in what order across the page. If you enter the PRTDBF command interactively, it will print a spooled file and then use the DSPSPLF CL command to display the spooled file.

A major advantage of this TAA tool is that you can use the OPNQRYF command as a front end to the print program. Thus, you can quickly specify selection and sequencing criteria and then use the print program to print the results. IBM-supplied tools such as DSPPFM, DFU, and RUNQRY don't work with OPNQRYF because they cannot share an open file (for more about this topic, see Chapter 20, "OPNQRYF").

To use the tool, you name the file you want to work with:

```
CRTPRTPGM   FILE(xxx)
```

By default, a "Z" precedes the file name you specify and the command submits a batch job that creates an RPG program named Zxxx. For example, if you specified FILE(FILEA), the print program would be named ZFILEA.

You only need to use CRTPRTPGM once for each file you want to work with. After the program is created, you can print by using the command

```
PRTDBF PGM(Zxxx)
```

Sample output for the PRTDBF command is shown in Figure 21.3a.

FIGURE 21.3a
Sample Output for TAA Tool PRTDBF

```
    4/11/93  12:08:35  SYSTEM1       Run ID-*NONE           PRTDBF
    File-FILEQ      Library-XXX          Member-FILEQ        Program
    SEQ-*ARR  L3CTL-*NONE        L2CTL-*NONE       L1CTL-*NONE

 *  CUST   CUSCDE  NAME                  ADDR                 CITY
    00003    B     Billy Smith           10 W Simpson         Wi...
    00001    A     Irene Arnold          522 Lexington Ave    Ne...
    00002    C     Jennifer Lattis       1900 Wilshire NE     Ro...
    00015    A     Johnny Johnson        200 N Broadway       Ro...
    00017    C     The Really BIG Co     White Gables Court   Ro...

  F3=Exit   F12=Cancel   F19=Left   F20=Right   F24=More keys
```

The PRTDBF command lets you decide which fields you want to print. For example, if you had specified

```
PRTDBF   PGM(Zxxx) FIELDS(*YES)
```

you would see the prompt shown in Figure 21.3b.

FIGURE 21.3b

Sample Prompt Screen for TAA Tool PRTDBF

```
File- FILEQ    Library- XXX        Select fields        Prt pos

Seq Ctl Field    Len  Dec  Text
___ __  CUST       6       Customer number
___ __  CUSCDE     1       Cust code
___ __  NAME      20       Customer name
___ __  ADDR      20       Address
___ __  CITY      20       City
___ __  STATE      2       State
___ __  ZIP        5       Zip code
___ __  TERR       3       Sales territory
___ __  CHRDAT     6       Date in character format
 .
 .

F3=Exit     F6=Use all fields       Help      ENTER-Refresh if changed
```

You can use the sequence column shown in the display to arrange the order in which the fields will be printed from left to right across the page. The exercises at the end of this chapter will give you the opportunity to see this tool in action; a must if you are to really appreciate its functionality.

The PRTDBF program created by the CRTPRTPGM command can be used for more than a front end for OPNQRYF. For example, if your end users need a simple query, you could

- Put up a prompt for a specific file and let the users decide which fields to print, what to select on, and how to sequence.
- Perform the selection and sequencing using OPNQRYF.
- Perform the display/printout with PRTDBF.

All of this could be done with a display file and a CL program. When using PRTDBF, keep in mind that it is not as efficient as a normal RPG program, so you shouldn't use it to print a lot of data.

Technical Tip

The CRTPRTPGM TAA tool gives you a quick way to look at data as printed output. It lets you control which fields are printed and the sequence of the printing. The command also works with OPNQRYF; together, the two commands form a powerful combination for working with data.

Exercise A Using the DSPDB TAA Tool

In this exercise you will experiment with various ways to display data, and you will compare the DSPDB TAA tool to the system command DSPPFM. If the DSPDB command does not exist on your system, see Appendix B. For this exercise, you will create a physical file using the format of the DSPOBJD outfile with a key on object name.

1. Use PDM and create a PF member named DSPOBJDP.
2. Enter the following DDS:

```
...+... 1 ...+... 2 ...+... 2 ...+... 4 ...+... 5 ...+... 6
     A          R QLIDOBJD                  FORMAT(QADSPOBJ)
     A          K ODOBNM
```

3. Create the physical file DSPOBJDP.
4. Use the DSPOBJD command to create an outfile of the objects in library QGPL. Output the data to the file you just created:

```
DSPOBJD  OBJ(QGPL/*ALL) OBJTYPE(*ALL)   +
           OUTPUT(*OUTFILE)             +
           OUTFILE(DSPOBJDP)
```

5. You'll need to be on the command entry display to do some of the later steps, so access it by calling QCMD:

```
CALL  QCMD
```

6. The DSPPFM command, which always displays the data in arrival sequence, can be used only against a physical file. Enter the command

```
DSPPFM  FILE(DSPOBJDP)
```

   You should see the data as it exists in the file (the records were written in order by object name within object type). Note that you can't read the packed fields and that it is difficult to tell where fields begin and end.

7. Use the DSPDB TAA tool:

```
DSPDB   FILE(DSPOBJDP)
```

Exercise A continued

Exercise A continued

You should see the first record (by key order) in the file with the field names highlighted and the data unpacked. The relative record number of the record is displayed in the upper right-hand corner. The display is not easy to read, but it is useful when you need to view data in a particular record.

8. Using the scroll keys (Page Up/Down or Roll Up/Down), you will advance through the data. Because you are processing the file in keyed sequence, the relative record numbers will not appear in order.
9. Press F3 to end the DSPDB command.
10. Request DSPDB again as

```
DSPDB  FILE(DSPOBJDP) FROMRCD(1)
```

You should now see the first relative record in the file; if you scroll through the file, you will proceed in arrival sequence.

11. Request DSPDB again and specify

```
DSPDB  FILE(DSPOBJDP) FROMKEY(*YES)
```

You should see a prompt displayed with the key fields of the file.

12. Enter MA as the key field and press Enter.

The first record displayed will be the object name that starts with MA or higher. You can scroll through the file from that point.

Exercise B Using the DSPDBF TAA Tool

The DSPDBF TAA tool provides a simplified interface, or front end, to the RUNQRY CL command. In this exercise you will compare the use of RUNQRY with and without the DSPDBF command. If the DSPDBF command does not exist on your system, see Appendix B.

1. Prompt for the RUNQRY command. Bypass the first parameter and enter DSPOBJDP for the value of the "Query file" parameter.

   File DSPOBJDP will be displayed with column headings. Command keys at the bottom describe how to shift the screen so you can see all the data displayed.

2. Now prompt for the DSPDBF TAA tool. Enter DSPOBJDP as the value for the "File name" parameter.

   You should see the same RUNQRY display. The DSPDBF command serves as a front end to RUNQRY, making the RUNQRY command easier to key. Normally, you would just enter

   ```
   DSPDBF  DSPOBJDP
   ```

Exercise C Using the CRTPRTPGM TAA Tool

The CRTPRTPGM TAA tool builds a general-purpose RPG print program to print a specific file. In this exercise you will use the tool to create a program that can be used over and over again for the same file. If the CRTPRTPGM command does not exist on your system, see Appendix B.

1. Prompt for the CRTPRTPGM program. You'll see several parameters; just take the defaults and specify DSPOBJDP for the value of the "File name to print" parameter. Then press Enter.

   By default, a "Z" precedes the specified file name (this makes it easier to remember which program will do your printing). You should see that the command submitted a batch job named ZDSPOBJDP.

Exercise C continued

Exercise C continued

You should specify this program name when you use the PRTDBF command.

2. When the program is created, enter the command

```
PRTDBF   ZDSPOBJDP
```

A spooled file containing your data should be displayed. The field names are used as the column headings, the packed fields are unpacked, and a decimal point will be shown if there are decimal positions.

3. Enter B (Bottom) in the control field to display the last page of the spooled file. The field names are printed just before the totals to help you see the values. You should see that the ODOBSZ (object size) field has some totals shown. For any decimal field, the data is always summarized.

The abbreviations on the left-hand side of the page are

Fn = Final total (sum of the field)
Av = Average (total divided by number of records)
Mn = Minimum value (smallest value in any record)
Mx = Maximum value (largest value in any record)

The final total will show the number of records printed (probably 60). The PRTDBF command is not the most efficient way to print your data; so rather than burn up CPU cycles, the PRTDBF NBRRCDS parameter defaults to *DFT. The default provides for 60 records if the command is in an interactive job and 1,000 records if the command is in a batch job. You should also see descriptive text that explains how to print all the records. If you want them all, specify NBRRCDS(*MAX).

If you are working on a 132-character display, there is no more data to see (you can't shift the screen as you can with RUNQRY). The printer layout is designed to be printed. Unlike RUNQRY, you can determine which fields you want to print within the 132-character boundary.

4. Use F3 to end the command.

You should see a prompt that asks whether or not you want to save the spooled file. The default is "N" for "No." You are looking at the prompt screen from the PMTOPR (Prompt Operator) TAA tool. By default, the spooled file will be deleted.

Exercise C continued

Exercise C continued

5. Press Enter to take the default.
6. Place the cursor on the PRTDBF command and press F4.

   You should see several parameters for which you can enter values.
7. Enter *YES for the "Prompt or enter field names" parameter and press Enter.

   You should see a multiple-page display containing all the field names for the file. You can select which fields you want to print.
8. Normally, I enter Xs next to the fields I want and then press Enter. Try this approach by picking a few fields (don't make them all consecutive) and then press Enter.

   The same screen should be redisplayed with the fields you selected at the top and sequence numbers filled in. You can now re-arrange the sequence numbers (using the Seq field) to control the order of the fields as they appear from left to right across the page.
9. Key some changes in the Seq field and press Enter.

   You should see a fresh display with the fields resequenced and with new sequence numbers.
10. Note the number for "Prt pos rqstd-" in the upper right-hand corner of the display. If this number is greater than 128, the number will blink at you because there isn't enough room to print everything. Each field will take up room for its column heading or size (whichever is greater), as well as space between fields. If a character field overflows, it will be partially shown. Numeric fields are never partially shown. If you forget some fields you wanted to print you can add them now. At this point you want to specify a sequence number and not "X." When you are satisfied with the display and have not made any changes, pressing Enter will cause the printed report to be generated. Press Enter.

    You should see the report with the left-to-right sequence of fields as you requested.
11. Return to the command entry display.

    You should see the PRTDBF command with FIELDS(*YES) followed by another PRTDBF command with the list of fields filled in for the

Exercise C continued

Exercise C continued

FIELDS parameter. The second command is what you really specified. It has been sent as a *RQS message type and then received. This causes it to exist on the display so that you can retrieve it (using F9=Retrieve) and execute the command again. (This concept was discussed in Chapter 6, "Miscellaneous Message Techniques"). This technique comes in handy with OPNQRYF: You can use OPNQRYF repeatedly and reuse the same PRTDBF command.

12. Use F9=Retrieve and duplicate the previous command (the one with the field names). Then press Enter.

    You should see the same report. Note that the data in the file is being presented in arrival sequence. This is the default for PRTDBF. You can specify that the sequence should be in the order of the file.

13. Place the cursor on the previous PRTDBF command and press F4.

    You should see the prompt filled in with your field names.

14. Enter *FILE in the "Sequence of the records" parameter and press Enter.

    You should now see the report in file sequence (ordered by object name). Note that system commands such as DSPPFM and RUNQRY always operate in arrival sequence. The PRTDBF and DSPDB commands let you see the data in either arrival or keyed sequence.

CHAPTER 22

The Program Stack

A key element of the AS/400 architecture is the program invocation stack (or program stack) — a list of active programs in a job, in the order in which they were called. (With the introduction of ILE — Integrated Language Environment — the term program stack will become call stack.) Programs on the AS/400 operate on a CALL/RETURN basis: One program can call another program, which can then call another program, and so on. When a program calls another program, the called program executes at a lower invocation level in the program stack. For example, consider the following diagram (all the programs are CL programs):

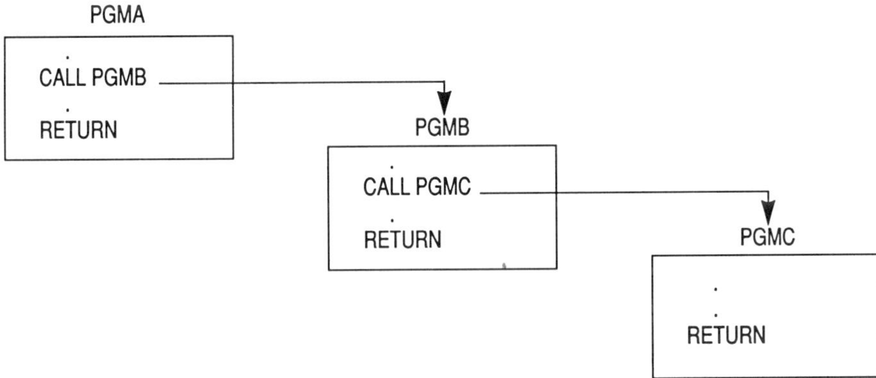

When PGMA calls PGMB, PGMA remains active, waiting at the CALL command until PGMB ends by executing a RETURN command. When PGMB ends, PGMA resumes at the instruction following the CALL command. When PGMB calls PGMC, at least three programs will be in the stack: PGMA, PGMB, and PGMC. But additional programs could be in the stack:

- Because other programs (normally IBM programs) may have executed ahead of PGMA in the stack (i.e., at a higher invocation level), or
- Because other IBM programs may execute after PGMC was called (i.e., at a lower invocation level), depending on what function(s) PGMC is executing

Only one program in the stack executes at a time, and the executing program is always at the lowest invocation level in the stack. In the example above, PGMA would not be aware of the number of programs below it in the stack; PGMA just waits for a return so it can proceed to the next instruction. As each of the programs in our example execute a RETURN, the program is removed from the stack.

The following diagram illustrates how the program stack functions when a program calls multiple programs:

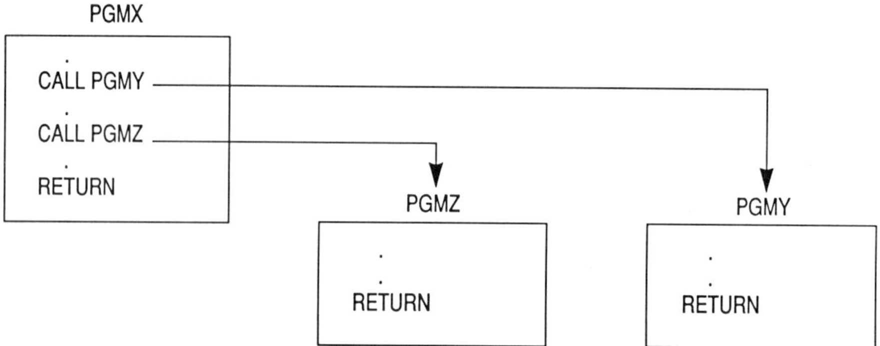

Remember that when a program ends, it is removed from the program stack. Thus, when PGMZ is called, PGMY is no longer in the stack. Because of this, both PGMY and PGMZ execute at the same invocation level.

The TFRCTL Command

The TRFCTL (Transfer Control) command is another way to call a program. Unlike the CALL command, which allows the calling program to remain active in the program stack, the TRFCTL command calls a program, passes control to the program, and then removes the calling program from the program stack. In our first example, if PGMB had used a TFRCTL command instead of a CALL command to call PGMC, then PGMB would have been removed from the stack. When PGMC ended by executing a RETURN, PGMA would have gained control.

If you use the TFRCTL command to pass parameters, you must follow strict rules. For instance, if PGMB in our first example had accepted a parameter list from PGMA and then used TFRCTL to call PGMC, PGMC must accept the identical parameter list.

I haven't used TFRCTL for a long time. From a performance viewpoint, one more program in the stack is not going to make a significant difference. And some of the original needs for TFRCTL (e.g., the

USEADPAUT — Use Adopted Authority — function) are supported with more straightforward solutions, described later in this chapter.

Many Ways To Return

In the previous examples, the RETURN command is used to end a program, but other options exist. Here are the normal ways to do a return:

- The RETURN command. You can have multiple RETURNs in the same program.
- The ENDPGM command. Normally, you specify ENDPGM at the end of the source, but the command may not be executed. You can specify ENDPGM in the middle of your source, but if you do, all the remaining source statements will be ignored by the CL compiler (they don't even appear on the compiler listing).

Technical Tip

You should use the ENDPGM command only to indicate that there are no more source statements in your program. The CL compiler ignores any source statements that follow an ENDPGM command.

- An implicit ENDPGM command. If you don't code an ENDPGM command, and the CL compiler finds no more statements to execute, an ENDPGM is implicitly understood and the program executes a RETURN. I prefer to code the ENDPGM command as a reminder that the program has no more statements.
- An escape message. When a program sends an escape message, the program ends, whether or not the program contains additional source statements. Chapter 2, "Sending Messages," explains this situation in more detail.
- SIGNOFF. A SIGNOFF command, which can be used only in an interactive job, not only ends the program, but also the job.

Should You Have More than One Return Point?

You can have only a single entry point in a CL program and you can't start in the middle of the program. But because any escape message will cause a return, it is perfectly normal to have multiple abnormal return points. If you prefer to have a single "normal" return point, then code it. Having done it both ways, my conclusion is that you must choose from the lesser of the following evils:

- More GOTO commands
- More DO group nesting
- Multiple RETURN statements

Of the three, I prefer multiple RETURN statements.

Technical Tip

You can't really have a single return point in a CL program because of the way escape messages are handled. You could have a single "normal" return point, but there is no performance advantage and trying to achieve a single return point can lead to an awkward coding structure.

Calling Your Own Program

It is possible for a CL program to call itself. This is known as a recursive call. Each time the program is called it starts with fresh variables and is placed in the program stack again (you could actually fill the program stack with the same program).

You can also call an active program that is further up the stack. For example, you could

```
Call PGMA

    PGMA calls PGMB

            PGMB calls PGMC

                    PGMC calls any program
                             PGMC (calls itself — recursive call)
                             PGMA (already active in the stack)
                             PGMB (already active in the stack)
                             PGMX (a program not active in the stack)
```

Regardless of how you call a CL program, you will get a fresh set of variables. Even if you are doing a recursive call, you don't get a chance to reuse the values from a program already in the program stack. Not all languages support a recursive call (e.g., RPG does not), and I have found that I rarely have a need for a recursive call.

Some Functions End When the Program Ends

When you design an application, you need to be aware that when a CL program ends (and is removed from the stack), various functions also end. Here's an overview of the important functions that will occur only when a program is in the stack:

- The system uses a work space to handle parameters passed from one program to another program. The called program actually changes the values directly in the calling program's work area. When the program ends, the work space is deleted and the variables are no longer available for use.

- You cannot call a CL program, have it perform an override, and then return and open a file with the override still in effect. The override is lost when the program is removed from the stack. For more information about overrides, see Chapter 18, "Overrides."

- If you use the DCLF and RCVF commands in your program, the first RCVF executed causes a file open. The file is automatically closed when the program reaches "end of file" or when the program ends. If you use the OPNDBF or OPNQRYF command in your program, however, the file remains open even if the CL program ends. You must close this type of file yourself (normally, by using the CLOF command).

- The program authority adoption function is in effect only when the program using the function is in the program stack. This function is discussed in the section "The Program Authority Adoption Function."

- Once a program ends, you can no longer access or clear messages from the program's message queue. The messages would be in the job log, but you cannot do anything with them. All you can do is remove messages from any inactive program. See Chapter 5, "The Job Log," for more information.

Note that most functions you might have a program perform are tied more to the job than to the program. For example, the CHGJOB command affects the entire job, not just the program in the stack; the QTEMP library exists for the job, the library list exists for the job, and so on.

Request Processor Programs

When you need to be sure that control returns to a specific program when an ENDRQS (End Request) command is executed or when a job is disconnected, you need to designate that program as a "request processor" program. If you include the following commands in a program, it will be a request processor program:

```
SNDPGMMSG   MSG('anything') TOPGMQ(*EXT) MSGTYPE(*RQS)
RCVMSG      PGMQ(*EXT) MSGTYPE(*RQS) RMV(*NO)
```

If you take option 11, "Program stack," on the DSPJOB command display, the column titled "Request level" will tell you whether or not a program in the program stack is a request processor. To really understand the function of a requestor program, see Exercise C at the end of this chapter.

The Program Authority Adoption Function

Program authority adoption lets you give a user temporary authority to accomplish a security-sensitive task. When you compile a program on the AS/400, you can supply a value for the USRPRF parameter of either *USER or *OWNER. The default value, *USER, tells the system to run the program using the authority of the user executing the program. A value of *OWNER tells the system to run the program using the program owner's authority, in addition to the authority of the user who called the program. This adopted authority remains in effect until the program ends. Any programs called by the program that adopts authority will also use the adopted authority unless you specifically block propagation of that authority with the CHGPGM (Change Program) command's USEADPAUT(*NO) parameter.

If all programs in the stack specify USRPRF(*USER), then the system checks authority against the profile of the user of the program. If a program in the stack specifies USRPRF(*OWNER), the system checks authority for that program and any programs lower in the stack against the profile of the owner of the program and the profile of the user. For example, if the program user has the right to add (but not delete) a record and the program owner has the right to delete (but not add), a program using the program authority adoption function could do both.

Most of the authority checking rules say that the first specific authority found in the "pecking order" is the one that is used. The "pecking order" is arbitrarily assigned by IBM (e.g., if a private authorization exists, it is used and not a public authorization). You can read more about the order of authority checking in the IBM *Security Reference* (SC41-8083).

Note that the program authority adoption function affects all programs lower in the stack. For example, in the following diagram, if the *user* running PGMA does not have authority to update FILEX, but the *owner* of PGMA does, PGMB would work successfully.

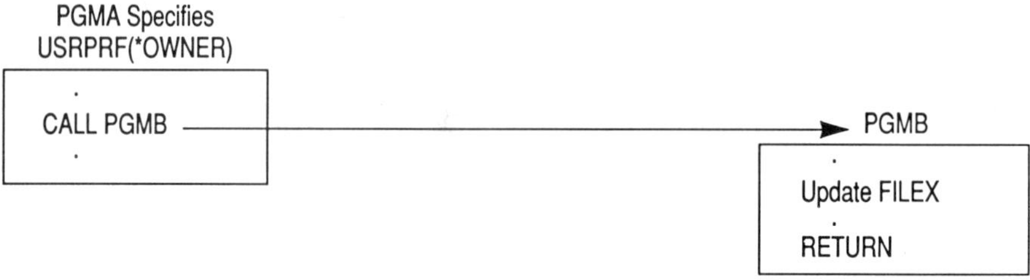

Advantages of Program Authority Adoption

Program authority adoption has several advantages:

- It minimizes the need for individual authorizations. Having many individual authorizations slows down the system, requires more time when saving authorities with the SAVSECDTA (Save Security Data) command, and gives you maintenance headaches (e.g., a user leaving the company might necessitate revoking many individual authorities).
- It is temporary. Unlike other forms of authorization, you can allow a user to do something in a controlled state that (s)he normally could not do. For example, if a user does not have *OBJMGT authority, (s)he can't clear a member. However, by specifying program authority adoption for an application that needs to use the CLRPFM command, a user of the program can be given temporary authority to use the command. Another solution would be to give the correct authorization to the specific user or to the public, but you may end up giving away more control than you would like (e.g., you may only want the file cleared when a user runs the application). If you use the program authority adoption function, you don't have to make everyone a security officer to meet your needs.
- It can be used in menu programs. Some users have a high-level CL program (i.e., a program high in the program stack) that acts as a menu and adopts the owner's authority. Therefore, every option executed from the menu operates under both the user's and the owner's authority. This avoids many of the potential authorization problems. An alternative is to have each option on the menu be a program authorized to individual users and each program may do an adopt. That way you can control who is authorized to high-level menu options. For example, you could have a menu option for Query/400 and accounts receivable, but you might want to provide program authority adoption only for accounts receivable.
- It adopts all existing special authorities. If the owner of the program has *ALLOBJ authority, for example, the user of the program can do whatever is needed (e.g., accessing all objects on the system).

Disadvantages of Program Authority Adoption

On the other side of the coin, program authority adoption also has disadvantages:

- You could be exposed to security problems. Writing programs that adopt authority can lead to security exposures. If your installation only allows production end users to access menu options for application functions (i.e., they are not allowed to access a command line) and you aren't concerned about programmers, security may not be an issue. But if your installation allows production end users to access a command entry line or you are concerned about the security of programmer actions, be sure to read Chapter 25, "Writing Secure Programs."
- Because of the dynamic nature of the program authority adoption function (i.e., object authority is based on the programs that are called), you have no way to display who has the authority to do what.
- A user could be given authority you don't want him or her to have. When a program adopts authority, programs lower in the program stack also adopt that authority. Because of this, a user might be able to perform a function that (s)he might not otherwise be able to do. The next section offers a solution to this problem.
- Adopted authority does not work with the SBMJOB command. When you use a SBMJOB command, the submitted batch job does not run under the adopted authority. The last section in this chapter offers a way to work around this problem.

THE USEADPAUT PARAMETER

The USEADPAUT parameter on the CHGPGM command can be used to "unadopt" authority specified by a program higher in the program stack. Let's say you have a program at a high level in the stack that has adopted QPGMR authority. Then at some lower point in the stack, you want the user of the program to be able to use the WRKOUTQ command to display the spooled files in the QPRINT output queue. The following diagram illustrates this scenario:

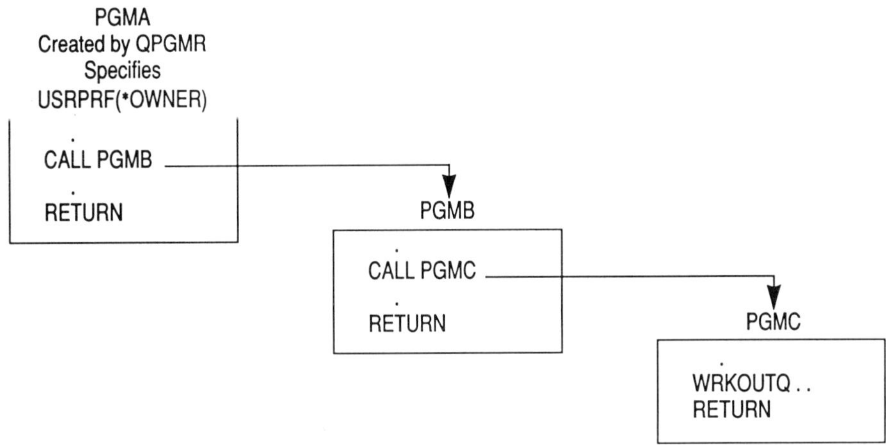

Because the user of PGMC is now running under the adopted authority of a user (QPGMR) who has the *JOBCTL special authority, the user of PGMC can now

- Look at anyone's spooled files
- Delete anyone's spooled file
- Enter additional commands on the command line
- Access additional objects

If the user profile of the user running PGMC is specified as LMTCPB(*NO), which is the default, the user can enter commands on the WRKOUTQ display command line (in this case, any command authorized to the user or to the programmer).

If you haven't changed the authorities shipped for QPGMR, the user could issue a PWRDWNSYS command or some other serious command. If the user profile is specified LMTCPB(*YES), the user can enter only fairly safe commands, such as DSPMSG and SNDMSG.

Note that specifying LMTCPB(*YES) only restricts the user's capability to enter commands on a command line. If a menu option exists, the user can execute any command (s)he is authorized to (most commands are authorized to the public). For example, from the WRKOUTQ display, the user could not key in the DLTSPLF command, but (s)he could use option 4 for the DLTSPLF command.

Technical Tip

If you are the security officer, be sure you understand the LMTCPB function, whether or not you use the program authority adoption function. You probably will want to limit the capabilities of some users. The CHKLMTCPB TAA

tool, discussed in Chapter 25, can help you determine which users are not limited and can limit their capabilities if you so choose.

In summary, if a user is specified as LMTCPB(*NO), then (s)he can access more commands and function than is desirable. If the user is specified as LMTCPB(*YES), his or her ability to enter commands is restricted, but (s)he can still delete someone else's spooled files. To fix this problem, specify the following command for the program that contains the WRKOUTQ command:

```
CHGPGM  PGM(xxx) USEADPAUT(*NO)
```

Because you don't know where your CL programs will be used, it is probably a good idea to move the WRKOUTQ command (or a similar command) to a separate program and specify the "unadopt" function, as the following diagram illustrates:

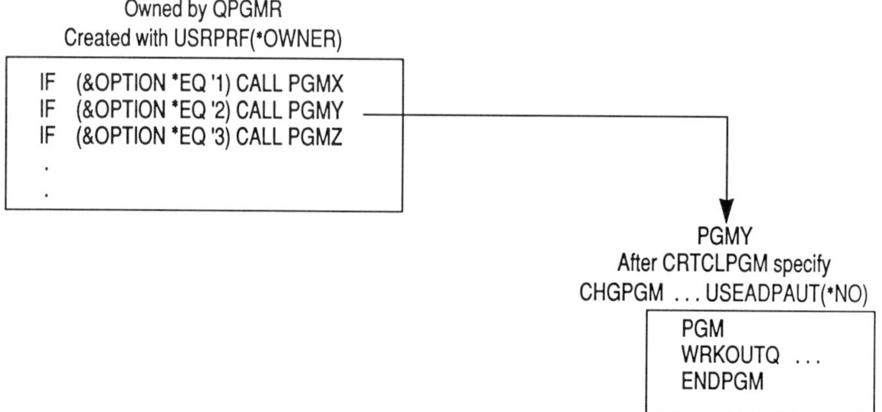

Note that the "unadopt" function affects the program for which it is specified and any programs lower in the stack (in this case, there are no more user programs).

You can also use the "unadopt" function for programs that support menu options. Let's say you have a menu that allows a user to perform a variety of production functions and then use a general-purpose function such as AS/400 Query. For production functions, the user may use physical files that (s)he should not use in Query. Or the user may be limited to use Query through a logical view that prohibits seeing certain fields in the physical file. Therefore, for the production functions, assume you want to adopt the authority of a more powerful user; but for Query, you want the user to operate under his or her own user profile. Given this scenario, your program would be similar to that shown in the previous diagram. The only difference would be that the program lower in the program stack would contain the STRQRY command instead of the WRKOUTQ command:

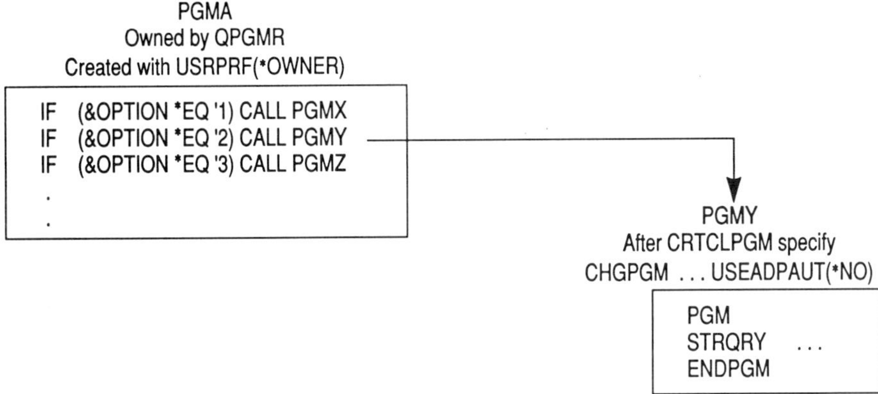

SUBMITTING A JOB WITH ADOPTED AUTHORITY

This section presents a technique that allows a submitted job to use the program authority adoption function. This method uses a program, essentially a command entry function, that adopts a programmer's authority. Because the program is accessible by the public (as well as by authorized users), you have some security exposure. However, if you do not allow production end users to access a command entry line, the solution works well.

I'll point out some things you can do to minimize the exposure and to track how the function is used. I have made the following assumptions: that the programmer who creates the program has the authority for what you want submitted to batch, and that the programmer does not have *ALLOBJ special authority. Here are the steps to follow:

1. Enter the source for a program named MYQCMD:

```
PGM
CALL      QCMD
ENDPGM
```

2. Create this program with USRPRF(*OWNER).

   At this point, any user who can access the program can enter commands under the programmer's authority. You can minimize the exposure by authorizing only certain users to the program. The reason the program cannot be private is that the user of the batch job must be authorized to use the program described in the subsystem routing entry. You could further minimize the exposure by doing the following:

— allow the program to run in batch only. For example, you could use the RTVJOBA command to determine whether the job is interactive or batch. If it is interactive, you could have the program send an escape message.

— log who called the program

— log the command that was executed

You could log the information via a journal using the SNDJRNE (Send Journal Entry) command (see Chapter 5, "The Job Log").

3. Create a special subsystem (you can use the same pool ID that you use for any batch work):

```
CRTSBSD  SBSD(xxxx)
```

4. Create a job queue and make it private (i.e., exclude the job queue from public use):

```
CRTJOBQ  JOBQ(PRIVATE) AUT(*EXCLUDE) ...
```

Making the queue private prevents total misuse of the function.

5. Add a job queue entry to the subsystem (specify a unique SEQNBR value):

```
ADDJOBQE  SBSD(xxx) JOBQ(PRIVATE) SEQNBR(Ø5)
```

6. Add a routing entry to the same subsystem and specify some unique CMPVAL data (I specified "ADOPT"):

```
ADDRTGE   SBSD(xxxx) SEQNBR(2ØØ)  +
            CMPVAL(ADOPT) PGM(xxx/MYQCMD)
```

7. Start your subsystem:

```
STRSBS   SBSD(xxxx)
```

Now you are ready to submit a job. When you specify SBMJOB, you need to use the same value for RTGDTA that was specified for the ADDRTGE CMPVAL parameter (ADOPT was used in the example). Normally, you would do the special SBMJOB in a CL program, but you can try it with the following SBMJOB command:

```
SBMJOB  JOB(xxx) CMD(xxxx)  +
          JOBQ(PRIVATE) RTGDTA(ADOPT)
```

The job is run under the user's profile. When the routing program starts, it invokes the QCMD system function. It will try to receive any request messages sent to the job. The command specified on SBMJOB is essentially sent as a request message to the job and is there for QCMD to process. Since program MYQCMD adopts authority, the user can run under both his or her and the programmer's authority.

Exercise A Displaying the Program Stack

In this exercise you will see the program stack in operation.

1. Access the command entry display:

   ```
   CALL  QCMD
   ```

   Note the "Request level" displayed in the upper right-hand corner of the command entry display. This is not the number of the program in the stack, but rather the number of the "request level." Only programs that are request processing programs are considered to be another request level and each request processor program in the stack is numbered.

2. Access the command entry display again:

   ```
   CALL  QCMD
   ```

   Note the "Request level" in the upper right-hand corner. It should have increased by one because QCMD is a request processor program.

3. Enter the DSPJOB command:

   ```
   DSPJOB
   ```

4. When the DSPJOB menu appears, enter option 11 to display the program stack.

   You should see the programs in the stack at the current moment and whether or not they are a request processor (those with numbers in the column "Request level" are request processors).

5. Return to the last command entry display from which you entered a command.

6. Press F3 to return to the first command entry display.

7. Enter the command:

   ```
   DSPJOBD  QBATCH
   ```

8. When the display appears, use the system request key to access the system request menu.

9. Enter a 3 to display your job.

10. When the DSPJOB menu appears, enter option 11 to display the program stack.

Exercise A continued

Exercise A continued

When the display appears, you should see that several IBM programs are in the program stack. The system uses the same "call and return" approach for its programs as it does for yours.

Exercise B Adopting and Unadopting Authority

In this exercise you will create a program stack of two programs and experience the capabilities of the program authority adoption function. To do the exercise you will need another user profile with very restricted capabilities. You may need to have the security officer create one for you. For this exercise, I assume that you are authorized to the STRDBG command and that you have *JOBCTL special authority; if not, certain steps will not make sense. I also assume that your installation has not changed the public authority to the commands STRDBG, DSPJOBD, and DSPMSG.

1. Use PDM to create a CLP member named TRYADOPT.
2. Enter the following source:

```
PGM
CALL       PGM(TRYADOPT2)
ENDPGM
```

3. Create the program.
4. Use PDM to create a CLP member named TRYADOPT2.
5. Enter the following source with the name of your output queue (or an output queue you can write to):

```
PGM
WRKOUTQ    OUTQ(xxxx)
ENDPGM
```

6. Create the program.

Exercise B continued

Exercise B continued

7. Enter the following commands to create some spooled files that can be deleted later:

```
DSPJOBD  JOBD(QBATCH) OUTPUT(*PRINT)
DSPCLS   CLS(QBATCH) OUTPUT(*PRINT)
```

8. Call program TRYADOPT:

```
CALL   TRYADOPT
```

   You should see a display of the output queue you named.

9. Enter DSPJOB on the command line.
10. When the DSPJOB menu appears, enter option 11 to display the program stack.

    You should see the programs TRYADOPT and TRYADOPT2 in the program stack. TRYADOPT is just waiting for a return from TRYADOPT2.

11. Return to the command entry line.
12. Either create a different profile or have the security officer do so. The profile should be specified as LMTCPB(*NO) (this is the default). Also, specify the INLPGM parameter as program TRYADOPT in the library where you created it.
13. Use system request option 1 to request "Transfer to an alternative job."

    You should see the sign-on prompt.

14. Sign on as the new profile.

    You should see the WRKOUTQ display.

15. On the command line, enter:

```
DSPJOBD   QBATCH
```

    This command should perform successfully because it is shipped with public authority.

16. Enter the STRDBG command and prompt for it (F4).

    If you created the user profile as described, you should not be able to enter the STRDBG command because it is shipped as private (the public is excluded from using it). You should see that you are not

Exercise B continued

Exercise B continued

authorized to the command. Because the programs in the program stack do not adopt any authority, the user profile is operating under its own authority.

17. Use the delete option (option 4) against one of the spooled files in the output queue. It shouldn't matter which one because the command should fail.

    You should see the confirmation display.

18. Press Enter.

    You should see a return to the WRKOUTQ display with a message that says you are not authorized to the spooled file.

19. Enter SIGNOFF on the command line.

20. You should now be back as the original user (the owner of the TRYADOPT program). Enter the command:

    ```
    CHGPGM   PGM(TRYADOPT) USRPRF(*OWNER)
    ```

    The program has now been modified to use the program authority adoption function. You should see a completion message stating that the program has been changed.

21. Use DSPPGM to see the current description of the program:

    ```
    DSPPGM   TRYADOPT
    ```

    The display should show the "User profile" entry of *OWNER. Note that there is another value titled "Use adopted authority," which is set to *YES. This is the USEADPAUT function, which may be specified on the CHGPGM command. When you create a program, the value for USEADPAUT is always *YES.

22. Use system request option 1 to request "Transfer to an alternative job."

    You should see the sign-on prompt.

23. Sign on as the new profile.

    You should see the WRKOUTQ display.

24. Enter the STRDBG command and prompt for it (F4).

Exercise B continued

Exercise B continued

You should now be authorized to the command because the TRYADOPT program is owned by a user who is authorized to STRDBG.

25. Use F12 to cancel the command.

26. Use the delete option (option 4) against one of the spooled files in the output queue. Pick out a spooled file you don't want because this time the command should work.

    You should see the confirmation display.

27. Press Enter.

    You should see that the spooled file has been deleted. Since you are now operating with the adopted authority of *JOBCTL, you have authority to delete anyone's spooled file. All the special authorities are adopted when you use the program authority adoption function.

28. Enter SIGNOFF on the command line.

29. You should now be back as the original user (the owner of the TRYADOPT program). Use CHGPGM to specify "unadopt" for the TRYADOPT2 program:

```
CHGPGM   PGM(TRYADOPT2) USEADPAUT(*NO)
```

30. Use DSPPGM to display the program:

```
DSPPGM   TRYADOPT2
```

    You should see that the value for "Use adopted authority" is *NO.

31. Use system request option 1 to request "Transfer to an alternative job."

    You should see the sign-on prompt.

32. Sign on as the new profile.

    You should see the WRKOUTQ display.

33. Enter the STRDBG command and prompt for it (F4).

    You should not be authorized to the command. The TRYADOPT program is still specified to use the program authority adoption function, but the TRYADOPT2 program is specified to operate under only the user's authority. Consequently, you are only a normal user at this point and the public is excluded from using STRDBG.

Exercise B continued

Exercise B continued

34. Enter the following command on the command line:

```
DSPJOBD   QBATCH
```

You should see the job description. Since your profile is not limited, you are able to enter any commands that are public.

35. Return to the WRKOUTQ display and use the delete option (Option 4) against one of the spooled files in the output queue. It shouldn't matter which one because this time the command should fail.

You should see the confirmation display.

36. Press Enter.

You should see that you are not authorized to perform the command. You are again operating under a normal user profile, with no adopted authority.

37. Enter SIGNOFF on the command line.

38. You should now be back as the original user (the owner of program TRYADOPT). Either change the new profile yourself or have the security officer change the profile to LMTCPB(*YES).

39. Enter the command

```
DSPCMD  CMD(DSPMSG)
```

40. Roll to the second page. You should see that "Allow limited user" has a value of *YES. DSPMSG is one of the few commands that IBM ships this way so that a user with LMTCPB(*YES) can still use it.

41. Enter the following command:

```
DSPCMD  CMD(DSPJOBD)
```

42. Roll to the second page.

You should see that "Allow limited user" has a value of *NO. This is the way most commands are specified, to prevent a user with LMTCPB(*YES) from using the command.

43. Use system request option 1 to request "Transfer to an alternative job."

You should see the sign-on prompt.

Exercise B continued

Exercise B continued

44. Sign on as the new profile.

    You should see the WRKOUTQ display.

45. Enter the following command on the command line:

    ```
    DSPMSG
    ```

    You should see that the message queue is displayed. This is a command with ALWLMTUSR(*YES) specified.

46. Return to the WRKOUTQ display and enter the following command on the command line:

    ```
    DSPJOBD   QBATCH
    ```

    You should see that the DSPJOBD command is not allowed.

47. Place the cursor on the error message and press Help.

    You should see an explanation of the problem.

48. Return to WRKOUTQ display and enter SIGNOFF on the command line.

    You should be signed off because SIGNOFF is also a command that is specified as ALWLMTUSR(*YES).

Exercise C Creating a Request Processing Program

In this exercise you will create a request processing program. Then you will use the ENDRQS (End Request) and DSCJOB (Disconnect Job) commands to see how they operate when a request processor program is in the program stack. For this exercise, assume that the source was entered for the two programs used in Exercise B. This exercise also uses the PMTOPR TAA tool; if it is not on your system, see Appendix B.

1. Call program TRYADOPT:

    ```
    CALL  TRYADOPT
    ```

    You should see the WRKOUTQ display.

Exercise C continued

Exercise C continued

2. Use system request option 2 to "End request" (the ENDRQS command).

   You should be returned to the command entry display, where you will see the message "Last request ... ended."

3. Place your cursor on this message and press Help.

   You should see that this is escape message CPF1907. It is not sent to either program TRYADOPT or program TRYADOPT2. Instead, it is sent to the first program higher in the stack that is a request processing program. We'll monitor for this message in the next step to show you how to recover.

4. Use PDM to create a CLP member named TRYRQSPCS.

5. Enter the following source:

```
           PGM
           DCL        &RTNVAR *CHAR LEN(16)
           MONMSG     MSGID(CPF1907) EXEC(GOTO RECOVER)
                      /* Make the pgm a request processor */
           SNDPGMMSG  MSG('DUMMYCMD') TOPGMQ(*EXT) MSGTYPE(*RQS)
           RCVMSG     PGMQ(*EXT) MSGTYPE(*RQS) RMV(*NO)
CALL:      CALL       PGM(TRYADOPT)
           RETURN
RECOVER:              /* TAA Tool command */
           PMTOPR     RTNVAR(&RTNVAR) LEN(1)            +
                        PROMPT('An End Request (ENDRQS) +
                        command has occurred.')         +
                        LINE1('M - Return to the menu') DFT(M)
           GOTO       CALL
           ENDPGM
```

   The SNDPGMMSG and RCVMSG commands must be coded in this manner to make the program a request processing program. Escape message CPF1907 occurs if the ENDRQS command is used. As mentioned, escape message CPF1907 is sent to the first program higher in the stack that is a request processing program. Identifying the program as a request processor tells the system that

Exercise C continued

Exercise C continued

- this program should be sent an escape message if ENDRQS is used and this program is the first program higher in the stack that is a request processor program.
- control should return to this program if the job is disconnected by the DSCJOB (Disconnect Job) command and then reconnected by a sign-on.

6. Create program TRYRQSPCS.
7. Call the program:

   ```
   CALL    TRYRQSPCS
   ```

   You should see the WRKOUTQ display.
8. Use system request option 3 to display the current job.
9. When the DSPJOB menu appears, request option 11 to display the program stack.

   You should see several programs in the stack, including TRYRQSPCS, TRYADOPT, and TRYADOPT2. The TRYRQSPCS program should have a number to the left for "Request level."
10. Return to the WRKOUTQ display.
11. Press Enter.

    You should return to the command entry display.
12. Call program TRYRQSPCS again:

    ```
    CALL    TRYRQSPCS
    ```

    You should see the WRKOUTQ display.
13. Use system request option 2 to "End Request" (the ENDRQS command).

    You should see the PMTOPR display. The TRYRQSPCS program successfully monitored for escape message CPF1907 and is now processing in the RECOVER routine.
14. Press Enter.

    You should see the WRKOUTQ display.

Exercise C continued

Exercise C continued

15. Use system request option 80 to “Disconnect job” (the DSCJOB command).

    You should see the SIGNON prompt.

16. Sign on again.

    You should see the system request menu with message CPC1194. This tells you that your job has been connected again and any sign-on information has been ignored. This means that your initial program or menu was not run. The system remembered where you were in this program (at the CALL to WRKOUTQ) and will return you to that point.

17. Press Enter.

    You should see the WRKOUTQ display again. Note that your program did not branch to the RECOVER routine. The disconnect function does not send an escape message. It just remembers where you were and restarts at that point (for the first request processor program). If the disconnect function had been caused automatically by the system value QDSCJOBITV (Disconnect Job Interval) or QDEVRCYACN (Device Recovery Action), you would probably not have been on the system request menu when the disconnect occurred. You probably would have been on the WRKOUTQ menu. In this case, you would have seen the WRKOUTQ menu when you signed on again.

CHAPTER 23

The CL Program Object

Three CL commands are important in the life of a CL program object: CRTCLPGM (Create CL Program), CHGPGM (Change Program), and CPROBJ (Compress Object). After you have created a CL program (using the CRTCLPGM command), you can use either the CHGPGM or CPROBJ command to modify the program. In this chapter I will discuss the more critical parameters for these CL commands, as well as several QUSRTOOL TAA tools that can help when you are working with program objects (e.g., when you need to replace, rebuild, or compress a program object).

In addition, I will discuss how you replace a program that is already in existence, and the different requirements for production and test environments. And I will present the results of live tests so you can see when it might be worthwhile to compress a CL program object.

But before we get into the commands and the tools, let's start with an overview of program and library objects.

THE PROGRAM OBJECT

The diagram on the following page illustrates the series of steps the system follows when it creates a CL program object.

The CRTCLPGM command processing program diagnoses your source and if it is error free, the compiler generates an intermediate level of code. This intermediate level of code is then passed to the Program Resolution Monitor (PRM), which is a common back end to many AS/400 compilers. The PRM produces a program template, which the CL compiler converts to object code.

The system deletes the intermediate level of code but keeps the program template as part of the program object. The program template is also defined as the "observability" portion of the object code. This is how you will see it described on commands and system output. The program template, or observability, isn't used during execution of a program (unless a debug function is used). Program observability, which is optional, provides for

- debugging the program (e.g., using the STRDBG command)
- pinpointing the statement number where a problem has occurred
- getting a formatted dump with the values of your variables

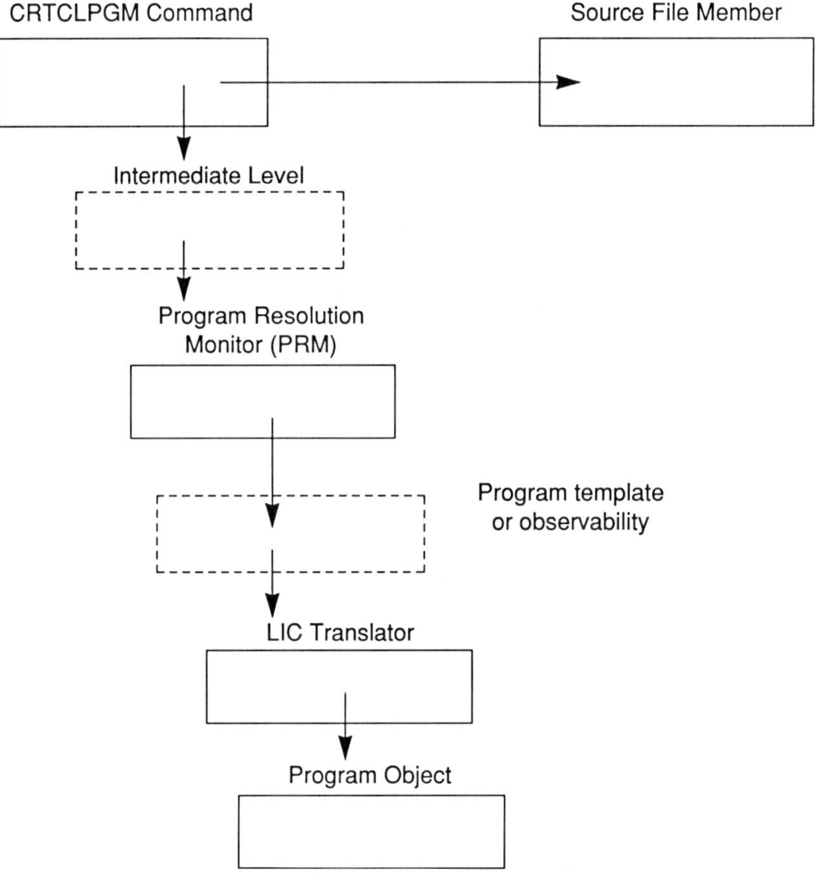

- displaying the current statement on the DSPJOB program stack display
- re-creating the object code without using your source
- changing a few parameters that are independent of the source (e.g., the USRPRF option)

The following diagram provides a conceptual view of a program object and its relationship to certain CL commands:

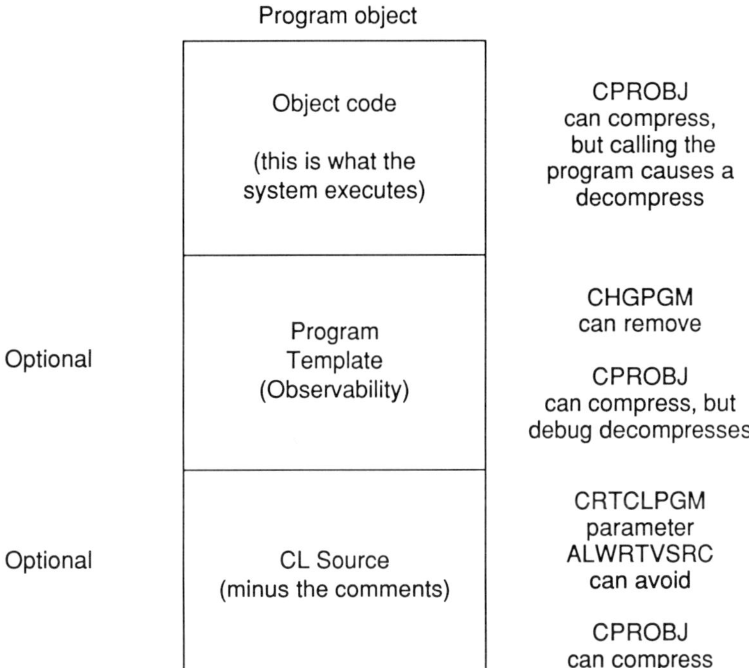

The Library Object

The program object is always placed into a library and each library includes a directory that contains high-level information about the objects in the library. You can't really see the directory itself, but you can see the *LIB object type, which is in QSYS for each library on the system. For example, the library object QSYS/QGPL (type *LIB) describes the QGPL library, and includes a directory of the objects in QGPL.

Every object that is placed in a library causes an entry to be created in the associated library object (i.e, in its directory). You cannot directly delete an entry in the library object; when you delete the object itself, the system automatically deletes the corresponding entry in the library object. In addition to knowing where every object is in the library, the library object (in the Object Information Repository) also contains high-level information about the object, such as its text description, source type, and last use date.

It's the number of objects, not the size of the objects, that determines the size of the library object (the number of members does not impact the library object size). Thus, if you have many objects in a library, the library object can be quite large. For example, consider two libraries on my system:

Library	Number of objects	Total size of library	Size of library object
1	25	36,000,000	125,000
2	1,120	11,700,000	1,100,000

The column "Total size of library" shows the total size of objects in the library. You will see this total if you use the DSPLIB command and print the output, but you will not see the size of the library object (in QSYS). When you want to find out the size of objects in a library, consider using the QUSRTOOL PRTLIBDTL (Print Library Detail) TAA tool. The TAA command provides more information than the DSPLIB or DSPOBJD CL commands and offers more selection criteria. PRTLIBDTL always includes the size of the library object.

Technical Tip

The PRTLIBDTL (Print Library Detail) TAA tool provides a good way to review information about objects in a library. The command offers many options and will always list the total number of objects in the library and the size of the library object.

The CRTCLPGM Command

Rather than cover commonly used parameters such as SRCFILE and SRCMBR, I'll discuss the parameters you may be less familiar with.

The USRPRF Parameter

When you create a program, the default on the CRTCLPGM command for the USRPRF parameter is *USER, which tells the system to perform authority checks based on the profile of the user who calls the program.

If you specify USRPRF(*OWNER), you enable the program authority adoption function, which tells the system to perform authority checks based on the combined authority of the user of the program and the owner of the program. The program authority adoption function affects all authority checking within the program and also affects any programs lower in the program stack. For more information about what happens when you specify USRPRF(*OWNER), see Chapter 22, "The Program Stack."

The Log Parameter

The LOG parameter controls whether or not you will allow CL commands to be logged if someone requests the function by specifying the CHGJOB LOGCLPGM option. The LOG parameter provides a good function, but it does not log all commands or parameter values. (I use the logging function in conjunction with the LOGCL TAA tool, discussed in Chapter 1).

Normally, I take the default (*JOB) for the LOG parameter when I create a program. The default says that the job will determine whether or not logging will occur. Then, when logging is turned on by a CHGJOB command (or by the LOGCL TAA tool), all CL programs for that particular job are logged.

Although logging can be helpful when problems occur, there are good reasons to turn off logging:

- It would make sense to prevent logging — by specifying LOG(*NO) — of security-sensitive programs. Not logging would make it less likely that someone could decipher the program's function.
- It would make sense to prevent logging of thoroughly tested CL programs that are called from other programs. For example, if you are having trouble with a program that calls some well-tested program, logging both programs might be confusing.

Technical Tip

If you are having trouble with one program, you can specify LOG(*YES), re-create the program, and then log only the commands from that program rather than all the programs in your job. You must re-create the program to change the LOG value.

The ALWRTVSRC Parameter

The ALWRTVSRC (Allow Retrieve Source) parameter determines whether or not your source will be stored in the object program. Specifying the default (*YES) wastes space in CL programs, but if you ever lost your source, you would be happy you took the option. By using the RTVCLSRC (Retrieve CL Source) command, you could retrieve the source code. You would lose only the comments contained in your source; they are not stored in the object program. If you specify ALWRTVSRC(*NO), you cannot use the RTVCLSRC command.

But you shouldn't be so extreme as to specify ALWRTVSRC(*YES) and then remove the source member. I prefer not to rely on the RTVCLSRC command: I don't want to lose my comments and I don't care for the way RTVCLSRC formats my source. My choice is to use the SRCARC (Source Archive) TAA tool daily to back up any source members that have been changed. The TAA tool provides a far better retrieval method than RTVCLSRC (see Chapter 28, "Setting up your Environment," for more information about the SRCARC TAA tool).

Technical Tip

Taking the default for ALWRTVSRC wastes disk space. If you have a good solution for backing up your source and you want to save space, it makes sense to specify ALWRTVSRC(*NO).

The TGTRLS Parameter

The TGTRLS (Target Release) parameter lets you create a program under a current version of the operating system that will execute under an earlier version. For example, if you are on V2R2M0 and want to create a CL program that must run on V2R1M0, you must create the program for V2R1M0 and then save it (using the TGTRLS parameter on a save command) so that it can be restored on V2R1M0. You can learn more about this parameter in the *CL Programmer's Guide* (SC41-8077).

Note that the version of the operating system under which a program is created is not a problem if you are creating a program on an older release that will run on a more current release. For example, if you are on V2R1M0 and want to create a program that will run on V2R2M0, you don't have to do anything special. You probably have many programs that were created on some prior release that are operating just fine on your current release.

The REPLACE Parameter

Replacing a program object that exists but that may be in use is always a challenge. The requirements differ for production objects and test objects. The needs also change depending on the type of object (a physical file has more challenges than a program).

Let's review the REPLACE option on CRTCLPGM:

- The default is REPLACE(*YES).
- If a program object of the same name doesn't exist in the library you specified, the create proceeds as if you had specified REPLACE(*NO). The attributes of the object come from the create command.
- If a program object of the same name does exist, the new source is used to create the program in a temporary place.
- If the create is not successful, you receive an error message and the old program still exists; it is not deleted.

- If the create is successful, the old program is moved to library QRPLOBJ and assigned an internal name. The text description of the object in library QRPLOBJ is changed to show the library and program name of the original program.
- Any security attributes specified for the old program are transferred to the new program. The AUT and USRPRF parameters on the CRTCLPGM command are ignored. Any authorities specified for the old program are transferred to the new program. The USEADPAUT value from the CHGPGM command is also transferred to the new program. No other attributes are transferred. Whatever you had specified for LOG, ALWRTVSRC, TGTRLS, et cetera, come from the current CRTCLPGM command and not from specifications for the old program.
- If the old object had been compressed, the new object is not compressed.
- If you attempt to replace an RPG program with a CL program, it works (the replace code is not sensitive to the type of program). The security attributes transfer as described previously; no error message is sent.
- Any user of the old program will continue to work with that version of the program, unaware that any change occurred. (S)he will not use the new version until (s)he calls the program again.

In general, specifying CRTCLPGM REPLACE(*YES) works well, but it is not perfect. Here are some points you need to keep in mind:

- In a test environment, it is quite normal to have a program re-creation attempt fail because of a source error. If you overlooked the error message that says your compile failed, you might think it worked. When you call the program again, you will get the old version (it still exists); you could spend considerable time debugging the old program before realizing what happened. In addition, you gain no advantage by cluttering up library QRPLOBJ with old versions of the same program.

  To avoid the possibility of inadvertently working with the wrong version of a program, and to avoid having to specify REPLACE(*NO) on every create command, I decided to do things differently — and automatically — for my test environment. I use the TAA tool SBMPARMS, which is described later in this chapter. You don't need any special comments in your source, but you must use the special batch program that is part of the tool. To use this technique for your test environment, create a data area in your library list:

```
CRTDTAARA   DTAARA(xxx/SBMPARMS) TYPE(*CHAR) LEN(1)  +
              TEXT('Used by SBMPARMS TAA Tool to  +
              cause REPLACE(*NO)')
```

The interactive program used by SBMPARMS looks for the data area. If it exists, it deletes the program object you are re-creating so that when the create command occurs in batch, the old object does not exist.

Technical Tip

Specifying REPLACE(*NO) for programs in your test environment can protect you from inadvertently working with the wrong version of a program and can keep you from cluttering library QRPLOBJ with multiple test versions of the same program. The SBMPARMS TAA tool can help you accomplish both these objectives.

- Except for security attributes, the parameters you specified for the old version of a program on the CRTCLPGM and CHGPGM commands are forgotten. You must specify the parameters every time you re-create the program, an error-prone process. However, two TAA tools — SBMPARMS and RPLPGM (described later in this chapter) — can help address this problem.
- In two situations, you can't change a program that someone is using and expect it to work. First, assume you need to change a parameter list used when PGMA calls PGMB. If someone is using either PGMA or PGMB when you start the re-create process, their program could end abnormally. Second, if an RPG program does a return with LR off and you re-create the program while it is being used, problems could occur. The potential problem lies in the fact that the open files and program work area (where field values are stored) available to the program as it was executing are no longer available when the new version of the program is called.

  Most programmers don't worry about these problems; they just replace programs and hope for the best.
- In a shop where programmers do considerable in-house programming, the QRPLOBJ library can contain many objects. Although library QRPLOBJ will be cleared by the system when you IPL, it isn't wise to clear the library indiscriminately because someone may be using an old version of an object that has been replaced.

But a TAA tool — DLTOLDQRPL (Delete Old QRPLOBJ objects) — is available that can help. When an object is moved to QRPLOBJ, the change date/time of the old object is updated. DLTOLDQRPL allows you to specify a time (the default is 10 hours) so that it is unlikely to delete anything still in use. You can run DLTOLDQRPL every night to clean up library QRPLOBJ and feel relatively safe about not deleting an object that someone might be using.

Technical Tip

If you don't IPL frequently, the DLTOLDQRPL TAA tool can help you keep the QRPLOBJ library clean without worrying about deleting an object that someone might be using.

The CHGPGM Command

The CHGPGM command mostly affects the program template, or observability, of an object program. Let's look at some of the parameters for this command.

The RMVOBS Parameter

The value you specify for the RMVOBS (Remove Observability) parameter determines whether or not an object program retains its observability. The default is RMVOBS(*SAME), which will leave the program as is, with its observability intact (assuming you have not previously removed it). If you specify RMVOBS(*ALL), your program object will be considerably smaller but you will lose useful capabilities such as program debugging, program dump, and program retranslation.

I recommend that you not remove observability unless

- you really want to save disk space, or
- you want to have a more secure program

If you do remove observability, be sure you have a good backup strategy and you can re-create the program object from source.

Technical Tip

For programs I develop for my own use, I take the default and retain observability of the program object. I would rather waste a little space and keep the benefits (periodically, I use the SQZPGMSIZ TAA tool, described later). For object code I develop for someone else's system (e.g., TAA tools), I believe that saving space is far more important.

The USRPRF and USEADPAUT Parameters

The USRPRF and USEADPAUT parameters control the program authority adoption function that is described in Chapter 22, "The Program Stack." The USRPRF parameter also is discussed in this chapter in the section "The CRTCLPGM Command."

If you have used the CRTCLPGM command to specify that a program execute under an adopted authority (USRPRF parameter of *OWNER), you can change the impact of this specification on a program lower in the program stack with the USEADPAUT parameter on the CHGPGM command. For example, if you specified USRPRF(*OWNER) on the CRTCLPGM command for PGMA but wanted PGMC (a program lower in the program stack) to operate under the authority of the user of the program, you could specify USEADPAUT(*NO) on the CHGPGM command for PGMC. The better you understand the USEADPAUT parameter, the more uses you will find for it (see Chapter 22).

The OPTIMIZE Parameter

The OPTIMIZE parameter forces the CL compiler to use a slower, but more optimal, translation from the program template to the object code. Specifically, when you specify OPTIMIZE(*YES), the system tries to optimize the register usage of the object program. Registers are internal hardware components that pertain to addressing main storage. Each register can address only so much main storage before it must be reloaded with a new offset. At times, considerable reloading occurs.

Some compilers are fairly liberal in their use of registers, and optimizing them (to reduce the amount of reloading) positively affects program size and performance. But CL program object code isn't that complicated. In a large CL program, most of the object program is made up of calls to other system functions, such as the command analyzer or command processing programs.

Consequently, there isn't much register usage within a CL program that can be optimized. My experience shows that requesting optimization on a CL program has little effect on either the size of the program or its performance.

Technical Tip

Don't expect much from optimizing CL programs. Because most functions are done externally to the object program, not much can be done to optimize the program.

The CPROBJ Command

The CPROBJ (Compress Object) command offers a significant benefit because you can compress all the major pieces of a CL program and save disk space.

If you take the default on the CPROBJ command of PGMOPT(*ALL), the entire object is compressed. If someone calls the program, the system must decompress the object code to execute the program. For some objects, the system does a temporary decompress, but for program objects the decompress is always permanent. This means that once the program is decompressed, it remains in its full size until you compress it again.

In the section "SQZPGMSIZ TAA Tool," I'll introduce a tool that will help you reduce the size of programs. Because a program can decompress the object code or the program template, you need to do a compress function periodically to keep your program objects at a smaller size.

You can also specify PGMOPT(*OBS) on the CPROBJ command to indicate that you want to compress only the program template portion of the program object. It makes sense to do this because the debug information lays dormant until you have a problem. Compressing the program template (i.e., the observability information) is one way to have your cake and eat it, too. You have a much more acceptable space overhead for retaining the observable portion of the program; and if the system needs to retranslate the program template, it can do it from a compressed version.

Displaying a Program's Attributes

Although the CL command DSPPGM does a good job of displaying the attributes of a program (e.g., all the attributes of a CL program are displayed), some terms used on the DSPPGM display can be confusing.

For example, the "User profile" option on the display refers to the program authority adoption function, which is set by the USRPRF parameter on either the CRTCLPGM or CHGPGM command. The "Use adopted authority" option on the display refers to the USEADPAUT parameter on CHGPGM command. Both of these parameters were discussed briefly earlier in this chapter and in more detail in Chapter 22, "The Program Stack."

Strange but true is the fact that you can specify USRPRF(*OWNER) and USEADPAUT(*NO) on the same program. These specifications tell the program to run under the authority of the owner of the program and to not adopt the authority of the owners of programs higher in the stack.

Technical Tip

Don't become confused by the DSPPGM display. The "Use adopted authority" option is mostly the inverse of the program authority adoption function and refers to the USEADPAUT parameter on the CHGPGM command. Authorization is handled separately. You can use the DSPOBJAUT command to see the authorizations of a particular program.

If you use the DSPPGM command to display the attributes of an RPG program, you will find that three values — IGNDECERR (Ignore Decimal Error), CVTOPT (Type Conversion Options), and ALWNULL (Allow Null Values) — are not displayed. A value on the DSPPGM display, "Fix decimal data," appears to be the same as IGNDECERR, but it refers to an attribute set by compilers of other AS/400 languages.

The hidden RPG values are kept as data values inside the program. But you can use the DSPRPGIGN (Display RPG Ignore Decimal Error) TAA tool to see the value of IGNDECERR, which is specified on the CRTRPGPGM command. To use this tool, your program must have observability. DSPRPGIGN goes into debug mode to show you the value of the ZIGNDECD field. If the value is 1, the program was created with IGNDECERR.

Technical Tip

The DSPRPGIGN TAA tool gives you a way to determine how the CRTRPGPGM IGNDECERR parameter was specified.

Retrieving a Program's Attributes

The CL command RTVOBJD returns a lot of general information about program objects. For example, the command provides information about the source member used, the create date, and the last use date. But if the RTVOBJD command doesn't provide information about the specific attribute you want, consider using one of two QUSRTOOL TAA tools:

- The RTVPGMA (Retrieve Program Attributes) TAA tool should do just what you want in a CL program. It works like any retrieve command. This tool is implemented using an API. It would be faster to use the API directly, but the RTVPGMA command is much easier to use.
- The CVTPGMA (Convert Program Attributes) TAA tool will give you an outfile of program attributes. You can work with a single program, generic programs, or all programs in a library.

Neither the RTVPGMA nor the CVTPGMA command will retrieve the special RPG values IGNDECERR, CVTOPT, and ALWNULL. These values are hidden from the system; only the RPG program knows about them. Before you use RTVPGMA or CVTPGMA, be sure another TAA tool (e.g., the PRTPRMPGM or RPLPGM commands described later in this chapter) might not better meet your needs.

Technical Tip

The TAA tools RTVPGMA and CVTPGMA will let you access the attributes of programs so you can work with the attributes in a program.

Printing a Program's Attributes

DSPPGM does a good job for a single program, but you have to look for the information you need. Sometimes you might want to know which attributes are not the default. Two TAA tools can help you address this issue.

- The PRTPRM (Print Parameters) TAA tool supports several commands that let you print information about parameters for most typical object types. The specific command from this tool that you want is PRTPRMPGM (Print Parameters for Programs). You can request a single program, a generic name, or all programs in a library. The PRTPRMPGM command gives you one line per program and one line for each parameter that is not the same as the IBM default on the CRTxxxPGM command. In addition, the command provides spooled output so you can use the scan capability of the CL command DSPSPLF. Thus, you zero in on the programs that have specified the parameter in which you are interested.
- The PRTPGMA (Print Program Attributes) TAA tool is designed specifically for program objects. You can request one program, a generic name, or all programs in a library. You can also request selection criteria, such as the ability to see only those programs that adopt authority. The printed output has a column for each major option.

Technical Tip

The TAA commands PRTPRMPGM and PRTPGMA can help you look for exceptions in your existing program attributes.

THE RPLPGM TAA TOOL

A series of RPL TAA tools exists for different object types. The RPLPGM (Replace Program) TAA tool addresses the need for replacing programs. It works against most types of programs (not just CLP-type programs). To use the command, you would code

```
RPLPGM  PGM(xxx)
```

where xxx is the name of the program. The command

- retrieves the current attributes of the program set by the CRTxxxPGM and CHGPGM CL commands
- for CL programs, specifies CRTCLPGM with the values of the retrieved attributes, and specifies REPLACE(*YES); this picks up any existing authority you have specified and moves the old program to library QRPLOBJ (assuming the create is successful)
- uses the CHGPGM command again if you had used one or more of the CHGPGM attributes on the old program

By default, the RPLPGM command uses the source from the member and source file that were used to create the existing object.

Note that the setting of the RPG internal attributes (IGNDECERR, CVTOPT, and ALWNULL) are not known and therefore are not picked up. If this might be a problem, don't use the RPLPGM command for RPG programs. Instead, you might find the SBMPARMS TAA tool helpful (it's discussed later in this chapter).

Technical Tip

The RPLPGM TAA tool works well any time you re-create a program. You only need to do use the CRTxxxPGM command once with the proper attributes (and optionally follow it with the CHGPGM command) and then use RPLPGM to handle any future source changes.

REBUILDING AN APPLICATION

Sometimes you need to change the definition of a database file (e.g., to accommodate the addition of a new field or to change the size of a field). When this happens, you often need to re-create logical files and programs to account for the new format. And, if you change a field's attributes, you may also have to change display files because you may be using the field with a reference function.

Typically, a change to an important file means a lot of searching and re-creates. Commercial software packages exist that address this problem, but I am not aware of any that have a better combination of capability and ease of use than the TAA tool RBLDBF (Rebuild Data Base File).

Assume you have to make a change to file FILEA. Assume that FILEA and all the associated application objects are in the libraries LIBX and LIBY. All you need to do is change the DDS source for FILEA and specify the command:

```
RBLDBF  LIB(LIBX LIBY) FILE(FILEA)
```

RBLDBF finds the logical files that are built over FILEA and uses the system cross-reference information to find out what programs use either the physical file or the dependent logical files. The command also finds any display files used by these programs and creates everything in the right order. All the re-creates are done in a separate library. A report is printed for what created successfully and what did not (sorry, it can't re-create a program if you lost your source). Before the re-creates occur, the RBLDBF command extracts the existing attributes so that these are specified on the create commands. And the command keeps your authorization structure the same, restarts journaling, and optionally copies the data.

When RBLDBF is done, you can look at the report provided and fix any problems. Then you use the RPLRBLOBJ (Replace Rebuild Object) command, which is part of the same tool. This command deletes your production objects and moves the re-created objects to the production library.

Technical Tip

The RBLDBF TAA tool greatly simplifies the task of making a database change.

The SBMPARMS TAA Tool

The SBMPARMS (Submit Parameters) tool lets you place the program attributes you want specified on the CRTCLPGM and CHGPGM commands into the source for the program. The TAA tool requires the use of special source comments and a special batch program that is part of the tool. The special batch program

- reads the first five statements of the source member,
- extracts any attributes from the special comments,
- generates the appropriate CRTCLPGM command,
- issues the CRTCLPGM command, and
- if needed, generates/executes the CHGPGM command.

The SBMPARMS command will work not only with the CRTCLPGM command but also with most of the create commands that use source. By using SBMPARMS to place program attributes in your source, you do not need to specify a create command's parameters every time you do a create.

The special comments that contain the attributes must exist within the first five statements of your source. The form varies depending on the source type you are dealing with. For CL programs, it should look like this:

```
*...+....1....+....2....+....3....+....4
/*PARMS USRPRF(*OWNER) LOG(*YES)  */
/*PARMS ALWRTVSRC(*NO) */
/*CHGPGM RMVOBS(*ALL)  */
```

The /*PARMS or /*CHGPGM option must begin in position 1. After that it is free form, but you must specify the keywords and the ending */.

SBMPARMS has instructions for how to use the function with either PDM or the Programmer's Menu. With PDM, you must create a special option and use it instead of the normal option to create. With the Programmer's Menu, you use a standard program name on the STRPGMMNU command's EXITPGM parameter.

Some initial setup is required to get SBMPARMS working and the attributes specified correctly in your source. But once you get there, you never have to worry about specifying the attributes again. You could use the PRTPRM tool (described earlier) to help you determine what attributes you have specified on existing objects.

SBMPARMS isn't just for CL programs; it works for most object types that are created from source.

Technical Tip

The SBMPARMS TAA tool lets you place the attributes that are specified on the CRTCLPGM and CHGPGM commands with the source for the program. The tool works for most create commands that use source.

SQUEEZING THE SIZE OF CL PROGRAMS

The table below indicates how specifying various options on the CRTCLPGM, CHGPGM, and CPROBJ commands might affect the size of a program. I ran these tests under Version 2, Release 2 of the operating system using two different programs. The first program contained 60 lines of code; the second contained 182 lines.

The program sizes shown were taken from the DSPOBJD command, which reflects the allocated space for the object. Allocations are done in page size increments (512 bytes). Thus, a simple change to the program probably won't affect its size much.

	— 60 Lines —		— 182 Lines —	
	Size	**Savings**	**Size**	**Savings**
All defaults taken on CRTCLPGM	18,432		44,544	
ALWRTVSRC(*NO)	16,384	11%	37,888	15%
CPROBJ PGMOPT(*ALL)	8,192	55%	16,896	62%
CPROBJ PGMOPT(*OBS)	14,336	22%	34,304	24%
CHGPGM OPTIMIZE(*YES)[1]	17,920	3%	44,544	0%
CHGPGM RMVOBS(*YES)	10,752	42%	28,160	37%
CHGPGM RMVOBS(*YES) and CPROBJ	8,188	56%	16,896	62%
ALWRTVSRC(*NO) and CPROBJ PGMOPT(*OBS)	12,288	33%	27,648	38%
ALWRTVSRC(*NO) and CHGPGM RMVOBS(*ALL)	8,704	53%	21,504	52%
ALWRTVSRC(*NO) and CHGPGM RMVOBS(*ALL) and CPROBJ	6,144	67%	10,240	77%

The SQZPGMSIZ TAA Tool

The TAA tool SQZPGMSIZ (Squeeze Program Size) can help you squeeze the size of programs. The command is designed to work on all program objects in a specified library. This is the kind of command you submit to batch.

Let's assume you have adequate backup of your CL source, you don't need the RTVCLSRC function, and you like the observability function for programs but you use it infrequently. Here's what you would specify to save a significant chunk of disk space:

```
SQZPGMSIZ  LIB(xxx) ALWRTVSRC(*NO) OBSERVE(*COMPRESS)
```

The SQZPGMSIZ command finds the program objects in the library specified and, for CL programs, re-creates them using the source member that was originally used. The CRTCLPGM command is specified with a value of *NO for ALWRTVSRC. The RPLPGM tool is used to replace the program so that no existing attributes are lost. For every program object (not just CL programs), the CPROBJ command would be executed with PGMOPT(*OBS) to compress observability.

The SQZPGMSIZ command prints a report that lists one line per program showing the size of the old and new programs and the difference

[1]The OPTIMIZE function didn't do anything for one of the programs and only a little for the other. As discussed earlier, you shouldn't expect OPTIMIZE to do much on CL programs. Because of this, I don't use OPTIMIZE on CL programs; it doesn't deliver adequate payback for the time it takes to run.

in program size as a percentage. Based on the results of the tests you saw in the previous section, you can expect to save about one-third the space of existing CL programs.

If you decided you didn't need the source in the CL programs or any program observability, you could save even more space. In this case, you would code

```
SQZPGMSIZ  LIB(xxx) ALWRTVSRC(*NO) OBSERVE(*REMOVE)
```

Based on the previous chart, you could expect about a 50 percent space savings for CL program objects. A companion command, DSQPGMSIZ (De-Squeeze Program Size), lets you restore observability by re-creating all the programs in a library.

Because the system will automatically decompress the observability portion of a program if debug is used, you should run SQZPGMSIZ periodically to return programs to their smaller size and to compress any new programs.

Technical Tip

The SQZPGMSIZ TAA tool can save you a lot of space with very little work and hardly any loss of function. You do lose the capability to retrieve CL source.

Exercise A Program Options

In this exercise you will create some programs and examine alternatives for compressing programs.

1. Use PDM to create a CLP member named TRYSIZ.
2. Enter the following source:

```
PGM
SNDPGMMSG  MSG(HI)
ENDPGM
```

3. Duplicate the SNDPGMMSG command 20 times (21 identical commands in all). If you've never used the SEU "Repeat" function, now is a good time to learn. Just key RP20 (repeat 20 times) over the statement number of the SNDPGMMSG statement and press Enter.
4. Create the program with all the defaults.
5. Use the DSPPGM command to display the program.

   You should see that the value for the ALWRTVSRC parameter is *YES, since the default was taken.
6. Roll to the second display, which shows the size of the program. On V2R2M0, the size is 11,776 bytes.
7. Return to the command entry line and enter the command:

```
DSPOBJD  OBJ(TRYSIZ) OBJTYPE(*PGM)
```

   This should show the same program size that you saw on the DSPPGM display.
8. Re-create the program and specify ALWRTVSRC(*NO).
9. Use DSPPGM to display the program.

   You should see that the value of the ALWRTVSRC parameter is *NO.
10. Roll to the second display, which shows the program size.

    On V2R2M0, the size is 11,264 bytes. About 500 bytes were saved by not storing the source with the program. You can't determine exactly how much space was saved because the system rounds the different pieces of program objects up to page boundaries. The amount of savings will vary because of this rounding technique.

Exercise A continued

Exercise A continued

11. Use CPROBJ to compress the observability of the program:

```
CPROBJ   OBJ(TRYSIZ) OBJTYPE(*PGM) PGMOPT(*OBS)
```

12. Use DSPPGM to display the program size.

    On V2R2M0, the program size is 8,704 bytes. About 2,500 bytes were saved by compressing the observability portion of the program.

13. Use CHGPGM to remove observability:

```
CHGPGM   PGM(TRYSIZ) RMVOBS(*ALL)
```

14. Use DSPPGM to display the program size.

    On V2R2M0, the program size is 8,192 bytes. About 500 bytes were saved by removing observability.

15. Use CPROBJ to compress the object code of the program:

```
CPROBJ   OBJ(TRYSIZ) OBJTYPE(*PGM) PGMOPT(*ALL)
```

16. Use DSPPGM to display the program size.

    On V2R2M0, the program size is 4,608 bytes. About 3,500 bytes were saved by compressing the object code.

17. Call the program:

```
CALL   TRYSIZ
```

18. Ignore the messages. Use DSPPGM to display the program size. On V2R2M0, the size is 5,632 bytes. The system has automatically decompressed the program. The program will remain at this size until you compress it again (there is no concept of temporary program compression, as there is with most object types).

Exercise B RPLPGM TAA Tool

In this exercise you will use the RPLPGM TAA tool to see how it can re-create a program with the existing options. If the RPLPGM command is not on your system, see Appendix B.

1. Use the CRTCLPGM command to re-create the TRYSIZ program (used in the previous exercise) without logging:

   ```
   CRTCLPGM  PGM(TRYSIZ) LOG(*NO)
   ```

2. Use the CHGPGM command to remove observability:

   ```
   CHGPGM  PGM(TRYSIZ) RMVOBS(*ALL)
   ```

3. Enter the command:

   ```
   DSPPGM  TRYSIZ
   ```

   You should see that the value of the "Log commands" parameter is *NO and that observability does not exist.

4. Use the GRTOBJAUT command to grant *USE authority to QSYSOPR:

   ```
   GRTOBJAUT  OBJ(TRYSIZ) OBJTYPE(*PGM) USER(QSYSOPR) AUT(*USE)
   ```

5. Use the DSPOBJAUT command to confirm that the GRT command worked correctly:

   ```
   DSPOBJAUT  OBJ(TRYSIZ) OBJTYPE(*PGM)
   ```

   You should see that QSYSOPR has *USE authority.

6. Use the RPLPGM TAA tool:

   ```
   RPLPGM  PGM(TRYSIZ)
   ```

7. Enter the command:

   ```
   DSPPGM  TRYSIZ
   ```

   You should see that the value of the "Log commands" parameter is *NO and that observability does not exist. RPLPGM has correctly picked up the existing attributes of the program and invoked CHGPGM.

Exercise B continued

Exercise B continued

8. Use the DSPOBJAUT command to confirm that the GRT command worked correctly:

```
DSPOBJAUT  OBJ(TRYSIZ) OBJTYPE(*PGM)
```

   You should see that the authorization is the way it was (QSYSOPR still has *USE authority). RPLPGM does a REPLACE(*YES) function, which causes the system to copy the authorizations to the new program.

Exercise C SQZPGMSIZ TAA Tool

In this exercise you will use the SQZPGMSIZ TAA tool to see how it can compress the size of CL programs without losing significant function (assuming your source is adequately backed up). We'll also use the PRTLIBDTL TAA tool to display the contents of a library. If these commands are not on your system, see Appendix B.

1. The SQZPGMSIZ tool can best be demonstrated if a separate library is created. Enter the command:

```
CRTLIB  LIB(TRYSIZ) TEXT('Try size options')
```

2. Move the object created in the previous exercise to the TRYSIZ library:

```
MOVOBJ  OBJ(TRYSIZ) OBJTYPE(*PGM) TOLIB(TRYSIZ)
```

3. Create another program in the TRYSIZ library. Use one of your own source members or enter the following command, which uses a source member from QUSRTOOL:

```
CRTCLPGM  PGM(TRYSIZ/TAACLPAC) SRCFILE(QUSRTOOL/QATTCL)
```

4. Create another program in the TRYSIZ library. Use one of your own source members or enter the following command, which uses a source member from QUSRTOOL:

```
CRTCLPGM  PGM(TRYSIZ/TAACLPLC) SRCFILE(QUSRTOOL/QATTCL)
```

5. Prompt for the PRTLIBDTL TAA tool command.

Exercise C continued

Exercise C continued

6. Note all the options you can use to print selected objects from the library. Enter the TRYSIZ library name in the LIB parameter (use defaults for the other parameters) and press Enter.

7. Display the spooled file that was created by PRTLIBDTL.

   Note the size of the objects and the size of the library object for the TRYSIZ library. When you save the library, you save all the objects as well as the library object.

8. Return to command entry and use the SQZPGMSIZ command:

```
SQZPGMSIZ  LIB(TRYSIZ) ALWRTVSRC(*NO) OBSERVE(*COMPRESS)
```

9. Display the spooled file that was created by SQZPGMSIZ.

   Note the size of the objects before compressing and the percentage of space gained. You can gain significant space savings without loss of function if you have adequate backup for your source.

10. Use DSPPGM to display the attributes of TRYSIZ:

```
DSPPGM  PGM(TRYSIZ/TRYSIZ)
```

   You should see that the program has been replaced, but the LOG attribute is still *NO as it was previously. The SQZPGMSIZ command uses the RPLPGM TAA tool to replace programs.

11. If you are finished with the exercise, delete the library:

```
DLTLIB  TRYSIZ
```

CHAPTER 24

CL Program Performance

In most cases, you probably can't squeeze much better performance out of your CL programs than you are already getting. For example, if your CL program is a front end to a high-level language (HLL) program that does most of the work, you won't gain much by tinkering with the CL program (although there are some things you can do that will improve the HLL program's performance). And if your CL program is only doing things that it needs to do (e.g., IF, DO, GOTO, ENDDO, CHGVAR), there is little you can do to make it more efficient. All these functions, which are performed internally by the created object code, perform efficiently enough.

In some cases, however, you can improve a CL program's performance. Here are some things you should be thinking about as you code your CL programs:

- Calls to system functions. Some CL commands (e.g., CHGVAR) do not call a command processing program (CPP). Most CL commands (e.g., OVRxxx, CALL, SNDPGMMSG, RTVxxx) result in a call to a CPP. Many of these latter commands will cause some disk access to occur. This becomes a performance concern if the commands will be executed many times (e.g., if the program is called many times a day). The solution, when workable, is to structure your code to avoid executing an unnecessary set of commands.
- Heavy overhead requests. Some CL commands that cause significant overhead are the ones that take a long time to execute interactively. These commands include

  — DSPLIB
  — Most requests to a multimember file; for example, DSPFD(*MBRLIST)
  — Any compiles
  — Any outfile request
  — RGZPFM

  Additional commands that cause significant overhead include

  — SBMJOB
  — Any open request
  — Creating files
  — Adding and removing members

> When you use a "heavy overhead" command, you need to ask, "Is this command necessary?" If you can avoid using a "heavy overhead" command, you usually can improve performance noticeably.

The next two sections will focus on performance gains you might find as you code a loop of instructions in a CL program and when you make iterative calls to a CL program from a HLL program. The last section of this chapter will discuss ways to code your CL program that can improve an HLL program's performance.

ITERATIVE PROCESSING IN CL

If you are going to perform a loop only a few times in a CL program (e.g., fewer than 10 times), optimizing the instructions isn't going to provide any significant performance payoff. It's only when your program needs to process the loop many times that trying to optimize your code makes sense.

To determine when you might think about improving performance, you need to think about how many times a day you will execute the loop. If a program is being called once a month, your potential for performance improvement is not as great as if it were being called multiple times per day. I use the following guidelines: If the loop is executed fewer than 10 times a day, forget about improving performance. If the loop is executed 100 times a day, I still wouldn't spend much time trying to optimize performance. If the loop is executed 1,000 times a day, I would be more careful with my code. And if the loop is executed many thousands of times a day, I would concentrate seriously on improving performance.

Here are some points to consider as you work to optimize the performance of your CL program:

- If at all possible, keep code outside the loop (I could make this same comment about any programming language). For example, if your program is reading database records and comparing for a date, use the CVTDAT command outside the loop to put the date in the same format as the database record. If your program executes a command only once per loop, it can make a difference in performance.
- Avoid using a "heavy request" command inside the loop. If the command you want to execute (e.g., SBMJOB, CRTPF) will cause many disk accesses, try to find a faster-performing solution. If you are not sure if the command you want to use is a "heavy request" command, compare the command interactively with a CHKOBJ of

an object you know exists. If you can see a difference in execution time, you probably are dealing with a "heavy request" command.

- Avoid repeated references to parameters that are passed to the CL program. Accessing a variable declared in another program has more overhead. If you have multiple references to this type of variable, move it to a variable declared within your program and reference that variable instead.
- Avoid repeated reference to a value specified with the substring function. If you are going to use the value more than once, move it to a separate variable.
- If you are testing a variable for several values, test the most popular one first and then use a GOTO to branch to a common point after all the tests are complete.
- If you are going to scan a variable that frequently is blank, compare for all blanks first. The system can compare one large variable faster than individual characters.
- If you are scanning a variable, you can avoid the "Am I at the end?" test inside the loop by moving the variable to a larger value and then placing the value you are comparing to at the low order of the new variable. For example, to scan a 20-character variable for an asterisk, you could code the following:

```
             PGM         PARM(&VAR1)
             DCL         &VAR1 *CHAR LEN(20)
             DCL         &VAR2 *CHAR LEN(21)
             DCL         &IX *DEC LEN(3 0)
             IF          (&VAR1 *EQ ' ') DO /* All blanks */
                         /*                    */
                         /* All blank function */
                         /*                    */
             ENDDO       /* All blanks */
                         /* Move to one position larger plus * */
             CHGVAR      &VAR2 (&VAR1 *CAT '*')
LOOP:                    /* Loop to find *     */
             CHGVAR      &IX (&IX + 1)
             IF          (%SST(&VAR2 &IX 1) *NE '*') GOTO LOOP
                         /* End of the loop */
             IF          (&IX *LT 21) DO /* Found an * */
                         /*                    */
                         /* Found * function   */
```

```
                    /*                  */
        ENDDO       /* Found an * */
                    /*                  */
                    /* No * exists      */
                    /*  function        */
```

In this example, there are commands before the loop starts and after the loop is complete to try to minimize the number of commands in the loop. The loop itself contains only two CL commands, both of which execute as generated code (they don't call any system function).

- Use odd-length decimal variables. The CL compiler uses packed-decimal values to perform arithmetic and it handles odd-length values more efficiently. For some variables, you may not have a choice; but for a variable that is being used as a work field (e.g., an index for a substring), be sure to use an odd length.
- Avoid operations that involve decimal variables with different numbers of decimal positions. Most of the time, your CL program decimal variables have only 0 decimal positions so they are all the same. CL will always perform decimal alignment on arithmetic operations. You are better off to keep everything with the same number of decimal positions inside the loop.
- If you have to read a lot of database records, CL is not as efficient as an HLL program. But if you have to perform a CL function for every record read, you will still be better off to read the records in CL.
- If you need to read a lot of database records in CL, consider using the OPNQRYF command to perform record selection; this will minimize the number of records your program must read. If the file is small or you can't make a significant reduction in the number of records, read it without using OPNQRYF.
- Avoid the use of the QCMDEXC command inside the loop; it adds overhead.
- If you need to call an RPG program repeatedly inside a loop, be sure the program returns with LR off (this keeps the RPG program active).
- If you need to call a CL program repeatedly inside a loop, it will cost you. Sometimes there isn't a reasonable alternative, but you might consider incorporating the functions in the main program to reduce the overhead of the CALL.

- If you call a program inside the loop, make it a qualified call (i.e., specify the name of the library where the program exists). If you don't want to hard-code the library name, use the RTVOBJD command outside the loop to return a variable that contains the name of the library and then use the variable as the library qualifier.
- If a user-written command must be executed many times, consider using a CALL to the CPP rather than to the command interface. You can't do the same thing with system commands unless an API is provided.

Iterative Use of a CL Function from an HLL Program

You usually can achieve greater performance gains with CL programs called iteratively from an HLL program than with CL programs used for other purposes. But the amount of usage is still a factor: The greater the iterative use of a CL program, the greater the chance of a performance payoff. I would consider using the following techniques to gain performance only if my CL program saw extensive iterative use:

- Use a compiled CL program instead of executing a command by using QCMDEXC; using QCMDEXC causes more overhead. You are better off to place a single command in a CL program and then call it from the HLL program, passing the appropriate parameters. This technique does not work if you are trying to do an override command and then open the file in your HLL program. Because the overrides are lost when the CL program is removed from the program stack, you must execute the QCMDEXC command from within the HLL program. For further understanding of this, see Chapter 22, "The Program Stack," and Chapter 26, "QCMDEXC and QCMDCHK."
- Avoid calling a CL program for functions you can code yourself. The classic example is the CVTDAT command. This is a nice CL command, but most of the functions can be done with a little bit of code in your HLL program.
- Use an API. The classic examples are the message-handling APIs. Use the API interfaces instead of calling a CL program.
- Use a direct CALL to the CPP instead of invoking a user-written command. CALLs are faster.
- Use a "requester type" job that is already active and waiting to perform your function; then send a request using a data queue.

HLL Program Performance

The most typical use of a CL program is to act as a front end for an HLL program. Typically, this means that your CL code does the following types of things:

- Checks for existence and authority to various objects
- Creates or allocates temporary objects
- Accesses system information (e.g., RTVJOBA)
- Issues override commands
- Performs OPNQRYF to select/sequence records
- Pre-opens files or requests shared opens
- Sends messages (errors or completion)

The following are the major things you can do in a CL program to improve the performance of an HLL program:

- When it makes sense, use OPNQRYF (see Chapter 20, "OPNQRYF"). OPNQRYF can have the best overall impact on your HLL program by minimizing the number of records your program has to read. To make OPNQRYF perform well on selection criteria, you may have to consider using permanent logical files with immediately maintained access paths.

- Use shared opens and pre-open files. This can have a very positive affect on quick response time. The performance of a full open has been improved over several operating system releases, but the shared open is still better.

  If your application has many HLL programs that all use the same database files, you can improve performance by using the OPNDBF command. Using a shared display file can also help. Normally, you would place all the display formats for an application into a single display file.

  In addition, you can retain the performance benefits of shared opens and reduced PAG size if you use group jobs in situations where a user switches between applications frequently.

- Use override options. The most significant of these is the database option for SEQONLY. Specifying a large block size for input-only or output-only files can do wonders to improve the performance of batch jobs. I have found that you can realize performance benefits by specifying a block size of up to 300 records.

- Avoid some override commands. Executing an override command does cost you. If you always request to override to the same value, you should make it a permanent file option. Creating a specific file instead of using an override can be helpful, but it probably is not worth the effort unless the file is used extensively.

- Avoid heavy overhead requests. Typical CL program functions such as SBMJOB and creating temporary files and/or members are heavy requests for the system to perform. If you do a lot of SBMJOB work, set up a never-ending program that will perform the work and communicate with data queue entries.
- If you use applications regularly that must create temporary files and members, you should consider creating permanent files and members for those applications. Creating files and members every time an application runs is costly in terms of performance. If you need a unique file/member for an application, take a look at the ALCTMPMBR (Allocate Temporary Member) TAA tool, which includes some files and members you might use and also provides a technique for assigning unique files and members to an application on request.

CHAPTER 25

Writing Secure Programs

The AS/400 has some outstanding security features, but it is not immune to break-in attempts (as I will demonstrate in a moment). And although you cannot prevent all break-in possibilities, you can make it more and more difficult for someone to break in.

In this chapter I will suggest roadblocks you can place in the path of would be break-in artists, discuss how to write a secure program, and introduce you to some QUSRTOOL TAA tools that can help you manage AS/400 security.

But first, let's start with an attention-getter.

ONE WAY TO BREAK IN

If I wanted to break into an AS/400, one method I could use would be to attack the system commands. For example, all systems have the library QSYS on their library list and in that library is the secured command CRTUSRPRF. If I can change the system portion of the library list, I can get into a position to do whatever I want on the system.

Here's the approach I would take: I would place a library (let's call it QSYSBOGUS) in front of library QSYS on the library list. Then I would place a user command named CRTUSRPRF in library QSYSBOGUS. I would simply duplicate the CRTUSRPRF command in library QSYS so the user command looked like the real command (including help text) and then I would change the CPP (command processing program) to one of my own programs (so far, I've taken about 30 seconds). Writing a bogus CPP would not be easy (the program has to accept the correct parameter list), but it would not be impossible.

Now, when the real CRTUSRPRF command is requested (hardly anyone qualifies the command name to library QSYS), the bogus CRTUSRPRF command would be executed instead of the real command.

The most clever thing the bogus command could do would be to invoke the system CRTUSRPRF command (it would appear to have worked normally), but it could also do something in addition.

Because the user who is running CRTUSRPRF must be authorized to it, I would know (s)he is probably the security officer (QSECOFR). I could actually determine in my bogus CPP (by using the RTVJOBA command) whether or not the security officer called the command and only do my "something in addition" if (s)he was QSECOFR.

I can think of some nasty things a programmer could do to the system under QSECOFR authority. Probably the sneakiest tactic would be to submit a batch job that would

- Create a program in an obscure library that calls QCMD, specifies USRPRF(*OWNER), and allows the public to use the program:

```
PGM
CALL        QCMD
ENDPGM
```

- Then remove the QSYSBOGUS library from the system portion of the library list.

Now a program would exist in an obscure library that would let a user do anything (s)he wants — and the system library list looks perfectly normal. When the new program is called, the command entry display would appear and the user would operate under the adopted authority of QSECOFR.

In reality, a normal user couldn't take control of your system in this manner because, by default, changing the system portion of the library list is not authorized to the public. But the scenario I've described does point out that the security officer has many major issues to consider.

Controls the Security Officer Should Insist On

In my opinion, the security officer should insist on the following controls:

- Create individual profiles with passwords that are required to change periodically.
- Restrict access to the system portion of the library list. This would include actions such as
  - — controlling who can change the system value QSYSLIBL. By default, this value can be changed only by a user with *ALLOBJ and *SECADM special authority.
  - — controlling who is authorized to the CHGSYSLIBL command. By default, the public is not authorized. While this command lets you change only the library list for your job, it is still a potentially dangerous authority.
- Avoid placing any library in front of QSYS on the system portion of the library list. If you do place a library there, prevent the public from adding objects to the library and carefully control what is in the library.

- Restrict authority for creating and changing subsystems. Routing entries are very security sensitive.
- Change the passwords for the shipped IBM profiles (especially QSECOFR and QSRV).
- Change the passwords for DST (Dedicated Service Tools).
- Use LMTCPB(*YES) for production end users.
- Limit the number of people in the QSECOFR group (if any).
- Limit the number of people with *ALLOBJ authority.
- Use Level 40 security. Level 40 security isn't as scary as it sounds and it can protect you from attempts to circumvent security. For more information about Level 40, see IBM's *Security Concepts and Planning* (SC41-8083).

Technical Tip

If you are the security officer, you certainly don't want to have to explain to management that a breach in security could have been prevented with Level 40. Level 40 is designed for your protection. Why not use it?

Menu-Level Security

Most AS/400 shops use some form of menu-level security for their production end users and feel safe in assuming that the user can choose only the options that exist on the menu. This approach is fairly clear and simple to implement, but there are some potential security loopholes to watch out for.

Most production end users aren't interested in "hacking" their way into the system, but let's look at an example of what could happen. Assume you take the defaults for most functions and you have an end-user display that has a command entry line on it. The production end user whose user profile is set to LMTCPB(*NO) could issue a command that would affect one of the programs on the menu. For example, imagine the thrill you would have figuring out what happened if your production end user issued the following override command and then called the Order Entry program:

```
OVRDBF  FILE(ORDERS) TOFILE(PAYROLL) LVLCHK(*NO)
```

Instead of adding "new order" records to the order file, the program would add records to the payroll file.

If you take defaults, nothing prevents a production end user from accessing the command entry display (QCMD) or any authorized program from the sign-on display and doing something like the previous override command example demonstrates.

Here's what you can do to secure your menus:

- Limit capabilities with the CRTUSRPRF LMTCPB parameter. The sign-on display lets an end user decide which program (s)he wants to run first. Normally, (s)he wouldn't enter anything and would be directed to his or her first menu. However, if the end user's profile is specified as LMTCPB(*NO), (s)he can decide to call any authorized program from the sign-on display. Unfortunately, the default for any new user profile is LMTCPB(*NO).

  You can use the TAA tool CHKLMTCPB (described later in this chapter) to find all the USRCLS(*USER) profiles and determine whether or not they have been specified as LMTCPB(*NO). You can use the same tool to change the specification. Another option is to use a personalized sign-on display that prevents a user from entering a program name (the *Work Management Guide* — SC41-8078 — tells you how to do this). But even if you use personalized sign-on displays, you should still be sure users are specified as LMTCPB(*YES) to limit access to a command entry line.

- Avoid any display for a production end user that provides a command entry line. If the user's profile is specified as LMTCPB(*YES), by default the user is allowed to use only a few commands (e.g., SNDMSG). This objective is complicated by the fact that 1) a program may adopt authority (see Chapter 22, "The Program Stack"), and 2) it's difficult to police what your programmers do when they create or change a command.

- Watch out for a function such as the Attention key. If you let your end users use the OA (Operational Assistant) Attention key function, they can get to a command entry line (they may have to request an Intermediate view of some of the displays). Fortunately, this type of Attention key handling program will not adopt authority, so the LMTCPB(*YES) user can enter only the commands that are specified as ALWLMTUSR(*YES).

  IBM doesn't ship many ALWLMTUSR(*YES) commands; the ones that are shipped are fairly insensitive, such as SNDMSG. However, this does not guarantee safety. Someone could change one of the more sensitive IBM commands, such as OVRDBF. Or how would you prevent a programmer from creating a seemingly innocent program with the following code and then creating a command interface and specifying ALWLMTUSR(*YES):

```
PGM     PARM(&CMD)
DCL     &CMD *CHAR LEN(500)
CALL    QCMDEXC PARM(&CMD 500)
ENDPGM
```

Now even the LMTCPB(*YES) users can execute any authorized command (most commands are public). Assume the name of the command is CMDENT. From a command entry display, the LMTCPB(*YES) user could enter

```
CMDENT  ('?OVRDBF')
```

and receive the command prompt for the OVRDBF command.

- Avoid providing indiscriminate authorization for debugging. By default, the STRDBG command is not public and you should be careful about who you authorize to use STRDBG. If a user has debug authority and has *CHANGE authority to the program (it's the default), (s)he can change the program's function. An exercise at the end of this chapter will demonstrate this potential problem.

Controlling Programmers

In most situations, programmers are trustworthy and you don't need to worry about controlling their actions. But if you want tight control over what programmers might do, you must

- Protect the data by using system security functions. If a programmer does not have authority to the data and if you are dealing with a program that does not use the program authority adoption function, the system will prevent the programmer from altering the data. It's much easier to protect the data than it is to write a program that a programmer can't fool with. If you want to prevent a programmer from fooling with a program, you must do the same things that are described in the section "Programs that Use Program Authority Adoption."
- Prevent a programmer from using the debug function. You would do this by specifying the program as *USE authority instead of the default of *CHANGE.
- For sensitive programs, specify CHGPGM USEADPAUT(*NO). This specification prevents the situation where a program higher in the invocation stack allows your program to operate under adopted authority.

Bogus Program Protection

Early in this chapter I used the technique of a bogus program to demonstrate how a programmer might break into the system. Now let's look at how to prevent a bogus program from gaining control of your system.

Remember that the easiest way to cause a bogus program to be invoked is to place the program in front of the real program on the library list. For example, assume I knew that a payroll clerk submits a batch job that does an unqualified call to PGMA. If I can place my own version of PGMA at the front of the library list, I can use the payroll clerk's authorization to do whatever I want that (s)he is authorized to do.

Consequently, if you want to make it difficult for a bogus program to gain control, you have to control the library list — both the system and user portion. Thus, the security officer must be sensitive to what libraries (s)he allows on the system portion of the library list, who can add programs to these libraries, and what programs exist.

Assuming you have control of the system portion of the library list, you need to set the user portion of the library list in the application to ensure it is not being tampered with. Chapter 26, "QCMDEXC and QCMDCHK," provides a technique for saving the current library list, setting it for your own use, and then resetting it to its original value.

Once you have control of the library list, you need to control what exists in the libraries. If you have a security-sensitive batch job, you should submit it using a qualified name such as LIB1/PGMA in the following command:

```
SMBJOB  CMD(CALL LIB1/PGMA)
```

Although using a qualified name isn't necessary if you are in control of the library list when the job is submitted, doing so places another hurdle in front of someone who is trying to write a bogus program.

If you are really concerned about the possibility of bogus programs, you also need to follow the suggestions described in the next section.

Programs That Use Program Authority Adoption

Although program authority adoption is an outstanding function, it can be a "cheater's paradise" for programmers. Writing a program that adopts its owner's authority and prevents a programmer from cheating is not easy. To prevent potential security problems when using the program authority adoption function — and when using a sensitive security function — you need to

- Be sure the security officer is following the suggestions outlined previously in this chapter. For example, it is important to control the library list.

- Use qualified names. With the exception of IBM system commands, you should always use qualified names. If you don't, you are exposed to the use of bogus programs or commands. For example, if you call a subprogram or use a user-written command (e.g., a TAA tool command), you need to qualify the library name:

  ```
  CALL  xxx/PGMX
  TAATOOL/ADDDAT  ...
  ```

  You cannot rely on using the CHGLIBL command to change the library list and protect the objects used within your program. If you code

  ```
  CALL  PGMA
  ```

  without specifying a qualifying library name, you take the default of *LIBL and use the library list. Thus, many PGMAs could be ahead of yours on the full library list. The libraries that could be ahead of yours include

  — Other libraries on the system portion of the library list. The public is authorized to add objects to libraries such as QSYS2 and QUSRSYS. Your security officer may also have added a library to the library list that is unique to your installation and may not have prevented the public from adding objects to it.

  — A current library. A user could have a current library, which by default will appear before your library, if you just do CHGLIBL with only the LIBL parameter.

  — A product library. Nothing prevents a user from creating a command in his or her own library and naming your security-sensitive program as the CPP. The user must be authorized to the program to gain access. When the command runs, his or her library is on the library list ahead of any of the libraries that you can control with CHGLIBL. The user can then place his or her own programs or files in his or her library with the same names as the ones you are using within your program. If you don't qualify the use of your objects, guess which ones get used.

Technical Tip

It is a misleading assumption to think you can avoid qualifying objects by controlling the library list with CHGLIBL. There are too many ways to place a library in front of the ones you think are in control.

- Use OVRxxx commands and specify SECURE(*YES). Even if you don't need an OVRxxx command, adding one with SECURE(*YES) prevents another program higher in the program stack from directing your program to operate on a different file. This is very important for programs that adopt the security officer's profile, because you want to be sure what these programs are doing. See Chapter 18, "Overrides," to learn more about specifying SECURE(*YES).
- Create sensitive programs, commands, and any "read only" objects as AUT(*USE), or at least prevent the public from having *CHANGE authority.
- For user-written commands that are used within the program, qualify the CPP name. This means the PGM parameter on CRTCMD or CHGCMD should be entered as

  ```
  PGM(xxx/yyy)
  ```

  The CPP has the same problem as any unqualified name. A CL program could qualify the name of the command so the right command definition object is accessed. But unless you qualify the CPP name, the system will search the library list to find the program.
- Use LOG(*NO) on the CRTCLPGM command. If you have a secure program, you don't want to give away any hints about what the program is doing.
- Use ALWRTVSRC(*NO) on the CRTCLPGM command. Again, you don't want to give away any hints about what the program is doing. Letting someone see the source would be like giving them a blueprint of a building and challenging them to break in.

KNOWING WHICH PROGRAM CALLED YOURS

If you have a sensitive program that should be called only by a specific program, it can be useful to determine the name of the calling program. Your program can determine the name of the program that called yours by sending a message to the previous program, receiving it, and then looking at the SENDER information. The code would look like this:

```
DCL         &SENDER *CHAR LEN(10)
DCL         &CALLER *CHAR LEN(10)
 .
 .
 .
SNDPGMMSG   MSG('DUMMY')
RCVMSG      PGMQ(*PRV) MSGTYPE(*LAST) SENDER(&SENDER)
CHGVAR      &CALLER %SST(&SENDER 56 10)
```

The variable &CALLER now contains the name of the program that called your program. This isn't a fail-safe technique, however, because you cannot tell which library the program came from; it could be another program of the same name from another library.

Masking Data

If one of your applications uses sensitive data in a database file (e.g., a file of passwords), you could mask the data so it would not be readable if someone displayed the file. Two QUSRTOOL TAA tools — SCRAMBLE and OR — can help you mask sensitive data.

The OR tool lets you "or" in bits based on a key that you supply. For example, you could "or" in bits and change the character "A" to the character "J." The "or" function is a typical bit-fiddling technique for masking data, by making a bit-by-bit comparison between two operands. For each bit position, the resulting bit is "1" if *one* of the corresponding bits in the operands is also "1".

The SCRAMBLE tool lets you scramble the bytes (e.g., byte 1 becomes byte 5) based on a key you supply.

Using both of these tools would make it difficult for someone to read the contents of a database file unless (s)he had the keys you used. An exercise at the end of this chapter demonstrates how to use these tools.

Other TAA Tools That Meet Security Needs

Several TAA tools are available that address security needs. To review the commands that are available, use the DSPTAATOOL command in member TAASUMMARY and look at the section on Security. The tools that can be of significant value to you include the following:

- DSPAUDLOG (Display Audit Log). You can use DSPAUDLOG to determine whether or not you can move to Level 40 safely and to monitor conditions while you are on Level 40. The tool works with the output of the audit log journal and lets you see all of the entries or select by type.

- DSPSECRVW (Display Security Review). This tool lets the security officer review the attributes of user profiles. It works with the outfile from DSPUSRPRF and allows you to select and sequence on various information. The tool acts as a general-purpose query over the outfile data and can eliminate the need to write programs to print special reports for the security officer or the auditor.
- DSPUSRAUT (Display User Authority). The system supports different levels of authorization for securing objects (e.g., object, authorization list, group profile, public access). When a conflict occurs, the system follows certain rules to determine which authority level is more important; but the information the system provides about authority levels is not presented in a meaningful manner. If your security structure is complex, trying to determine "Who can do what?" or "What can the public do?" can be difficult. The DSPUSRAUT tool helps answer these questions. The tool is actually three commands:
  - CVTUSRAUT captures information about your security environment and builds a database file in the sequence in which the system will apply its rules.
  - DSPUSRAUT lets you query the information provided by CVTUSRAUT, so you can answer questions such as "Who is allowed to do what?" DSPUSRAUT supports an optional outfile so you can capture in a database file what you see on the display.
  - CMPUSRAUT lets you compare the outfile created by DSPUSRAUT at two different points in time. This function lets you easily see changes in your authorization structure.

Technical Tip

If you are dealing with a complex security structure, you'll want to take a look at the DSPUSRAUT TAA tool.

- DSPPWD (Display Passwords). On the S/38, the security officer could review user passwords. The AS/400 prevents this review by performing a "one-way" encryption of the passwords. Although, this technique is much safer, many security officers liked the old approach. If you want to display passwords, you can do it with the DSPPWD tool. The AS/400 operating system provides a system value (QPWDVLDPGM) that lets you access passwords as they are being changed. The intent of the system value is to let a user program perform additional validation checking. DSPPWD uses this "hook" to capture the passwords.

If you control the function (see the documentation for DSPPWD), only the security officer can review passwords. Note that it takes an overt act on the security officer's part to invoke the DSPPWD function. Unless (s)he changes the QPWDVLDPGM system value, the DSPPWD tool won't do anything.

- PRTSECVIL (Print Security Violations). If you are not using Level 40 security, the place to look for security violations is in the QHST file. You can access the violations with the PRTSECVIL tool; it knows the message ID ranges to look for.
- CHGLIBOWN (Change Library Owner). This tool lets you ensure consistent ownership of all objects in a library or to change those that are owned by a particular user.
- (Check Limited Capability). When a new user profile is created, the default is USRCLS(*USER) and LMTCPB(*NO). When a user's capabilities are not limited, (s)he can enter any command on a command line display and can decide on the sign-on menu what initial program (s)he would like to run. For most production *USER types, you want to specify LMTCPB(*YES). CHKLMTCPB will find the users who are not limited and supports a "force" option that changes the specification to LMTCPB(*YES).

Exercise A Authority to Debug

To show you what it takes from an authority viewpoint to debug a program, you will create a simple program and then change the authority so you can act only as a public user. Some of these steps will work only if you do not have *ALLOBJ special authority; if you do, you could use a second profile.

1. Use PDM to create a CLP member named TRYSEC1.
2. Enter the following source:

```
PGM
DCL         &NAME *CHAR LEN(10)
CHGVAR      &NAME 'SMITH'
SNDPGMMSG   MSG('Give ' *CAT &NAME *TCAT ' a $1000 raise')
ENDPGM
```

3. Create the program.
4. Call the program:

```
CALL   TRYSEC1
```

   You should see the message that says "Give SMITH a $1000 raise."

5. Use EDTOBJAUT to change the authority:

```
EDTOBJAUT   OBJ(TRYSEC1) OBJTYPE(*PGM)
```

   You should see yourself as the owner and that you have *ALL authority to the object.

6. Position the cursor to the *ALL authority value and blank out the field. Press Enter.

   The screen should be refreshed, and you will not be shown as having any specific authority (don't worry, as the owner you can restore your authority to the object).

7. Return to the command entry display. If you do not have *ALLOBJ authority, enter the command:

```
DLTPGM   PGM(TRYSEC1)
```

Exercise A continued

Exercise A continued

The DLTPGM command should fail because you no longer have *OBJEXIST authority to the object. Because you are the owner, you can grant yourself this authority (we'll do this later). Some users remove the owner's *OBJEXIST right to critical master files to prevent an inadvertent deletion.

8. Enter the command:

```
STRDBG  PGM(TRYSEC1)
```

9. Assuming the SNDPGMMSG command is statement number 4.00, enter the following:

```
ADDBKP  STMT(400)
```

10. Call the program:

```
CALL  TRYSEC1
```

You should see the breakpoint display at statement 4.00.

11. Press F10 to access the command entry display.

12. Enter the command to change the variable value to your own name:

```
CHGPGMVAR  PGMVAR('&NAME') VALUE(xxx)
```

13. Press F3 to return to the breakpoint display.

14. Press Enter to continue.

You should see that you are about to get a good raise. Using debug is valid because the public has *CHANGE authority to the program. In many installations, production users can't enter commands and if they could they are probably not authorized to STRDBG (it is not public). However, programmers can do interesting things with supposedly secure programs.

15. End debug with the command:

```
ENDDBG
```

16. Now let's change the program to allow the *PUBLIC *USE authority. Since you are the owner, access the edit object authority display:

```
EDTOBJAUT  OBJ(TRYSEC1) OBJTYPE(*PGM)
```

Exercise A continued

Exercise A continued

17. Position the cursor to the *PUBLIC user and change the *CHANGE value to *USE.

    If you have *ALLOBJ authority, the next step is not going to work as described because you will have authority (you could try it as a user without *ALLOBJ authority).

18. Return to command entry and enter:

    ```
    STRDBG  PGM(TRYSEC1)
    ```

    You should see a message that says you are not authorized to debug the program. When you take the default for creating programs, (AUT = *CHANGE), you are really enabling anybody who is authorized to debug to do interesting things.

19. Put yourself back in charge by accessing the edit object authority display again:

    ```
    EDTOBJAUT  OBJ(TRYSEC1) OBJTYPE(*PGM)
    ```

20. Use Function key 6 to add new users. When the display appears, enter your name and *ALL for "object authority." Press Enter. You now have control of the object again.

Exercise B SCRAMBLE and OR TAA Tools

The SCRAMBLE and OR TAA tools let you mask data so it will not appear to be what it really is. For example, if you were keeping a database file of passwords, you could mask them so that someone reading the file could not tell what they really were (or at least they would have to work hard). In this exercise you will use the SCRAMBLE and OR tools; if they do not exist on your system, see Appendix B.

1. Use PDM to create a CLP member named TRYSEC2.
2. Enter the following source (if you were really going to use this code, you would probably want to qualify the library for the TAA tool commands):

Exercise B continued

Exercise B continued

```
PGM
DCL         &INPUT1 *CHAR LEN(256)
DCL         &INPUT2 *CHAR LEN(256)
DCL         &OUTPUT *CHAR LEN(256)
DCL         &OUTPUT2 *CHAR LEN(256)
DCL         &USER *CHAR LEN(10)
DCL         &NEWVAR *CHAR LEN(10)
RTVJOBA     USER(&USER)
SNDPGMMSG   MSG('Before-' *CAT &USER)
            /* Random upper shift entries as code */
CHGVAR      &INPUT2 '*%_#(*@+$&'
OR          INPUT1(&USER) INPUT2(&INPUT2) OUTPUT(&OUTPUT) LEN(10)
CHGVAR      &NEWVAR &OUTPUT
SNDPGMMSG   MSG('After OR-' *CAT &NEWVAR)
            /* Use same upper shift characters for */
            /*   the secret code                   */
SCRAMBLE    INPUT(&OUTPUT) OUTPUT(&OUTPUT2) LEN(10) SCRCDE(&INPUT2)
CHGVAR      &NEWVAR &OUTPUT2
SNDPGMMSG   MSG('After SCRAMBLE-' *CAT &NEWVAR)
            /* Now bring it back */
SCRAMBLE    INPUT(&OUTPUT2) OUTPUT(&INPUT1) +
              PROCESS(*UNS) LEN(10) SCRCDE(&INPUT2)
OR          INPUT1(&INPUT1) INPUT2(&INPUT2) OUTPUT(&OUTPUT) LEN(10)
CHGVAR      &NEWVAR &OUTPUT
SNDPGMMSG   MSG('Bring back alive-' *CAT &NEWVAR)
ENDPGM
```

3. Create the program.
4. Call the program:

```
CALL  TRYSEC2
```

You should see a message containing your user name. Then you'll see the result after your user name has been OR'd with the secret code placed in the CL program. This will probably result in some nondisplayable characters. Then you will see the result as the SCRAMBLE command scrambles the same bytes. Finally, you should see the results when the data is unscrambled and the secret code is OR'd back in to create your name again. The SCRAMBLE and OR tools can be very helpful in masking data you don't want other users to see.

Exercise C CHKLMTCPB TAA Tool

You will need *ALLOBJ special authority to try the CHKLMTCPB tool. If the CHKLMTCPB tool is not on your system, see Appendix B.

1. Prompt for the CHKLMTCPB command.

   You should see that the default is to "check" only.

2. Press Enter.

   CHKLMTCPB will send messages for every *USER type specified as LMTCPB(*NO). You should consider changing these profiles to LMTCPB(*YES). You can do this with the *FORCE option. For a more detailed discussion of the LMTCPB parameter, see Chapter 22, "The Program Stack."

Exercise D PRTSECVIL TAA Tool

The PRTSECVIL TAA tool will show you a list of the security violations that have occurred. If you are using security Level 40, you should use the DSPAUDLOG command instead. However, the security violations are still logged to QHST and you can follow the exercise. You need to have *ALLOBJ authority to follow these steps. To access the information for PRTSECVIL, the CVTQHST TAA tool will be used. In addition, we'll use the DSPDBF TAA tool to look at the data. If the CVTQHST, DSPDBF, and PRTSECVIL commands are not on your system, see Appendix B.

1. Use the DSPOBJD command to identify the QHST files in QSYS:

   ```
   DSPOBJD  OBJ(QSYS/QHST*) OBJTYPE(*FILE)
   ```

   You should see a display. Write down the name of one of the files (not the last one).

2. The QHST files have fixed-length records of 142 bytes each. Each message takes one or more records. To give you an idea of what the file looks like, enter the following DSPDBF tool with the QHST file name you wrote down:

Exercise D continued

Exercise D continued

```
DSPDBF  FILE(QHSTxxxx)
```

You should see the data, but there is only a single field to the file and the data would be difficult to process in this manner.

3. We will use the CVTQHST TAA tool to make a normal database file of one record per message. Use the name of the QHST file (the one you wrote down) in the CVTQHST command. Write the output to a library on your library list:

   ```
   CVTQHST  QHSTFILE(QHSTxxxxx) QHSTPLIB(yyyyy)
   ```

   The CVTQHST command makes a normal externally described file with one record per message. The data is written to the QHSTP file in the library you named.

4. Use the DSPDBF tool to look at the QHSTP file:

   ```
   DSPDBF  FILE(QHSTP)
   ```

   You should see an externally described file with unique fields for the different parts of a message. If you want to write a program against QHST, using CVTQHST first can make it a lot easier.

5. Enter the command PRTSECVIL to find the security violation messages in the QHSTP file:

   ```
   PRTSECVIL
   ```

6. A spooled file will be created. Display the spooled file.

   You should see one line for each message, which is a security violation. This provides a good report for reviewing violations that have occurred.

CHAPTER 26

QCMDEXC and QCMDCHK

In this chapter we will look at the functions provided by QCMDEXC and QCMDCHK — two IBM-supplied programs that let you generate a command string on the fly.

QCMDEXC

QCMDEXC executes a CL command. Normally, when you use variables in a program, you simply specify them. For example,

```
CALL  PGM(&PGM)
```

You could use QCMDEXC to perform the same function by building a command string:

```
DCL     &CMD *CHAR LEN(100)
  .
  .
  .
CHGVAR  &CMD ('CALL PGM(' *CAT &PGM *TCAT ')')
CALL    QCMDEXC PARM(&CMD 100)
```

The first parameter for QCMDEXC is the command string; the second parameter is the length of the command string. With QCMDEXC, you want the command string to look exactly as if you had entered it on a command line.

Obviously, you wouldn't want to use QCMDEXC unless it was necessary. Let's look at a few cases where QCMDEXC would be useful:

- Some RTV commands provide a return variable for a parameter originally entered as a list. Using the return variable as is, however, can get you into trouble because it comes back as a single value.

  A classic example of a parameter that is entered as a list is the LIBL parameter on the CHGLIBL command. If you operate interactively, you could specify

  ```
  CHGLIBL  LIBL(LIB1 LIB2 ...)
  ```

  or, in a CL program, you could specify variables:

  ```
  CHGLIBL  LIBL(&L1 &L2 ...)
  ```

Let's assume you want a program to retrieve the current library list (using the RTVJOBA command), temporarily change it, and then restore the library list to its original setting (using CHGLIBL). You might think you could code

```
PGM          /* Incorrect code */
DCL          &LIBL *CHAR LEN(275)
RTVJOBA      USRLIBL(&LIBL)
   .
   .
   .
CHGLIBL      LIBL(&LIBL)
```

But this technique won't work, because the CL compiler isn't smart enough to know what to do. At execution time, you'll see the general escape message CPF0001 ("Error found on command") and the diagnostic message CPD0078 ("Value 'xxxx ' is not a valid name"). The diagnostic message indicates that you are trying to place the entire &LIBL variable (275 bytes comprising several library names) into the first entry in a list (i.e., the first entry for a library name).

You could use a substring function to extract the name of each library from variable &LIBL, but this would be too much work and you would have to ensure that no blank names exist on the CHGLIBL command. It would be much easier to use QCMDEXC, as the following code demonstrates:

```
PGM
DCL        &LIBL *CHAR LEN(275)
DCL        &CMD *CHAR LEN(500)
RTVJOBA    USRLIBL(&LIBL)
  .
  .
  .
CHGVAR     &CMD ('CHGLIBL LIBL(' *CAT &LIBL *TCAT ')')
CALL       QCMDEXC PARM(&CMD 500)
```

In the code above, when the RTVJOBA command returns the library list, each entry includes a 10-byte character name followed by a blank. The CHGVAR command builds the command string that will be executed by QCMDEXC.

- If you are using a command that has many variations, it would probably be easier to build a command string and execute it using

QCMDEXC than it would be to code the many different commands. For example, you might use OPNQRYF as a front end to an application program that presents a display so a user can specify selection criteria. Because the user may not select all the fields you may be better off to build a command string using OPNQRYF. This may not be easy, but the alternative (coding separate OPNQRYF commands for every possible combination) can be a lot worse. You can find more code similar to the example above with the DSPSPLCTL TAA tool command. The source is in member TAASPLIC3 in file QATTCL.

- Sometimes you want a program to submit a command to batch or execute it, depending on whether your job is already running in batch or is running interactively. For example, assume you have a CALL command with a complex parameter list (made up of variables). Rather than use two sets of code, you can build a command string in a variable, then use either the SBMJOB command or a CALL to QCMDEXC with the command. For an example of using QCMDEXC in this situation, see Chapter 8, "Retrieve Commands."
- QCMDEXC can also be used in a high-level language program such as RPG. Chapter 18, "Overrides," provides examples of using QCMDEXC in an HLL program.

QCMDCHK

QCMDCHK, which supports the same two parameters as QCMDEXC, performs syntax checking for a single CL command, and optionally prompts for, but does not execute, the command.

The purpose of QCMDCHK is to let you "sanity-check" a command entered by a user even though you do not intend to execute the command until later. The command could be executed later in the same program, submitted to batch, or placed in a database file to be executed at a later date.

For example, assume that you want a program to prompt for the SAVOBJ command but not execute the command until later. Your code might look like this:

```
DCL          &CMD *CHAR LEN(500)
  .
  .
  .
CHGVAR       &CMD ('?SAVOBJ')
CALL         QCMDCHK PARM(&CMD 500)
  .
  .         /* Cmd is now in the &CMD var */
  .          /* Do other work and then */
CALL         QCMDEXC PARM(&CMD 500)
```

Using QCMDCHK is not a good choice if you expect to find errors when you execute the command, because you have little control over the command string. You can present the error messages to the user, but it is not easy to reprompt for the original command with the values keyed by the user. You would have to scan the returned command string and put in the ? character where it was needed.

For example, assume you prompted for the SAVOBJ command with selective prompting (using ? values) and the user enters several values. The selective prompting values are removed when the command string is returned. If you later try to execute the command and discover errors, what do you do? If you try to reprompt with your original command, you would lose all the user entries. If you try to reprompt with selective prompting, you would have to scan the command string and insert the proper value. If a program will prompt a user for only one or two values, I prefer to use the PMTOPR TAA tool (see Chapter 13, "Communicating with a Workstation Operator").

Combining the Use of QCMDCHK and QCMDEXC

Here is a technique that uses both QCMDCHK and QCMDEXC I've found useful on occasion. This technique doesn't provide the best user interface for handling errors, but it is simple to use.

Assume you have a menu where the user can request an option that is a command. When the user selects the option, you want to use selective prompting to prompt for the command. When the command completes, your program displays the menu again. At that point, the user might like to perform the same option again. Rather than having the user key in all the parameters again, a little bit of code can reprompt with the information used on the last command.

Assume the command you want to prompt for is INZTAP. Here is the code I use (this is abbreviated to simulate only a single menu option):

```
         PGM
         DCL      &INZCMD *CHAR LEN(200)
LOOP:             /* Process the INZCMD option */
         IF       (&INZCMD *EQ ' ') DO /* First time */
         CHGVAR   &INZCMD 'INZTAP'
         ENDDO    /* First time */
         CHGVAR   &INZCMD ('?' *CAT &INZCMD)
         CALL     QCMDCHK PARM(&INZCMD 200)
         MONMSG   MSGID(CPF6801) EXEC(DO) /* F3 */
         RETURN
         ENDDO    /* F3 */
         CALL     QCMDEXC PARM(&INZCMD 200)
         GOTO     LOOP
         ENDPGM
```

The code first tests whether or not the user has used this option on the menu before. If not, the INZTAP command (with no parameters) is used to initialize the command variable. A question mark (?) is then concatenated in front of the command string. The question mark tells the system to prompt for the command. When QCMDCHK calls the command, the user sees the INZTAP prompt and keys in the values (s)he wants. QCMDCHK returns the command string to be executed and QCMDEXC executes the command.

When the program branches back to the top, it finds a value (the previous command string executed) in variable &INZCMD; so it places a question mark in front of the value and calls QCMDCHK again. The user sees the same prompts (s)he entered previously and can either change the values or press Enter.

If the prompter catches an error (e.g., the user enters *YSS instead of *YES for the CHECK parameter), the error-handling facility provided by the prompter is adequate; the user simply corrects the problem and continues.

If the command processing program catches an error (e.g., the user enters an invalid device name), the call to QCMDEXC fails. If users of the code described above are programmers, a simple error-handling technique would be adequate: Monitor for any error from the command, receive the escape message, and then display the message on the menu.

This combined use of QCMDCHK and QCMDEXEC is not perfect, but it does work around the fact that QCMDEXC does not return the command string when it's used with selective prompting. By using QCMDCHK as well, you can capture the command string so you can use it again.

Exercise A Using QCMDEXC

In this exercise you will practice building a command from a string using a parameter passed to your program. You will use QCMDEXC to execute the command.

1. Use PDM to create a CLP member named TRYQCMDEXC.
2. Enter the following source:

```
PGM      PARM(&OUTPUT)
DCL      &OUTPUT *CHAR LEN(7)
DCL      &CMD *CHAR LEN(500)
CHGVAR   &CMD ('WRKDSKSTS OUTPUT(' *CAT &OUTPUT *TCAT ')')
CALL     QCMDEXC PARM(&CMD 500)
ENDPGM
```

   Note how the command string is built. You must use an apostrophe to identify the literals and the concatenation function.

3. Create the program.
4. Call the program as

```
CALL  TRYQCMDEXC PARM(*)
```

   You should see the WRKDSKSTS display.

5. Now call the program as

```
CALL  TRYQCMDEXC PARM(*PRINT)
```

   A spooled output file named QPWCDSKS should have been created.

6. Now let's try the RTVJOBA and CHGLIBL functions. First we'll try the function that doesn't work. Use PDM to create a CLP source member named TRYLIBL.
7. Enter the following source:

```
PGM
DCL       &LIBL *CHAR LEN(275)
RTVJOBA   USRLIBL(&LIBL)
          /* Pretend you changed the library list */
          /* Now change it back */
CHGLIBL   LIBL(&LIBL)
ENDPGM
```

Exercise A continued

Exercise A continued

8. Create the program.
9. Call the program:

```
CALL  TRYLIBL
```

You should receive escape message CPF0001. The preceding diagnostic message will tell you that the value for the LIBL parameter is invalid. You can't use a variable that contains a list in a parameter that is expecting a list. The command expects only a single value to each entry, but in this case the command receives multiple values for the first entry.

10. You can get this to work with QCMDEXC. Modify the source as follows:

```
PGM
DCL       &LIBL *CHAR LEN(275)
DCL       &CMD *CHAR LEN(500)
RTVJOBA   USRLIBL(&LIBL)
CHGLIBL   LIBL(QTEMP)
DSPLIBL
CHGVAR    &CMD ('CHGLIBL LIBL(' *CAT &LIBL *TCAT ')')
CALL      QCMDEXC PARM(&CMD 500)
DSPLIBL
ENDPGM
```

11. Create the program.
12. Call the program:

```
CALL  TRYLIBL
```

You should see the library list displayed with just QTEMP in the user portion. This was caused by the first CHGLIBL command. Your program then restores the library list to its original setting with the CHGLIBL command executed through QCMDEXC. You should see that the second DSPLIBL command has reset the library list as it was originally.

CHAPTER 27

APIs

An API (Application Programming Interface) is any request that cannot be executed from a command prompt or a menu. APIs let you access certain parts of the operating system that might be difficult or impossible to access using other methods. To facilitate performance, an API generally is in the form of a callable program.

System APIs — for example, call interfaces to system functions such as QCMDEXC and QDCXLATE — have been around for some time. The term API came into use when IBM began adding more call interfaces to certain system functions. I will use the term API to refer to the call-level interfaces provided by IBM. You will find that APIs are quite prevalent on the AS/400.

In some cases, you will find that both a CL command and an API exist to perform the same function. For example, you can get a list of objects or members from the outfile support on the DSPOBJD and DSPFD commands, as well as through API support. In a few cases, you will find only an API. For example, an API is available to retrieve the attributes of a job description, but there is no system command RTVJOBD. And in many cases, you will find only a CL command. Although there are many APIs, there are even more CL commands.

If you are a typical AS/400 programmer who uses RPG and CL, you most likely will use basic APIs such as QCMDEXC and QDCXLATE that are fairly simple to use. You would be less likely to use advanced APIs, which have more complex interfaces that are harder to use. Although no clear distinction exists between "basic" and "advanced" APIs, I would say an API is "basic" if it uses a simple parameter list and it doesn't require a data structure.

Most of the advanced APIs are described in the *System Programmer's Interface Reference* (SC41-8223). This is a very heavy manual not only in size, but also in content. The interfaces have been designed not for the average AS/400 programmer, but for software developers who need to program at a different level of the system. Most typical AS/400 programmers will probably never need to code an advanced API. That doesn't mean you can't gain the benefits of an advanced API, but most programmers will do so through higher-level interfaces.

Many commercial software developers use advanced APIs for a variety of needs, and certain TAA tools also use advanced APIs. When the

RTVJOBD TAA tool was first developed, for instance, it used the DSPJOBD command to create a spooled file and then read the information from the listing. Because the tool read the information from the listing, it was English-language dependent. Now the RTVJOBD tool uses an IBM-supplied API, which improves performance, eliminates the possibility of the printed listing format changing on a new release, and eliminates the English-language dependency.

While it is true that call-level interfaces are more efficient than system commands, most applications will have little to gain in performance by using an advanced API rather than a system command.

Now that I've tried to convince you not to use APIs directly for most normal use, let me discuss a few ways to use APIs in CL programs.

Single-Function Advanced APIs

A single-function advanced API is simply a call with a parameter list that returns information to your program in a data structure. The QUSRSPLA program, which provides the attributes of a spooled file, is a good example of a single-function API. The RTVSPLFA TAA tool uses this API. RTVSPLFA provides a command interface so that you can specify one or more return variables. You don't have to know anything about the API to use RTVSPLFA. The CL program for RTVSPLFA is TAASPLFC in member QATTCL in library QUSRTOOL. If you have created the DSPTAAMBR TAA tool on your system, you can look at the source for RTVSPLFA by using the command

```
DSPTAAMBR  MBR(TAASPLFC) SRCFILE(*CLP)
```

The parameter list passed to the QUSRSPLA API does the following:

- Identifies the spooled file for which you want the attributes. You have to be very specific (i.e., use a qualified job name plus the spooled file name). In some cases, the API will support special entries for the "internal ID" of a spooled file. You determine the spooled file's "internal ID" by performing some other API first. For example, you can access the list of spooled files in an output queue using the QUSLSPL API and then using the "internal ID" to access the attributes of a specific spooled file.
- Describes the data structure name that will be used to return the spooled file attributes. The attributes are returned in a variable you name. You then must use the substring function to extract the information you want from the variable.
- Describes how to format the data structure. You do this by specifying a format name. Many of the APIs support multiple data

structure formats; the format you choose depends on the amount of information you want returned. Some formats have only basic information, but they can be accessed faster than a format that contains all the information. You should ask only for the name of the data structure format that will return the minimum amount of information you need.

- Describes how you want to handle errors. You can choose between exceptions (escape messages) or return codes; I prefer exceptions when coding in CL.

The *System Programmer's Interface Reference* (SC41-8223) describes which formats exist and the layout of each format. The data structure is returned to your program in a single variable, and you use the manual to determine what information you want and where it is located in the data structure. The information in the data structure is described with an offset beginning at 0, because this is what some languages require. For CL, you need to add 1 to every offset to access the data. For example, the *System Programmer's Interface Reference* will tell you that for the QUSRSPLA API, the SCHEDULE (file available) value for a spooled file is located in format SPLA0100 at offset 110 and is 10 bytes long. You would access the information starting at position 111:

```
CHGVAR   &SCHEDULE %SST(&DS 111 10)
```

Most of the numeric information in the data structure is kept in binary format, so you need to convert it to decimal (using the %BIN function) to work with it. If you look at member TAASPLFC, you can get an idea of what you must code to access the information.

List-Function Advanced APIs

Most of the "list" APIs are designed to return a list of things such as objects or members. These APIs place the information in a special object type called a "user space." You have to create the user space (or use an existing one) and identify it when you use the API. After the API places the data in the user space, you must use

- other APIs to access (or in some cases change) the user space.
- pointers to the user space. CL does not support the use of pointers.

Each entry in the list that is returned is a fixed-length data structure beginning at a specific location. You shouldn't code directly to where the list starts because it may change on a new release. The length of each entry may also change. What you should do is access the information from the user space that tells you

- where the first entry starts
- how many entries exist
- the length of each entry

Then you process the information by coding a loop to access each entry. The API format that you've used then describes the layout of each entry so that you can access the individual fields. The following diagram illustrates how a user space for a list looks:

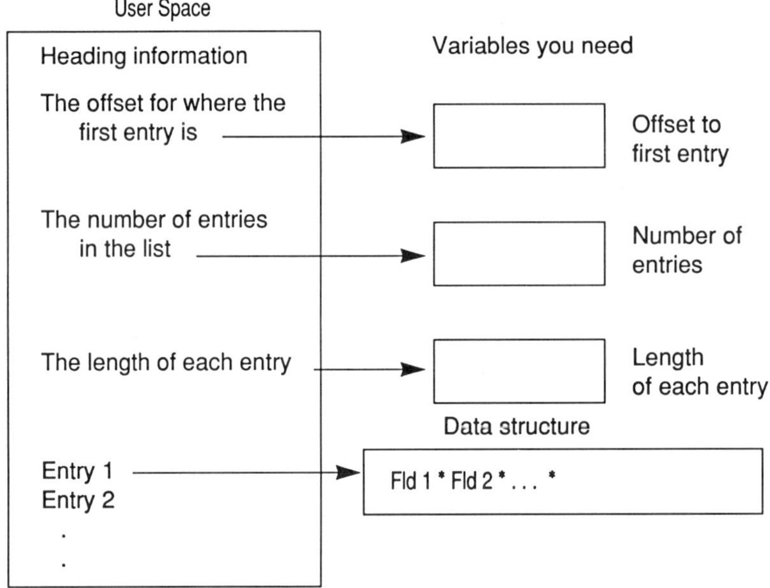

In CL, it is a challenge to access information in a user space because you need to work with binary values and other things that are foreign to most CL programs. To lessen the challenge, I wrote some TAA tools. The tools don't operate as fast as coding the interfaces directly, but they make it a lot easier to use the technique. For most uses, you will probably find that performance is adequate. Three TAA tools are involved:

1. CRTUSRSPC (Create User Space). This tool is a command interface to an API that creates a user space.

2. RTVUSRSPCI (Retrieve User Space Initialization). After the user space has been created, RTVUSRSPCI returns three values (start position of the first entry, the number of entries, and the length of each entry).

3. RTVUSRSPCE (Retrieve User Space Entry). You use this command in the loop within your program that processes each entry. Simply plug in the variables returned by RTVUSRSPCI (start position and length) and name the variable that will contain the data structure for the entry. The command automatically adds the entry length to the start position and returns that value so it is ready to use for the next entry. All you have to do is
   - count each time you go through the loop.
   - only process the rest of your loop if your count is less than or equal to the number of entries in the list (returned from RTVUSRSPCI).
   - extract the information you want from the variable you named as the data structure. Because each data structure format differs, you will need to refer to the *System Programmer's Interface Reference.*

You will find the code for the RTVUSRSPCI TAA tool in documentation member RTVUSRSPCI in file QATTINFO in library QUSRTOOL. Simply copy the code and provide the specifications that meet your needs. The specific example used by RTVUSRSPCI (Figure 27.1) is to access the *JOBQ objects in library QGPL and send a message for each — not the most exciting implementation, but basic enough to help you understand the technique.

The basic code provided for RTVUSRSPCI does not do much with the object that was found. In a more typical example, you would then use another API to access the specific information about the object.

Technical Tip

If you want to work with the "list" APIs, take a look at the RTVUSRSPCI TAA tool. It can make your life a lot easier.

As a final note, when you work with user spaces, you may find it helpful to be able to display the contents. The TAA tool DSPUSRSPC can do that for you; it displays the contents in both character and hex format.

Technical Tip

To help you learn more about what a user space looks like, or if you are having trouble using user spaces, use the DSPUSRSPC TAA tool to display the contents of the user space.

Figure 27.1
Code Provided in Documentation Member RTVUSRSPCI

```
             PGM
             DCL          &ENTLEN *CHAR LEN(4)
             DCL          &NBRENT *DEC LEN(9 0)
             DCL          &FULLSPACE *CHAR LEN(20)
             DCL          &FULLOBJ *CHAR LEN(20)
             DCL          &OBJ *CHAR LEN(10)
             DCL          &LIB *CHAR LEN(10)
             DCL          &SPACE *CHAR LEN(10)
             DCL          &SPACEL *CHAR LEN(10)
             DCL          &OBJTYPE *CHAR LEN(10)
             DCL          &STRPOS *CHAR LEN(4)
             DCL          &RTNVAR *CHAR LEN(1000)
             DCL          &COUNT *DEC LEN(9 0)
                          /* Create space using TAA command */
             CHGVAR       &SPACE 'SPACE2'
             CHGVAR       &SPACEL 'QTEMP'
             CRTUSRSPC    USRSPC(&SPACEL/&SPACE)
                          /* Next two CHGVARs build up 20 byte    */
                          /*   variables as needed for the CALL   */
                          /*   to QUSLOBJ                         */
             CHGVAR       &FULLSPACE (&SPACE *CAT &SPACEL)
             CHGVAR       &FULLOBJ   ('*ALL      QGPL')
                          /* Call to QUSLOBJ is the API to fill   */
                          /*   the space with an object list. It */
                          /*   requests the *JOBQ objs in QPGL.   */
                          /*   OBJL0100 is the format name of the*/
                          /*   list produced.                     */
             CALL         QUSLOBJ PARM(&FULLSPACE 'OBJL0100' +
                            &FULLOBJ '*JOBQ')
                          /* Retrieve the initialization values   */
                          /*   as described in this tool          */
             RTVUSRSPCI   USRSPC(&SPACEL/&SPACE) STRPOS(&STRPOS) +
                            NBRENT(&NBRENT) ENTLEN(&ENTLEN)
LOOP:                     /* Start processing loop                */
                          /*   Count and check for total in list */
             CHGVAR       &COUNT (&COUNT + 1)
             IF           (&COUNT *LE &NBRENT) DO /* Pcs entry    */
                          /* Retrieve the entry using TAA cmd     */
                          /* The &STRPOS value is initially set   */
                          /*     by the RTVUSRSPCI cmd. On each   */
                          /*     use of RTVUSRSPCE,               */
                          /*     the next &STRPOS value           */
                          /*     is automatically returned.       */
                          /* The ENTLEN is the same for each use */
             RTVUSRSPCE   USRSPC(&SPACEL/&SPACE) ENTLEN(&ENTLEN) +
                            STRPOS(&STRPOS) RTNVAR(&RTNVAR)
                          /*   Extract fields from RTNVAR         */
                          /*   The format of each list differs.   */
                          /*   See the list data section for the */
                          /*   API that you are using             */
```

Figure 27.1 continued

FIGURE 27.1 *Continued*

```
CHGVAR      &OBJ %SST(&RTNVAR 1 10)
CHGVAR      &LIB %SST(&RTNVAR 11 10)
CHGVAR      &OBJTYPE %SST(&RTNVAR 21 10)
            /* This example only sends a message   */
SNDPGMMSG   MSG(&OBJ *CAT &LIB *CAT &OBJTYPE)
GOTO        LOOP
ENDDO       /* Process entry */
            /* RTVUSRSPCE defaults to return with   */
            /*    LR off to allow faster access.    */
            /*    When the loop is complete, use    */
            /*    SETLR(*ON) or RCLRSC.             */
RTVUSRSPCE USRSPC(&SPACEL/&SPACE) ENTLEN(&ENTLEN) +
              STRPOS(&STRPOS) RTNVAR(&RTNVAR) +
              SETLR(*ON)
ENDPGM
```

DUPLICATING A SPOOLED FILE

Several APIs allow you to access a spooled file and rewrite the information. These APIs are used by the TAA tool DUPSPLF (Duplicate Spooled File), which consists of two commands:

1. DUPSPLF. This command uses the API interfaces so you can duplicate a spooled file and not lose any characteristics. You can use the same spooled file name, a new name, a different output queue, et cetera. After the file is duplicated, you can use the CL command CHGSPLFA to change many of the new spooled file's attributes. But you can't change attributes such as LPI or CPI after the file is written because they might affect how many characters fit on a line (the line overflow would differ) and how many lines fit on a page (the heading might have to appear at a different place). With DUPSPLF, the owner of the new version is always the same as the owner of the old version.

2. DUPSPLF2. This command duplicates the spooled file by using the CL commands CPYSPLF and CPYF. It is much slower than DUPSPLF, but because you are reprinting the data, you can write to a new printer file and change any of the attributes. For example, you can redirect the output to a separate DRAWER. Depending on which attributes you want to change and how they will affect your listing, the DUPSPLF2 command can either work the way you want or make a mess of your output. Because you use normal system functions, the owner of the new version is the user who executed DUPSPLF2.

The CL code to call the APIs to perform DUPSPLF is complicated. For example, a series of APIs must be called in the right sequence and with the right parameter list. To see a correct use of the DUPSPLF command, look at member TAASPLDC in file QATTCL in library QUSRTOOL.

CHAPTER 28

Setting Up Your Environment

Setting up the right programming environment — that is, using the system and its functions in a way that best suits you — can make you more productive. In this chapter, I will talk about how I have set up my programming environment and why.

Although what I do works for me, that doesn't mean the approach I take is right for you. Establishing an effective programming environment is certainly a matter of personal choice and my intent in this chapter is only to share personal choices I have made. If you like what you are doing and it works well for you, by all means stick with it.

PERSONAL LIBRARY

For most of my coding work, I use a personal library that contains both source and objects. I use this personal library as my current library. The current library concept is an outstanding function on the AS/400. You don't have to worry about where your objects go when you create them, and the library is in the right place on the library list. I specify the CURLIB parameter (where xxxx is the name of my personal library) on the CHGLIBL command in my initial program:

```
CHGLIBL  CURLIB(xxxx)
```

PERSONAL OUTPUT QUEUE

I have my own output queue in my library. I rarely print my compilation listings, but I do use DSPSPLF to look at a lot of spooled files. If I need to print something, I spool it to my output queue and then move it to a "hot queue" (one where a spool writer is active).

SINGLE-THREAD JOB QUEUE

Being a one-thing-at-a-time kind of person, I prefer to work with a single-thread job queue (only one job can be executed at a time). When you submit several batch jobs to a multi-thread job queue, you can never be certain about the sequence in which they might be executed. When I don't care about the sequence and I have long-running batch jobs, I use a regular batch queue where multiple batch jobs can run concurrently.

JOB DESCRIPTIONS

I use unique JOBDs (Job Descriptions), but only for batch work. My user profile uses the default (QDFTJOBD) for JOBD. I have unique JOBDs, but I don't use one of them in my user profile because I want several options so that I can differentiate between what I do interactively and what I do in batch. For interactive work, I use an initial program to set my options (see the section "Initial Program").

My normal job description for batch work is set to establish my output queue and the job queue that I use. In addition, I specify INQMSGRPY(*DFT), which says that any batch job that sends an inquiry message gets the default response. I prefer to abort a job rather than hold the batch job queue for any of my work.

Technical Tip

I don't like to let the job queue "hang" while waiting for a response to an inquiry message. I prefer to provide a default response (by specifying INQMSGRPY(*DFT) for my JOBD) and go on to the next job. For most other JOBD options, I take the defaults.

I use a separate job description for logging. It is the same as my normal JOBD, but it is specified to log all the commands. I use it when I need more information about what is happening in batch. I specify LOG(4 0 *SECLVL).

Technical Tip

It's handy to have a JOBD that specifies logging so you can get additional debugging assistance when submitting a batch job.

HANDLING MESSAGES AT MY WORKSTATION

Most of the messages I receive are from batch jobs saying they completed normally or abnormally. If I set my message queue to break mode, I would be interrupted when these messages arrive. If I set my message queue to notify mode, I would have to keep requesting DSPMSG to see what happened.

Rather than take either one of these options, I have chosen a middle ground provided by the STSMSG TAA tool. This command lets me turn the batch job completion messages into status messages. I get the messages, but I don't get interrupted. And if I miss seeing a status message, I can still find it in the message queue. You use the STSMSG tool by coding

```
CHGMSGQ  MSGQ(xxxx) DLVRY(*BREAK) PGM(TAATOOL/TAAMSGDC)
```

I place the CHGMSGQ command in my initial program and I specify MSGQ(*USRPRF) on the command. The STSMSG tool is sensitive to the batch completion messages (CPF1240 and CPF1241). If any other message appears, I get interrupted.

If you work in an environment where you are interrupted by other messages (for example, if you send files to other systems with SNADS, the SNADS messages can be particularly annoying), you can make a copy of the TAAMSGDC source, add your own message IDs, and handle them in the same manner as the batch completion messages.

Technical Tip

The STSMSG TAA tool is one of my favorites. You can increase your productivity by controlling messages that might otherwise interrupt your work.

Group Jobs

As a programmer, I always have multiple things I want to see at the same time. To meet this need, you can use option 1 (Transfer to secondary job) on the System Request menu or you can use an Attention key handling program to transfer to a different group job. I prefer to use an Attention key handling program. You can set up an Attention key handling program in one of two ways:

- to allow you to toggle between two group jobs, or
- to display a menu of existing or possible group jobs

I like to keep things simple, so I prefer to be able to toggle between group jobs. I set up the Attention key handling program by using the TAA tool ATNPGM (Attention Program). A simple way to set it up is to specify it in your user profile as

```
CHGUSRPRF  ... ATNPGM(TAATOOL/TAAATNAC)
```

Or you can set up the Attention key handling program with the SETATNPGM command in your initial program:

```
SETATNPGM  PGM(TAATOOL/TAAATNAC)
```

After you have used either one of these options, simply press the Attention key when you want to toggle to a different group job. Sometimes I like to have several jobs I can switch to. I use the System Request option 1 and I can then do two additional group jobs.

Technical Tip

Group jobs can be a great productivity aid. If you want a simple approach, use the ATNPGM TAA tool.

PDM Versus the Programmer's Menu

Gosh, I hate to admit it, but I use the Programmer's Menu, which was carried over from the S/38 to the AS/400. I use PDM, too, but not as frequently.

PDM works well if all your source for a given application is in a single file. I have unique source file names such as QCLSRC for each different type of source. I don't like having to switch to a different source file with PDM; it seems slow and awkward.

If I had started out on PDM or if I had all my source in a single file, I would probably be a major fan of PDM.

User Profile

When setting up my user profile, I take the default for most parameters. I use an initial program to set options and specific JOBDs (described earlier) rather than specifying the same options in the user profile. Here's what I do specify in the user profile:

- INLPGM. See the next section.
- OUTQ. I use the user profile OUTQ parameter when the system I am working on is used for receiving SNADS spooled files (in that situation, you need to define an output queue). For the systems where I don't use SNADS, I take the default of *WRKSTN.
- ASTLVL. I use *INTERMED.
- KBDBUF. I use *TYPEAHEAD.

Initial Program

I specify an initial program named SETUP in my user profile; the program is in my library. I perform the following functions in my SETUP program:

- CHGLIBL. I name the library list I need, which includes the TAATOOL library, and the libraries QGPL and QTEMP. I specify my personal library as my current library on the CURLIB parameter. If you have a current library, you don't need to name it in your library list (it is there by default).
- CHGJOB. I specify my output queue (OUTQ parameter). The wait

time I specify on the DFTWAIT parameter (3 seconds), may be too short for your environment. The default is 30 seconds; I specify a shorter value to cut down on the wait. If I can't allocate a resource, it probably won't be free in 30 seconds, so why wait that long?

- I specify a PRTKEYFMT format of *NONE. If I include any displays in my documentation, I don't want headers and borders.
- CHGMSGQ. I use this command to set my *USRPRF message queue to break mode for the STSMSG TAA tool (described earlier). If I am already signed on a different workstation, the CHGMSGQ command will fail with the escape message CPF2451 ("Message queue allocated to another job"). I monitor for this condition and just ignore it. Before my initial program runs, the system has already sent me a message stating that my message queue is in break mode elsewhere.
- SETATNPGM. I use this command to set my Attention key handling program for the ATNPGM TAA tool.
- STRPGMMNU. As I mentioned earlier, I use the Programmer's Menu. On the STRPGMMNU command, I specify SRCLIB, OBJLIB, and JOBD for my standard values. I also specify EXITPGM(TAATOOL/TAASRCDC), which is the SBMPARMS TAA tool described in Chapter 23, "The CL Program Object." If I was using PDM, I would probably bring up the WRKMBRPDM display.

Here are the basic commands I use in my SETUP program (I've used the library name MYCURLIB for the current library):

```
        CHGLIBL    LIBL(QGPL QTEMP TAATOOL) CURLIB(MYCURLIB)
        CHGJOB     OUTQ(MYCURLIB/xxxx) DFTWAIT(3)     +
                     PRTKEYFMT(*NONE)
        CHGMSGQ    MSGQ(*USRPRF) DLVRY(*BREAK)        +
                     PGM(TAATOOL/TAAMSGDC)
        MONMSG     MSGID(CPF2451) /* Ignore */
        SETATNPGM  PGM(TAATOOL/TAAATNAC)
PGMMNU: STRPGMMNU  SRCLIB(MYCURLIB) OBJLIB(MYCURLIB) +
                     JOBD(MYCURLIB)                   +
                     EXITPGM(TAATOOL/TAASRCDC)
        MONMSG     MSGID(CPF3220) EXEC(GOTO PGMMNU)
```

Performing Standard Routines

As part of my setup program, I submit a standard batch job when I sign on for the day for the first time. My setup program uses a data area to determine whether or not it's the first time I've signed on each day:

```
DCL         &DATE   *CHAR LEN(6)
DCL         &SIGNON *CHAR LEN(6)
  .
  .
  .
RTVDTAARA   DTAARA(SIGNON) RTNVAR(&SIGNON)
RTVSYSVAL   SYSVAL(QDATE) RTNVAR(&DATE)
IF          (&DATE *NE &SIGNON) DO /* First time */
SBMJOB      CMD(...)
CHGDTAARA   SIGNON &DATE
ENDDO       /* First time */
```

The batch job executes routines I want performed daily only when I first sign on. The types of things the batch job causes to happen are

- Cleanup. This deletes things that are some number of days older than the current date.
- Refresh. I have some "where used" type functions that require certain database files to be rewritten to represent my current structure.

BASIC DISPLAYS

I start with the Programmer's Menu and then use the F10 command key to access a command entry display, if needed. The command entry display accessed via F10 acts the same way as if you had called QCMD. A slight difference is that any commands you enter from the command line on the menu are considered to be at the same level as those you enter from the F10 command entry display. I usually keep one group job on the Programmer's Menu and one on the command entry display.

I don't particularly like the command line on PDM or on most IBM menus. When you use this type of command line, messages are changed (the type and who sent them) and you can't see all the messages on one display (see Chapter 1, "Monitoring for Messages"). I use the basic command entry display and the functions that go with it. You can access the command entry display from PDM (using a command key). This display presents messages as they are sent and does not change them.

KEEPING YOUR OUTPUT QUEUE CLEAN

The default for how the AS/400 presents output is *FIFO, which means the oldest spooled file is displayed first; the most current one is displayed last. Consequently, if you are reluctant to delete your spooled files, and you want to display your most current spooled file, you might have to scroll through several displays to find it.

My approach is to delete old spooled files regularly. I don't clean up my spooled files every time I work with them, but I rarely let the display go more than one page before I clean up.

You can keep your spooled files under control by creating a special command that deletes all your spooled files, or by using the delete option on WRKSPLF/WRKOUTQ.

By keeping your spooled files to a manageable number, you can find the one you want more quickly and you can more easily avoid the possibility of displaying an old version of a spooled file by mistake.

I have several functions that compile many objects from source and therefore generate many spooled files. I prefer to use a DLTSPLF command as part of the create process. If the object creates successfully, I automatically delete the spooled file.

Backup

I don't ever want to be in the position where I have to re-create several days worth of coding, so I back up my source at least once a day. For this purpose, I use the SRCARC (Source Archive) TAA tool, which lets you have multiple versions of source online in a compressed format.

Rather than saving individual source members, you save the archive, which is one large member. Consequently, the save takes less time than normal because the save operates at close to device-rated speed on a large object. The save also takes less media than a normal source file because the member headers are not written. You can update the archive while programmers are editing their source files.

I keep a few months' worth of source updates in the archive, which lets me access an earlier version of source code without having to restore any media. Although I don't "bring back" an old version of source frequently, I have occasionally brought back the current member after accidentally deleting it or simply because I wanted to start over.

Technical Tip

If you need a good method of backing up your source, consider using the SRCARC TAA tool. It has many advantages and few restrictions.

Displaying Source

Because I mainly use the programmer's menu, I use the TAA tools DSPSRCMBR or DSPTAAMBR. These tools invoke SEU, but ensure "browse mode." Using "edit mode" can get you into trouble sometimes, especially if your fingers accidentally hit the wrong keys.

I also use two other TAA tools frequently: DSPLSTCHG (Display Last Change) and PRTSRCSUM (Print Source Summary). These two tools are not on PDM, but you could define options for them.

The DSPLSTCHG command (Figure 28.1a) is part of the RTVLSTCHG TAA tool. If you can't remember whether or not you made a change to your source, or if you need to be reminded of the last change made, DSPLSTCHG will find the most recent changes and display them.

FIGURE 28.1a
DSPLSTCHG TAA Tool Prompt Screen

```
                    Display Last Change Date (DSPLSTCHG)

Type choices, press Enter.

Source file name . . . . . . . .   __________   Name, *CBL, *CL, *CLP...
  Library name . . . . . . . . .     *LIBL_____   Name, *LIBL
Member name  . . . . . . . . . .   __________   Name

                                                                     Bottom
F3=Exit   F4=Prompt   F5=Refresh   F12=Cancel   F13=How to use this display
F24=More keys
```

Figure 28.1b provides an example of what DSPLSTCHG will show you.

The PRTSRCSUM command (Figure 28.2a) provides a better solution than DSPFD *MBRLIST for reviewing your source members.

The PRTSRCSUM command's output provides more information and the command offers several selection criteria so you don't have to look at every member in the file. Figure 28.2b shows sample output from the PRTSRCSUM command.

FIGURE 28.1b

Sample DSPLSTCHG Display

```
                      Display Last Change Date

Member . . . . . . . . . . . . . . . . . . . . . . :          TAAMBRDC

File . . . . . . . . . . . . . . . . . . . . . . . :          QATTCL

Library  . . . . . . . . . . . . . . . . . . . . . :          QUSRTOOL

Last change date . . . . . . . . . . . . . . . . . :          921208

Count of stmts with last change date . . . . . . :              5
Record count in member . . . . . . . . . . . . . :            146
Text characters found. . . . . . . . . . . . . . :             *NO

            First 5 statements that have the last change date

         2.00        PGM  PARM(&FULLFROM &FULLTO *CPYDATE
         3.00               &BLKSEUDAT)
         7.00        DCL  &BLKSEUDAT *CHAR LEN(8)
        87.00        IF   (&BLKSEUDAT *EQ '*INCLUDE') DO /
        89.00        ENDDO  /* Use 999999 */
```

FIGURE 28.2a

PRTSRCSUM TAA Tool Prompt Screen

```
                    Print Source Summary (PRTSRCSUM)

Type choices, press Enter.

Source file name . . . . . . .    __________    Name, *STD, *QATT, *CBL...
  Library name . . . . . . . .      *LIBL_____  Name, *LIBL
Generic member name (no *) . .    *ALL______    Name, *ALL
Chg bar date (YYMMDD)  . . . .    *NONE_____    Number, *NONE
Print changes only . . . . . .    *NO_          *YES, *NO
Actual last change date  . . .    *NO_          *YES, *NO
Blank SEU dates  . . . . . . .    *INCLUDE      *INCLUDE, *DROP
Space after detail line  . . .    1             1, 2
Print file name  . . . . . . .    QPRINT____    Name
  Library name . . . . . . . .      *LIBL_____  Name, *LIBL

                                                                  Bottom
F3=Exit   F4=Prompt   F5=Refresh   F12=Cancel   F13=How to use this display
F24=More keys
```

FIGURE 28.2b
Sample PRTSRCSUM Output

```
3/25/93    9:04:23
SYSTEM1          Print Source Summary fo ...
           CHGBARS-*NONE
MBR-*ALL             CHGSONLY-*NØ         ACTLSTCHG-*NO                 ...

           Source    Number     Create              Change    Change
Member     type      records    date                date      time      ...

TAACMDBD    DSPF           55   92/Ø4/13            93/Ø1/17  18:51     ...
TAADBFCD    DSPF          111   92/Ø4/13            93/Ø1/17  13:28     ...
TAADBFED    DSPF           18   92/Ø4/13            93/Ø1/17  13:26     ...
TAADBFID    DSPF           7Ø   92/Ø4/13            93/Ø1/17  13:26     ...
TAADBFJP    PF             22   92/Ø4/13            93/Ø1/17  13:26     ...
TAADBFOL    LF              2   92/Ø4/13            93/Ø1/17  13:27     ...
TAADBFOP    PF              3   92/Ø4/13            93/Ø1/17  13:27     ...
```

PRINTING SOURCE MEMBERS

Both SEU and PDM support a print function, but I prefer the format supported by the TAA tool PRTSRCF (Print Source File), which lets you flag recent changes.

I don't print many compilation listings, but I do print a lot of source. The PRTSRCF command (Figure 28.3) lets me specify a change date so I can flag all the statements that were changed after a particular date.

COPYING COMPLETE SOURCE MEMBERS

Although I use the CL CPYSRCF command, more often I use the TAA tools DUPSRC (Duplicate Source), CPYGENSRC (Copy Generic Source), and CPYCHGMBR (Copy Changed Members).

The DUPSRC command (Figure 28.4) provides prompts for the member name first, which saves a few keystrokes. I've made mistakes with the CPYSRCF command because it requires so many keystrokes. But the DUPSRC command provides some protection because it defaults so that it will not write over an existing member.

The CPYGENSRC command (Figure 28.5) copies source from multiple files based on generic names you specify.

The CPYCHGMBR command (Figure 28.6) copies source based on the change date of the member or the most recent date on which a source statement was changed. Because many functions affect the member level

FIGURE 28.3
PRTSRCF TAA Tool Prompt Screen

```
                      Print Source File Member (PRTSRCF)

 Type choices, press Enter.

 Member name . . . . . . . . . .   __________     Name
 Source file name . . . . . . . .   __________     Name, *CBL, *CL, *CLP...
   Library name . . . . . . . . .     *LIBL_____   Name, *LIBL
 Output queue . . . . . . . . . .   *JOB______     Name, *JOB
 Chg bar date (sysfmt)  . . . . .   *NONE___       Number, *NONE
 Chg bar character  . . . . . . .   *              Character value

                                                                      Bottom
 F3-Exit   F4-Prompt   F5-Refresh   F12-Cancel   F13-How to use this display
 F24-More keys
```

change date (e.g., RST, MOVOBJ, CPYF), the SEU statement date can provide a more accurate reflection of what happened. Being able to copy

FIGURE 28.4
DUPSRC TAA Tool Prompt Screen

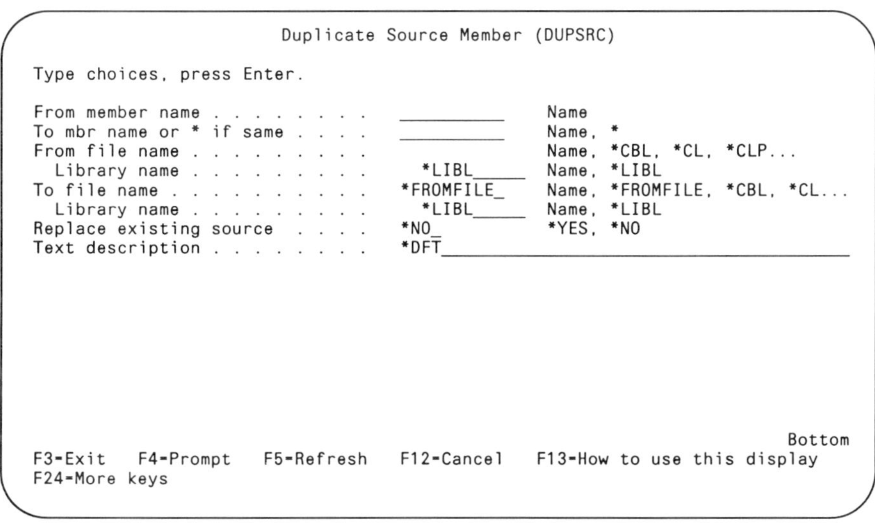

```
                      Duplicate Source Member (DUPSRC)

 Type choices, press Enter.

 From member name . . . . . . . .   __________     Name
 To mbr name or * if same . . . .   __________     Name, *
 From file name . . . . . . . . .                  Name, *CBL, *CL, *CLP...
   Library name . . . . . . . . .     *LIBL_____   Name, *LIBL
 To file name . . . . . . . . . .   *FROMFILE_     Name, *FROMFILE, *CBL, *CL...
   Library name . . . . . . . . .     *LIBL_____   Name, *LIBL
 Replace existing source  . . . .   *NO_           *YES, *NO
 Text description . . . . . . . .   *DFT________________________________________

                                                                      Bottom
 F3-Exit   F4-Prompt   F5-Refresh   F12-Cancel   F13-How to use this display
 F24-More keys
```

FIGURE 28.5
CPYGENSRC TAA Tool Prompt Screen

```
                    Copy Generic Source (CPYGENSRC)

Type choices, press Enter.

Generic name (no *) . . . . . . .   __________    Character value
From source file name . . . . . .   __________    Name, *STD, *QATT
From library . . . . . . . . . . .  *LIBL_____    Name, *LIBL
To source file name . . . . . . .   *FROMSRCF_    Name, *STD, *QATT, *FROMSRCF
To library . . . . . . . . . . . .  *LIBL_____    Name, *LIBL
Remove FROMLIB members . . . . . .  *NO_          *YES, *NO

                                                                        Bottom
F3=Exit   F4=Prompt   F5=Refresh   F12=Cancel   F13=How to use this display
F24=More keys
```

source based on the SEU statement date can be very helpful. The same option also exists on the PRTSRCSUM command.

FIGURE 28.6
CPYCHGMBR TAA Tool Prompt Screen

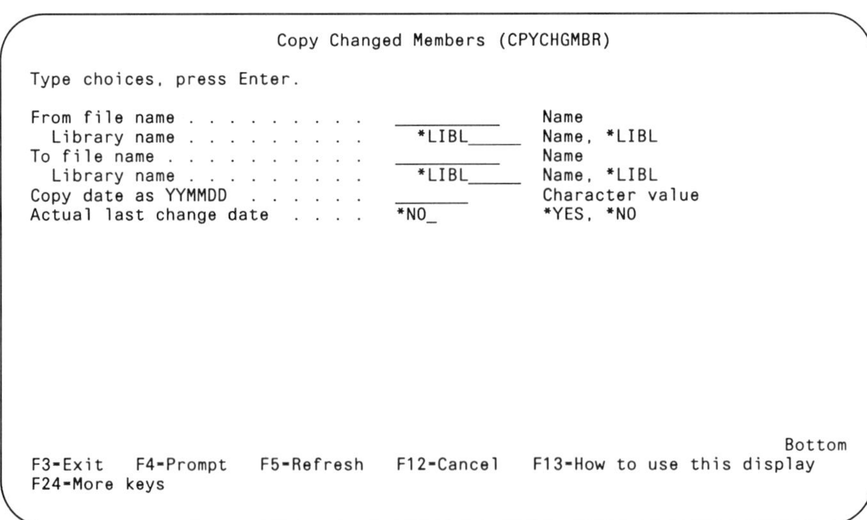

```
                    Copy Changed Members (CPYCHGMBR)

Type choices, press Enter.

From file name . . . . . . . . . .  __________    Name
  Library name . . . . . . . . . .    *LIBL_____  Name, *LIBL
To file name . . . . . . . . . . .  __________    Name
  Library name . . . . . . . . . .    *LIBL_____  Name, *LIBL
Copy date as YYMMDD . . . . . . .   ______        Character value
Actual last change date . . . . .   *NO_          *YES, *NO

                                                                        Bottom
F3=Exit   F4=Prompt   F5=Refresh   F12=Cancel   F13=How to use this display
F24=More keys
```

Moving a Source Member

If you have a source member in the wrong file, you can move it with the TAA tool MOVM (Move Member). The MOVM tool (Figure 28.7) uses a simple combination of the CPYSRCF and RMVM CL commands to perform the function.

Figure 28.7
MOVM TAA Tool Prompt Screen

```
                         Move Member (MOVM)

Type choices, press Enter.

From file name . . . . . . . . .   __________   Name, *CBL, *CL, *CLP...
  Library name . . . . . . . . .     *LIBL_____ Name, *LIBL
To file name . . . . . . . . . .   __________   Name, *CBL, *CL, *CLP...
  Library name . . . . . . . . .     *LIBL_____ Name, *LIBL
From member name . . . . . . . .   __________   Name
To member name . . . . . . . . .   *FROMMBR__   Name, *FROMMBR
Replace if TOMBR exists  . . . .   *NO_         *YES, *NO

                                                                  Bottom
F3=Exit   F4=Prompt   F5=Refresh   F12=Cancel   F13=How to use this display
F24=More keys
```

Removing Source Members

From your own experience, you probably know that it's just as easy to remove source you want as it is to get rid of source you don't want — and it happens despite all the confirmation displays.

One reasonable solution for this occasional problem is the TAA tool CNFRMVM. The CNFRMVM command displays a prompt with as much information about the member as can fit on one screen, plus the first five statements from your source. Using this command, you must press a command key (not just the Enter key) to delete your source, which makes the command safer than other methods.

If you want to delete both objects and source, the TAA tools DLTPGMSRC, DLTCMDSRC, and DLTFSRC can do the job for you. Simply describe the object and these commands will delete the object and the source used to create the object. These commands don't offer any confirmation displays, so you have to be careful. I use these commands to help clean up after writing a test case.

Exercise A Using the STSMSG TAA Tool

The STSMSG TAA tool turns batch job completion messages into status messages. I specify STSMSG in my initial program, but here we will use it interactively. The STSMSG function is performed by the TAAMSGDC program. If TAAMSGDC does not exist in the TAATOOL library, see Appendix B.

1. Enter the command:

   ```
   CHGMSGQ  MSGQ(*USRPRF) DLVRY(*BREAK) PGM(TAATOOL/TAAMSGDC)
   ```

2. Enter the command:

   ```
   SBMJOB  JOB(DSPJOBD) CMD(DSPJOBD QBATCH)
   ```

   When the job completes, you should see the message "Batch job completed normally" (CPF1241), which was sent to your display as a status message.

3. Enter the command:

   ```
   DSPMSG
   ```

   You should see the same message. Sometimes you may miss the status message, but the original message is still in your message queue.

4. Enter a SBMJOB command for a program that doesn't exist:

   ```
   SBMJOB  JOB(BADPGM) CMD(CALL XXXYZ)
   ```

   When the job completes, you should see the message "Batch job completed abnormally" (CPF1240), which was sent to your display as a status message.

   The STSMSG tool, a good productivity aid, operates on the two completion message IDs as demonstrated above. If you want other message IDs handled in the same way, see the discussion in the STSMSG member in the QATTINFO file in library QUSRTOOL.

Exercise B Using the ATNPGM TAA Tool

The ATNPGM TAA tool lets you toggle between two group jobs. The ATNPGM function is performed by the TAAATNAC program. If TAAATNAC is not in the TAATOOL library, see Appendix B. For the attention program to work properly, you set it in your initial program or in your user profile. In this exercise, we will use the user profile.

1. Enter the command:

   ```
   CHGPRF  ATNPGM(TAATOOL/TAAATNAC)
   ```

2. Sign off your workstation.
3. Sign back on.
4. Enter the following command to determine which group job you started with:

   ```
   DSPJOBD  JOBD(QBATCH)
   ```

5. When the display appears, press the Attention key.

   You should flip to a new group job and see your initial display (this tool works correctly only if QCMD is the routing program).

6. Press the Attention key again. This should flip you back to the DSPJOBD display.
7. Press the Attention key again and you will flip back to your initial display.
8. Enter the DSPMSG command.
9. When the display appears, press the Attention key.

   Nothing should happen. A few system functions — DSPMSG is one of the more common ones — mask the Attention key so it is not active.

10. End the DSPMSG display.
11. Press the Attention key again.

    You should flip back to the DSPJOBD display. The Attention key can be pressed only when the screen is available for input. This differs from

Exercise B continued

Exercise B continued

the System Request key, which lets you interrupt any function while it is running. Using the Attention key is much safer; you should avoid interrupting a running function because doing so can cause problems in your other job or when you return as a result of locks set or assumed.

Exercise C Using the DSPLSTCHG TAA Tool

The DSPLSTCHG TAA tool helps refresh your memory about changes you might have made to a member. If the DSPLSTCHG TAA tool is not on your system, the tool you need to create for this exercise is RTVLSTCHG (see Appendix B).

1. Pick a source member you have changed recently and call the following command:

   ```
   DSPLSTCHG  SRCFILE(xxxx) MBR(yyyy)
   ```

   A display will appear that provides information about the last time you changed the member. You should see a count of how many statements were changed the last time you modified the source and up to the first five statements that were changed.

Exercise D Using the PRTSRCF TAA Tool

The PRTSRCF TAA tool lets you print a source member and optionally flag all the statements that were changed after a specified date. If the PRTSRCF command is not on your system, see Appendix B.

1. Pick a reasonably sized source member and a date in the past that will let you see the statements that have changed since the date you specified. Use the CHGBARS parameter on the PRTSRCF command to specify the date to compare to (enter the date in job format). Enter the command:

```
PRTSRCF  MBR(xxx) SRCFILE(yyy) CHGBARS(nnnnnn)
```

2. A spooled file should be created. Use the DSPSPLF or WRKSPLF command to view the file.

   You should see a listing of the source. Any statements that were made on or after the date specified on the CHGBARS parameter should be flagged with an *.

Exercise E Using the PRTSRCSUM TAA Tool

The PRTSRCSUM TAA tool is designed to print a better listing than DSPFD *MBRLIST. It prints one line per member with more information than DSPFD *MBRLIST and it provides selection options. If the PRTSRCSUM command is not on your system, see Appendix B.

1. Enter the PRTSRCSUM command against a small source file. Specify a "Change bar date" that will let the tool flag any members changed after the date specified (it's always in YYMMDD format):

```
PRTSRCSUM  SRCFILE(xxxx) LIB(zzz) CHGBARS(yymmdd)
```

2. A spooled file should be created. Use the DSPSPLF or WRKSPLF command to view the spooled file.

   You should see a listing for each source member. The format of the listing has more information than DSPFD *MBRLIST. The members that were changed on or after the date you specified have been flagged.

Exercise E continued

Exercise E continued

3. Try the command again, but request a listing of only the source members changed since the date specified:

```
PRTSRCSUM  SRCFILE(xxxx) LIB(zzz) CHGBARS(yymmdd) CHGSONLY(*YES)
```

4. Use the DSPSPLF or WRKSPLF command to display the listing.

   You should see only those members that have been changed since the date you specified.

5. The CHGBARS date is being compared to the member level change date. The member level change date can be changed by a variety of functions (e.g., MOVOBJ, CPYSRCF, RST) and may not reflect the actual last SEU change. If you want only those members that have changed based on the SEU statement date, specify:

```
PRTSRCSUM  SRCFILE(xxxx) LIB(zzz) CHGBARS(yymmdd)      +
              CHGSONLY(*YES) ACTLSTCHG(*YES)
```

   Because every source statement must be read, this technique runs slowly; but it can give you a truer picture of changes that have occurred. If you have source members that have all zeros in the change date, the BLKSEUDAT parameter will let you include or drop these members.

Exercise F Using the DUPSRC and CNFRMVM Tools

The DUPSRC TAA tool simplifies duplicating source code. The CNFRMVM tool minimizes the possibility of removing source code you really want to keep. If these commands are not on your system, see Appendix B.

1. Prompt for command DUPSRC.
2. Enter the parameters to duplicate one of your members to a new member name in the same file. The default for text description is to use the existing member description.
3. When you press enter, DUPSRC should execute by internally invoking CPYSRCF.
4. Press F9=Retrieve and try the command again. The command should fail because the default is REPLACE(*NO). This prevents you from deleting existing source.
5. Prompt for command CNFRMVM.
6. Enter the name of the member you just created.
7. When you press Enter you should see a prompt with high-level information about the member at the top of the display and the first five statements from the member at the bottom of the display.
8. Press Enter again.

   You should see an error message that says you must press a Function key (F6 or F12). Requiring a Function key minimizes the problems you can get into with mindless responses in the type-ahead buffer.
9. Use F6 to remove the duplicate member.

CHAPTER 29

Debugging

As one wag said, "I may not be an expert at writing programs, but I sure get a lot of practice debugging them." Most of us get a lot of practice debugging, but that doesn't mean we use all the functions available to help us. Let's review the various levels of debugging assistance provided by the system to see what tools exist that can help you.

ENTERING CL COMMANDS VIA SEU

The SEU syntax checker is very helpful when you are entering CL commands; it prevents you from making silly mistakes. The CL syntax checker is turned on only when you identify the member you are editing as a CLP type member. The prompter support, which provides a good deal of validity checking, is outstanding for avoiding problems that might occur when entering keywords, parentheses, and * values.

THE COMPILER LISTING

Most compiler errors are denoted by message IDs that start with CPD (the complete message text appears after the statement in error — unlike RPG), so an easy way to find the errors in your listing is to scan for CPD. For the scan to work properly, you must enter CPD in uppercase letters. You can scan for CPD by using the SEU split-screen browse function for a spooled file, or by using the DSPSPLF command.

Technical Tip

To speed the debugging process, scan for CPD when you are looking for errors in a CL compiler listing. Most compiler errors are denoted by message IDs that begin with CPD.

Because the compiler places an * in front of source statements in error, you also can find errors on your compiler listing by searching for an * in position 1. You can use the SEU browse function to search for an *, but it is awkward; you must enter the * in quotes on the Find Options display and specify the "To column" as 1.

Although the compiler will find some errors for you, such as a GOTO where the label doesn't exist or a variable that isn't declared, it won't find them all. For example, the compiler offers no help in finding unbalanced sets of DOs and ENDDOs or in determining where your DO groups are.

However, a TAA tool, DSPCLPDO (Display CLP DO Groups), can help. DSPCLPDO finds the DO groups and identifies them with 1s, 2s, et cetera, to depict the nesting level. DSPCLPDO not only finds the unbalanced DOs and ENDDOs more easily, but it can also help you understand the program's logic.

Technical Tip

When you need help determining the correctness of your DO groups, turn to the DSPCLPDO TAA tool. DSPCLPDO not only finds the unbalanced DOs and ENDDOs but it can also help you understand the program's logic.

Logic Checking

If a program you are running ends abnormally or simply produces the wrong result, you may find that logging the CL statements will help you find the problem quickly. You specify logging with the LOGCLPGM(*YES) parameter on the CHGJOB command.

Most commands are logged with the actual values of the variables and not the variable names. Unfortunately, logging does not capture the values on CHGVAR statements and it does not show you the parameter values passed on a CALL command.

Nevertheless, logging is an invaluable debugging tool. I use logging so often I have placed a shorthand command (called LOGCL) in QUSRTOOL to specify logging. To use this tool, you simply code

```
LOGCL
```

After you run your program, press F10 to display the detailed messages, which will include those generated by LOGCL. The LOG parameter on LOGCL defaults to *YES.

I have been able to debug many programs by just logging the CL statements. For more information about logging, see Chapter 1, "Monitoring for Messages."

Technical Tip

The LOGCL TAA tool is a valuable debugging aid that can give you information quickly about what's happening in your CL program.

Program Dump

A program dump gives you a complete "snapshot" of a program at a specific moment in time. For example, it will capture messages sent to your program message queue and the values of variables.

You can request a program dump by responding with a "D" from the CPA0701 inquiry message (Error detected at statement ...) if an unmonitored error occurs in a CL program. To automate the process, you can set your job attribute so that your program will automatically respond with a "D." This is an effective technique for batch jobs (see Chapter 1, "Monitoring for Messages").

You can also request a program dump by using the DMPCLPGM command. If you have a serious debugging problem, placing a few DMPCLPGM commands in your CL program can help.

Display Job Menu

The DSPJOB command menu can be helpful if you are trying to understand your environment. The menu options that display which files are open, which overrides exist, which locks are in effect, or that display the job log can sometimes help you pinpoint a particular problem.

The real question is, "How do you say DSPJOB at the right time?" For interactive jobs that present a display, you can take option 3, "System request," when the display appears to access the DSPJOB menu. If your job does not provide access to a menu, you can use the system debug facility to cause a breakpoint. For batch jobs, it isn't as easy, but debug can still be used.

I have found the DSPJOB "open files" display to be helpful when I know a file contains data, but I can't seem to read it. The "open files" display tells you which file and member you really have open.

System Debug Facility

Although the system debug facility is a great tool, it can be difficult to work with. For example, you must place quote marks around CL variables (e.g., '&VAR1'); you may find the array of command parameters (some of which don't apply to all situations) confusing when prompting for a debug command; and the messages generated by the debug facility are sometimes confusing.

To help you avoid some of the difficulties of working with the system debug facility, a TAA tool is available. The BKP tool, which is a set of commands (BKP, TRACE, STEP, DBGVAR, and CHGDBGVAR), works for any program type.

The BKP tool offers several advantages: It uses a data area in QTEMP that remembers what BKP command you entered last; you don't need to enter the quote characters for variables (or the & character that precedes the variable name); the command prompts, which don't support as many irrelevant options, are much easier to use; and special messages are sent to assist you in the overall process.

Exercise B at the end of this chapter will step you through the use of the BKP tool.

Technical Tip

If you are looking for a simpler form of debug, give the BKP tool a try.

Debugging Large Program Variables

The system debug facility is awkward to use if you have a large variable to be displayed, because the system truncates the value. To keep this from being a problem, while you are debugging, you could send a message to yourself that contains the untruncated value of the variable. This technique was discussed in Chapter 5, "The Job Log," as a way to provide an audit trail. You send such a message by using the TOPGMQ(*SAME) parameter on the SNDPGMMSG command:

```
SNDPGMMSG  MSG(&BIGVAR) TOPGMQ(*SAME)
```

You can leave this command in the program and then remove the message with a cleanup RMVMSG command at the end of the program. For example, if you normally clean up the job log with a RMVMSG CLEAR(*ALL) command, the command will take care of your audit trail message for you. If you want the message in the job log, just change the command to have it sent to TOPGMQ(*PRV).

Adding Test Statements

Sometimes I like to add test statements to my program. For example, if I am working with a complex program, I may include test statements to assist me in debugging. This may be as simple as sending a message that says "I got here," or displaying the current value of a variable.

When I add a test statement, I include a comment that tells me it is a test statement; this helps me later on when I'm cleaning up the program. I use the following convention:

```
/* TEST */  Some command
```

A typical test statement would look like this:

```
/* TEST */  SNDPGMMSG  MSG('OBJ-' *CAT &OBJ)
```

The SNDPGMMSG command sends an informational (*INFO) message to the program that called your program (if you operate from the command entry display, you would see the message). I like to include something unique in the message (e.g., 'OBJ-') to tell me when during the program the message was sent.

You can also use the test statement technique if you want to see a value at some position deep into a variable. You can extract a value and send it in the same command. For example, to extract positions 501 to 600 and send the data as an informational message, I would code

```
/* TEST */  SNDPGMMSG  MSG('POS 501-600=' *CAT +
                          %SST(&BIGVAR 501 100))
```

Technical Tip

It's easy to add test statements that help you debug your program. So that you can find the test statements quickly when you no longer need them, consider using a preceding comment that identifies the test statement.

Exercise A Using DSPCLPDO

In this exercise you will use the DSPCLPDO TAA tool; if it does not exist on your system, see Appendix B. The DSPCLPDO TAA tool, which lets you view a CL program's DO group structure, is helpful for fixing problems caused by unbalanced DOs and ENDDOs or for understanding a program's logic.

1. If you have a favorite complex CL source member with nested DO groups, use it instead of the TAADBFOC member (TAADBFOC is the CL source for the PRTDBFEXP tool). Enter the command:

   ```
   DSPCLPDO  MBR(TAADBFOC) SRCFILE(QUSRTOOL/QATTCL)
   ```

   On the display, you will see the DO groups numbered according to nesting level.

Exercise B Using BKP

In this exercise you will use the BKP TAA tool; if it does not exist on your system, see Appendix B. The BKP TAA tool is a series of commands that act as front ends to the debug commands supplied by the system. To try this tool, you need a simple program to work with (any program type will work).

1. Use PDM to create a CLP member named TRYBKP.
2. Enter the following source:

   ```
   PGM
   DCL        &VAR1 *CHAR LEN(5)
   DCL        &VAR2 *CHAR LEN(3)
   CHGVAR     &VAR1 'ABCDE'
   CHGVAR     &VAR2 'XYZ'
   SNDPGMMSG  MSG('Variable 1-' *CAT &VAR1 *CAT  +
                '   Variable 2-' *CAT &VAR2)
   ENDPGM
   ```

3. Create the program.

Exercise B continued

Exercise B continued

4. Access a command entry display (e.g., CALL QCMD).
5. Call the program:

```
CALL   TRYBKP
```

   You should see the message that contains the value of ABCDE and XYZ sent at the end of the program.

6. Now prompt for the BKP command. You will see a display that looks like this:

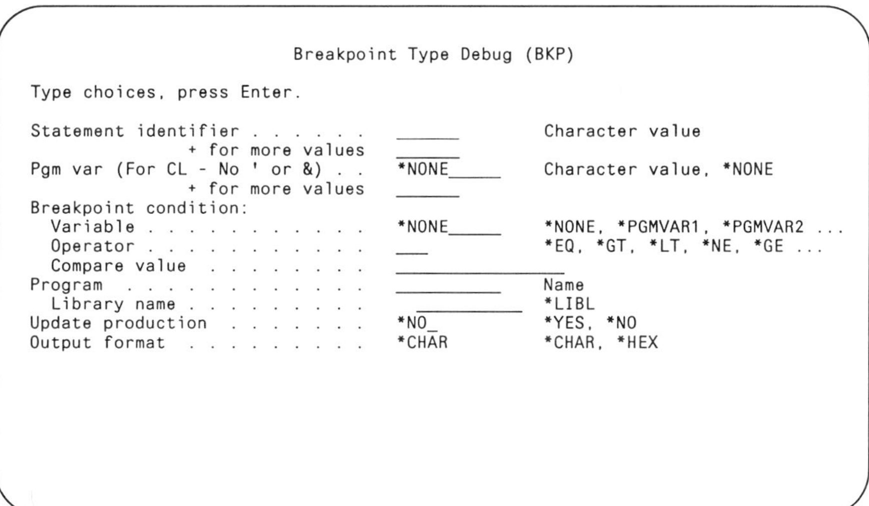

```
                          Breakpoint Type Debug (BKP)

Type choices, press Enter.

Statement identifier . . . . . .   ______        Character value
               + for more values   ______
Pgm var (For CL - No ' or &) . .   *NONE_____    Character value, *NONE
               + for more values   ______
Breakpoint condition:
  Variable . . . . . . . . . . .   *NONE_____    *NONE, *PGMVAR1, *PGMVAR2 ...
  Operator . . . . . . . . . . .   ___           *EQ, *GT, *LT, *NE, *GE ...
  Compare value  . . . . . . . .   _______________
Program  . . . . . . . . . . . .   __________    Name
  Library name . . . . . . . . .     __________  *LIBL
Update production  . . . . . . .   *NO_          *YES, *NO
Output format  . . . . . . . . .   *CHAR         *CHAR, *HEX
```

7. First, let's make a typical mistake to show how easy it is to recover. Assume we want to see the value of &VAR2, which is set at statement 5.00. Specify 500 as the statement identifier for the breakpoint (this is a mistake because the breakpoint occurs before the statement is executed; not afterward).
8. Now enter the program variable for &VAR2. Note that the prompt text tells you to enter it without the & and without quote marks.
9. The next parameter allows you to condition the breakpoint to occur only when your selection criteria is met. Skip this parameter. Enter the name of the program (TRYBKP) in the Program parameter. Press Enter.

Exercise B continued

Exercise B continued

You should see the following statement on the command entry display:

```
BKP   STMT(500) PGMVAR(VAR2) PGM(xxx/TRYBKP)
```

Note that the completion message says debug mode has been entered and the breakpoint is set. With BKP, you don't have to call STRDBG; you just start with your breakpoint statement.

10. Now call the program:

```
CALL   TRYBKP
```

You should see the breakpoint display at statement 5.00. The variable is blank, however, because we should have specified statement 6.00.

11. Press Enter to end.

12. To perform the breakpoint at the correct statement, specify

```
BKP   600
```

A data area in QTEMP, shared by all the BKP tool commands, contains the information from your last BKP command. All you have to do is name the new statement. Note that ending debug doesn't delete the data area. If you didn't debug again for several hours, the information would still be in QTEMP.

13. Now call the program:

```
CALL   TRYBKP
```

You should see the breakpoint display with the value of &VAR2 (equal to XYZ).

14. Press Enter to continue.

15. Sometimes a trace is helpful when you are debugging. Prompt for the TRACE command. It looks like this:

Exercise B continued

Exercise B continued

```
                         Trace Type Debug (TRACE)

 Type choices, press Enter.

 Statements to trace:
   Starting statement identifier    *ALL__         Character value, *ALL
   Ending statement identifier  .   ______         Character value
                 + for more values _
 Pgm var (For CL - No ' or &) . .   VAR2______     Character value, *NONE
                 + for more values _
 Program  . . . . . . . . . . . .   TRYBKP____     Name
   Library name . . . . . . . . .   MYLIB______    *LIBL
 Update production  . . . . . . .   *NO_           *YES, *NO
 Output format  . . . . . . . . .   *CHAR          *CHAR, *HEX
 Maximum trace statements . . . .   1000           Number
```

You should see that prompts are already filled in for the program variable and the program name. The maximum number of trace statements has been increased from the STRDBG default of 200.

16. Enter the statement numbers you want to trace, starting at 400 and ending at 800. Press Enter.

    Note that the command was returned and the helpful completion message tells you to run your command and then use DSPTRCDTA.

17. Now call the program.

    ```
    CALL  TRYBKP
    ```

18. When the program completes, use DSPTRCDTA to look at the trace output:

    ```
    DSPTRCDTA
    ```

    Each use of BKP or TRACE ends debug and starts it again. You create a clean coding environment when you use BKP or TRACE as your last debug statement. But you always need to remember to end debug when you are done.

Exercise B continued

Exercise B continued

19. I sometimes forget the zeros when I request a breakpoint and I specify 6 instead of 600. Let's see what happens:

```
BKP  6
```

You should see an error message that says something like "Do you really mean 600?".

The BKP tool also supports three other commands:

— The STEP command executes one command at a time (you can name a range of statements). Although it can be helpful, it is awkward to use. The STEP command causes a breakpoint on each statement. On a 5250-type display, you have to hit reset when the breakpoint statement appears, then access the F10 command entry display to display variables.

— The DBGVAR command can be accessed only from the F10 command entry display. The command is similar to the CL command DSPPGMVAR, except that DBGVAR will display all the variables that were previously described. From the F10 command entry display, you just enter

```
DBGVAR
```

— The CHGDBGVAR command is similar to the CL command CHGPGMVAR, except that it is easier to enter values into the prompt.

20. Feel free to try these commands; you will find documentation for them with the BKP tool (see Appendix B).

21. When you are done, enter the ENDDBG command.

CHAPTER 30

Cross-Reference Techniques

Programmers typically need to answer questions such as

- What programs call program AAA?
- What programs update file BBB?
- What programs use field CCC?
- Where have I used the DDD command or keyword?

To answer some of these questions requires the use of high-level language programs rather than CL programs, but most of the cross-reference support I talk about in this chapter can be used for either.

You have a choice when you try to answer questions such as those listed above: You can work against source code or object programs. Each approach has its advantages and disadvantages.

The major advantage of working against source code is that you can look for more detailed information, such as field names, keywords, and command names. The major disadvantage is that the source code you are scanning may not accurately represent the related objects.

The major advantage of working against object code is that you are using current information. The disadvantages are that multiple steps may be required to get the information you need, or that you may not be able to get the information you need. For example, to answer the question, "What programs call the program AAA?" you need to run a "where used" report. The system stores the information you need for this report in the OIR (Object Information Repository), which is part of the library description object for each library in QSYS. When a program is created, most of the objects the program uses are captured and placed in the OIR. You get the information out of the OIR with the DSPPGMREF (Display Program References) command. The data is written to an outfile and then you can write programs or query the information.

The problems with this approach are that

- You must take time to run the DSPPGMREF command and then run a query against the outfile created to collect the information you need. (See the section "The DSPPGMREF Command.")

- The information obtained is not very detailed. You can only cross-reference the use of programs, files, and data areas. You can't get down to the level of field names, command names, or keywords.

- If you use variable names, the information isn't meaningful in the cross-reference. For example, if you use the following CALL command:

  ```
  CALL   PGM(&PGM)
  ```

  the system cross-references the variable name (&PGM) and not the name of a specific program.

Scanning Your Source

I have found that scanning source is the best technique for obtaining the cross-reference information I need. It works reasonably fast and you can scan for command names, keywords, or any string of data. If you take the time to set up the DSPPGMREF command properly, the command will work faster than scanning the source, but it offers fewer capabilities. Regardless of the information I am trying to find, I prefer to scan the source rather than use the DSPPGMREF command.

PDM supports the FNDSTRPDM (Find String Using PDM) command, which lets you search for character or hexadecimal strings, but I don't need all the options supported by this command and I don't care for the output format. My favorite method for scanning source is to use the SCNSRC TAA tool.

The SCNSRC TAA tool works as fast as anything else against source members. You specify what you want to scan for (the ARGUMENT) and it prints one line with the member name, statement number, date of change, and the first 70 characters from the statement. For example, if you coded

```
SCNSRC   FILE(xxx) ARGUMENT(CCC)
```

you would get a list of every source statement that contains the string CCC. The one restriction is that the argument you are scanning for must be contained in a single source record.

Technical Tip

The SCNSRC TAA tool is my favorite method of scanning source. I like the function, performance, and format.

Three other TAA tools build on the SCNSRC command:

- The SCNALLSRC command is of value only if you use standard source file names, such as QCLSRC or QRPGSRC. You indicate which source files you want to scan by specifying one or more source types (e.g., *CLP, *RPG) and the command submits a batch job. The batch job invokes SCNSRC for each source type you have named.

- The SCNTAATOOL command works like SCNALLSRC, except it is specifically designed for the QUSRTOOL source files. You specify one or more source types and SCNTAATOOL submits a batch job. The batch job invokes SCNSRC for each source file you specified.

- The SRCARC tool supports several functions, including scanning source code. The SCNSRCARC command, part of the SRCARC tool, provides the fastest way to scan source code. See the next section.

The Fastest Way To Scan Source

The Source Archive (SRCARC) TAA tool supports several useful functions (e.g., archiving and backing up source code), but we will focus here on its capability as a source-scanning tool.

To use the SRCARC tool for scanning source, you first need to use the UPDSRCARC command to place the source into an archive. This command compresses multiple members and versions into a single member; a "header" file keeps track of each version. The section "Setting Up a Source Archive for Static Source" explains how to create a source archive.

Once the archive has been created, you can use the SCNSRCARC command to scan your source. The following is the format of the SCNSRCARC command:

```
SCNSRCARC  ARGUMENT(ZZZZ) ARCFILE(xxx/yyy) SRCARCLIB(www)
```

The ARGUMENT parameter is the value you want to scan for. The ARCFILE parameter describes the source file in the archive that should be scanned; the default is for all files. The SRCARCLIB parameter describes the library that contains the source archive.

In this case, the command would create a spooled file that lists each current member in the archive that had ZZZZ in the source.

The combination of archived source and the SCNSRCARC command provide the fastest way to scan source because

- only a single member must be opened, rather than every member in a source file; the process of opening and closing members is relatively slow and reducing the number of opens delivers a major performance payoff.

- fewer database records must be read. This technique packs several source statements into a single archive detail record. This reduces the number of records, which means fewer database calls are required to access the records.

- fewer bytes must be scanned. The archiving process squeezes out blanks, so the scan function has much less data to look at. The RPG operation code SCAN is used to scan the archive record.

Despite its speed, the scanning function has a few disadvantages:

- The listing only tells you which member has the argument you specified. It doesn't count the "hits" and it doesn't know which statement the "hit" occurred on. SCNSRCARC only knows that the string exists at least once in the member. For many functions, however, just knowing the member that has a "hit" is satisfactory. For example, if you are trying to copy existing source, the member name is adequate. Assume you have scanned the archive and you have found some source in MBR22 that you want to copy to MBR1. You would access MBR1 via SEU and then use the F15 browse/copy function and name MBR22. Then you would scan MBR22 for the same argument until you found the source you wanted to copy.
- After setting up the archive, you need to run the UPDSRCARC command whenever your source changes so the archive remains current.
- You can't scan for an argument that includes consecutive blanks because the archiving process eliminates blanks. Scanning for multiple blanks normally isn't a problem. Most of the time you will be looking for a name that doesn't contain blanks.
- The argument you scan for must be completely contained in the original source statement (i.e., all characters must be on the same line).

Setting Up a Source Archive for Static Source

If you have static source on your system (i.e., source that doesn't change often) that you would like to scan on occasion, it makes sense to set up a source archive to take advantage of the fast scan provided by the SCNSRCARC command.

First, you need to create the SRCARC tool if it has not already been created. Then create an archive in a library (only one archive per library). You can more easily remember where the archive is if you put it in the same library as the source.

Let's step through the process. I'll assume that you want to archive the QUSRTOOL source files so you can scan them, but you can use the same technique for any source.

1. Create the source archive:

```
CRTSRCARC  LIB(QUSRTOOL)
```

2. Run the update command. You need to name the source files you want to archive. In this example, I have not named all the source files in QUSRTOOL, but rather the ones that I would be interested in. This is a long-running command so you should submit it to batch.

```
UPDSRCARC  SRCFILE(QATTINFO QATTCMD QATTCL     +
             QATTDDS QATTRPG) SRCLIB(QUSRTOOL) +
             SRCARCLIB(QUSRTOOL)
```

When the UPDSRCARC command completes, you are ready to scan the source. Assume that you would like to scan the QUSRTOOL source for CLP type members to find any use of the API that accesses the list of spooled files in an output queue. You'd like to see an example of how it is coded and perhaps copy some of the code.

You would refer to the *System Programmer's Interface Reference* (SC41-8223) to find the name of the API program (QUSLSPL) you want to scan for. You would then use the following command:

```
SCNSRCARC  ARGUMENT(QUSLSPL) SRCTYP(CLP) SRCARCLIB(QUSRTOOL)
```

A spooled file will be created with one line of information for each member where at least one "hit" was found. You then use the normal SEU scan function on the member to look for the information you need.

If you receive an update to QUSRTOOL, or if some other source you have archived is updated, you must run the UPDSRCARC command again; otherwise your archived source will not match the original source. Before you run the update, you need to clear two members (the files that make up an archive):

```
CLRPFM   FILE(QUSRTOOL/SRCARDP)
CLRPFM   FILE(QUSRTOOL/SRCARDH)
```

Technical Tip

If you have static source on your system that you would like to scan occasionally, it would make sense to set up a source archive (using TAA tool SRCARC) to take advantage of the fast scan provided by the SCNSRCARC command.

THE PRTCMDUSG COMMAND

Although I prefer to scan the source, the IBM-supplied PRTCMDUSG (Print Command Usage) command can be useful. PRTCMDUSG lets you search CL programs for one or more commands. The command works fairly fast, and it works even if you have created a program with RTVCLSRC(*NO).

PRTCMDUSG only provides the names of the programs that contain the command(s) you are looking for. You can't use PRTCMDUSG to determine where you have specified a keyword or an object name.

THE DSPPGMREF COMMAND

When you need to cross-reference the objects referenced by one or more programs in one or more libraries, the DSPPGMREF (Display Program References) command can come in handy. The DSPPGMREF command will build an outfile that you can then query against. The typical command to build an outfile for library LIB1 would be

```
DSPPGMREF  PGM(LIB1/*ALL) OUTPUT(*OUTFILE) OUTFILE(LIB1XREF)
```

DSPPGMREF will only let you name a single library for each use of the command (you can specify *LIBL). However, you can use the command multiple times (each time naming a new library) and have all the output directed to the same outfile.

For each program in the library specified, the outfile will contain one record for every object referenced; but for CL programs, only three object types are considered: files, data areas, and programs. For example, if a CL program did the following:

- one RTVDTAARA
- one OVRDBF
- two CALLs

the outfile would contain four records for the program. Note that the outfile will not contain a record for any commands specified, any message files referenced, or any data queues referenced.

The outfile information can be confusing, so let me comment on the important fields:

- WHPNAM. This field contains the name of the program that uses the referenced objects.
- WHFNAM. This field contains the name of the referenced object (e.g., the file used by the program). Normally, this is the field you want to select on.
- WHOBJT. This field contains a one-character code that identifies the referenced object type. The codes are

F = File
D = Data area
P = Program

- WHFUSG. This field contains a one-character code that indicates how the file was used. The codes are

1 = Input
2 = Output
3 = Input and output
4 = Update
8 = Unspecified

Because you sometimes get a combination of the codes (e.g., a 6 would mean "Output and Update"), interpretation of this field can be difficult. If the code is 8, which normally stands for "Unspecified," it means a command such as OVRDBF specified the file.

Now let's step through a simple example of using the DSPPGMREF command and of querying the generated outfile. You will need the CRTPRTPGM TAA tool to create a general-purpose print program so that you can look at the data.

1. Use DSPPGMREF on a library of your choice:

```
DSPPGMREF  PGM(LIB1/*ALL) OUTPUT(*OUTFILE) +
               OUTFILE(LIB1XREF)
```

2. Use the TAA tool CRTPRTPGM to create a general-purpose print program:

```
CRTPRTPGM  FILE(LIB1XREF)
```

3. Specify the following commands to run OPNQRYF (you can also use the TAA tool QRYF) with the general-purpose print program. You need to specify the object you want to reference (in the example code it is xxxx):

```
OVRDBF   FILE(LIB1XREF) SHARE(*YES)
OPNQRYF  FILE(LIB1XREF)  +
           QRYSLT('(WHFNAM *EQ "xxxx")')
PRTDBF   PGM(ZLIB1XREF)  +
           FIELDS(WHFNAM WHOBJT WHFUSG WHPNAM)
```

You will get a listing of all the programs that use the object you specified.

If you think you'd like to use this solution more than once, you should take the time to follow the next set of steps. We'll create a CL program and command that will let you look at any cross-reference file created using the DSPPGMREF command. To improve the performance of the CL program, we'll create the DDS for a physical file that you can use to create any file for DSPPGMREF output.

1. If you already have a file named LIB1XREF (or whatever name you used in the example above), delete it:

   ```
   DLTF  FILE(LIB1XREF)
   ```

2. Use PDM to create a PF member named PGMREFP.

3. Enter the following DDS source. This specifies the outfile and format name of the DSPPGMREF file and then places a key over the referenced name. This will allow OPNQRYF to use the access path for a faster selection.

   ```
   A          R QWHDRPPR                 FORMAT(QSYS/QADSPPGM)
   A          K WHFNAM
   ```

   You don't need to create the PGMREFP file. We'll use the PGMREFP source to create as many cross-reference files as you need.

4. Create a physical file with the name you want and specify the source you just entered. In the code shown, I use the file name LIB1XREF. If you use a different name, you need to change it throughout.

   ```
   CRTPF   FILE(LIB1XREF) SRCFILE(xxx) SRCMBR(PGMREFP)
   ```

5. Use the TAA tool CRTPRTPGM to create a general-purpose print program against the file you just created. This will submit a batch job to create the program.

   ```
   CRTPRTPGM  FILE(LIB1XREF)
   ```

6. Use DSPPGMREF to output records to the file you just created. If you specify a large library, this will be a long-running command and you should submit it to batch.

   ```
   DSPPGMREF  PGM(xxx/*ALL) OUTPUT(*OUTFILE) OUTFILE(LIB1XREF)
   ```

7. Use PDM to create a CMD source member named DSPCRSREF.

8. Enter the following source:

```
          CMD        PROMPT('Display Cross Reference - xxx')
          PARM       KWD(OBJ) TYPE(*NAME) LEN(10)          +
                       EXPR(*YES) MIN(1)                   +
                       PROMPT('Referenced object name')
          PARM       KWD(FILE) TYPE(QUAL1)                 +
                       PROMPT('DSPPGMREF outfile')
QUAL1:    QUAL       TYPE(*NAME) LEN(10) DFT(LIB1XREF)
          QUAL       TYPE(*NAME) LEN(10) DFT(*LIBL)        +
                       SPCVAL(*LIBL *CURLIB)               +
                       PROMPT('Library name')
```

9. If you are not using the name LIB1XREF, scan the source for that string and change the value to the name you are using.

10. Create the command:

```
CRTCMD  CMD(DSPCRSREF) PGM(DSPCRSREFC)
```

11. Use PDM to create a CLP member named DSPCRSREFC.

12. Enter the following source. I'm using the TAA tool QRYF with the command BLDQRYSLT. We'll sequence the information on the usage of the object.

```
PGM         PARM(&OBJ &FULLFILE)
DCL         &OBJ *CHAR LEN(10)
DCL         &FULLFILE *CHAR LEN(20)
DCL         &FILE *CHAR LEN(10)
DCL         &LIB *CHAR LEN(10)
DCL         &QRYSLT *CHAR LEN(2000)
CHGVAR      &FILE %SST(&FULLFILE 1 10)
CHGVAR      &LIB %SST(&FULLFILE 11 10)
OVRDBF      FILE(LIB1XREF) TOFILE(&LIB/&FILE)               +
              SHARE(*YES) SECURE(*YES)
BLDQRYSLT   QRYSLT(&QRYSLT) SELECT((WHFNAM *EQ &OBJ F2))
OPNQRYF     FILE((*LIBL/LIB1XREF)) QRYSLT(&QRYSLT)          +
              KEYFLD((WHFUSG))
PRTDBF      PGM(*LIBL/ZLIB1XREF) FIELDS(WHFNAM              +
              WHLNAM WHOBJT WHFUSG WHPNAM WHLIB WHTEXT)     +
              NBRRCDS(300) TITLE('PRTDBF Command output ') +
              FILE(&LIB/&FILE)
CLOF        OPNID(&FILE)
DLTOVR      FILE(&FILE)
RMVMSG      CLEAR(*ALL)
ENDPGM
```

The BLDQRYSLT command (part of TAA tool QRYF) generates the value for the QRYSLT parameter to be used in OPNQRYF. In this case, the BLDQRYSLT command specifies selecting records equal to the referenced name passed in from the command. The PRTDBF command (part of TAA tool CRTPRTPGM) prints a listing with the field names specified. The program (ZLIB1XREF) was created in a prior step.

13. If you are not using the name LIB1XREF, scan the source for that string and change the value to the name you are using.
14. Create the program. Now you are ready to give it a try:

```
DSPCRSREF  OBJ(xxxx)
```

You should get a report that identifies all the programs that use the object you specified. If you specified a file, the programs appear in usage sequence.

Note that the object name does not distinguish by object type. We could have added a command prompt for this, but you'll see the object type in the report. You could improve the error-handling for the DSPCRSREF command by adding the standard error-handling code presented in Chapter 4, "Standard Error-Handling Routine."

You now have a utility command that is crude, but effective. You can run a batch program every night or once a week to rebuild the outfile from as many libraries as you want.

Exercise A Using SCNSRC

In this exercise you will use the SCNSRC TAA tool to look for a character string in a source file; if SCNSRC does not exist on your system, see Appendix B.

1. If you have a favorite source file and something to look for, use it. Otherwise, do the following to scan for all the places where the DSPFFD command is used in the QUSRTOOL source file QATTCL:

```
SBMJOB  CMD(SCNSRC FILE(QUSRTOOL/QATTCL) +
          ARGUMENT(DSPFFD)) JOB(SCAN)
```

2. When the job completes, use WRKSPLF to look at the listing.

   You should see one line for each source statement that specifies the DSPFFD string. The listing identifies the member, the statement, and the change date and includes 70 bytes from the statement itself. Note that you not only found the places where the command was specified, but also any time the string DSPFFD was found. I find this helpful. The nice thing about SCNSRC is that you get a readable listing and it works whether you are looking for an object name, a field name, a command name, or a keyword. If you want to scan a QUSRTOOL source file, the better command to use is SCNTAATOOL. It will do the SBMJOB for you and provide better defaults.

Exercise B Using PRTCMDUSG

In this exercise you will use the system command PRTCMDUSG to determine all the CL programs in TAATOOL that use the DSPFFD command. I'll assume that you have created all the TAA tools. If not, you need to use some other library and you may not find any use of DSPFFD. Instead of DSPFFD, you could use a command that you know does not appear frequently.

1. Enter the command:

```
SBMJOB  CMD(PRTCMDUSG CMD(DSPFFD) PGM(TAATOOL/*ALL)) JOB(USG)
```

2. When the job completes, use WRKSPLF to look at the listing.

   You should see one line for each program that uses the DSPFFD command. PRTCMDUSG runs faster than SCNSRC, but you don't get as much information and the only thing you can look for is command name usage.

Appendix A

How I Code

In answer to the many programmers who have asked how I code, I will reveal all my major secrets:

- steal from things that work
- be persistent
- try to think about what might happen
- test, test, test
- remember that code always needs to be maintained

Of course, how you or I code depends greatly on personal preference. What I offer here are simply my preferences; if you like what you are doing, stick with it.

Machines Are Relatively Cheap

I don't mind recompiling. I often make a single change and then recompile and test it. That way I can focus on a problem and make sure I have solved it correctly.

If you work with huge programs, however, you probably can't afford to do this. I operate in an environment where a lot of machine time is available to me. I would have to operate differently if machine time were at a premium.

Machines are relatively cheap in comparison to the expense of a skilled programmer. Thus, good response time and good compilation time are keys to programmer productivity. In fact, as the low-end AS/400 models have significantly improved in performance, having a separate system for program development is a lot cheaper than it used to be and a lot more productive than you might think.

Should You Design a Program?

Because CL programs tend to be small (in comparison to other programs) and the ones I design tend to follow a similar pattern, in most situations I just "have at it."

The obvious weakness of the "have at it" approach is that without knowing exactly where you are going you could end up with a significant rework project on your hands. But I take this approach because, like many programmers, I don't necessarily know what I want until I see something in action and have used it for awhile; then I can describe what

I like and don't like about a solution. I find it much easier to critique something that exists than to plan what it should be. And if I have to throw away a 150-line CL program, I believe the effort was worth it if it helped me understand the path I need to take. Because I have a reasonable degree of experience, my throw-away rate is low.

Of course, for large projects, you have to plan; you can't just "have at it."

WHY START FROM SCRATCH?

Coding into an empty SEU display is no fun. Copying existing code is the best way to be productive. When I start a new source member, I use the DUPSTDSRC TAA tool, which lets me copy existing source and set up the source member with statements appropriate for the type of source I am going to use. To set up a new CLP member, I would specify

```
DUPSTDSRC    MBR(xxx) SRCTYPE(*CLP) +
               TEXT('...') SRCFILE(xxx)
```

It is generally much easier to delete statements you don't want than to key new code. The DUPSTDSRC tool describes how to change the source so you can personalize it for your needs.

In addition to copying from your own source or from source other programmers have written, you can copy and use source contained in many QUSRTOOL tools.

Several TAA tools also have documentation that includes CL code. You need to access the correct member in file QATTINFO in library QUSRTOOL and then copy in the CL code. The format of the commands is as if you had used the prompter. Three TAA tools are designed specifically for copying — in fact, they don't have any other source members (they are described further in Chapter 9, "Subroutines," Chapter 17, "Outfiles," and Chapter 4, "Standard Error-Handling Routine"):

- CLPSUBR How to code a subroutine in CL
- CLPOUTFILE How to code to read an outfile
- CLPSTDERR Standard error handling

If I want to use some existing source but I'm not sure where it is, I like to use the TAA tool SCNSRC to scan an existing source file. This tool is described in Chapter 30, "Cross-Reference Techniques."

USING A STANDARD HEADING

I find it helpful to have a standard heading at the beginning of my source that contains comments about the program. Consistency is more important than the standard used.

My approach is not very elaborate. Normally, I use only one comment statement, but I do include the member name as the first comment. The DUPSTDSRC tool will include the member name as the first comment for you. For commands or key application programs that I invoke directly, I may include information about their purpose and about subprograms or objects they use.

How I Find the Command I Want

I often know there is a system command, a QUSRTOOL command, or a user-written command that does what I want, but I can't remember the name.

If it's a system command I want, I can access menus that start with CMDxxx. For example, if I want to find a spool command, I specify

```
GO  CMDSPL
```

to view a list of the spool commands or sublists of the command groups I should look at.

If I'm trying to find a TAA command, I use the DSPTAACMD TAA tool. You also can use this technique for system commands or user-written commands. See the section "Remembering Command Names" in Chapter 14, "User-Written Commands."

Entering Keywords

I don't enter keywords on every command. For frequently used commands (e.g., DCL, CHGVAR, IF, GOTO), I just key as fast as I can. I find the format readable.

Throughout this book, you have seen me use the following format:

```
DCL      &FILE *CHAR LEN(10)
CHGVAR   &VAR1 'ABCDE'
IF       (&VAR2 *EQ '*YES') DO /* Yes value */
GOTO     NXTCMD
```

Placing all the keywords in the statements just adds clutter for commands that I see over and over again.

For commands I don't use often, I prefer to use keywords. Sometimes I key them, but most often I use the prompter.

The IF Command

Typically, I use a DO command on an IF statement. Unless I am going to use simple CHGVARs or a GOTO, I like the DO group function. All the commands are in a nice, neat column (as an RPG programmer, my eye is trained to read down columns).

When coding an IF statement, I try to immediately add the ENDDO statement. Thus, I would begin the DO group with

```
IF    (&FAIL *EQ 'X') DO /* Failure occurred */
ENDDO  /* Failure occurred */
```

Then I go back and insert the commands I want to execute inside the DO group. This approach cuts down on the number of mismatches between DOs and ENDDOs. Note that I put the same comment on both the DO and the ENDDO. This makes the code more readable.

Some programmers indent their DO groups, but I don't like indentation because

- you lose the capability of the prompter or you spend a lot of time shifting your statements to indent.
- you have to run some program against the source to format it. The source looks different during maintenance.

I don't use many nesting levels (about three deep would be a lot for me). For code with many nesting levels, I use the TAA tool DSPCLPDO to help me find any mismatches (it also numbers the DO groups).

I have never understood the fuss over the use of a GOTO command. In my opinion, a well-placed GOTO that is properly documented to branch to a unique set of logic is a blessing.

The ELSE Command

I don't use the ELSE command often. Typically, I repeat the IF command and change the operator. The method you choose depends on which you believe offers the best documentation. If I have a lot of statements before the ELSE, I would rather see another IF statement to refresh my memory about what the code is doing.

Using Comments

The best place to document a program is in the program itself. A few well-placed comments can aid my memory and help someone who has not seen the code before. For large programs, I usually include an overview section that describes the program's structure.

I try to comment more about "why" I am doing something than "how" I am doing it. Most of the "how" is fairly evident with CL programs; the "why" may not be as obvious.

Although SEU does not make this an easy task, I put my comments in lowercase to provide a contrast with the code, which is in uppercase. My eye is well-trained to read lowercase as comments or message text. Uppercase means code to me, and I like the sharp contrast between the two.

External Documentation

External documentation for a program that describes the major interface (the command or major program that should be called) can be helpful to someone who uses the function. I like to put this level of documentation online so users can find it easily.

Typically, I describe the objects used, the structure (what program calls what program), and the details of the external parameters. I believe that is enough information to get a user started; after that, the code is its own best documentation.

What My Programs Look Like

Because CL lacks subroutines, I seldom use a mainline approach when coding. My CL programs all tend to follow the same structure:

- Check the parameters
- Check for the existence of and/or allocate critical objects
- Send escape messages for errors
- Do overrides if needed
- Send status messages if meaningful
- Do the processing function
- Send completion or error messages
- Clean up
- Include the standard error-handling routine

Taking a Piecemeal Approach

Unless I'm coding a simple program, I code the program a piece at a time and then test each piece as I continue building the program. I do this for two reasons:

- The concept of "code a little, test a little" works well for me and I do a better job of testing. My mind stays focused on smaller entities. I can "see the code" better and I am more likely to test all the conditions.

- I find it discouraging to face a huge pile of source that has never been tested and that I'm having trouble getting to work properly. I need feedback that says "That worked, good for you"; then I can go on to the next piece.

My Testing Approach

I check the error conditions first. Therefore, I try things I know shouldn't work so that I don't forget to test them. I often change the error text after I see the message displayed. By testing the error conditions first, I avoid the temptation to ignore possible bad results.

I don't use a lot of test data for most testing. I try to exercise everything, but normally I can do this by varying the same test data. The more test data, the more chance there is of errors in the test data itself, which complicates debugging. When I think the program is working, I may run it against more test data.

Getting Unstuck

We all get stuck sometimes, ending up with code that should work, but doesn't. After I've tried all the normal things (I've looked at the code again, debugged, read the manual) and I'm still stuck, what do I do?

My experience suggests that the problem is usually something extremely basic: I'm accessing the wrong file, misspelling a name, or submitting an incorrect parameter list. Therefore, I review the basics to make sure that the structure is in place for my code to work.

I often explain what I am doing to my imaginary friend (I'm Calvin, he's Hobbes). If that doesn't work, I try to get away from the problem for awhile, coming back later with a fresh perspective. If that doesn't work, I ask one of my peers for help.

What I Do When I Think I'm Done

When I think I am done with my code, I step through the following checklist:

- Test commands. I have discussed how I sometimes use commands to help me test a program (see Chapter 29, "Debugging"). Now I need to remove them from the final version of my code. Using a standard convention for coding the test commands helps when it's time to remove them.
- Extraneous DCLs. These appear as messages in the compilation. I just delete the variables I don't need.
- Job log. What messages appear in the job log when the program works correctly? I prefer to keep the job log clean. I may have to go back and get rid of some of the messages caused by the program (see Chapter 5, "The Job Log").
- Completion messages. If I need a completion message, is it coded as type *COMP? I like completion messages and normally use them unless I have a low-level command or program that isn't executed directly (e.g., IBM doesn't send a completion message from the CHGVAR command and I don't send one from the TAA tool EDTVAR). If you have a function that is called only from a CL

program, a completion message may create extra clutter. See Chapter 2, "Sending Messages."

- Status messages. If a program's response time is longer than seems reasonable, a status message gives me a "warm fuzzy" feeling; I know the program is doing something appropriate. I've also found logic bugs by running interactively and watching the status messages. See Chapter 2, "Sending Messages."

- Audit trail. Is this a program where I need to leave something other than a completion message as an audit trail? If so, what should I do? A variety of audit trail functions are available for use. It may be as simple as putting a time stamp in a record's date field; or it may be an entry in the job log, a message to a message queue, or a transaction record written to a file.

  A good, seldom-used technique is to write an entry to a journal. The SNDJRNE command is ideal because the journal entry automatically includes a lot of information about my job without requiring additional work on my part. See Chapter 5, "The Job Log."

- Escape messages. Are the error conditions being sent as escape messages? I may look at the code to answer this question, rather than run additional tests.

- Performance. Is performance what I would expect? Sometimes performance is easy to measure; other times, if my program front-ends some function, measuring performance is more difficult. But having this question on my checklist makes me think about performance.

- Recovery. How would I recover if the application blew up? This is the most difficult of all questions to answer. Most of the time I can't do much, but sometimes I can provide for a reasonable degree of recovery. I keep in mind that the normal human reaction is to try it again (people generally are eternally optimistic). If my code will recover if it is restarted at the beginning, I'm probably doing the right thing.

- Cleanup. I want to be sure I have not kept anything locked, even if I end abnormally. This means that if I allocated anything, I must remember to de-allocate. Most of the system functions will take care of themselves, but anything you allocate can cause problems (see Chapter 11, "Allocating Objects"). The TAA tool ALCTMPMBR is an exception. Although this tool will allocate temporary members, it doesn't matter if you leave them allocated because the lock will be released at the end of job.

If I create something in QTEMP, I normally don't bother to delete it. Unless I create something very large, I would rather waste temporary space and provide faster response time by avoiding use of the delete commands.

- Program comments. Have I included comments that will help me or somebody else maintain the program? Have I pointed out the "whys" rather than the "hows"?
- External documentation. If I plan to provide external documentation about a program, I do it when my mind is still fresh from the coding effort. As I document something, I am often reminded of situations I haven't coded for. This often forces me back into the program; it can be an iterative process.
- Final review. I like to wait a few days and then re-read the documentation and the code. The period of time I wait should not be too short or too long; I need to get away from the code for awhile, but not so far away that it looks new.

  During this final review stage, I usually add comments that explain the code better or clarify the documentation. And I often find additional coding I should do (e.g., some function I haven't handled but should have) or "dumb" things I have done that I need to change. In some shops, other programmers may be able to join in this review.

Here's a summary of my "when it's all done" checklist:

- Do test commands need to be deleted?
- Do extraneous DCLs need to be deleted?
- Is the job log clean?
- Are any completion messages needed?
- Are any status messages needed?
- Is an audit trail needed?
- Are escape messages sent for errors?
- Is performance adequate?
- Is special recovery needed?
- Is any cleanup needed (e.g., de-allocate objects)?
- Have program comments been included?
- Is external documentation needed?
- Has the code been reviewed one last time?

And yes, I do have the checklist taped to my workstation. I never outgrow the need for good fundamentals.

Coding for the Long Term

It probably goes without saying that I read every line of code I write many times over the life of any given program. I read it when I'm developing a program, when I'm fixing a problem, and when I'm making an enhancement. Because I may read the code months, or even years, later, I think it is worthwhile to

- include comments that explain how the code works
- use simple techniques that will make sense years later
- ensure, to the best of my ability, that my code is bug-free

That last item — ensuring bug-free code — is a challenge. It definitely costs more (in man-hours) to fix code than it does to develop code. But based on my experience, I can conclude only that I should have spent more time testing code. We all know the hindrances to effective code testing: schedules, work pressures, and the simple fact that looking at the same code over and over becomes boring.

I'm still looking for the magic wand that can cast a spell on my code and make it perfect. Let me know if you find it. In the meantime, I will have to settle for a happy medium between a reasonable amount of testing time and a reasonable amount of fixing time.

Appendix B

QUSRTOOL

QUSRTOOL, an optional library shipped with the AS/400 operating system, provides example tools and programming techniques (known as TAA tools) that may help you operate your system or develop software. This appendix will focus mostly on the TAA tools. The AAAMAP member described in the "Documentation" section of this appendix provides information about the TAA tools, and about other code that exists in QUSRTOOL. As you use tools from QUSRTOOL, here are some important points to remember:

- By default, QUSRTOOL is installed when you install a new release.
- As of V2R2M0, the library comes in a "packaged" state. You must "unpackage" most of the source files (see the section "Unpackaging QUSRTOOL").
- File names start with QATT (e.g., QATTINFO, QATTCL, QATTRPG).
- You must create the objects. Subsequent sections in the appendix describe programs that do the "creates" for you.
- A disclaimer with QUSRTOOL essentially says that "What you see is what you get." APARs are not accepted for QUSRTOOL.
- PTFs are rarely provided for anything in QUSRTOOL. This means that if incorrect code is shipped during the release, it will not be fixed by a PTF or any PTF cumulative package. Any corrections to the code will not be made until the next release. For information about an informal update program, see the section "Informal Updates to QUSRTOOL."
- The code is essentially public so you can borrow or modify whatever you want. The source code is copyrighted only to prevent someone from selling it.
- On each release, the entire QUSRTOOL library is replaced. Therefore, if you modify any of the code, either don't make the modifications to QUSRTOOL or be able to make the same changes on the next release.
- Included in QUSRTOOL are the TAA tools. These are the ones I

personally worked on and am the most familiar with. TAA doesn't stand for anything; these letters were assigned only as a naming convention to the source members I worked on.

- I will use the terms "TAA tools" and "non-TAA tools." The TAA tools have a common create function (CRTTAATOOL); the non-TAA tools have individual create steps.

THE PURPOSE OF QUSRTOOL

QUSRTOOL contains practical tools that work. The tools can

- help make you more efficient.
- provide solutions not provided by the system. This was the original intent of the forerunner of QUSRTOOL (the TIPSTECH library on the System/38). That library was born out of frustration that IBM developers couldn't work fast enough to satisfy all the user requests for function.
- prove educational. Many programmers have told me they learn a lot about the system by looking at the source code in QUSRTOOL. The system is so rich in function that we often miss the significance of some function unless we see it in a situation we can understand. Other programmers have told me they look at the tools to get an idea of how to approach a problem. When we're lost, we all need direction and QUSRTOOL can help get you going.
- tickle your imagination. Often we just need an idea or a technique to help us solve some problem. Stealing ideas and techniques is the foundation of good programming.

WHAT IF QUSRTOOL IS NOT ON YOUR SYSTEM?

The QUSRTOOL library is shipped as part of the operating system. If you received your OS/400 release from IBM, you can mount the IBM distribution tape and use the command GO LICPGM. The item to look for is not described as "QUSRTOOL," but as the "Examples Tools Library." To install the library, select the option "Examples Tools Library" on the Install Licensed Programs prompt screen.

UNPACKAGING QUSRTOOL

As of V2R2M0, IBM ships QUSRTOOL in a "packaged" state. This means that the source files (except for QATTINFO) were saved to save files and the save files were shipped in QUSRTOOL. The save files have the same name as the source files. This method has several advantages:

- The new release is installed faster.
- The QUSRTOOL library does not take up as much room on the system for those customers who don't want to use it but install it anyway by default.

The instructions for how to "unpackage" QUSRTOOL may change in a future release. If you are on a release later than V2R3, be sure to check the installation instructions that come with the media.

If you are on V2R3, the simplest solution is to unpackage all the source files, which will take several minutes. To unpackage the source, use the following commands:

```
ADDLIBLE  LIB(QUSRTOOL)
CALL      UNPACKAGE PARM(*ALL 1)
RMVLIBLE  LIB(QUSRTOOL)
```

Documentation

The documentation you need for QUSRTOOL is online in the file QATTINFO. There is no IBM manual for QUSRTOOL, nor do I think you need one. The QATTINFO source file contains some members you should be familiar with:

- AAAMAP. This is the controlling member and it provides an overview and general instructions. AAAMAP also provides a detailed road map to non-TAA tools.
- AAAREADME. This describes new non-TAA tools that appear in the current release and any significant changes to previous non-TAA tools.
- AAAUPDATE. This describes the TAA tools that are new for the current release, plus enhancements and fixes to existing tools.
- TAASUMMARY. This describes the TAA tools by category and gives you a one-paragraph description of each tool.
- TAAUPDATE. If you installed an update, this describes the new tools, enhancements, and fixes that are included.

The DSPTAATOOL Command

One of the first tools you should create (if you don't create all the tools) is the DSPTAATOOL command, which provides a simple way to look at the documentation for any tool. DSPTAATOOL is only a shorthand to invoke STRSEU and place you in browse mode (you can't change anything). If you don't have SEU on your system, DSPTAATOOL invokes the DSPPFM command.

The default for the source file is QATTINFO in QUSRTOOL, which is where the documentation exists. DSPTAATOOL can be used for any tool (not just the TAA tools). A typical command would be

```
DSPTAATOOL   TOOL(ADDDAT)
```

You can also print the documentation for any tool or all the tools by specifying OUTPUT(*PRINT). Printing the documentation for all the tools will require a lot of paper.

How To Get Started

As mentioned above, member AAAMAP in QATTINFO provides an overall discussion of QUSRTOOL. You can read it by entering

```
DSPTAATOOL   TOOL(AAAMAP)
```

AAAMAP contains a discussion of QUSRTOOL, the disclaimer, the copyright, overview information, and a one-paragraph description for each non-TAA tool. An important section in AAAMAP that follows the one-paragraph descriptions explains how to start using a specific non-TAA tool.

A chart shows the non-TAA tool name on the left, followed by the documentation ID, the documentation member, and the install member. For example, if you wanted to read more about the "Converting Office Documents to SEU Text" non-TAA tool, from the chart you would find the name of the documentation member (TOFINFO) and then enter the command:

```
DSPTAATOOL   TOOL(TOINFO)
```

The TOFINFO member provides more information about the "Converting Office Documents to SEU Text" non-TAA tool and explains how to create it. Most of the non-TAA tools provide an install program that you create first and then call to create the objects (normally, you don't issue the CRTxxxPGM command directly).

The documentation for the TAA tools, described as "Programming and system management tips and techniques," is contained in member TAASUMMARY. The documentation for non-TAA tools and TAA tools is separated because there are a handful of non-TAA tools and more than 300 TAA tools, and the TAA tools have their own method of documentation and creation.

TAASUMMARY

Member TAASUMMARY in file QATTINFO is the controlling member for the TAA tools. The first page provides highlights of the TAA tools. Here's what you will find in TAASUMMARY:

- The first section lists the tools by category. The categories will help you answer a question such as "Is there a tool that does ...?" The categories are divided into sections such as Spool, Data Base, Source. A tool may appear in multiple categories. The following is an example of the category listing:

```
Job accounting:

    PRTQHSTANL     Print QHST analysis
    PRTJOBACG      Print job accounting

Job log:

    CHKSAVRST      Check save/restore job log
       .
       .
```

- The second section provides a one-paragraph description for each tool in alphabetical order. For example,

```
PRTQHSTANL
                   Print QHST analysis. Analyzes the information
                   found in QHST. The major analysis is based on
                   the CPF1164 job completion message. These are
                   summarized by day, by completion type, and by
                   user. Other significant messages are listed
                   and counted. A general count is provided for
                   each unique message ID. This can be used for
                   a basic form of job accounting.
PRTPGMA
                   Print program attributes. Prints the common
                   attributes of a program, generic programs or
                   all programs ...
```

- TAASUMMARY also references the CRTTAATOOL member, which you use to create one or all of the tools.

TAA Tools Require the RPG Compiler

The RPG compiler is a prerequisite for the TAA tools. With one exception (see the section "The DUPTAPIN Tool"), no other licensed programs are required. Of course, you do need OS/400.

Many of the TAA tools create RPG programs. If you don't have the RPG compiler, you could have someone else create the object code for all the tools and then save the libraries TAATOOL and TAASECURE. You could then restore these libraries on your system.

Most of the tools will work using this technique. There are some authorization lists that you will need, but you can either work around these or create them yourself.

The CRTPRTPGM tool creates an RPG program when you run the tool. This tool requires the RPG compiler to be available at run time. It is possible for some tools that do not require the RPG compiler to be created with individual create commands, but this approach is not as easy as using the CRTTAATOOL command.

The CRTTAATOOL Command

The CRTTAATOOL member describes how to create one or all of the TAA tools. You may want to read about some of the options in the documentation. The command prompt looks like this:

```
                    Create TAATOOL objects - TAA (CRTTAATOOL)

Type choices, press Enter.

Tool name . . . . . . . . . . .    __________     Name, *ALL
Library to create files in. . .    *NONE_____     Name, *NONE
Source library. . . . . . . . .    QUSRTOOL__     Name
Command library . . . . . . . .    TAATOOL___     Name
Restart name if TOOL(*ALL). . .    *NO_______     Name, *NO
Restart after named tool. . . .    *NO__          *YES, *NO
Remove observability. . . . . .    *YES           *YES, *NO
Allow retrieve of CL source . .    *NO__          *YES, *NO
Compress objects if TOOL(*ALL)     *YES           *YES, *NO
```

To create the CRTTAATOOL command, take the following steps (in the section "Updates to QUSRTOOL," I'll discuss what to do if you have an update to QUSRTOOL):

1. Create the library TAATOOL (this is where the objects for the tools will be placed):

```
CRTLIB  LIB(TAATOOL) TEXT('Library used for TAA tools')
```

2. Create the base program:

```
CRTCLPGM  PGM(TAATOOL/TAATOLAC) SRCFILE(QUSRTOOL/QATTCL)
```

3. Call program TAATOLAC (this is a long-running program so you probably want to submit it to batch):

```
SBMJOB  JOB(CRTTAACMD) CMD(CALL PGM(TAATOOL/TAATOLAC))
```

Program TAATOLAC will create the CRTTAATOOL command and the programs that will allow you to create the tools.

Steps 2 and 3 must be done on every release unless you receive an update.

The CRTFILLIB Parameter

Whether you create all the tools or certain tools, the CRTTAATOOL command requires that you name a library for the CRTFILLIB (Create File Library) parameter. Some tools create files that will eventually contain your data.

These files should be placed in a library that you back up regularly. You can create a special library for these files or you can place them in an existing library. You cannot name the TAATOOL library.

Creating All the Tools

I recommend that you create all the TAA tools; the task is easy, but it will take time. A lot of CRTxxx commands must be executed. On a low-end AS/400 dedicated to the job, it will probably take five or more hours; on a high-end AS/400 dedicated to the job, it will take less than one hour. Creation of all the tools would be a good job to run overnight. You need to create the tools on every release.

The tools will not take up much space on your system. The object code is compressed so that the libraries are less than 15 MB. Creating all the tools on each release

- makes it much more likely that someone will use a tool (because it is already created).

- avoids problems caused when one tool requires another. Some of the tools use other tools and therefore the dependent tools must be created first. If you create the tools individually, you will run into prerequisite problems. If you create all the tools, the tools are created in the proper order to avoid this problem.
- ensures that all fixes and enhancements are applied to the tools. Because the tools are never PTFed, the only way to get fixes and enhancements into the tools is to re-create them from the new source.

I know of no security exposures if you create all the tools. Some of the tools perform security-sensitive functions, but it takes an overt act by the security officer to allow use of these tools.

Technical Tip

You should create all the TAA tools. By doing so, you'll avoid many potential problems and learn more quickly which tools you might need.

To create all the TAA tools, take the following steps (if you have an update to QUSRTOOL, follow the instructions that came with the update and not the remainder of this section):

1. You must be the security officer or a user with *ALLOBJ authority to create all the tools.
2. If you have never used the TAA tools, I suggest you start by taking the defaults for most of the options on the CRTTAATOOL command (you must name a library for CRTFILLIB).
3. Enter the following command:

```
SBMJOB  JOB(CRTTAATOOL) CMD(CRTTAATOOL TOOL(*ALL) +
          CRTFILLIB(xxxx))
```

You can create the TAA commands in a library other than TAATOOL, and after you have experience with the TAA tools you may want to do this. The TAA tool MOVLIBOBJ will move all the command objects for you. See the discussion in member CRTTAATOOL.

Steps To Take if CRTTAATOOL Fails

If CRTTAATOOL fails, you'll need to look at the job log to determine what went wrong. Here are a few typical problems users have experienced when using the CRTTAATOOL command:

- All the source files were not unpackaged. On the job log, you'll see an escape message stating that a program failed to create and a preceding diagnostic message (CPF4156). This tells you that you attempted to open a file that was not a source file. To recover, see the section "Unpackaging QUSRTOOL" and start over.
- The code shipped from IBM is incorrect. Either the code won't compile, a member was not shipped, or the wrong member was requested to create. If you get an update, this should fix the problem. In the meantime, you can create the remaining tools by following the procedure described below.
- A command in a library that is ahead of TAATOOL on the library list is using the same name as a TAA tool command, but the parameters differ. For example, you may have your own tools library on the system portion of the library list. If a command exists in your library with the same name as a TAA tool, you can have problems. You can create the remaining tools, but you have a naming problem that only you can solve.

If the procedure blows up in the middle of creating all the tools, you may be able to fix the problem that caused the tool to fail or you may just want to bypass the tool that cannot be created. In either case, CRTTAATOOL has a restart capability to allow for this.

On the CRTTAATOOL command, two parameters control restart. Assume the procedure blew up on the tool PRTLIBDTL, but you have fixed the problem and now want to restart at PRTLIBDTL. Restart with

```
CRTTAATOOL  TOOL(*ALL) CRTFILLIB(xxx) RESTART(PRTLIBDTL)  +
              AFTER(*NO)
```

If you can't fix the problem with PRTLIBDTL, restart at the tool after PRTLIBDTL:

```
CRTTAATOOL  TOOL(*ALL) CRTFILLIB(xxx) RESTART(PRTLIBDTL)  +
              AFTER(*YES)
```

The Libraries Used

The library structure for QUSRTOOLs looks like this:

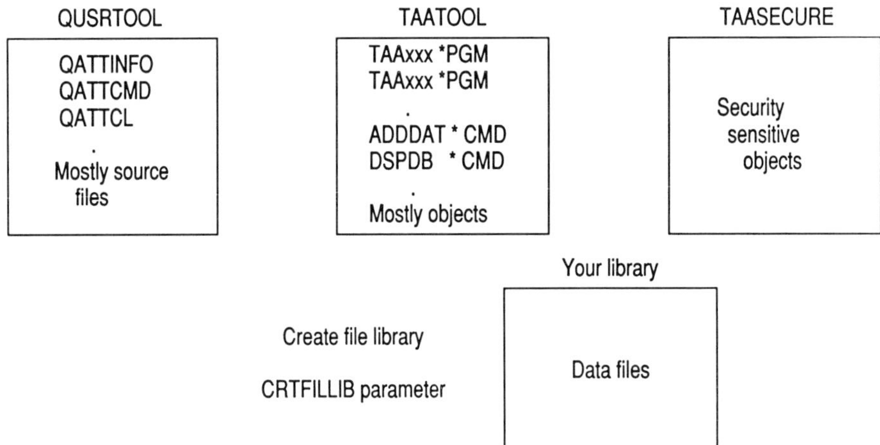

The libraries are

- QUSRTOOL. This approximately 40 MB library contains the source files (e.g., QATTINFO, QATTCMD). If you create all the objects, you probably still want to have the documentation file (QATTINFO) online. A few tools use source members in the other files during the execution of the tool. Most tools do not use any source after the tool is created. You could remove the members to save space or you could use the SRCARC tool to create a condensed, online archive of the source.

  You only need to back up the QUSRTOOL library once per release or after you install an update. It is rare that a PTF changes QUSRTOOL so it normally does not need to be backed up after installing a PTF cumulative package.

- TAATOOL. This 10-15 MB library contains most of the object code. The library never needs to be backed up if you don't mind re-creating the objects, if required. I back up my TAATOOL library only when I save all my libraries.

- TAASECURE. This approximately 1/2 MB library is used for security-sensitive tools. For example, the DSPPWD tool places data in this library.

- Your CRTFILLIB library. This approximately 1/2 MB library contains files that will have your data for certain tools. This library should be backed up regularly.

- Other libraries. Some tools require that special libraries be created.

Adding TAATOOL to the Library List

The library where the TAA tool command definition objects exist must be on the library list for you to execute a TAA tool. If your commands are in the TAATOOL library, then TAATOOL must be on your library list.

Some tools don't have commands, and to use them you normally qualify the program name with the TAATOOL library.

Informal Updates to QUSRTOOL

Informal updates may be available for QUSRTOOL. There is no guarantee of this, but it has been going on for several releases. The updates include fixes, enhancements, and new tools. Each update is cumulative for a release (meaning the most recent update contains all the prior updates for the same release). There is a unique update for each release.

To determine if you have the update, enter:

```
DSPDTAARA  DTAARA(TAATOOL/TAATOOL)
```

If no data area exists, you don't have the update. If the data area exists, it will tell you at the top of the display if the update was installed and what release it was for. If the first 100 bytes of the data area are blank, you have never installed an update.

To determine whether or not an informal update is available from IBM, you need to contact your IBM SE. Your SE may already have the update. If not, ask your SE to send a note to

```
QUSRTOOL at RCHASA04
```

When a new release of the operating system is being developed, there is a cutoff point for QUSRTOOL updates that occurs early in the cycle. After that point, no changes are made to the release for QUSRTOOL.

Because the informal update contains fixes, enhancements, and new tools, you will find that the latest informal update for one release is probably more current than the IBM distribution tape for the next release. To stay current with QUSRTOOL fixes, you should see if there has been an informal update at least once per release.

For supported releases, a single library (TAAUPD) is shipped with save files for the supported releases. A menu is provided. You access the menu as follows:

```
CALL  TAAUPD/TAATOLHC
```

I recommend you take option 1, which lets you install the update and create all the tools. It will determine which release you are on and restore the correct save file, and then do the entire install and create process for you.

Technical Tip

Because of the early cutoff date for changes to QUSRTOOL, you don't get the most current level of code when you install a new release. If there has been an informal update for QUSRTOOL, you should get it at least once per release. This will fix most of the problems you may encounter with the tools. No PTFs are shipped for QUSRTOOL.

What You Should Do on a New Release

Unlike OS/400 system code, which ships replacement objects, QUSRTOOL is only source. Because of this, the fact that QUSRTOOL is refreshed by an install of a new release does not mean you automatically have the benefit of the new code. You must re-create everything on a new release if you want fixes, enhancements, and new tools.

The create process for TAA tools is driven by the CRTTAATOOL command and the programs behind that command. You must re-create the CRTTAATOOL command and its associated programs before you can re-create the tools you are using.

The best approach is to get the latest update, as described previously, and take the option to install and create all the tools. If you don't get an update, you need to start over. Because only source is shipped, you should repeat Steps 2 and 3 described in the section "The CRTTAATOOL Command." You don't need Step 1 to create the TAATOOL library. Here are the steps to follow:

- Create the base program:

```
CRTCLPGM  PGM(TAATOOL/TAATOLAC) SRCFILE(QUSRTOOL/QATTCL)
```

- Call program TAATOLAC (this is a long-running program so you probably want to submit it to batch):

```
SBMJOB  JOB(CRTTAACMD) CMD(CALL PGM(TAATOOL/TAATOLAC))
```

After taking these steps, you must re-create the tools you are using — or better yet, create all the tools.

What if a Tool Doesn't Work?

First, determine whether or not you have the latest update to QUSRTOOL. If you don't, get the update (described previously) and see if the update fixes the problem. In most cases, you have probably run into a problem that has already been fixed. I recommend creating all the tools with each update because sometimes the problem is with a prerequisite tool and not the tool that you are invoking.

If the update does not fix the problem, you need to do one of the following:

- Have your SE send a note describing the problem to

  ```
  QUSRTOOL on RCHASA04
  ```

- Mail a description of the problem (include IBM branch and SE name) to

  IBM
  QUSRTOOL
  Dept 469
  Hwy 52 and 37th St
  Rochester, MN 55901

  You have no guarantee that IBM will fix the problem, but so far the results have been good.

One of the major reasons the QUSRTOOL code carries a disclaimer is that it does not undergo the rigid testing that normal system code goes through. Normally, for QUSRTOOL tools a single person (e.g., myself) develops and tests the tool. This procedure keeps the cost low, but makes it more difficult to produce a high-quality tool.

If the developer moves to a new job and no one claims ownership of his tool, IBM will probably remove it from QUSRTOOL. This has already happened to a few tools. But assuming you are running with the latest update, the quality of the QUSRTOOL code is usually very good.

If This Book Doesn't Agree with Your QUSRTOOL

This book was written during the V2R2M0 timeframe. Tools and enhancements to tools are mentioned that do not appear in the IBM distribution tape for V2R2M0; but they are in the latest update for that release. If you are on a release later than V2R2M0 or have the latest update to QUSRTOOL, you should see all the tools/enhancements described.

However, this does not mean there won't be further changes to QUSRTOOL. Also, the system may be enhanced, which may cause some of the tools described in this book to be outdated or to be out of synch with the system.

The DUPTAPIN Tool

The DUPTAPIN command is the only TAA tool dependent on the PL/I compiler. The DUPTAPIN command uses two small PL/I programs to read a 32 KB record. If you specify CRTTAATOOL TOOL(DUPTAPIN), the PL/I programs will not be created even though the source exists.

You can get the object code for this tool in one of two ways:

- Find a PL/I compiler and create the programs yourself.
- Get the update for QUSRTOOL. The update contains the object code and automatically moves the programs into the TAATOOL library as part of the install process.

The DSPTAACMD Tool

More than 350 commands are associated with the TAA tools (some tools have multiple commands), so remembering them is out of the question (the operating system has about 900 commands, so the TAA commands add about 40 percent more).

The DSPTAACMD tool will help you work with the commands. DSPTAACMD lets you search for command names and helps answer the question, "Is there a tool that does ...?" For example, if you want to find all the TAA tool commands that start with the verb RTV, you would specify

```
DSPTAACMD  CMD(RTV)
```

This will bring up a subfile of all the commands starting with RTV:

```
                             Display TAA Commands

Type options, press Enter.
   1=Dsp TAA tool   2=Prt TAA tool   3=Command prompt   8=Attrib
   9=Dsp Obj Descrp

Opt  Command     Type  TAA   Text description
 _   RTVBIGPARM  CMD    Y    Retrieve big parameter - RTVBIGPARM
 -   RTVCLSA     CMD    Y    Retrieve class attributes - RTVCLSA
 -   RTVCMDA     CMD    Y    Retrieve command attributes - RTVCMDA
 -   RTVDAT      CMD    Y    Retrieve date in various formats - RTVDAT
 -   RTVDLTRCD   CMD    Y    Retrieve deleted records - RTVDLTRCD
 .
 .
 .

F3=Exit         F6=Dsp TAA Summary
```

Once you find the command you want, you can use an option to display the documentation for the tool, print it, or prompt for the command.

The TAA tool commands follow a naming convention similar to that used by system commands (e.g., OBJ for object, LIB for library). If you wanted to find all the TAA tool commands that have LIB in them, you would specify

```
DSPTAACMD  CMD(LIB) SCAN(*NAME)
```

Sometimes you may be looking for a word such as "queue," but you may not be sure how it is abbreviated in the command. You can scan the text description of the commands by specifying

```
DSPTAACMD  CMD(QUEUE) SCAN(*TEXT)
```

By default, the DSPTAACMD command works only with the TAA commands. If you like the approach, you can add commands from other libraries (including QSYS) to the file that is used; see the discussion that accompanies the DSPTAACMD tool in QATTINFO.

Technical Tip

The DSPTAACMD TAA tool helps you quickly find the TAA command you need.

The DSPTAAMBR Command

If you want to look at the source for one of the QUSRTOOL tools, the DSPTAAMBR command can save you many keystrokes. The documentation for a particular TAA tool describes the source members used to create that tool. For example, the documentation for the ADDDAT tool tells you that the CL source member name is TAADATAC. To use a minimal number of keystrokes to look at that source, you would specify

```
DSPTAAMBR   MBR(TAADATAC) SRCTYPE(*CLP)
```

or just

```
DSPTAAMBR   TAADATAC *CLP
```

The DSPTAAMBR command invokes SEU in browse mode; if you don't have SEU, the DSPPFM command is used.

Changes to QUSRTOOL

QUSRTOOL is not as firmly fixed as the operating system between releases or informal updates. You do have some exposure if you use the commands in production functions because there may be changes on the next release. The following types of changes may occur:

- The system may supply a function that was being provided in QUSRTOOL. For example, in a previous release, the CVTBINDEC command was replaced by the system function of %BIN in CL programs. The CVTBINDEC command was left in QUSRTOOL with a statement that it would be withdrawn in the following release. This provided one release to clean up any use of the QUSRTOOL command. In another case, the RTVOBJD command was replaced by a system command of the same name, but some of the parameter names differed. This caused a problem for certain uses of the QUSRTOOL command. The QUSRTOOL version was removed on the same release that the system command came into existence.

- Some of the tools use spooled output from system commands to access information that is not available in any other manner. The system may change the format of the output on a new release. In most cases, any changes are found when testing QUSRTOOL for the new release and the source code is revised to match the new format before the code is shipped. However, you must re-create the source on every release to account for these kinds of changes. In some cases, the system changes the format after QUSRTOOL is frozen for the release. If that happens, the tool isn't going to work unless you get an update.
- As with system support, there are a minimal number of changes and deletions to QUSRTOOL for a variety of reasons. The TAA tool changes are documented in the member AAAUPDATE. You should review this on every release to determine what has changed.
- Any fixes or enhancements are always shipped by modifying the source. For this reason, you should re-create all the tools (or all you are using) on each release.
- IBM may withdraw a tool or make changes to a tool on any release. Because the source exists on the previous release, you might consider keeping a copy of the source from the prior release to protect your use of certain tools, or you might consider incorporating the code into your source files and creating the tool using different names and libraries. However, in most cases, you don't need to take this approach. The vast majority of tools will work the same on the next release or they will include enhancements that are upwardly compatible.

Exercise A Using the CRTTAATOOL Command

Even if you create all the tools via the update (you don't enter CRTTAATOOL directly), you should still be familiar with the TAA tool command. If the CRTTAATOOL command does not exist on your system, see the section "The CRTTAATOOL Command."

1. Prompt for the CRTTAATOOL command. I'll only comment on a few parameters. The others are explained in the online documentation for CRTTAATOOL. The two RESTART parameters were explained earlier in this appendix.

   The last three parameters have to do with compressing the size of the object code. By default, the programs are created without observability. Thus, if you are trying to debug a tool, you will have to re-create it with RMVOBS(*NO). To save space, the CL source (by default) is not placed in the object program. If you create all the tools, the default for CPROBJ is *YES, meaning that the object size is further reduced. The system will automatically decompress the object if you use it.

2. Even if you created all the tools, you can re-create an individual tool using CRTTAATOOL (if the tool already exists, you will need proper authority). Enter the command:

   ```
   CRTTAATOOL  TOOL(LOGCL)
   ```

   While the tool is being created, you should see a status message:

   ```
   LOGCL tool objects of SET10 being created
   ```

   The tools are arranged in sets to ensure that the prerequisite tools are created first. Set 10 contains the simplest tools.

Exercise B Using the DSPTAATOOL Command

You use the DSPTAATOOL command to look at documentation for TAA tools. If the DSPTAATOOL command does not exist on your system, you can create it using the CRTTAATOOL command.

1. Enter the command:

   ```
   DSPTAATOOL  TOOL(AAAMAP)
   ```

   You should see member AAAMAP, which is the controlling member for documentation in QUSRTOOL.

2. Roll to the section that contains one-paragraph descriptions of the tools. Find the description for "Converting Office Documents to SEU," and assume you want to read more about this one.

3. Roll further to the section that describes the documentation member name for each of the non-TAA tools.

   You should find that the member name you want is TOFINFO.

4. Return to the command entry display and enter

   ```
   DSPTAATOOL  TOOL(TOFINFO)
   ```

   You should be looking at the documentation for the "Convert Office Documents to SEU" tool. The documentation will describe the tool and explain how to create and use it. You can use DSPTAATOOL against any member (TAA or non-TAA). DSPTAATOOL is just a shorthand to put you in browse mode in SEU.

5. The TAA tools differ from the non-TAA tools in that they use a documentation member that is the same name as the tool. Assume you want to see the documentation for the ADDDAT TAA tool; you would enter

   ```
   DSPTAATOOL  TOOL(ADDDAT)
   ```

6. Return to the command entry display and enter

   ```
   DSPTAATOOL  TOOL(*SELECT)
   ```

   This brings up the "Work with Members Using SEU" display. You can now access any member, but you should avoid updating the source.

7. Return to the command entry display and prompt for the DSPTAATOOL command.

Exercise B continued

Exercise B continued

You can see that you can print a tool using OUTPUT(*PRINT) if you want hard copy. There is also an option to print documentation for all the tools, but this takes a lot of paper.

8. Assume that you want to look at all the TAA tools that have something to do with writing or working with commands. Enter the command to look at the TAASUMMARY member:

```
DSPTAATOOL  TOOL(TAASUMMARY)
```

9. Roll until you come to the section "Command aids."

   You should see a one-line description for each tool. Looking at member TAASUMMARY can help answer the question, "Is there a tool that does ...?" If you can get to the right category, you can quickly make a determination.

10. Pick one of the tool names and scan for it using the SEU scan function. For example, you might scan for ADDDAT.

    You should eventually come to the one-paragraph description of the tool (this brief summary may be all you need, thereby saving you from having to print the complete documentation for a tool). Printing out a copy of TAASUMMARY is a reasonable thing to do to give you a hard-copy version to refer to.

Exercise C Using the DSPTAACMD Command

The DSPTAACMD command can help you find command names when you have only a partial idea how they are spelled. If this tool is not on your system, you can create it using the CRTTAATOOL command.

1. Assume you want to find all the commands that start with CVT; you would enter

   ```
   DSPTAACMD  CMD(CVT)
   ```

   You should see a subfile displayed of all the TAA tool CVT commands.

2. Assume you are interested in reading further about the CVTMSGF command (you may need to scroll through the subfile to find the command name). Enter the option to prompt for the command.

   You should see the CVTMSGF command prompt. Return to the subfile display.

3. Enter the option to display the documentation (Dsp TAA tool).

   You should see the documentation for the CVTMSGF tool. Return to the subfile display.

4. Enter the option to print the TAA tool.

   You should see a message that the tool was printed. Return to the command entry display.

5. Some TAA tools do not have command interfaces. Enter the command:

   ```
   DSPTAACMD
   ```

   You should see the tools that are run just by calling a program.

6. Sometimes you may be interested in all the TAA tool commands that have the abbreviation SRC in them. Return to the command entry display and enter the command:

   ```
   DSPTAACMD  CMD(SRC) SCAN(*NAME)
   ```

   You should see the subfile with just the command names that have SRC somewhere in the name.

Exercise C continued

Exercise C continued

7. Return to the command entry display. When you don't know the abbreviation for the command you want, you can scan the text description of the command. For example, assume you wanted to see all the commands that have the word "member" in them. You would enter

```
DSPTAACMD  CMD(MEMBER) SCAN(*TEXT)
```

You should see the subfile filled with the commands that have "member" in the text description.

Exercise D Using the DSPTAAMBR Command

The DSPTAAMBR command provides the simplest method for looking at the source of a member in QUSRTOOL. If this tool is not on your system, you can create it by using the CRTTAATOOL command. If you have SEU on your system, the DSPTAAMBR command uses SEU's browse mode to display the member; if SEU does not exist, the DSPPFM CL command is used. For this exercise, we will assume you want to look at the CL source for the PRTSRCF tool, which prints a listing of the source in a member.

1. You first need to know the name of the CL source member. To find this name, use the DSPTAATOOL command to look at the documentation for PRTSRCF:

```
DSPTAATOOL  TOOL(PRTSRCF)
```

2. Scroll through the documentation and you will come to a section titled "Objects used by the tool." The PRTSCRF tool is comprised of a command, a CL program, and an RPG program. You can see that the CL program source is named TAASRCJC.
3. Prompt for the DSPTAAMBR command. You can see that you can use the command for any type of source, but it is most useful for QUSRTOOL source because you can use a shorthand for the type of

Exercise D continued

Exercise D continued

source. For example, the command will interpret the value *CLP as file QATTCL. Therefore, you simply enter

```
DSPTAAMBR  MBR(TAASRCJC) SRCFILE(*CLP)
```

You should be looking at the CL source for the PRTSRCF tool.

Index

*ALLOBJ special authority, 393, 450
for CHKLMTCPB TAA tool, 454
for creating all TAA tools, 532
limiting, 441
for PRTSECVIL TAA tool, 454
*BCAT operator, 25
*CAT operator, 25
*CHANGE authority, 443
*EXCL locks, 201, 204
*EXCLRD lock, 223
*EXT message queue, 235-237
*FIFO, 478
*JOBCTL authority, 158
*SHRNUP lock, 203, 220
*SHRRD lock, 204, 222, 223, 224, 229
*SHRUPD lock, 222, 224
*TCAT operator, 25
*USE authority, 443
? (question mark), in selective prompting, 234

A

Access paths, 336-337
building, 336-337
keyed, 337
OPNQRYF command and, 338-339, 350
choosing best, 351
searching for, 351
performance, 337-338
Active
jobs, 199
objects, 197, 202
programs, 193
users, 125
ADDDAT (Add Date) command, 138-139, 144
uses, 138-139
ADDDTAARA TAA tool, 206
exercise, 216-217
uses, 206
ADDLFM command, 336-337
Adopt. *See* Program Authority Adoption
ALCDBF (Allocate Data Base File) command, 205
ALCOBJ (Allocate Object) command, 75
completion messages and, 203
database files and, 204
default class wait time, 201
escape messages and, 8, 203
CPF1002, 202
exercise, 210-214
locking objects and, 198
monitoring error conditions and, 8
unobtained locks, 202
ALCTMPMBR (Allocate Temporary Member) command, 298, 300, 303-305, 309
files/members, 437
parameters, 303
uses, 303
using, 304, 305
Allocating objects, 193-217
database files, 204
all members of, 205
device files and, 204
manually, 200-205
problems, 219-232
data areas, 220
display files, 220
library lists, 222
logical files, 222
physical files, 224-225
printer files, 220-221
programs, 221-222
source files, 222-223
spooled files, 221
user profiles, 222
restore commands and, 227
SAV commands and, 227
system defaults, 193
what you can/cannot do with, 201
See also Objects
Allocation requests, 196-197
ALWRTVSRC attribute, 160
APIs. *See* Application Programming Interfaces (APIs)
Application Programming Interfaces (APIs), 113-114, 465-472
advanced, 465-466
list-function, 467-469
single-function, 466-467
CL commands and, 465
command line processing, 290
defined, 465
invoking, 199
job names and, 199
outfiles vs., 297
system, 465
TAA CVT commands and, 299
AS/400
override processing on, 325-326
Query, 341
AS/400 Programming: Reference Summary, 297
ATNPGM (Attention Program) TAA tool, 475-476
using, 487-488
Attention key handling program, 475
Attributes
displaying, 417-418
retrieving, 418-419
file, changing, 317
printing, 419
Audit trail, 24, 99-101
code for, 100
permanent, 100-101
system time and, 142
temporary, 99-100
Authority
adopted, 393-395
See also Program authority adoption function
adopting, 397-402
changing, 226
debugging, 433, 450-452
locking requirements, 219
unadopting, 397-402
Authorization lists, 226

B

Backup
  code, 479
  spooled file, 96
Batch jobs
  avoiding SBMJOB and, 156
  default wait time, 201
  preventing simultaneous submission of, 196
  sending message to submitter of, 36-37, 46
  standard, 477-478
  See also Jobs
Binary format, accessing data in, 55-56
Binary tree, 337
BKP TAA tool, 190, 495-496
  defined, 498
  using, 498-502
BLDCALL command, 156-158
  key commands, 157-158
  restriction, 158
  using, 157
  for using same parameter list, 187
BLDPRTIN (Build Print Line) command, 278-280
  combined with PRINT, 280
  command prompt, 278-279
  numeric fields passed to, 278
  sample CL code, 279-280
  uses, 278
BLDQRYSLT command, 354-355
  exercise, 365-366
  power of, 355
  prompt, 354
  QRYSLT parameter, 354
  return variable, 354-355
  See also QRYF command; QRYF (Query File) tool
Break-handling programs, 121
BRKMSGQN command, 121
Bubbling up messages. *See* messages, resending

C

CALL command
  coding parameter list on, 181
  for executing same program, 158
  maximum number of parameters on, 186
  programs invoked by, 47
  reducing overhead of, 434
  same parameter list on, 187
  user-written commands vs., 249, 435
Calling
  other programs, 383-384
  own program, 386
  program that called your program, 113
Call stack, 383
  See also Program stack
CAPJOBA (Capture Job Attributes) command, 159
  RTNJOBA command with, 159
  using, 164-165
CHGBIGPARM command, 187
CHGDSPF (Change Display File) command, 220
CHGDTAARA (Change Data Area) command, 75, 205
  *SHRNUP lock, 220
CHGJOB (Change Job) command, 93
  executing, 95
  INQMSGRPY(*DFT) parameter, 119
  LOGCLPGM(*YES) parameter, 494
  RTVJOBA command with, 158-159
  RUNPTY parameter, 158
CHGLIBL command, 159
  CURLIB parameter, 473
CHGLIBOWN (Change Library Owner) command, 24
  function of, 449
CHGMSGD2 command, 116
CHGMSGD (Change Message Description) command, 116
CHGPFM (Change Physical File Member) command, 224
CHGPGM (Change Program) command, 407, 415-416
  OPTIMIZE parameter, 416
  program size and, 422-423
  RMVOBS parameter, 415
  USEADPAUT parameter, 390-393, 416, 417
    *NO value, 443
  USRPRF parameter, 416, 417
    *USER value, 388
CHGPRTF (Change Print File) command, 93
  MAXRCDS parameter, 220
CHGSPLFA (Change Spooled File Attributes) command, 221
  using, 471
CHGSYSLIBL command, authorization for, 440
CHGVAR command, 160-161, 183
  message ID MCH3601 and, 161
CHKACTOBJ command, 197-199
  *DEVD objects and, 198
  *LIB objects and, 198
  database files and, 198
  exercise, 215
  function, 197
  for locking/unlocking objects, 198
  object types supported by, 198
  PGM objects and, 198
  uses, 199
CHKACTPGM (Check Active Program) command, 194-197
  ALLOCATE keyword, 194
  disadvantage of, 197
  exercises, 207-209
  function of, 194
  in interactive program, 195
  PGM keyword, 195
  uses, 197
  using, 195-196
CHKDAT (Check Date) command, 140
  using, 140
Check list, 520-522
CHKGENERC (Check Generic) command, 263-264
  optional return values, 263
CHKLMTCPB (Check Limited Capability) command, 391-392, 442
  exercise, 454
  security and, 449
CHKOBJ (Check Object) command
  CPP, 32
  errors and, 3
  using, 5
    advantages, 5
  when to use, 5
CHKSYSCND command, 122-123
  uses, 123

using, 122
CL commands. *See* Commands; *specific CL commands*
CLCTIMDIF (Calculate Time Difference) command, 143, 148
uses, 143
Cleanup routine
adding, 85-88
job logs, 96, 101-104
message monitoring in, 78
RMVMSG CLEAR(*ALL) and, 78
standard error-handling routine, 77-78
CLNTAATEMP command, 305
Closing a file, 387
CLPOUTFILE TAA tool, 300, 309
CL Programmer's Guide, 200, 201, 233, 412
CL programs
calling CL programs, 434
calling RPG programs, 434
code functions, 436
database records, high volume and, 434
de-squeezing size of, 424
inquiry message, 18-20
logging, information, 22
parameters, referencing, 433
performance, 431-437
code for improving, 331-432
HLL programs, 436-437
iterative processing and, 432-435
optimizing, 432-435
register usage optimization, 416
replacing RPG programs with, 413
squeezing size of, 422-423
uses, 436
variable scanning and, 433-434
variable testing in, 433
See also Programs; RPG programs
CLPSUBR tool, 169, 175
using, 169
CLR command, creating, 252
CLRLIB (Clear Library) command, 105
CLROUTQ command, 252-253
CLRPFM (Clear Physical File Member) command, 224, 389
error conditions on, 7
execution, before, 7-8
overrides and, 322
CMDLINE TAA tool, 290-291
functioning of, 290-291
menu support, 291
message handling and, 291-292
using, 296
CMD statement, PROMPT parameter, 251
CMPDAT (Compare Date) command, 139-140, 144
return values, 139
using, 140
CMPDTA parameter
with CPYF command, 10
function of, 9-10
with MONMSG command, 9-10
CNFRMVM command, 485
using, 491
Command definition object (CDO), 250
illustrated, 251
Command definition statements, 250
ELEM, 265
for lists, 264
parts of, 250
source code for, 267
Command entry display, 478
accessing, 478
Command interfaces, 249
advantages, 249
See also Commands
Command lines
processing, 290-291
requesting, 290
using, API, 293
Command processing program. *See* CPP
Command prompt
for CPYF command, 262
display, 251
PARM statements and, 254
QUAL statements and, 254
text, 251
See also Commands
Command prompter, 297
OPNQRYF QRYSLT parameter and, 344-345
SNDPGMMSG MSG parameter and, 38
Commands
APIs and, 465
building, from string, 462
entering, via SEU, 493
execution time, long, 431
monitoring, 3
overhead, heavy, 431-432
TAA, standards, 251
user-written, 249-268
constants in, 266-267
CPP name qualification, 446
decimal and character parameters, 259
defined, 250-251
disadvantages, 249-250
duplicating standard command source, 260
examples, 267, 510
expressions and, 261
generic names and, 263-264
identifying, 251, 517
lists and, 264-266
multiple, 266
with no parameters, 252-253
relational and range checking, 260
required parameters (MIN parameter), 257-258
restricted list of values, 259-260
return variables and, 264
simple object name as parameter, 253-254
special value conversion in, 262-263
when not to use, 249
writing, 250-260
See also Command prompter
Comments, 518
Commitment control, 228
Compiler listing, 493-494
Completion messages, 23-26
CPYF, 66
decimal value in, 25-26
example, 25
exercise, 486, 488
function name in, 25
OPNQRYF, 352
receiving, 48-49
removing, 51
resending, 53
exercise, 64-65

sending, 24-25
simple, 38-39
using a count in, 40
variable name in, 25
See also Messages
CPA0701, 12
default, 12
'D' response, 14
low-level, 12-13
responses to, 12
second-level text, 12
CPA5305, 225
CPC1221, 55
CPC2191, 105
CPC2955, 56
CPF0000, 6-9, 97
with CLRPFM command, 8
good use of, 8-9
misuse, 6-8
monitoring for, 6-9
at command level, 8
at program level, 8-9
without EXEC parameter, 7
CPF0864, 271-272, 299, 307-308
CPF1002, 202
CPF1005, 203
CPF1085, 202
CPF1164, 105
CPF1240, 36, 475
CPF1241, 36, 475
CPF1392, 118
CPF4174, 342
CPF4520, 342
CPF9898, 40, 42, 80, 198
MSGDTA parameter and, 29
uses, 29, 30
using, 28-29
when not to use, 29-30
CPI9801, 34, 35
CPP, 250
CHKOBJ, 32
CL commands not calling, 431
DLTDTAARA, 106-107, 108
name qualification, 446
passing parameters from commands to, 181
for RTV commands, 160-161
user-written commands and, 249
CPROBJ (Compress Object) command, 407, 417
PGMOPT parameter, 417
program size and, 422-423
CPYCHGMBR (Copy Changed Member) command, 482-484
CPYCL (Copy CL) command, 170, 176
against same source, 173
CRTCPYCL command and, 174
eliminating special comments and, 174
"end of file" and, 172
options, 173
temporary member split, 172
using, 172-173
CPYCL (Copy CL) TAA tool, 170-174
commands, 170
functioning of, 171-173
STRCPYCL comment, 171-174
uses, 170
using, 176-179
See also CPYCL (Copy CL) command; CRTCPYCL command; Subroutines
CPYF (Copy File) command, 223
*NOCHK and, 306
CMPDTA parameter, 10
command prompt, 262
completion message, 66
DUPSPLF2 and, 471
error-handling of, 10
escape messages for, 4
failure, 10
FMTOPT(*MAP) parameter, 301
OPNQRYF command and, 341
CPYFRMOUTQ command, 96
CPYFRMQRYF (Copy From Query File) command, 341-342
CRTFILE(*YES) parameter, 368
exercise, 368-369
CPYGENSRC (Copy Generic Source) command, 482
CPYJOBLOG (Copy Job Log) command, 356-357
benefits, 357
exercise, 366-367
using, 356
CPYSPLF (Copy Spool File) command, 272
to database file, 61
using, 471
CPYSRCF (Copy Source File) command, 169, 223, 227, 482
Cross-reference techniques, 503-512
CRTCLPGM (Create CL Program) command, 407, 410-415
ALWRTVSRC parameter, 411-412
*NO value, 412, 413, 446
*YES value, 412
disk space and, 412
function, 411
AUT parameter, 413
LOG parameter, 410-411
*JOB value, 411
*NO value, 411, 446
*YES value, 411
function of, 410-411
placing parameters in the source, 421
program size and, 422-423
REPLACE parameter, 412-414
*NO value, 412, 413, 414
*YES value, 412, 413-414
TGTRLS parameter, 412
USRPRF parameter, 410, 413, 417
*OWNER value, 410
*USER value, 410
See also Program object
CRTCMD (Create Command) command, 252
PGM parameter, 252, 253
CRTCPYCL command, 170, 176
CPYCL command and, 174
function of, 173-174
CRTMNU (Create Menu) command, 285
&MENUL parameter, 288
&MENU parameter, 288
PGM parameter, 288
TYPE parameter, 285-286
*DSPF value, 285-286
*PGM value, 286
*UIM value, 286
CRTPRTPGM command, 306, 355-356, 374-376, 509
advantages, 374-375
exercise, 358-361, 379-382
function of, 374
OPNQRYF and, 374
PRTDBF and, 374-376
uses, 376

using, 375
See also PRTDBF command
CRTRPGPGM command, IGNDEC ERR parameter, 418
CRTTAATOOL command, 530-533, 541
CRTUSRPRF command, 439
LMTCPB parameter, 442
CRTUSRSPC (Create User Space) TAA tool, 468
CVT commands, 298-299
APIs and, 299
reading tool descriptions for, 298
spooled files and, 299
TAA tool, using, 314-315
CVTDAT (Convert Date) command, 131, 432
*CYMD date format and, 132
abuse of, 133, 435
for date conversion, 133
TOSEP parameter, 133
using, 133
CVTDSKSTS command, 314-315
CVTMSGF command, 120
CVTOBJLCK (Convert Object Lock) command, 202, 204
CVTOUTQ command, 299, 314-315
CVTPGMA (Convert Program Attributes) command, 418-419
special RPG values and, 419
uses, 418, 419
CVTQHST TAA tool, 454
CVTSYSSTS (Convert System Status) command, 273

D

Data
displaying, 371-379
extracting, 53-55
masking, 447
Data areas
allocation problems, 220
for indicating jobs in use, 196
updating, 205-206
Database files
access paths for, 337-338
ALCOBJ command and, 204
allocating, 204
all members, 205
changing authority and, 226
changing definition of, 420-421
CHKACTOBJ command and, 198
converting
message file to, 120
to spooled files, 272
deleting, 198
multimember, 227
reading, 271-272
exercise, 281-282
SECURE(*YES) and, 321
See also Logical files; Physical files
Data Management Guide, 317, 322
Data structures
with packed-decimal fields, 187
passing, 186-187
Date, 131-140
ADDDAT command, 138
century support, 134
checking, 140
comparisons, 134, 139
conversion, 133
exercise, 144-148
fields, 135
passing, 182
spelling options from RTVDAT, 137
system values, 131
time stamp, 142
See also Time
Date formats, 131-133
choosing, 134-135
CYYMMDD, 135-136
advantages, 135-136
disadvantages, 136
in packed format, 136
favorite, 135-136
QDATE, 132
RTVSYSVAL and, 132
SQL, 134
See also Date
DCLF command, 269, 270
accessing display file, 287
outfiles and, 297, 299
program stacks and, 387
using, without processing file, 270
DDS
DATFMT keyword in, 134, 135
using, 135
indicators for command keys in, 287
printer files and, 326
retrieving source, 305, 316
SQL date formats in, 134
De-allocation, 75
object, 78
Debugging, 493-497
authorization for, 443, 450-452
BKP tool, 495, 498
compiler listing and, 493-494
display job menu, 495
DO groups, 494, 498, 518
large program variables, 496
logic checking and, 494
program dump and, 495
speeding, 493
system debug facility and, 495-496
test statements and, 496-497
Device files
allocating, 204
SECURE(*NO) and, 321
DFU, OPNQRYF command and, 341
Diagnostic messages
multiple, 73
processing, 73
resending, 71
sending, 73
See also Messages
Display files, 270, 285-296
allocation problems, 220
CL and, 285
HLL program and, 285
menus, using, 294-295
sending messages and, 287-288
See also Files
Display Program Messages display, 235
Displaying data, 371-405
DSPDB command, 371, 377
DSPDBF command, 373, 379
CRTPRTPGM command, 374, 379
DLCDBF (De-allocate Data Base File) command, 205
DLCOBJ (De-allocate Object) command, 202-203
completion messages and, 203
escape messages and, 203
exercise, 210-214

uses, 202
using, 203
DLCTMPMBR command, 304
DLTCMDSRC TAA tool, 485
DLTDTAARA (Delete Data Area) command, 106
completion message and, 107
CPP, 106-107, 108
running, 108
DLTF (Delete File) command, 198
DLTFSRC TAA tool, 485
DLTOLDQRPL TAA tool, 415
DLTPGMSRC TAA tool, 485
DLTSPLF command, 391
DLYCMD command, 231-232
uses, 231
DMPCLPGM (Dump CL Program) command, 76, 495
using, 79-80
Documentation
comments, 518
external, 519
DO groups, 494-498
DO logic, negative, 11
DSCJOB (Disconnect Job) command, 402
DSPAUDLOG (Display Audit Log) command, 447
security Level 40 and, 454
DSPCLPDO (Display CLP DO Groups) TAA tool, 494
uses, 498
using, 498
DSP commands, OUTPUT parameter emulation, 155
DSPCRSREF command, 510-512
DSPDBD (Display Data Base Definition) command, 356
DSPDB (Display Data Base) command, 371-373
exercise, 377-378
prompt, 372
sample output, 372
uses, 373
using, 371
DSPDBF command, 314-315, 373-374, 454
exercise, 379
parameters, 373
prompt, 373
sample output, 374
uses, 374
using, 373
DSPFD (Display File Description) command, 93, 298
model files and, 298
reading outfile from, 308
TYPE parameter
*MBRLIST value, 298
*MBR value, 298
using, outfile, 311-313
DSPFFD command, 297
uses, 302
DSPJOB command, 495
DSPJOBLOG (Display Job Log) command, 98
to spooled file, 61
DSPJRN (Display Journal) command
outfile, 305-306
outfile fields, 302
journal entry, 305
output journal entry, 305-306
using, 306
DSPLSTCHG (Display Last Change) command, 480
display, 481
using, 488
DSPMSGD (Display Message Description) command, 114
menu, 54
QCPFMSG default and, 114
DSPMSGDTA TAA tool, 55
using, 56
DSPMSGTXT (Display Message Text) command, 114-115
function of, 114
DSPOBJD (Display Object Description) command, 299
for finding "MSGF" object types, 114
DSPPFM command
DSPDB TAA tool vs., 377
OPNQRYF command and, 341
source data and, 223
use of, 371
DSPPGM (Display Program) command, 418
values, 418
DSPPGMREF (Display Program References) command, 503, 508-512
disadvantages, 503-504
example, 509
outfile fields, 508-509
using, 508
DSPPWD (Display Passwords) command, 448-449
DSPRPGIGN TAA tool, 418
DSPSECRVW (Display Security Review) command, 448
DSPSRCMBR command, 480
DSPTAACMD command, 314-315, 539, 544
DSPTAAMBR command, 480, 539, 545
DSPTAATOOL command, 298, 314-315, 447, 527, 542
DSPUSRAUT (Display User Authority) command, 448
DSPUSRSPC TAA tool, 469
DSQPGMSIZ (De-Squeeze Program Size) command, 424
DUPMSGD (Duplicate Message Description) command, 115, 116
TOID parameter, 115
DUPSPLF TAA tool, 221, 471-472
DUPSPLF2 command, 221, 471-472
DUPSPLF command, 221, 471
DUPSRC (Duplicate Source) command, 482
using, 491
DUPSTDSRC (Duplicate Standard Source) command, 69-70, 82
creating menus with, 289-290
exercise, 207
source type *MNUC, 289, 290, 292
source type *MNUD, 289, 290, 292
using, 169, 260, 516

E

EDTOBJAUT (Edit Object Authority) command, 226
EDTVAR (Edit Variable) command, 25, 144, 175, 216, 311
existence of, 40
function, 25
using, 26
ELSE command, 518
Ending a CL program, 385
ENDPGM command, 385
using, 385

ENDRQS (End Request) command, 387, 402
Environments
 capturing, 159
 setting up, 473-485
Error conditions
 for application, 1
 from command entry display, 16-18
 on CLRPFM command, 7
 standard routine, important aspects of, 71-73
 for system, 1
 testing, 3
 See also Monitoring
Error-handling
 from command entry display, 16-18
 logic, 14-15
 in production applications, 80-81
  standard routine vs., 81
  user decisions and, 80
 recovery routine and, 76-77
 standard routine, 69-92
  advantages, 69
  cleanup routine, 77-78, 85-88
  copying, 70
  de-allocation and, 75
  deleting objects and, 75
  duplicating, 69-70
  error switch testing, 78
  external failures and, 76
  feedback and, 75-76
  functioning of, 71-75
  loop, 72
  modifying, 75-76
  not included in, 76-77
  production application routine vs., 81
  program dump, 76, 79-80, 89-92
  program structure, 70-71
  removing messages and, 77
  STDERR1 label, 71-72
  STDERR2 label, 72, 74
  STDERR3 label, 75
  template, 70
  using, 82-84
 strategy, 2
Error messages, 181
Errors
 CHKOBJ command and, 3
 coding for, 2
 unexpected, 5
 See also Error-handling
Escape messages, 23, 26-33
 ALCOBJ command and, 8, 203
 for CPYF command, 4
 DLCOBJ command and, 203
 ending program and, 385
 IDs, 2
  list of, 3
 impromptu messages and, 28
 monitoring for, 2-3
  CPF0001, 4
  CPF9801, 5
 not monitoring, 3-5
 to program message queue, 27
 receiving, 49
 removing, 51
 resending, 32-33
  code for, 51
  exercise, 63-64
 sending, 26-33
  exercise, 40-42
  SNDPGMMSG command, 27
  with variables, 42-43
 text, 28
  library name in, 30-31
  member name in, 31-32
 unmonitored, 71
 See also CPF0000; CPF9898; Messages
Expressions, 261
 as parameter values, 261
External message queues
 clearing, 236
 creating, 34
 inquiry message to, 236
 sending messages to, 23
 using, 244-247
 for workstation operator communication, 235-237
EXTLST (Extract List) command, 265-266
 &CURNBR variable, 265-266
 uses, 266
 versions of, 265, 266
Extracting data, receiving messages for, 53-55

F

Feedback, providing, 75-76
Fields
 date, 135
 key, 348-350
File attributes, changing, 317
File processing, 269-283
 restrictions, 269-270
 See also Files
Files
 database
  access paths for, 337-338
  ALCOBJ command and, 204
  allocating, 204, 205
  changing authority and, 226
  CHKACTOBJ command and, 198
  closing, 387
  converting, to spooled files, 272
  deleting, 198
  message files converting to, 120
  multimember, 227
  opening, 271
  random processing, 273
  reading, 271-272, 281-282
  SECURE(*YES) and, 321
  writing to, 274
 DCLF statement, 270
 device
  allocating, 204
  SECURE(*NO) and, 321
 display, 270, 285-296
  allocation problems, 220
  CL and, 285
  HLL program and, 285
  sending messages and, 287-288
 logical
  allocation problem, 222
  ASP, 336
  creating, 335
  MAINT parameter, 335-336
  with no key fields, 271
  specifying, 335-336
 menus, using, 294-295
 message
  converting to database files, 120
  overriding, 116-118
  OVRMSGF specification and, 117
 physical

accessing, 335
allocation problem, 224-225
arrival sequence option, 335
keyed sequence option, 335
SIZE parameter, 225-226
printer
allocation problem, 220-221
DDS and, 326
defining, 326
externally described, 326
printing from a CL program, 275
using unique, 325-326
source, allocation problem, 222-223
spooled
allocation problems, 221
backing up, 96
converting to database file, 272
creating, 95
deleting, 100
duplicating, 471-472
overriding attributes, 326-327
reading, 272-273
SPLRNAME attribute, 326-327
USRDTA attribute, 327
temporary, creating, 437
See also File processing; Outfiles
FMTDTA command, 274-275
for physical sort, 340
sort specifications, 274
FNDSTRPDM (Find String Using PDM) command, 504
FROMRCD parameter, 262

G

Generic names, 263-264
GO ASSIST command, 96
GO command, 289
for accessing CL program, 288-289
for invoking menus, 285-286
using, 294
GOTO command, 167
on MONMSG EXEC parameter, 10
subroutines and, 169
Group jobs, 475-476
Guide to Programming Displays, 286

H

HLL programs
controlling file open in, 324-325
display files and, 285
iterative use of CL function from, 435
OPNQRYF and, 436
passing parameters between, 181
performance, 436-437
QCMDEXC in, 459
See also RPG programs
HLRMVMSG command, 104

I

IF command, 167
subroutines and, 169
ILE (Integrated Language Environment), 167, 383
Impromptu messages, escape messages and, 28
"Include" function, 170
Initial program, 476-477
INQMSGRPY, 12
*DFT value, 12, 14
*SYSRPYL value, 14
saving current value of, 119
setting to original value, 119
Inquiry messages, 12-13
CL program, 18-20
disadvantages, 13
handling, 13-14
modifying, 118-120
See also CPA0701; Messages
Installation, new release, 232
Integrated Language Environment. *See* ILE
Interactive jobs, termination of, 97
Interactive programs, CHKACT PGM command in, 195
INZTAP command, 460-461
Iterative processing, 432-435

J

Job accounting journal, 100
setting up, 101
Job descriptions, 474
JOBDs (Job Descriptions), 474
Job log, 93-112
audit trail, 24
permanent, 100-101
temporary, 99-100
cleaning up, 96, 101-104
exercise, 110-111
RMVMSG CLEAR(*ALL) and, 102-103
RMVMSG PGMQ(*ALLINACT) and, 103-104
defaults, 94
defined, 93
deletion, 100
example, 105-109
PGMA program message queue in, 109
PGMB program message queue in, 109
subprogram invocation in, 108
forcing, 97-99
generation, 93
LOG attribute and, 96-97
messages, minimizing, 102-103
output queue, 93-94
single/separate, 96
partial, 95
displaying, 111-112
program message queue relationship, 94
reading, 24, 105
review, 105-109
spooled, 93
Job queues, single-thread, 473
Job submitter, 36, 46
Jobs
active?, 199-200
with adopted authority, 393-395
default response mode, 120
group, 475-476
interactive, termination of, 97
LOG attribute, 96-97
types of, extracting, 163-164
See also Batch jobs; Job log
Journals, 100
audit, 100
system job accounting, 100
setting up, 101

K

Keyed access path, 337
Key fields, OPNQRYF command and, 348-350
KEYVAR parameter, 56-57
RCVMSG command, 57
SNDPGMMSG command, 56

using, 57

L

Last message, 48
Level 40 security, 441
Libraries
current, 445
in front of QSYS, 440
list function, 30-31
name in message text, 30-31
personal, 473
product, 445
program objects in, 409
qualified names, 445
Library list
allocation problems, 222
controlling, 445
function, 30-31
objects on, 31
retrieving, 458
security, 444
See also Libraries
Library objects, 409-410
contents of, 409
size of, 409
See also Libraries
List APIs, 467-469
list entries, 467
user space, 467-468
working with, 468, 469
Local data area (LDA), 186
Locks, 201
*EXCL, 201, 204, 223
*EXCLRD, 223
*SHRNUP, 203, 220
*SHRRD, 204, 222, 223, 224, 229
*SHRUPD, 222, 224
data area, 205-206
device file object, 204
function of, 219
object types not supported, 201
programs, 193, 207
releasing, 202-203
types of, 201
unobtained, 202
LOG attribute, 96-97
LOGCL TAA tool, 18, 22, 494
Logging, 494
function, 22
job descriptions and, 474
See also Job log
Logical files
allocation problem, 222
ASP, 336
creating, 335
MAINT parameter, 335-336
*DLY value, 336
*IMMED value, 335-336
*REBLD value, 336
with no key fields, 271
specifying, 335-336
See also Database files; Files; Physical files
Logic checking, 494

M

MCH3601, 161
Members, name in message text, 31-32
Menus, 285-289
CL code for, 286-287
command line processing, 290-291
creating, 285-290
with CRTMNU command, 285-289
with DUPSTDSRC TAA tool, 289-290
GO command to access CL program, 288-289
message handling and, 291-292
program message queue subfile and, 291-292
SDA and, 286
securing, 441-443
simple, 286-288
using display file, 294-295
See also CRTMNU (Create Menu) command
Message data, 54
accessing, 66-67
Message description, 53
Message files
converting to database files, 120
DSPMSGTXT command, 114
overriding, 116-118
OVRMSGF specification and, 117
See also Files
Message handling
advanced topics, 56-62
See also Messages
Message key field, 56-57
Message queues
external, 23
clearing, 236
creating, 34
inquiry message to, 236
using, 244-247
for workstation operator communication, 235-237
FIFO order processing, 58
program, 23, 47
escape messages to, 27
illustrated, 47
job log relationship with, 94
old messages and, 58
removing messages from, 50-51, 103-104
subfile, 291-292
QSYSMSG, 122
QSYSOPR, 120-125
reading through, 58
user, 23
Messages
automatic responses, 118
binary format and, 55-56
bubbling up, 51, 53
completion, 23-26
decimal value in, 25-26
example, 25
exercise, 486, 488
function name in, 25
OPNQRYF, 352
receiving, 48-49
removing, 51
resending, 32, 53, 64-65
return types, 59
sending, 24-25
simple, 38-39
using a count in, 40
variable name in, 25
diagnostic
multiple, 73
processing of, 73
resending, 71
sending, 73
duplicating, 115
error, 181
escape, 23, 26-33
ALCOBJ command and, 203
DLCOBJ command and, 203
ending program and, 385
impromptu messages and, 28
monitoring for, 2-3

to program message queue, 27
removing, 51
resending, 32-33, 51, 63-64
sending, 26-33, 40-43
text, 28, 30-32
unmonitored, 71
finding, 114
handling, at workstation, 474-475
impromptu, 28, 35
inquiry, 12-13
CL program, 18-20
disadvantages, 13
handling, 13-14
modifying, 118-120
menu, 291-292
modifying, 117-118
inquiry, 118-120
monitoring for, 1-22
in cleanup routine, 78
exercise, 21-22
generic range of, 9
nonaccessible, 60-62
old vs. new, 58
processing, 58
receiving, 47-67
by message type, 49-50
to extract data, 53-55
last, 48-49
process of, 48-56
to remove them, 50-51
to resend them, 51-52
unable to, 60-62
removing, 77, 101-104
with RCVMSG command, 101
with RMVMSG command, 101
request, 126-130
manipulating, 128
returning commands as, 128-130
responding automatically to, 118-120
sending, 23-46
to active users, 125-126
completion, 24-25
escape, 26-33
to job submitter, 36-37, 46
to message queue, 99
overhead and, 24
status, 34-36, 43-44
status, 23, 34-36
blank, 34
clearing, 34
displaying, 34
impromptu messages and, 35
preventing display of, 36
removing, 35
sending, 34-36, 43-44
shutting off, 44-45
using, 35
system, capturing, 121-123
in TAATOOL library, 30
text, changing, 115-116
See also specific messages
Message techniques, 113-130
Monitoring
for CPF0000, 6-9
for CPF0001, 4
for CPF9801, 5
for messages, 1-22
in cleanup routine, 78
escape, 2-3
exercise, 21-22
for generic range of, 9
for positive condition, 10-11
program-level, 11-12
EXEC parameter and, 11
Monitor message process, 15
MONMSG (Monitor Message) command, 1
CL commands monitored for, 3
CL program inquiry message, 12, 18
CMPDTA parameter, 9-10
CPF0000, 6-8
EXEC parameter, 10
in program-level monitoring, 11
function of, 2
generic range, 9
message IDs and, 5
messages you shouldn't monitor for, 5
MSGID parameter, 71
MSGTYPE(*EXCP) and, 49-50
multiple, 6
negative logic, 10-11
at program-level, 11-12, 72
MOVCHRDEC command, 186-187
MOVM (Move Member) TAA tool, 485
MSGCTL command, 124-125, 225
function of, 124
MSGID return variable, 59

N

New release, installing, 232

O

Object Information Repository, 409
Objects, allocating, 193-217
database files, 204
all members of, 205
device files and, 204
manually, 200-205
problems, 219-232
data areas, 220
display files, 220
library lists, 222
logical files, 222
physical files, 224-225
printer files, 220-221
programs, 221-222
spooled files, 221
user profiles, 222
restore commands and, 227
SAV commands and, 227
source files, 222-223
system defaults, 193
what you can/cannot do with, 201
Objects
controlling, 193
de-allocating, 78
deleting, 75
"IF active" test, 193
library, 409-410
contents of, 409
size of, 409
locking, 198
locks, 201
data area, 205-206
function of, 219
object types not supported, 201
releasing, 202-203
types of, 201
program, 407-424
qualifying, 445
types of, allocation problems with, 219-226
unlocking, 198

in use, 197-199
See also Objects, allocating
Open data path (ODP), 342
Opening a file with OVR, 326
Operational Assistant
Attention key function, 442
job log defaults and, 94
OPNQRYF command, 128, 338-339, 341-369
access paths and, 338-339, 350
choosing best, 351
searching for, 351
ALWCPYDTA(*OPTIMIZE) parameter, 340, 351, 352
calling program second time and, 343
calling program with incorrect name/parameter, 343
from command entry display, 342-343
exercise, 358-361
complexity, 341
CPYFRMQRYF command, 370
CPYJOBLOG tool, 358, 368
CRTPRTPGM tool, 357, 360
debug mode, 352
errors, 342-343
feedback, 354
FILE parameter, 351
front-end processing, 341
full opens and, 350
HLL programs and, 436
interactive, 366
JORDER(*FILE) parameter, 351
key fields, 348-350
ascending order, 349
descending order, 349
multiple, 349
as variables, 39
in record format being queried, 349
variable, 349
KEYFLD parameter, 349-350
elements, 349
MAPFLD parameter, 348
defining new field on, 350
prompting for, 348
message feedback, 352
ODP, 342
reading contents of, 369
OPTALLAP(*YES) parameter, 351
performance, 338-339, 350-352, 434, 436
for physical sort, 340, 351
points to remember about, 341-342
print programs and, 355-356
prompting for, 346
QRYF tool, 354-357
QRYSLT parameter, 343-348
apostrophes and, 343
command prompter and, 344-345
complex selection statements, 347-348
concatenation for, 345-346
decimal variable and, 346-347
double quote marks and, 345
function of, 343
parenthesis and, 347-348
size, 343
using, 344-348
records, reading and, 434
response time and, 350
running against production version, 351
shared file requirement, 341-342
system functions not working with, 341
temporary files and, 351
typical errors, 344
using
in CL program, 362-363
from command entry display, 342-343, 358-361
key fields, 348-350
See also CPYJOBLOG command; CRTPRTPGM tool; QRYF (Query File) tool
OR TAA tool, 447
exercise, 452-453
Outfiles, 297-316
ALCTMPMBR tool, 303
APIs vs., 297
CLPOUTFILE tool, 300
coding, 297-298
copying to permanent files, 301
creating, 358-361
creating/reading, in same program, 299-300
DCLF command and, 299
defaults, 301
DSPFD, using, 311-313
DSPJRN, 305-306
DSPxxx command and, 299
fields in, 302
names, 302
format consistency, 301
information updates and, 301
with LVLCHK parameter
*NO value, 300-301
*YES value, 301
model files, 297-298
MONMSG MSGID(CPF0864) command and, 299
names of, 297-298
OPNQRYF and, 302
OUTMBR parameter and, 301
OVRxxx command and, 299
SECURE(*YES) parameter, 301-302
processing, 307
RCVF command and, 299
requesting, 301
required commands for, 299
reusing, 306-308
system commands supporting, 298
using, 300
exercise, 309-311
when to create, 297
See also Files
OUTPUT parameter, 155
Output queues
cleaning up, 94
job log, 93-94
single/separate, 96
keeping, clean, 478-479
personal, 473
Overrides, 317-334
automatic removal of, 318
cascading and, 322-323
CLRPFM and, 322
commands ignoring, 322
exercises, 328-334
to different file, 333-334
to QPRINT at different levels, 330-333
to same file, 328-330
functions of, 317
merging rule, 320
occurrence of, 317-318
on AS/400, 325-326
precedence rule, 319-320

programs in program stacks and, 319
program stacks and, 387
second, in program, 318-319
working with, 317-324
Overriding
message file, 116-118
spooled file attributes, 326-327
OVRDBF command, 273
POSITION parameter, 273
SECURE(*YES) parameter, 301-302
SHARE(*YES) parameter, 341
OVRMSGF (Override Message File) command, 116
message file specification and, 117
using, 117-118
OVRPRTF (Override Print File) command, 95, 98
OVRxxx command
for overriding to different file, 317
SECURE(*NO), 320, 321
default, 322
SECURE(*YES), 320, 321, 446
default, 322
illustrated, 322
understanding, 321
specifying, 320

P

Parameter list
changing programs and, 414
coding, 181
on SBMJOB and CALL commands, 187
Parameters, passing, 181-191
character values and, 182-183
size of, 185
without quotes, 190-191
to CL programs, 185
from command entry line, 182-184
rules, 182-183
from command to CPP, 181
data structures and, 186-187
dates, 182
between HLL programs, 181
large, 187, 188-189
LDA and, 186
longer than 32 bytes, 188-190
methods of, 181-182
number of parameters and, 185
numeric values and, 183
performance, 433
from one program to another, 181
to RPG programs, 185-186
to submitted jobs, 181-182, 184-185, 187
switches, 182, 183
8-byte, 183-184
See also specific parameters
Parameters
expressions as values for, 261
See also Parameter list; Parameters, passing; *specific parameters*
PARM statements
CONSTANT parameter, 266
MIN(1) value, 257
modifying, 254
order of, 181
RANGE parameter, 260
TYPE(*GENERIC) parameter, 263
Passing parameters, 181-191
character values and, 182-183
size of, 185
without quotes, 190-191
to CL program, 185
from command entry line, 182-184
rules, 182-183
from command to CPP, 181
data structures and, 186-187
dates, 182
between HLL programs, 181
large, 187, 188-189
LDA and, 186
longer than 32 bytes, 188-189
methods of, 181-182
number of parameters and, 185-187
numeric values and, 183
from one program to another, 181
to RPG program, 185-186
to submitted jobs, 181-182, 184-185
switches, 182, 183
8-byte, 183-184
See also Parameter list; Parameters
Passwords, 441
See also Security
PDM, 476
command entry display access, 478
command line, 478
FNDSTRPDM command and, 504
PDM User's Guide and Reference, 127
Performance, 431-437
Personal library, 473
Personal output queue, 473
Physical files
accessing, 335
allocation problem, 224-225
arrival sequence option, 335
keyed sequence option, 335
SIZE parameter, 225-226
See also Database files; Files; Logical files
Physical sort, 339-340
methods, 340
OPNQRYF command for, 340, 351
PMTOPR command, 99, 237-240, 402
functioning of, 237
LEN parameter, 238
prompt display, 239
RTNVAR value, 238
using, 238
exercise, 247-248
validity checking, 240
levels, 239
Printer files
allocation problem, 220-221
DDS and, 326
defining, 326
externally described, 326
using unique, 325-326
See also Files
Printing, 275-278
source members, 482
Print programs, 355
creating, 355-356
PRINT tool, 276, 277-278
ACTION parameter, 278
combined with BLDPRTLIN, 280
TITLE parameter, 278

using, 278
Production applications
handling errors in, 80-81
standard routine vs., 81
user decisions and, 80
program dump for, 79-80
Program authority adoption function, 388-390
advantages, 389
disadvantages, 389-390
LMTCPB function and, 391
program stack and, 387
rules, 388
security and, 444-446
submitting a job with adopted authority, 393
USEADPAUT parameter and, 390-393, 416
USRPRF parameter and, 416
See also Authority
Program checklist, 520-522
Program dump, 79-80, 495
adding, 89-92
modifying standard error-handling routine for, 76
Programmers
controlling, 443
environment for, 473-485
Programmer's Menu, 476, 478
Program message queue, 23, 47
escape messages to, 27
illustrated, 47
job log relationship with, 94
old messages and, 58
removing messages from, 50-51, 103-104
subfile, 291-292
Programming: Reference Summary, 2, 152
Program object, 407-424
conceptual view, 409
in libraries, 409
observability, 415
optimizing register usage, 416
printing attributes, 419
replacing, 412
retrieving attributes, 418
of same name, 412
See also Objects; Objects, allocating
Program observability, 407
functions of, 407-408
template of, 408
Program Resolution Monitor (PRM), 407
Programs
active?, 193-197
allocation problems, 221-222
attributes
displaying, 417-418
printing, 419
retrieving, 418-419
break-handling, 121
calling
name of, 113, 446-447
other programs, 383-384
own program, 386
compression alternatives for, 425-426
initial, 476-477
modifying, 407
previous, 27
replacing, 407, 413
request processor, 387-388
creating, 402-405
structure, 519
See also CL programs; RPG programs
Program stack, 383-395
DCLF/RCVF commands and, 387
displaying, 396-397
functioning of, 383-384
illustrated, 384
functions ending and, 386-387
overrides and, 387
program authority adoption function and, 387
returning from a program, 389
USRPRF(*USER) parameter and, 388
See also Programs
Prompting
for library name, 258
for objects, 258
for OPNQRYF command, 346
MAPFLD parameter, 348
selective, 233-235
exercise, 241-244
question mark (?) in, 234
special characters in front of parameters, 234
using, 235
values, 233
PRTCMDUSG (Print Command Usage) command, 508
using, 514
PRTDBF (Print Data Base File) command, 356, 374-376
CRTPRTPGM command and, 374
QRYF command and, 356
sample output, 375
uses, 376
See also CRTPRTPGM command
PRTLIBDTL (Print Library Detail) command, 410, 428
PRTPGMA (Print Program Attributes) TAA tool, 419
PRTPRM (Print Parameters) TAA tool, 419
PRTSECVIL (Print Security Violations) command, 449
exercise, 454-455
PRTSRCF (Print Source File) command, 482
using, 489
PRTSRCSUM (Print Source Summary) command, 480
output sample, 482
using, 489-490
PTFs, dedicated systems and, 232
PWRDWNSYS command, 391

Q

QACGJRN, 100
QADSPOBJ, 297
QAUDJRN, 100
QCMD, 126, 395
security, 442
QCMDCHK, 459-460
parameters, 459
QCMDEXC and, 460-461
use of, 459
using, 460
QCMDEXC, 99, 126, 324-325, 457-459
exercise, 462-463
in HLL programs, 459
inside loop, 434
parameters, 457
performance, 435
QCMDCHK and, 460-461
uses, 457-459

using, 458
QCPFMSG, 48
changing message descriptions and, 117
contents, 114
defaulting to, 114
QDCXLATE, 465
QPGMR authority, 390-391
QPGMSGF, 114
QPJOBLOG file
OUTQ parameter, 93, 95
value, 94-95
QPRINT, 155
QRPLOBJ library, 414, 415
clearing, 414
keeping clean, 415
QRYF command, 128-129, 352-354
entry display, 129
function of, 352, 354
KEYFLD parameter, 354
as totaling function, 356
MBR parameter, 354
prompt, 353
PRTDBF command and, 356
quote marks and, 352
screen, 129
using, 354
exercise, 364
QRYF (Query File) TAA tool, 352-355
exercise, 364
See also BLDQRYSLT command; QRYF command
QSYS library, 52
libraries in front of, 440
QSYSMSG message queue, 122
creating, 122
QSYSOPR message queue
capturing critical messages with, 121-123
managing, 123-125
multiple-person surveillance of, 120-121
QTEMP library, 85
ALCTMPMBR and, 303, 305
cleaning, 105
cleanup messages, 105
deleting from, 8
outfile in, 303
QTIME, 141
9-character time value for, 141
QUAL statements, 254
separate defaults and, 255
using, 255
Queues. *See* External message queues; Job queues; Message queues; Output queues
QUSCMDLN, 290
using, 293
QUSRSPLA, 466
parameter list, 466-467
QUSRTOOL
CRTTAATOOL, 530-533, 541
DSPTAATOOL, 527, 542
examples, 267-268
informal update, 535
just discussion, 525-540
libraries used, 533-534
retrieve commands, 160-161
TAASUMMARY, 528
See also TAA tools

R

RBLDBF (Rebuild Data Base File) command, 421
RCLRSC (Reclaim Resource) command, 342, 343
RCLSTG command, 231
RCVF command, 271, 281
outfiles and, 299
program stacks and, 387
RCVMSG (Receive Message) command, 48
default, 58
function of, 48
KEYVAR parameter, 57, 72
at label STDERR2, 74
loop, 60
MSGDTA parameter, 52, 55, 59
layout, 55
MSGFLIB parameter, 52
MSGID parameter, 52, 59
MSGKEY parameter, 57, 59
MSG parameter, 53, 59
MSGTYPE parameter
*COMP value, 49
*EXCP value, 49, 50, 72
*LAST value, 48, 49
PGMQ parameter, 62
*PRV value, 113
*SAME value, 48
removing messages and, 101
RMV parameter, 33
*NO value, 59, 72
*YES value, 50
RTNTYPE return value and, 58-59, 74
SECLVL parameter, 59
SENDER parameter, 113
SNDMSGFLIB parameter, 52
TOPGMQ parameter, 62
Records
blocked, 302
journaled, 306
Recursive call, 386
Register usage, 416
Removing messages, 101
Request messages, 126-130
manipulating, 128
returning commands as, 128-130
See also Messages
Request processing programs, 387-388
creating, 402-405
Restore commands, allocation and, 227
Restricted state operations, 230-232
defined, 230
Retrieve commands, 151-165
writing your own, 160
RETURN command, 384-385
multiple, 386
using, 385
Return variables
RTV commands and, 151-152
RTVMBRD, 152
RTVOBJD, 153
user-written commands and, 264
RGZPFM command, 224
RMVM command, 336-337
RMVMSG (Remove Message) command, 101, 496
CLEAR parameter, 77, 78, 101
*ALL value, 102-103
PGMQ parameter, 62
*ALLINACT value, 103-104
*PRV value, 104
TOPGMQ parameter, 62
RPG OPEN operation code, 318
RPG programs
to call CL programs, 318
file open in, 324-325
internal attributes, 420

passing print lines to, 276-277
replacing, with CL programs, 413
See also CL programs; HLL programs; Programs
RPLCMD (Replacement Command) command, 253
RPLPGM (Replace Program) command, 174
exercise, 427-428
function of, 420
RPLRBLOBJ (Replace Rebuild Object) command, 421
RSTD keyword, 260
RSTWHLACT (Restore While Active) command, 230
RTNJOBA (Return Job Attributes) command, 159
CAPJOBA command with, 159
RTNTYPE return value, 59-60, 74
codes, 59
RCVMSG command and, 58-59
RTNVAL function, 264
RTVCLSRC (Retrieve CL Source) command, 411
RTVDAT (Retrieve Date) command, 137-138, 144
return variables, 137
using, 137-138
value attributes and, 152
RTVJOBA (Retrieve Job Attribute) command, 113, 151
CHGJOB command with, 158-159
for determining environment, 156
DSP command (OUTPUT) emulation, 155
exercise, 163-164, 209-210
uses, 154
using, 154-155
RTVJOBD TAA tool, 466
RTVJOBSTS (Retrieve Job Status) command, 199-200
using, 200, 209
RTVMBRD (Retrieve Member Description) command, 151
description prompt, 151
MBR(*FIRST) parameter, 152, 154
prompting for, 151-152
retrieving text value on, 152
return variables, 152
RTNMBR parameter, 31, 154
uses, 152
using, 152-154
RTVOBJD (Retrieve Object Description) command, 151
century support and, 134
exercise, 162
return variables, 153
RTNLIB parameter, 31, 153-154
uses, 152-153, 418
using, 152-154
RTVPFSRC (Retrieve Physical File Source) command, 305-306
advantages, 316
using, 316
RTVPGMA (Retrieve Program Attributes) command, 79, 160, 418-419
PGM parameter, 79
special RPG values and, 419
uses, 418, 419
using, 89
RTV (Retrieve) commands, 151-165
CPP for, 160-161
prompting for, 151-152
QUSRTOOL, 160-161
return variables and, 151
writing own, 160-161
See also specific RTV commands
RTVSPLFA TAA tool, 466
RTVSYSVAL (Retrieve System Value) command, 131, 151
date formats and, 132
returning values with, 152
system time and, 141
RTVTIMSTM (Retrieve Time Stamp) command, 142-143, 148
time stamp formats, 143
RTVUSRSPCE (Retrieve User Space Initialization) TAA tool, 469
RTVUSRSPCI (Retrieve User Space Entry) TAA tool, 468
documentation member code, 470-471
RUNQRY (Run Query) command, 371
DSPDBF TAA tool vs., 379
OPNQRYF command and, 341

S

SAVCFG command, 230-231
SAV commands
allocation and, 227
default lock state, 219
SAVWHLACT (Save While Active) option, 227-229
SAVLIB command, ACCPTH(*YES) parameter, 336
SAVSECDTA command, 230-231
SAVSYS command, 230
SAVWHLACT (Save While Active) command, 229-230
uses, 229
SAVWHLACT (Save While Active) function, 227-229
commitment control and, 228
functioning of, 227-229
seize operation, 228
SBMJOB (Submit Job) command, 394-395
avoiding, if in batch, 156
CMD parameter, 181, 184, 188
using, 185
for executing same program, 158
LOG parameter, 93
performance, 437
same parameter list on, 187
SBMPARMS command, 253-254, 413, 421-422
batch program, 421
initial setup, 422
instructions, 422
in replacing programs, 414
uses, 421, 422
SCAN function, 506
Scanning a variable, 433
SCNALLSRC command, 504-505
SCNSRCARC command, 505-506
ARGUMENT parameter, 505
using, 506-507, 513
SCNSRC command, 504
SCNTAATOOL command, 505
SCRAMBLE TAA tool, 447
exercise, 452-453
Security, 439-449
bogus program protection, 444
breaking in and, 439-440
calling program name and, 446-447
controls, 440-441

Level 40, 441
masking data and, 447
menu-level, 441-443
program authority adoption and, 444-446
programmer control and, 443
QCMD, 442
TAA tools, 447-449
See also Passwords
Security officer controls, 440-441
Security Reference, 388
Selection techniques, 335-340
Selective prompting, 233-235
exercise, 241-244
question mark (?) in, 234
special characters in front of parameters, 234
using, 235, 461
values, 233
Sequencing, 335-340
arrival sequence, 335
keyed sequence, 335
one thousand or more records, 352
SETUP program, 476-477
commands, 477
functions, 476-477
SEU
to edit members, 223
entering CL commands via, 493
prompting for OPNQRYF from, 346
split-screen Browse/Copy function, 169
disadvantages of, 170
SIGNOFF command, 385
SNDBRKACT command, 125-126
SNDBRKMSG (Send Break Message) command, 125
SNDJRNE (Send Journal Entry) command, 394
SNDMSGSBM command, 37, 46
SNDPGMMSG (Send Program Message) command, 497
*LIBL, 52
KEYVAR parameter, 56, 130
MSGDTA parameter, 29
MSGID parameter, 28
MSG parameter, 24, 75
command prompter and, 38
MSGTYPE parameter, 24
*COMP value, 24
*ESCAPE value, 40
PGMQ parameter, 62
TOPGMQ parameter, 27, 62
*SAME value, 99
SNDRCVF command, 287
SNDUSRMSG (Send User Message) command, 236-237
DFT keyword, 237
implementation of, 236
lowercase responses and, 236
using, 237, 244
SORTDB TAA tool, 282-283
Sorting, 339-340
physical, 339-340
methods, 340
OPNQRYF command for, 340, 351
specifications, 274
Sort User's Guide and Reference, 274
Source archive, 506-507
Source code
backup, 479
proven, reusing, 169-174
scanning, 504-506
source archive and, 506-507
static, 506-507
subroutine, 169
for TAA commands, 267
working against, 503
Source files, allocation problem, 222-223
Source members
copying complete, 482-484
displaying, 479-480
duplicating, 169, 491
moving, 485
printing, 480, 482, 489
removing, 485, 491
SPLCTL command, 96
Spooled files
allocation problems, 221
backing up, 96
converting to database file, 272
CVTOUTQ tool, 298, 314
creating, 95
deleting, 100
duplicating, 471-472
overriding attributes, 326-327
reading, 272-273
SPLFNAME attribute, 326-327
USRDTA attribute, 327, 333
See also Files
SQZPGMSIZ (Squeeze Program Size) command, 415, 423-424
exercise, 428-429
functioning of, 423
using, 424
SRCARC TAA tool, 173, 227, 230, 505
for picking up changed source members, 411-412
for scanning source, 505
for source backup, 479
uses, 505
Standard error-handling routine, 69-91
advantages, 69
cleanup routine, 77-78
adding, 85-88
copying, 70
de-allocation and, 75
deleting objects and, 75
duplicating, 69-70
error switch testing, 78
external failures and, 76
feedback and, 75-76
functioning of, 71-75
important aspects of, 71-73
loop, 72
modifying, 75-76
not included in, 76-77
production application routine vs., 81
program dump, 76, 79-80
adding, 89-92
program structure, 70-71
recovery routine and, 76-77
removing messages and, 77
STDERR1 label, 71-72
STDERR2 label, 72
RCVMSG at, 74
STDERR3 label, 75
template, 70
using, 82-84
Standard routines, 477-478
Status messages, 23, 34-36
blank, 34
clearing, 34
displaying, 34
impromptu messages and, 35
preventing display of, 36
removing, 35
sending, 34-36

exercise, 43-44
shutting off, 44-45
using, 35
See also Messages
STRCPYCL comments, 171-174
inserting, 171
multiple, 171
STRKEY command, 274
STRMSGCTL command, 124
STSMSG TAA tool, 36, 474-475, 486
using, 475
Subfiles, 270
Submitting a job with adopted authority, 393
Submitter of a job, 36, 46
Subprograms, 167
Subroutines, 167-179
CLPSUBR tool, 169, 175
defined, 167
IF/GOTO commands and, 169
structure for, 168
subprograms vs., 167
typical approach to, 167-169
using, 175-176
See also CPYCL (Copy CL) tool
Subsystems, authority restriction for, 441
Switches
8-byte, 183-184
passing, 182, 183
System date. *See* Date; Date formats
System debug facility, 495-496
System errors, 1
System functions, 226-232
System messages, capturing, 121-123
System Programmer's Interface Reference, 114, 465, 467, 507
System time. *See* Time
System values
date, 131
time, 141

T

TAAATNAC, 487
TAAMSGDC, 486
TAASPLFC, 466-467
TAATOOL library, 30
messages in, 30
TAA tools, 25
ADDDAT, 138-139, 144
ADDDTAARA, 206, 216-217
ALCDBF, 205
ALCTMPMBR, 298, 300, 303-305, 309, 437
ATNPGM, 475-476, 487-488
BKP, 190, 495-496, 498-502
BLDCALL, 156-158, 187
BLDPRTIN, 278-280
BRKMSGQN, 121
CAPJOBA, 159
CHGBIGPARM, 187
CHGLIBOWN, 24, 449
CHGMSGD2, 116
CHKACTOBJ, 197-199, 215
CHKACTPGM, 194-197, 207-209
CHKDAT, 140
CHKGENERC, 263-264
CHKLMTCPB, 391-392, 442, 449, 454
CHKSYSCND, 122-123
CLCTIMDIF, 143, 148
CLNTAATEMP, 305
CLPOUTFILE, 300, 309
CLPSUBR, 169, 175
CMDLINE, 290-292, 296
CMPDAT, 139-140, 144
CNFRMVM, 485, 491
CPYCHGMBR, 482-484
CPYCL, 170-174, 176-179
CPYFRMOUTQ, 96
CPYGENSRC, 482, 484
CPYJOBLOG, 356-357, 366-367
CRTPRTPGM, 306, 355-356, 358, 374-376, 379-382, 509
CRTTAATOOL, 530-533, 541
CRTUSRSPC, 468
CVT commands, 298-299, 314-315
CVTDSKSTS, 314-315
CVTMSGF, 120
CVTOBJLCK, 202, 204
CVTOUTQ, 299, 314-315
CVTPGMA, 418-419
CVTQHST, 454
DLCDBF, 205
DLCTMPMBR, 304
DLTCMDSRC, 485
DLTFSRC, 485
DLTOLDQRPL, 415
DLTPGMSRC, 485
DLYCMD, 232
DSPAUDLOG, 447
DSPCLPDO, 494, 498
DSPDB, 371-373, 377-378
DSPDBF, 314-315, 368, 373-374, 379, 454
DSPECRVW, 448
DSPLSTCHG, 480-481, 488
DSPMSGDTA, 55, 56, 66
DSPMSGTXT, 114-115
DSPPWD, 448-449
DSPRPGIGN, 418
DSPSRCMBR, 480
DSPTAACMD, 314, 538-539, 544
DSPTAAMBR, 480, 539, 545
DSPTAATOOL, 298, 314-315, 447, 527, 542
DSPUSRAUT, 448
DSPUSRSPC, 469
DSQPGMSIZ, 424
DUPMSSGD, 115, 116
DUPSPLF, 221, 471-472
DUPSRC, 482, 483, 491
DUPSTDSRC, 69-70, 82, 169, 207, 260, 289-290, 292
EDTVAR, 25-26, 40, 66, 144, 175, 216, 311
EXTLST, 265-266
HLRMVMSG, 104
LOGCL, 18, 22, 494
message IDs, 30
MOVCHRDEC, 186-187
MOVM, 485
MSGCTL, 124-125, 225-226
OR, 447, 452-453
OUTPUT parameter support, 155
PMTOPR, 99, 237-240, 247-248, 402
PRINT, 276, 277-278
PRTDBF, 356, 374-376
PRTLIBDTL, 410, 428
PRTPGMA, 419
PRTPRM, 419
PRTSECVIL, 449, 454-455
PRTSRCF, 482, 489
PRTSRCSUM, 480-482, 489-490
QRYF, 128-129, 352-355, 364
RBLDBF, 421
RPLCMD, 253
RPLPGM, 174, 420, 427-428
RTVDAT, 137-138, 144

RTVJOBD, 466
RTVJOBSTS, 199-200, 209-210
RTVPFSRC, 305-306, 316
RTVPGMA, 79, 89, 160, 418-419
RTVSPLFA, 466
RTVTIMSTM, 142-143, 148
RTVUSRSPCE, 469
RTVUSRSPCI, 468, 470-471
for saving while active, 229-230
SAVWHLACT, 229-230
SBMPARMS, 253-254, 413, 421-422
SCNALLSRC, 504-505
SCNSRC, 504, 513
SCNTAATOOL, 505
SCRAMBLE, 447, 452-453
security, 447-449
SNDBRKACT, 125-126
SORTDB, 282-283
source code for, 267
SPLCTL, 96
SQZPGMSIZ, 415, 423-424, 428-429
SRCARC, 173, 227, 230, 411, 479, 505
STRKEY, 274
STRMSGCTL, 124
STSMSG, 36, 474-475, 486
TAASUMMARY, 528-530
WRTDBF, 269, 307
WRTSRC, 269, 274-275, 282-283
Temporary files, creating, 437
Testing approach, 519
Test statements, 496-497
examples, 496
using, 497
TFRCTL (Transfer Control) command, 126, 384-385
uses, 384
using, 384
Time, 141-143
audit trail and, 142
calculating differences, 143
exercise, 148-150
in milliseconds, 141
system values, 141
time stamp formats, 143
See also Date

U

USEADPAUT parameter, 390
User profiles, 476
allocation problems, 222
parameters, 476
SETUP program, 476-477
User spaces, 467-468
displaying contents of, 469
illustrated for list, 468
User-written commands, 249-268
command prompt text, 251
constants in, 266-267
CPP name qualification, 446
decimal and character parameters, 259
defined, 250-251
disadvantages, 249-250
duplicating standard command source, 260
expressions and, 261
generic names and, 263-264
identifying, 251
lists and, 264-266
multiple, 266
with no parameters, 252-253
object name as parameter, 253-254
relational and range checking, 260
required parameters (MIN parameter), 257-258
restricted list of values, 259-260
return variables and, 264
special value conversion, 262-263
special values for names, 258-259
using qualified names, 254-257
when not to use, 249
writing, 250-260
See also Command definition statements

V

VALUE keyword, 260
Variables
decimal, 434
odd-length, 434
scanning, 433-434
testing, 433

W

Work Management Guide, 100, 122, 152, 442
Workstation operator
communicating with, 233-248
controlling, entry, 234
WRITE statements, 326
WRKMSGD command, 115, 119
WRKOBJLCK (Work with Object Locks) command, 202
WRKOUTQ command, 390-391
CHGPGM and, 392
display command line, 391
WRKSPLF command, USRDTA parameter, 327
WRKSYSSTS (Work with System Status) command, 272
WRTDBF command, 269
ACTION(*WRTCLOSE) parameter, 307
WRTSRC command, 269, 274-275
exercise, 282-283
uses, 275
using, 275

Also Published by ***NEWS 3X/400***

APPLICATION DEVELOPER'S HANDBOOK FOR THE AS/400

*Edited by Mike Otey, a **NEWS 3X/400** technical editor*

The handbook explains how to effectively use the AS/400 to build reliable, flexible and efficient business applications. It serves as a guide for incorporating features such as commitment control into existing applications and it provides both step-by-step instructions and handy reference material. Contains RPG/400 and CL coding examples and tips. the *Application Developer's Handbook* is an easy-to-understand reference that can be used in all phases of the application development process. Includes diskette.

800 pages, 49 chapters, 7"x9"

CONTENTS: Historical Perspective • AS/400 Architecture • Security Concepts • Object Authorization • OS/400 Security exposures • User Profiles • Library Standards • Work Management • Controlling Output • Journal Management • Commitment Control • Job Accounting • Message Handling • Disk Space Management • Physical File Structure • Logical File Structure • File Overrides • File Sharing • Database Normalization • Relational Database Principles • Join Logical Files • Using OPNQRYF • SQL Embedded Statements • Controlling Object Locks • Concurrent File Updating • Creating Commands • Command Principles • Validity Checking Programs • Return Variables • Designing Commands • CL Programming Style • User Interface Design • Creating Standard AS/400 Panels • Virtual Subfiles • Group Jobs • UIM Help for Commands • Efficient Workstation Programming • Windows with DDS • Subfile Record Retrieval • Side-by-Side Subfiles • UIM Help for Programs • Using PDM • Customizing PDM • CL Programming Techniques • CL Programming Style • RPG Programming Style • COBOL Programming Style • Using the Integrated Debugger • Appendices (QUSRTOOL, API's, The Complete CVTOUTQ Command)

POWER TOOLS FOR THE AS/400

*Edited by Dan Riehl, a **NEWS 3X/400** technical editor*

This one easy-to-use source unlocks the secrets of time-saving shortcuts, gives you solutions and tips from the experts. Edited for professionals, all the best AS/400 tips and techniques are conveniently organized, indexed, and cross-referenced, with diskette containing all programming code.

713 pages, 24 chapters, 7"x9"

CONTENTS: HLL Tips • The OPNQRYF Command • String Manipulation • Display Files • Data Files • Data Areas • Data Queues • Messages • Graphics • Debugging • Documentation • System Configuration • Group Jobs • Managing Output Queues • Working with Objects • Change Management • Managing Resources • Disaster Recovery • Security • Job Accounting • PC Support • OfficeVision/400 • Communications • System Programming • Appendices

C FOR RPG PROGRAMMERS

*By Jennifer Hamilton, **NEWS 3X/400** author*

Expand your RPG knowledge to include the currently demanded C programming skills. Because this book is written from the perspective of an RPG programmer, you can easily adapt to C without returning to the basics. *C for RPG Programmers* includes side-by-side coding examples written in both C and RPG to aid comprehension and understanding, clear identification of unique C constructs, and a comparison of RPG opcodes to equivalent C concepts. Also, both the novice and experienced C programmer will benefit from the many tips and examples covering the use of C/400.

250 pages, 23 chapters, 7"x9"

CONTENTS: Overview • Data Types • Expressions • Statements • Arrays • Structures & Unions • Functions, Scope, and Storage Class • Separate Compilation and Linkage • Parameter Passing • Pointers • Pointer Arithmetic • Using Pointers • The Preprocessor • Type Conversions and Definitions • Stream I/O • Error Handling • Dynamic Storage Allocation • Recursion • Programming Style • The Extended Program Model • Interlanguage Calls • C/400 File I/O • System C/400

COMMON-SENSE C
Advice and Warnings for C and C++ Programmers

*by Paul Conte, a **NEWS 3X/400** technical editor*

C is not a programming language without risks. Even C experts rely on careful programming, lint filters, and good debuggers to handle problems common to C. This book helps prevent such problems by showing how C programmers get themselves into trouble. The author draws on more than 15 years of experience to help you avoid C's pitfalls. And he suggests how to manage C and C++ application development.

96 pages, 9 chapters, 7"x9"

Contents: Preface • Introduction • Common Mistakes and How to Avoid Them • Foolproof Statement and Comment Syntax • Hassle-Free Arrays and Strings • Simplified Variable Declarations • Practical Pointers • Macros and Miscellaneous Pitfalls • C++ • Managing C and C++ Development • Bibliography • Index • Appendix (C Coding Suggestions)

AN INTRODUCTION TO COMMUNICATIONS FOR THE AS/400

By Ruggero Adinolfi
*Technical editor, John Enck, a **NEWS 3X/400** technical editor*

This guide to basic communications concepts and how they operate on the IBM AS/400 helps clarify an increasingly complex subject. *An Introduction to Communications for the AS/400* outlines the rich mix of communications capabilities designed into the AS/400 and relates them to the concepts that underlie the various network environments. This book helps you, as an MIS professional, prepare for future AS/400 developments and new application potentials.

196 pages, 13 chapters, 7"x9"

CONTENTS: Introduction to Data Communications • Communications Fundamentals • Types of Networks • OSI Reference Model Architecture • Systems Network Architecture • PU 2.1, LU 6.2, and APPN • Networking Roles • The AS/400 as Host • Communications in APPN • Traditional SNA Networks • OSI • TCP/IP • The AS/400-DEC Connection • Appendices • Glossary

CONTROL LANGUAGE PROGRAMMING FOR THE AS/400

By Bryan Meyers and Dan Riehl

This comprehensive textbook on CL programming for the AS/400 is a boon to students who plan to initiate careers as AS/400 programming professionals. Bryan Meyers and Dan Riehl, with 20 years' experience in CL programming between them, write from an up-to-the-minute knowledge of the skills required in today's MIS environment. Students without prior knowledge of CL will learn the basics quickly. As the book progresses methodically to more complex processes and concepts, it guides readers smoothly toward a professional grasp of CL/400 programming techniques and style.

500 pages, 26 chapters, 8-1/2"x10"

CONTENTS: What is CL? • Command Structure • Command Parameters • Command Line Operations • Compiling and Running a CL Program • The Parts of a CL Program • Declaring Variables • Manipulating Variables • Program Logic Expressions • Controlling Workflow • Error Trapping • Parameters • Retrieving and Changing External Attributes • Files and Data Areas • Advanced Message Handling • Advanced File Techniques • Command Prompting • Using IBM-Supplied Programs • Displaying and Changing Command Attributes • Job Logs • Testing a CL Program • User-Defined Commands • Command Definition Statements • Command Processing Program • Advanced Command Facilities • Appendices (Most Often-Used CL Commands, PDM, SEU, Bibliography, Glossary)

DESKTOP GUIDE TO CL PROGRAMMING

By Bryan Meyers

This first book of the *NEWS 3X/400 Technical Reference Series** is packed with notes, short explanations, practical tips, and CL code segments you can use in your own CL programming. You can easily find answers to most of your everyday questions about CL. A complete "short reference" lists every command and explains the most-often-used ones, along with names of the files they use and the MONMSG messages to use with them.

205 pages, 36 chapters, 7"x9"   On-line Windows Help Diskette

CONTENTS: Introduction • CL Coding Style Standards • Declaring Variables • Using the CHGVAR Command • Using Expressions • Character String Expressions and Concatenation • Using the %SUBSTRING Function • Binary Values and Hexadecimal Notation • Using Data Areas • The CALL Command • Passing Constant Parameters Between Programs • Using Hexadecimal Notation To Pass Decimal Parameters • Using the TFRCTL Command • Command Prompting Allocating Objects • Using File Overrides • Date Format Conversion • Using a Message Monitor • Sending and Receiving Messages • Types of Messages • A CL Standard Error-Handling Routine • Using Break-Message-Handling Programs • Processing Outfiles • Retrieving Job Attributes • Retrieving Object Descriptions • Retrieving Member Descriptions • Retrieving User Profiles • Retrieving the Name of the Current Program Using OPNQRYF • Using CL's Built-In SQL Functions • Processing a Qualified Name • Processing Lists • Debugging a Batch Job • The LODRUN Command • System Values • Hexadecimal Collating Sequence • CL Command Summary

*Other books so far scheduled as part of this series (available before the end of 1995) include *Desktop Guide to Programmers' Tools, Desktop Guide to RPG/400, Desktop Guide to ILE RPG, Desktop Guide to DDS,* and *Desktop Guide to Client Access/400.*

IMPLEMENTING AS/400 SECURITY

By Wayne Madden, a ***NEWS 3X/400*** *technical editor*

All of the hard work you put into your MIS operation is endangered if system security is substandard or outdated. But everything you need is here to achieve or upgrade security of your AS/400 without struggling for hours searching through manuals and wondering if you have all the bases covered. Expert Wayne Madden shares his know-how, makes recommendations, and leads you through all the necessary steps in one easy-to-read volume. Security implementation utilities are included on accompanying 3-1/2" PC diskette.

286 pages, 13 chapters, 7"x9"

CONTENTS: Security at the System Level • The Facts About User Profiles • Object Authorization • Database Security • Network Security • Evaluating Your Current Strategy • Establishing and Controlling System

Access • Building Object and Role Authorizations • Security Implementation Examples • Is Your Strategy Working? • Status Auditing • Event Auditing • Appendices, References, Figures and Tables

NEWS 3X/400's DESKTOP GUIDE TO THE S/36

*By Mel Beckman, Gary Kratzer, and Roger Pence, **NEWS 3X/400** technical editors*

The definitive System/36 survival manual, this book includes practical techniques you can apply today to supercharge your S/36, whether you have a long-term commitment to the S/36, or you just want to get the most from the system as you prepare for migration to another machine.

Starting with an overview of the S/36's capabilities and limitations, *Desktop Guide to the S/36,* gives you the information you need at your fingertips for maximum system performance tuning, effective application development and smart Disk Data Management. A diskette containing ready-to-run utilities will help you save machine time and implement power programming techniques such as External Program Calls. Finally,, the book includes a chapter reviewing two popular Unix-based S/36 work-alike migration alternatives.

350 pages, 21 chapters, 7"x9"

CONTENTS: Introduction to S/36 Architecture • S/36 Memory Management • Disk Data Management • S/36 Models and Configurations • The Importance of Memory and Disk Space • Other Configuration Considerations • How External Program Calls Work • A Comparison of EPC Vendor Offerings • Implementing Modular RPG Applications • Using DBLOCK and IBLOCK Effectively • Understanding the Storage Index • Disk Data Management Tips and Techniques • Disk Cache • How to Use SME • Assessing the Need for More Memory • Achieving Acceptable Response Time • Harnessing Assembly Routines • Profiling and Advanced Debugging • Achieving Upward Compatibility • The AS/400 • The UNIX Alternatives • Diskette Included

OBJECT-ORIENTED PROGRAMMING FOR AS/400 PROGRAMMERS

*By Jennifer Hamilton, **NEWS 3X/400** author*

If you are an AS/400 programmer who wants to understand the increasingly important topic of object-oriented programming, then this is the book for you. *Object-Oriented Programming for AS/400 Programmers* explains basic OOP concepts, such as classes and inheritance, in simple, easy-to-understand terminology. The OS/400 object-oriented architecture is used as a basis for the discussion throughout so that an AS/400 programmer familiar with the OS/400 object model will find the discussion easy to follow. The concepts presented are reinforced through an introduction to the C++ object-oriented programming language, using examples based on the OS/400 object model.

114 pages, 14 chapters, 7"x9"

CONTENTS: Introduction and History • Encapsulation • Abstraction • The Object Model • Using Objects • Classes • Inheritance • Polymorphism • a Final Comparison • Object-Oriented Programming Languages • Classes in C++ • Using C++ Classes • Derived Classes in C++ • Additional C++ Constructs • Appendix: The Object-Oriented Architecture of the AS/400 • Glossary • References

PROGRAMMING IN RPG/400

*By Judy Yaeger, Ph.D., a **NEWS 3X/400** technical editor*

An illuminating textbook on RPG/400 satisfying a long standing need for comprehensive instructional material in this highly specialized subject area. The book gives students a thorough understanding of how to use RPG/400 effectively in a variety of applications. Heavy emphasis is placed on top-down, structured programming and modular design. Questions and exercises follow each chapter to reinforce learning.

430 pages, 13 chapters, 8-1/2"x10"

CONTENTS: Introduction to Programming and RPG • Getting Started • Arithmetic and Assignment Operations • Top-Down, Structured Program Design • Externally Described Files • File Access and Record Manipulation • Introduction to Interactive Applications • Tables and Arrays • Advanced Data Definition • Interactive Applications — Advanced Techniques • Byte- and Bit-Level Operations • Inter-Program Communications • Looking Backward: RPG II • Appendix A: Developing Programs on the AS/400 • Appendix B: Introduction to SEU

THE QUINTESSENTIAL GUIDE TO PC SUPPORT

by John Enck, Robert E. Anderson, Michael Otey, and Michael Ryan

This comprehensive book about IBM's AS/400 PC Support product is required reading for anyone who works with PC Support — and for anyone who wants to learn about this invaluable connectivity resource. *The Quintessential Guide to PC Support* defines the architecture of PC Support and its role in midrange networks, describes PC Support's installation and configuration procedures, and shows you how you can configure and use PC Support to solve real-life problems.

325 pages, 11 chapters, 7"x9"

CONTENTS: PC Support to the Rescue • Connectivity Options • Hardware Installation • Software Installation on the AS/400 • Software Installation on the PC and PS/2 • Configuration Overview • Terminal Emulation Scenarios • Using the AS/400 as a Server • Client/Server Applications Using Data Queues • Coexistence with NetWare and Windows • Advanced Options and Considerations • Appendices • Diskette Available

S/36 POWER TOOLS

*Edited by Chuck Lundgren, a **NEWS 3X/400** technical editor*

Five years' worth of articles, tips, and programs published in *NEWS 3X/400* from 1986 to October 1990, including more than 280 programs and procedures. Extensively cross-referenced for fast and easy problem-solving, and complete with diskette containing all the programming code. Winner of an Award of Achievement from the Society of Technical Communications, 1992.

747 pages, 20 chapters, 7"x9"

CONTENTS: Backup and Restore • Communications • Data Conversion, Edits, and Validation • DFU, SDA, and SEU • Diskettes • DisplayWrite • Documentation • Files • Folders • IDDU and Query/36 • Libraries • MAPICS • Performance • POP • Printers • Programming • Security • System • Tapes • Workstations • Appendix

STARTER KIT FOR THE AS/400, SECOND EDITION

An indispensable guide for novice to intermediate AS/400 programmers and system operators

by Wayne Madden

with contributions by Bryan Meyers, Andrew Smith, and Peter Rowley

This second edition of the *Starter Kit for the AS/400* not only contains updates of the material in the first edition, but also incorporates new material that enhances its proven value as a resource to help you learn some of the basic concepts and nuances of the system — information that will make your job easier and increase your comfort working on the AS/400.